SAGE was founded in 1965 by Sara Miller McCune to support the dissemination of usable knowledge by publishing innovative and high-quality research and teaching content. Today, we publish over 900 journals, including those of more than 400 learned societies, more than 800 new books per year, and a growing range of library products including archives, data, case studies, reports, and video. SAGE remains majority-owned by our founder, and after Sara's lifetime will become owned by a charitable trust that secures our continued independence.

Los Angeles | London | New Delhi | Singapore | Washington DC | Melbourne

ART AND SCIENCE OF MANAGEMENT IN THE DIGITAL ERA

ART AND SCIENCE OF MANAGEMENT IN THE DIGITAL ERA

INDIAN SPIRITUAL WISDOM FOR MANAGING SUSTAINABLE GLOBAL ENTERPRISE

R. P. BANERJEE

SAGE | spectrum

Los Angeles | London | New Delhi
Singapore | Washington DC | Melbourne

First published in 2020 by

SAGE | spectrum

SAGE Publications India Pvt Ltd
B1/I-1 Mohan Cooperative Industrial Area
Mathura Road, New Delhi 110 044, India
www.sagepub.in

SAGE Publications Inc
2455 Teller Road
Thousand Oaks, California 91320, USA

SAGE Publications Ltd
1 Oliver's Yard, 55 City Road
London EC1Y 1SP, United Kingdom

SAGE Publications Asia-Pacific Pte Ltd
18 Cross Street #10-10/11/12
China Square Central
Singapore 048423

Published by Vivek Mehra for SAGE Publications India Pvt Ltd. Typeset in 10/12 pt Minion by AG Infographics, Delhi.

Library of Congress Control Number: 2020943104

ISBN: 978-93-5388-507-6 (PB)

This work is dedicated

to

all those who consider it
as having provided any kind of support
or guidance, either in principle or in practice.

CONTENTS

LIST OF ILLUSTRATIONS

Figures

Tables

LIST OF ABBREVIATIONS

3Cs	Commitment, coordination and cooperation
AFM	Atomic force microscope
AGM	Annual general meeting
AI	Artificial intelligence
ALR	Absolute liquidity ratio
AR	Autonomous response
ATR	Acid test ratio
AUR	Asset utilization ratio
BEP	Break-even point
BMCs	Bricks-and-mortar companies
CBA	Cost–benefit analysis
CBP	Composite behaviour patterns
CCDRS	Collective context for discrete response system
CEOs	Chief executive officers
CFO	Chief financial officer
CKO	Chief knowledge officer
CMO	Chief marketing officer
CNS	Central nervous system
COGM	Cost of the goods manufactured
COGS	Cost of goods sold
CPV	Customer perceived values
CR	Conscious response
CRM	Customer relationship management
CSR	Corporate social responsibility
CSV	Customer-skimmed value
CTO	Chief technology officer
CTR	Capital turnover ratio
DER	Debt–equity ratio
DFL	Degree of financial leverage
DLS	Dynamic light scattering
DMD	Discriminating market dynamism
DOL	Degree of operative leverage

DSR	Debt service ratio
EBDIT	Earnings before depreciation interest and tax
EBIT	Earnings before interest and taxes
EBT	Earnings before tax
EFA	Education for all
EPS	Earnings per share
ESG	Environment, social and governance
FATR	Fixed asset turnover ratio
FCS	Functional coordination system
FDD	Financial due diligence
FG	Finished goods
FMCD	Fast-moving consumer durables
FMCG	Fast-moving consumer goods
GDP	Gross domestic product
GEC	Global economic and financial concern
GP	Gross profit
GVC	Global value chain
GVGV	Give value to get value
GWC	Gross working capital
HNWI	High-net-worth income
HR	Human resources
HRIS	Human resource information system
HRP	Human resource policy
ICT	Information and communications technology
IJV	Intuitive judgemental view
IRR	Internal rate of return
ISKCON	International Society for Krishna Consciousness
IT	Information technology
ITES	Information technology-enabled services
LNWI	Low-net-worth income
LTIS	Linear time-invariant system
MFCs	Mixed form companies
MNCs	Multinational corporations
MNWI	Middle-net-worth income
MRI	Magnetic resonance imaging
MROCE	Marketing return on capital employed
NA	Net value of assets
NEC	National economic and financial concern
NFDD	Non-financial due diligence
NPR	Net profit ratio
NPV	Net present value
NW	Net worth

PAT	Profit after tax
PDI	Power distance index
PET	Positron emission tomography
PLC	Product life cycle
PR	Proprietary ratio
QR	Quick ratio
R&S	Reserve and surplus
RE	Retained earnings
RFM	Rational functional method
RKM	Ramakrishna Mission
RM	Raw materials
ROCE	Return on capital employed
ROE	Return on equity
ROI	Return on investments
RONA	Return on net assets
ROS	Return on sales
RSG	Relative sales growth
SAB	Scenario analysis for business
SBU	Strategic business units
SCN	Suprachiasmatic nucleus
SEM	Scanning electron microscopes
SMEs	Small and medium enterprises
SRS	Situational response system
STM	Scanning tunnelling microscope
SWOT	Strengths, weaknesses, opportunities and threats
TEM	Transmission electron microscopes
TNC	Training needs analysis
TNCs	Transnational corporations
TPLC	Technology-driven product life cycle
TSC	Technology and services companies
UN	United Nations
UNDP	United Nations Development Programme
UNESCO	United Nations Educational, Scientific and Cultural Organization
UNICEF	United Nations Children's Fund
UVS	Ultraviolet visible spectroscopy
WCTR	Working capital turnover ratio
WIP	Work in progress
XPS	X-ray photoelectron spectroscopy
ZOD	Zone of discretion

PREFACE

Thousands of basic works on 'management' are available in different languages. Although the fundamentals are elemental in nature, the learners and practising managers should continuously sensitize themselves with the fundamentals to have an edge on time and change. The human society is now on the threshold of a massive change. Technology has penetrated into almost all aspects of human life—be it personal growth, organizational development and transformations in the market and society; in every aspect of human life, everywhere and every time, the spirit of human being has to come up to become an overarching control over the factors of technology.

It is in this respect that the present work is not only important but also an urgent contribution to the pool of knowledge and a guide for the human society in general and organizations in particular. Managers are thus not only executives and small leaders in the context, but they also have to become an element of illumination, creating pathways to the aspects of consumption, making and providing things and offers to people.

A manager thus performs the roles of a leader, consumer, buyer, maker, worker, messenger, advisor and guide to all others. Until the current period, self-management has been an untouched dimension of management. Now onwards, it is going to be the core of corporate management.

This work shall prove to be a handbook for most learners and practising managers for the new dimension as stated.

I suggest the new-era managers and learners to be thorough with this new dimension of management.

Acknowledgements

I convey my thanks to the publisher for the publication. I also offer thanks to Mr Lintu Majumder, Ms Rupa Dutta, Mr Shanti Gopal Hazra, Mr B. S. Yadav and Mr Babulal Patra for helping me in typing and structuring the manuscript. Thanks are due to my wife, Mrs Sipra Banerjee, son, Dr Debajyoti Banerjee, and daughter-in-law, Dr Dimple Banerjee, for their continuous support to complete this work. Thanks are also due to all others who really matter.

OBJECTIVE OF THE BOOK

Thousands of titles are available globally to discuss the issues of management from theoretical and practical perspectives. However, a wide gap existed before this work between what was available and what required to be made available. Few highlighting points will make it clear. Among many such points, commendable and more important issues are as follows:

- Management thoughts have been based on either unitary or collective experience of thinkers, practitioners or authors.
- The intrinsic spiritual identity of human beings has never been integrated with the issues of managing enterprises.
- Theories have been founded on the historicity of practices involving selected enterprises.
- Systems, structures and procedures of managing enterprises have become more important than the core contents of human beings.
- Customers have been considered as the units of commerce and an objective has been set to skim off surplus from the individual or the groups of customers.
- Business gets priority over other broader concerns including the concern for the world and society.

These are a few and relevant observations that have actually skewed the objective function of the management thoughts and philosophies.

This book emphasizes on the core spiritual identity of human beings. It highlights the aspects of digital and latest technology on the one hand and attempts to combine these with several millennia-tested spiritual principles of sustainable living. It recommends corporate strategies in a different way, goes beyond the pleasant limit of prevailing management thoughts and recommends a superior way to develop excellence in management for any kind of enterprise in the world.

CHAPTER 1

INTRODUCTION

In the Realm of Business Heroism

Whether a business can be best visualized and developed by a person qualified in the theories and practices of management or by a person with strong intent to do and deliver is a matter of a century-old ongoing debate. The world society has observed a large number of very successful business leaders who have reached the summit of achieving resources, properties, power, money and recognition. This has been perceived as the phenomenon of the 'rule of heroes'. A business hero is someone who has attained the height of a mountain of achievements in resources, money and honour. Heroes of the corporate world are worshipped in the corporate corridors and shop floors. They rise up to the position of any benchmark so that heroism is worshiped across.

A hero is someone who is super equal among the equals. They can think and do ahead of others and are ambiguous in thoughts, appearance and reality in most of the cases. What they would do is a matter outside the ambit of thoughts of others. They are like father-leaders, who can win lots of challenges, of course in their own way. They demand obedience and effectiveness from all individuals around them. They offer grace to others at will and can attempt to damage the cause of others. They are like a conservative father in spirit—caring to the obedient but offensive to someone distancing from.

Fordism

Henry Ford, at his time of emergence, became a legend and a name to pose faith and respect and have dedication in the work assigned to a large number of workers and technical persons. His great grandson, Alfred, became a devotee of the International Society for Krishna Consciousness (ISKCON) and joined the work of the monastery, having received the name Ambarish Das from the monastery. As one of those corporate leaders who are destined to be one of the wheels of change in business and industry, Ambarish found it a better role to take care of the social responsibility of the company, as a devotee of the monastery. Henry Ford had another similar personality in the Asian continent, in India, J. R. D. Tata. Both Ford and Tata were very close to the common workers, technicians and other general employees of their respective companies during their periods of corporatization. Both were heroes of their respective groups of companies, which went far ahead of the boundaries of the respective companies.

Ford not only became a pattern in manufacturing in the automobile sector but also created a phenomenon in the industry in general in American industrialization and also in many parts of the world for industrial emergence. Fordism, as it has been termed by many leading thinkers and practitioners in the world, is a pattern in manufacturing which is essential to drive the wheels of industrial growth.

Fordism became very attractive in Russia as an intrinsic principle of growth and to drive the wheels of growth forward. Vladimir Lenin, after the 1917 occupying power of the Russian Empire and subsequently post 1922 as the great empire of the Soviet Union, having attached many adjoining nations by applying force, had focused on industrialization of the Russian region.

Fordism had a strong underlying following in Russian industrialization during the period of rule by V. Lenin until 1924 and subsequently by Joseph Stalin until the mid-1950s. It was liked and indirectly followed by Russian authorities during the period of autocracy, as their pattern of governance was dictatorial imposition of decisions on the system. To the dictators of Russia, it had created a perception of similarity of the pattern of governance of their state and Fordism. They had perceived Fordism as a sort of 'industrial dictatorship'.

Henry Ford did not behave and act as a dictator; of course, he also did not have managers to run the business. His spirit was like that technicians and workers do the work, so having a set of people called managers is not essential; rather, it may erode the resources of companies and sometimes misdirect the wheel of the growth of the company. So he was strong in his belief that the decision would be his own or of his close people and others would execute the way they were expected to.

Fordism became a system of having an enterprise with a large number of workers and many technicians and no manager. Non-managerial people in an enterprise, as Henry Ford had his faith in his manpower policy in the enterprise, were enjoying good amount of success with Detroit nooks and crannies being on talk about Fordism. The Great Depression had pushed the scale of growth down, but the subsequent period of the Second World War had pushed up the Fords up with an internal transformation by the grandson of Henry Ford, Henry Ford II could make turn around post Second World War.

Henry Ford II took the responsibility as early as mid-20s of his life after his father, Edsel Ford's, sudden death at an early age during the Second World War. Henry Ford II had a strong, intelligent mind. He made a massive turnaround in the company by taking a decision to have managers in place. Each manager was attributed with the charge of a business unit and the responsibility to make that business successful.

Henry Ford II started having managers in place to run the business. He had segmented the group's business among different special areas. Each segment was made almost independent at the responsibility of a manager. Henry Ford II had sourced the persons for the managerial positions from the set of successful managers of leading competitors such as General Motors and others in the automobile sector. This again became to be known as Fordism II. This led to a dramatic transformation of the profitability of Ford Motor Company.

Detroit came back on wheels after a period of one and a half decade of slow fever in business. Whereas the early Russian industrialization was inspired by Fordism, Fordism II had inspired neo-Americanism, triggering a massive fast forward in the American industry during the post-Second World War period.

Features of Fordism II

Principles put forward by Henry Ford II were as follows:

- Independence of decision, execution and control by managers under the overall guide of the objectives, mission, vision and philosophies of the company
- Managers were entitled with the task of making plans, getting investments, executing the plans through market-driven activities, and drawing and using resources of all kinds to benefit the company and all its stakeholders
- Mass production and economies of scale in every major activity involving technology and process that emerges out of global initiatives of different categories of people
- Automation in manufacturing, distribution, marketing and many other functions
- Manager-driven functions of enterprises
- Large number of shareholders
- Stakeholder capitalism satisfying different groups of stakeholders' expectations of value gains

Heroes of business, as most of these people are identified as, lacked in the principle of distributive justice for people who are either elemental entities of the business or recipients of the business output in the world. Business required spreading out to carry the effective attributes forward. This as a philosophical factor required to be explored philosophically.

Surprisingly, to the benefit of the large number of emerging and ongoing consumers, 'management' as a discipline has emerged as one of the strongest economic forces in a way far away from the core philosophical spirit of the ideal enterprise of today.

'Management' as a function has emerged from the managerial mindset to a superior one gradually. The age of computers began with the power of multiplying the human capacity. Globally, the power of computers started giving amazing results. Computer-driven manufacturing replaced the mechanistic ways through the power of technology to do things non-manually yet human-driven.

In the initial period, the power of computers was not much; however, over a period of time, it yielded enormous power in the hands of organizations and societies. Computer-coordinated manufacturing, distribution, designing, preserving and so on, on the one hand, and creating effective tools for decision-making, on the other, became the strengths of the entities using it.

The era of the Internet has actually further pushed up the forces of digitalization. The Internet has provided new tools, new ways and methods to connect, new factors of business and an overall new way of life. People have come forward globally to use computers of different types and the Internet. Digitalization has advanced further with smart mobile phones. The era of smartphones, as it is called now, has created a new approach of living, a new kind of taste of life, and new ways to interact with the society and the market.

The market as an identified place has almost become an old concept. Now the market is on the palm of people. With smartphones in hand, people may reach any end of the market in the world, transacting on e-commerce platforms. Now companies can reach out to consumers with a plethora of schemes and offers to attract the interest of the consumers, and hopefully select the items of consumption that satisfy their intent and preferences.

Consumers were considered most important half a century ago. Now the consumer power has grown to such a proportion that all activities, industries and businesses have to make or break on the basis of the collective intent of the consumers. The consumer power has now become so strong that it guides, drives and reorients the focus of investments in any business and industry.

Emergence of Consumer Capitalism

When consumers become the critical entity of a business, the system, structure, process, contents and all arrangements focus on the choice, taste, preference and need of the consumers. Consumers' knowledge of the product and services is the basis on which the company should thrive, and above that, the company should also fully understand the perception of the consumers about the things and entities which concern the product and service being offered by the company.

The preference vetted by the consumers leads to an accumulated impression of the company and its product or service. This accumulated impression leads to the making of a brand and taking the brand ahead of its time. A brand thus formed offers to the consumers a series of assurances. Some of the important assurances that a brand offers are as follows:

- It assures that the quality of the product or service shall be based on certain accepted standard as expected by the consumer.
- It assures the conformity of the actual offers to the mentions made by the company.
- It creates a flow of relations with the stream of things as per the norms and standards of the company.
- It attracts a kind of relationship with the consumers by maintaining the flow of relations between the consumers and the company that offers the product or service.
- The brand established in the minds of the consumers relates its message to different segments of the market, making ease of funds for investments in expansions, diversifications, acquisitions, mergers, R&D and new project investments.
- Consumers' preferred brands induce mass investors to invest in the brand so favoured by the consumers. So the shares of such brands get a high degree of attention from the mass investors in the capital market. The obvious impact of that goes into making the company's value high with the secondary market showing attractions for investments in that share. The corporate value increases sharply because of the higher degree of consumer preference for a particular brand and company.

Assimilation of value by the company and the brand thus gets triggered by consumer acceptance and preference. With consumers by its side, the company can make inroads into the investment market, financing market and so on. Also the company has a better chance and ability to enhance its boundary of business and activity. With this new dimension and new horizons before the company, capital asset formation by the company becomes relatively easier.

Bill Gates has suggested a combination of market objectives and social objectives. In a conversation with Michael Kinsley, Bill Gates suggested,

---

As I see it, there are two great forces of human nature: self interest, and caring for others. Capitalism harnesses self-interest in helpful and sustainable ways, but only on behalf of those who can pay. Philanthropy and government aid channel our caring for those who can't pay, but the resources run out before they meet the need. But to provide rapid improvement for the poor, we need a system that draws in innovators and businesses in a far better way than we do today. (Kinsley, 2009, p. 10)

Corporate profit maximizes with maximum participation and support from the consumers. However, a moderate level of assured participation by the consumers and perceptive participation by a new set of consumers inspire the corporate activity to the extent that helps to satisfy each one's selfish interest in the first place. However, the issue of extending the hands of care by the market to those who deserve the care remains untouched.

Manager Drives the Wheel of the Organization

One understands the essence of business once the participation in the decision-making becomes wider from the end users of the business. Any business needs to have certain spread in terms of the quality of involvement and perceived ownership of it.

A person develops better attractions, responsibilities and thrusts for business once they are endowed with the share of ownership. As one of the owners, the responsibility of the person becomes double—on the one hand, as a customer, trader, employee or any other stakeholder, the person has a moral binding to do good to the company; on the other hand, as a manager, they have to do and get done by others the best for the company.

However, the emergence of 'management' as a thought and practice has made dramatic transformations in the scenario of world business. Modern management is known to be an agent of the owners of an enterprise. The owners are the shareholders, each of whom the company owes the initial capital fund to start, run and transform the business. The prevailing idea is that since shareholders have invested their money to start the enterprise, they are the owners and most important elements in the entire gamut of things for a company.

The power of initial money is considered the most powerful element in a business. So, a business works as a representative of the shareholders. The 'management' of a company, thus, performs as the agent of the group of people considered as owners, as their fund goes into the shareholding of the company. Managers, starting from the top executive position to the most junior one, are the agents of the owners.

At the end of the year of performance, the management has to submit the entire work report, things achieved and lost, and the financials. Financials are considered very important by the shareholders, who want to see how much their investment has grown. This growth is actually shareholder income. As it is known, a shareholder, or any person, has the opportunity to invest in any share in the capital market.

By investing in the share market, the investor expects capital gain or dividend yield. Dividend yield is the percentage gain by the shareholder on the invested money. Capital gain is the gain earned by selling the shares held in the market and earning a margin from there. In both the cases, the effective management of the enterprise makes the ways for the gain.

The efficient management of the company by the managers and their corporate colleagues can take a company to a superior height or gradually pull it down to the business debris. The entire process has now become dependent upon the consumers of the products or services offered by the company. The vehicle of growth is actually in the hands of the consumers. The 'management' which understands it better would do better. 'Consumer first, consumer second and consumer next' is the predominant legend today.

Managers have their selfish interests of getting more money and, through managerial activities, fulfilling their dreams and objectives of lives. The manager who finds the work rewarding enough to get delight from is one who puts in most of their human energy into the work, system and process. With the efficient delivery of the work as the manager, one can create higher degree of opportunities for people having the intent to work and earn. Consumers fulfil their selfish interest by virtue of their being in the domain of the company.

'Commitment, coordination and cooperation' (3Cs) are expected to become the wheels of change in the new era of business. Competitions in the market shall have more focus on understanding, belief and preference than the quantitative factors of the market.

Companies open their windows of good wishes throughout the span of their presence in the market. By virtue of the delightful consumption by a person, a fragment of opportunity opens up. Effectively, the wheels of change are triggered by the fulfilment of customer interest.

Thus, it is a nicely woven texture of economic and social possibility that creates the chance to elevate the condition of the human society. A manager performs a social role much more than most others. They perform their own role and thus push the wheels of growth forward.

Management has attained a system outlook. The system, structure and procedure involved in the art and science of management have been assumed to be effectively rewarding if they follow the patterns of having certain elements, which are as follows:

- Planning
- Organizing
- Coordinating
- Communicating
- Controlling
- Feedback and reengineering

Scope of Plans So Far

It has been widely observed and also proved that most functions of management defeat the factors of planning. Most of the manufacturing and distribution functions depend on some kind of planning. Without the edge of planning, organizations cannot expect to deliver the output on the desired time frame. This is, of course, driven by the demand and expectations of the recipients, the customers. In the ultimate analysis, all plans are dependent functions of the changing demands and expectations of the consumers of products and services. It covers the spectrum of production, distribution, financing, investments, R&D, reorganization, strategies and stakeholder policies, and so on. Management actions are seldom confined within the contours of plans; rather, they follow the pathways of emergent plans, which are actually non-plans in nature. With the situations emerging continuously, most plans are actually affected by the forces of disruptions where the input factors and the conditions of actions may require changes—from incremental or minor to massive or major. However, planning as a process helps organizations profusely to the extent of understanding the resources, utilizing the resources, and adding value to and by the resources. The process of planning lets the managers understand the worth of the following:

- Material resources
- Financial resources
- Human resources

Whether the resources are good or bad in the real sense of the term is known only when the managerial intervention into the resources can make it work. Resources are good if these are capable of generating value. However, it is not the resource alone but the art and science of making the resource utilizable and worthy which turns as the most important dimension than the bare resource left in the debris of time-burned-valued items. Only the art and science of management can make the resources working and rewarding most effectively.

Unutilized money is also like a material resource left untouched. Managerial intervention finds out the optimum solution to how a financial resource can be made to yield the most significant return in a given prevailing situation. Financial resources can be made to grow through any means that the manager makes it happen. The scenario in which the management functions becomes very important for the same. A manager needs to consider the scenario and create the optimum pathways to utilize the intrinsic value of each to multiply the worth of the elements.

Left to the person's emotions and prejudices, an individual may function to the required spirit or not. A manager finds the way forward to stimulate ideas, trigger energy, sensitize creativity and tune the person to the dedicated work of the organization. This yields highest possibility of gains and value for the organization, person, stakeholders and world as a whole.

Once the organized efforts take shape, the manager can win the race of the corporate world, with the entire scenario and context supporting the cause to fulfil the objective.

The scenario has changed during the recent period.

The global society has now gone in favour of the digital way of living. Although a compulsive phenomenon, it has actually created a new love for the digital ways in all or most of our activities. Digital pushes the society to be either in solitude or in a small combine of close connects on the one hand and the world at large on the other. The context becomes such that right from the point of manufacturing through the points of distribution and finally at the end of consumption, the spirit of association becomes different.

The digital society follows the principles of 'less physical, more virtual'.

Therefore, the organization has to find out ways to be more mechanistic and process driven in the business process than any time before.

With a mechanistic and process-driven business, the organizations have to depend on internal people more on aspects which connect the internal people with the external. In fact, an individual's role as an employee is destined to change sharply.

In a digital society, organizations will require the following:

- Each manager will become an ambassador of the company.
- All functional activities will merge to perform as a holistic 'consumer-centric function'.
- Instead of working within separate domains, each manager will be required to be equipped with a cross-functional entity.
    - The managerial role shall have a less distinct identity from the blue-collar roles.

- The issues of trust, trustworthiness, honesty, sincerity, integrity and commitments will become values of very high importance in the realm of business transactions and interactions.
- The 'human edge' in business will be considered very important, as equal as the 'product edge'.
- The quality of interactions by the company people will be considered with equal emphasis with that of the quality of product or service.
- The role of a manager shall undergo a fundamental change. They will have a more advisory role to the company than any time before.

A new manager's commitment shall be to:

- Serve the consumers with better ideas
- Guide them with critical inputs of knowledge regarding the concerned product or the service
- Be more impersonal in behaviour and interactions than before

Therefore, the digital-era manager will be a person with less of selfishness and more of self-giving.

An ideal manager in the digital era will be a person with spiritual understanding. The usual approach of manpower management does not understand and appreciate the core dimension of spirituality.

Self-management tools and attitude become some of the most important aspects of the becoming of a digital-era manager.

It is in this context that the need for a new focus on management is essential. This work has been designed on that basis. Hence, it is going to satisfy the need for basic inputs to manage enterprises in times to come.

Reference

Kinsley, M. (Ed.). (2009). *Creative capitalism*. Simon & Schuster.

CHAPTER 2

ORGANIZATION: THE ANTHROPOMORPHOLOGY

Concept of Organization

An organization is a combination of living and inanimate entities and elements. An entity is formed across certain ideas, principles, plans or doctrines with the legal guidance for its formation. Entities formed as an organization are of different attributes and qualities. The usual way has been a mix of structured and unstructured elements bonded together for its formation. Usually, it requires a good number of people to make and run an organization; however, one single person may get an organization started successfully. Normally, in the process of its making and being, more and more biological entities should be present in the organization.

Definition of Organization

Early definitions of organizations were concerning the economic identity. Mostly, it has been thought of rendering economic benefits to the society and nations. Many organizations did develop their economic models to drive decisions concerning the formations of organizations towards effective actions and results. However, the right definition should be as follows: An organization is an entity formed by a single individual or a group with a purpose and having the required drive and activities towards fulfilling the purpose.

Thus, an organization has to serve the appropriate role to add value to the society and the world through its existence. Small or large, each organization has to perform and deliver as per its role. In its pursuits to fulfil its own objective, the organization should keep in perspective the concerns of the society and the world. The purpose of an organization, among others, could be:

- Economic
- Commercial
- Business
- Political
- Human
- Environmental
- Cultural
- Leisure
- Aesthetic
- Legal

- Professional
- Philosophical
- Religious
- Social
- Spiritual

Whatever be the nature of an organization, it should focus on the choice of its objective and then do everything possible and drive the journey of the organization towards effectively achieving the targets.

Any organization, thought to be of economic identity used to deliver goods is expected to provide value to others. Economic decisions involve expectations towards involving the economic actions for making decisions regarding organizations at any point. The economic identity of an organization would influence each decision in the organization towards having economic gains. The value created by an organization in its products and services is just the value that attempts to be distributed among its stakeholders. Thereby, the economic priority for an organization creates a condition which would render the activity to deliver proper values to the stakeholders.

Views of organizations are changing with added priorities; the priority which otherwise would emphasize the roles of consumers, people involved, the society, the world system and nations gets subordinated. Organizations need to identify the role beyond the limits of the current period. The future has to be in the focus for organizations—the shape of things that are expected to be in place in future are the desired outcomes of the impacts of all different types of forces from within and outside. Impacts from the society, nations, environments and all corners and impacts from within, all put together shall make an organization a sustainable and continuing entity.

The idea of triple 'P' of Milton Friedman has captured a dominant position in the minds of leading people in the world. The concept suggests and recommends our concern for three different but interrelated parameters. These three Ps are as follows:

- Profit
- People
- Planet

Whereas profit or surplus is basic to the functioning of an organization, it needs to take appropriate care about the 'people' within the organization or those who are supporting the organization in any way. These could be by way of consuming or buying the products or services of the organization or investing in the organization. Organizations thrive on the basic and fundamental resources of this planet, either consciously or unknowingly. It is therefore advised that the organizations should take care of the planet. Each organization should have the issues of giving back to the planet to the extent it is possible in its active agenda.

An organization is formed by people with the objective of a continuing identity. In the current period, it is created with an objective to make a sustained effort to make it grow with an objective to accumulate value and create an additional value. Value generated in this way would sum up to have a new identity. The face, shape, dimensions and even contents may undergo changes or transformations in the context of the society from where it operates and the overall context of the market and the environment. In fact, organizations are the subsets of the markets, whether it is the domestic market or the global market, partners of the market process and market's functioning influence always upon organizations. The economic choice of organizations thus passes through pushes and pulls across its having a lot of functioning constraints and impacts. That is one of the important reasons why organizations attempt to focus on areas and things outside their own boundaries.

Perceptions about organizations and the real identity of organizations do vary in most places. The outward look of a person and the actual position or description of position of a person may also vary. In fact, in a larger number of cases it varies. However, perceptions play a very important role in understanding an entity in general and an organization in particular. The excellence of an organization in real economic terms and that in the form of its physical entity work as such to fit in the changing scenario of the environment.

In order to have a real identity of an organization, let us look into certain dimensions of an individual—probably to draw an idea from the profile. An organization is a cluster of many elements—materials, financials, attributes and volumes. An individual lives on the inputs for life, sustenance and projections into the future. A balanced life will consider factors contributing to the physical aspect and other factors contributing to factors responsible for the mind as well. A balanced life will consider the environment and situation around as important. An individual needs to establish relations of various types with relevant people and entities. They become successful with a planned and strategic approach of life. They need to garner strength and energy in life to coordinate with the world of understanding the principles of good life.

A good life is one which is good to a person and to the people and entities the person is and expected to be associated with. It always makes a wide planning of the self. Whatever a person does should prove to be positive to their surroundings—the family, society, nation and world. It is the bottommost fact that a life is proved good when it is in a position to draw success through actions and plans in life. Actions in life may be those which are based on basic plans or are poised to make things orderly and available on the streams of life. Actions should prove success. An individual may strive for success through any means. This is quite a large number of cases happening. There is another approach of life which does not eye on success at any cost or by any means; rather, it looks for perfection in life. Perfection is the art of doing things in the best possible way while maintaining the norms and ethical standards of functioning. An individual needs to attain perfection in mind for an efficient and smooth attainment of perfection in their actions and behaviour. Perfection in action and behaviour would require an environment which proves conducive to the basis of performance. Thus, a person has to be equipped with the knowledge and values which would develop enough skills to develop things, contributing towards attainment and keeping up with the objectives of perfection.

It is thus the prerogative of the person to maintain a kind of poise within, which would balance between the rational, measurable and quantifiable parameters of life, on the one hand, and the subjective and intuitive parameters on the other. A proper balance between these two aspects of life makes the life based on themes of perfection. This life is good in all respects.

Theory of Organization

An organization is a mix of subjective and objective attributes contributing towards a purposeful growth and existence. In other words, an organization is a purposeful entity with almost all aspects of life. It has to move forward in terms of its basic identity. It has to induct into its functioning aspects which are either connected or not connected for the time being. It can find its roots in the aspirations or the promises of its formations. Sometimes it may be defined properly, but in most cases it may not be properly defined in specific terms.

The basic ideas or aspirations behind the formation of an organization are called seeding, which makes and creates the character of the organization. The purpose for which an organization is created sets the tone of the organization. However, in the course of its functioning as an entity, the organization may make significant changes in the process and thereby create the basis for ongoing changes as well.

Types of Organizations

The basic ideas across which organizations are usually formed may be grouped into certain categories.

Some of the highlighting categories may be as follows.

Gainful Organization (Profit-making)

An organization formed by a person or a group of persons with the purpose to create gains over a period of time through its own or allied activities is a gainful organization. The objective of gain could be achieved through direct or indirect actions of the organized entity.

The term that is usually used for gains is 'profit'. Scholars, thinkers and practitioners have collectively identified making profit as the objective of gainful organizations. In fact, the usual objective has been to maximize profit. In order to maximize profit, an organization has to look into various aspects of it at the same time. Some of the highlighting areas for achieving profit maximization are as follows.

Cost Optimization

The cost of production of goods or delivering services should always be attempted to optimize. The idea is that with the same customer value and consumer happiness having maintained, the organization needs to see that all elements of costs are maintained at such a level that the products or services transacted bring in a favourable margin to the extent that market competition is properly taken into account, factors for sustainability are looked into and market share is increased with a positive transactional balance in each or most of the transactions. Profit maximization as a policy requires proper utilization of assets; contribution of maximum value by people; adherence to the environmental, social, cultural and legal imperatives; and judicious utilization and transformation of the intangibles associated with the organization.

Revenue Maximization

Products and services offered by an organization need to be coordinated in such a manner that it enhances the revenue of the organization. Increased power of earning may be created through the existing business or by a way of expansion into new business opportunities. A new product or service taken into a new market would make diversification happen properly.

Whether it is the existing business or a new one, each element of transaction should take care of the cost of goods sold or the cost of services provided, component of investments made into the business that goes with each transaction, cost of the logistics transportations, parking of products or getting into services that are connected with business options—all these have to be looked into from a revenue perspective with a motto to create maximum inflow of funds through business.

The revenue maximization principle indicates the extent of revenue for the organization through the business process or the allied activity which would create positive business value in any way. The concept of positive business value attempts to create an understanding in such a manner that the business transacted contributes any of the following:

1. Surplus in terms of business transaction in monetized terms of actual real currency valuation
2. Added intangible, which implies having penetrated into a territory or domain uncharted so far with an intent to generate additional business value in future
3. Dominance over any or many market factors such as channel of distribution, coverage of territories with future prospects and reaching out to new zones of the market
4. Getting identified with the forward technology and advanced modernism for a superior market positioning
5. Getting identified as the benchmark product or service to create a new face of the organization
6. Knowledge- and creativity-driven structure and shape of the organization
7. The most or one of the most socially, culturally or environment-friendly organization

Business value maximization contributes to not only the business wealth but also the social wealth. Business valuation process may not be in a position to offer increased value in a real tangible term for the current period, but it may create a basis and a scenario wherein the business is poised to get a dimension which would liberate the business from the constraints it suffers from; cracking bottlenecks for the business is one of the ways which may create a larger canvas of the business in a new paradigm, which would benefit all the stakeholders of the business from real perspectives. The value calculated in physical material and financial terms may not remain the only component of it. However, both perceptive and reference values of the organization act on the fate of the organization for a better presence in the domain of its current market and the prospects in the future market conditions as well.

Reward Orientation

Organizations aspire for rewards from relevant sources. Rewards generate an additional value for the organization. A better way of positioning is actually through rewards from an appropriate or a relevant forum. A reward has to be based on certain attainments or achievements in the business process or its allied activities. For example, a company producing industrial items having industrial sales only may not have social relevance that way. The society in general does not help in the process of its business transactions. However, with social awareness and collective respect for the company, the impression creates an influencing parameter over the mind of those deciding on the products or services offered by the organization. Thereby, the business prospects, and even the actual ones in the current period for the company are enhanced by social recognition. The concept of corporate social responsibility (CSR) has brought in the way and opened up opportunities for the same.

Social recognition of an organization for being friendly with the society makes a new pathway, adding to the existing ones for horizontal and vertical growth of the organization. Whereas the horizontal growth is expanding into business that was hitherto uncharted for, the vertical growth is always an expectation of the existing business to grow into. Rewards spread the positive parameters about the organization. This could be initiating, undertaking or participating into any of the activities that would contribute to the growth and expansion of the organization. Apart from the social esteem and social recognition of the organizations, recognition from the market, market associations and activities related to the thoughts and activities of the markets are expected to play a great role in establishing credibility of the organization.

Gainful organizations may try to create new intellectual and knowledge bases for organizations. Knowledge is an important component of organizations in the current period. It is the foundation of the methods and processes of organizations. A new type of business process or having adopted new methods of business operations brings in lots of new ideas and methods. With new ideas and methods in place, the facts about the organization change. Knowledge-based organizations grow in terms of wealth and possibly contribute to higher business volume and turnover, mostly with a higher degree of profit. New ideas, methods and processes properly patented bring in a lot of new opportunities in terms of its added market value.

Gainful organizations which are listed with the capital markets aspire to grow in capital gains for the investors in shares. Capital gain is earned in those cases where the investor having invested in the share of a company finds a better selling price of the same share if sold in the stock market. Perceptions about the company on the one hand and the company fundamentals on the other talk about the value of the company in the context of corporate valuation in general and valuation of the company in particular.

Rewards have a push effect on organizations. The push is for the period of a year and sometimes for years to come. Awards are thus considered market-driven inputs and indirect investments into the growth profile of the organization.

Neutral Organization (Non-profit)

Apart from the gain-seeking approaches, there are other approaches in maintaining the organization's values. Gainful organizations actually create the corporate climate. The corporate climate with competitions in products, services, deliveries, prices, quality and other relevant parameters makes the corporate market. The corporate market thus combines factors that coordinate and satisfy the demands of consumers and buyers on the one hand and satisfy the demands of the providers of the products and services through supplies on the other.

There remain a large number of organizations which cater to the idea of 'distributive justice'. Global wealth needs to be reached by everyone. The concept of economic justice is still far reaching. Distribution of economic value among people on the earth is the concern. In the first half of the 21st century, a large number of children living with their families in shanties, slums, canals, forest areas and hills and on roadsides, riversides and other areas do not get proper food, have no shelters over their heads, hardly get any medical support, do not receive education and have no amusement in life—many of them live in different parts of Asia, Africa, South America and even in some parts of the most advanced world. Deprived of the logical share of their basic support for living a usual life, these are the people who account for well above two billion of people of different ages and other demographic identities.

Nations have not developed options for a new set of organizations which do not belong to the government, nor are they functioning as gainful organizations. This category of organizations is non-government in nature. They perform the roles of extended governments, wherein the social commitments of the governments otherwise have the responsibility of the governments and societies being undertaken by these types of organizations. Among many responsibilities, these organizations are known for their active role in the following areas:

1. Education and health for underprivileged children living in slums, pavements, canals, hills and forests and areas with barren lands and on riverside and those living in families affected by poverty
2. Food for the hungry people of the world, also providing their clothing and shades over heads
3. Helping women and children who are deprived of their rights to come forward with encouragement, support and vital resources

4. Eradicating social evils and establishing fair norms for them
5. Creating the basis of self-supporting works and activities for those who deserve them the most
6. Creating a sustainable basis of growth of individuals through a sustainable world created out of the existing natural inputs

Neutral organizations do not aspire to have gains through their activities. These organizations are expected to work for enhancing the boundaries of their activities. The support received from around including those from the governments and societies are directed towards the purpose of its coming into existence.

Purposeful Organization (Objective-oriented)

There is yet another variety of an organization which is neither after gains nor is neutral in its nature. These organizations do have their own philosophy, objective and identified vision. The purpose of their formation is to fulfil the objective identified as the purpose of their being. Usually with philosophical bent of mind and objective, a purposeful organization is formed. The usual method of operation is to structure a mission of its formation. The mission identified in philosophical terms usually has the following streams for action:

1. Spreading the ideas of the founding father to the wider groups, people and places. The span of spread is sometimes global for certain organizations, whereas the spread or attempt to spread as such may attempt to change or transform the focus of life, attitude to life and approach to life. It may attempt to help a society to sustain or transform its structure suited to the ideas and philosophy of the said purposeful organization.
2. Creating or attempting to offer certain civic services including education and health to people. Purposeful organizations would continue to join the process of social care on the one hand and offer their philosophical or spiritual doctrines on the other.
3. Constrained by their own doctrines, purposeful organizations develop their own priority. In most cases, the charitable activities undertaken by them have underlying objectives of taking care of the spread of ideas and doctrines. Although the doctrines are in most places presented as impersonal, non-parochial, impartial and pure, many of these organizations have proved that the mission for charity through which they create their identity of moving forward targets most beneficiaries being brought to the fold of their doctrines or faiths.

Purposeful organizations are mostly faith-centric. The central agenda is to see that their faith has a larger following through the offerings of their charity. However, the spread of faith provides, in many cases, a higher degree of goodness than before. This higher degree of goodness, though coloured by a particular doctrine or faith, goes beyond the usual matrices of our living process. Societies across the globe, high or low in economic standards, receive lots of mental peace and support having been with these practice schools of faith. Generic ideas of peace go around the calming of minds through a process of detachment with the factors of life and consecrating upon a superior entity, which would provide essential components of support for life.

Doctrines and faiths, at times, contradict with each other. The faith has got the essence of life from a particular point of view; however, it may lead to a total isolation or partial isolation from the mainstream of life. Isolation in segments or parts is an adjustment with the existing stream of things. In this context, the priority goes to the organization carrying the message than to the one carrying pure faith advocated by the founding great minds.

Doctrine of Faith

Organizational priority over the faith ultimately reduces the doctrine or the faith to a tamed condition. It is a gradual process of joining hands with the reality around, which may look forward to prioritize the scope of activity and receive influencing impacts from the society and the world. However, there are a handful of these types of organizations who have not only survived but grown steadily over a period of more than a century. Let us discuss in brief the case of one such organization each during the prehistoric Vedic period in India and another organization started more than 12 decades ago.

The history of the prehistoric Vedic period organization harps on the system of living and coordinates with the society and civilization created by people and processes around. People and process in place form integral components of the society. This story is of a great Indian Vedic sage, Yajnavalkya. He developed a monastery across his living. This was known as 'ashram' or hermitage. The primary purpose of this hermitage was to spread the core wisdom, the wisdom of god—realization of the supreme truth through learning, self-study and practice. The process of learning has to be one that identifies a central focus. The central focus is the core divinity. The Supreme god has to be understood and realized through one's own study and understanding the truth that is not only the empirical understanding and realization alone.

Yajnavalkya was a teacher in essence. A teacher with excellence in wisdom has so many areas of spread of truth. Truth that he maintained was an earned and evolved way of unfolding the truth. In his monastery, he was pivotal in inducting the students chosen in a way that they have chosen objectives of good in life. Good in life has to be understood by the aspirants. How was it made and realized through the journey was left to the individual aspirant for wisdom.

About 10,000 such disciples were with him. Each had to spend a period of 12 years. Days were charted in a reutilized manner. Each day, a student had to perform the assigned duties, involve in interaction with the nature and have certain activities which contributed to the well-being of the team. The student had to learn from teaching, do self-study, interact with people around, be in touch with the nature and take care of the physical health in such a way that generates and spreads the message of intrinsic learning.

This effort was around the teacher. The monastery, as an organization, was informal yet formal. Morning prayer, meditation and chanting, all these were the elements of collective programmes. Each person had to perform certain activities which were economic in nature. Other activities included being with the nature and with the society. The formal structure of the organization was understood in terms of their individual capacity to understand. The period of monastic education was identified, yet it was made often to take into account the individual differences in personal attributes.

The structure of the monastery of Yajnavalkya was as follows:

1. *Identity of the organization:* It was developed around the sage and teacher, Yajnavalkya, and named after him. The teacher himself was always the central attraction and the most important in most periods.
2. *Type of the organization:* It was a monastery where all students and aspirants of wisdom were to stay for a continuous period of 12 years to complete their effort to learn the truth. Deliberations or hearing were not enough. Each element of learning was required to internalize through the process of meditation or that of introspection.
3. *Method of functioning:* In the monastery, everyone was inducted as a member of a larger family, a family that is broad based enough to accommodate each person of the monastery in the larger identity of this informal organization. They had the options of collective eating, collective daily activities and self-initiatives towards functioning. Organizations that are poised like this always have a unique mode of functioning.

4. *Benefits accrued:* It was a purposeful organization. The central focus or the sage was to spread the message across, the message of supreme oneness which forms the core truth in this case. The idea of supreme oneness required to be perceived by different students from different angles. Oneness viewed by a person appears skewed and the oneness experienced by them is getting into the truth of the same. Each participant of the programme of study, apart from their core objective of studying, used to learn their ways of living. Experiential methods of study being individual specific, the emphasis was on developing a unique and good character to deliver through a series of good behaviour. The process being experiential, each individual had to learn things with individual perspective. But at the same time, the individual had to be in the mix of others—teams formed of a good number with a given agenda to perform and deliver. Thereby, they learnt collective living and objectives of being in the society with all the tenets of formation and maintenance of the society. Although in the midst of others in their activities, the participants had individual correlation with the master, as the master had ways to look into the functioning of each of them.
5. *Final objective:* The master had the final objective to see and ensure that each one of his students attain the wisdom of truth. It is this wisdom which was pivotal in spreading his doctrine of truth. Thus, each participant, on completion of the study, became self-realized of the supreme truth.

In the final convocation of the batch of students or disciples, the award was given in the form of a declaration by the master. This event appeared after 12 years of the induction of the person to the stream. However, if anyone fails to fulfil any of the criteria, he had to pass through another set of learning. The period of this varied from person to person. The approach to judge was twofold: one was the learning contents and the other was the character and behaviour of the person. Most cases of non-fulfilment were the overall attitude and certain other specific aspects of the character of the individual. Everything being favourable, cases were there when a student was denied of the award of the declaration of wisdom because of non-fulfilment of certain basic and required approached to the wide nature and the entire creation.

The organization of this kind was based on the fabric of respect, love, faith and dedication. Faith was first practised as faith in one's own intrinsic. Once the faith in the intrinsic is established, faith in all others including in the doctrine and the fundamental philosophy of the monastery were considered primary.

This organization used to follow certain styles in functioning:

- *Communication:* It used to follow unstructured, informal and verbal communication. In many cases, the core spirit was communicated through non-verbal ways. It was left to the realization of the person to understand the spirit of expectation and thus communicated to the appropriate person in the proper context.
- *Control:* The organization had the informal method of control. It was not the dictates but the voice unexpressed throughout. The control mechanism was expected to be the coordinating aspect of the organization. Being fully principle-centric, the organization used to give importance to the adherence of principles set for everyone. The twin purposes of control are principles of existence on the one hand and the quest for expansion of the same on the other.
- *Coordination:* The organization used to maintain the system of coordination through the mutual relationship established in the entire organization. So the duties of each person and the individual responsibilities were instantly understood by each person. Coordination was thus mutually supportive.

The master was considered as the nucleus of the organization. It was a dynamic situation. Whereas the learners were in the process and habit of learning throughout, the master was also constantly engaged in the additional and incremental learning. The objective and direction of this dynamism was aimed at the absolute truth. The discovery of the supreme truth was always incremental in the system. The master, already a realized person, had in his possession the supreme truth. But as the realization of the truth is unending, the master used to engage himself in further exploration of truth in his own way. As and when a new discovery was there, the master used to distribute the new discovery of truth to the aspirants of the system. The organization was knowledge-centric and wisdom-focused.

Purposeful organizations are diverse in their nature. Although they are diversified in their approach, functioning and profile, they have certain things in common. Most of these organizations are sustainable and have strong concern for wider mass of people. Most of these are founded on the basis of certain principles and perform on the basis of those principles. These organizations, though driven initially by one or a few great minds, function in an impersonal way and driven gradually by those people who are believers in those principles and sometimes may be respectful to those sets of principles. Either way, they devote to the doctrines of the founding personalities. This way, the governance of these purposeful organizations progresses and proceeds forward in the realm of destiny of life. During the pre-modern and modern periods, some of these organizations have risen, which are still on the growth path. Let us have somewhat highlighting discussions of these organizations and select one of those organizations carrying the impressions of the 19th and 20th centuries. The first organization identified is Ramakrishna Mission (RKM) and the second one is ISKCON. These two organizations belong to the same category of being purposeful in nature. The first one was formed in the year 1897 and the other one was formed in 1966. There remains a gap of nearly 70 years between the formation periods of these two organizations. The founders of these two organizations were two great personalities, Swami Vivekananda and Srimad Prabhupada.

Principles on which these two organizations are based have wide differences. Swami Vivekananda had established RKM and Ramakrishna Math to spread the message of Sri Ramakrishna, the great master of its founder and the principal idol. On the other hand, Abhay Charanaravinda Bhaktivedanta Swami (known as Prabhupada or A. C. Bhaktivedanta Swami) started the Hare Krishna movement. Swami Vivekananda (prior to being a monk named Narendranath Datta) became a monk at his early age. He did not marry, whereas Prabhupada was married (born in 1896, married with Radharani Devi in 1918) and had sons, Vrindavan Chandra De, Mathura Mohan De and Prayag Raj. Swami Vivekananda was actually a messenger of Sri Ramakrishna, whereas Prabhupada was actually a messenger of Shri Krishna Chaitanya Mahaprabhu. Swami Vivekananda had formed RKM with the twin objective of spiritual upheaval in the pathways of Vedanta, whereas Prabhupada had formed the International Society for Krishna Consciousness with a view to propagate Vaishnavism in the ways Bengal's 'Bhakti' Movement (devotional movement). The former was formed in India, whereas the latter was formed in the United States. The former being 70 years senior in age has proved its power to sustain over a period of more than 12 decades, having spread in many places in the world. The latter being just over five decades in existence has proved a very rapid growth in terms of its presence and getting connected to people. Whereas the former has grown slow and among the elite and middle segment of population mostly, the latter has grown among masses in various parts of the world, having reached the highest of being the second largest entity. The founder of the former actually had his journey from 1886, the year of departing of his master Sri Ramakrishna from his mortal existence, until 1902, the end of the mortal journey of the founder, whereas the journey of the founder of the latter was from 1966 until 1977, the year of his leaving the physical abode.

The founder of the former had basic inclination towards Vedanta—the philosophical view that considers god to be formless, eternal, omnipresent and omniscient—therefore, temples were without any form of god of eternity, but rather with the form of his master to have the basic and central figure in the idol of his master, Sri Ramakrishna. This is considered as an influence of the model of Buddhist way of functioning, the formless realized in the form of the person of Sri Ramakrishna. The latter organization did not consider the idol and form of the founder or his supreme master, Shri Krishna Chaitanya Mahaprabhu; rather, the forms and idols of Lord Shri Krishna and Sri Radhika Devi were established as the central figures in the temples. The supreme master of Prabhupada, Shri Krishna Chaitanya, had always immerged his consciousness in thoughts and consciousness of Lord Krishna and Sri Radhika Devi. That is why the idols of Lord Krishna and Sri Radhika Devi had been positioned as the central images and central deities. The images and idols of Shri Krishna Chaitanya Mahaprabhu had been placed additional to the central deity, and the idol of Prabhupada was positioned as further addition to these. The concept is that of Shri Krishna Chaitanya Mahaprabhu, wherein Mahaprabhu always visualized the Supreme one—the Brahmin in the form of Sri Krishna—Radhika Devi. Krishna–Radhika to them are in a form omnipresent and omniliving. They are present in every form, every life and for that matter everywhere. Visible in form, Krishna–Radhika are present in all lives, all perceptions, all understanding and all realizations. Being omnipresent and omniscient, they are present in all visible forms in all human consciousness. The divine consciousness thus merges with the human consciousness. The presence of the consciousness revives the human spirit, rejuvenates it and infuses divine spirit in the person. The mixed conditions of human spirit turn pure and noble in character. The human condition of a mixed nature turns unique and becomes a pure one without any kind of association with wrong and negatives. The person turns into a devotee of god. A devotee is one with total mind devoted to the spirit of god. Simplicity being the basic pattern of their character, the person is expected to be free from their ego. The ego self-tempts mind to consider oneself special because of whatever they possess. Their idea and design of the world are those of a position where they find a special status of their presence. A devotee is a soft, docile, simple person, who is pure in heart and mind, not greedy, devoid of anger, does not become jealous of others, and is never a prey to the desires for material gains and possessions; however, the position of the person is thus now converted into the symbol of purity. The devotee is a very special personality for the world and lives a lie of creative contribution to the world. They are selfless and for the world. They create a cohesive situation for every good element in the world. They with their selfless approach dedicate themselves for the cause and benefit of others.

A true devotee is non-egoistic, tolerant and truthful. They do all kind of work considering those as the work endowed with by the god. They do the work as inspired and intrinsically guided by the spirit of divinity from within. They work for and on behalf of their master. They think that the work that is endowed to them is the work given to them by their god, which is divine work to them. Their role is to perform under the invisible command of their god. As the performer of the assigned work, their duty is to see that the work is performed to the best of it. Being committed to the work alone, they wish to endow the outcome of the work to the master they have thought as the leader of the work.

A purposeful organization usually allows the performer do a better work than the other variety of organizations which have not yet been able to develop their purpose for organizations. A purposeful organization could be of any basic identity—whether gainful, neutral or the other type. A recent study by Robert E. Quinn and Anjan V. Thakor (2018, p. 78), titled 'Creating a Purpose-driven Organisation', reads, among other aspects, as,

According to economists, every employer faces the 'principal agent problem', which is the standard economic model for describing an organisation's relationship with its workers. Here is the basic idea: The Principal (the employer) and the agent (the employee) form a work contract. The agent is effort-averse. For a certain amount of money, he or she will deliver a certain amount of labour and no more. Since effort is personally costly, the agent underperforms in providing it unless principal puts contractual incentives and control systems in place to counter that tendency.

For a purposeful organization, the workplace is made attractive for the workers to make it a better place of work and then the workers try and devote to work in a better way. The purpose-driven organizations are expected to be of a superior type, delivering more energy into the system and creating a higher perspective for the system. The steps as suggested by this team, based on their research, are as follows: To envision an inspired workforce, to discover the purpose, to recognize the need for authenticity, to turn the authentic message into a constant message, to stimulate individual learning, to turn mid-level managers into purpose-driven leaders, to connect the people to the purpose and finally to unleash the positive energies. Finally, the team concludes with the following terms: 'So purpose is not just a lofty ideal; it has practical implications for your company's financial health and competitiveness. People who find meaning in their work don't hoard their energy and dedication. They do more—and they do it better' (Quinn & Thakor, 2018, p. 85).

DTE Energy, formerly known as Detroit Edison Energy, a company at Detroit in Michigan engaged in power, industrial projects, natural gas pipelines, gathering and storage of energy, marketing and trading, serves more than 2 million customers with a revenue base of more than 12 billion US dollars and total assets of nearly 30 billion US dollar. It has done extensive research on the issue of the 'purposeful organization'. The conclusion on the basis of this research conducted in the United States shows that employees are more intensely integrated with the system and the work when they are involved intimately with the purpose of the organization but being one with the purpose of their organization. Once the purpose of existence of the organization is settled and accepted by the people in the organization, the work gets a new dimension; when the purpose of the organization and that of the person are either homogenous or the same, the performer gets a higher level of motivation to deliver the work.

The finding of another important research on the healthcare industry has proved that passion and perseverance turn into a higher degree of performance. *Harvard Business Review* has published a paper by Thomas H. Lee and Angela L. Duckworth (2018), which reads:

High achievers have extraordinary stamina. Even if they're already at the top of their game, they are always striving to improve. Even if their work requires sacrifice, they remain in love with what they do. Even when easier paths beckon, their commitment is steadfast. We call this remarkable combination of strengths 'Grit'.

Grit predicts who will accomplish challenging goals. Research done at West Point, for example, shows that it's a better indicator of which cadets will make it through training than achievement test scores and athletic ability. Grit predicts the likelihood of graduating from high school and college and performance in stressful jobs such as sales. Grit also, we believe, propels people to the highest ranks of leadership in many demanding fields.

Like the previous case of making purposeful organization's basic purpose one with that of the performer, in this current research about the high achievers, grit of higher goal identifies high achievers. These high achievers do sacrifice in many aspects; they undertake a challenging work and deliver at a speed and dimension much ahead of others. Dedicated in their approach, they remain in love with the work, the organization. They are committed and dedicated. They love the work and the organization and are least concerned about their personal selfish interest. Grit operators are not only achievers in all respects, but they also keep on scaling higher and higher paradigms in their own ways to reach higher levels of business volume, business value and business coverage. The person also grows high in their personal life.

There are special types of people who work together to form teams. They are likely to possess certain basic traits with a certain degree of emphasis on them. Some of the their highlighting attributes are as follows: dedicated to work, have desire to work hard, have the urge to develop and learn continuously, and have a strong idea about the purpose. A person should have the sense of equating the purpose with the sequence of work, which thus makes a new scheme of priorities for the work connected and synchronized with the purpose of the organization. This has been further identified by Thomas H. Lee and Angela L. Duckworth (2018, p. 102) as follows:

If 'Gritty' individuals and teams are to thrive, organisations need to develop cultures that make them, in turn, macrocosms of their best teams and people.

So, organisations may benefit from making their goal hierarchies explicit. If an organisation declares that it has multiple missions, and can't prioritise them, it will have difficulty making good strategic choices.

Another danger is promoting a high-level objective that people won't embrace. In health care making cost cutting or growth in market share the top priority is unlikely to resonate with care givers whose passion is improving outcomes that matter to patients.

These teams are compatible with the basic view of commitment to the purpose and principles of the organization. The range and depth of commitment depend on the degree and extent of the sense of oneness with the organization; oneness does not necessarily mean being a part of the ownership of the company but belonging to the stream of activities and the flow of work for the organization. It is thus the closeness identified in terms of the priority activities and flow of actions to make the organization grow in the current period and sustain in the long run. Organizations in the corporate sector with ideas of gain have to see the light of success through the market indicators on the one hand and financial indicators on the other.

An individual performer in the system can go beyond just the immediate demand of the work context when the person has just been in tune with the design and purpose of the work. The performer then performs as an insider and as a person belonging to the stream of owners of the enterprise. Values that drive this consciousness in the person of the performer can be automatically gifted in their personality. Or otherwise, these values need a strong and sustained process of grooming. These elements of grooming go beyond the usual learning process and have to be through total involvement of the person in the system. Corporates do this through incremental gains in the process of earning benefits from the system, wherein it attempts to acquire things thought in principle.

Recent studies have finally converged to certain values and principles which are not common in the set of gainful organizations or even mostly in neutral organizations. The examples of two organizations that have purposeful existence actually represent certain types wherein the intrinsic qualities called *daivi guna* (divine attributes) are prominent.

Case Analysis of Purposeful Organizations

Cases of purposeful organizations as mentioned earlier have different origins. The first case about RKM shows that it originated in India with the concepts, principles and philosophies that have their origin in India as well. The second case, that of ISKCON, shows that it originated in America but was based on the philosophy and principles which are practised and cultivated in India throughout several millennia. Both have certain principles and values in common. Some of the highlighting common values pursued by both are as follows:

1. Dedication to the cause, resulting in the dedication to the spirit of the organization
2. Self-giving and attitude of sacrifice through selfless initiatives
3. Tolerance, endurance and resilience in the context of the work
4. Drive the engine of the organization towards the purpose
5. Make motivated and inspired efforts to expand the sphere of the organization in a manner that is synchronized with its purpose
6. Try to make creative contribution to expand the cause of the organization further to meet the increased requirements therefrom
7. The person acts as if they own up the work and the organization
8. Decisions are distributed across so that everyone is empowered to take decisions on their own for the best fulfilment of the organization
9. Constantly strive to add vital resources to the organization to make its purposeful existence more vibrant
10. The individual in this system shall enhance the scope of basic principles and values of the organization through living up those values and at the same time spreading the values across and throughout

The main attractions of the two organizations mentioned with a brief about them are the way of life based on the core principles and beliefs. They are based on the lives of their founding fathers and the principles they lived on. Those who have faith in those values and principles resolved to dedicate themselves for the cause of the organizations. In the current examples of two organizations, the grit individuals are all totally dedicated. They join the organizations as monks of the respective order. Monkhood is adopting a new form of life. Leaving aside the social living, these people adopt the monastery as their new homes. They wear a new type of robes suited to their ways.

These grit people who have left their personal contexts and joined the monasteries consider this as the new phase of life. A new identity is created for each, having given a new name. It is expected that these people do not keep themselves connected with their previous phase of life. New thoughts, ideas, styles of life, focus of life and objective of life make them highly motivated, efficient grit people. But the difference between those in the corporate sector working in their respective organizations for benefits is based on the focus and objective. Whereas both the categories of people have many common attributes, the differences are also remarkable. Monks in organizations, Rama Krishna Mission (termed as 'one') and ISKCON (termed as 'two') have superior positions with respect to certain values. They deliver superior value to the respective organizations and place themselves in the track of time to keep themselves updated. There are some distinguishing parameters between highly motivated and effective people in organizations one and two on the one hand and those of organizations in the corporate sector on the other. Some of the highlighting differences are as follows:

1. Although both types of people with grit quality have dedication for the cause of their organization, the type one and type two are truly dedicated to their organizations and their spirit. Their dedication is not affected by any changes in the material conditions.
2. Although both the categories have the element of self-giving and attitude of self-sacrifice, types one and two grit people are more intense in their spirit of sacrifice and its implications.
3. Although tolerance, endurance and resilience are common to both the categories, the quality and degree of tolerance, endurance and resilience are more intense in one.
4. Both the categories have purpose-oriented activities, but in the case of categories one and two, the extent of sustainability and effectiveness is more with a higher degree of orientations.
5. In the corporate world, motivation is associated with some kind of gains or achievements. These could be tangible or intangible or both.

When it is tangible, it brings in financial and/or material gains. However, if the gains or returns are intangible in nature, awards or rewards are in the forms of recognitions. However, those who are in the first or second category of organizations are totally dedicated. They do not have any kind of expectations. They draw bliss in the scope to be a messenger to establish, propagate and spread further the doctrines of the founding fathers. These make them always inspired to move forward and further to broad-base the application of the founding father's philosophy in the world.

6. Creativity is an intrinsic factor of a person. This is a commonly used and referred aspect of corporate management. The corporate approach to creativity contributes to incremental addition to the series of products and services.

Creativity is established through the set of thoughts, ideas, ideals and principles. Modern scholars have defined creativity as a combination of innovation and discipline. The corporate culture should promote creativity. However, this needs appropriate merit, skill, knowledge, passion and intent of the individuals involved in creative activities. This is sometimes through incremental or continued innovation. The factors of innovation turn out to be corporate value engineering. Let us add up issues which are pertinent to the scheme of things, which could be a combination of full range of products or services. Even on the issue of product segment or service segment, incremental addition gradually adds to the fulfilment of the new requirements of the market. Companies set aside their funds and other benefits to respect those contributions. The corporate world looks for meeting the requirements of the markets and tries to update the products or services accordingly.

Tvam agne brijina bartaning narah
Sakamanu piparshi bidathe bicharshane
yah shurasata paritakamye dhane
Dabhro bhishichat samrita hamsi bhuyasah.

(Rigveda 1.131.6)

I bow my head in total ovation to god. As we lack in the complete range of knowledge that you endow man with.

We solicit your presence in the realm of truth and wish to act accordingly things on the principles of truth.

In all situations or conflict you protect us providing inspiration for truth. You protect us always in all incidence of departure from truth. You inspire us and infuse strength in us to position us in the path of your truth.

Sages of the ancient Vedic era had their ultimate objective to understand the required basis of the truth of market and do things in such a way that it fulfils the objective of the company in the prevailing context of the market. Creativity or incremental innovation, whatever be the context, it is a positive value addition to the corporate. Value addition is surely physical and material in nature. Value engineering could be a sure growth track and multiplication in the business volume and business value.

Whereas profit-seeking corporates look for incremental value addition through a new face and contents of the products and services, purposeful organizations have a different way to understand that and make the creative additions to their contents and approaches. Truth remains the main focus for them. The process of unfolding truth as they have adopted in their organizations is intrinsic to the individual's initiative for the same. No reward or return is expected in any way by the true seekers of truth. It is, thus, the creative contributions which are all pure in nature. The discovery of truth of divinity, both intrinsic and extrinsic, remains within the scope of the person's domain of research or exploration for the same. Although there is no material addition of value, the intrinsic value of the organization enhances through identification of a new form of values. Surrender to god and consecration create a new identity through an enhanced set of values. These are all spiritual in nature. Purposeful organizations create an intense impact through these types of creations.

7. Attitude to work and work environment are very important for all types of organizations. Core people in purposeful organizations consider the given work as their own work and perform with utmost honesty and sincerity. However, gainful organizations usually function through allocation of work among people relevant for the work. Compensation in financial terms is associated with elements of work up to a level of fixed targets. Additional compensation in terms of financial reward or non-financial reward is associated with additional work beyond the assigned targets or limits of works assigned in terms of the volume or value of the work.

In both the cases, the person acts as a performer. However, the corporate world tries to integrate the scope of work with the persons involved. Lots of motivational models are in place which companies keep on trying through applications in such cases. However, all these motivational models fail to offer the desired results in most of the cases. The cost of having motivation in place is really very high. For every extra bit of things, the additional cost of involvement is higher than the usual. However, sometimes the gains to the organization are just little incremental and in some other cases it could be a multiplier, also bringing in fabulous gains for the organization. But still, distance remains between the work and the performer. Work, along with the flow of work and the desired destiny for the work, makes the context of the work mixed one. The performer sees the work from a distance in the beginning, and in the end the work has to get associated with the person or the performer.

The scenario becomes different in the case of purposeful organizations. Here, a person combines their feelings, emotions and aspirations with work. The performer carries an intrinsic feeling of the following:

Karmanayae vah adhikarah astu maa phaleshu kadachanah.

You have all the rights for doing the work yourself but do not aspire for any resultant personal gain out of the said work.

This principle has been conveyed in the Bhagavad Gita in the process of advices offered by Lord Krishna to his disciple Arjuna in the context of the war IN Kurukshetra as stated in the great epic, the Mahabharata.

A dedicated person belonging to the group of purposeful organizations therefore dedicates the work to eternity and does not expect to extract any benefit out of it. Then what is the factor of motivation for the person? This question has an ongoing obvious answer in the context of the work which elaborates that the person has a wholesome dedication to the cause, principle and spirit of the organization; therefore, the work pertaining to it remains a work intrinsic to the person and thereby it also becomes the best of its kind and always adds up to the basic spirit of the organization and thereby makes it truly holistic.

8. Decision-making is a distributive approach expected of the systems for the best implementation of the decisions into action. The corporate context maintains various approaches to select decision alternatives of different situations and approaches. The most important way forward for a corporate is to collect ideas and inputs, but the decisions for actions are taken keeping in mind the objective function of the organization.

Both decision hierarchy and work hierarchy are taken into account to take care of the flow of information available in the system for the best possible decisions in a particular set of realities. In the decision hierarchy, the most remarkable aspect is that involvement is considered with priority. Corporate decisions may adopt a distributive approach. The distributive approach involves most or all to take part in the process of decision. This process could be based on a rational approach, which would take the relevant parameters into account. The actual decision may or may not be based on the inputs. So the rational parameters have to consider all the aspects of rationality and its relevant related inputs.

Major decisions are coordinated and derived from the core objectives; however, companies may proceed to take decisions on a strategic platform in ways that are different from those of the basic principles and objectives. Fundamental differences occur between the gain seekers and purposeful organizations. The gain seekers bank on the expertise and knowledge of the market, whereas the purposeful organizations have wisdom focus in decision-making. Wisdom is the wholesome knowledge of the extrinsic and intrinsic twined together. Knowledge is the sum total of the understanding and facts behind the lives and the universe. First, one has to understand the visible and tangible aspects of the universe and penetrate deep inside the realm of things, leading to its proper understanding.

Yah vidyat sutram bitatam
yasmin notah prajah imah,
sunyam nah sutrasyah yoh vidyat
sa vidyat Brahmanam mahat.

(Atharva Veda, 10/8/37)

A person who has been able to understand and unfold the secret of the science and facts about the creation, he may attain the competence to glimpse the invisible, the creator behind the creation.

Knowledge derived from our understanding of the universe from the aspects of visible and tangible revelations creates the basis of our understanding of the creation in a way but establishes only a fragment of the wholesome truth that is revealed through our existence. The Vedic sages talk about life as a whole. The visible and tangible on the one hand and the invisible and intangible on the other together make the content of knowledge more or less total. However, the total truth still remains uncovered. Whatever we call intangibles in our normal parlance is something that connects with our empirical mind. Empirical aspects of our mind carry the reflections of the external world. Many times, this mind acts as a mirror of the outside world. Wisdom is experientially understood and realized in the world within.

9. Adding to the vital resources of the organization is one of the most important corporate objectives. Scholars have identified innovative cultures as a highly recommended system for organizations of a large or global scale. However, words of caution and in a way giving cognisance to the other side of the coin have also emerged as important. Gary P. Pisano (2019, p. 62), a professor of Harvard University, in his article 'The Hard Truth about Innovative Culture', has spelled out as the following:

A tolerance for failure requires intolerance for incompetence. A willingness to experiment requires rigorous discipline. Psychological safety requires comfort with brutal candour. Collaboration must be balanced with individual accountability. And flatness requires strong leadership. Innovative cultures are paradoxical. Unless the tensions created by this paradox are carefully managed, attempts to create an innovative culture will fail.

It can be argued, as Pisano has also picked up the points from management literature, that tolerance for failure, willingness to experiment, psychological safety, and highly collaborative and non-hierarchical organizations are the main components of innovative organizations. But unless each of these practices has balancing aspects and acts, they cannot be looked into as complete systems that benefit both employees and individuals associated with the organizations or not.

Enhancement of employees' personal worth could be through the process of career development or training development. The pool of knowledge and expertise earned as such contributes to the total amount of knowledge at a given point of time within a given area of territory or the society. Benefit accrues to the organization only when the value-added person contributes back to the organization with a view to apply the earned knowledge and expertise down to the system in a way that is best recognized as distributive knowledge and knowhow. Things pertaining to the knowledge and expertise could be deliverable and transferable to a certain extent, and the same cannot be obtained through a reserved flow of things. Other aspects of the distribution of knowledge and elements of experience are shared; still, the performance is one of the most important parameters in the corporate world, which is measured through rational parameters unique to the organization. As has been observed by Gary P. Pisano (2019, p. 65) on the corporate culture for competence-linked decisions,

---

People who don't meet expectations are either let go or moved into roles that better fit their abilities. Steve Jobs was notorious for firing anyone he deemed not up to the task. At Amazon, employees are ranked on a forced curve, and the bottom part of the distribution is culled. Google is known to have a very employee-friendly culture, but it's also one of the hardest places on earth to get a job (each year the company gets more than two million applications for about five thousand positions). It, too, has a rigorous performance management system that moves people into new roles if they are not excelling in their existing ones. At Pixar, movie directors who cannot get projects on track are replaced.

Effectiveness in corporate context is measured on the basis of the output given in financial or economic terms with respect to the inputs into that. People working at the upper level of hierarchy have to be more focused in their contribution to the company. Upper-level people in organizational hierarchy are more into leadership functions than just managerial functions. Even the most employee-friendly organization has to see the level of effectiveness of the concerned employee from the perspective of the organization's objective, mission and vision. From this perspective, vital resources are added to the organization. This way, the total knowledge content of the organization enhances gradually. The technological content, the content of value, remains either at the same level or enhances gradually. An increase in value makes the system gradually dependent upon those people who have achieved more than the expected value for the organization. Vital resources added to the existing level of resources bring in new prospects and possibly new identities. New prospects would always create the ways to add more and more in the same context. An organization looking for incremental additions of vital resources would look into the superior prospects for vital resources from the company and thereby create an additional value for the society or the broader entity of a nation or the world. An addition to economic value is expected to create a multiplier that impacts the system in such a way that the context of life in the new situations has to be benefited either ways. Value addition through this material arrangement or some kind of arrangement for services would provide a new meaning to life and activities. A new meaning has a new face, a new kind of revelation. So the value of the organization changes and in a way changes the brand and factors that make the pattern of the organization evolve. The features of brand also change. The symbol, identity and total contributions from the organization also change. This is how the changes through a vital addition finally affect the identity, functioning, takeaway and support to the society and system, and the world changes forthwith or on a gradual scale.

It occurs in a different way with purposeful organizations. In the case of a purposeful organization, the important operators for the organization breed in the effect of vital additions to the organization through the methods as mentioned below, adopting either any one of these or a combination of these:

a. Creating a platform with an objective to multiply the benefits or the value to be offered to a specific segment of population or groups of entities.
b. Creating a message which would contribute the benefits and effects of an individual or collective motivation in a way that boils down to situations poised to affect the equality by establishing a network of superior equality in the society, nation or world.

c. Creating front-runner organizations which would make the system and the net effects better by operating as unique or special subsets to the organization. This would mean that the organizations developed in such a way feed the system through their enhanced and broad-based presence.

In a way, the agenda is to magnify the scope of work of the purposeful organization in such a way that properly feeds and provides with the value primarily held by the mother organization. Multiplying the scope is actually multiplying the coverage of providing benefits across so that the unique message of this purposeful organization spreads across motivating people to be one with or to join the stream of activities with a view to further spread the philosophy or principle of this organization.

Addition of vital resources is actually now creating a vital message and extending the philosophy and principles of the organization to the meaningful application of the philosophy or the principle thus identified. This, however, may weaken the strength of the philosophy in terms of its purpose and basis of functioning. A purposeful organization creates enduring presence among those who have come to their fold to have the core aspects of their principle or philosophy, getting spread on the one hand and making the presence of these effective elements in such a way that provides new inputs for creating basis for a new situation on the other.

A purposeful organization stands way ahead of the gainful in creating social forces to add vital resources in order to have a superior value organization in place. Both gainful and purposeful organizations function in their ways to enhance the total value and identity of either of them.

10. Enhancement of the scope and purpose of values of organizations applies to both the sectors. Whereas the scopes are the same for organizations, the identity of purpose could be different. In this context, purposeful and gainful are totally devoted to the cause of each of the organizations. These similarities make distinguishing factors towards enhancement of the purpose on the one hand and leading that to perfection on the other. Organizations of these types are dedicated to the cause of the basic objective of each. In the structure of these organizations, issues that lead to transformations are always subject to undergo significant changes; thereby, not only the external identity but also the process and content of the organizations undergo changes.

Purposeful organizations create philosophical oneness with the broad universal reality. The cosmic reality thus opens up the contents with all aspects of the universal truth for us to realize. Vedic sages visualized this truth having been present through the cosmic system as follows:

Utedanim bhagavantah syamoth
Prapitwa Utah madhye ehanham
Uta udita madhavantah suryasya
Bayam devanam cha sugati syam.

(Yajur Veda, 34/37)

This world's nature has things which you do possess also.

Live in total harmony with them and
experience the grace of god in the vast sweetness of the universe.
Be blessed by the continued love of god.
The sweet down is continuously ushering the spirit of the nature.
The midday dazzling rays of sun shall strengthen your system.
The serene beauty of nature shall enhance the music.
That our soul rhythms with and
get back to lap of our universal mother in her unique creation
of this nature.

The philosophical view of a purposeful organization of uniqueness in approach has to be experienced and realized with appropriate sensitization of truth within. The cosmic truth which remains as a fact of life in the nature as a part of the universal truth requires experiential understanding of the same. God's grace in the form of the unique providence of nature earth on one hand and the impacts of invisible spirit of the creator as attached thereon is in need of understanding. The grace of god as reflected through his creation—the air, water, light, plants, animals, man of varied nature and other things of creation—including the inanimate things, all provide, radiate and distribute either together or discretely in the realm of the prevailing truth of creation. As it stands now as the revealed truth, one has to penetrate deep inside to consider the presence and existence of the inner truth and to penetrate into the realm of inner consciousness and to unfold the contents of inner consciousness towards the fulfilment of the wish of the creator. Having made this creation, the creator intends that the entire creation rhythms with him.

The world of modern corporations reflects certain realities which are cut off from the cosmic reality. The broader presence of these elements in the world rhythms a unique type of characteristic features, which are integral to the system and are apart from the objectives and philosophies or mission and visions of the organizations. A study conducted by *Harvard Business Review* on the best and topmost performing 100 chief executive officers (CEOs) of the world reveals certain basic trends followed by the best performing topmost ranked CEOs of the world. Turbulent times of economies and markets make the corporate leadership difficult and sometimes impossible to penetrate the focus shifts to steadiness and stability in the face of market chaos and forces opposing the steady progress of organizations forward.

In turbulent times, steadiness and stability can be significant virtues. These qualities are evident in the 100 men and women who have achieved a spot in HBR's 2018 ranking of the world top-performing CEO's. They face an array of outside forces—savvy competitors, demanding customers, and profit hungry investors, political and economic headwinds. Nonetheless their companies have shown a remarkable ability to sustain momentum.

One of the tests of any leader is how he or she adapts to a shifting environment. Among the biggest shifts companies face right now is in the global political environment. The rise of populism as a potent force is most apparent in the election of Donald Trump and Great Britain's departure from the European Union. For business leaders, especially in manufacturing, this has brought the threat (and sometimes the reality) of tariffs and trade wars, along with industry specific opportunities and challenges.

(*Harvard Business Review*, 2018, pp. 38–39)

Corporate focus is to always stand erect in the marketplace in the face of all odd things and different kinds of resistances that would always contribute to the basic make-up of the corporation. Profit-hungry investors and shareholders who have invested money in the equality of the organizations compel the CEOs to undertake such initiatives as to cherish and fulfil the essential spirit of organizations. In this approach, the focus of the organization is on satisfying the investors of all kinds, the institutional or individual investors always trying to fulfil the ideas of organization, and at the same time satisfying the demands of different stakeholders—shareholders, employees, customers, government and society—and apart from these, satisfying the demands of others connected with the system. While the organization requires servicing all the various groups of stakeholders, it has to fulfil the expectations of the different groups outside the purview of general stakeholders. Environment, social and governance (ESG) concerns have come over as very important in the face of emerging realities. Therefore, the leaders of business organizations have to maintain the demands of all stakeholders through an act of efficient balancing between and among conflicting and contradicting demands and then going beyond the boundary of the logical and normal demands of the groups inside. The concern for environment is now universal, and the concern for societies at the same time creates an appropriate and comprehensive focus on all aspects of corporate governance.

In their efforts to satisfy all different stakeholders in the way, they are always contended in the process to make them satisfied—happy and delighted. A corporate should try to fulfil all different demands of the stakeholders for its survival and growth. Broad-basing the ideas of the organization through different performing options, the CEOs have to be in a position to have it understood in such a way that the boundary of the operation has to be beyond the current period and move into the areas unknown or uncharted, which means getting into the future with the contents of the current period. This carries the legacy of the current period to combine the impacts of the past and current period coupled with the expectations of the different stakeholders through a continuous process that attempts to understand the various aspects of the corporation. Vedic sages had fully advocated the merit of carrying forward the virtues of the past to benefit the world in the current period and that of the future as well. A Vedic sage says,

Yatha iha anupurvam bhabanti
Yatha atha eva ritubhih yanti sakam
Yatha nan purvam aparou jahatu eva
Dhatasam yushi kalpah esham.

As the time passes one after the other, a new day carries forward the results of the previous day. The new season carries forward the resultant impressions of the previous season. Similarly, the successor should understand and accept the legacy of the predecessor. Let us all carry forward virtues that our elders have liked up to. For if the universe ordained, bet this be the order of the day, perpetually.

The process of carrying forward things of the current period to the periods in the future forms a part of the stakeholder services in the organizations. If we understand the presence of virtues in the living of our previous or ancient generations, we understand the impact of lineage in the making and formation of personalities who embody the virtues of the past and add the best things of the current period to chart out the optimum and most feasible dimension of coming up and formation of the inner spirit for the future range of activities through impacts of the future generations.

Goodness in life can prevail through all kinds of activities in both corporate and personal contexts. This aspect of the social life and connected realm can be considered as somewhat the basis of the new era.

The new-era organization would succeed the most through the process of balancing on the one hand and adopting the clear message for the benefit of the new world on the other. The world that we are acquainted with has made its wheel corrosive, having lost the process of smooth transition from the previous to the next position on the time frame. The time that completes its round and the time that knocks at the door of life have to be combined for this.

The rocky world has to learn the process and art of getting into the new life. The new life needs to correct its corrosive nature to make its wheel of progress smooth. This condition of human civilization has been identified as the human condition which has lost its spirit of making things smooth for human progress. The urge of human progress has been towards making a world that would be free from the differentiating parameters which would be in a way transformational. The act of transformation has to be taken into account in a way that positions a man as different from the creatures of the animal world. Compassion, integrity, self-giving love, honesty, cooperation, care, concern and fellow feeling, all these are intrinsic attributes of human beings, which differentiate a man from other creatures belonging to different species. The sense of love, compassion, feeling—these factors of human heart are lost in the process of civilization. As has been observed by a great poet, T. S. Eliot (2004, p. 72), the world has turned heartless:

> Here is no water but only rock
> Rock and no water and the sandy road
> The road winding above among the mountains
> Which are mountains of rock without water
> If there were water we should stop and drink
> Amongst the rock one cannot stop or think
> Sweat is dry and feet are in the sand
> If there were only water amongst the rock
> Dead mountain mouth of carious teeth that cannot spit
> Here one can neither stand nor lie nor sit
> There is not even silence in the mountains
> But dry sterile thunder without rain….

The observation of this great poet carries a strong sense. The progress which we earmark as the progress in the lives of the organizations and various segments of stakeholders associated with the organization is nonetheless a tangible progress that attempts to ease the lives of men on earth. This has surely brought in a higher degree of comfort, better facilities for movement, ease of work, technology-supported activities of life, better medical support, longer life, better quality of food, diversified aspects of living satisfaction and happiness derived from material possessions, wealth and tangible components of living. Still, the human journey through the pathways of civilization has been very stressful and straining, leading to lack of peace and permanent joy in life.

Material possessions can be achieved by virtue of a person's knowledge content. Knowledge earned through a process of continued competition in life brings in the factors for knowledge in life. It may be unique and a winner through a series of specific competitions in the society and life. The uniqueness of knowledge gets revealed through the uniqueness of the scope for its application in life and society. Knowledge of material science makes a person fit for the material domain of our existence. Knowledge for social, cultural, anthropological, psychological, biological, medical, technological, environmental, cosmic, water, ocean, air, gaseous, plasma and all other aspects of living make a person competitive enough to stand in life. Any of these areas is so wide and vast that it can contain all the treasures of life and enhance the span of life through a higher degree of satisfaction and enjoyment for life. The concepts and actual happenings of satisfaction and enjoyment help the biological functions to sharpen and thus bring in a higher span of existence. Material prospects of life are thus very important and make life stronger enough to move up and sustain for a longer period.

It is indeed the fact of the flow of life of human being in the world has become more smooth and stronger which is revealed through the facts that the average life of man has increased significantly. Not only that the span of life has increased, but the quality of life has also advanced. Now it is the higher basis of living that has provided with lots of satisfaction and joy. Life has become easier and man has higher options for getting medical support, higher scopes for better living, increased contents of life in terms of a higher degree of sources for information, more options to earn knowledge, more opportunities for fulfilling material desires of all kinds and fulfilling the urge to know the not yet known, the discoveries of so far unearthed, to scale high and high in the sky exploring the infinite sky on the one hand and penetrating deep down the bed of the seas and oceans for getting across the infinite pool of resources to fulfil the dream of human conscious mind, on the other.

Whatever be the gain or achievements in life, the loss of life is even greater. Life has gained profusely all aspects of material comforts and gains. However, the other aspect of life is also very remarkable. Life has lost touch with things that are natural in its origin. Things of nature have lost connections with day-to-day lives of man. Rapid urbanization has captured the modern minds. People have chosen urban living as a better choice, a superior destination in place of their previous context of living, which used to make lives associated with the elements of the earth. The lap of Mother Nature is no longer in a position to attract most minds; rather, most people prefer to move away to form close connection with the material comforts and material achievements. The balance in living, thus, is lost. Life has to depend on artificial contents. It is artificial contents of living that has embraced the lives of modern people and thus modernism has come forward as an opponent to Mother Nature. Thus Mother Nature has to reach out to people to deliver things to meet the demands of people through multiplier systems.

The multiplier systems are thus killer of the ambience and equations which make life pleasant. Life's condition was suppressed down to artificial supports to augment different functions of life on one hand and thus, push life to an end where the extrinsic are so much organized in a nice context but the intrinsic are burned to destruction of poise, peace and bliss of life. The inner peace, poise and bliss are lost in the face of rapid impacts of greed, selfish tendencies, wants and desires. All these are very high and always grow for the satisfaction of the next level of desire and want of life. If one desire gets fulfilled, it does not mean that it is lost; rather, the desire satisfies one end of it and then pulls in the next level of desire. The desire of a particular level is satisfied, breeding in the desire for the next higher level. The desire of one level needs to the fulfilled through not only providing the elements required for meeting desire. In that place, we need to see that desires of all kinds are frozen. They need to be set aside.

With desires which are vibrant in life, people develop a sense of deprivation through a consistent method of having a desire in place, fulfilling a part of it and then seeing a gap between the onset and development of it. A desire turns into greed once it happens in a way that creates a sense of deprivation—a significant gap between what is expected to obtain and what is actually obtained. This gap solidifies, strengthen and moves to the next level of need turned into greed. But the problem lies with the mode and process of the modern civilization.

Corporate organizations are the principal agents of the society and the world to carry forward the agenda of the modern civilization to create a need-based demand or demands that do not arise from needs. Needs are sometimes inherent in human system and sometimes they are added through the lanes of corporate process and progression. A demand is the initiator to the process of corporate agenda. All supplies of products, instruments, items and elements depend on the demand for each. Services provided are subject to the need felt for those. Need is the driving force. Corporates are happy with a higher degree of need. A higher level of need breeds in a higher demand. Each segment of products and services is positioned through a different mix of promotions or campaigns to attract the attention of people. Products and services are thus spread further through the depth and breadth of demands. This is a chain stimulator to the desires of people. Desires enhance through this process of corporate promotions. The result of this is satisfaction among many and accumulation of gradual dissatisfaction among even a larger number of people. Deprivation looms large. Desires mounting on one another increase the demand for the products and services on the one hand and impact the minds of many with the sense of deficit for not having that or not being able to procure and consume those on the other. Stress creeps in the deficit minds. A person becomes prey to the onset and process of stress.

References

Eliot, T. S. (2004). *The waste land* (p. 72). Faber and Faber.

Harvard Business Review. (2018). The best-performing CEOs in the world 2018. *Harvard Business Review* (November–December), 38–39.

Lee, T. H., & Duckworth, A. L. (2018). Organizational grit. *Harvard Business Review, 96*(5), 98–105.

Pisano, G. P. (2019). The hard truth about innovative culture. *Harvard Business Review* (January–February), 62.

Quinn, R. E., & Thakor, A. V. (2018). Creating a purpose-driven organization. *Harvard Business Review* (July–August), 78.

CHAPTER 3

THE ART AND SCIENCE OF MANAGING ORGANIZATIONS

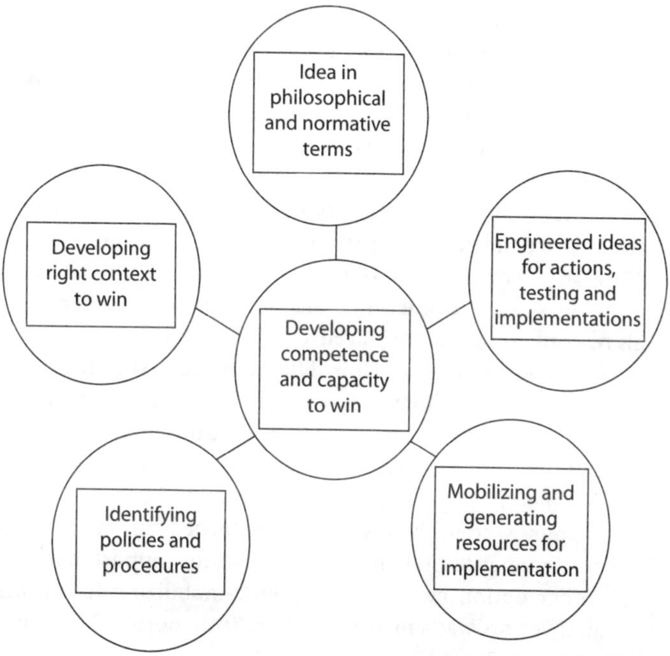

M4: First Design of Management

Management Begins with Man at the Core

Big or small, global or local, whatever be the feature and dimension of an organization, whether it is a new or an old organization, whatever be the age of the organization, man is at the core of management. In an organization of any kind and any dimension or duration, man is at the centre stage. Man being a psychosomatic entity, the rise of an organization depends on the ascendance of man in progression of the human journey forward.

All the management functions begin with an 'idea'. Whether it is a new business or an old or matured business, it is an idea that can make it grow or push it down to dooms. An idea is a product of human consciousness. It arises out of thoughts, dreams, observations, experiences, interactions and other similar human features. Management as a discipline begins with human ideas. Success and sustainability depend on the emergence of an idea.

Ideas are driven by dreams in most cases. However, there are many sources of getting ideas. Experiences in life may develop reactions to different experiences and incidents. They contribute to ideas when proved negative in life. Reactions to the uncomfortable experiences may develop more intense contents of ideas. A promising mind develops well-structured ideas and leads them towards an action agenda. In the world of industry, there are many examples of developed companies and organizations of large types and dimensions. India stands as a leading market and society where there are several such examples. In the background of Tatas having set up the first iron and steel factory in Jamshedpur, India, there was a historical piece of advice by a great monk of India, Swami Vivekananda, on board on a voyage from India to Japan. In Dhirubhai Ambani's endeavour to start diversified manufacturing and petrochemicals, the refusals by bankers to finance played a great role.

'Ambani', known better as Dhirubhai, was the first Indian industrialist to appreciate the ordinary investor and his needs. Asked once what the secret of his success was, he answered, 'One must have ambition and one must understand the minds of men.' His support for small shareholders stemmed from personal experience. First, he knew what it was like to be poor. Second, banks had often turned him away when he badly needed money to build his factories. So, for support, he turned to the only other option he had: 'The public-mobilizing funds directly from small investors was a major departure from normal practice at the time' (Pirama, 1997, p. 5).

Ambanis were the first large group of companies having initiated public participation in a large number towards ownership through each small investment. This had created broad-based, mass-based ownership of their group through shareholding distribution. Shareholding of a company creates a broad base of ownership. A company's ownership goes to all shareholders in the proportion of the share held by each. When shares are distributed around, with the ownership, the sense of belonging with the company also gets distributed. More people coming into the bracket of ownership mean more people standing by the company and its brand. A shareholder effectively acts as a sure multiplier of the goodness message of the company. They are usually expected to spread the message of company's quality in products and/or services and the power of brands, and highlight the goodness of its products or services as against the competitor brands. Public participation in the shareholding of a company enhances the chances of mass marketing or at least wider marketing. Larger the participation in shareholding, better the scenario for customer integration. The idea of involving a large number of people implies being transparent on the details of technology, process, materials, resources, utility, service and the process as a whole.

Ambanis were the first in modern India to involve large-scale mass investment in the primary shares of the companies. Public participation in business through distribution of ownership in the form of publicly available shares was a great step adopted by Ambani. Share participation in industrial organizations implies two different ways of enhancing corporate prospects.

These are as follows:

- Large ownership base of the organization facilitates public investment in the activities of the organization.
- Broad base of ownership spreads and strengthens the goodness of the brand, products and services throughout the market and economy.

If we want to refer to those achievers in the world who have moved up in the ladders of life, we find many legends having achieved and created benchmarks for the world. Zubin Mehta became legendary in conducting music; Muhammad Ali became the most famous boxer; William Shakespeare in drama, T. S. Elliot in English literature, Saint Paul and Swami Vivekananda in spiritual thoughts for the masses, Albert Einstein and Enrico Fermi in physical science, all of them individually pioneered their ideas and driven that to the realization and acceptance of the world. In the later period, particularly the period after the Second World War, close to 1940, the emergence of collective thoughts and practices came into the world stage. The emergence of new-generation technology had transformed the manufacturing system and the art and science of human living. Life's expectations had transformed accordingly.

Einstein indeed stands like a giant amid the pantheon of scientific figures of the twentieth century; his ideas unleashed a revolution whose changes are still being felt into this new century. What he did was to take our commonplace nations of space and time and completely alter their definitions. The evolution of physics in many ways traces this changing conception of space and time. And each adjustment in our world view—our cosmic frame of reference—brought with it an accompanying change in the physics of handling that new framework. It is the start of every physicist's musings: an attempt to track an object's motion in space and time. These intangibles are given names. Such as miles and seconds, and ever since Sir Isaac Newton all ready analyzed that falling apple, scientists believed that they finally understood the true meanings of those descriptive words. (Bartusiak, 2017, p. 5)

It is rare to find mega personalities like Albert Einstein in the modern period, particularly in the current scenario of the world. However, in the field of business, through commercial innovation of knowledge, huge magnitudes of breakthrough have been made. These have transformed the lifestyle, manufacturing process, business industry, way of living and focus of the world society. Management thoughts of pre-tech days need to be transformed accordingly. Pre-tech management's focus was on planning; now it cannot be so.

Peter Drucker had travelled in his thoughts up to the realm of objectives. Objectives that Drucker could think of have been basically synthesized with the traditional ways to manage an enterprise. These thoughts updated up to Drucker's addition of objective to it can be termed as the 'pre-tech management thought'.

Pre-tech indicates the period prior to the spread of the modern form of technology as it is in force already in the world now. Now the manufacturing end of a product involves less number of people; on the other hand, the distribution, marketing and servicing ends of the enterprises are out to involve people in those areas. People have gone to the finishing and consumption ends of products and services than in the making and manufacturing of it. It is enough of evidence across the world that people have taken a back seat at the producing end and have allowed machines with intrinsic automation to take up its place throughout.

This is simply another way of saying that a business must be managed by setting objectives for it. These objectives must be set according to what is right and desirable for the enterprise. They must not be based on the experiment or an adaptation to the economic tides. Managing a business cannot, in other words, depend on intuition. In fact in the modern industrial economy with its long time span between a decision and the ripening of its fruits, the intuitive manager is a luxury few companies, large or small can afford. And profit in a well managed business is not what one happens to make. It is what one sets out to make because one has to make it. (Drucker, 1986, p. 60)

In the context of Indian consumption, the emergence of Titan was a new taste. It paved the way to have a transformation from the existing mechanical variety of watches to a digital watch. Xerxes Desai pioneered in creating this new variety in the Indian consumption scenario with the first mover advantage brought in. Under the creative leadership of Xerxes Desai, Titan had the advantage of creating a space for wrist watches and other varieties. Wrist watches, jewellery and eyewear are the three major areas where Titan could establish its excellence in the eyes of Indian customers. In a similar manner, Tanishq and Titan Eyeplus got themselves into the mind space of consumers with the new aesthetic view and perception about the new product. The perceived space in the mind of people became that of respect and excellence. The perspective power of customer observation was made to be deeply foreseen in the Indian consumer market. It not only created brands having made a breakthrough in the marketplace but also paved the ways for the emergence of the special position of respect and love among the minds of consumers for watches, jewellery and specs.

Ideas drive down to imagination and creativity. The factors of imagination are those which are really associated with the formation of emotions that drive the issues of selection and purchase. People match their expectations with the providence or supplies in the market. Products catch the attraction of consumers in the physical or mental space. Combined impressions of such attractions create demands at the collective level. There are certain kinds of impressions which find common features with those impressions generated in other areas. A new product has to identify those factors within people's mind which are urgent or important in their approach and functioning. This importance has to be taken forward by the providers of products or services through induction of new products or services.

Xerxes Desai's grand imagination and creativity manifested itself in many ways. Perhaps the most visible of these was the very fertile partnership he built with his creative partner, the advertising agency Ogilvy & Matter. The early catalogue type advertisements of Titan watches were imaginative in themselves because such lush advertisements had never been seen in our country before. Then, he partnered with agency to take an astounding leap of creativity, which has rarely been seen in India. In a country where virtually no one understands or follows western classical music, he readily agreed to the use of Mozart's twenty-fifth symphony as the signature music of Titan. (Bhat, 2017, p. 101)

Markets are full of products or services that are currently present in terms of their prevailing identities. However, there are situations when markets are driven by new ideas and ways of having the products or services. An idea taken up by companies and operators becomes live with its translated form of a product or service. The product or service is expected to carry the image or impression arising out of the idea which had seeded the concept towards the formation of a product or service. The idea which is developed carries the impression of people and their expectations. The product or service may not be compatible with what was the essential expectation of people. It may drive further down to see that expectations are met initially at the level of the available offers and then at an enhanced level of the maturity of the underlying concepts into the forms of matured products or total services. This is how an idea gets translated into a physical material entity which can be offered to people for their consumption. The impact of globalization takes our ideas to different horizons to respond to various aspects of human living. A new technology developed by any entity anywhere in the world will actually impact the consumer choice in any other part of the world. The world has developed a wide range of similarity across the living style, quality of life and expectations in life. People on earth respond in a particular way with a lot of similarity from any part of the world.

Corporate activities are spread among various functions. Most important among these functions are marketing, finance, manpower, manufacturing, distribution, supply chain, retail, sales, administration, accounts, legal and other departments, which function distinctively, separated from each other, yet each one is connected with the other to deliver a proper value to the company. However, only the marketing department is equipped with appropriate customer orientation. In order to orient the entire company towards customers, each department should have the chance to understand them. Customer-focused decisions are the best of all varieties of decision-making. Data-driven insights provide inputs for leadership decisions. In all situations, the activities of companies attain perfection when these are based on customer taste, preference, choice and recommendations. The technology and process need to be reoriented in tune with customer-focused decisions in the enterprise.

Consumer neuroscience applies the principles of neuroscience to understand how the human brain responds to marketing stimuli, including advertising, packaging, point-of-sale material and product formulation—done in technologically advanced rigs where the science of EEG (electro encephalography, or the recording of electrical impulses along the scalp) is used to understand how a consumer reacts to a television advertisement. Unlike the conventional research, the consumer does not need to answer questions here. The consumer's brainwaves, when seeing an advertisement or a pack design, are captured using a wired cap placed on the head. This cap reads brain pulses 500 times a second and there is also a camera which tracks eye movements. (Bhat, 2017, pp. 134–135)

Brands and products are physical or intangible impacts on a constant scale over the mind of people. Any organization, whether it is for profit or not for profit, has to create its acceptability among people. For the corporate sector, profit is an inseparable aspect. The process of corporatization is actually a process in which people are involved in its functioning or output with a concern to create acceptability in terms of its design of products or services in such a fashion that its impact would be financially remunerative. Not only that, it should get the business running by creating surplus from operating. This surplus is normally construed as a profit generated from business. Business gains surplus only when it has adequate acceptability in the product or service market. It means that the concerned customers should find adequate interest in this business and buy their products or services at the mutually acceptable or market-driven prices. Customer orientation of each business is fundamental in its winning. That is why each one needs to update the business position from the customer's point of view.

'Share a Coke' was a campaign launched by Coca-Cola in 2013. This was a campaign specifically for the UK market. Coke began making and selling Coke cans which carried names written on it. It identified 150 names from the country. These were considered most popular among people in different areas. These names were drawn from popularly known people who were adored for their achievements in various walks of life. Each of these names was liked by a large number of people. With the product in hand, the consumer developed delight in appreciating it by identifying oneself as the identity of the famous name as identified in the product through the name that was scribed on the can.

This campaign, titled, 'share a coke', delighted consumers who lined up to buy cans carrying their own name, or perhaps the name of their spouse, partners, mom or dad. A year earlier (in 2012), the same idea had been a smash hit in Australia, where it had first been launched. In Australia, young adult consumption of coke had increased handsomely by around seven percent, after the launch of this campaign and traffic at coke's Facebook page had grown dramatically as well.

There were similarly positive results in the UK too. Consumer perceptions of brand improved on virtually every metric. The buzz around the brand was fabulous and coke suddenly appeared to be enjoying many more young adults. So, thousands of consumers, the mere thought of finding their own names (or loved names) on the iconic coke cans was simply magical. (Bhat, 2017, pp. 214–215)

Even prior to this experiment there was a 'get well tins' experiment run on tomato and chicken soup. In 2010, Heinz had launched the campaign. The company, already known for its tomato and chicken soup, had run the campaign to enhance the market share at a rate higher than the usual. The cans of soup were personalized by making labels bearing the slogan of 'get well' with a name written on that. Consumers were given a call to indicate their individual names while booking the orders for soup. The booking made online carried the names of the consumers. This paved the way for sharing customer names with the company and thereby allowing Heinz to gain a large number of new customers who took keen interest in possessing the soup can with their own names written on it. The personal involvement attached through this method appeared to those customers as a shower of good wishes, which kept on reminding them of the personalized service of the company that captured the heart and intent of the person. It was actually soul-filling for the consumers, and the brand got associated with the consumers' minds, giving appropriate emphasis on the total quality and affinity for the brand. This has spoiled the chain of connection and relations with the core value of the product and the perceived value by the operators of the market relevant for that product at the current period.

Most of the successful companies in the world depend on profit orientation through their strategies and actions pertaining to customer centricity. Companies oriented to customers need to develop appropriate eyes and ears to catch the flavour of customers' mindset, which is turned to be in a place in the market. Companies having oriented themselves to the market learn dynamics from the market about how they should respond to the market forces. This element of learning is common to all.

Customer-centricity and revenue growth go hand in hand. Overperforming companies are for more obsessed with customers than their mediocre peers. Customer-centricity is no longer an option, it is an imperative.

Three key dimensions of customer-centric growth in companies include: (a) the creation of total customer experience at all touch points, rather than just providing customers functional products and services, (b) a total obsession with customers across the organization, and (c) a strong customer insights engine within the organization, with data as its clean fuel.

A strong customer insights engine can be created by the insights and analytics function having a seat at the top table of the organization and also by unlocking the power of data. (Bhat, 2017, p. 130)

Functional areas in a business should be conversant with the customer demands. How a customer should respond to the action of a company and how they actually respond is a matter which is the practical point of understanding. The usual functional divisions of a company are normally apart from the continuous understanding of the choice, taste and preferences of the customers. With the change in time, customers keep on changing their positions with respect to a certain range of products or services. These products or services are usually governed by the laws and principles of the market. Sometimes customers get attracted to the products or services because of certain psychological factors; however, in other cases, they are driven by material parameters. Material parameters of choice may make the customers sensitive to them for a short term or for a long term. When the customers find more than one product in a particular category with variations in certain material aspects, they tend to exercise their choice in terms of one or more of those attributes. Once selected, they may not continue in general for a long period; however, there could be certain subjective factors which would make the selection durable.

In their endeavours to understand the factors leading to the exercise of the customers' choice towards buying products or services, certain factors figure out as important. Some of the important parameters are discussed below.

Understanding Customer Choice in Business and Society

- *Psychological factors* associated with the total product or service based on the perceived utility and goodness of the products or services.
- *Prices of those products with respect to the quality of the products or services.* At the same level of quality and availability, higher prices would tend to lower the demand for the products or services.
- *Distribution and logistics factors are important from the perspective of movement of products and spread of the services.* Better distribution and logistics for the product and ease of availability and scope for easy consumption would always make the product more attractive to the customers. This holds equally good for the services.
- *Material content of the product and effective utility of the services create the basis for a higher level of consumption of the product or service.*

Better contents of the products and attributes of services would make products more acceptable to the customers and consumers.

- *Underlying technology in making the products or services has a strong impact on the design, specification, finishing, packaging and basis of providing the services and creating the products.* Superior technology used in making the products and arranging for the services does create a better market for those products or services.
- *People involved in the selling, distribution, post-sale services and making of the product or those involved in the services matter a lot in the marketability of products or those services.* People inside the organizations do influence people as customers or consumers. When the vibration and consciousness of people within organizations do match with the consumers and the said range of products or services, the products or services move better in the market.
- *Favourable social and economic climate would always make products more and more attractive and services receive better attraction in the market and economy.*

Companies can follow certain principles to develop customer-centric attitude and orientations. However, there are various ways to design a customer-centric approach depending upon the following elements of the organizations:

- Objective of the enterprise
- Nature of the business or activity
- Demographics relevant to the enterprise
- Social–cultural–economic–fiscal–political–generic environment in which the organization is destined to function

Customer-centric attitude and orientation are difficult to prescribe and measure. However, some of these could be as highlighted in generic terms, which are mentioned below.

Highlights of Customer-centric Approach in Business and Society

- *The urge to know things from the universe of knowledge is important as* the knowledge acquired by a person is just a fragment of the total knowledge of the universe.
- Identify the gap in the existing pool of knowledge at the individual and collective levels. After the gap of knowledge is identified, there should be a positive initiative to fill it by acquiring a new set of specific knowledge.

- With the knowledge augmentation, the individual or group of individuals may grow overconfidence. For any organization in any context, anywhere in the world, this overconfidence is detrimental. Constant identification of the knowledge gap and augmenting knowledge thenceforth should be adopted as the process throughout.
- Constant inquisitiveness and probing into the market situations on the one hand and taking proper initiatives to implement those inputs into the affairs of business make the business grow properly.
- *Think smart, act proper:* Companies and organizations of all colours and varieties should try to proceed beyond the current limits of thoughts and activities. As an individual in the company and many individuals collectively within the said organization do not think that way.
- Organizations should create proper sensing systems through their eyes, ears and perceptive mechanisms. Each unit of an organization should develop its own way to understand the mind and consumption orientation of the customers.
- *Welcome the new emergence:* Organizations should learn to welcome the new. Particularly, the technology used for making the product or providing the service should be constantly updated. With the emergence of a new technology, the products and services take a new shape. It generates a new taste, new way of living life, new habits, new methods and new approaches to discover and takes forward a new agenda for implementations. This creates a new generation of business.

References

Bartusiak, M. (2017). *Einstein's unfinished symphony*. Yale University Press.

Bhat, H. (2017). *The curious marketer: Expeditions in branding and consumer behaviour.* Penguin Random House.

Drucker, P. F. (1986). *The practice of management*. Hasper.

Pirama, G. (1997). *Business maharajas*. Penguin Books.

CHAPTER 4

MANAGEMENT: SITUATIONAL RESPONSE SYSTEM

Organic ways to identify the process of human decision-making may be split between two levels based on the patterns of the response to the external stimuli. Basically, two types of responses are valid for the human system. These are: (a) conscious response (CR) and (b) autonomous response (AR). The AR system is basically comprised of a network of immune and fluid control system which keeps life safe and makes it easier in terms of the creation of an automatic system of behaviour of human organization.

The autonomous system is something that constantly monitors the entire biological and physiochemical system of a human organization. The whole human system has a well-guarded mechanism, which tries to identify any input factor which would identify any element that proves harmful or a potential problem for the life. As soon as anything harmful is perceived to be in the vicinity, life attempts to take care of that. The first protection is offered by the auto-immune system. Sometimes human emotions drive through a situation which stands beyond the logical limit of the human identity.

CR is based on reasons and general rationality. The general rationality is based on the choices, needs, preferences and understanding. There are the following situations:

- Urgent need for a certain activity
- Certain compulsions in life
- To complete the unfinished task
- To work for implementing new ideas
- To identify things available and visible around
- To identify financials for a work or endowment
- To calculating possessions and acquisitions
- Behaviour in a prescribed situation
- To collect and remember information
- Days' work schedules
- To learn agenda and process agenda
- To recognize the things around
- To create plans for days, months, years and longer terms

- To assimilate things from around
- To know the secrets about the world
- To gather knowledge of the world of matter and non-matter
- To connect memory with the forward thoughts

Collective Context for Discrete Response System

A discrete response system pertains to human behaviour with respect to the factors and stimuli which are basically differentiated by time, space, characteristic parameters or any other parameter which would involve the features and attributes in a manner that clearly indicates the uniqueness or identity of the element or entity for that matter. Whenever there is an elemental identity or a kind of identity which has universal presence in all, the fact of its being eliminated and unique is maintained to the extent that its features are apparently different from each other. But this apparent difference may not remain valid for a further period in the time scale of life. However, there are living cells and organic entities which function in a manner that appears to be unconnected to each other and stands apparently not connected with the system as well. In the language of mathematics, this has been transformed into a system called discrete linear time-invariant system (LTIS). This system plays a key role in designing most of discrete time-invariant entities function in a manner that resembles the flow of dust particles in cyclonic air or in a flow of light weight particles in a manner that appears to be a flow like molten of liquid materials but occurs in a way that are connected with each other on the basis of some principles but are actually different from each other. Flow of light as a bundle of minute particles collected together through a stream of things which support and fulfil the concepts of continuity in discrete phenomenon. Particles flow in a discrete manner as a part of the dynamism that concerns the discrete time signal in a composite. A visible phenomenon of a large number of pet animals passing through a corridor connecting their herds and gazing fields is in a random flow of discrete entities in a coordinated manner. If the elements in this flow are different from each other, the flow is judged in terms of linear discrete elements getting processed through a method of continuity. This continuity is a process. The flow of nerve signals in a human system follows at times of uncertainty this method of dynamism in its existence. Variables which are tuned to this flow or are connected with this flow make a system that embarks on the mechanism of 'being discrete yet functioning in a rhythm that makes a unified system'. This discreteness satisfies both the principles of linearity and time invariance. The invariance on a time scale can be thought of having the same kind of a feature in a sequence of space. Thus, the phenomenon, by obeying the principle of linearity, may involve into a non-linear curvature, which basically leads to spherical patterns as a continuous formation.

Intuitive or Perceptive Response System

The faculty of perception keeps a person ahead of their parallels. Often, the other observers or listeners miss the abilities to see, hear, have feelings or understand things, owing to being less observant, insightful, less capable or interested in knowing. Strong intuition is present in some, whereas the level of intuition is less in others. Professor Mark D. Hauser, Director, Cognitive Evolution Laboratory of Harvard University, attempted to identify certain factors which could be construed as the universal perspective capacity. According to him,

---

An alternative to the view of morality as emotionally driven comes from thinking about the problem in the same way that the linguist Noam Chomsky has thought about language—an alternative that I have adopted in my own research. This idea supposes that all humans are equipped with a moral faculty, a cold computational system that evaluates the moral permissibility of an action based on what an individual believes and intends, together with an evaluation of how his actions cause particular consequences, some good, and some bad. Thus, in the same way that a Chomskyan perspective proposes a universal grammar to account for the similarities in structure and pattern of acquisition of all languages, as well as to the nature of neural breakdown, so too many we propose a universal grammar to explain similar aspects of our moral system. Only recently this view has been explored on empirical grounds. (Charter, 2010, p. 130)

Perception involves two aspects of the same reality. One of this is the visible or empirical reality; the other one is the eternal dimension. The same truth reveals in differentiated form in different situations or to different people. Perception takes beyond the limits of our normal way of understanding things. To perceive is one way of getting into the doctrine of the world of invisibles and playing into the court of the world of visible things. The world of visible is confirmed by its existence through the organs of senses, whereas the world of perception is based on the understanding of the inputs which come out of the inner domain of an individual. On the one hand, intuitive understanding is based on the knowledge of things, which is important for snapping the things within and outside. The world of works is apparently based on the rational and scientific principles which are actually turned to the principles of action in the world. On the other hand, the spirit of work is based on certain other principles which have the roofs ingrained in the nature. These are universal principles. The inherent principles of this universe are based on the principles of life and sustainability. Certain unseen methods and principles are there in the living and growth of this universe, which need to be discovered and applied as the governing principles of life. Collective living—live and let live—should be the universal spirit of things and life. Intuitive or perspective response system (IPRS) is formal and informal at the same time and is based on the universal spirit.

Perception plays an important role in social life and the interactions between individuals and the society on the one hand individuals and activities on the other hand. Corporate decision-making is based on a rational process mostly involving empirical scientific methods, but many of the important decisions are based on perceptive and intuitive methods. Intuitive methods are based on subjective understanding. Knowledge and expertise that remain at the base of the subjective understanding of things play an important role. Perceptions and intuitions are important in human life. Intuitions act as a guiding instrument in many situations. This is particularly very important in sudden incidents, quick transactions and critical situations. Groups of people busy in certain activities are involved in situations where a collective initiative is dependent upon intuitions and perceptions which anchor in the group dynamics.

Composite Behaviour Patterns

Human behaviour is a product of a comprehensive impact of the intrinsic dimensions of the person on the one hand and the impact of the inputs from the external world on the other. The basic set of attributes is understood from the factors of impact within and the factors of impact outside. The basic genealogical attributes' function is the life based on the total attributes of the intrinsic world and those derived from the outside world.

The way we experience the world is misleading. It feels like a one way process: light reflected from objects outside in the world strikes our eyes, signals are transmitted to our brain and we then see the objects. But how is it possible to have hallucinations, to see something when no signals are striking eyes? The answer is that perception is a two way process. The crude light signals striking our eyes are never sufficient to tell us what is out there. We have to interpret the signals on the basis of our long term experience and our current expectations. Then our brain can predict what signals should strike our senses. Our predictions will not be quite right. But errors are vitally important since they enable us to improve our guesses. (Charter, 2010, p. 195, quoting Chris Frith)

As has been identified by Professor Frith, the short-term and long-term experiences of human beings play an important role and shape the course of responses based on the basic inputs which the person inherits in the formation of life. The neural networks present in the human brain preserve the information at different points and situations in an autonomous manner as also in a conscious way. Composite behaviour occurs when the human mind is free from all impacts but consolidated on the chosen input signals from where the behaviour arises.

The human biological system depicts various layers of decision-making and coordination. This applies to a general natural system and remains an influencing force for all different types of future activities. The biological patterns are obviously structured in a pattern that contributes to the strength and inspiration to good attribute. The general natural system if adopted makes a system sustainable to the extent that creates and maintains the vital to make an organization grow on the path of accomplishment to fulfil the expectation of the makers of the enterprise. The progress of an organization takes place through addition and adoption of a new range of products and services through a method and basis that certainly involves the subjective approach of the organization.

The conventional tools we all learned in business school are terrific when you are working in a stable environment, with a business model you understand and access to sound information. They are far less useful if you are on unfamiliar terrain—if you are in a fast changing industry, launching a new kind of product, or shifting to a new business model. That is because conventional tools assume that decision makers have access to remarkably compute and reliable information. Yet every business leader we have worked with over the past 20 years acknowledges that more and more decisions involve judgements that must be made with incomplete and uncertain information. (Courtney et al., 2013, p. 64)

Management Process: Traditional View

Traditional thoughts of management involve certain steps. These are as follows:

1. Planning
2. Organizing
3. Coordinating
4. Communicating
5. Controlling
6. Feedback

Every act of management is supposed to involve a planned process. Traditional thoughts of management begin with plans. Planning is a process in most of the cases. It is also unitary. For a large system, it may involve many functional divisions. For a unitary system, however, it has to be comprehensive. In a small unit or a small activity, even functional planning is involved. The objective of the activity or the entire set of inputs needs to be coordinated. Functional plans are meant for understanding the situation in the current moments and extending the factors towards a period in future. Factors present and the impacts of the process in the future reasonably guide the contextual change. An organization of any type gains life's form through this method. This process may be all-inclusive and comprehensive.

Plans are settled facts with respect to certain decisions. Decisions are made of available variables in the process. Ideas contribute to various activities. Generating ideas is the fundamental and starting point of management as a key to planning. Generating ideas is the starting point. All ideas do not materialize into the doctrine of work. Most of them die out. Among the various ideas generated, some see the light of implementation. When an idea gets a seeding, it needs to be substantiated through the process of seeing the light of days. Refining of ideas requires refreshing questions which would always try to explore through the ideas and see the prospects that ideas would generate pathways to actions for implementations in the given context. As observed by Brooks and John (2018, p. 63),

---

Questions are such powerful tools that they can be beneficial perhaps particularly so—in circumstances when question asking goes against social norms. For instance, prevailing norms tell us that job candidates are expected to answer questions during interviews. But research by Dan Cable, at the London Business School, and Virginia Kay, at the University of North Carolina, suggests that most people excessively self-promote during job interviews. And when interviewees focus on selling themselves, they are likely to forget to ask questions—about the interviewer, the organisation, the work—that would make the interviewer feel more engaged and more apt to view the candidate favourably and could help the candidate predict whether the job would provide satisfying work. For job candidates, asking question such as 'what am I not asking you that I should?' Can signal competence build rapport, and unlock key pieces of information about the position.

Sometimes, or most times, the way questions are put across leads to the understanding of the intrinsic dimensions of ideas. Once the ideas are allowed to unleash, the scope to implement those ideas increases. After we get the ideas, the phase for making plans begins. For the same kind of things to be done, a number of ideas arise. Now the question is: How to identify the right idea? In order to select one of the many ideas, the following methods are usually adopted.

Selecting Ideas for Implementation

- Rational functional method (RFM) to identify the best idea
- Intuitive judgemental view (IJV) to select an idea

Scanning of ideas requires either of the above-mentioned methods to come to a clear understanding on the outcome of the application of those ideas. RFM may be applied through any of the biological patterns of command and control system: functional coordination system, situational response system (SRS) or collective context for discrete response system (CCDRS). The other method may involve an IPRS or composite behaviour patterns (CBP). Whereas most companies in the professional world depend on the ideas generated in the system, the new economy organizations, in particular bank on ideas to make the business grow. It is in this endeavour that new economy companies give most prominence to ideas. While structured methods are there to test the ideas, there is hardly any method available to get ideas unleashed.

Ideas are human specific. These can be obtained by means of threats, coercions or even persuasions. The best ideas are products of free minds and free environments. However, a mind with an inbuilt quest to search things of either intrinsic or extrinsic elements to discover certain aspects of truth may do so in any environment. Research organizations attempt to understand truth in a structured manner.

Hierarchy in Organizations

The command and control system in an organization paves ways to structured assessments of ideas but hardly gets new types and faces of ideas. Bureaucracy can assess ideas but cannot create ideas. Gary Hamel puts across the matter as follows:

Though mindful of its evils, many people believe bureaucracy is unavoidable. Dimon remembers an outside adviser who defended it as the 'necessary outcome of complex business operating in complex international and regulatory environments'. Indeed since 1993 the number of manager's supervisors and administrators in the U.S. Workforce has grown by more than 100%, while the number of people in all other occupations has increased by just 44%. In a survey by Harvard Business Review, nearly two-thirds of respondents said their organisations had become more bureaucratic in recent years. Peter Drucker's prediction that today's organisations would have half as many layers and one-third as many managers as their late-1980s counterparts were woefully off the mark. Bureaucracy has been thriving. (Hamel & Zanini, 2018, p. 52)

Ideas Form the Seed of Any Business

Any activity requires an idea or a set of ideas in the background. An experienced wind has the scope to form one or more ideas which have the potential to prove success, whereas fresh minds have the potential to develop ideas that may take any shape. Failure may occur in both the cases. However, amid failures of a large number of cases of getting ideas, there are a handful of ideas that see the light of success. Some of these ideas get success in a short while, whereas other get success in the long term. The depth and spread of success for different ideas differ widely. Whereas ideas can be inclusive of elements from around and within, they can be exclusive as well. Intuitive ideas are sometimes realistic and again may be based on dreams. Big dreams push forward to develop big ideas. Dream-driven ideas carry the potential to be vast in their philosophical backdrop or idealistic context. Dreams drawn or infused from various aspects make the idea see the light of success. This success depends on the conformity of the elements which have a real basis for any agenda that requires to be put forward. Big dreams drawn from the facets of life push through big ideas. In the case of Reliance Industries, an idea had played a very basic role. Mr Dhirubhai Ambani had the dream to develop a world-class company with world-class technology, world-class manufacturing process and world-class quality of output, maintaining world-class process in the internal system.

This example has been identified by Piramal (1997, p. 8) as follows:

Dhirubhai's modern way of thinking brought into play his second achievement: the idea that Indian manufacturing could and should be world class. He was the first industrialist in India to build facilities which could be compared to the best internationally, both in terms of volume of production and quality of output. 'My commitment is to produce at the cheapest price and best quality. He insisted time and time again. 'Think big, think fast, think ahead,' he would exhort colleagues.

Before getting into the major business of petrochemicals, which achieved the final magnitude and awesome gains, Mr Ambani did burn his fuel of life in tiny to medium to semi-large enterprises, involving trading, merchandising and distributing activities. The dream of a mega scale and international standardization help streaming of ideas when these are generated in the mind of thinkers and people of promised activities.

Dreams are usually unstructured. In his analysis of dreams, Sigmund Freud has identified a dream as either a reflection of or something drawn from the cultivated thoughts of significance or the spirit of things associated during the works and activities of life. Whether these are drawn from within or are a reflection of cultivated thoughts, actions or experiences, dreams are the elevators to a particular scale of achievements in life. Ideas may be self-generated, crafted based on part inputs available, or gifted or transferred by someone. Knowledge of things or of unknown aspects may contribute to the formation of certain outlines of ideas. Rest is the initiative of the person designing the ideas.

Certain ideas are tested on floor by the person and certain ideas could be there which start getting implemented as soon as those are formed. Intuitive picking up of things towards having the ideas in place of the running stream of works may work wonders. Many such amazing achievements have occurred in the event of crafting ideas towards getting success.

Scientific ideas may emerge out of the sequence of events or set of the flow of reality apparently available, or it could be a culmination of rational elements of life to achieve a certain basis of life which would leave apart inputs to a better life. Certain aspects of the universe that are not yet properly known remain a question before scientific minds. These are ideally minds which are open to understand those phenomena of the universe which matter to us. Gravitation, for example, is a mystery before the scientific minds throughout; however, the impact of the force of gravitation on certain particles or entities is unitary or composite forces. Sometimes exploring the facts about it may lead to intuitive decisions in the field of science.

Scientific ideas may or may not evolve through a structured process. However, each scientific process has its own unique ways of getting the physical truth out of its natural sequence to a form that could benefit the human society in any way. In this way, changes in a scientific process have to account for the so-far undiscovered elements of the physical identity of reality. Missed-out dimensions of the scientific truth are always open to new discoveries. The ideas missed out at one stage of scientific development get revealed at the subsequent phases of development. One such case of missed-out dimensions as not thought of by Sir Isaac Newton but later noticed by Albert Einstein is as quoted below:

Of course, the anomalous precession of mercury was already known, and general relativity could explain it. But Einstein also predicted another effect, which Newton and others had once pondered but never pursued. As soon as physicists reliably thought of light as a wave in the nineteenth century, they generally assumed that it was different from matter, that it was immune from gravitational attractions. General Relativity, on the other hand, asserted that light must be bent that is, be attracted by massive objects like the Sun, just like matter. More than that, the attraction would be twice the bending calculated when Newton's law of gravity is used. The extra contribution comes from the wrapping of space-time, especially near the mass, an effect that Newton's theory couldn't account for at all. (Bartusiak, 2017, p. 48)

Scientific ideas keep on changing. Ideas of science change with respect to time and advancement of knowledge. The wave theory of light could explain things more or less, except for certain questions and mysteries which could not be explained altogether. The general theory of relativity tried to give answers to those questions in its own way. Matter is subject to the pulls of gravity. However, the gravitational pull on light is only possible when it is exposed to large objects of masses like the Sun or large-sized stars. Light has been identified as a particle called photon. Being massless, when it is made to pass through large objects with a gravitational pull of huge magnitude, the pathway of the flow of large beam of light gets pulled towards the large-sized objects of the magnitude of the Sun, large stars and so on. This beam of light that flows through comprises of a large bundle of photons particles. Although considered massless, light quanta of photons do possess the characteristic features of a particle or a group of particles. Thus, there has been a fundamental change in the pattern of thoughts about a very basic cosmic endowment, light. Scientific ideas, thus, keep on changing even at the fundamental level. At each stage of the emergence of scientific thought, the basic premise of structured rational view of things has to be reviewed as new ideas that attempt to replace the existing ideas and are quite often developed in the intuitive way than through rational methods.

Sixth Sense of Business

Intuitive ideas of things and forces in a business develop over a period of time. Those who have experienced a business know how the business forces work on the aspects and practices of business. Listening to business helps us develop and earn the *sixth sense of business*. Every business practice has some unstructured and unidentified aspects of the business. The rhythm of business is actually heard by those who have really absorbed the process of business. Practitioners in business, particularly the managers and business leaders who have been able to get into the work and transaction of business, develop certain added faculty which can make them enjoy the what about of business through a vision of the future. A vision is what presumably pierces through all barriers to see the likelihood of the things in future. This is actually called the prophetic vision. Prophetic vision is seeing through the barriers of time. It is actually seeing the apparently unseen, hearing the apparently unheard and feeling the causative vibrations of transactions through a method of detached understanding. In other words, 'intuitive decisions are important component of decision-making.'

The faculty of sixth sense is developed through certain steps, which are as follows:

- Intuition
- Intention
- Creation
- Informal communications
- Conformity
- Adoption to practice through gradual inclusion of the ideas

Whatever be the shape of things, it is always taken into the realm of things as if tested throughout in organic ways. The tasting process, however, requires the rigour of firmness in the understanding of things. In his own biography, the book titled *Made in Japan*, Mr Akio Morita (former Chairman of Sony Corporation), while explaining the process Sony Corporation could adopt, has emphasized the spirit of the sixth sense of business as one of the most important ways to take a brand, an enterprise, forward.

Two options were available before the company:

- To produce in Japan and sell abroad with the tag 'Made in Japan'
- To produce at the destination and sell in its market

The process was to apply technical tools and arrive at the right decision, whether to have the Japanese brand produce in Japan and sell in Europe through the identity of 'Made in Japan' or bring the technology and get things manufactured at the destination and sell in regions around.

Final Recommendation for Decision

Usual technical tools had confirmed the first mode of business, which means to produce in Japan and sell abroad with the tag 'Made in Japan'.

The final decision by the company was the other way round, that is, to produce at the destination country and sell in that and adjoining regions. This was based on the intuitive judgements. Intuitive judgements require a huge amount of real-life experience of the entire business and most parameters of the markets. Otherwise, the decision may be subject to a lot of dark areas in the business process, leading to business loss or business debacle. A mix of proper knowledge of how a business functions and experience of the business from the core of it makes the personality of leadership of the business competent to take a decision on the basis of intuitive judgement.

This decision could lead to a wide business with enduring and long-term existence and growth in the west.

Intuitive judgement supports the wider perceptive basis of understanding things. This, at the same time, triggers off new opportunities. Once an idea takes its grounding and seeing, opportunities do open up for the stream of other related activities. Planning comes after ideas. Once an idea is coined, then only the plans may be made to fulfil the idea and drive the action forward.

Management decision-making has two broad components as has been highlighted and explained before. However, there are other methods which have also delivered good or sometimes great achievements in business. Rational decision science generally considers the past behaviour of a business in a particular context and builds on that to create a forecast or predictive model for the future of the business. Among other models which have created a huge pathway in organizational management, the most important one has been *principle-driven or philosophy-driven organizational management.*

Examples of such organizations have been given in the context of sustainability. Examples of the RKM and ISKCON have been mentioned in that context. It depends on the strength of the concept or the philosophy that whether it is going to be durable and successful as well.

References

Bartusiak, M. (2017). *Einstein's unfinished symphony.* Yale University Press.

Brooks, A. W., & John, L. K. (2018). The surprising power of question. *Harvard Business Review* (May–June), 63.

Charter, R. (2010). *Mapping the mind.* Phoenix.

Courtney, H., Lovallo, D., & Claske, C. (2013). Deciding how to decide. *Harvard Business Review* (November), 64.

Hamel, G., & Zanini, M. (2018). The end of bureaucracy. *Harvard Business Review* (November–December), 52.

Piramal, G. (1997). *Business maharajas.* Penguin Books.

CHAPTER 5

LEADER MANAGER: ART AND SCIENCE OF MANPOWER MANAGEMENT

The art and science of manpower management mostly concern human beings. Traditionally, it has been termed as 'manpower'. Although the term has actually a narrow focus in managing human beings in organizations, on a usual scale, it has the same meaning for human beings in general, as a man and a woman both meant by the term 'manpower'. The prerogative of a manager is to have certain understandings in the art and science of functioning. Some of the important elements of that understanding are as follows:

- The primacy of the factors related to human beings in the business or organizations.
- Understanding of the dynamics of human beings as an entity and human organism from the fundamental perspective of the world of work and living.
- Role of a person in an organization.
- Synchronizing the requirements of a role in the organization and the actual capacity and attributes of the individual in the organization.
- Identifying the job and role responsibility and selecting the right persons accordingly.
- Developing a proper system of information of human power in the organization, identifying the gap that remains from the ideal set-up, becomes important.
- Identifying, sourcing, inducting, properly developing and deploying human power in appropriate positions in the organizations.
- Motivating employees to devote their energy and mind towards obtaining productivity as an individual and the functional groups in the organization.
- Swinging the ball of corporate agenda to roll faster with a higher level of efficiency, productivity, effectiveness and dedication towards achieving the corporate goal needs to be reviewed.
- Tuning people towards creating a synchronized environment within the organization so that the human energy finds total involvement in the affairs of the organization towards fulfilling the objectives of the enterprise.

- In order to survive the competitions in the markets, the organization should have such manpower that has the required excellence to thrive the wheel of growth amid all competitive forces present in the market.
- Organizations should create an exit barrier by way of creating additional space for added mental satisfaction of the employees.
- Adaptation to technology should always be the mindset of the top management, and the manpower plans should be designed in accordance.
- Corporate manpower policy should have the policy of encouraging people to learn continuously.
- Learning organizational environment should be created to sensitize the opening up of individual potentials under the corporate umbrella coverage.
- Ethical rectitude should be the agenda of the manpower department for which the organizations should develop a corporate policy for organizations.
- Manpower policy of the organizations can be oriented towards the ecological competence of the world system.
- Human attitude of service can be infused in the manpower of organizations.
- Leadership is realizing the intrinsic potentials of a person and transforming the personality to make the prospects reveal into the practice of life.
- Human resources (HR) has to identify the elements of commonness among the people and foster these elements forward.
- Diversity sometimes leads to the conflicts of attributes in groups with diverse identities; human resource management (HRM) as a function has the responsibility to put across the elements of diversity for creating cohesion among these elements of diverse identity.
- Homogeneity in the spirit of work and collective thought has to be one of the important areas of focus for the HR manager.
- Discipline in terms of time to be devoted to work has to be made very essential for an HR manager.
- The spirit of work has to be transformed into the spirit of dedication, and the HR manager requires to be a person having enough capacity to induce motivation among the people of the organization.
- Reward and remuneration are automatically associated with the system and organization involving any kind of manual process or human intervention.
- Continuous improvement in personal skills and attributes becomes an integral component of the corporate organization.
- Concern about the quality of work done or the quality pursued is an automatic contribution of the person; HR function needs to identify

that concern in the individuals and try to enhance the content of that in all possible ways.

- Every person working in an organization has a proportionate responsibility towards the well-being of the organization; an employee should be made to understand the same.
- Rights of an employee should be conversant with the duties undertaken by every employee of the organization; the HR function has a strong responsibility for that. Each person in the organization should develop a feeling of belongingness and take care of the duty first and assert the authority with responsibility.
- Extra-organizational inclinations should be kept aside, and a person belonging to an organization needs to work with full loyalty to the organization.
- Individuals should develop matching involvement to the work of the organization, devoting their full mind towards the work and development of the organization.
- The private interest of the employee should take a back seat, prioritizing the interest of the organization.
- Collective consciousness of the people in the organization should develop the collective power to create a new destiny for the organization and prepare the individuals in accordance.

Factors for Managing the HR Function

Certain common factors are very important for a manager leader of the HR function. These are some of the composite elements of the whole managerial functions for which a person is destined to address the issues of the core functions of the corporate managerial activities. The HR function, so to speak, involves the intrinsic aspects of an individual and the extrinsic component of it. The intrinsic aspect is solely dependent upon the understanding of the nature of the intrinsic contents and at the same time to focus on the company's fundamentals to connect the intrinsic contents of a human being with the goals, plans, strategies, possibilities, prospects, constraints, obstacles, challenges, opportunities, emerging dimensions and so on. This could be in concern with the industry to which the company belongs, the economic region within which the company works or a part of the global environment that the multinational company works in touch with.

Basic Factors for Efficient Management of HR in an Organization

A manager needs to understand the basic imperatives of managing HR in an organization. The basic factors can be divided into three broad

Figure 5.1 Trio Parameters of Managing HR

categories. The trio parameters essential for clear understanding in the beginning are as follows (Figure 5.1):

- Analysis of the external environment of the company, spanning across the socio-economic and market-driven environments in which the company operates. Also, the trends of the socio-economic patterns, environmental factors, natural disasters, any emergency and any other type of exigency.
- Analysis of the internal environment of the company, spanning across the objective of the formation of the company, the core philosophy of the company, shareholding pattern, ownership pattern, company's policies towards the broader environment in general and policies towards efficient manpower management.
- The academic attainment, professional attainment, competence, character, attributes, skill set, values, possibilities, potentials, prerogatives, aspirations, motives, choice, taste, preferences, wishes and objectives in the life of the individual engaged or to be engaged in an organization.

Basic activities as per the usual understanding of the HR function are mentioned in the following section. Although there is a general understanding of the same, the focus or emphasis is related to various variables. Human resource information system (HRIS) has the potential to bring home the impacts of different parameters of the industry, competition, economy, regulator, fiscal, socio-political scenario and any situation having an impact on the business and value of the organization.

Understanding of the Basic Function of an HR Manager

Once the policy of managing HR is identified and the policy is dovetailed to fit in the corporate strategy of the organization, the regular functional activity of an HR manager sets in. As the regular functional activity of an HR manager is focused on to the immediate and short-term period, it is required to be properly placed within the broad gamut of the overall philosophy and values of the company. Given this background, the immediate call of the HR manager stands as shown below.

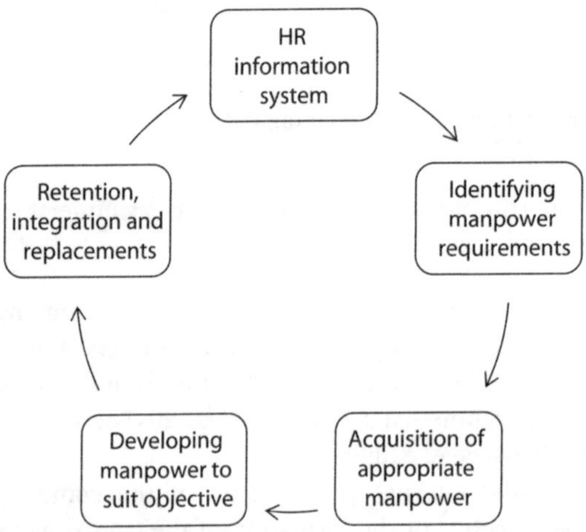

Although these functions are all between the individual and organization, it is an essential mix of things that the manager of the manpower function has to deliver and discharge in the functional domain of the manpower management.

Human Resource Information System

HRIS forms the basis of managing the corporate HR function. It gathers information about the manpower possessed by the people in the organization. Primarily, with this objective, HRIS was identified to be in place. It is a computerized system for keeping the set of information about the manpower of the organization which is globally located and spread across the people of the world and working in the organization throughout the world. According to this system, the process would be identified as the guiding source of input that would create the basis for global-scale management of the HR function of the multinational functional organization. This information system is primarily known as the information provider; however, this goes far beyond the boundary of the factors of information and becomes a true source of the crafting of the strategy.

HRIS is responsible for gathering, holding, processing, assimilating, analysing and distributing information. It is also responsible for reverse utility, management control, manpower compatibility and utility, performance and reward management, role- and scenario-matching, special purpose functions, financial and fiscal compliance, cost efficiency, profit centre, value and resource optimization, investment analysis, capacity utilization, product/service orientation, customer interaction, sales orientation, marketing competence, motivating and training people, functional development of people, professional development of people, developing and maintaining integrity, ethical foundation and ethics function of the organization.

The HR analysis, developed by the HRIS, is actually a basis of the total analytic of the manpower of an organization. It is not just the set of information; rather, it is a kind of dynamics of knowledge that not only maintains the inputs of knowledge but also maintains a creative platform for knowledge for an organization. It requires a large unit of inputs that are essential for the organization to garner and to analyse the basis from there. It is actually a set of data or a dynamic framework of the application of the data making an ongoing basis of the same for the benefit of the real essence of the understanding of the basis of the flow of certain attributes of organizations.

HRIS is a pool of knowledge that could be known as the basis of the application of the same pool of knowledge that is available in the organization. Knowledge is an available basis of the manpower. This information system gets the organizations the way to select and decide on the inputs of the knowledge for the best utilization of the HRIS in the context of the organizations in the world. Although scaled for a global organization, it is universal in the factors of manpower management in the context of the world.

HRIS, a knowledge-based system, is a complex model of a set of information that requires the utilization of the system of the organization that has the basis of the contents and complexity in it. The knowledge-based system is always probing into the realm of the inputs through a different mode that makes it always accessible to the framework and utilizes the strength of the content for the benefit of the purpose of the organization. A minimum amount of requisite information can also be the basis of a focused organization. However, for a large organization, it grows into a gradual complexity of the system. Complexity is in the aspects of searching, retrieving, testing, selecting, applying and assimilating in the patterns of the organization. The entire mechanism of the knowledge retrieval system is actually a basis of the near outer-inner dialogue for the organization. The computerized system, initially developed as HRIS, was actually an expert mechanism with somewhat complex algorithms that can be assimilated and disseminated towards the optimum acknowledgement of the process and its total effective application in the context of the organization. However, with the further development of the system, this expert system has attained the proportion of an artificial intelligence (AI) in place for the organization. HRIS has already become an effective contribution of the AI in practice for organizations.

This smart and expert digital system containing several millennia strong data stores for the organization can be easily retrieved into the proper set of advisory inputs for use in the organization. The processing capacity of the organization's data source and its effective utilization in the context of strategy formation are essential.

The smart system has been contextually included in the dynamic framework of the software and its mode of applications in the context of the organization. The information system uses inputs that are versatile in terms of effectiveness and scope. It can be applied for an industry, an economy and larger context of identifying HR. It depends on the nature and extent of data input into the system whether it can be of use for larger canvas of global spread. Larger the capacity of the computing system, stronger is the basis of the input factors for the organizations in the domains.

The human environment is always dynamic. The changing scenario is common always. It is drawn from the similarity of the functions of the human brain. Neurons are the right factors for the organizations in the context of work and activity. The complexity of the neurons performs a certain set of input data and finally gets back to direct decisions in the context of human activities. In fact, it is the day-to-day activities of a person which come out as a function of the complex system of the neural mechanism. Neural network contributes to the direct, easy and focused choice of the person in the individual context of the person and the collective context of the people in terms of the people in the organizations. It performs the same way as the new ways of living the individual life of organizations. It is always a systemic approach that can make things smarter, in a way, to make a better choice for the human being. As the human brain works in a dynamic frame of things, the HRIS works in the same dynamic way. As such, the dynamism works in the pattern that is usual for the organic system to make things happen; in the fashion, it attempts to retain and retrieve the inputs towards making a new way to create the designs of the system.

This system is actually always changing and making inroads into the process of the prior happenings, but the creative contribution of each of the inputs have to be in place for a better solution. It has certain important features. Some of these features are as follows:

- HRIS is designed to add, integrate and redesign the input factors to have the right terms of inclusion of those factors in the ongoing activities of the organizations.
- Any change in the strategies of the organization has to be included in the activities and plans of action as depicted through this information system.
- Data science, applied to the big database, would apply automatically in a way that provides the inputs for the dynamic platforms of the systems. It may recognize data into various categories, linear and non-linear. If it is not a linear or otherwise, the data inputs of the systems would apply into a collated system of the organization that devotes to its orientation of being into a space of the system of the organization.
- Data inputs into the system always make it happen in such a way that retrieving is contextual and situational as and when it occurs for the benefit of taking a final choice in the context of an organization.
- A conceptual cluster of knowledge is essential to analyse, apply and then keep in the data source of the organization in question.
- Frequency of retrieval and changes in the contexts are essentially inbuilt in the HRIS for use in the current period or future.

The set of algorithms could be of two-tiers or multi-tiers in the systems. Multi-tier algorithms would imply the random distribution of inputs. This can be used to assess the performance of a large sales force of a multinational multiproduct megacorporation spread across various parts of the world. Each national-level entity of this megacorporation has its unique impact on the various attributes and influencing parameters drawn from various aspects of the markets and economies and the global trends of the same.

'Technology of real essence required for the implementation of HRIS is AI and various aspects of its applications in the field of business and enterprise.'

Knowledge enterprise also helps in the augmentation and growth of required and added knowledge content of competent persons in the organization. It refers to the physical system of acquiring knowledge through formal and traditional ways. The manual information system is available and in force for a small- and medium-size domestic companies. Most companies follow this process and are always making the basis of a new-age learning organization through traditional ways.

Identifying Manpower Requirements

The requirement of manpower in an organization is done in a segmented manner. The process followed is essentially spread across the various functions, cultures, activities, territories, dimensions, legal environments, political environments and overall objectives of the company.

The combination or mixture of career elements in an organization is actually important to understand to decide on the type of person for a specific role. This requires some of the highlighting aspects as follows:

- Description of the role—this requires the identity of the role in the context of the work and the organization
- Identifying required attributes and attainments to fit in the role with all its considerations
- Maintaining the work process so that the optimization of time and energy spent into the system is considered pertinent
- Selecting the right framework of the induction process so as to make it worthy of the ideas and strategies of the organization
- Budgetary implications of the process and the role–person compatibility within the boundary conditions of the company
- Role identity for the future period—considering the market trend of the role and estimating the trend of its movement forward
- HR analytics to identify at what level of knowledge and mix of experience the person is expected to deliver the best result
- Fixing the company's policy with respect to the orientation to train people once on board or get them ready to mix
- Having the design framework for the manpower mix in a particular function and offering the individual an opportunity to grow within
- Identifying corporate values and creating a requirement of that mix of value and skill in the individual

Choice Matrix for Individuals in an Organization: Acquisition of Appropriate Manpower

Based on the type of role, the acquisition process occurs. It could be at the bottom or directly at the top of the hierarchy. The method is a matter of choice by the organizations.

Acquisitions are tuned to the specific requirements and attributes of a person. Usually, acquisitions are a market-driven process where

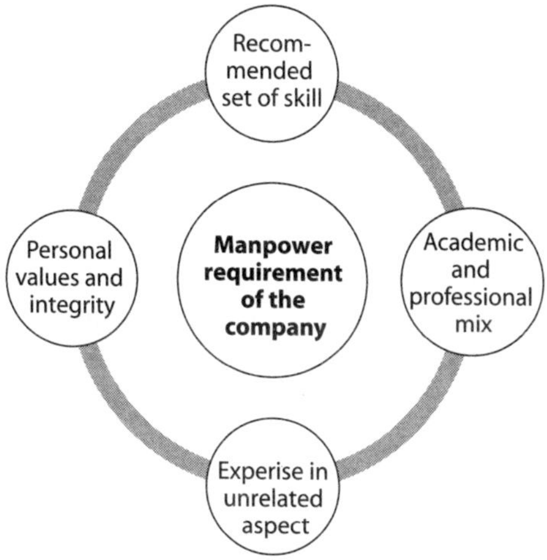

logically the best persons as per the choice matrix are obtained through the recruitment activities of the company. Many cases are visible where the company does not take the burden of doing the entire gamut of activities leading to sourcing the right person to fit in the right position in a given context of the externals and the objectives of the company.

As shown above, the following are the areas that the HR manager should take care or do the oversight control when it is outsourced to some organization professionally competent to handle the same.

These aspects are as follows:

- To prepare a recommended set of quality, skill set, attributes, personality matrix, experience, expertise, personal values, personal integrity, personal choice, taste, preference, orientation and attitudes to life.
- Academic and professional mix as specifically required to deliver the best result being into the position of the company. The market standard for the same would be essential for the HR manager to understand the benchmark in this agenda and set action plans in accordance.
- Multi skilling is one aspect of the job but in most of the middle and senior positions or strategic positions of a company, the manager has to have extra potentials to handle eventualities in the process of taking the corporate agenda forward in the most efficient manner as compared to similar others in the market. Therefore, the company would look into the potentials in the person to take care of things which arise as and when situations prevailing around undergo a lot of

changes in the factors of activities of the company. That is why companies would look for additional potentials or extra competencies of the person in a particular role.

- Each company must develop its own philosophy of being and the outlook or the reason for being into existence in the market. The company's own policy of values and ethics should be explicitly made available to the public. The HR manager should be conversant with the implications of the employee not fitting into the corporate values system of the organization. Each individual inducted in the company in the middle of the hierarchy or a senior level should be tested on the generally pursued values with respect to the factors of activities in an organization and the specific aspect of personal integrity.

Once these parameters are taken care of, the company obtains the best mix of a person to grace the position. Thus selected, the person is expected to be of best rewarding to the organization.

Companies have the right and prerogative to continually develop the persons having positive attitudes towards the organization on areas of skill development and technology upgradation. A knowledge-based enterprise would always look into the attitude of the person towards:

- Learning for organizational development continuously with a view to contribute through work for the organization in the current period and the future—c11.
- Learning for personal attainment without any kind of concern for the benefit provided to the organization—c12.
- Be positive in the work and assignments and try best to deliver as far as possible—c21.
- Be into the work and assignments without anyway committing to the delivery of that in the context of the company or the work situation—c22.
- Open to the challenges in the works and assignments—c31.
- Given a situation with a certain amount of challenges makes the person psychologically averse to the content and domain of the work—c32.
- Oriented to accept personal difficulties even to benefit the organization—c41.
- Will to deliver as per the remunerations available in the system—c42.
- Finds it committed to the organization as it is said to be the place where the intrinsic value of the organization is actually the motive force behind the person being into it and focus on the organization as the place which is as close to the person as the personal entity of the

person's intrinsic is. Being trustworthy and having trust on the system and organized entity in which work is being done—c51.

- The person thinks that financial value is the measuring element and not the pleasure of being into the fathom of the organization—c52.
- An insider and at home in the organization of work—to grow with it in all respects, to be with the well and wane of the organization equally and to be by the side of the organization during the trying times of the market and the society—c61.
- The organization is viewed as the steppingstone in the ladder of career. The person has a self-view of an outsider and finds in it a place until the career objective is fulfilled and an alternative of matching prospect is available in the market within the reach of the person at the run time. The person is an agent and element of trade in the market to push forward the personality in the manpower market for the purpose of obtaining the highest trade value from the market. The person is thus focused on the financial valuation of the personal career and poised to be a tradable commodity in the market wherein the commodity is placed on sale at any financial value significantly higher than the existing one. Values, culture, integrity and love for the organization are measured by this person in terms of the financial value attained now and the prospective financial value for the future—c62.

The above analysis puts across opposing tendencies of a human being in the context of work and habit of the human being in the context of the current world. The set of attributes which have been mentioned above follow a particular pattern. It is that all second numerical, as mentioned, being '1' denotes the positive attitude of a person in the organization. The other variety that is where the second numerical is '2' denotes attitudes which are treated negatively in the context of the organizations. This means that 11, 21, 31, 41, 51 and 61 refer to the positive attitudes of a personality, whereas 12, 22, 32, 42, 52 and 62 represent the other set of attributes considered negative for any organization.

'Attitude makes a difference in an organization. An HR manager has to possess a strong positive attitude and identify people to work in the organization with the strength of positive attitude.'

Training and Development Function of an HR Manager

Training and development occupy one of the most important functions of an HR manager. The purpose of this activity is to keep the manpower updated to the need of the present time and possibilities for the future.

Basically, this activity is done through the institution of a learning organization to act as a facilitator of the program of training and development. Also, this activity provides a unique opportunity to the employees and members of tenured staff to access the avenues of development of the organization.

In order to impart training and develop the person holistically, the organization needs to follow certain procedures. Some of the highlighting areas of these procedures are as follows:

- *Training needs analysis (TNA):* This is obviously the foremost activity to understand the need in specific terms against the designated people in the organization. This requires a thorough analysis of the existing quality matrix of a person and the gap as understood by the experts in the system. The objective of this activity is to identify what is the type of training needed and why.
- *Training to satisfy the objective of the organization:* Whether the training is going to satisfy the company's objectives in a particular functional area or not is the core issue. However, the company may like to have a proactive approach in this.
- *Creating a focused group to face future challenges:* In order to create a focused group of people competent to face future challenges of the market, a company may like to develop a new team to become what the company expects them to be.
- *Technology and machine learning:* This is particularly an issue in the field of technology learning for the concerned manpower for future requirements. As the shape of technology is changing fast, creating an advanced team to fit in the future requirement is a proactive stance of the company.
- *Application areas:* The field of such technology application could be in the processes, systems, structures of business, communications, features of the business, new designs for products, AI for functional activities, a new combination of languages, new business model and so on.
- *Formulation of training agenda:* A company needs to formulate a training agenda and its contents for each field of activity.
- *Placing the trained personnel on board:* This requires placing the trained personnel in the right positions and activities with the new set of responsibilities.
- *Test of assimilation:* It is the training imparted to people in organizations.
- *Budgetary implications:* Budgetary implications of the training and the prospects for revenue generation through that require to be planned for.

- *Training and development:* These are the institutional activities within the organization which assess their ongoing impact in the productivity, efficiency and effectiveness of persons in the organization. Training and development have an impact on the profitability of the company and the brand value as well.
- *Employee motivation study through training:* It is given to those having trained and the others outside the coverage of the training program of the company.

Trained persons should perform better and different than others, maybe to create an emotional impact on the entire organization. This should be revealed through the periodical or annual performance appraisal of employees in the organization.

Performance Appraisal: A Knowledge-based Action

'Organizations in the world are trying to move forward with the agenda of acquiring and disseminating knowledge. Proper performance appraisal requires a knowledge-based application.'

Knowledge is an ongoing responsibility of an HR manager to ensure that a proper understanding and appreciation of knowledge takes place in oneself. Also, the need to forward the elements and inputs of knowledge in the personality of the managers of different functional areas in the organization needs to be understood. Knowledge has a general connotation widespread in the world of learning, but in the context of work, it is more inclined to the scopes for application than just normative aspects of it. Thus, the concept of 'knowledge' needs to be reviewed in the context of the work and organizations.

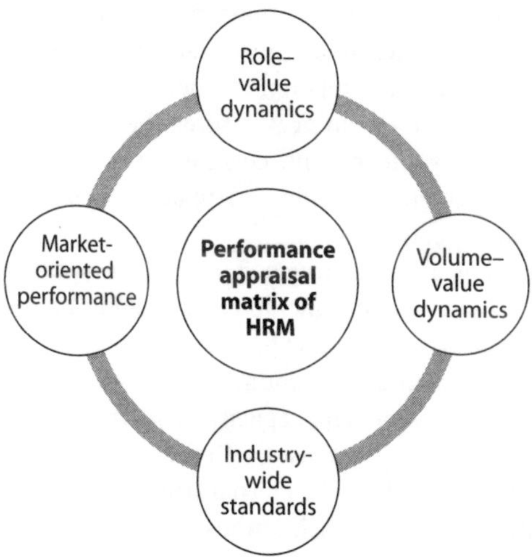

Types of Knowledge

There are two broad types of knowledge essentially present. These are:

- *Eternal knowledge:* This refers to the knowledge of the ultimate truth of existence. Eternity is something that is neither influenced by the passage of time nor by any incident of occurrence in the world, either in the present, past or future. Eternal is infinite and absolute. Knowledge of that absolute is possible through the intrinsic process of realization of God, the supreme as a part of self-management.

  The realization of absolute truth may have any nature, the formless void as an existence, void with any symbol, void absolute, any form of God, any form of the descend from God or in any other way to understand the truth of existence which is the actual reality of life on earth and presence in the universe. However, for all practical purposes, people tend to avoid this aspect of our understanding of knowledge to avoid any controversy or not to involve in anything that does not have corporate or organizational relevance.

  Eternal knowledge is personal to every individual. If a person embodies the same, the character of that individual elevates to the character of a divine personality. It makes the individual automatically full of honesty, integrity, truthfulness, cooperative, dedicated and selfless in work and life.
- *Empirical knowledge:* Knowledge is roughly a combination of an act, a fact or body of facts and principles as accumulated by humans. Normally, it is understood as having familiarities with certain things—concepts, facts, procedures, languages, abstracts, places, ideas, customs, theories, principles, identities, subjects, objects, personalities, products, services, associations, nations, environments, climate, nature, air, earth, water, small things, large things, technologies, practices, business, industry, relations, understanding, perceptions, art of life and the science of physical nature, chemicals, mechanics, electronics, electricity, life, oceans, cosmos, technology and human creations of instruments, machines, artefacts, objects and many other innumerable aspects.

  Knowledge is assumed to get stored in the complex structures of neurons. Neurons are innumerable, assumed to be several trillion in numbers. Each is connected with other segments. An average human brain is assumed to be of around 3.3–3.5 pounds in weight. It is assumed to possess the data capacity of several million or trillion in bits. This data capacity increases with the cultivation of the functions. For a person in search of the eternal truth and doing regularly deep concentration through meditations and other deep devotional modes, the data capacity enhances infinite times. Therefore, the knowledge possessed by a truly spiritual person is infinite. A truly realized person acquires and possesses knowledge that covers in principle the entire range of empirical knowledge and in addition, spiritual knowledge, as well.

Empirical knowledge may be:

- Factual Knowledge
- Perceptive knowledge
- Hypothetical knowledge
- Heuristic knowledge
- Meta knowledge
- Epistemology of knowledge

Factual knowledge: This aspect of knowledge depends on the elements of data and information. Data leads to the formation of knowledge, but it is itself is not knowledge. It is an input to build knowledge. Similarly, information is also an input to the creation and development of knowledge. Whereas data bring in objectivity in the knowledge, the information could be either objective or subjective in nature.

When applied to performance appraisal, data refers to the quantitative description of the work performed as against the set target for the same. The magnitude of work, frequency of work breaks, frequency of new work adaptability, the quantum of work units performed within the specified time limit and so on.

Apart from the fact of life, job- and work-related information is required to assess the factual knowledge. This has an information component. A wide dimension of this information pertains to the qualitative aspect of the work. For the work performed by the individual, a company needs to set standards for maintaining quality.

Quality standards may be as per the norms of the industry, any other broader entity or the market also. Conformity to quality is the desired task for the individual. However, any deviation from that has to be measured in both qualitative and quantitative terms.

The deviations and departures are actually measured to identify the position of the person in the quality matrix for the work. If the work involves participation in a process or a dynamic system, in order to measure it properly, a random scheme is recommended in most of the cases. The work and activities of the executives of most companies operating at multinational or transnational scale are standardized. Therefore, the performer is aware of the individual role in delivering the work and its domain of activities. The standard thus set is something to follow.

If the individual has the knowledge about the objective of fulfilling the agenda for work and action, then they need to know the target of the work, standards of performance, quantum of work, frequency of output, volume of output and specific quality of output so that the person has the opportunity to keep track and comply.

Perceptive knowledge: In medical transcription, a combination of data and perception is presented in the fact sheet of the patient. The fact sheet, thus, involves the available data about the physical condition of the patient, for example, measures of temperature, blood pressure, drugs taken; basic statistics of the patient and other factors of the person also contribute to the data to be provided to the doctor. However, the doctor also needs from the patient the perceptions about the condition of health, the mental framework, personal understanding and so on.

Knowledge of this aspect of the patient contributes to the perceptive knowledge for the case. When the patient provides a personal understanding of the case, it contributes to the perceptive knowledge. Perceptive knowledge, thus, depends on the prejudice, belief and individual psychological background of the person.

Perceptive knowledge is used in various multi-product, multi-located, and multinational corporations (MNCs) in the world. Perceptions of the senior or top management play a very important role in the performance measure of middle-level or senior-level executive in many companies.

The kind of perception thus formed may be out of any incident, the response of the individual in any matter of importance or some other relevant matter. Perceptive knowledge plays a very important role in the case of the performance appraisal for senior management and sometimes for middle-level executives also.

Hypothetical knowledge: A hypothesis is a justified belief that is not known to be true. It is a belief which is backed up with some supporting points relevant to the subject of knowledge. A hypothesis may or may not be true in the ultimate analysis. Supporting evidence for the hypothesis may be just a fragment of what the real position of the thing or the fact is all about.

In a unionized work environment involving a large number of workforce, sometimes the hypothetical approach plays an important role in performance management in general and performance appraisal in particular.

Heuristic knowledge: A heuristic is a special type of knowledge used by modern enterprises and academics to solve many complex issues that come across. It is a type of knowledge used to make good judgements, develop tricks and have thumb rules used to simplify a complex problem. For example, in locating a fault in a desktop computer, the expert may like to understand the nature of the problem through a description of a layperson who is the user of the computer. The expert then comes to an approximate point of the fault and then attempts correction. Alternatively, the expert applies the usual experiential judgement in identifying the problem.

For a series of cases in large number, statistical measures are better applied in the hands of corporate management to take care of the issues of performance appraisal and performance management. Multiple variables in standard setting and standardizing become a matter of importance in this case.

Application of heuristic methods in identifying the real nature of the performance trends of a large number of people in a factory or a large distribution system is helpful.

Meta knowledge: Meta knowledge is the knowledge about the varieties of knowledge. Alternatively, it is the knowledge about what we know in essential terms about the subject of knowledge.

The central knowledge reservoir of a company develops the meta knowledge with a view to keep track of the practice, procedure and policies pursued by the segments of the company. Different aspects of the elemental knowledge meet the reality of the company where the segments of the company make it to the desired outcome in the company.

Meta knowledge applies to large-sized organizations with multiple business lines spread across large-geographical areas involving many regulatory and social realities.

Epistemology of knowledge: Epistemology is the study of the nature of the knowledge acquired. It is the knowledge type and knowledge mix that pertains to the work and activities in a specific context of the work.

The computerized database would depict the connection and degree of divergence among the policies pursued in different places of the same entity. This enables the management of the company to adopt a better strategy for managing HR.

Strategic Business Unit (SBU)

Nowadays, HRM is considered as an SBU that not only gets on board manpower but also develops it with potentials to earn value for the organization much more than usual. Like other functional activities, internal customization proves a rewarding tool for HR managers. The efficient strategic move makes the HR function dynamic and a front runner for the organization.

Three Hundred Sixty Degree Appraisal System

This is one way to create a holistic organization where people develop an informal cord of relations and makes the flow of work better and smoothly. An individual in an organization is assessed, according to this system, by all others within the entity as also by those who are associated with the organization. This system attempts to collect inputs for the appraisal from all levels and corners of the company.

Everybody in the company has the scope to talk about the other. Therefore, the system has the versatility to make an agenda move across the company. This system has certain effects which are better than other methods.

Some of the advantages of this system are as follows:

- Enhances collectivism within the company
- Enhances the level of motivation
- Allows better team performances
- Better understanding among employees
- Reduces the stress potential in the work
- Better productivity in the organization
- Superior quality of individual output
- Reduces interpersonal conflicts
- Better conformity to budgetary and regulatory implications

Self-managing Work Teams

The objective of the HR function should be to see that the core functionaries develop skill sets so as to become a self-manager. This person understands clearly the corporate objective and sets the motion on the wheel in such a way that fulfils the corporate agenda and matches with the objectives.

A self-managing executive uses the corporate resources in such a way that it allows optimization to work always in terms of costs and expenditures and attempts to maximize the flow of revenues to the company.

A self-manager is essentially an entrepreneur with the strength of mind and power to create avenues of business within the defined parameters of the company. Resources required for the same are considered inputs and absorbed in the cost parameters of the company. The entrepreneur manager would go a long way to make the business turn better in terms of productivity and profitability.

Strategic Orientation in Manpower Management

Organizations follow certain core strategic process to skim off the advantages that are available in the markets. Some of the highlighting aspects pursued by many MNCs are:

- *Follow the sun policy:* This is actually used in the trade process pursued by transnational corporations (TNCs) and MNCs across the globe. The objective of this method of business process is to see that the business can continue without pause and sleep. Areas of specific applications are investment funds getting continuous benefits of investments across the globe from the sunrise zone and continue with the sun, passing the net balance of the investment from the east to the extreme west and come back to east.
- *Global investments through 'follow the sun policy':* A global fund manager can begin with investments for day trading in Osaka Exchange, then moves the fund to Mumbai via Singapore, then proceeds to London and moves forward to Chicago. Again, they may come back to Osaka via Toronto. The same kind of routing can be followed by product distributions across the globe. Manpower movement should match the scheme of business and follows the same policies in these kinds of global business.
- *Outsourcing:* Getting a service or a product from external sources has become a business pattern nowadays. This has become very prominent in manpower for a company or industry. Usually, when in a new territory which is yet to standardize the manpower and labour laws and rules and where there is a business point to understand the sociocultural or political scenario, companies take less burden of the manpower and tend to outsource the activity to chosen enterprises. The regulatory implications of such employments lie with the third party, which is engaged by the company to take care of this activity. However, people engaged in such have to deliver work as per the norms and standards of the first party. Although the person is legally an employee of the third party, for all practical purposes, the person is considered as the official authority of the first party for the segment of work assigned. Actually, the intrinsic purpose is to observe the quality of performance of the individual with a view to select the one who has the mix of attainments and attributes as expected strictly by the first party.
- *Offshoring:* The development of stable, secure and high-speed data transfer enables companies to do offshoring across the globe for business. It is the outsourcing of an activity or a function to a wholly owned company or an independent provider in a country. Information and communications technology (ICT) has made a strong sense of this type

of doing global business. Companies create a competitive advantage in terms of savings on the related investments and overheads in the related countries of doing business. Freight and container services across the globe, supported by financial risk management through insurance and reinsurance make this business happen profitably. Manpower connected with this business requires being conversant with global business process, norms and standards.

- *The technology of manufactures, operations, distributions, communications, control, R&D, mergers and acquisitions, takeover, diversification, product development, market development and so on:* All these keep on changing with the passage of time. Manpower management requires being adaptive to the changes in the parameters and be on the threshold of the change always. It talks about the dynamism inbuilt in the manpower management system and processes.

Leader in Action: Cosmic Spirit in Management

Cosmic Ways

Organizations throughout the world perform in a way that fits in and suits the basic objective of the organization, and the objective remains in the fundamental design of the entity. Each organization performs its functions in a way that leads to the uncovering of the hidden dimensions of it. The hidden part of it draws from the surrounding guiding environment on one hand and the nature on earth on the other.

Organizations can draw heavily from the basic ways of functioning of the natural world. In a way, the basic understanding of the rules and ways of functioning of lives contribute a lot towards making a sustainable structure and sustainable model of the organization. Nature has created ways and options for creatures to make the defence more effective and to engineer the functions of life in a way that enhances its effectiveness on the pathways of aligning stakes for its life and create a way for safety and victory.

Sustainability and winning become simultaneous with this organization and its connected horizon of sustenance. Nature has maintained lives of species for centuries, millennia or ages beyond that. Through the same way, the sea creatures have maintained their pathways of winning and sustaining, defeating all evils and all hindrance to their lives.

The hammerhead shark patrols from reef to reef, looking for skates and rays. She sees her world through an electromagnetic vision that shows her only the fish – visualized by the signals generated by the electric currents coursing through their nervous systems. She carries her electromagnetic sensory organs on opposite sides of her winged head; this positioning allows her to triangulate her scanning, giving her stereoscopic sense of the living environment. She follows her flattened snout from one stimulus to the next, watching for fish no longer able to keep up with their schools or no longer able to keep hidden – easy targets, easy meals. She is oblivious to anything else – anything without a nervous system. Now she senses the presence of a bass in the middle distance, and her course automatically comes around in that direction. (Daubert, 2006, pp. 6–7)

As some of the sea creatures develop their horizon of existence through sustainability and winning, certain types of special attainment and development make them competent to survive longer than the real essence of life. Sea creatures, like the creatures on the soil surface, create their territory of life and growth.

With the expansion of certain sensor and communication functions, some of the sea creatures have their winning dominance in their horizon. This makes the lives more competent to survive and grow. Nature has a unique design in which each of the species has its ways to look forward to its subsistence, and through that, it ensures dominance in its horizon.

Some of the sea creatures are luminescent in their organic makeup. These are creatures that can generate light rays and emit certain other types of rays which are not visible but at the same time make it applicable towards a better living and better scope for a larger span of living supports. This support provides the species with the scope for creating coexistence and collaborative presence in the universe. Although conflict remains among creatures for their struggle for existence and growth, the ultimate rule or norm of the global nature is to coexist through mutual dependence.

Natural Choice

Natural choice and natural makeup of the living kingdom as also things present in the non-living material world exhibit and follow a particular arrangement and pattern. The patterns are thereby uniform and universal. This universality is overarching and prevalent in all aspects of living and material creations. Entities that follow these principles of universality are better off than those who do not follow.

Organizations are managed and maintained in so many ways which cannot be listed down in one place. However, those organizations that have preferred to pick up the attributes of universality and follow those in their plans of action have proved better sustainability and continue for a longer period than others.

Organizations have to pass through ups and downs based on factors which could originate from inside or such other factors that originate from outside—such as the economic and market-driven situations.

A unique call of the emergence of an Indian brand in the United Kingdom reflects valuable message as:

First, my vision for the company never wavered. I wanted to create the finest Indian beer and sell it everywhere. With determination, my team and I turned Cobra into a household name in Britain, and that strength of brand helped us through tough times; during none of the crises did our sales decline.

At the same time we have been creative and flexible—willing to constantly adapt, learn, grow and innovate. That's the heart of successful entrepreneurship: knowing where you want to go but staying open to different ways of getting there. (Bilimoria, 2018, p. 34.)

This is about a company which had to pass through a lot of challenges from domestic and international areas. The factors which made the emergence happen were based on the points of convergence on the strength of some such attributes.

Decision parameters: Determination, constant adaptation, learning, growing and innovating are the factors which were accepted and made to be a part of the decision choice and actions of companies which tried to have a better standing in the market through its position of winning and continuance for a longer period. Determination, as the leader of the organization has observed, played a strong role in the makeup of things. The leader tried to become competent enough to understand the underpinning of the facts and effects of the market and economy.

Decisions of the leader should be such that they take the organization forward in the pathways of generic universal principle which the entire creation adopts as one of those guiding policies.

When it comes to the material facts of the world, adopting things from around becomes important for a leader. However, from this kind of implementation, one can proceed forward to lead an organization. This approach of a leader allows the living world a unique learning from the stories of lives. Thereby, the person gets a chance to apply key points of observations to their immediate agenda of action.

Learning as such is a constant factor, and it allows corporate leaders with responsibilities and duties to explore the adaptation of things considered very pertinent to the growth of the entity. In this process of learning and adaptation, factors which may contribute to the growth of the entity and face the challenges imposed by the market and economy can be met with some degree of success.

Cosmic inspiration: It is the context where entities are actually tuned to the effective rhythm and vibrations of the cosmic system. In the cosmic system, when learning takes place in the context of an entity, factors leading to growth open up. However, basic attributes which nature nurtures for its continuation of making lives and allowing passages of lives through the constancy of time to the eternity understands the spirit of things that have happened in the course of cosmic progress.

Another key element of our success has been integrity. Throughout the life of Cobra, I have been surrounded by loyal partners, employees and family – especially my wife, whom I met one year after I started the business. They stuck with me and the company through thick and thin, and I am immensely grateful. As a group, we have always adhered to strong moral principles. Even when others didn't play its straight, we did. In my opinion, it is better to fail doing the right thing than to succeed doing the wrong one. (Bilimoria, 2018, p. 35)

Not only growth happens here in life, but also things responsible for creating hindrance and obstruction to the process of growth are identified on specific notes and obtains learning elements and learning messages from them. These factors, which are considered as basics, are not always applicable in all situations of the organizational makeup.

Loyalty to the leadership has been observed in this case study as one of the most important attributes for the people in an organization to grow high in the success matrix of an organization. Loyalty to the organization turns out to be loyalty to the leadership and principles of the organization. Apart from loyalty, another important attribute is the integrity of the person in an organization.

Loyalty and integrity: Loyalty and integrity are usually considered as normal attributes of people in the organizational context. However, whenever any kind of crisis looms at the face of an organization, it has to adhere to certain basic principles of operation and functioning. These are usually those principles and attribute that are universal in their nature and applications. Attributes which pertain to a single individual are applicable to larger entities of the proportion of an organization. Whether the organization is passing through its normal days with everything smooth or it is in a condition that points out to the series of

Design of Winning Organization

unutilized resources for survival or growth or in a condition of chaos, loyalty and integrity play a very important role.

Growth of an organization through learning and innovation happens in normal situations of market and economy. However, when organizations are in transition or transformation, or when the market and economic conditions present gloomy contexts, organizations fall prey to that.

A chaotic condition or even usual volatility of markets, the support that is provided through the usual process of learning and innovation, seldom creates competence for growth and win the competition and challenges of the markets. Situations that compel organizations to look at the basics, demand review of its fundamental principle and policies. Determination, loyalty and integrity have been identified by some organizations as a set of remedy in this context. Determination, loyalty and integrity are the factors intrinsic to individuals. However, the context around within the organization and outside has to make somewhat conducive to the actions of the organizations for the current period and beyond.

Prophetic vision: Organizations need leaders with prophetic vision and positions. A prophet is one who is not only conversant with the periods that pertain to current situations but also open to visualize situations, which may occur in the future. A corporate prophet has a sixth sense, strong enough to sense the conditions of business.

This requires a projective understanding of economic and market conditions which are relevant to the scope of activities of the organization.

A prophetic vision should be based on certain basics. The sixth sense is, in fact, going beyond the usual five senses. These first five senses that we are in constant use are factors of the following organs: vision, hearing, smell, taste and touch.

The prophetic sense is actually attributed to the next, the sixth, which is beyond the common-sense perceptive capacity of the person. Prophetic approach to the senses is categorically different and can be classified as mentioned in Table 5.1.

Ideation: It is generating ideas forms one of the most important elements of growth. An idea forms an integral component of living. Every human being creates and nurtures ideas. Ideas could be anything, it may drive the person down to the low levels of attainment, it may also push the person to sky-high. Incremental ideas may add up to a great idea leading to a great change or transformation in the existing system or creation of new structure and discovery of the intrinsic, inner dimensions or the inner reality of the cosmic system or a part of it. An idea may arise out of our endeavours to develop the same, or it may be something that gets transmitted through the journey of lives and the lineage.

If the connection between hateful acts across the countries and between trauma and distrust over generational time is real, how do the ideas and feelings persist? How might they be passed down from one generation to the next? Can the personal qualities of a great -great - great grandfather, like his faith in people or his suspicion of them, really influence the feelings of his descendants today? (Kennelly, 2015, p. 150)

Different forms of ideas stimulate different kinds of energy into the system. Actions propelled by that energy takes different forms and makes a new identity for a renewed set of activities. Ideas lead to actions, and that ultimately lead to growth and developments of systems and organizations. Ideas that contribute to the growth are essential materials to win.

Ralph Waldo Emerson raises the question, 'why should not we also enjoy an original relation to the universe?' Maybe we can, but it will surely help if we can identify what has passed down to us and what we have freely chosen ourselves.

Actually, ideas contribute to the new formations. These formations may have arisen out of the existing or maybe directly vetted by an existing set of ideas. In the market and economy, ideas create and make differences. Market and product differentiation and diversification are all outcomes of the impact of ideas. In order to survive through growth,

Table 5.1 Prophetic and the Sixth Sense of Business

Usual	Prophetic
• *Vision:* To see all, from the visible and oriented to the extrinsic and focused in the current period.	• *Vision:* To see the entire and beyond; invisibles and the inner aspects
• To see a tree and within the horizon and the outer	• *Visibility:* To see the outer and the roots, the current, the beyond visibility and things within the domain
• *Hearing:* Hear the noise, hear the audible, hear rhythms of the tangible and the gross	• *Hearing:* To hear the rhythm and the unheard, the soundless rhythms of the unuttered words
• The usual way to understand things, such as applying data science and variables used in the data science are very essential.	• Smell feeble and dormant, smell the prominent ones also those elements which have surfaced already. Smell the hidden agenda, the thing undercover.
• Perceptions in the context of the business and for the fulfilment are very widely captured in the framework of the business applying the tools of managing enterprises.	• The sixth sense unfolds. The sixth sense of the business understands things through the vision and applying wisdom.
• Subjective understanding of things and incidences are judged against the object-oriented analysis for the same.	• The business decision occurs in the context of the world of incidents taking place around for the organization.
• Business analytics has a major role to guide the organization towards arriving at an optimal decision matrix in the context of the external designs of the market and the economy.	• The sixth sense makes a difference in the process and outcome of the decision. It originates from the prophetic mind but applies to all situations of business life.
• Coordination among practitioners drawn from different functional and normative areas of thoughts and practices. Decision-making involving many people would be placed under the choice of the leader to select the best.	• The sixth sense of business paves the way for the top management to explore the new horizon of growth and sustenance. Although the decision is by the wise personality; the execution is widespread involving many.

organizations are bound to make changes in the structure of functioning, including changes in the design of the organizational setup.

Manpower distribution in the organizations has a certain basis. The basic reason and focus of organizations are those which attribute to the core competence of individuals, and the required competence for the work in the organizations.

Each work as a unit defines a certain set of competence required in the person doing the work. If, goodness rests and develops while doing the work, the scope for change and development remains always open in the system for making the work more rewarding to the organization and be successful. Ideas inherited through lineage, as genealogists have suggested, add up to its strength is application.

Organizations encourage the generation of ideas throughout its life cycle. Ideas for the entire organization to follow and apply pertain to the corporate level or pan-organizational structure and activity. This leads to the change of corporate strategy and strategy for the entire organization. However, the impact of this change of strategy applies to all aspects of the organization. This includes, among other things, situations that pertain to internal and external factors. The human factor plays a strong role here.

Ideas can help scientists understand data and can also prevent them from seeing what is under their nose: either way, they are essential to how science works.... Organisms are not machines, even if they work on physical principles and share some features with devices we have invented.

The genetic code is not literally a code and it is like a language. It is a process that enables organisms to carry out particular functions by turning stored information into structures or actions, using evolved systems of control.

Future will inevitably contain opportunities and challenges.... By revealing and cracking genetic code, science has shown itself capable of revealing life's greatest secret. But science cannot tell us what to do with the secret, nor ensure that the knowledge and technology that flow from it are used for the greatest good of the many and with the least damage to the planet.

(Cobb, 2015, pp. 313–314)

As it has been correctly mentioned, organizations that refer to the health of the concerned market and economy sometimes take a corrective course through technology. The behaviour and impact of this technology have to fit in the human system. In case the factors of induction of new technology do not fit in the competency, in the eyes of modern analysts, those people turn redundant and surely the case for their exits are recommended.

Organizations opt for a new process and new technology to fit in the internal situation. However, if the new process or the new situation remains external to people of the organization, the very purpose of value engineering for the organization has to be protected as the induction of new technology may create a lot of people unfit for the said organization.

If it so happens that the organizations create situations which can embrace the existing people also through a process of skill augmentation and skill enhancement, then the organizations offer a new structure and shape to all by providing opportunities to deserving people to enhance their skill and develop competence to cope with a new productive system. This new productive system can go far way to contain everyone through renewed skill enhancement and accommodate things that are hitherto considered away from the process and the system.

The basic awareness of the changes in strategy and process needs to be applied as and when the organization takes a call about it. Ideas play a very important role in giving a new shape to the organizations by way of inducting a new technology and process and of course, a new system. Ideas stand as the stimulating factor or sometimes just a sensation input for many including those who fall short of organization of expectations. It is, thus, imperative that an organization keeps getting ideas from around and implementing the chosen ideas into action.

Resource and wealth in action: Natural providence of wealth is basic. On the strength of whatever nature has provided beneath the soil, at the seabed, on the soil surface, in the atmosphere, mid-air and the infinite sky, the added strength and quality of resources have been achieved by the human endeavour.

The human world has made lots of transformations in the systems and structures with the application of human intellect and competence. Capital is formed out of the natural capital, available in the form of resource. Usually, resources are classified in various ways. However, major ways to classify wealth and resources are material, financial and HR. Material resources can be many, present in many forms. The major divisions in material resources are natural material resources and made up material resources. Looking at it from a different angle, the material resources can make up to the formation of the capital of different kinds. The three major classes are identified as follows:

- The primary capital
- The secondary capital
- The tertiary capital

Natural resources, including minerals, seabed plants and creatures, forests, soil, water resources—all these put together make the natural resources. Natural resources are primary in their entity. Any productive resource that is derived out of the natural resource is secondary, and the resources which are extracted or made available from the secondary are tertiary.

Material resources are converted to the utility value with respect to the inputs provided. Minerals, for example, converted to industrial outputs may act as secondary resource to generate resources further. In the ancient world, as compared to the West now, the awareness was less.

For a long time there was strife between the rich and the poor. For the state was oligarchic in all ways, and the poor, along with their wives and children, were enslaved to the rich. And they were called 'clients' and 'sixth partners', for it was at this rate that they worked in the fields of the rich. All the land belonged to a few people; and if the poor did not render their dues, they and their children could be sold overseas. And before Solon, all loans were made on the security of the person; but he became the first champion of people. (Magill, 2000, p. 803)

Ancient Greece and Rome had the system of human trade in addition to certain kinds of trading in the social context that had prevailed upon. Ancient Greece and Rome had equated land and other natural resources to have values related to human beings.

Loans and debts were always equated to men and women, and in case of unpaid loans and debts, the rich persons, who were the owners of lands and natural resources, used to capture people as slaves.

The market for slave trading turned into international, making people available in place of unpaid loans and selling them as merchandise to overseas traders against value. The rich people thus used to gather more resources through slave trading throughout.

The Employee Speaks

Certain common concerns are now a day universal in the world or work and business. Wherever the person is located in the world or whichever the business is, the concerns are usually the common in type and pattern. Some of these are as follows:

- *Human resource policy (HRP):* Company should adopt a proper policy for managing HR. This is a standard document, usually projected in the form of a manual, which should include important aspects of the contract between the person and the organization. HRP should include, among others, the important aspects which are in usual expectations of an employee. Aspects of concerns are many, however, the most important is the 'policy manual with legal status, rights and privileges' of a standard employee.

- *Recruitment policy:* This indicates the methods, financials, contents, procedures, fairness, attitudes and values involved. It has an organization chart depicting hierarchy, job descriptions of each role.
- *Financial package:* Pay and perks related to the job, incentive schemes for any kind of work involving qualitative involvement, components of pay, policy on chances of increase in financials and other terms are included in the financial package. It also includes promotion policy, retirement policy, policy for termination/resignation.
- *Discipline rules:* This indicates on-the-job discipline, transactional discipline and relational discipline. It has ethics policy, interpersonal ethics, work ethics, an organizational initiative for ethics, business and transactional ethics.
- *Interpersonal policy:* This policy includes conflict resolution mechanism, dynamics of shop-floor worker—supervisory staff relations.
- *Gender policy:* This policy indicates the rights and privileges of women in work policy and protection of the rights of women.
- *Health support policy:* It includes ongoing health-related support scheme and schemes towards health hazards of employee and dependents.
- *Health support policies:* This is for self and family sickness support in terms of pay off, insurance support and other supports.
- *Leisure policy:* This includes annual or biannual policy on entertainments and leisure travels by the employee and family.
- *Motivational policy:* This policy has financial schemes of motivation, non-financial schemes of motivation.
- *Employee higher education policy:* This includes scopes for enhancing educational qualifications while on board of the company and presence of good schemes to support the education of dependent children, particularly overseas employees in foreign nations.
- *Learning and experiencing options:* It includes ongoing learning and learning on deputation.
- *A policy of training and development:* This has a frequency of chances, quality of training, the impact of training on elevation or better terms of employment
- *Technology policy:* This has scopes offered by the company for technology learning and experiencing while in employment.
- Policy on socializing, extra-professional/entertainment policies, policies on personal/organizational/national/natural exigencies, policy on mergers and acquisitions and policy on corporate restructuring.
- *The financial and other rewards from the employment:* Rational approach in reward management with a structured mechanism for

the incentive and other receivables from the company makes an employee convinced about the financials and career path.
- Nature of contract for employment.
- Content of the job or tasks to perform.
- The culture and spirit of the HR organization and the corporate.
- The frequency and pattern of changes in the job description and contents.
- Career prospects in the employment.
- The growth prospect in the employment.
- Kind of people to work with and work for.
- Philosophy and values of the organization.
- Industry or the sector of the economy in which the organization belongs and future prospect of that industry or sector of the economy.

All these points are relevant when the person, the organization looks for or inducts, is of strategic importance to the organization. Otherwise, it turns the other way around. The demand and supply matrix of manpower in an economy determines the approach and orientation of the person towards the employment or that of the organization towards the employee or the person.

In an economy, where jobs are in abundance and the supply of right manpower is short, the bargaining power is in the hands of the competent manpower. However, if the availability of jobs is less than the usual requirements, the bargaining power shifts to the employer. Persons without the right set of required qualification, skill or expertise do not have the same kind of privilege in a job market. Unskilled workforce always faces the fate of becoming a tool in the hand of the forces of the market settlers. Collective bargaining power allows them the way to have the right path of achievement, the right place to work and the right mix of job details. Not being ready for the job market, though, makes a person prone to the impact of the forces of the market, still way out for this category is the collective force of the working community of a particular nature.

This is primarily the market of blue-collar labour. For the white-collar category, the market response is more of individual orientation than that of the other category. For people with highly specialized knowledge and expertise, the bargaining power is huge and mostly in the hand of the person.

Mobility in the job market enhances the spirit of the market. However, a job market with too many shifts or changes makes it prone to risks. Too high frequency of entry and exit in jobs make the market volatile. A volatile market is always problematic for both the person and the organization.

Whatever be the situation, once inducted, the employee needs to be nurtured for obtaining the best output. Then only, the person is supposed to be motivated to give out the best for the organization. The collective contribution of such motivated people forms the core strength of the organization. For this purpose, organizations pursue motivational programs to achieve gain.

Employee Motivation in Organizations

Motivation is an important aspect of corporate management. It makes a huge difference between a motivated and unmotivated group of people in an organization. A properly motivated person can contribute immensely to the growth of the company. Persons motivated can go beyond the schedules of work, assignments or duties. Self-motivation is likely to set in a person who is highly motivated with things in the company.

A self-motivated person actually works as a manager—entrepreneur within the ambit of the organization. The boundaries of that organization may even be crossed by the self-motivated person to undertake new types of challenges of the market. At times, undertaking challenges mean to the companies a leap forward to take the mantle of the organization to a height not thought of before. Economic, social, political, environmental or situational opportunities may pave the way for an enthusiastic manager to move up fast to the race with the existing operators through developing uniqueness in the offers of the company. The manager may not hesitate and wait for the green signals by the board or the top management for the same. However, the result of such operations should be convincing enough to prove the intent of the manager.

In a fast-changing scenario of the world, it is essential, sometimes, that the company leaves the major decision-making with the operating managers at the segments of business. The manager, thus, receives the mandate of doing as a leader and gets enough chance to prove the merit of the mandate.

Employee motivation has different meanings and many ways of understanding. However, it can be seen through a standardized and defined way. The existing options and practices are somewhat normative for organizations across the globe and somewhat self-engineered. Although it has been mentioned quite often that the practice follows concepts, here we find that the concepts put across and mentioned as such lack in the potent to sustain the issues of motivation in perpetuity.

Definition of Motivation

Motivation is a beam of emotions that sensitizes additional flow of energy—adrenalin in the volume, content and quality of involvement—in the world of thought and works by a person or a group of people transcending the usual limits and barriers in varying degrees. Motivation is the art of selfless and dedicated contribution to the world of thought and work.

There are various approaches and definitions of motivation presented by practitioners and scholars. However, the final score on it boils down to the selflessness and dedication, which has not been properly noticed as yet. Motivation has a strong intrinsic component which the companies need to understand. What the corporate world has been pursuing by and large is the extrinsic elements of personalities. The intrinsic aspects are partly covered in the process, leaving the most precious intrinsic elements aside.

A duly motivated person becomes a self-starter in the organization who performs with a persistent level of high energy and coordinated decisions in tune with the goal of the organization.

A higher level of energy devoted to the activities of the organization by a manager makes a churning effect on the morale of employees and the stakeholders of the organization. It rolls forward the wheels of the organization in a definite momentum to catch hold of things hitherto considered beyond its horizon of accomplishments.

Theories of Motivation

Most theories of motivation, which are actually spoken about and regarded as the dominant theories of the same, have one common principle underlying the concepts. This common belief is about the identity of a human being. It has been widely considered that a human being is actually a needing animal. Need is considered as fundamental in human being. It is assumed that motivation arises out of the fulfilment of the needs. Needs are spread across different varieties and categories.

Model of Hierarchy of Need by Abraham Maslow

Out of the most widely discussed theories of motivation, Maslow's theory is regarded as the most widely referred to. Abraham Maslow had designed the human need in several categories. There are basically five such categories. The sixth one has been added later. The first five have been designed in the shape of a pyramid with the basic physiological needs at the bottom of the pyramid.

In the sequence of ascending order, the needs in the 'pyramid of needs' are as follows:

- Self-actualization
- Esteem
- Social
- Safety/security
- Physiological

(The needs are arranged in the ascending order of a pyramid with physiological at its base and actualization at the apex).

The sixth or the topmost one is considered as *intrinsic value*. The concept of intrinsic here is actually based on the externalities of the person and draws from the parameters of need which are less expressed and more understood.

Physiological: This refers to the needs that are mentioned as having originated from bodily requirements, such as hunger, thirst, sex, shelter, wear and related items.
Safety/security: This refers to the security of the job in an organization, sense of security in the context of work, perception of security in the society and environment. People are more prone to explore the physical and perceptive notion of security and safety by people in the organization.
Social: This includes the society of people around the person in the organization. People expect a society within organizations of such a kind where the informal relations of friendship and cooperation is established and maintained. An attractive environment of the workplace is satisfying to people.
Esteem: Recognition from others and competent authorities, acclaims in the workplace or from the society, industry and competent sources act as motivators for work in an organization. Factors such as independence in work and power to take decisions play an important role in motivating people. Defined zone of discretion (ZOD) for the person is again a strong motivator when the domain is wider enough to assert individual strength of character and qualities.
Self-actualization: Accomplishing the hidden potentials of the person, creating proper perspective and scenario congenial to the proper growth of the person are some strong motivators for the organization. Realizing the perceived potentials in the self-chosen ways by the person makes the person motivated. The way individuals think about themselves is unique in attributes. Most persons have expectations of this self-identified uniqueness which get recognized and fulfilled by the organization or the system. Once this expectation is satisfied, the person feels very dear to the company and is said to devote to the cause of the organization strongly.

The model of Abraham Maslow is founded on the basic assumption that human being is a variety of animals with a bundle of needs arranged in a particular range of hierarchy. A base-level need fulfilled means the attention of the person moves up to the next higher level. Similarly, for other levels, it is connected in the hierarchy in the same pattern.

Two-factor Theory of Frederick Herzberg

The basic hypothesis of the psychologist Frederick Herzberg is about a person's relation to the work and the attitude to the work and workplace. According to the result of Herzberg's study, the two-factor theory was put forward by him. These two factors are as follows:

- *External factors:* These are primarily having dissatisfying characteristics in a job context. These are also known as *hygiene factors*. Once these hygiene factors are fulfilled, people will not feel dissatisfied. Some of the things that are usually considered as hygiene factors are company policy and administration, supervision, salary and perks, the culture of the company and working conditions.
- *Intrinsic factors:* These are *motivating factors* or *motivators*. Once these factors are properly fulfilled, the person feels motivated in the context of the organization and the work. Some of the highlighting issues that individuals are sensitive to are career advancement, recognition, responsibility, scopes for personal growth and achievement are usual expectations of the persons in an organization. Once fulfilled, the company or a segment of it gets satisfied executives to work with a lot of high level of motivation.

The most interesting part of Herzberg's two-factor theory is that if hygiene factors are satisfied, these do not get people motivated—these turn into 'no satisfaction' elements. Whereas once the hygiene factors are properly fulfilled, and the motivating factors are satisfied, the person becomes strongly motivated.

Not a Needing Animal, Human Being Is Potentially Divine

The models of motivations have a common underlying belief that 'human being is a special category of an animal with special needs', or most precisely, they view the human being as needing animals. This view contradicts the basis of being 'human' and not an animal.

An animal is known for certain habits, characters and behaviours. Nurtured and trained by human beings, some animals which are brought to human homes as pets are seen to develop certain attributes of humans. Pet birds flute as human talks and sound like humans in some cases. Pet dogs have a better capacity to learn human norms and patterns of behaviour. Even there are cases of trained dogs who can understand the situation and minds of their masters. Pets develop sentiments close to humans and behave in such a fashion as if they have certain attributes and habits which can be branded as quasi-human attribute and habits. There are cases of pet lions, snakes, tigers and certain other variety of animals known for their having killer faculty and tendencies. However, for this category, the results in most of the cases are disastrous.

Being in the midst of animals, there are also lots of examples of human beings nurtured by animals. Stories of elephants having shown and maintained affectionate care to small child somehow fallen inside deep forest and offering full protection to the child until the child is returned to the places nearby localities are available. Also, similar other stories are available in many parts of the world, especially in and around deep forests of Amazon and other major forest areas.

However, these are sporadic in nature and do not show any pattern. There are special cases also in literatures to understand the unified spirit of the nature. Even though animal habit explores across the nature to trace elements of selfish gain, there are exceptional cases as well. Although animal habit is structured across various items of needs, the animal needs can be sequenced as well. Some ideas of animal needs are as follows:

- *Hunger:* Endless hunger is satisfied through some means and from anywhere. Usual methods of satisfying hunger are applying force and power. Force and power are for every creature to apply, irrespective of the context or the target of the animal. The target could be common among many. The rule of jungle is 'fight to win' and 'win through any means'. 'If it requires to kill any creature which comes on the way, do that'—this is another dominant philosophy maintained by the animal world.
- *Safety:* Each creature in the forest or any jungle wants to safeguard itself through some means. There is some way to naturally protect every creature, however, animals behave through group formations to safeguard their mutual interests and protect themselves. Safety is a general concern of every creature and it is a usual way to respond by all animals either in the jungle or out of it. Pets are quasi-animals as they inhibit some of the human traits. Being in the jungle, an animal is survival minded. Darwinism exactly fits in the animal world though it has been recommended for the human world. In the animal world, all needs are not greed. However, to fulfil the need, the animal cultivates greed to possess through any means. An animal attribute is thus full of arrogance, anger, destructive, selfish and unending hunger.
- *Dominance:* An animal wants to create its own dominance in the process of ongoing life. An animal habit has the tendency to create a dominant position in the approach. Animal fights tooth and nail to win that dominance in its own world. Either it wins or perishes in the fight. Animal dominance has a jurisdiction within which it is always the king of its own territory. An animal maintains its territory by any

means. A street dog creates its dominance by littering across to establish its own smell as the boundary of its dominance. A lion asserts its kinghood within the sphere up to which its roars reach. Within the kingly area of the lion, it is the lord and it does not tolerate any other dominance within that.

- *Spreading:* The animal habit is to spread its impact throughout the zone of its influence and make others accept the fact of its spread over there. However, other creatures wait for the opportunity to put down and destroy the prior one in any way.
- *Winning:* An animal habit knows less of cooperation and more of conflict. Factors of conflict are implicit in animal behaviour. However, within their own group, they behave as closely connected. Any external entity within their domain causes anger in the animal, and it reverses with arrogance and attempts to destroy. The lion does not stop until it wins the fight. In the process, it may lose life also, but it does not give up.

Joy of Doing, Joy of Being in the Company and Joy of Giving

Although theories of motivation focus on the needing character of the human being, many actions and behaviours show that humans are not the needing animals rather human being is a superior entity. A human being is superior in terms of the qualities of life. However, it is a measure of the number of people being really different from the basic tenets of animal attributes. It depends on the condition of society, where the dominance of needing persons varies over the period. Actually, human society has a unique mix of people with animal-like habit and character and the opposite—divinely character.

About the animal-like character, there is a nice description in the Bhagavad Gita. Lord Krishna says to Arjuna (in Sanskrit):

Ahamkaram balam darpam kamam krodham cha samshrita
Mam atmam pardeheshu pradishantu abhyasuyakah.
(Gita, 16/18)

Having possessed egoism, power, insolence, lust and wrath, people develop animal-like characters. They hate divinely personality and cannot recognize the presence of noble attributes within the self.

Animal attributes are present in the personality of individuals. These attributes on one hand and the divinely attributes on the other in a mix of personality makes a common human person. The usual human character with a mix of divinely and demonic attributes are in abundance in every organization.

The demonic dominance in characters reveals the personal values of individuals with a higher share of attributes oriented to greed, anger, arrogance, hatred, lust, covetousness, jealousy, envy and so on. From this point of view, the impact of the needing model of Maslow or the hygiene-motivator model of Herzberg become very useful.

However, for organizations having the intent to grow in perpetuity with the moral and ethical basis of doing things, it is essential to go beyond the need-driven thinking for a human being. A human being has a different dimension which is much superior to the need-based thoughts about a person.

Needs are there to survive, grow and win. But people may get a higher level of satisfaction by establishing self-identity with superior things. The joy of giving is something which makes the person not only happy but also satisfies some of the intrinsic expectations of a person. The joy of goodness makes a person liberated from the impacts of the demonic attributes, at least, partially.

When a person receives the receivables from an organization or some individual, it provides the satisfaction of having fulfilled the demand. But when the person can offer something to someone without any prejudice to the thing, it provides joy to the giver. The joy of giving is much superior to the plans to collect, receive and demand.

Giving is possible only when the person has withdrawn any kind of greed across the elements or items of giving. Giving becomes a divinely quality if it does not carry along any calculation for getting things in return. A person has to identify if there is anything which can be given.

In the ultimate analysis, a person would find that there are a lot of things every individual possesses, which can be an important gift from a person.

What can a common person give out in an organization?

The usual notion of wage earners centres on a sense of deprivation. People prefer to think of the gap in possession than possession. The gap is felt in two ways. First, the gap is understood by the person in general in the context of the world and work. Second, the gap is actually a comparative understanding. This is the perception of the relative position of a person with respect to others in similar or aligned roles in the same industry or on the similarity drawn in any way.

Psychology of trade unionism is thus a collective way to understand the gaps on a collective scale and then attempting to redress the gap in the manner chosen by the combination or the majority of the labour forces in an entity or across the entity. The efforts to standardize the rewards for work in the form of pay and perks is actually generalizing the nature of the work and contributions by individuals in the context of work.

Trade unionism holds good in a system-based process industry where the impact of the work is such that the factors for individual differentiation are really minimum. Work has a role to play in the approach of the collective initiative through trade union process.

If the nature of the work is faceless, trade unionism has a strong place. If each person has the same chance of contributing similar or the same output in the system through the machine-driven activities, then the work is standardized. For a standardized activity, the principle of 'equal pay for equal work' holds good. Here, the trade union has a strong case to interfere in the affairs of the company through the organized moves with a view to correct the system in the event of anything having departed from the standard norms and practices.

As the responsibilities grow within an enterprise, the tasks start becoming unique in nature. Individuals holding the positions and responsibilities where decision-making is a part of the task, uniqueness occurs there. This unique person cannot be 'me too' in the organization.

Tom Peters has coined an interesting observation about the art of managing enterprises. Tom Peter has mentioned about Peter Drucker's own observation about the nature of corporate management. Let us quote Tom Peters to get the flavour of his thoughts directly as:

'Peter Drucker's assessment of his most important contribution: management as a liberal art.'

At a seminar in 1999, the moderator asked Peter Drucker, generally considered the father of modern management thinking, what he thought was his most important contribution to the field of management.

Peter Drucker replied:

'I focused this discipline on people and power; on values, structure, and constitution; and above all, on responsibilities—that is, I focused the discipline of management on management as a truly liberal art.'

In recent years, consistent with Drucker's view, I have focused on shifting the MBA from master of business administration to master of business arts. (Peters, 2018, p. 35)

Tom Peters's own understanding of and advocacy of 'management' as a function echoes the same tune as that of Peter Drucker. Tom Peter defines 'managing' as:

Managing: As the pinnacle of human achievement. The greatest life opportunity one can have; mid-to long-term success is no more and no less than a function of one's dedication to and effectiveness at helping team members grow and flourish as individuals and as contributing members to an energetic, self-renewing organization dedicated to the relentless pursuit of excellence. (Peters, 2018, p. 32)

Unleash Your Power to Inspire: *Ananda* (Bliss) Is the Basis of Real Joy

The joy of giving comes from the spirit of sacrifice. The spiritual understanding of the human being is that every human person is potentially divine. Therefore, if the intrinsic divinity is sensitized, the person develops the capacity to overcome the barriers of life.

Usual human understanding of self is that of the need-based orientation of life. However, once the door of realization opens, a person opens up the doors of the discovery of the intrinsic potentials lying dormant within. It is like the green cover over the petals of a lotus. Once the morning sun rays offer touch on the surface of the green cover of the lotus, it starts opening up—unfoldment starts. Gradually, it blossoms into a huge lotus with magnificent petals. Now, the lotus is fully open into the world and life.

Similarly, when the intrinsic goodness of a person is sensitized to open up, the person can taste the elements of joy in the real sense of the term. It is the inner sense of bliss that can elevate a person from the narrow thinking of being a 'small', 'powerless' and 'helpless' to elevated self-realization of 'broad', 'resourceful' and 'self-sufficient' personality.

The corporate world is founded on principles of give and take—this is, of course, the fundamental mechanism of commerce. However, the person, who wants to elevate to a real corporate leader to sustain, needs to transcend this notion. The person would find a huge amount of energy, joy and perpetual inspiration to be able to develop joy in others.

Basis spiritual identity of a person lies in the *ananda* (bliss) of existence. The cause of life lies in *ananda*, the progression of life occurs in *ananda* and the destiny of life is also *ananda*. It is *ananda* that can bring up the most fundamental strength and vitality of life. *Ananda* offered to a person is reciprocated back to the giver.

This has been nicely described in Upanishad, one of the core spiritual sources of India, as:

Ananda bramha eti byajanyat
anandat hi eva khalu emani bhutani jayante

anandena jatani jivanti
anandam prayanti avishanti eti. (Taittiriya Upanishad, 3/1)

Know for certain blissfulness is divine. This entire creation takes place through bliss. The creation grows in search of the intrinsic experience of bliss. The progression of the created is also unknowingly towards the same bliss.

A manager transcends to a leader when this blissfulness is experienced in life. One of the best empirical ways is to be a giver. Giving principle offers the context of bliss. Once the person takes a call of giving, the person gets elevated to a broader personality and surely grows into a leader.

Be a giver to become a corporate leader.

A manager becomes a leader by becoming a broader personality of a leader.

The common issue that may come in the mind of a manager as a question, 'what do I have that I can give?'

Among many points to answer the following are surely the answers to the question, as mentioned below.

A manager, or for that matter, every person in the organization is endowed with many important treasures in possession. Among these, the following are just a few highlights:

- Every person possesses intrinsic strength—you possess the same as well. You can transcend your personal mental barrier and contribute immensely.
- Cultivate the will to do things beyond the horizon of the task, you will find, winning is possible and easy.
- You have surplus potentials, start cultivating that. You will find you cannot remain just a surplus taker, rather, you turn into a surplus giver.
- You can give out your encouragement through your own deeds. Be a unique driver and force in tune with the spirit of the organization, you will find, many behind.
- You have infinite inner potentials, cultivate your creative potential, contribute your positive imagination, your power of innovation, your strength of goodness and spread across for the growth and emergence of the organization, you will find that you are blessed with bliss and peace; your action, character inspires all around to move further than expected and reach goals beyond that set to achieve.

You do not just motivate, rather you become a continuous source of inspiration by giving your surplus of intrinsic energy for the emergence of the organization. You benefit the human society at large for perpetuating further and better.

References

Bilimoria, K. (2018, November–December). Cobra's chairman on turning an Indian beer company into a global brand. *Harvard Business Review*, p. 34. https://hbr.org/2018/11/cobras-chairman-on-turning-an-indian-beer-into-a-global-brand

Cobb, M. (2015). *Life's greatest secret: The race to crack the genetic code*. Profile Books.

Daubert, S. (2006). *Threads from the web of life: Stories in natural history*. Vanderbilt University Press.

Kennelly, C. (2015). *The invisible history of the human race*. Penguin Books.

Magill, F. N. (ed). (2000). *The ancient world*. Fitzroy Dearborn Publishers.

Peters, T. (2018). *The excellence dividend*. Nicholas Brealey Publishing.

CHAPTER 6

EMERGENCE OF MANAGEMENT THOUGHTS AND PRACTICES: FROM VEDIC TO ROBOTIC ERA

The Vedic (Wisdom) Era

Thoughts and practices established in the modern era could get the opportunity for validation less than a couple of centuries only.

Ancient Indian civilization had a system and practice of management which was remarkably at such a superior height that even the current thoughts and practices are yet to reach that standard. The entire Vedic period followed principle-centric practices in life. The practices that Vedic sages have established were far reaching in their impacts and effects. The impact was, by far, the longest in the human context. The formal academic method of history, primarily developed as an offshoot of the prevailing models of academics, has adopted a view that chosen sources of inputs to history are only limited to be considered as references. That is the reason why the academics have hardly touched upon the real sources of history of the ancient Indian civilization.

In fact, the ancient Indian civilization is the birthplace of a mature civilization on earth. The Vedic wisdom stands as the root of the world civilization. The Vedic wisdom of seeking truth in life became the essence of the spirit of all civilizations. At a much later phase, the European hemisphere got the touch of the quest for the eternal truth in empirical life through the seeking of truth by Socrates and by his followers—Plato and Aristotle. The scientific civilization of the West is based on later modifications of the spirit that Socrates could realize in his life. Western ideals have followed the Aristotelian principles of crating individuality through the cultivation of individual heroism more. René Descartes's principle of *cogito ergo sum*, meaning I think, therefore I am, has prioritized the role of 'me' in the whole chain of relations in the human society. Therefore, the individual has been identified as the most important element in the whole measure of things. Thus, the greed and desire of individuals play the most important role in the whole set of things, which means that the wish, desire, taste, preference and choices of individuals are the most important things. The role of the society and others becomes subordinate to that of the individual. This spirit of living is yet to pass the test of time.

It has completed a journey of slightly over a century, whereas the Vedic spirit of life lasted for over several thousand years very successfully. The basic spirit of the Vedic wisdom was dedicating the human life towards attaining or realizing the spiritual truth in life. Yet the Vedic sages and people of that civilization had devoted their lives into regular activities of life as a normal person. That spirit cannot be exactly replicated in the modern era. However, the basic underlying message of that great civilization which has the record of coordinating human life's activities for over several thousand years most effectively can be replicated in the modern period. This requires the intent of modern man towards that direction. A manager can play a very important role in establishing that. If the human objective is to create a happy, balanced, harmonious and just society, it has no other option but to establish a society and a transaction system in the world based on the Vedic spiritual principle. This principle has been highlighted under the title 'Wisdom Era'.

Evolution of Management Thoughts

The phases of management thoughts and processes are as follows:

- The wisdom era of spiritual human emergence
- The era of heroism and dominance of strength
- The era of collectivism through cultural interactions
- The era of scientific materialistic rational
- The era of cohesion through process impersonalization
- The era of human behaviour and human dominance
- The spiritual–scientific management of holism
- The era of autonomous individuality

The Wisdom Era

The Vedic period in India scaled the wisdom era. The impact of the Vedic principles got spread throughout the world through commercial connections of the European region via the Middle East. India's philosophies got spread in various parts of the world. Ancient India was known in the entire world as the place with huge reserves of gold and precious materials. Savages in the world who lived on looting the sea and making sudden attacks on the coastal regions and places could get in touch with them. In India and around the Indian Ocean, the European pirates and Arabian looters were widely known during the early period of human history. The Indian civilization during the Harappa and Mohenjo-daro periods was the pinnacle of scientific and technological achievement in the history of human journey through the paths of the world. This period had revealed advancement of the society based on the spirit of the Vedic principles of life. The Vedic period spans through a long journey of nearly 15,000 years.

The wisdom era is the longest period of the span of an era in the human civilization. This era can be divided into two segments. These two segments are as follows:

- The Vedic era spanning up to the war of the Mahabharata. This period can be termed as the era of pure wisdom.
- The post-Mahabharata war period, which can be termed as the era of applied wisdom.

Both these eras were under the philosophical influence of the Vedic ideals. The basics of the Vedic philosophy were widely covered in the life and activities of people in the world during this period of several thousand years.

Era of Pure Wisdom

The pure wisdom era was principle centric. The society was structured across spiritual principles in life. All actions were basically drawn through coordinated ways in such a fashion that the principles became a set of doctrines having the power to govern, coordinate and control. Certain principles that were construed as dominant and most important among all others are as follows:

- Truthful in thoughts, words and actions
- Faithful in the intrinsic contexts and the inner self
- Wisdom seeking towards realizing the cosmic spirit
- Affirmation to the things to be undertaken through a challenge
- Cooperation in the context of work in the world
- Honesty in character and behaviour in the context of the world
- Caring for the people of the world, particularly the deserving ones
- Compassion for the weaker ones in the society
- Sincerity in thoughts and actions in the context of the world
- Integrity in personality being non-discriminative, synchronized in thoughts and words

The pure wisdom era was basically a values-centric era. All actions and initiatives arise out of the fundamental attitude of life, which is centric to principles. The principles are basically noble principles. So all activities of life used to move around these noble qualities. Vedic way was the path of the movement in life to get into the realm of noble effects of the actions in the world that spontaneously give rise to some good effects of life.

Era of Applied Wisdom

Examples of the applied wisdom-centric pattern of living were vibrant in India during the ancient post-Vedic period. Living examples of that were made into the practice of life for several millennia before the pre-historic period as documentation could surface in. During the Harappan civilization, those Vedic principles were adhered to. The art of collective living through a process of mutual cooperation, understanding and civilized living were practised in the Harappan culture in India. Certain aspects of technological wonders and impact of scientific minds were visible during the post-Vedic period, glimpses of which have been there in Harappa and Mohenjo-daro. During this period, the society had developed a unique form of collectivism. Spirit of collectivism was visible in the living system developed. Glimpses of this are visible at the sites of Harappa. Some of these are as follows:

- Structured homes built with stones and some metallic artefacts
- Wide roads constructed with solid materials for durability
- Wide wells constructed where pure water was made available for the drinking and personal use of people
- Wide bathing wells which were used by a large number of people at a time
- Language for communication and connections among people for well-being of all
- Principle of life: *Sarve bhavantu shukhinah sarve santu niramaya*

The pyramids of Egypt and the Great Wall of China are among the indicative and penetrative aspects of life and living left behind the examples of the global society. These ideas got spread through the ideas developed and cultivated during the pre-historic and early historic period.

The basic idea of Vedas was echoed during the early Christian period. This has been depicted in the 'Divine Comedy' by Dante.

Glimpses of this are revealed in the following realization of the spirit:

How I entered there I cannot truly say. I had become so sleepy at the moment when I first strayed, leaving the path of truth.

A bitter place! Death could scarce be bitterer. But if I would show the good that came of it I must talk about things other than the good.

But my own wings could not take me so high. Then a great flash of understanding struck my mind, and suddenly its wish was granted. (Dante)

Dante's realization was intrinsic in the core understanding of individuals.

This realization was based on the following parameters:

- Faith in the Supreme Spirit for life's emergence
- Individual urge for goodness for the collective
- Intrinsic guidance by the supreme light
- Inner strength for winning life's aspirations

The emergence of 'heroism' in the entire land of Europe was an immediate consequence of the principles lived on and the attributes of life developed out of the cultivation of certain core principles, applied in the respective manners. Dante had identified the spirit of goodness through the faith that he had garnered during the set of drives initiated in life one after the other.

Faith in the Supreme Spirit derives the guidance from within to deliver collective good and live a life that refers to the inner strength of man towards greater accomplishment.

An arrogant and egoistic person may garner some kind of momentary heroism. This heroism in life can be accomplished to some extent but fails to provide goodness to a larger set of people or a larger section of a community or the mass. This requires a humble personality, not a humbug.

A unique example of such a mind is seen in the personality of a monk of global acclaim and a person who had won the mind and heart of millions and also seeded the becoming of a long-term institution that has already survived the threats and pressures of different forces over a century and a half as of now and is poised to take off beyond the boundaries of centuries. This great person is Swami Vivekananda, who mentioned his own way to project the idea of universality as:

I have travelled all over the world; I have been among the very worst kind of people—among 'Carnivals'—and I have never seen the man who is not at least my equal. I have done as they do—when I was a fool. Then I did not know any better; now I do. Now they do not know better; after a while they will. Everyone acts according to his own nature. We are all in the process of growth. From this stand point one man is not better than another. (Swami Vivekananda, 1900)

Principle-centric view of life requires the resilience and wideness of view and mental framework. Cultivation of 'goodness' within one's own self is important for accomplishing this principle in life, not only to cultivate individual goodness but also to spread the spirit of goodness through the faith in the Cosmic Spirit and the role of everyone in the design of the same spirit.

Goodness dominating in the mind and thoughts of the leaders of society transforms the social consciousness from merely driven by the collective interest of the group they belong to and serving the smaller domain to a wider interest that benefits many more people in the process of their living. The wisdom era, thus, had revealed the true spirit of human existence from one extent to the other delivering things in such a manner that used to benefit the larger mass of people going beyond the immediate boundary of beneficiaries out of that action. This could bring in the series of thoughts and actions that have always tried both ways—to benefit the immediate set of responsible centres and to go beyond the immediate boundary of concern and create a momentum for the rolling forward of the spirit of goodness towards the broader extent of the society to better the life and aspects of human living in general.

A humble mind actually helps those who have deviated from the path of fairness to do things that are undesired. It develops and transmits the power to transform forward and create a global society based on the spirit of fairness.

Ancient civilization in India did translate the spirit of wisdom in several ways. The major streams were grouped through some broad divisions and expressed through six different schools of philosophies called *sharadarshana*. The major objective of all these was to understand and develop realization of god in different ways, see the impacts and presence of that realization in different ways and finally cultivate the doctrines in such a way that the major schools of such doctrines offered by the Indian civilization have bearing and impacts on the thoughts of goodness developed and cultivated by people of the world in different ways.

Basic Six Indian Philosophies

The five major streams of Indian philosophy are as follows:

- Vedanta (the unified spirit of universality)
- Shakti (the strength and force of being and becoming)
- Bhakti (the stream of devotion and dedication)
- Samkhya (the nature of universal with the spirit behind)
- Buddhist thoughts of goodness of life through good thoughts and acts

Vedanta believes in the existence of god as an invisible force that remains and resides in everyone and everything, that is, all living and non-living objects as a subtle, invisible strength that acts as the supreme strength of life, the world and the universe. The Supreme is:

- Omnipresent
- Omniscient
- Universal

This invisible strength, though common in all, does not interfere in the thoughts, actions and pledges of life. Man has been gifted with a free mind and the individual capacity to think and act in his own ways but is always coordinated and guided by the spirit behind. The invisible universality becomes activated through the spirit of life within and connects the same with the world around.

Doctrines of strength and devotion demand the universal spirit to be revealed in terms of forms of existence and refer to the forms of god. Strength originates from the form of god for human action through faith, self-confidence and enduring divine action through the ideas of goodness prevailing around. The cosmic nature brings in the doctrine of cosmic rationality, where the earth system always tries to indulge in the enjoyment of certain types of impersonal elements of dormant goodness, and to bring forth the aforementioned dormant goodness into the visible, tangible action of life.

Thus, the doctrine tries to push and connect human awareness to the supreme well-being of everyone and establish a path of continuity towards creating a homogeneous human society for creating a world society that attempts to nurture human objective to have a good life and bring forth goodness for others around as well. This tends to create a mental framework that supports everyone and attempts to provide goodness to the entire human society and civilization.

Strong reflections of the original thoughts of goodness structured across several streams are observed in certain basic thoughts of the Chinese civilization. There emerged certain schools of thoughts in ancient China that resembled the spirit of goodness as proclaimed by the Vedas and attempted to make enduring impacts on the human society. At the core of these thoughts the impact of the Vedic ideas has been very much visible.

The highlighting streams of these ancient Chinese thoughts are as follows:

- The school of Confucianism: promoting sense of right and wrong
- The school of Taoism: Lao-Tze's doctrine of self-effacements
- The school of Motism: understanding basic utilitarianism
- The school of Yin-Yang: discovering the law of nature to follow

Brief mentions about these could be as follows:

The school of Taoism urged the unity of spirit to men. It advocates that all activities should be in harmony with the unseen and with abundant liberality towards all things in nature.

As to practice some thinkers accept the orderly sequence of nature from Ying-Yang school for living and maintaining the process of good life in society and the earth system.

The Confucian school identifies the right and distinguishes it from the wrong. It develops the right ways to think and act.

With the identification of utility of thoughts and actions, Motism combines with the school of law and school of names.

With the changes in the seasons, these schools, thus, combine with the spirit and work for the betterment of the society. In accordance with the changes in the seasons and changes in the natural contexts, these views act for the development of the natural objects.

This achievement fits everywhere. The applications of such ideas are made in such a way that they are simple and easy to carry out.

Performances lead to the culmination of the objective of life and thus the objective of the society.

The good thinkers used to perform but little, yet the achievements generated are numerous.

The Vedic spirit of dedicated and collective work was applied for making the great Chinese wall. However, it failed to create a society with absolute values at the centre of civilization to remove discriminations.

The Vedic spirit was primarily bringing our minds together for a greater benefit of the people on earth. The following verse of the Rig Veda focuses on the spirit:

Sam gachhadhvam sam vadadhvam sam vo manamsi janatam.

Meaning: Let us unite our minds together let us all speak the same tongue.

This talks about bringing individual minds together and developing common agenda and voice in life and works. This Vedic view of collectivism was a unique advancement in the ancient world. This got spread over a period of time in Asian, Arabian and European regions within the pre- and post-Christ periods.

The impact of the thoughts developed during the wisdom era were percolated down towards creating new set of things which provided guidance for creating a better society through making of better organizations. Historically, the emperors ruling throughout ages have banked on the doctrine of heroism and the emergence of some great personalities.

In the early age, the Western world witnessed the rise of individual hero in the personalities who were primarily invaders of different areas of the world and made empires as a result of these invasions.

Alexander's invasion of the Eastern world created the situation that could provide a solution to the scheme of things. Alexander's individual learning, as a student of Aristotle, was to develop individual heroism. This concept of heroism was different from the Platonic doctrine of ethics. Heroism could establish a durable context if it had pursued certain fundamental principles of righteousness. Principles of righteousness and values of noble character could create a long-term and enduring context of the world. Alexander's heroism focused on achieving and winning things in any way and to take back precious wealth and resources to benefit his people and himself at the cost of devastation and destruction of the places thus battled through for the purpose of winning in any way.

On the other hand, the war at the Kurukshetra coordinated by the great warrior Arjuna was for the purpose of establishing righteous principles for the society and human lives. The hero had to undertake destruction of many to fulfil the righteous objectives of life.

Alexander's objective was to amass wealth and resources apart from capturing areas of the world for dominance. That means this concept of heroism was dominated by power instinct.

Arjuna's objective was to fulfil the objective of god in destroying the evil forces and establishing the power of good and values. He used to adhere to the principles of ensuring well-being for all.

Alexander's approach was dominance by his own spirit of heroism and personal ego in these actions throughout.

Arjuna's approach was to support the cause of god who was personally supporting and helping his cause throughout.

The Savage Faces of History: Negative Heroism

Historical development of the world next was a mix of negative heroism and collectivism dominated by negative heroism. During the Vedic period, the proper idea of collectivism was developed. Vedic collectivism was based on spirit of goodness and the urge to do well to all. It was never aimed at creating any problem for the life of anyone and there was no killing or causing harm to anyone else for converting their faith to one's own in any way.

Although heroism can be fulfilling throughout, with the possession of strength and the power of applying that strength towards fulfilling the desires, it proves fatal to human existence. There were real savage forces during different phases of history that have cared little for being direct or background killers of great masses of people in order to force their own doctrines in the society.

This has been witnessed during the medieval period in India. The Moghuls and Pathans could enter in India basically because of the kindness and openness of the society maintained by the kings with liberal gifting attitude. These kings of India had never thought of applying the strength of muscles against people and have atrocities in the outlook. Having penetrated somehow, these invaders came with a small mass of savage power to capture a part of India as they knew about the country's possession of great wealth. Eventually, for over generations they applied all bad tactics to acquire wider range of land in India. Once they started making inroads, the ugly faces of those savage aggressors got revealed. The two most savage kings of that origin were Babar and Akbar. Both had acquired power through unethical means and applied the power against the Indian masses. Both Babar and Akbar were killers of thousands of populations in the act of fulfilling their agenda of mass conversion to the faith they belonged to. In order to do that effectively, they started demolishing the temples and shrines of India. Many of these temples and shrines were in place for thousands of years and were considered as the most auspicious by the people. Demolition of temples, forcing the masses to get converted to their faith or else to pay heavy prices including personal torture on their ladies and death at the end. This period of the Middle Ages is the real period of Black stint in India.

Similar Black era was there in the early modern and modern eras in Europe. The periods of Adolf Hitler in Germany, Joseph Stalin in Russia and Mao Zedong in China were such periods when a large mass of people were crucified to be punished for not getting converted to their respective faiths.

India has always, from the ancient to the modern period, honoured the principle-centric view of life and allowed multiplicity of faith in the society. Highlighting features of the Indian civilization have been in place during the entire period of its existence except for the period of the foreign origin forces in place. The Bhagavad Gita has depicted the Indian spirit in a focused manner.

In the example of Arjuna, since the real objective was impersonal and involved god's presence, the actions were cherished and the impact of the achievement was enduring and long term.

Principle-based heroism can only bring in long-term goodness for the entity and for everyone else these set of initiatives and actions. Goodness for all brings in sustainable results.

This era of goodness did not sustain over a long period after the Vedic era. The concepts did sustain in a sporadic manner in the history of human civilization. Not as a whole for a continued period but as a concept which could be applied in different phases of human history until the current period. Gradually, the proportion of good and well-wishers of everyone has been going down, replacing collective initiative with individual initiatives, where individuals are immersed in good thoughts and spirit of divinity.

Scientific Materialistic Rational View and Cohesion through Impersonalization

The era of collectivism and the scientific materialistic approach were spelled out by many scholars of management as follows:

- The scientific management approach
- The general administrative approach

Scientific Management Approach

Fredrick Winslow Taylor advocated the principles of scientific management which he had published in 1911. They are as follows:

- Identifying the elements of work and creating a structured method to replace the rule of thumb method with a rationally coordinated method.
- Management and workers are identified as distinctly different entities.
- Workers are to be hired on the basis of the real requirement of the work. They will be trained to develop the skills required of them to accomplish the work in the best possible ways.
- Management should cooperate with the workers in the best possible ways to see that the work is done in accordance with the expressed requirement of the work.
- Principles of scientific rational should govern the approach of work and the context of the work.
- Work and responsibility should go hand in hand. Management should develop the schedule of work to be done by the workers.
- Management should take the responsibility of the well-being of the workers in the interest of work.

F. W. Taylor had appreciated the efforts of the president of the United States, Theodore Roosevelt, on his policies of conservation of national resources. Theodore Roosevelt considered the conservation of national resources as preliminary in developing national efficiency. Taylor identified that a right man can not only be searched out but also be developed. The goal of work should be to develop efficiency.

Taylor had identified some principles with the following highlights:

- Inefficiency looms largely in works and activities that can be reversed
- Extraordinary man or unusual personality may be searched out from the society to deliver more efficiently, but it is better to develop a systematic management system rather than waiting for the extraordinary persons in the society.
- The best management is a science. It should depend on clearly defined laws, rules and principles. This implies the belief that the best way to enhance the efficiency in utilizing the natural and national resources is to adopt the science of management. Management is a true science, which should be based on the structured and defined laws, rules and principles. This can be applied in the context of individuals, enterprises of any size, any type, any context, any home, any social entity, any firm, churches, small businesses, philanthropic institutions, educational institutions and even governments.

The greatest contribution of Taylor was the motion and time study. It attempted to identify the areas of loss of human energy in the system and generate better output through schemes of incentives for initiatives.

General Theory of Business Administration of Henri Fayol

A mining engineer and director of mines, Henri Fayol, had published his work in French, later on translated into English, which was a pioneering work on general theory of management and administration. Fayol had identified five primary functions of management which are valid to date as well. They are as follows:

- Planning
- Organizing
- Commanding
- Coordinating
- Controlling

Fayol had visualized and advocated for the following.

1. *Division of work:* Specialization in the workforce to enhance productivity of the organization.
2. *Authority and responsibility:* Responsibility should be connected to authority so that the person can perform effectively.
3. *Discipline:* This promotes right conduct of people in an organization with mutually respectful attitude to develop cohesion among people in the organization.

4. *Unity of command:* The decision should flow as orders from defined unitary sources to avoid any conflict of focus in the work and agenda of the organization.
5. *Unity of direction:* Departments or groups in an organization should be directed to fulfil the desired objective or goal of the work.
6. *Subordination of individual interest to general interest of the team or the organization:* This applies to everyone in the organization right from the top in the hierarchy to the bottom-most level.
7. *Remuneration:* Fair wage for the work delivered by a worker or a person in the organization is a must for the best results.
8. *Centralization and decentralization:* This implies the attitude to increase the involvement of subordinates in the decision-making process
9. *Scalar chain:* Defined line of authority from the top management to the bottom-most level to convey assignments and for better effectiveness of the work procedure
10. *Order:* People, materials, machines and everything in the organization should have an identified place. Systematic arrangement of men, machine and materials is essential for any size and type of organization, and it should be treated as vital for large production or manufacturing entities.
11. *Equity:* Justice should be in force for everyone in the organization. Each person should feel equally important in the organization to be fully contributing to the productive system.
12. *Stability of tenure of everyone:* Tenure of a person working in the organization should be identified so that the person has a feeling of stability. Also, the plans for replacements should be in place to take care of any important position having fallen vacant for any reason.
13. *Initiative:* High levels of initiatives are expected of employees with decision-making and planning agenda.
14. *Esprit de corps:* This advocates the idea to promote team spirit. Team spirit in an organization enhances harmony and unity among people in the organization. Thus, the output is always higher.

The general administrative approach of Henry Fayol and Max Weber attempted to identity the hand and body movement of the worker to fulfil the work. It had the intent to develop the following: rationality, predictability, impersonality, technical competence, authoritarianism, collective spirit to combine with each other and join hands with others to accomplish the assigned work. Also, they suggested marginal changes in the design of work.

The general administrative approach requires managers to understand the company, the work and the worker in terms of each element to categorically suit the purpose of the work and the organizations. As mentioned before, the elements identified by Henri Fayol played a very important role in the emergence of management thoughts and practices, some of the elements that this approach had in its prerogative are mentioned here again as a measure to explain each item of his thought in the following sequence.

1. *Division of work:* Through this division the company can create specialization in actions for better ways to get the output and better results.
2. *Authority:* Authority lies with the manager. With this right, the manager tries to give orders for the work and receives the output suited to the purpose of the organization.
3. *Unity of command:* There should be an identified and single source of authority and the orders should come from the same source of power. This develops the spirit of work in a coordinated way.
4. *Unity of direction:* The direction and objectives of the work done by the workers should be the same as that of the one chosen by the organization.
5. *Discipline:* The rules and regulations imposed on the organization on one hand and that of the said organization needs to be adhered to. This helps the organization to achieve properly coordinated business of the organisation.
6. *Priority of the general interest over individual interest:* This implies that the individual interest of the person should be always subordinated to that of the organization and the interest of the larger group of people within the organization.
7. *Remuneration:* Fair wage commensurate with the degree and quantum of work should be given to the worker and the regulatory stipulation for the same be adhered to.
8. *Scalar chain:* The direction of control and coordination should be top-down towards the shop floor and the person involved in the work.
9. *Centralization:* Decision-making should be top-down. However, participation of the worker in the process of decision-making should be oriented towards the centralization of the work design.
10. *Equity:* The organization should promote an equal approach towards all. Equity in the views and approach of the people in the organization should be ensured. For the work of a particular design and content, the wage or remuneration of the person be established or ensured.
11. *Order:* Scheduling of materials is required in the place at the time of manufacturing of a finished goods. Man and materials which are required in the manufacturing process be oriented to the needs of people.

12. *Initiative:* When the plans and actions are in place, the effort that one should be recognized in the light of the work should be accomplished. Once the effort of the person is recognized, the person gets additional energy in delivering work to be highlighted for that.
13. *Stability of tenure:* Once the worker and duration of a particular work are identified, it is now the responsibility of the organization to define the tenure of the person.
14. *Esprit de corps:* For a team to deliver the best output, there is a need to develop the spirit of teamwork. Whenever the team spirit for the work is discovered, the output ranges the highest.

The above-mentioned approaches gave shape to the organizational development. Structured mechanisms have paved the way to look into the behaviour of people connected with the organization.

One of the most important aspects of the functioning is the urge to understand the people. Those who are working with the organization should be understood. How much is the level of involvement of the organization in the process of the work is very important as this would clearly identify the level of energy the person would be devoting to the work of the organization.

The work of the organization, demands understanding of the spirit of underlying work. This is actually the level of motivation. A motivated person delivers the most. They deliver the work in such a way that they work beyond the usual limits of human potential. The behavioural era of management emphasized on taking ownership of the work and contributing the best in the best possible manner.

The Era of Human Behaviour and Human Dominance

Elton Mayo, a professor of Harvard University, after having examined the work situation at a major industrial enterprise in the United States came to the conclusion that the group behaviour of individuals in an organization plays an important role in the productivity of the organization. The Western Electric Company in Illinois, United States, had engaged Elton Mayo to advise the company on the Hawthorne experiments as well as to understand whether the context of work and workplace behaviour of people collectively impact the output of the organization or not.

Hawthorne experiments were conducted in the company with a control group with a constant intensity of shop floor lighting and the experimental group was exposed to variable intensities of light at different points of time. The objective of this study was to find any connection between the two. Hawthorne experiments could not establish any relation between the lighting intensity and worker productivity. Finally, it was found that some other factor might be responsible for low productivity. Elton Mayo and his associates came to the conclusion that group behaviour plays a major role in changing the work behaviour of individual workers. Incentive schemes also play an important role, but factors such as group pressure, acceptance and security have a better impact. Elton Mayo observed that money was less a factor in determining output than group attitudes, standards and security. Behaviour and attitudes of people are closely related and group factors affect individual behaviour significantly.

People Behaviours Approach

This approach basically happened on this identity of a worker or an employee of any identity in organization. Robert Owen's contribution during the late 1700s was remarkable, as he observed that worker's condition of work should be a matter of concern for the identity. Owen's observation and recommendation included the following:

- Deplorable working conditions should be changed to better conditions
- A better condition of workplace promotes better output of the organization
- Organizations should invest money to improve the condition of labour and the place of work
- Better workplace creates basis for wider growth of the organization

Hugo Munsterberg had advocated for industry-wide psychology. During the early 1900s, he suggested the need for wide study of people at work to understand how people respond to the condition and context of the work. His basic recommendations were as follows:

- People at work should be studied using scientific parameters and the results be quantified for decisions
- Psychological tests be done for selection of people in organization
- Employees be trained to tune to the orientation of the organization
- Human behaviours in organizations be studied to understand the sources of motivation for the people at work

Mary Parker Follett during the same period as that of Hugo Munsterberg identified the need to understand group behaviours in an organization. Follett identified the following:

- Organizations need to be understood from the point of view of individuals and groups

- Group behaviour needs to be understood in the organizational context
- Groups properly energized can contribute better to the organization
- People-oriented views to be given higher importance than the structured, impersonal scientific management practices
- Group ethic should be identified for the groups within the organization

The workplace issues were better understood through Hawthorne studies. This was conducted at the Western Electric Company in Cicero, Illinois, United States, during the mid-1920s. The study initiated with the workplace highting level and to understand the industrial output as a result of that started in 1924, the experiment concluded with the impact of workplace light on the productivity. Workplace lighting was gradually lowered, and it was found that productivity decreased. However, with slight reduction in light productivity remained the same. Whenever the bright lighting was reduced to the level of moonlight there was significant reduction in the productivity. Another experiment was synchronizing the impact of sound and habit through external means; collective and group activities were studied and the pattern of behaviours was precisely understood and recorded. Later, the experiments on the work design, group activity, remuneration to work, workplace culture, working condition, length of work and rest and so on were conducted by the Harvard professor, Elton Mayo, and inferences were drawn from them. During the early 1930s, Chester Barnard made a significant contribution to the evolution of management thoughts. Chester Bernard identified that:

- An organization needs to be considered as on open system like a society.
- An organization requires cooperation both from the people who work within and those who are associated with it.
- A manager needs to communicate the objective of the organization to all workers and see that the communication has been effective.
- A manager needs to stimulate high levels of efforts among employees and workers.
- As a social system, organizations should have means to have dialogue with people and make them confident about the association with the place of work and the organization.

Elton Mayo observed the following:

- Peoples' behaviour and attitude towards work are closely related
- Money is a factor up to only a certain level

- Group behaviour impacts on individuals are significant in the organization
- Group dynamics of affirmations helps to increase productivity
- Security and group attitude play an important role in determining and maintaining the quality and quantum of output
- Human behaviour, both at the individual and group levels, plays a general role in identifying the higher achievement by the organization

Later developments included that of leading thinkers and real practitioners in the global context. The later schools of thought have relied on the quantitative dimension of management. This had in focus the concerns of the stakeholders in business. By and large, the main stakeholders in business are as follows:

1. Shareholders
2. Customers/Consumers
3. Employees
4. Government
5. Traders/Financiers/Creditors
6. Society
7. People

Each segment of the stakeholders has its own way of looking at the business. Each segment looks at the business from its own perspective and expects the outcome as per its intrinsic relation with the business.

Shareholders: When a company is born, it needs initial investment to establish it, and to get it on feet. Initial investment usually comes from a group of people who are the owners of the enterprise. The enterprise grows in dimension through interactions in the market, thereby requiring significant amount of reinvestment into the business. This is done through many ways. Out of these diverse options, one option is to broad base the corporate activity through public participation in the pattern of shareholding. This makes the ownership of the company distributed to many in the proportion of the shares held by each.

A shareholder is the owner of the company. They invest money in the basic functioning and activities of the company. Money invested by the shareholder comes in the record of the company as its own fund. That means the fund provided by the owners. The shareholders enjoy equal status with respect to the company, in the proportion of the money invested in the company. Shareholders do not get back the interest on money from the company. They have two types of gains through investment in the shares of a company. These gains are as follows:

1. Dividend yield
2. Capital gain

Dividend yield: Dividend is the share of profit earned by the company at the end of the period of operation. Companies do the assessments of the current and past performances and plan out for the future, sitting in the annual general meeting (AGM). If they have earned some profit, then they decide to plough back a part of it for growth and expansion of the company and set aside another component for the purpose of marketing including sales promotion, advertising, schemes and apart from these costs of obsolescence should be maintained at a level of optimum or less than the optimum.

- Less amount to be given to the government in the form of taxation and other fiscal responsibilities.
- Lesser expenses towards manpower development, acquisition and maintenance costs.
- Lower involvement towards social and environmental liabilities.
- Higher brand value, higher perceptive value in the stock markets and greater access to national and international opportunities.

The customers/consumers would expect from the company in the following ways:

- Best price vis-à-vis the quality of the product or service
- Best quality vis-à-vis the price of the product or service
- Higher utility of the product or the service
- Higher degree of satisfaction with the product or service
- More quantity at the same price
- Higher access to a large range of products or services to choose from
- Better quality people to interact with while buying the products or services
- Better attention through realigning with the intrinsic expectations of the consumer
- More visibility and wider acceptability of the brand endorsed by the customer or consumer
- Higher degree of flexibility in the configuration of the product or service
- Lesser magnitude and extent of wastage and higher degree of salvage from the product or service
- Elemental delight present in the product or service
- Scope of brand association or band ownership

Each item of expectation has a cost involved in its accomplishment. Shareholders always draw their happiness from such actions of the company. The shareholders would always expect that companies spent less to earn more and create more surplus. With more surplus in hand, companies will find higher demand for the shares in the share market. So the scope for higher capital gain will be available for investors or traders in the share market. Also with higher net profit allocable, surplus for distributions among shareholders will be more, thus companies will issue higher amount of dividend per share from the company.

Employees of the organization think of their contribution in the process of business as the most important. Employees expect the following:

- Higher pay and benefits from the company for the same level or work for the company
- Higher scope for professional and skill development at the cost of the company
- Better terms of employment with the company
- Higher scope for growth within the hierarchy of the organization
- Partial ownership of the company through possession of some of the equity shares of the company
- Higher level of recognition within the company

Employees expect things which are logical in their approach. Each of these demands and expectations has a cost involved. Shareholders always expect that the employees get optimum or the minimum amount against their complete contributions as per expectation.

Government: Government expects to benefit from the business in two broad ways—economic and monetary benefits.

Monetary benefit: This occurs through the benefits earned from the company. With the functioning of the company, government earns fiscal benefit from the business operations and outputs.

When the company makes profit, a part of the gross profit (GP) after deduction of all other items makes the government's taxation. Taxations as applied to the case of the company need to be paid to the government. With growing and profitable business of the company, government earns higher corporate tax. In addition to this, the employees receive payments from the company, higher the capacity of the company, higher would be the payments received by employees and direct taxes from the individuals would be higher also.

Economic benefit: Companies contribute to the state and the society in different ways, some of which are as follows:

- Companies offer employment to the people in the society.
- With growth and expansion of the company, employment potential of the company increases.

- Companies undertake certain responsibilities of the society under their corporate social responsibility programme.
- Companies undertake environmental responsibility.
- Products or services of the companies need the market and the traders to help the customers and consumers in getting products or services at the desired level of exchange of value.
- Companies involve logistics, supply chain, distributors, retailers and large number of people involved at each stage contributing to the economic value of the state.
- Companies collectively help develop market for the products or services bringing in higher economic value for the state.
- Companies create professional climate in the area that helps generate a social climate conducive to the growth of educational and health facilities of the region.

Traders/Financiers/Creditors: Traders, creditors and financiers expect the company to perform in such a way that benefits them but at times at the cost of other stakeholders.

- They expect their money to be returned with desired appreciation in such a manner that fulfils the terms of contract for the trade finance or trade credit.
- They expect quicker repayment of the finances given to the company. With quicker repayments to be made to the company, the short-term liquidity of the company is of concern. Companies should have adequate short-term liquidity. This means the company should have sufficient current assets of the current liabilities.

Society and people: Apparently, the society in general and people at large are not connected with the enterprises. However, the rise of modernism in human activity and technology-driven civilization, companies should adhere to the concerns of the society. The general concerns of society and people are as follows, each of which means cost of the company:

- Business should adhere to the principles of ethical transactions.
- Companies should fulfil the concerns of the society before they earn or attempt to earn profit
- Companies with whatever origin should abide by the social norms and practices governing activities in the society
- The products or services offered by the companies should not violate the general expectations of the societies. The cultures and rituals followed by general mass need to be respected by the companies.
- Societies with mixed or differential demographics would expect companies to have a generic view and attitude about business.

- Societies and people would expect more economic support in terms of higher employment of people.
- More involvement in the economic design of the societies in terms of higher of business through people and organizations of the society
- Participation in the voluntary activities to help societies sustain the weaker people living in.

Role of the Manager

The manager is a bridge between the owners and the market.

Step 1: To understand the company through its

- Mission
- Vision
- Objectives
- Short- and long-term plans

Step 2: To understand the environment in which the company is doing or supposed to do business through

- Economic environment
- Social environment
- Cultural environment
- Political environment
- Technological environment
- Special issues concerning many

Step 3: To understand and develop plans and strategies with a view to make the business happen and with the market response and customer favour through

- Plans to achieve the mission and objectives
- Develop policies and broad guidelines with regard to doing business through proper decisions and executions
- Design programmes to take business forward, make the products and services accepted by the customers and create attractions across the products and services, thus to earn value more than the value that has gone into business through investments and financing
- Develop budgets and do business in such a way that the gains out of the business are usually more than that stipulated in the business
- Develop procedures to do the business based on norms and standards
- Evaluate performance of everyone to see that each one has contributed not less than desired performance for the company

The manager should be aware of the following issues concerning the company:

<table>
<tr><th colspan="4">Resources</th></tr>
<tr><td>Material</td><td colspan="3">• What are the material resources available with the company
• How to make use of the existing material resources
• What additional or new material resources are needed for the business
• Develop short- and long-term plans to utilize the material resources in the best possible manner
• Continuous updating on the need for and use of material resources</td></tr>
<tr><td>Human</td><td colspan="3">• What are the requirements of manpower
• Skill and values of the manpower needed
• Enhancing efficiency and effectiveness of the manpower
• Getting manpower properly motivated for the best output
• Engineering creativity among people
• Team cohesion for the best output and integrated response for the growth of the company</td></tr>
<tr><th colspan="4">External Resources</th></tr>
<tr><td rowspan="3">Short-term financial resources</td><td colspan="3">Current assets to be monitored through major items of business</td></tr>
<tr><th>Cash</th><th>Inventory</th><th>Receivable</th></tr>
<tr><td>Manager must keep watch on the liquidity balance through regular monitoring of expenditure and income</td><td>Inventory be managed in such a way that business can service the market demand yet mention optimum investment in inventory</td><td>Manager should try to bring back liquidity through regular recovery of the business receivable which occur on sales made but payment not obtained</td></tr>
<tr><td>Fixed assets and brand value</td><td colspan="3">It is the fundamental responsibility of the management of a company that the brand value is created and made to grow higher also to see that long-term assets, fixed in nature, are created adequately. A manager has to follow the same principle and policy.</td></tr>
<tr><td>Long-term financial resources:</td><td colspan="3">• The equity fund being company's own fund needs to be seen and utilized carefully
• Manager should look into long-term value creation for the company through branding and creating long-term fixed assets
• Debt intake should be opportunity only and all risk factors that arise out of debt intake be kept on vigil</td></tr>
</table>

References

Dante. *The divine comedy*. 1-1-10/12.

Swami Vivekananda. (1900). *The ideal of universal religion*. Lecture at California Unitarian Church, Pasadena, CA, USA.

CHAPTER 7

DECISION AND ACTION SCIENCE: THE BIOLOGICAL WAY

Management Decisions

Study and practice of management go hand in hand. Historically, there have been a large number of cases where the practice of management has emerged out of the blue. In the beginning of industrialization and the Industrial Revolution, the methods of co-ordinations of enterprise management were mostly individual driven. The advent of steam engine in its primitive form was an idea about using the water power through heating. The developments gave rise to the Industrial Revolution during the 18th century. James Watt's contribution to the development of the steam engine was the real breakthrough. He developed the external combustion system and later on developed a parallel system, which made the engine work for wheel movements successfully. The force produced by steam pressure pushes the piston back and forth inside the cylinder. The force thus produced works on a connecting rod and flywheel. It is made to work on the system in such a way that it develops a relational force and makes the wheels rotate, and it works on the principle of transforming the heat energy into mechanical energy. It was made to drive the wheels of carts making the cart into a rapid movement vehicles, and in its matured condition getting this applied into a better facility to move forward through developing railway wagons. With the development of steam engine, gradual transformation started off rapidly among the industrial enterprises formed. The impetus was there in the European spirit of doing new things, discoveries and inventions. However, major thrust came from England. The Industrial Revolution required a strong financial backup and adequate resources for growth and sustenance. European initiatives in Germany, France and Italy were mostly driven by indigenous resources, but the focus of the Industrial Revolution shifted to England. This was primarily driven by a new set of resources garnered by the British initiatives through their new domain of business with India. East India Company started to focus on dominating the Indian subcontinent with direct help and participation of the government of Great Britain. East India Company's initiatives were joined by many companies and initiatives from various corners of Europe, particularly France, Italy, Germany, Denmark and small- or medium-capacity initiatives from Great Britain. Although historians are yet to do justice on the depiction of the real flow of resources towards the Industrial Revolution that took place in Europe, no doubt at all that it was India, if not alone, but mostly. Business with India helped the British and other European enterprises to invest in need areas of growth. A new industrial set-up grew out of the previous. The textile industry was, among others, the most prominent one to come forward with new productive approaches and develop a higher level of manufacturing mechanism through development of new type of machines replacing the pure manual production.

Management Thoughts

Thoughts and practices of management keep on changing. They change over a period of time. Also, the thoughts and practices change with respect to the geographical locations and other major variables. However, slow and small changes remain unnoticed until identified by some special factors or parameters. Impacts of social culture, current of events, economic conditions, collective wishes, lifestyles, dominant trend of public motives and various other attributes play an important role in the choice of a decision model. Work process or the system of work changes because of many factors. From the early period of human civilization, the process of getting work done through minimum human labour has been strived for. It is an intrinsic human nature that attempts to broaden the horizon of human involvement and human activities. According to the *World Development Report, 2015*,

> *Individuals are not calculating automatons. Rather, people are malleable and emotional actors whose decision making is influenced by contextual cues, local social networks and social norms, and shared mental models. All of these play a role in determining what individuals perceive as desirable, possible, or even 'thinkable' for their lives.... (World Bank Group, 2015, p. 3)*

The structured view about management is just slightly over hundred years old, but the view of management was prevalent in all phases of human activity. The earliest form of unit management in society, groups and states was diverse in nature, with changes in the pattern of living and the outlook of life in various phases undergoing various changes. The changes were structured and unstructured at the same time. With the structured changes, the approach was to create a system and arrangement that would benefit the spirit of living. Changes have occurred throughout human history towards making an essential change in the views of life.

Mental models and social beliefs and practices often become deeply rooted in individuals. We tend to internalize aspects of society, taking them for granted as inevitable 'social facts'. People's mental models shape their understanding of what is right, what is natural, and what is possible in life. Social relations and structures, in turn, are the basis of socially constructed 'common sense', which represents the evidence, ideologies, and aspirations that individuals take for granted and use to make decisions—and which in some cases increase social differences. (World Bank Group, 2015)

The art of organizing has been organic in nature, and that is why the organizing faculty has always been prevalent and active in the journey of human beings. Human journey is essentially undertaken in nature. But at the same time, human journey has been collective as well. Even though it is considered collective, it happens sometimes such that the human mind has a tendency of seclusion. Although a human being wants to be in the company of others and in communion with others, at the core of the being, it always contains both. While collective living or being amidst others is a unique trend, it makes the human mind inclined towards the intrinsic identity of man. At the deeper core of being, the person understands, on the one hand, the need to become twined with the spirit and approach of collectiveness, and, on the other hand, the urge to be within the biological identity of being in touch with the spirit of the person at the movement when things are settled on a dynamic frame and support the ongoing passage of life forward. It is, thus, in tandem with the continuity and flow of the spirit of life that makes it happen in natural emergence, otherwise the spread of the essence and spirit of life makes the span of influence of a life on the surroundings significant always.

The Biological Pattern

A human being is basically driven by the inner biological arrangement of things. Any stimulus created from outside impacts the human system as long as the person is open to the context of the external stimulus. With the changes in the pattern of the stimulus, the response also changes. Gradual learning effect makes or attempts to change the pattern of response of the individual in accordance with the changes in the factors of the stimuli. It is the primary task of human neural system to make significant inroad into the functional habits or discrete functions in an organization so that the functional attributes are transformed in the process of life. Thus, the functional aspect of a person has approximately two coordinates to control the entire biophysical activities. Human mind, the functional organization of a human, on the one hand and the groups of human beings on the other always cluster around to cater to a purpose that always takes into account the factors which are imperatives of the human system. The purpose of the human cluster is either driven by undefined urge or sometimes by the necessity felt at the inner core of the being. The urge to have the human actions in seclusion, on the one hand, and that of making the collective living worthy, on the other, can make things possible in a way which may be desired by one individual and may not be acceptable to others. Collective entity grows out of human tendencies to make the matter to be felt and realized in a way considered significant by the most.

The biological pattern of a human system gives rise to the nature of our thinking and activities based on the thinking as that may happen in a sequential pattern or is a discrete pattern in life. Sequential arrangement in life occurs through the understanding of commonness. Common patterns or common parameters impact in the process of thinking of a person. Whether it is sequential or discrete in nature, the biological context of a person ultimately coordinates with the factors of growth on the basis of mutual understanding of things.

Factors that emerge as the common elements in collective lives are some of those which are actually destined to be the real-life factors for the emergence of commonality.

Six patterns emerge in the biological system as common pattern. These patterns are as follows:

1. Command and control system
2. Functional coordination system
3. Situational response system
4. Collective context for discrete response system
5. IPRS
6. Composite behaviour patterns

Command and Control System

Human activities are coordinated and controlled through the central nervous system (CNS). The synchronization is done through time scale and spread of situations and with the help of a control mechanism. Work is done by the outer body and functional coordination is done thereunto. But behind the work performed by the limbs, there remains the background coordination of the system in such a way that best befits the system towards making it always promising and effective. With this effective and promising system in place, the functional organs are better off, and they perform in a more effective way. Human brain coordinates the activities in a pattern which has a rhythmic connection with the cosmic rhythms. The cosmic rhythms are understood by the organic system automatically.

Located in an area of the human brain, called hypothalamus, a large group of neurons consisting of many thousands of nerve cells perform the function of a biological clock. This is not only in tune with one person's own system to take care of, but it also keeps parity with the demands of the cosmic system. This control centre has overarching control over the entire biological system to make it tuned to the cosmic nature. The neurons are contained within suprachiasmatic nucleus or SCN. This SCN is connected with functional organs. SCN has direct connection with our sense organs, particularly eyes, and organs coordinating external senses. This causes an impact on the functioning of the organs. Although located in SCN in the hypothalamus, their network is spread across the entire biological system of the body. Command and control work for the entire system.

Figure 7.1 shows the connection between SCN and the functional cells spread across the body. These together make the command and control system functional in a human organic scheme.

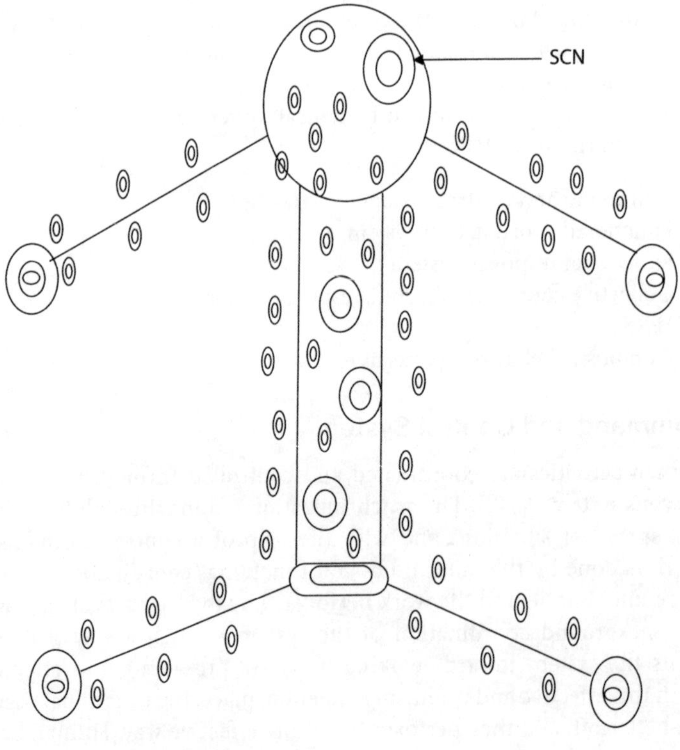

Figure 7.1 Schematic Sketch of CCS

CCS: Management Thoughts

Management thoughts have diverse basis. However, the CCS orientation contributes a definite mechanism to run and drive an organization towards achieving the desired result. These factors are applicable in different fields of management practice, with being most successful in the following categories of organizations:

- Large size manufacturing organizations with many departments and functions of activities
- Multinational companies doing any kind of business and having various national locations
- Large distribution and logistics house with a wide network to cover the distribution, ideally on a global scale
- Services organisation with the service calls from many and diversified locations
- Large banking and financial company with wide national and global network
- Government departments having diverse responsibility centres distributed over a large geographical area

The Process

Level 1

- Establish CCS (A)
- Classify activities according to their functional identities (B)
- Geographical classification (C)
- Technology-aligned classifications (D)
- Culture-specific classification (E)
- Skill-specific classification (F)
- Investment-linked classification (G)

Level 2

Establish network of relations and control in different combinations, such as:

Set 1. A to and fro (B + C + D): Applies to MNC in general
Set 2. A to and fro (B + D + F): Applies to MNC in knowledge and technology
Set 3. A to and fro (D + F): Applies to domestic and regional companies
Set 4. A to and fro (B + D): New generation companies
Set 5: A to and fro (B + C + D + E + F + G): Universally applicable

Set 6. A to and fro (B + G): Banking, finance, risk and investment companies

Any of these sets should work for all, however, they would better fit the types of organisations as mentioned.

There could be other combinations as well.

Central control should be with A in all situations.

However, in all situations, a combination of things may be tried.

Functional Approach

Like the biological process, the management process should also begin with the basic objective of the organization. Based on the corporate objective, the plans of actions and agenda should be drawn up to satisfy the objectives.

The similar scheme of things is present in all creatures, small or large. Also, in a human body, the command and control network is present in all cells and stored in the human genome as well. Any message that is collected by any living cell of the body is transmitted to SCN for whatever response it wants to transmit down to all connected cells. On the other hand, SCN keeps up with its receiving points and terminals to receive stimulus and instantly decide on the response and then put the response forward.

Commands thus generated based on the input factors are distributed across for actions and implementations. The functional organs perform in accordance with the reality generated and perceived by the system. CCS is function-oriented and makes organs function in its own way. The pattern of biological clock is basically indicative and suggestive, but its impacts are oriented towards the performances and works initiated by different organs and functional systems of the body. Thus, CCS is both unitary and collective depending upon the requirements of the situations.

Functional Coordination System

Human brain has a unique functional coordination system. The brain divides itself into central points of control and coordination and develops through appropriate identification system which remains in constant communication with the functional organs of the human system. First of all, the sections or segments pertain to a cluster of activities, however, recent research has revealed the fact that in case of urgency, the functional organs do respond in a manner that best connects through a cyclic impulse system wherein absence of any control point is partially met with increased and wider or dispersed positioning of other control points.

The Human Brain				
↓	↓	↓	↓	↓
Cerebrum	Cerebellum	Diencephalon	Brainstem	Network of neuron within and spread down
(a)	(b)	(c)	(d)	(e)

Cerebrum			
↓	↓	↓	↓
Frontal Lobes	**Parietal Lobe**	**Temporal Lobe**	**Occipital Lobe**
• Largest lobe • Coordinates behaviour • Motor skills • Problem-solving • Judgement • Planning • Attention • Emotions • Impulse control • Located in the front	• Located behind frontal lobe • Organizes information into sensory patterns • Interprets sensory information • Forwards information • Reactions on emotional inputs	• Located at ear level on either side of of brain • Coordinates specific functions • Visual memory • Verbal memory • Interpreting emotions	• Located back • Understanding visuals • Reading & learning • Interpreting visual imprints in brain • Different aspects of vision • Quality in visuals

1. *Cerebrum:* It comprises these four lobes and is the largest part of the brain. It is formed by two hemispheres, each one roughly half of whole of cerebrum. The two halves are separated by longitudinal fissure. The lobes are present in both hemispheres and their functions have been mentioned earlier. However, there lies some qualitative difference between the lobes. The right hemisphere is more inclined to wholesome inputs and thoughts, ideally, with an emphasis on the intuitive; however, the left is more oriented towards rational, quantification, measurability and logic.
2. *Cerebellum:* It is located just below the occipital lobe and forms the major part of the hindbrain. The dominant functions of cerebellum are as follows:
   - Fine motor skills coordinating with exterior organs such as hands and feet. Coordination with smaller and finer movements for all the functional activities of the body and the entire system.

- Maintains equilibrium and posture of the organic system. Maintains balance of the body and the entire organic system.

3. *Diencephalon:* Located at the base of the brain, diencephalon maintains a strong communication function. This is divided among the following three important segments and activities.

Diencephalon		
Thalamus	**Epithalamus**	**Hypothalamus**
↓	↓	↓
• Involves in maintaining Consciousness • Sleep Control • Memory –short term maintenance and retrieving.	• Connecting between different junctions, nodes and points in brain • Limbic System coordination • Memory – long term • Behaviour – consistency and regulation.	• Physiological cycles sleep-wake etc. • Appetite – generate and regulates • Body temperature maintenance and Regulation • Hormones Control release, production and assimilation.

4. *Brainstem:* Located at the front of the cerebellum, the brainstem forms a major component for maintaining the functions of life. Brainstem is connected to the spinal cord. Through the brainstem the connection that is developed is known in the medical and spiritual world very specifically. Brain stem is divided among three principal segments which are: (a) midbrain, (b) pons and (c) medulla oblongata. The brainstem is identified as the principal centre for coordinating with major biological functions like the cardiovascular system. This makes life's activity smooth and regenerates vital whenever the chances for the erosion of vital occur in a context that requires urgent intervention. The brain stem can offer new vital to the major input of life.

Brainstem		
Mid Brain	**Pons (middle part of Brain Stem)**	**Medulla Oblongata**
↓	↓	↓
• Eye Movement • Vision – Processing • Vision – Recognition • Hearing	• Origin of some cranial nerves • Nerves connecting different parts of brain	• Lowest part of brain • Coordinates cardiac system and functions of heart

• Auditory Recognition	• Facial Movement • Sensory information-modulation and transmission	• Coordinates the lungs – the breathing and air circulation • Sneezing and swallowing

The brainstem, particularly the medulla oblongata, makes the fundamental coordination between the cardiac system and the entire process of breathing. In addition to the basic function of maintaining the normal movement of the cardiac system, it attempts to coordinate with the *pancha prana vayu*, or five different types of energy flows, that embrace different human organs to perform the coordinating and revitalizing functions of the living entity.

a. *Prana vayu:* Draws in air to stimulate head, brain, nervous system, bone marrow, vision, hearing, sensing and thinking, setting on the control systems through mind organs and psychic process.
b. *Aparna vayu:* Sustains the entire cellular functions of the body, excretion, gender-specific functions, urinary functions, kidneys and organs around and below the naval system.
c. *Samana vayu:* Sustains the entire control region of the body, the metabolic system, cardiothoracic functions, lungs, liver, spleen, stomach, gall bladder, intestine and cardiovascular system.
d. *Udana vayu:* Sustains the entire cellular functions of the body, nervous coordination, vascular coordination, endocrine balance, mineral balance, chemical balance and coordination among different physiological functions.
e. *Vyana vayu:* This maintains the warmth and heat of the entire body, stimulates *tejah* or energy for work and thought, connects all functions through autonomous mode and specific functional energies. Connects the empirical body with the pure soul, the *atman* residing within.

5. *Network of neurons within and spread down:* Neural network has been devised artificially to fathom the wonder of the brain system for the benefit of human activity. Human knowledge is restricted up to the present period. The past is known in two different ways: first, direct knowledge where personal involvement was available and second, indirect knowledge where personal involvement was not available. These two apply for the current period also. Most of the incidents of the current period are not happening with the person. Rather, the person has very less information towards forming the direct knowledge. In fact, indirect knowledge of the past and present period is most prominent and abandon. Whenever we have direct knowledge,

the same is always tinged with the colours of our mind at that moment. If the mind is calm and quiet, then we tend to get most of the knowledge of the past and the present. If the mind is occupied by anger, jealousy, depression, obsession, arrogance, greed, covetousness, lust, energy or it is swayed by the temporary joy of winning, grabbing, possession, gains, favours, esteem or any other similar factor, then at that point it fails to get hold of the most part of the knowledge of the past and the present. We have the capacity to garner only infinitesimal fraction of the knowledge of reality of the past and the present through the method of direct knowledge. Most part or almost the entire spectrum of knowledge is either indirect or based on the perspective and understanding of things whenever it is applied. Guess or perception being the basis of knowledge, we gather it in a composite manner. This composite method of winning and gaining knowledge is a mix of direct and indirect methods with the focus on the spirit of goodness which has to be combined with the spirit of things to gather knowledge in totality.

Knowledge of the past and the present has a traditional way of developing and storing. However, there is no way to have the knowledge of the future. Knowledge of the future is obtained through extrapolation of the trends of the past and the present drawn into the realm of the future. The future is unpredictable in general. However, the present as a continuation and extension of the past remains vibrant as a set of things, entities and situations can be drawn based on perspective understanding, guess or assumptions. Fuzzy logic, fractal geometry and theory of chaos play a major role in this. The recent development of the AI and its partial application through neural networking system work as a vibrant method to understand the future and know it partly in a way better than other methods and approaches.

The Artificial Neural Networks

Our brain is comprised of different elements of which some understanding is required for all individuals in management. Human brain contains billions of cells of nano magnitude and other small dimensions which perform the role of coordination and contribute to our understanding of the future. Neurons are competent and capable of creating and emitting soft electrical signals and connect with all relevant cells of the brain, it is connected central nervous system and the connected organs spread out to the entire body via the vertebral column. The brainstem connected with the bone marrow within vertebral column makes things happen in such a way that the information generated can be processed in a meaningful manner to the system. The human system of gathering, storing, processing and disseminating information is imperative to the knowledge of the things yet to occur.

Neural networks are one of the most advanced scientific methods to predict the future. This is particularly applicable in the prediction of prices of shares and different financial products in the context of the capital market. In the entire structure of the neuron, the functioning occurs in two broad manners:

1. External to internal
2. Internal to external

1. *External to internal:* External stimuli reach the brain in the form of an electrical signal. This signal is usually received by the dendrites when these are significant. Dendrite acts as a receptor and transmits the impulse received to the main body of the neuron. Cell body of neuron then does total processing within itself or collaborates with other neurons. It may so happen that immediate requirement arises for the neuron to collect the same information from other sources or other neurons also. Neuron cell body after processing the signal may like to create an output which is forwarded to other neurons through its connecting mechanisms of axons. The neural output is now forwarded through the axon to the next or other neurons for any further processing of signals or forwarding the impulse to the organs or limbs for response through the mechanisms of CNS.
2. *Internal to external:* Inputs may be generated by the thinking mind also. The thinking mind creates structures that are suitable for decision science. It requires making things happen in a desired manner. Decision parameters do evolve in the brain, require impulse at dendrites and assimilation or mutations in the cell body of neutrons, and then pass through axons to the proper brain segments of brain for action.

Reference

World Bank Group. (2015). *World development report, 2015: Mind, society and behavior*. The World Bank.

CHAPTER 8

PRACTICE OF MANAGEMENT: DEVELOPING ACTION PRINCIPLES FOR PRACTICE

Definition of Management

Management is identifying the objective of an entity, aligning all resources and strengths towards fulfilling the objective through creation of value, providing fulfilment of all concerned and safeguarding the enterprise from risks of all kinds in a given context in real time and continuing in perpetuity.

There could be various ways to define 'management' for practice and execution. However, certain fundamental norms could be considered as underlying basics to deliver better results in a given context. 'Management' is inherent in a human system as a structured mechanism to provide guidance and leadership based on somewhat rational parameters essential in the world of business and society which have attained an extreme form of complexity in its structure and dynamism.

Management is a multifunctional activity. It is not a linear subject. It involves almost every aspect of human thoughts and aspirations ingrained in a human system. Management as a subject of study includes all disciplines of study, in general, and specific aspects of human growth, in particular. While learning or teaching the subject of management, one needs to learn or teach the following broad areas of knowledge, among many others:

- Nature of human being as a resource
- Technology and process for manufacturing, packaging, storing, distribution, logistics, financing, accounting, control and so on
- Resources of various types like material, finance, knowledge, derived or inherited property, goodwill, network or connections for business and activities or something else of that kind
- Fiscal policies of the government, other government policies, social and cultural norms
- National, regional and global environment relevant to business or activity of the organization
- Subjects such as marketing, finance, systems, psychology, statistics, mathematics, economics, communications, quantitative techniques,

computing, analytics, forecasting, strategies, legal issues, culture studies, environmental studies, relevant literatures, social norms, philosophy, spiritual principles, and ethics and values are all relevant in the study of management
- Existing norms, practices of business, historical emergence, position of business and organizations
- Global trends of business and enterprising
- Decisions and patterns of actions of global institutions, organizations and so on

Management is primarily the art of thinking, deciding and doing, and surviving, sustaining and winning. While the management practice is on, certain tools and techniques are involved. The art and science of management varies from one organization to the other and from one situation to the other in the same context and period of time.

For example, the techniques used in manufacturing are the process of distribution, the methods and outputs in a factory vary with the degree of human involvement in the process. Machines and tools used in the manufacturing depend primarily on the quality of manpower involved in it. Machines, tools, techniques are just fragments of management as a medium of action. The most important aspect of management is human being. Dictionaries have collectively defined management as a set of activities that consolidates actions driven by man to fulfil the objectives and dreams set in the process of doing things to optimize the use of resources and create value in the process of delivering and actualizing the potentials of people involved.

Management involves techniques and scientific tools to fulfil the objectives identified. However, management makes the basic functional distinction in terms of the capacity and effectiveness towards bringing maximum human involvement. It allows people to cherish the blossoming of their hidden potentials. Management attempts to sensitize human potentials. The roar of machines needs to be properly coordinated. Machines and the technology have to serve the company, the society, the nation and the world. In order to derive maximum value out of the investments in the machine, process and technology, management needs highest human energy in the system.

One of the core responsibilities of management is to identify the right man for the right work. Right man at the right place brings the basic responsibility of each management function, and the motivation level of people involved plays an important role. Highly motivated people play the most important role in creating maximum value for a company or any type of organization. Highly motivated people are properly inspired to take the agenda forward. With the same level of resources and input value, a set of highly motivated people can deliver higher level of value for the world.

There could be organizations basically dominated by machines and underlying technologies. However, there are other types of organizations dominated by people. Process-driven, large organizations depend less on manpower than labour-driven organizations. Mega production or mass production requires automated activities in managing enterprises. While high-tech companies need competent people to coordinate and control, the role of machines is still the driver of good output as per designs of the enterprise. Even in organizations using robotics or drones, the role of competent human being as managers or leaders of the organization becomes very vital.

Characteristics of a World-class Organization

For an organization to become a value creator, it has to apply rational judgement for selection of the type of tools of management and things relevant for decision-making and action. There are various levels of choice matrix for the same. The important areas of the choice matrix are as follows.

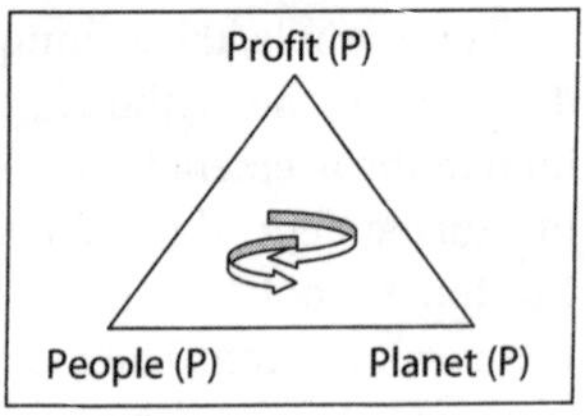

- Profit
- People
- Planet

This is the Triple 'P' model as highlighted by Milton Friedman. While crafting plans and developing strategies for managing enterprises, concern for Triple 'P' is important. Profit or creating surplus is essential for the survival and growth of any organization. The concern for people inside the organization and those outside is very important. People inside the organization are the employees, including workers, labourers and managers, whereas those outside are primarily the customers and consumers.

A manager has to keep managerial focus on people of all types and at the same time the world as a whole. Their focus should be on the stakeholders of the organizations. Stakeholders are basically the following (however, when it comes to specific areas of transactions, several other entities are included in the stakeholder model):

- Shareholders
- Employees
- Customers
- Government
- Society
- World

Apart from the stakeholders of the organization, the manager has to keep in mind corporate responsibility and duty towards the world as a whole. Concern for the environment and helping to maintain balance in the entire ecology are also a part of the long-term agenda of a successful company.

Purpose of an Organization

The purpose of an organization lies in its desired role to play in the economy and society. Identifying the role may be done through discussion of certain issues. However, the issues could be based on the core objectives of the organization. For example, the issues could be something drawn from the existing framework or from outside the purview of the entity. The purposes of forming, sustaining and making an organization grow may be as many as one can think of; however, broadly speaking, they are grouped under those oriented to make profit and others which do not want to make profit.

From the point of view of purpose, organizations may be grouped into the following two basic types:

- For-profit organizations
- Not-for-profit organizations

For-profit Organizations

Profit is usually defined as the excess of revenue earned over the cost and expenditures required to make the revenue earned by the organization. However, while computing the cost impacts of the revenue, the cost of capital and investment, opportunity costs, and implicit costs are all considered. Revenue may come from the operations directly or indirect revenue from other activities is also considered.

Organizations that seek profit may be further divided into four broad categories:

Category 1: High profit, high concern
Category 2: High profit, low Concern
Category 3: Low profit, high concern
Category 4: Low profit, low concern

The organizations that want to make profit while keeping high level of concern for the people or high level of concern for the planet are guided by the concept of Triple 'P', as was put forward by Milton Friedman.

Worldwide, there are certain categories of organizations which try to maintain proper balance among the factors of Triple P. All these P's are important in the society for a sustainable growth of economy. Profit is essential for any organization with a view to move forward meeting all responsibilities. Organizations have to fulfil the primary responsibility towards the people associated with. The world at large needs sustenance of the society.

Each organization needs to shoulder the concern and responsibility of the world. This green nature, air, water and all other natural resources need to be maintained. The water balance, purity of air and fertility of the soil need to be maintained.

Profit-making companies or organizations should take care of the distributive justice to various stakeholders involved. Stakeholders are usually the shareholders, the employees, the customers, the governments, the society and other investors in the activities of the organization, apart from the environment and the world.

Not-for-profit Organizations

Not-for-profit organizations are those which have undertaken certain set of responsibilities that aim at fulfilling the core objectives of their existence. Organizations promoted by the governments come under this category quite often. While maintaining its social objective and responsibility towards delivering certain services to the society, governments tend to undertake the responsibility of economic value which involves functions and activities suited to the short-term promise or the long-term objective of the said governments in position.

Economic development through government intervention in most of the countries occurs that way. Infrastructure developments in many countries in a few selected areas do occur in that way. For example, the railways in the world have always proved to be a high-investment growth area. Initial investment in these areas is massive.

Creating railway routes through laying of railway tracks require a mega-scale activity that does not promise a direct pay back within a short period. Not only laying of railway routes but also creating the power supply system, making of the railway coaches, rail engines and a large number of products which are required as associated products for the running of the trains are always required for the industry.

Governments do not explore any direct way to recover the investment in the short-term period. However, with the laying of railway tracks and having the trains on it to run fast from remote areas to metropolises carrying the agricultural goods, rural or urban outputs to the principal hub of business, and carrying large number of people from one place to the other to deliver their individual and collective output places the economy of the nation at a higher level. Economic transactions are higher and the result of this higher level of economic transaction is the spread of economic benefit to people living at the length and breadth of nations.

The economic agenda of nations is structured to engage the government's initiative and resources in order to benefit from the long-term economic gains derived from such activities. Each of these activities generate certain value that goes to the fund of the state as a higher level of fiscal income. Governments garner higher fiscal income in the short term out of their long-term investments in the economy. On a short-term direct assessment, the investments range much higher than the income generated during the said period. Direct comparison of the amount of money put in and that gained from the industry directly through operational services in the short term proves non-rewarding. However, over a long-term period this becomes rewarding. The other gain for the nation is development.

Economic development being a promise and agenda of the government gives priority to long-term agenda while keeping an eye on the work and agenda for the short term. Social organizations with a purpose are also not for profit, in most of the cases. But they drive the activities through creating additional value to sustain the next level of agenda of action in the focus.

Broad environment, in which companies and organizations perform, matters a lot for the entities. These may be entities which are within the economic influence of the nation. A favourable broad environment brings forth the understanding of the fulfilment of the broad objectives that organizations put forth in their active lives. However, management of these organizations would involve understanding the true spirit of the objective and creating agenda in tune with that to fulfil the core objectives of the companies or other types of the organizations.

For a new entity, the idea that comes in the mind of promoter or promoters of the idea has to remain vibrant and compatible with the scenario prevailing. Global, national and local trends have to be understood in realistic terms to go ahead with the idea of setting up of an organization.

A new entity should identify the relevance of the entity in the space of the economy, market and society. If an idea is taken forward to establish a social, religious, charitable organization, it needs to have proper answer to certain basic questions. Relevant among these questions are a few most important ones, which talk about the locator or character of the organization in the appropriate space in the society, nation or the world.

Some of the major questions that these organizations should have rational answers for are stated below:

1. *Purpose:* Does the purpose of the organization match with the broad purposes highlighted by the society or it matches with the aspects of happiness and well-being of the society? Purpose should be clearly understood by the future managers.

2. *Concern:* Concerns for the customers and people in general should be identified constantly. It needs to be seen whether the new entity fits in the gamut of concerns in the society. If it does, then the organization has a strong hope.
3. *Gap or space:* Each society and market moves through the passage of time in a way that accommodates new entities by allowing space in their minds. Organizations need to identify the market gap or space by understanding the position and allowing a new product or service to have space for its products, services or activities. The products, services or activities thus make it relevant at higher degree marketing, a good amount of prospect for the new entity.

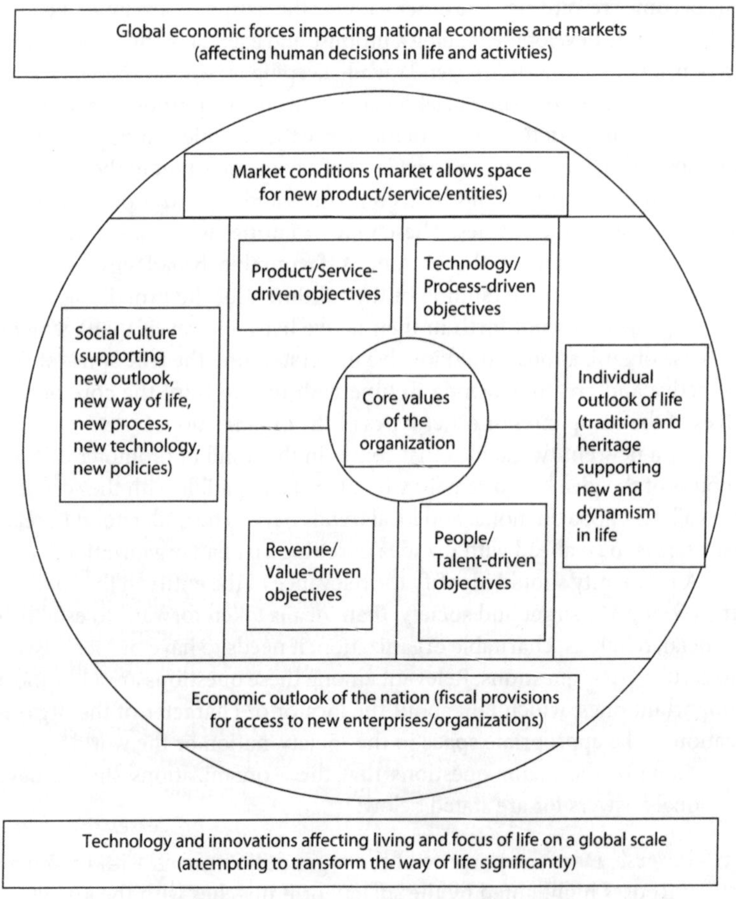

Contextual Analysis of Global Organization

Managing Global Corporations: Basic Issues

Important issues in forming and managing a global-scale organization are usually the following:

- Whether the organization is likely to fulfil any relevant need of any group or many groups of people in the world.
- Whether the organization serves any purpose of the society or the market (or any segment of the market).
- Whether the objective of the organization has any or somewhat relevance in the current context of the local or global situation (chance of fitting in the gaps available).
- Whether the organization is likely to contribute effectively towards creating and maintaining value in the economic or financial terms (short term or in long term).
- Whether the organization has the potential to develop things providing goods to human beings in any way either at the current period or in future period.
- Whether the organization has already contributed or is likely to contribute the philosophical basis of any aspect of human survival and growth.
- Whether the organization is catering to the historical need of any society or any market in the world.
- Whether the organization has the strength and potential to create value in any terms—material, finance, knowledge, wealth, human and cosmic.

The issues mentioned above could be the relevant questions an entity should be prepared to introspect and answer before trying to expand, diversify, broad base, globalize and open up new entities beyond the existing parameters. Market is the entity which comprises the buyers, sellers, regulators, visitors, onlookers, networkers, policymakers and other relevant groups of people. Consumers form the most important component of the markets. Consumers may or may not be the customers but either from the front of the transaction process of the market or from the back, they assert most influence on the market.

While a decision is taken, certain relevant variables are considered for the achievement in the process of taking up the lessons from the historical impacts of those variables in the process of human life and activities. It is important that management thoughts and processes take into account all these variables as important for reaching a fine decision in terms of setting up a new enterprise, getting into new business or new activities leading to the formation of a new identity.

The core value of an organization is to create an identity for it. For example, the mission statement of 2019 of Apple Inc. (AAPL) states, 'Apple designs Macs, the best personal computers in the world, along with OSx, iLife, iWork and professional software. Apple leads the digital music revolution with its iPods and iTunes online store.'[1]

The mission and vision statement of Amazon, 2019, shows, 'Our vision is to be earth's most customer-centric company; to build a place where people can come to find and discover anything they might want to buy online.'[2]

The mission statement of Nestle 2019 says, 'Nestle, the world's leading nutrition, health and wellness company. Our mission of "good food good life" is to provide consumers with the best tasting, most nutrition choices in a wide range of food and beverage categories and eating occasions, from morning to night'.

The mission statement of Panasonic Corporation (formerly, Matsushita Electric Corporation), Japan, says,

---

A business won't survive without profits still; profit is not the sale purposes of business improving people's lives through creating goods needed for society through providing wholehearted services are vitally important. After all, business in ultimately for the betterment of our society. That is where the mission and value of every business exist. If business underscored by the mission is conducted forcefully, it will generate appropriate profits as a natural result of being supported by the society.

Try anything well beyond your own strengths and you're likely to fall. Aim short of your abilities and your talents will be unused, your work less than satisfactory. Examine yourself; therefore, try to find how you work best. Evaluate your strength and your weakness objectively.[3]

Tata Group philosophy is follows:

'In a free enterprise, the community is not just another stakeholder in business but is in fact the very purpose of its existence'. The five core Tata values underpinning the way we do business are as follows:

- Integrity—we will be fair, honest transparent and ethical in our conduct, everything we do must stand the test of public scrutiny.
- Responsibility

---

[1] https://www.apple.com/

[2] https://www.amazon.com/

[3] Kenosuke Matsushita, founder of Panasonic Corporation (panasonic.com)

- Excellence
- Pioneering
- Unity pioneering[4]

The mission statement of ITC says, 'To enhance the wealth generating capability of the enterprise in a globalising environment, delivering superior and sustainable stakeholder value. ITC is a board managed professional company, committed to creating enduring value for the shareholder and for the nation'.

The core values of companies have actually gone beyond the scope of business of the company or the organization; it has included the concerns of the society, the nation and the world at the same time. However, in order to fulfil the core values or the objectives of the company or the organization, the following areas of concern should be always kept in mind:

- Profit from operation (look into the trend of net profit and GP)
- Efficiency of performance (cost-efficiency, time management, create satisfaction)
- Stakeholder gains:
  - Sustained gains for shareholders
  - Customer value growth and customer delight
  - Employees gain in career growth, potential of employees to find opportunities to take shape
  - Government gains in fiscal benefit and economic benefit through more employments, more opportunities for the market, more options provided to the people
  - Society gains better product or service with competitive price and recommendable qualities
  - Investors gain in timely and appropriate servicing of their funds invested. Investment paves the ways for further investment opportunities

Apart from this, the company/organization need to put emphasis on various aspects of the following factors:

- *Technology:* To examine the level of technology constantly and try to move to a better and optimal one
- *Strength:* Creating consistent and fundamental strength of the company/organization

[4] https://www.itcportal.com/

The CRAMEL Model

C—Capital: To maximize the utility of funds for business
R—Risk: To contain and optimize the risk of business
A—Asset: To see that assets created in the organization are utilized properly to fulfil the core objectives of the organization and support the concern for people and plant.
M—Management: To develop a management philosophy and get this philosophy imbibed by all such that it always benefits the people inside the organization, customers and consumers.
E—Earnings: To see that earnings for the organization get continuity and maintain adequacy and growth over a period of time.
L—Liquidity: To make plans in such a fashion that organization is able to maintain adequate liquidity always.

Profit-oriented companies and organizations need to identify the appropriate business model so that each activity of the company is preordained to make a positive balance for the company. The business model should incorporate the following factors and attempt to have answers to those issues that might arise meanwhile (Figure 8.1).

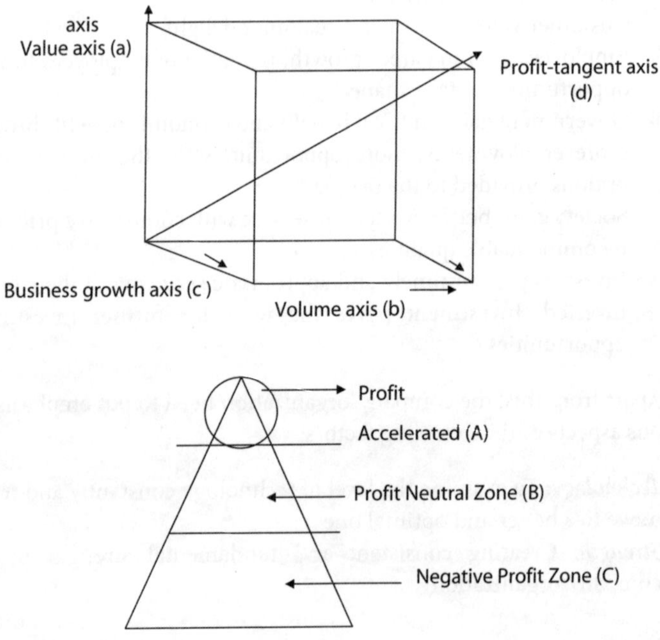

Figure 8.1 Pyramid of Profit-making

Pyramid of Gains

Profit equation: A > (B + C) (magnitude only)

Certain ranges of products/services are enjoying the scheme of:

No profit, no loss: This requires social support in terms of government or charity funding to make the organization grow.

Certain other ranges of products are there which push companies to negative profit. The top-end value mix of products creates so much gain that offsets the profit neutrality and loss incurred in other range of products.

This is strategic homogeneity created by the company. Strategic homogeneity requires the functional perspective, whereas the loss incurred in financial terms is made to offset by the gains earned through any other set of products or services on offer by the company.

Cross-subsidization

When a company wants to perform the role of social changing, it may do so on its own through a process of 'discriminating market dynamism (DMD)'. DMD can be accomplished by following certain steps in business, highlights of which are mentioned below:

- Segment the market across the purchasing power of focused customers at the bottom level of market operations (to keep in mind that company cannot afford to risk its existing and potential markets and customers
- Forecast expected revenues from the total market and its segments
- Markets need to be segmented first between the assured minimum market and expected trend of the markets; then within each of it to segment the customers based on the category of economic capacity or buying behaviour of the customers
- Assess the option to raise the entire or most part of the expected profit from the top end of the market and offer the product or the service at the bottom end of the market at very thin margin to enable the operators maintain profit yet provide good product/service to the deserving people at affordable prices
- Adjust and correct any gap that arises in the revenue which has direct bearing upon the profitability of the enterprise

DMD needs dynamism of the market and can be applied only in a dynamic market.

DMD can be applied to infrastructure business, among many others. Many of the infrastructure organizations engaged in housing may adopt mass housing using the DMD method. This would obviously elevate the brand strength of the organization. Other industries where DMD can be applied easily include automobiles, textiles, pharmaceuticals, health care, transport and so on. For example, mass housing requires low pricing, sometimes even reduced with thin margin of profit and marginal loss in certain ranges. The profit made through the transaction of a high-end, high-volume range of products or services provides additional profit, the magnitude of which stands more than the sum of loss and profit continues in many aspects of business.

Customer-focused Profit Drive

A manager should take care of the views of others about the initiatives of the company. The major areas of managerial concern should be as follows:

- How do the customers and consumers view the initiatives and offers through the products and services of the company?
- How do the shareholders, investors, facilitators and transactors view the company?
- How does the society in general view the company?
- How do the employees view the company?
- How do the governments view the company?

Through creating customer satisfaction and identifying long-term association with the brand, there are various ways of looking at this concept. The approach would depend on the structure and condition of the market. Market structures could be defined from the point of view of customers or from the point of view of the companies. The same can be viewed from the perspective of industries and governments or societies. For example, from the social angle, customer-driven approach is identified through the following ways:

1. Social view of companies

Socially Responsive Companies	**Companies Sensitive to Social Cause**	**Companies Involved in Social Development**
• Companies which have policies to be open to social cause particularly to the major concerns of the society for survival and emergence	• Roots of the social objectives may be lying somewhere in the environmental areas, social structure or homogeneous condition of the society	• Helping the weaker part of the society to come up to the standard of the stronger part of the society.

• Social dynamics of regional culture to help rise to the global culture	• Supporting the quest and helping in restructuring social cause towards unity	• Identifying ways to develop sustainability

2. Government's view of companies

- Companies obliging to fiscal demands
- Companies doing business on fair basis, that is, ethically
- Companies supporting the economic concern of the nation—both on short- and long-term scale
- Companies supporting in social cohesion
- Companies helping in environmental optimization
- Companies supporting the concerns for value and benefit distribution through a process of distributive justice
- Welfare of workers or employees and welfare of support system properly maintained or not
- Law of the land regarding manpower, process, business operations, market interactions and so on maintained or not

Market-driven Companies

Companies having market orientation need to focus on customers. Whether individual or collective within a large group, the customer focus is central to any corporate.

Customer-oriented Actions by Companies

- Frontline people of the company, the channel members and retailers are the most important and direct sources for gaining knowledge about existing customers. However, in order to know the potential customers, the company needs to follow a certain process to get the most of it.
- Broad understanding of customer categories
- Value perception from customer categories
- Level of interactions with the customers needed

Customer Demographics		**Customer Psychographics**		**Customer Value Chain**	
Strong back-ground customer identity	Weak back-ground flexibility	Highly inclined strong Brand loyal	Moderated and less searching through market veins	Positive cash flow in distribution network and direct or e-commerce	Short-term funding through business process cycle

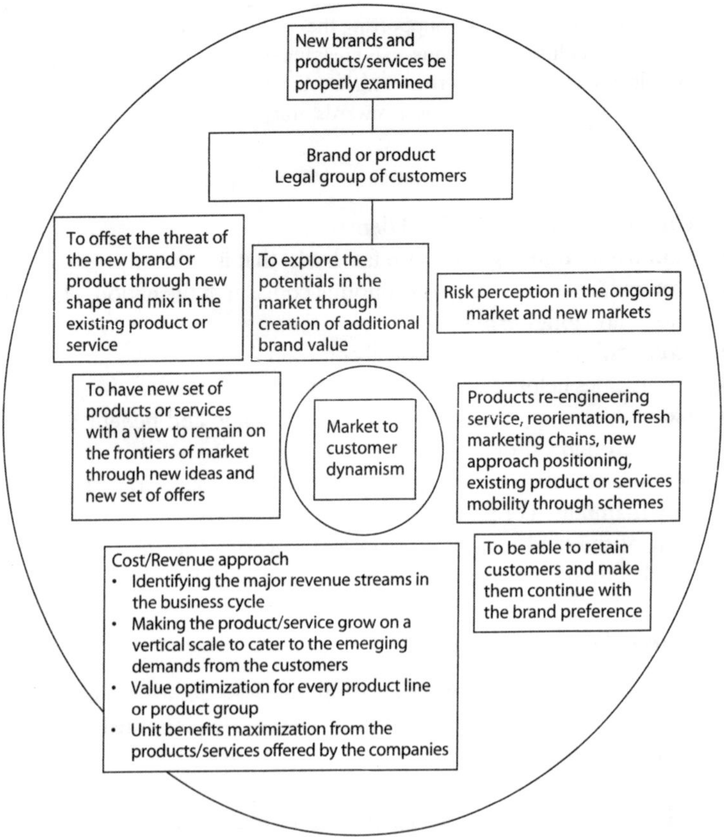

Knowing the Customer

Whenever a company is desirous of developing long-term strategies for corporate survival or growth, it should attempt to understand the process of creating a value chain based on the demographic, psychographic and social factors that matter to the revenues and earnings of the organizations. Quantitative data for customers may not reveal the actual position of demand for the products or the services of the company. However, it gives a somewhat proper idea about the pattern of acceptability of the products and services.

CHAPTER 9

REVENUE MANAGER: MANAGER MAKING ORGANIZATION PROFITABLE

Revenue: The Life Blood of Business

Revenue is the most important element of a business. It has to be in place to start a business, to run it and to make it grow. Managed properly, revenue generates surplus. Lack of proper revenue management can be suicidal for a company. Proper revenue management yields to better positions of a company, whereas mismanagement may pull the company down to shutting its doors.

Better revenue under a given situation puts across better opportunities to create, expand, multiply and re-engineer business. Proper management of revenue satisfies the customers, shareholders, fiscal authorities and employees and helps the company to fulfil the responsibilities towards the society, environment and the world.

Revenue generates and maintains liquidity of an organization. It provides the inputs to maintain solvency of a company. It creates the basis for sustainability and can restrict the process leading towards bankruptcy of a company.

Proper revenue management means proper cash flow decisions, optimum position of the working capital of a company and at the same time proper investment, financing and dividend decisions. It implies proper management of manpower in the company, optimum resource creation and utilization for the current and long-term period of a company and at the same time appropriate match of the risk-return position of the company.

Revenue maintained properly yields optimum gains for the shareholders and investors of the company. Even though revenue is at the centre of the business, so far, business scholars have hardly given adequate attention to the concerns of revenue directly.

Revenue for HRM Function

A new-age manager should keep in mind the utmost importance of revenue management in business. If someone is performing the marketing function of the business, they should make primary plans in terms of the revenue in the business or the aspect of the business they are concerned with. Similarly, a human resource manager is supposed to see that functions associated with recruiting, training, development, redeployment, multi-skilling, technology pitching, cultural configuration, role reversal and other activities associated with manpower management should be performed with optimal resource utilization for the company.

Revenue for Finance Function

The finance manager should be aware of the role of revenue in all aspects of financial management. Revenue maximization includes the aspects of cost and expense minimization for a given scenario of managing finances for a company in a given context of the market. Three major decisions that a finance manager needs to be careful of are: investment decisions, financing decisions and dividend decisions. In all these functions the role of revenue is primordial. While making the investment decisions, the most important role is played by revenue as the basis of selecting the investment as an option is based on the stream of revenues that are expected during the future period.

Whether the stream of revenues has the capacity to service the cost of investment in the shortest period of time or not is the basic indicator to invest in a long-term investment in an existing company or a new company. The financing decision of a company is also dependent upon the capacity of the stream of revenues in the short term to pay off the rent of such finances.

With adequate surplus yielded through enough revenues generated in business, a company can take dividend decisions compatible with the net surplus earned through revenue maximization principles.

Revenue for Marketing Function

A marketing manager should look into the prospect of earning of the sales revenues while planning for promotions, distributions and other functions. Any promotional scheme is scheduled on the basis of revenue plans for the said area of business. A company undertakes advertising, branding, campaigns and other related activities on the basis of the expected flow of revenues from the impact of those marketing activities. While identifying the basics of marketing through four Ps (product, price, place and promotion), a marketing manager is supposed to identify price plans compatible with the factors of the market.

Some of these important factors in marketing function which require proper management of revenues are as follows:

- Competition analysis (on all factors of product, price, place and promotion) for the existing market condition and the possible changes in the structure of the market

- Forecasts about the next phase of the market (both in terms of the quantum and value of sales and also the velocity of product movement in the market
- Chances of intruding of new technology—for adoption on a short- or long-term basis
- Market dynamics, particularly, the degree of external influence on the market
- Strength of the distribution system, in general, and channel chain, in particular
- Product development, market development or diversification activities
- Market research, in general, and consumer research, in particular, for the generic market or any specific segments of it
- Recruiting appropriate territory-based professionals, product- or service-based professionals, and sales and marketing professionals

Even though revenue has such immense importance, the finance profession has hardly taken due cognizance of the same while managing finance. That revenue management has not received proper concern of the professionals throughout the world can be inferred from the number of publications, research papers and documents published on revenue management unlike those on other areas of financial management.

While the traditional approach of financial management was based on the single principle of minimization of cost in the procurement of funds and optimum use of such funds, the later developments, particularly, in the latter half of the previous century, are focused more on certain other areas given as follows:

1. Investment decisions
2. Financial decisions
3. Dividend decisions

The need for an inclusive treatment of these finance functions being incontestable, the eagerness of the professionals for spreading their knowledge in these fields have tended to push the other critical function of finance, the management of revenue, to the back seat. Obviously, certain actions such as expansion, reorganization, merger, acquisition, modernization and allied organic growth require amounts of fund with separate consideration from outside. Decision-making on procurement of funds then becomes an important issue.

When there is a demand in the market in terms of procurement of funds, suppliers of money rush in. Then it becomes a matter of making a choice among available alternatives to make an investment. It may be the other way round also. With progress of technology and horizontal integration of markets, the options before the investors began increasing, leading to the importance of investment decisions.

Again, for various reasons including increase in demand, newer opportunities having been available in the market, the question of financing began haunting the minds of the professionals. This coupled with the internal demand for financing various items and activities, the emphasis on financing became obvious. Further, with the onset of market economy, the importance of securities market has been felt by everybody.

While the price movement of scrip is seen by many as a reaction to the health conditions of the company, the questions of valuations of the scrip have been attempted to be resolved by many through the dividend decisions of the related company. Dividend decisions have become important in the context of the changed ownership patterns. If the company is unable to maintain a high share price in the market through appropriate dividend decisions and related actions, then the act of the managers of the company go against the interests of the shareholders leading to a shake-up in the ownership patterns.

The above discussion shows the importance of investment, financing and dividend decisions. But, in the process, we tend to ignore the quality of actions taken in day-to-day functioning of the financial activities of the company. It is this day-to-day functioning of the company in the field of finance that is called the working capital management. Working capital management is again imperative of the aspects of management of revenue.

The question of possible revenue inflow determines the quantum, content and speed of the investments in the working capital of a company. In an intrinsic sense, working capital should include all sorts of funds nurtured and garnered by the company at any point of time. Revenue from any source whether it is the mainstream business, additional components of business or diversified portfolio of business requires to be optimized in real time and in terms of real value.

That means the portion of long-term finance with which current work is being run, the intrinsic fund of normal day-to-day functions as well as the potential activities arising out as effects of the day-to-day functions initiated as causes now are all to be clubbed under working capital. In fact, nearly 50 per cent of the job hours of finance professionals are invested in managing working capital. If we consider the finance functions as such, the total job hours, in most of the organizations, invested usually in managing the working capital is roughly 60–70 per cent. Time wise, and also value wise, working capital management consumes most of these as compared to other areas of financial management. Managing revenue is a primary activity in the efficient management of working capital.

Let us look into the functions of finance with a focus on the roles expected of it.

Ordinarily, the desired role of finance is to fulfil the objectives set by the proprietors and entrepreneurs. The single objective of shareholder's 'wealth maximization' cascades down to the level of the agents (managers and professionals who run the show) of the company, which are classified between two areas of focus.

These objectives are as follows:

1. Wealth maximization
2. Profit maximization

In order that the wealth or value of the company is maximized, we have to take care of the effect of time on value. An amount of ₹100 accruing after a period of one year does not carry the same meaning as in the current period. This shows that wealth has to be measured in terms of the time value of money. The present value of future potentials, that is, the present value of the stream of net income that the scrip is going to generate in the future period is to be considered as the worth of the company. This could be based on the estimation done by the holder of scrip of the company. This shows that there should be discrimination between financial actions that are going to generate positive cash flows (income over incipient or incurred costs).

A financial action that has got the potentials of generating positive net present value (NPV) is only accepted. In case alternatives are available in a particular financial initiative, the one with the best possible gains in terms of NPV is considered for acceptance.

Between two mutually exclusive projects, having the same amount of initial investments, same time span estimated for completion, belonging to the same industry and operating at the same level of technology, the question of short-term management of fund becomes the most important and instrumental in getting positive NPVs.

Investment Decision Worked Out

Let us take the example of a company listed in the stock market. The name of the company is Mishra Ltd. It is a diversified industrial house. Its finance professionals are currently evaluating investment proposals submitted by two different divisions.

- The personal computer division has put forward a proposal to produce a new version of the laptop which is expected to have four years of life (because of the rapid changes in the field of computers and electronics, the life expectancy is short). But the project would require one-year time to get the production facilities set properly.

- The manufacturing division, which wants to have a new facility to manufacture the latest version of textile machine with computerized operation system, would require the same amount of investment and the life expectancy is five years.

The finance division, in its efforts to evaluate these two projects, has received the following cash flow estimations furnished by the departments.

Year	Laptop Division	Textile Division
0	−1,000[a]	−200[a]
1	−1,000[b]	+400
2	+900	+450
3	+900	+1,000
4	+900	+1,000
5	+900	+750

Notes: [a]Initial investment.
[b]Additional investment required to finish the project.

Conditions: Now the finance department has to procure ₹2,000 million for either of these projects and the amount is supposed to be returned by both the laptop and textile divisions more than squarely.

If the finance division calculates the outcome based on the payback period, that is, the period of time in which the initial investment is returned, it would find that for the two projects these periods are as follows:

- *Payback period for laptop division:* 3 years, 2 months and 20 days
- *Payback period for textile division:* 3 years, 1 month and 24 days

It means that the two projects promise to pay back in almost the same period of time with difference of almost one month. Promises made by the projects would become futile if there is any lack of efforts in the short-term management. For example, in the laptop division, let us say, the components would come from the United States and they are faced with problems like any disaster of international proportion, and there is a delay in supplies by six months. This means that for components, either in the years of commissioning or in the subsequent year, the gap of six months results in the accruing of funds by the same time. So for the laptop division, at the commissioning stage, it would cost the company ₹1,000 million multiplied by half of the annual rate of interest at which the company had procured the fund. The second effect being the extension of project life from 3 years, 2 months and 20 days to 3 years, 8 months and 20 days. That means a viable project would lose its intrinsic viability.

The firm may take an alternative stand if it can foresee the problem in obtaining components from overseas. It may go for maintaining a buffer stock of the components as a measure of safeguarding against the incidental impacts of the supplies. This again is a costly proposal, as the investment which could be made after a while was likely to be made at a point much early for which the company would require additional amount of fund.

Further, this shows that investment decisions cannot remain indifferent of the short-term aspects of managing finance which contributes to the optimum policy decision or final judgement. An investment decision can produce results only if it stems from a proper management of working capital.

Now, the company has to examine the role of working capital management in financing decisions. In corporate financing, we do examine various mixes of alternatives.

There can be internal source of financing, that is, through ploughing back of profit into the business. The second option could be to issue common stock for a long-term spectrum. The third option could be to get debt through long-term or flexible bond issues or getting finance from the financial institutions. The issue could be viewed as a problem, analysing and working out trade-off between two or among many alternatives.

Some of the issues confronting the business firms are as follows:

- Should the firm plough back most of its earnings in the business, or should it pay them out as dividends?
- In case additional investment is required, should the firm finance it through issue of more shares or should it borrow?
- In case it decides to borrow funds from external sources, should it borrow for a short term or for a long term?
- Instead of borrowing the required amount of funds from the financial institutions, should it obtain from the common investors by issuing bonds? If so, should it issue long-term bonds and come under a long-term commitment or should it issue a flexi bond wherein the investors feel more freedom to choose among alternatives?

There are a number of other issues, or trade-offs, that come up in the process of financing of a project or a scheme.

Let us now examine these financing decisions in the light of the short-term management of finance.

In the example of Mishra Ltd, we found that both the laptop and textile divisions want ₹2,000 million as an immediate financing need. In a market where corporate taxation is present, dividend against the shares is costlier than the interest payments against the bonds or loans taken from financial institutions. If the interest rate is 10 per cent per year for a period of 10 years, on a flat rate, the total sum of interest will be the amount equal to the original investment of ₹2,000 million.

However, this whole amount is deducted from the revenues earned by the company in the corresponding years to arrive at a net profit. Tax is charged on this net profit to get the after-tax profit which is the fund available for the shareholders. In the absence of any decision to plough back this fund as 'reserve and surplus (R&S)' by keeping them, the whole amount is supposed to be distributed to the shareholders.

Now the question is how much surplus or profit the organization is supposed to earn in order to make either of the above-mentioned plans to succeed. It is again the function of short-term management of finance that is instrumental in finalizing that. For example, in the case of Mishra Ltd, if unrealized sales are abnormally high, say 50 per cent of sales and the total expenditure is at 75 per cent of total sales, then the company will enjoy a book profit of 25 per cent but at the same time will suffer an amount of cash deficit of 25 per cent of sales.

The unrealized amount of sales is termed in accounting parlance as 'sundry debtors'. It is one of the major components of the working capital of the firm. While cash is flowing in the arteries and veins of the organization, it gets converted into items of sales and then through sales kit is returned either as cash or as sundry debtors. It is a matter of fact that unless the company gets a good management for its working capital, even an impressive sales volume and value could result in an actual cash loss for the company. But the book profit would invite taxation and then paying dividend from the residual 'after-tax profit' might prove fatal to the company.

The other side of the problem is unless there is a legacy and inherent indication about a good dividend, the company will lose financing options. This is again true in the case of getting fund through bond issues as well as direct loans obtained from the financial institutions. In both the cases, the ultimate measure is the actual net inflow of cash (cash inflow in excess of cash outflow) for the period under consideration.

The above analysis establishes that whatever be the case, financing decision can attract funds from potential sources. Finally, coming to the dividend decision, we find that dividend is a function of cash profit which the company is able to generate.

Again, as we have already discussed, earning profit is a function of short-term management of finance. This could be achieved in the following two ways:

- Optimization of cost
- Maximization of sales volume and values

Cost optimization is again a function of short-term financial management. Rationalizing liabilities in the short-term period is one of the most important items. Short-term liability can be considered as the book-source of short-term finance, until it is converted. The moment it is paid, the accrual dissolves and the book-finance turns into costs for the period under consideration. This is how management of short-term liability can be instrumental in maximizing profit.

The other option is the most positive, that is, increase of sales in real terms. This means having earned an amount of sales is not enough, the amount has to be realized in practical terms also. The amount of sales made through credit needs to be collected as per the terms of sales. If not realized within stipulated time, that sale becomes redundant. Company loses the required revenue. In both the cases, it turns into the question mark and creates negative impact on revenue estimation of the company, thus, the profitability is directly affected.

Revenue management, as it has been identified through the analysis made above in the management of funds, has been therefore the backbone of the financial management. We have seen that with the three major functions of finance profession—investment decision, financing decision and dividend decision—the success of all depends very much on the success of the working capital management for the corresponding period.

Revenue, considered as circulating main fund and capital, has been termed as 'life blood' of corporate enterprises. It is true for every stage, size and form of enterprises. A grocery firm cannot survive without proper management of the amount of cash and commodities which it carries. A manufacturing firm cannot maintain cycle without adequate cash to obtain the feeding items for the cycle. Insufficient management of working capital can lead to bankruptcy of the organization through phases of illiquidity and insolvency. In fact, in India, enterprises in the public as well as private sectors are being confronted with the problems of working capital. Industrial sickness in India and in many developing countries is mainly because of the lack of proper attention in the sphere of working capital management. Revenue management is, therefore, important for corporate survival and needs to be carefully maintained and managed.

Operating Cycle Concept

The operating cycle concept of a company talks about the period for which the amount of cash which is originally put into the business is returned squarely. It is essentially a cash-to-cash cycle. Initial investment of cash is used to create inventories and through the sales of these inventories cash is returned to the same source with some appreciation. If the amount of cash invested originally can be multiplied for a number of times, surplus is also increased. The objective of drawing operating cycle for an enterprise is to see that whatever money goes into investment and financing in a company, gets returned with due appreciation within the period of operation of the business. Each segment of the operating cycle is important from the perspective of business and enterprise.

Initial cash (C) is used to buy raw materials (RM).

RM is fed into the machine for conversion, this is known as work in progress (WIP), finally, the output is obtained as the finished goods (FG) from the manufacturing cycle.

This FG is now subject to sales. Planned output can be placed in the market for direct sales. However, if plans are not charted the right way, the output may require being stored for certain period until it finds the opportunities in the market for sales.

Sales can be transacted in the cash market to obtain direct cash, whereas if sales are through credit, the company has to wait during the credit period until it is likely to get cash from the buyer. Once full cash is received from the market, the operating cycle gets completed.

Each segment of this operating cycle is important. Two variables are very important here: time and cost. For each segment of this operating cycle, time required to finish needs to be minimized to bring efficiency in the system. On the other hand, if demand for the product is high, sales can be made immediately after the product is produced. In fact, there could be a situation of high market demand for a product when the company can demand advance money from the marketing channel partner for forwarding that product to them quickly. If the advance is such that the cost of RM or a significant part of it is recovered, then the company enjoys a better financial margin through the sales procedure. Prudent management of the business cycle, in a market-friendly way can create better fortune for the company. Focusing on the components of business with the revenue motive paves the way for better profitability for the company.

In fact, the modern concept of managing revenue originated from the old Yankee trading systems when the Yankee peddlers would sell goods located in wagons to gain some margin. Goods located in wagons were termed as current assets and the investment made in that were rotated a number of times to get a formidable margin.

A very simple example would explain this concept. Say, Rashmi has hired a car at ₹1,000 a day to sell a bottled natural perfume at ₹200 per bottle at doorsteps of the householders. Rashmi buys a bottle from wholesaler at ₹100 and sells at ₹200 per bottle. Assuming that Rashmi spends ₹10 towards cost of distribution of each bottle, in this case, the profit per unit is 90 per cent of investment into one unit. But for Rashmi, earning a profit is solely dependent on her volume of transaction. If she buys one bottle of perfume per day, the financial position for her is as follows, assuming that distribution cost can be turned insignificant once volume of business rises significantly.

Case I	Investment made by Rashmi	Returns to Rashmi
	Car rental = ₹1,000 Goods bought = ₹100 Total = ₹1,100	Items sold = ₹200 Total = ₹200

This shows that even if cent per cent profit margin is there, the unit cost to Rashmi, ignoring other cost, is ₹1,100 if she buys one item and sells the same. If instead, Rashmi is able to buy 10 bottles of perfume and sell them at the stipulated price, ignoring other costs, the financial position of Rashmi will be as follows.

Case II	Investment made by Rashmi	Returns to Rashmi
	Car rental = ₹1,000 Goods bought = ₹1,000 Total = ₹2,000	Items sold = ₹2,000 (10 × 200) Total = ₹2,000

In the second case, we find that Rashmi is able to square up the amount of investment at the end of the day. She breaks even the costs but is unable to earn profit. For Rashmi, in this example, the cycle of operation is one day. Say, now after she is able to sell 20 bottles per day. In this case, her initial investment remains the same as she buys 10 bottles by cash and the rest 10 on one-day credit from the wholesaler. But with the extended market, her customers also demanded credit. She could get cash payments from 10 and the rest 10 promised to pay after 2 days. So for Rashmi the cash flows are (assuming she is only able to invest ₹2,000) as follows.

Case III

Day 1. Rashmi invests:	For car rental	₹1,000
	For 10 bottles	₹1,000
		₹2,000

Rashmi gets credit for 10 bottles		₹1,000
	Total	₹3,000
Returns to Rashmi in cash (10 × 200)		₹2,000
Outstanding for 2 days (10 × 200)		₹2,000
	Total	₹4,000
Day 2. Rashmi invests:	For car rentals	₹1,000
	Repays for 10 bottles purchased on the first day	₹1,000
		₹2,000
Gets credit for 10 bottles		₹1,000
Returns to Rashmi (10 × 200)		₹2,000
Day 3. Rashmi invests:	For car rental	₹1,000
	Repays for 10 bottles	₹1,000
		₹2,000
	Gets credit for 10 bottles	₹1,000
Returns: Rashmi gets payment for sales made on the first day		₹2,000
Sells 10 bottles		₹2,000
		₹4,000

Now, at the end of the third day, Rashmi is able to come to the end of cycle which she has been able to generate. She can now set ₹1,000 aside and initiate business with the balance amount of ₹3,000 to repay the goods bought on credit by ₹1,000 and the balance of ₹2,000 could be treated as her initial investment again as in the case of the first day's investment in Case III. Thus, Rashmi had operating cycle of 3 days and at the end of per operation, she gained ₹1,000. If we consider a year to be of 360 days, then Rashmi is having a rotation or turnover for her business as follows:

Rashmi can earn a profit of 120 × ₹1,000 = ₹120,000 at the end of the year just by making an initial investment of ₹2,000.

The simple example of Rashmi shows how rotation is important. The higher the rotation, the greater is the margin. In the last example, Rashmi had her inventory of FG (bottled perfume), sundry creditors (credits received by her from the wholesaler) and sundry debtors (credits offered by Rashmi to the customers).

This can be shown in the loops operating cycles as follows.

Operating Cycle of Simple Trader

A trader buys FG to deliver to the customer.

This involves buying finished products to be forwarded to the relevant market.

The trader may make somewhat cosmetic change in the outer look or packaging of the product. Trader may add some new feature to the product so that apart from the intrinsic demand for the core product, it can attract new consumers and new users in terms of the better marketability of the product.

In this situation, the trader, apart from investing in buying the product, makes some calculated expenses on the augmentation of the product. This supports the business in terms of higher volume of sales. Therefore, the additional expense converts the product into a value-added product. With this additional expense made on the product, the trader's profit margin becomes higher. This discussion assumes that other factors in the market remain static.

Operating Cycle of Trader: With Credit at Both the Ends

Now, let us imagine that Rashmi gets the confidence to have her manufacturing facility. She plans to have a facility whereby she buys perfume in bulk in a huge container, get empty bottles and in her own bottling plant she makes the finished products.

She gets the bulk supply of RM on credit for a period of one month, again since the production is also bulk, she had to make arrangements for selling perfume bottles in bulk to the small traders who had to be given a credit period of one month.

- Credit provided by the supplier of RM = 1 month
- Credit period provided to the small traders who are buyers of the finished product in packs of few dozens to sell through retail counter = 1 month

In this case, operating cycle takes a different shape with more steps involved in it.

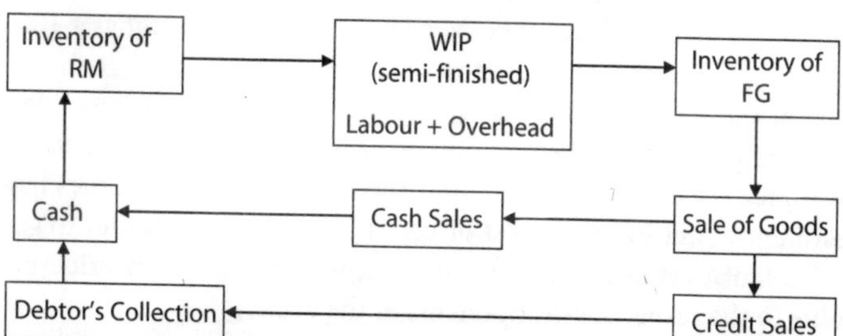

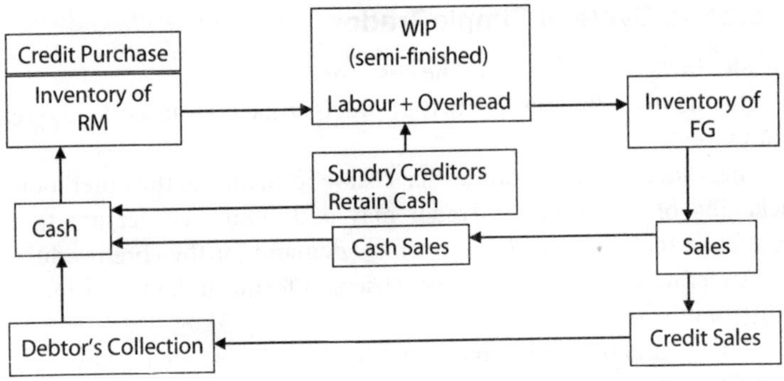

Operating Cycle of a Manufacturing Firm: With Credit Options at Both Ends

Operating Cycle of a Manufacturing Firm: With Credit at Both Ends Plus Market Borrowals

As shown in the above explanation, the total operating cycle breaks into the additive and subtractive components as follows:

Operating cycle = Inventory conversion period plus receivables collection period less payables deferral period.

Again, inventory conversion period consists of the following periods:

RM holding period plus RM in the process (WIP) plus inventory storage period as FG.

Operating Cycle: Conceptual Framework

The method of getting revenue estimation through the operating cycle analysis is to get the period of blockage of the fund first and then convert the period of blockage into cash money or near cash instruments, equivalent by multiplying this with the unit investments.

The ordinary method of doing this exercise takes care of the unit approximate but cannot be treated as accurate. Investment at the unit level arises widely at stages. For example, if the product enjoys a 100 per cent markup, then the unit investment at the FG level is more than double of that at the RM level. This is simply because RM gets value added by labour and overhead in the process before it turns into a FG at cost. Then only, under the existing scheme unit investment in RM becomes half of investment under FG at market price. This shows that in order to get an actual calculation of the operating cycle, we should assign value-based weights to the respective components of the cycle.

We have seen from the above analysis that an operating cycle has got various components. These can be identified as something through various stages also.

Starting from cash and back to cash, there can be five stages of revenue mentioned as follows:

1. Cash stage
2. RM/Accounts payable stage
3. Work-in-process stage
4. FG stage
5. Accounts receivable stage

The period of an operating cycle can be calculated as the summation of periods for which cash has been blocked at other stages of the cycle. A mathematical relationship for this shall have the following shape:

$$OC = P_m + P_p + P_f + P_d - P_e$$

where OC stands for the operating cycle,
P_m stands for the period for which cash is tied up as RM,
P_p stands for the period for which cash is tied up in the work in process (this includes material plus average of labour and overhead required in the process),
P_f stands for the period for which cash is locked up as FG in the system.
P_d stands for destination period and
P_e stands for the period of earning.

Now, once we have come to know about the complete cycle, we have to learn how to get a measure of the cycle.

The operating cycle is normally expressed in terms of days. The components of operating cycle can be calculated as differently.

This means that the material stage represents the number of days for which the company's RM remains in that stage.

The period for process can be defined as the number of days which the company takes for the RM to be converted into FG.

This can be calculated as the value accrued during the entire process.

The period for FG storage is defined as the number of days for which FG are stored in the company before selling them.

This can be calculated using debtor's model.

The period for debtor's stage is defined as the number of days for which the company is supposed to finance the sales transacted by it.

This can be calculated as:

$$Dp = \text{Debtors Period} = \frac{Sd}{Sg} \times 360 \text{ days}$$

Sd = Debtors (Sales on Credit)
Sg = Gross Annual Sales
360 = Days considered in a year

Finally, the period for creditor's stage is defined as the number of days for which the company enjoys credit for buying RM from the suppliers.

This can be calculated as:

$$Pp = \text{Creditors Period} = \frac{Sc}{Cp} \times 360 \text{ days}$$

Sc = Sundry Creditors
Cp = Credit Purchase (Annual)
360 = Days considered in a year

Having defined the various storage periods, namely the components of the operating cycle at each stage, our focus now goes to one finer aspect of the concept of operating cycle.

While computing the periods for each stage we have used in the denominators, the unit costs or values appropriate to the respective levels.

This needs corrections. Because 10 days in the stage of RM does not have the same meaning as 10 days in the stage of sundry debtors. At the former stage, the value held is that of RM and at the later stage it passes through WIP where labour and overhead are added to and then finally with the markup being added to that, the product comes at the stage of debtors. So at every stage if we get the unit-level cost or value that is shown in the denominators as fraction of the unit selling price, then we get the 'uniformity factor' for each stage of the cycle and the summation of the product of the respective periods with the factor gives rise to the actual operating cycle for the company.

Then corrected operating cycle for the company would be:

$$\text{Net OC, NOC} = Ip + Dp - Pp$$

where

Ip = Inventory Conversion Period = Period of Conversion for (Rm+WIP+G)
and so, IP = [S – (Cr+Cp)]/Cg × 360 days

where

S stands for sales price per unit,
Cr stands for per unit cost of RM and storage,
Cp stands for per unit process cost which includes the material consumed plus half of the labour and overhead
and Cg stands for unit cost of goods sold.

This analysis considers the relative importance of various components of working capital in the operating cycle of the business.

Case on Operating Cycle

Rashmi Ltd in its different units is maintaining the following cost and production data:

Average monthly production = 1,000 units
Time periods at different stages are as follows.

Stage	Unit A (in months)	Unit B (in months)
RM stage	3	4
WIP stage (processing)	2	2
FG stage	2	2
Sundry debtors	1	2
Sundry creditors	1	1.5
Delays in payments of wages	0.25	0.25

The cost data are as follows for both the units.

Direct materials = ₹40 per unit
Direct labour = ₹20 per unit
Direct overhead = ₹10 per unit
Total = ₹70 per unit
Selling price per unit = ₹140

Based on the method mentioned in the above data, we can calculate the fund required for both the units of Rashmi Ltd as follows.

For Unit A (period in months)

	Material	Labour	Overhead
RM stage	3	–	–
WIP stage	2	1	1
FG stage	2	2	2
Sundry debtors stage	1	1	1
	8	4	4
Less			
Sundry creditors	1	–	–
Delay in wage payment	–	0.25	–
Total	7	3.75	4

So the requirement of working capital for Unit A comes to:

Materials: At the rate of ₹40,000 per month for 7 months = ₹280,000
Labour: At the rate of ₹20,000 per month for 3.75 months = ₹75,000
Overhead: At the rate of ₹10,000 per month for 4 months = ₹40,000

Total = ₹395,000

For Unit B (period in months)

	Material	Labour	Overhead
RM stage	4	–	–
WIP stage	2	1	1
FG stage	2	2	2
Sundry debtors stage	2	2	2
	10	5	5
Less			
Sundry creditors stage	1.5	–	–
Delays in wage payment	–	0.25	–
Total	8.5	4.75	5

So the requirement of working capital for Unit B comes to:

Materials: At the rate of ₹40,000 per month for 8.5 months = ₹340,000
Labour: At the rate of ₹20,000 per month for 4.75 months = ₹95,000
Overhead: At the rate of ₹10,000 per month for 5 months = ₹50,000

Total = ₹395,000

We could get the same result if we had used uniformity factor at the sales price for the blockage of material, labour and overheads.

The received calculation for the requirement of fund then would be as follows:

For Unit A
So working capital requirement per unit month can be estimated.
Then, total requirement of working capital = ₹395,000

For Unit B
So fund required per unit month can be estimated.
Then total working capital required = ₹485,000

(We should remember that while calculating the WIP period, material is taken in full, labour and overheads are averaged for obvious reasons as these two are spread over products with level of completion to near full finished stage.)

Let us pick up the example of one of the top-ranked private-sector organizations by sales turnover during the year 2020, the Mata Engineering Company Limited. This organization, known as MEC could be taken as one following standard practices, also setting standard, and is worth examination.

Estimation of Operating Cycle for MEC Ltd for Six Years

Data source: Company reports and publicly available data.
(The period of study is six years ending in 2019)

- The estimation of operating cycle can be calculated as follows:
  Net operating cycle (NOC) = Inventory conversion period (ICP) + Book debt conversion period (BDCP) – Payables deferral period (PDP)
- Inventory conversion period (ICP)—this consists of the following four parts:
  a. Raw materials conversion period (RMCP)
  b. Stores, spare parts and consumable tools conversion period (SSCCP)
  c. Work-in-progress and stock-in-trade conversation period (WIPSCP)
  d. Finished goods conversion period (FGCP)

These can be calculated using relevant data as per the indications given above.

a) RMCP
b) SSCCP
c) WIPSCP
d) FGCP
BDCP
PDP

Revenue management as a focus helps to identify the following:

- Areas of strength of the business the company is in
- Areas where the company needs to assert focus to get rid of factors having pooling down impacts
- Areas of business segments which the company can put further assertions for superior business gains

From Table 9.1, we get a complete picture of operating cycle maintained by one of the widely acclaimed private-sector organizations. We have shown how this cycle could be derived directly from the published financial date of the company.

While calculating the operating periods under various stages of production, sales and realization of cash, we have taken care to see that all important items that could consume fund are properly included in the process.

Table 9.1 Various Components of the Operating Cycle of MEC

	Item	Y1	Y2	Y3	Y4	Y5	Y6
1.	RMCP	32	29	26	34	37	30
2.	SSCCP	150	145	140	166	165	148
3.	WIPSCP	71	108	105	118	59	35
4.	FGCP	5	4	5	5	4	4
5.	BDCP	148	142	140	128	117	76
6.	PDP	136	194	172	123	158	97
7.	NOC	270	234	244	328	224	196

This calculation and the exposition of net operating cycle provide us a good amount of clarity regarding the flow of revenue throughout the process. We can now identify the areas of strengths and weaknesses in the system with a view to getting them corrected, if possible.

It has been found that the company takes more time in finishing the manufacturing activities than distributing the same to meet the market demand. The very fact that FG lie in the stores for a very short period of few days shows that the products enjoy comfortable market demand.

There could be two issues at this point, the answers to which could provide a fresh guidance to the company for an alternative approach.

They are as follows:

- To try and reduce the manufacturing period
- To try and reduce the period for selling activities

If we can have a fresh light thrown on the first issue, we find that stores and spares consumption period is the highest.

Next comes the processing period. As long as there is no change in the underlying technology, change in the processing time becomes very difficult, at least in a big way. But then, a careful observation of RMCP, SSCCP and WIPSCP shows that there could be one effort, based on historical data to try and crash each component to the extent of minimum possible crashing time.

For example, in case of RMCP, we find that over a period of six years, the processing period ranges between a minimum of 26 days and a maximum of 37 days. While the company has been able to maintain a certain bandwidth for RMCP, possibility of the reduction of the RMCP period could not be ruled out.

If we take a conservative stand, then possibly we can think of maintaining RMCP at least at half of its present level. For all practical purposes an approximation can be made here and cut down the minimum level by a period of 20 days without much risk.

If we plan to crash RMCP by 20 days, then the whole range of RMCP becomes 12, 9, 6, 14, 17 and 10 days, respectively, for a period from Y1 to Y6. Of course, the entire set of things related to availability of RM and the timely supply of it would become very important.

So if the objective function is considered as the crashing of the operating cycle at the RM stage by 20 days, that would mean synchronization of RM, a systematic and defined flow in the appropriate level of quality of it and finally a system to absorb the shocks, if any, for non-supplies.

Synchronization demands a cross-company network of relationship based on complete trust, cooperation and mutual sharing of fortunes. A companywide strategy should be crafted in such a way that strengthens the brand positioning of the company, on one hand, and at the same time enhances the revenue at the current period. The company needs to take care of the short-term interest of all the stakeholders and take the mantle of the company ahead of time for a better fortune in the periods to come. That means the company has to create the revenue that supports its long- and short-term objectives.

Next arises the question of crashing the operating time taken at the stage of stores and spares. Although maintaining a particular level of stocks in stores and spares is a function of the product and manufacturing cycle in which the company is in, it can be considered to be an item or a stage of production where the idea of crashing of time cannot be ruled out.

An examination of SSCP shows that stores and spares conversion period ranges from a minimum of 140 days to a maximum of 166 days. Again following a conservative approach, a crashing by half of the existing periods could be advised. A business and the manufacturing system based on 'excellence', skill and cross-company trust and cooperation can definitely go even further to get the time period reduced by maximum period.

Crashing by 100 days could be visualized as the safe period by many standards. Then the length of the cycle at the stage of stores and spares would come to 50, 45, 40, 66, 65 and 48 days, respectively, from Y1 to Y6.

A similar argument is not being applied to WIPSCP which is mostly a function of the level of technology that the company is working with now. But there could be bandwidth of operating period from where crashing of total of 120 days, at least, from the operating cycle for manufacturing activities may not be difficult to achieve. Then for the company during the period under study, the operating cycle pertaining to manufacturing of products would come to 133, 162, 151, 198, 141 and 93 days, respectively.

If we accept this logic, then the company should not think of deferring the payments for supplies of RM, stores and spares beyond the period of its remaining in the same form in the premises of the company. This shows that if the company could achieve this objective, it could offer the suppliers of RM, stores and spares beyond the period of its remaining in the same form in the premises of the company.

This shows that if the company could achieve this objective, it could offer the suppliers of RM, stores and spares a period of credit not exceeding 133 days during Y1. That means the supplier would also benefit from the systems actualization (a process where the right approach is undertaken by the system at the right time) of the company.

This analysis can be extended to the areas of activities relating to sales, distribution and realization of money back from sales account.

The example of MEC Ltd is an eye opener for us, which shows that even one of the best performances leaves certain avenues to work on, if the OC concept is adopted.

Working Capital Leverage: Walker's Theory

The theory of working capital leverage, as propounded by E. W. Walker, is a very useful tool in the hand of a marketing professional to decide on the optimum sales quantum in a given particular context of the market and at a given scenario of the company.

Making sales through market drives is usual for companies. However, the choice of the sales manager sales has to be made based on the prospects of making profit or adequate surplus through making the sales for the company in particular situation of marketing. At times, the company has to take a decision of halting the sales drive. This is because at that point and beyond, making sales further may prove negative to the company. If beyond this point the sales process is continued as before, it may lead to erosion of the brand strength of the company. Walker's theory, thus, creates a strong support system to the company by protecting the worth of the company in the right context.

The paper 'Towards a Theory Working Capital' was published by E. W. Walker in the *Engineering Economist* in 1994. Walker had suggested the theory of working capital in four parts for the efficient management of short-term finances as against other financial and business parameters of the company. Walker's principles are mentioned below:

- *First principle:* If working capital is varied relative to sales, then the amount of risk that a firm assumes is varied and the opportunity for gain or loss is increased.
- *Second principle:* Capital should be invested in each component of working capital as long as equity position of the firm increases.
- *Third principle:* The type of capital used to finance working capital directly affects the amount of risk that a firm assumes as well as the opportunity for gain or loss and cost of capital.

- *Fourth principle:* The greater the disparity between the maturities of a firm's short-term debt instruments and its flow of internally generated funds, the greater is the risk and vice-versa.

Principles mentioned above can be worked out to develop a relationship which shows how working capital invested in a company is connected with the short-term result of the company. The same can be established through the analysis of leverage.

Here, investment in working capital is assumed to have an impact on the returns on capital employed. A portion of the capital employed is seen fixed in nature, the other part, the component as working capital is made variable in the short-term period. Leverage analysis shows whether through the changes in the variable component, the company can earn a substantial gain or not.

This analysis can be made as follows:

Let C_W = The amount of working capital employed.

Here, we use the concept of gross working capital (GWC), which means current asset is equated to the quantum of working capital.

C_F = Investment in next fixed assets (value of fixed asset less depreciation)
C_E = Earning before interests and taxes (EBIT)
L_W = Degree of leverage of working capital

Definition: Degree of working capital is defined as the percentage change in the return on capital employed (ROCE) as a result of one percent change in working capital.

So total capital employed, $C_T = C_W + C_F$
And ROCE = C_E / C_T

The impact of change in the investment in working capital on the return can be understood by considering a change occurring in it.

Let us assume that the change be a decrease, to begin with
let C_W = The decrease in working capital.
Then, percentage decrease in working capital, $C_W = C_W / D_W \times 100$.

Now, the moment the working capital changes, there occurs a corresponding change in ROCE in the system.

So the new ROCE = $C_E / (C_T - D_W)$
(This means there is an increase in ROCE.)

So the increase in ROCE = $C_E / (C_T - D_W) - C_E / C_T$.

Then, percentage change in ROCE = $D_W \times 100 / (C_T - D_W)$.

Now, degree of working capital leverage,

LW = (% change in ROCE) / (% change in working capital)
or $L_W = C_W / (C_T - D_W)$.

This means that the break-even condition for working capital leverage is to have a decrease in the working capital by an amount equal to the fixed capital.

Now, let the change in working capital be a fraction (say, x) of its originals level.

Then, $\Delta C_W = x \cdot C_W$

And let y be the ratio of net fixed assets to gross working capital. Then,

$$C_F/C_W = y \text{ or } C_F = y \cdot C_W$$

Now, $L_W = C_W / (C_T - \Delta C_W)$

$$= C_W/(C_F + C_W - \Delta C_W) = C_W/(y \cdot C_W + C_W - xC_W)$$

$$= 1/(y + 1 - x)$$

Thus, if $L_W > 1$

$$= 1/(y + 1 - x) > 1 \text{ or, } 1 > (y + 1 - x) \text{ or, } x > y$$

If, $L_W = 1$, then,

$$= 1/(y + 1 - x) = 1$$

$$\text{or, } 1 = (y + 1 - x) \text{ or, } x = y$$

and $L_W < 1$ means,

$$= 1/(y + 1 - x) < 1 \text{ or, } < (y + 1 - x)$$

$$\text{or, } x < y$$

It is obvious from the above analysis that if the change in the working capital is more in magnitude than the ratio of net fixed assets to working capital, then working capital leverage can have a positive value.

That means when the change in working capital as a ratio of the original level of working capital is more than the ratio of net fixed assets to working capital, then we can expect to get ROCE at a rate higher than the rate of change of working capital. A 1 per cent change in working capital under condition of $x > y$ results in more than 1 per cent change in the return on the total capital employed in the business.

The working capital leverage analysis shows how responsive the return of a company is to the changes in the levels of working capital. This explains why certain industries are more responsive to working capital management than others.

Industries requiring less investment in fixed assets would be more responsive to the positive leverage of working capital.

Industry groups which are more responsive to short-term finances than heavy industries such as steel, cement, automobiles, manufacturing and electronics are as follows:

- Service industry
- Hospitality industry
- Health industry
- Education and training
- Trading
- Logistics and supply chain
- Consulting
- Information technology (IT) and information technology enabled services (ITES)
- Agricultural and rural marketing
- Non-governmental organization and social service organizations
- Cultural organizations
- Organizations for social and personal care
- Municipal services
- Plantation industry
- Metal fabrications
- Agro products

According to the theory of Walker, a decrease in the GWC will induce increase in the return. In the relationship for leverage if we see the effect of increasing GWC, we find

L_W varies with GWC in the reverse manner.
From this analysis it is oblivious that

This shows that reducing GWC is to the advantage of the company.
Again, as the value of x increases, there is an increase in the leverage.

Since x is a fraction, it should increase within the limits of $0 < x < 1$.

Now, let us examine the mathematical criterion for maximisation/minimisation.

$$L_W = 1/(y + 1 - x) > 0 \text{ (For all practical purposes)}$$

Taking the first order derivative of L_W with respect to x, we get

$dL_w/dx = [1/(y + 1 - x)\,]^2 > 0$ shows that L_W is an increasing function of x

Taking the second order derivative, we get,

$$d^2L_W/dx^2 = 2/(1 + y - x)^3 > 0$$

Hence, the rate of increase of L_W with respect to x is positive. So, L_W increase at an accelerated rate if x is decreased. This means with tighter controls on working capital management, company can enhance its returns even more. If, however, x is increased, we find

$$L_W = 1/(y + 1 + x)$$

$$dL_W/dx = -1/(1 + y + x)^2 \text{ or, } \quad d^2L_W/dx^2 = 2/(1 + y + x)^3 > 0$$

This proves again that an increase in x decreases L_W at a faster rate. Then the company needs to take care of this aspect very much as increase in the GWC could prove negative responsiveness for the net return on the total capital employed by the company.

According to Walker's principle, the company's gain or loss potential increases with the amount of risk it is prepared to undertake. With higher level of risk, company's gain may be high, so will be loss. But at a higher level of risk, the responsiveness increases. With a flabby working capital company's opportunity to gain is very less. Then the question arise, what the minimum level of working capital can be. Can there be a zero level of working capital? If working capital is infinitesimally small, then the gain or loss potential is near infinity. With the increase in the level of working capital, the gain or return potential on the total investment reduces. Company can maintain some level of profit even at that point but that does not favour a sound principle of management.

Return Potential vis-à-vis Level of GWC

In the principles postulated by E. W. Walker, we have seen that the leverage increases with the reduction in the level of working capital. A reduction in the current asset is reduced, after a certain point of time the business may become insolvent also. In this situation, the capacity to meet the claims of the suppliers as well as the ability to provide fund for activities are lost, leading to a survival risk for the firm.

It is a matter of fact that profitability of the organization increases with risk. For example, holding a high level of cash would improve a healthy situation for the company so far as liquidity is concerned, but then it reduces profitability as cash maintained is idle. Procuring more funds as debt means inviting more risk, but it raises the rate of return.

Looking at the problems of risk and return from a broader perspective, we find that investing in advanced technology means undertaking challenge in shorter period but then it opens up the avenue of creating new markets, increased usage and wider acceptability of products or services.

This discussion draws our attention to a direction where the finance professional is supposed to find out a trade-off between the profitability and risk. The problem boils down to finding out the risk intake capacity of a profit-hungry company.

Risk–Return Trade-off for Revenue Management

While the companies continue with the effort to maximize their profit, optimization of costs at all actions and practices has to be maintained. The maximization of shareholders' wealth depends on the trade-off between risk and profitability.

The optimal balance between risk and profitability that maximizes shareholders' wealth is obviously expected to be reached by the company. This optimal balance is called risk–return trade-off. This trade–off between the level of risk and the consequent return earned by the company becomes the focus of the company almost every time. Risk is associated with almost every initiative of the company. This is more pertinent and visible when there is a financial or operational initiative of a new or a challenging category.

The risk is experienced by the company in the following two aspects:

- The operating risk
- The financial risk

Operating risk or business risk depends on the levels of operation. It focuses on the volume of business vis-à-vis the gross and net returns earned by the company. On the other hand, the financial risk is a function of the capital structure of the company. Financial risk varies with the intake of debt from the market for the company. Walker proposes that with the increased dose of working capital, there should be additional space created in the capital structure of the company for gathering higher equity base that maintains the intrinsic balance in the system.

Measuring operating risk involves proper idea about responsiveness of the gross profit by the changes in the levels or scales of operations. Analysis of cost, volume and profit is good to understand this and through that analysis we can develop relations and models for operative leverage. Since this is essentially a relative measure, it involves a degree of achieving. This is called degree of operative leverage (DOL).

On the other hand, measuring financial leverages involves finding out the responsiveness of the earnings to the shareholders to the changes in the capital structure and corresponding changes in the interest costs.

There are levels of operations where the profitability is more than at other points. This depends on the extent of fixed assets used in the operations, then the fixed costs associated with them will tend to push up to the break-even point (BEP) of operation. BEP is a point of operation where the total cost of business equals the total revenue. If the fixed asset created for the operation is more than the optimum requirement for a particular industry in a given context and mix of business, then profitability of the company is affected. Capital-intensive companies have a general tendency of keeping in higher levels of fixed assets to explore business opportunities from the changing scenarios of the markets.

The profitability becomes higher once BEP is reached. A highly capital-intensive company tends to have a higher BEP than less capital-intensive companies. Usually, for a highly capital-intensive company involving automated systems, labour is much less, correspondingly, the requirement for working capital is low. This situation is explained through the concept of DOL which is defined as the percentage change in the earnings before interest and taxes (EBIT) that results from 1 per cent change in units sold.

DOL can be expressed as follows:

$$\text{DOL} = Q\,(P - V) \,/\, (Q\,[P - V] - F)$$

where the legends stand for:

Q = Quantity produced
P = Price per unit
V = Variable cost per unit
F = Fixed cost

DOL = (% change in operating profit) / (% change in sales volume)

$$\text{Initial profit} = Q\,(P - V) - F$$

Change in volume = ΔQ, change in fixed cost = nil

Therefore, change in operating profit = $\Delta Q\,(P - V)$
% change in operating profit = $\Delta Q\,(P - V) \times 100 \,/\, (Q\,[P - V] - F)$
% change in the sales volume = $\Delta Q \times 100 \,/\, Q$

Therefore, DOL = $\Delta Q\,(P - V) \times 100 \,/\, (Q\,[P - V] - F) \div \Delta Q \times 100 \,/\, Q$
$= Q\,(P - V) \div (Q\,[P - V] - F)$

Therefore, if F is any positive quantity, then DOL will be greater than 1. However, in the absence of any fixed cost in the organization, the value of DOL is 1.

DOL is normally greater than 1. It can be 1 only when there is zero fixed cost. Again, in abnormal situation of negative fixed costs for a particular period, the value of DOL can be less than 1. Let us examine the situation with the help of an example.

DOL analysis shows that the company, the finance professionals need to balance risk and return in such a way that the operations are well within the angle of incidence, which means that they are being able to fetch profit, that too at such an optimum point where a change in sales by 1 per cent would give rise to a change in the returns by a higher percentage.

If the company fails to operate at the BEP level or higher than the BEP level, then it enters into the zone of business risk. The most important point is in its efforts to cross BEP, if the company just fails to achieve it, the risk is the highest. Just below BEP if the sales are increased by 1 per cent, the returns will be reduced by a rate much higher than that.

Under a given business context and set-up, the company can think of having different kinds of financial structures to suit the strategies of the company.

Business risk is intrinsic with a system for a company. At different levels of investments for the growth of the company, the amount of revenue spent on the fixed costs creates opportunities for the company. With a higher level of fixed cost, the company can expect increased rate of profit from the current business and may expect the same to occur in future, given all other relevant parameters remaining the same.

Financial risk, on the other hand, indicates the scope of the company to create opportunities for earning more than usual. The responsiveness of earnings available to individual shareholders per share to the gross income at the level of EBIT is identified through the analysis of financial risk. This responsiveness is determined through degree of financial leverage (DFL).

Degree of Financial Leverage

DFL shows the extent to which funds with fixed charges are used in the company operations. Operating leverage determines the mix of fixed assets and GWC, whereas financial leverage shows how these assets are being financed. The use of funds at a fixed cost offers the actual state of the responsiveness.

DFL is defined as the percentage change in earnings per share (EPS) of the company as a result of 1 per cent change in the level of EBIT.

DFL = (% change in EPS) / (% change in EBIT)

Following the same notations we have used so far, we get,

$$\text{Operating profit} = \text{EBIT} = Q\,(P - V) - F$$

Say, ΔEBIT is the change in the operating profit,
then % change in EBIT = ΔEBIT × 100 / EBIT.

$$\text{EPS} = (\text{EBIT} - I)\,(1 - t) / N$$

where I = Total interest
N = Total number of shares
t = Tax rate

$$\text{then } \Delta\text{EPS} = \Delta\text{EBIT}\,(1 - t) / N$$

(since I is constant here)

so % change in EPS = ΔEBIT $(1 - t) \times 100 / N \div$ (EBIT $- I) (1 - t) / N$
$= \Delta$EBIT $\times 100 /$ (EBIT $- I$)

therefore, DFL = ΔEBIT $\times 100 /$ (EBIT $- I) \div \Delta$EBIT $\times 100 /$ EBIT
= EBIT / (EBIT $- I$).

This shows that the presence of any amount of debt makes the value of DFL greater than 1. So any amount of debt can leverage the financials of the company. However, the amount of debt intake should be so carefully chosen that the interest payable is reasonably lower than EBIT of the company. Otherwise, the company runs the risk of not being able to control finances. This situation for any company is the situation of financial risk.

The analysis shows that DFL can become 1, only when there is no debt, that is, when I is 0. In all other situations, DFL should be greater that unity. The higher the value of 'I', greater is DFL. Favourable leverage occurs when the firms procure more funds on debt or through issue of bonds. If the proportion of GWC is unduly high in the asset mix, company loses the benefit of getting returns to the shareholders multiplied through unit changes at the level of EBIT.

According to Walker's principles of working capital we have seen that for an enhancement in the investment in working capital, Walker has suggested a matching enhancement in the equity base of the company. But then, enhancement of equity base does not prove worthy to the company as it does not enhance the benefit to the shareholders.

The debt alternative is not always helpful to the company. If EBIT falls below a certain level, then company may like to prefer other options like preference or equity participation. This can be shown through the following analysis.

We can write,

$$\text{EPS} \times N = (\text{EBIT} - I)(1 - t) - \text{Dp}$$
$$\text{or EPS} = ([\text{EBIT} - I][1 - t] - \text{Dp}) / N.$$

Where N = Total number of shares
DP = Preference dividend

The relationship between EBIT with EPS shows that with the growth in the value of EBIT, a company can go for preference issues. There are points on the EBIT scale of the company where it is really indifferent about choosing between two alternatives—debt and preference. Again, down the line when EBIT registers a lower figure, then equity stands as the only favoured option.

Assessment of Revenue from Different Perspectives

There are two approaches in the proper management of revenues. It is not only for the assessment of the current position but also to examine the positions that might occur in future. For both aspects, the matter requires thorough analysis based on the relevant data of the enterprise. Given the relevant boundary conditions of the environment, one can predict the likelihood of doing good or bad business in the relevant market.

It can lead to a good and reliable level of estimation for a company's journey forward. Whether the company has a reasonable level of prospect in doing the business or in investing in the business needs to be explored properly. In the event of having multiple opportunities in business, the option that is likely to yield the best output requires to be chosen for making the investment. For the existing business, analyses of results among all segments are required to properly assess that which segment of the business is better than the other.

The business segment that has better prospect to grow deserves to scale up. This may require additional investment to move up for new and better technology, better manpower, better process arrangements, sharper and faster machineries and superior distribution system. R&D activities to make continuous improvement in the core or augmented products and to attract better market information are one of the areas of concern for an existing business. This is why a business requires additional long- and medium-term investments to remain competitive in the market.

A manager has to develop proper insight to assess the situations prevailing and the likelihood of obtaining proper responses from the relevant business channels and partners to extract the best out of the conditions and situations prevailing in the market.

They may like to assess the conditions of their own enterprise or, for that matter, any enterprise to see whether it has good prospect or good condition to thrive through for a reasonable period of time.

For any organization, the assessment may include the following three broad aspects:

- Health of an organization or prospects in a project for short term
- Health of an organization or prospects in the project for a long term
- Examining the entire matters of the organization from diverse angles to see whether any valid chance is there for incidence of bankruptcy or loss of all hopes of survival of the organization. This applies to projects as well. For projects we need to see its validity of coming into existence and chances of continuation. In short, the expected life of the project needs to be assessed.

Accounting Tools for Assessment

Three major areas can be mentioned as collectively contributing to the complete understanding of the health of an entity. These areas are as follows:

- Liquidity
- Solvency
- Profitability

The main point of concern of the shareholders is to see that safety for the current period is ensured. Not only that the prospects for enhancing shareholder value is of utmost importance, but liquidity ratios are also essential for understanding the conditions in the current period. The position of liquidity of an organization can be assessed through the following three parameters:

- Working capital
- Liquid ratio or acid test ratio
- Current ratio

Working Capital

The following two concepts are valid about the assessment:

- Gross concept
- Net concept

The gross concept says that the working capital is equal to the current assets of the organization. To take a simple view about the matter, we find that major items of current assets matter the most. Let us concentrate on the major items only. A manager has to set priorities in every functional decision. Their role is to identify major areas of decision-making so that every aspect of the corporate functions is taken into account.

Major items which are covered under current asset and current liabilities are as follows:

Current Asset (CA)

- *Inventory:* Including RM, WIP and FG (M)
- *Cash:* Cash in hand and cash at bank including near cash instruments created which are tenured for getting converted to cash on the tenure terminals (C)
- *Sundry debtors or bills receivables:* Sales transacted but money not yet realized makes this account head (D)

Therefore, CA = M + C + D.

Current Liability (CL)

- *Sundry creditors or bills payables:* Materials (say, RM) received but not yet paid for makes this account (SC)
- Salary, wage and other statutory payments made due beyond stipulated time frame (S)
- *Bank overdraft:* Short-term finance taken from banks or other financial institutions to meet immediate short-term requirements of the company (OD)

Therefore, CL = SC + S + OD.

Ideally, salary, wages and so on may be included in the overall estimation of the sundry creditors.

$$GWC = CA$$

Net working capital, WC = CA – CL

It is important to understand that investment in working capital should be optimized. A company should have only adequate amount of working capital, neither too high nor too low. Each component of working capital requires investment into it. Therefore, the company should come up with proper plans so that none of the items is held for a period more than the least period or the most optimum period for that component.

Efficiency of managing working capital thus lies with the efficiency of using the investment in working capital faster and higher degree of rotation of the working capital fund. Inventory, for example, is crucial for making sales. But company should plan investing in inventory of those items which have demands in the market. That means, where the product is not required to store at all or if stored, then for a short term only.

With the transaction of sales, the inventory item becomes cash of any form. This cash can now be invested in areas of business where market demand is as high as before or even higher. Sundry debtors or receivables are the amount of money invested that is subject to be realized back after a gap period. If this gap can be shortened, it is good for the business. On the other hand, for any company, if the sundry creditor account can be extended further, it proves good for the company. So reduction in the period of receivables and extending the period for payables make the company's position better.

Overall efficiency of managing working capital can be understood better with the following ratio:

Working capital turnover ratio = Net sales / Working capital

This can further analysed by examining certain other ratios which are:

inventory turnover ratio, creditors turnover ratio, debt collection period and cash turnover ratio.

Let us take an example to see how the decision on liquidity is appropriated. Assume the following figures for a company PQ Ltd.

Figures in '000 dollars.
Inventory = 800
Cash = 400
Sundry creditors = 800
Sundry debtors = 800
Bank overdraft = 200

In order to assess the liquidity position of the company, the following ratios are required to be analysed:

- Current ratio (CR)
- Acid test ratio (ATR) or liquid ratio (LR)

CR = Current assets (CA) / Current liabilities (CL)

Ideally, all items under CA and CL should be for short term, maybe a year or one-and-a-half year. This ratio is a good indicator of liquidity of any organization.

Usually, the value of CR is assumed to be around 2 or within a range of 1.5–2.

$$\text{ATR} = (\text{CA} - \text{Inventory}) / (\text{CL} - \text{Overdraft})$$

While assessing ATR or LR, the lesser liquid items like inventory is deducted from CA and slightly longer duration element of CL like bank overdraft (OD) is deducted from current liability to obtain a picture of the real short-term liquidity condition of the company.

In general, for any company in normal condition of the market, the value of LR is assumed to be 1 or around 1.

The value of CR and LR as mentioned above are indicative but not compulsive. It varies from one industry category to the other.

Let us now examine the condition of the case of PQ Ltd based on the figures displayed above.

For PQ Ltd we get:

$$\begin{aligned}\text{Current asset} &= \text{Inventory} + \text{Cash} + \text{Sundry debtors}\\ &= 800 + 400 + 800\\ &= 2{,}000.\end{aligned}$$

Current liability = Sundry creditors + Bank overdraft
= 800 + 200
= 1,000.

Therefore, CR = CA / CL = 2,000 / 1,000 = 2.0

This shows that the company enjoys a very ideal position in terms of the overall liquidity of the company.

Let us examine the position of liquidity using acid test ratio to take a final view about the liquidity of the company.

ATR = (CA – Inventory) / (CL – OD)
= (2,000 – 800) / (1,000 – 2) = 1,200 / 800 = 1.5

In this case, partial anomaly is seen from the above, as ATR shows higher figure. This means somewhat corrective measure is needed to bring parity to the liquidity position of the company in terms of overall liquidity indicator and its acid test. The position should be further explored for managerial action in this case.

Managerial Choice of Action for PQ Ltd

- Bank OD needs to be paid off at the earliest
- Outstanding in the form of sundry debtors needs to be recovered as soon as possible
- Inventory needs to be further looked into through rigorous analysis that would make it a company with level of inventory just needed for the market
- The level of cash needs to be reduced to match with just immediate requirement. Cash requires servicing the growth of business more than other purposes.

All these can be included in the absolute liquidity ratio (ALR).

ALR = (Cash + Bank + Marketable securities) / (Liquid liabilities)

This should range between 0.5 and 1.0.

Other ratios that are indicative of the management of components of working capital are as follows:

Debtors turnover ratio = (Net credit sales) / (Average debtors + Average B/R). Objective of this ratio is to see that it is kept optimum at a given context of the market and the business.

Creditors turnover ratio = (Net credit purchase) / (Average creditors + Average B/P)

Objective of this ratio is to explore the limits of tolerance of the market for obtaining credit on the things purchased from.

Where B/R stands for bills receivables and B/P stands for bills payables.

For inventory management we can use the following ratios to maintain a balance in the inventory.

Inventory Turnover Ratio = (Cost of goods sold during the period / Average inventory at cost)

Liquidity ratios collectively indicate the position of management of current period finances of the company. If the company can manage well the current period finances, then it has the option to fetch profit at the end of the accounting period. Having a good level of liquidity for the company is important even from branding point of view. The entities who supply RM, consumables and other materials or services and the customers of goods and services, as well as people connected to the fiscal and regulatory services collectively contribute to the creation and maintenance of good impression for the company.

Usually, market-based companies have a common objective of any of the following two:

- Profit maximization
- Wealth maximization

In general, both have a common agenda of creating surplus through activities of the company. Making profit is always the core direction of any company and for that matter for any type of organization. Organization having social objective or not-for-profit organizations also need to create positive revenue through all the operations. Surplus is required to make the wheels of the organization run smoothly and to take it forward.

Therefore, profitability is important for all types of organizations.

One of the most important indicators for profitability is to see whether relative to investments the activity generates adequate surplus.

Profitability Ratios

$$\text{GP ratio} = (\text{GP} / \text{Sales}) \times 100$$

Although there is no benchmark for this ratio, one general indicator is to see that the gross rate generated by the business goes ahead of the rates any kind of market investment may fetch from the market.

$$\text{Net profit ratio (NPR)} = (\text{Net profit / Net sales}) \times 100$$
$$\text{Operating profit ratio} = (\text{Operating profit / Net sales}) \times 100$$

Operating profit is the earnings before tax or EBT of the company.

Both NPR and operating profit ratio are very important from the point of view of the company.

Company can keep track with these two parameters of the profitability of functional activities. It may give indications as to any corrective action that may be required for the company.

Management of the company and its shareholders are eager to understand the relative and absolute returns from the business. Investors would take more interest in the company where they find higher level of profit options from their investments. Thus, the share price of the company increases and thus the company is elevated to a higher value company in the market.

One of the most important measures of the profitability in the eyes of the investors and shareholders of the company is ROCE.

$$\text{ROCE} = (\text{Operating profit / Average capital employed}) \times 100$$

Operating profit can be worked out from the business as its EBT.

Capital employed is best worked out from assets.

$$\text{Gross capital employed} = \text{Fixed assets (FA)} + \text{Investments (In)} + \text{Current assets (CA)}$$
$$\text{Net capital employed} = \text{FA} + \text{In} + \text{WC}$$

Where working capital, WC = CA – CL.

Shareholders are interested to see whether they have continuous and increasing gains from the investments made in the shares.

$$\text{Return on equity capital (REC)} = (\text{NP} - \text{SP}) / \text{ESC} \times 100$$

where NP is net profit

$$\text{Statutory payment (SP)} = \text{Income tax} + \text{Preference dividend}$$
$$\text{ESC} = \text{Equity share capital.}$$

$$\text{Earnings per share (EPS)} = (\text{NP} - \text{SP}) / \text{NES} \times 100.$$
$$\text{NES} = \text{Number of equity shares.}$$
$$\text{SP} = \text{Income tax} + \text{Preference dividend.}$$

$$\text{Return on investment (ROI)} = (\text{Net operating profit}) / (\text{Capital employed}) \times 100.$$

Shareholders would always expect higher value of EPS, ROI and ROCE.

Du Pont Control Sequence

This is a control chart that connects the final corporate objective with ground-level functions of the company. Final objective of the company is to generate adequate profit so that the shareholders finally earn their desired or more than expected gains through the business operations of the company. Highest returns for the shareholders are possible only when the company maintains the stream of positive returns throughout the entire business process.

ROI has to be supported by NPR and CTR.

Where NPR = (Net profit / Sales) × 100

$$\text{Capital turnover ratio (CTR)} = (\text{Net sales} / \text{Capital employed}) \times 100$$

Higher ROI becomes assured when both NPR and CTR are favourable.

NPR should be supported by strong operating ratio.

$$\text{Operating ratio} = (\text{Operating cost} / \text{Net sales}) \times 100$$

Expenses ratio needs to be properly taken care of to make the operating ratio increase substantially.

$$\text{Expenses ratio} = (\text{Expenses on each product or service} / \text{Its sales}) \times 100$$

Minimization principle is followed for expenses ratio. Lower expenses and lower operating costs are instrumental in contributing towards making ROI higher.

NPR contributes to the increase of ROI and requires total support from CTR.

CTR is supported by fixed asset turnover ratio (FATR) and working capital turnover ratio (WCTR).

$$\text{FATR} = (\text{Net sales} / \text{Fixed assets}) \times 100$$
$$\text{WCTR} = (\text{Net sales} / \text{Working capital}) \times 100$$

WCTR has four components which are as follows:

- Inventory turnover
- Debt collection period
- Cash turnover
- Creditors turnover ratio

Du Pont sequence gives a comprehensive basis of factors collectively contributing to the overall gains of the shareholders. Whether it is assessed using ROI, ROCE or is a measure of EPS, the revenue manager needs to focus on the efficiency of each of the components to finally reach a point where shareholders feel comfort and encouragement to invest in the activities and new areas of investments in the company open.

Shareholder Gains

An investor in the shares of a company expects two types of income from the investment of the shares. These are as follows:

- Capital gain
- Dividend yield

Capital gain: This is the amount of gains secured from selling the shares in possession in the market at a price which is higher than the price at which it was purchased. Each share has a book price. Dividends that are announced by the company are disbursed on the basis of the book value of the share. However, if a company performs well or if the company has good prospect in the market because of internal or external factors, then its share price in the capital market rises. This leads to the capital gains for the investors. Certain factors can be roughly identified as those which influence the share price of the company in the stock market. These are as follows:

- Company fundamentals proving very strong and prospective for the future
- Technology upgradation, automation, diversification, breakthrough in R&D, product leadership, market leadership, brand augmentation and so on
- Market having turned strong and favourable with sharp rise in the demands for the products
- Favourable fiscal conditions or favourable conditions for production, distribution, supply of right manpower and right sociopolitical conditions
- Global scenario turning favourable for the industry and so on

Company Fundamentals

A unique way to examine the company fundamentals is to see the position of the company from the point of view of its functioning in the immediate prior period. This is done through certain analysis, many of which have been mentioned already. There are certain other areas of concerns.

In order to have a total view about the company fundamentals, we need to do the following analysis in any sequence:

- Liquidity analysis
- Solvency analysis
- Profitability analysis

Liquidity analysis and profitability analysis have been explained above. Solvency analysis is explained as follows.

Solvency Analysis

Solvency refers to the ability of the company to meet the short-, medium- and long-term obligations. The liquidity ratios indicate the management methods to coordinate and control the parameters and aspects of business in such a fashion that the short-term obligations are met properly. Good liquidity management takes care of the medium-term obligations as well. However, the long-term obligations are overarching in the company. They influence all the functions whether in the short, medium or long term. Generally, solvency refers to the long term, and therefore, is better seen from the perspective of the long-term obligations of the business.

Basically, the following ratios are used to judge the solvency of a company:

- Debt–Equity ratio (DER)
- Debt service ratio (DSR)
- Proprietary ratio (PR)

DER relates to all external liabilities to the company.

Various ways are adopted to calculate DER.

DER = Total debt taken by the company / Total equity of the company

Ideally, companies try to maintain the value of DER as 2.

However, for an opportunistic market, a company may like to take slightly more debt from the market to keep up with the pace of change with respect to the conditions of the market at that point of time.

From a different perspective, DER is defined as

DER = Total outsider's fund / Shareholder's fund
PR = Shareholder's fund / Total assets
DSR = EBIT / Fixed interest charges

Shareholders look for receiving dividend from the company more earnestly when the increase in share prices in the market is not satisfactory.

However, in case of a booming market condition, the focus of investors is casted more on the capital gain than the income through dividend. An example may clarify this point better.

Assume an investor 'P' has significant investments in two companies. These are Company A and Company B. Following are the facts of the case:

Company A
Book price of a share = ₹10
Current market price of a share = ₹850
Share price one month before = ₹750
Number of shares owned by 'P' = 40,000

Company B
Book price of a share = ₹10
Current market price of a share = ₹12
Share price one month before = ₹12
Number of shares owned by 'P' = 40,000

Both the companies have called general meeting in Mumbai on the same day and same time, 10 days from now to decide on the following agenda:

The main agenda of 'A' and 'B' is same and reads as: 'To decide on the dividend to be announced (suggestive notes recommend either 10% or 12% dividend to be announced for immediate disbursements)'.

The investor 'P' can influence the decisions at the floor of the general meeting of both the companies as he holds significant share blocks.

'P' has to decide on where to go. It cannot physically attend meetings of both the companies at the same time. Both the companies have obtained legal support for voting on presence only. Decide and recommend 'P' where to go.

In this case we need to assess the gain now and the prospects.

Gain now from the meeting is meagre. Whether the dividend is 10 per cent or 12 per cent, it comes to a figure of either ₹1.0 or ₹1.2 per share. 'P' finds that 'A' has higher prospects of capital gain, as the market prices of shares are steadily rising, so it cares less for the small difference in dividend rates. However, for Company 'B', the share prices in the market are unfavourable being static for a month. Logically, only gain 'P' can expect is from the dividend income as of now. So 'P' should attend the meeting of 'B' and try that the dividend rate is made 12 per cent. This gain is the only income from the investments in 'B'. However, for both the companies, 'P' has expectations for earning capital gain and dividend yields. 'P' shall wait for the opportune moment to back out from its investment in 'B' and make more investments in 'A'.

Shareholders' Analysis of a Company

Shareholders want to look into the intrinsic potential of the company and its current performance in the given conditions of the markets. The approaches mentioned above are good indicators of a company and through analysis the shareholders may also like to be apprised of the company and invest in accordance.

There are various kinds of operators in the share markets. Some are actual investors in nature and others are traders in the market. Traders keep the market liquidity strong, whereas the investors provide the volume and value of the market products.

For investors a unique way to understand a company is to see that short- and long-term health of the company goes well. A strong and comprehensive measure for that is mentioned in the CRAMEL model given below.

CRAMEL Model

C—Capital: Objective is to see the adequacy of capital. Shareholders would examine whether with the capital the company has created appropriate assets on long-term basis or not. The assets thus created should be properly utilized. Two types of ratios are important here to examine: DER and asset utilization ratio (AUR). Optimum measure for DER is 2:1. AUR should be high and indicate maximum utilization by the company under a given boundary condition.

R—Risk: The company should not be averse to risk, rather it should have risk appetite to the extent permissible under given circumstances. Degree of financial leverage indicates the extent a company should go for accepting risk and thrive on to skim off higher degree of surplus in a given condition of the market.

A—Assets: A company should maintain a balance between fixed assets and its working capital. Unnecessary holding of higher level of current assets at a given level of business operation pushes the company's profitability down. Shareholders would like to see that the company maintains the right level of liquidity, utilizes fixed assets to the maximum extent and reaches the right level of profitability. Also, the shareholders would like to see that the company develops market reputation and does proper branding for that as well.

M—Management: Quality of management is a factor that spreads through various means in the market. It is actually the good will and brand strength which are known either widely or in a focused manner. Bankers and investors in fixed interest bearing instruments get to know the details about management through the credit score of the organization under that management. Consistency in making regular payments in the instruments obtained is the indicator of the goodness of a management. Quality of a management depends on the profiles of the organizations run by the management. Not only the credit score but also the accounting reports placed with the taxation and other fiscal authorities are also a parallel indicator to the goodness of a management.

E—Earnings: Revenue model ensures the earnings of a company. No company can sustain with only accumulated money. Companies should go on earning with continuity. Continuity in the earning is supposed to ensure the ability of the company to meet the running expenses. Once the running expenses are taken care of, the company can think of setting aside some fund for the future. Companies can create short-term financial instruments with the continuity of earnings. Companies in the financial sector are also supposed to have straight knowledge of the affairs of personal finances. In the case of personal finances, one should have the knowledge of the ways to understand the stream of inflows of funds and the ways to make efficient use of the flow with a view to create wealth out of the flow of cash.

L—Liquidity: Liquidity is very important for a company. Maintaining liquidity keeps the company upright in the presence of the short-term transactions in the organizations. Appropriate liquidity ratios support the organizations with the right assertions about the liquidity position of the company. A combination of CR and ATR provides a comprehensive view about the liquidity of the company. Proper level of liquidity allows the company to service the short-term obligations of the company and then contribute effectively towards the profitability of the company.

Proper analysis through the CRAMEL model can make the shareholder and investor understand the position of the company directly from the overall perspective. This, apart from the other relevant methods of control, makes the manager also understand their own company or any other company for that matter.

While the CRAMEL model offers a good approach to examine the health of a company, tools for financial control should adequately be in hand of the manager. The tools mentioned so far offer sufficient mechanism to understand a company and coordinate its activities immensely. However, budgetary control is one area which helps the manager to have in place the activities in sequence of their importance and go for enforcing control as per the stipulations of the budgets.

CHAPTER 10

INVESTMENT AND RISK DECISIONS

Each company or firm operates in the midst of several constraints and conditions. The constraints and conditions may be intrinsic to those entities or explicit in the boundary conditions provided by economy and markets (Figure 10.1).

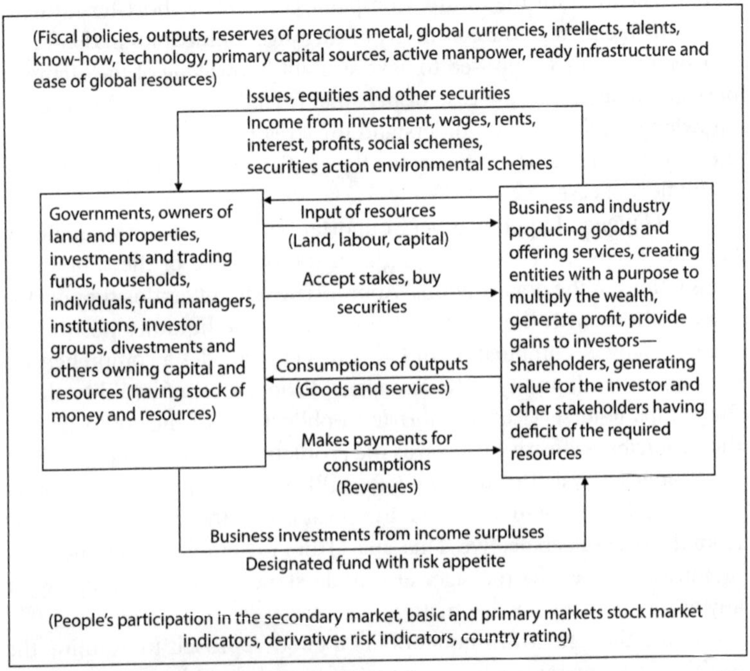

Figure 10.1 Boundaries of Economy

Cushions of the Markets

Each entity, whether manufacturing or services or busy in the field of social support or social activity, has to depend on the condition of the economy and that of the relevant market. Basic inputs and impetus come from households. Households are expected to make some amount of saving—small or big—from the incomes made by them. Accumulated savings of the households form a fund. Funds were kept idle long back, but in the modern society, funds always look for some gains. If it is in banking organizations, funds would expect some gains with very low risks involved in that. Banking organizations are required to make bulk investments in business activities. A business obtains investments from households, banks and other organizations. Funds could be available with other sources, such as governments, owners of land and properties, investment and trading funds, individuals, fund managers, institutions, investor groups, disinvestments, and other capital resources owned by anyone. Households provide workers, managers, technicians, knowledge providers, facilitators, creative persons, entrepreneurs, traders and consumers to work in the business and industry. Funds and resources are required by business and industry to grow. However, once the funds are raised, the business has the responsibility to return the fund with gains to the providers of that fund. Business and industry make payments of salary, wages, rents, interests, dividends and accruals of different types to households.

The money that households receive from firms to make payment for their resources is their income. The money that households pay to firms in order to buy products or receive services is the expenditure. It is always expected that households peg their expenses to the income and that income is expected to be more than the expenses. The difference that households get as income in excess of expenditure is considered as the savings of that households. Again, households' income is actually considered as overall costs to the business, industry and firms. On the other hand, households' overall expenditure is construed as the revenues of the firm and business. When we look at the aggregate picture, we find that the firms keep on receiving support for their financial and wealth needs from the households, society, governments and individuals, but the firms are required to constantly live up to the level of constant and continuous expectations of the consumers. People from the households and institutions become the consumers and users of products and services, while the business and firm sectors are in deficit as they require cash against the providence of products and services. Firms and businesses require additional cash, which is why they issue securities to obtain funds. Business and firms extend their ownership to others by obtaining funds through issue of equity, collect funds against issuing bonds and other certificates. Business and firms collect funds through loans and other securities and provide for each unit of fund received through return in some form, either interest, dividend, or rent or return in other forms and ways. The firms usually use the concept of cash flow to understand the condition of the business and assert control over the entire business or activity.

Let us take a simple example to understand what cash flow is and how to make use of it for the betterment of the business. Let us consider the example of TBK Ltd, a company that produces and sells consumer goods. It has its own machines to produce outputs. The figures available are: earnings = E, depreciation = D, interest = I and tax = T.

Gross sales	=	10,000,000	(Total)
Less: COGS	=	4,000,000	
EBDIT = Gross surplus	=	6,000,000	(From total business)
(Earnings before depreciation interest and tax)			
Less: D	=	1,000,000	(Machine installed at 5 million with a life expectation of 5 years so each year depreciation is 1 million)
EBIT	=	5,000,000	
Less: I	=	1,000,000	
EBT	=	4,000,000	
Less: Tax (T at the rate of 25%)	=	1,000,000	
Earnings after tax (EAT)	=	3,000,000	

Cash flow: CF = EAT + D = (3 + 1 = 4 million).

EAT is available to shareholders for keeping some amount as R&S to finance expansions, diversifications, value engineering, technology upgradation and so on. Let us assume that TBK Ltd decides to hold back at the rate of 2:1. So the company retains ₹2 million as R&S and distributes to shareholders ₹1 million as dividend. Assume the company has 0.1 million shareholders. So each of these shareholders receive dividend of ₹10 per share.

Issues of Liquidity

For any organization, availability of cash is of utmost importance to run the activities properly. The term 'liquidity' is used to mean the availability of cash once it is needed for the use of business. Generally speaking, funds that are available with the households are sensitive risks. Households dislike lending their savings to firms, as they are not sure about the chances of getting those funds back with some reasonable appreciations. Households have appetite for liquidity. They want the funds to come back to their hold once those funds are required. Corporate or firms cannot return the funds that easily. If the funds are taken against bonds or debt instruments, they have a fixed time period or tenure of maturity. Households or their investors can expect their investments back only when the designated maturity occurs. However, if the funds are invested as the equity shares of the companies, then the investor has to wait for the AGM of the shareholders of the company. At the AGM, if a proper announcement of dividend is made, then the investor gets back the amount of the dividend at the rate of announced thereof. If the investor has to withdraw from the investment for any reason, then he has the option to sell his shares in the secondary market. If the investor gets satisfied with the pay-off offered by the company to them in the form of dividend and if they are assured of the continued prospect of the company in terms of the market impact or the company's actions about the continued appreciation or prospects for gains through the dividend pay-offs, then they may like to retain the investment in the company for longer period than expected. This is how the company can expect to have a better financial position through a better cash flow.

Firms, on the other hand, can expect to retain the borrowed fund or the funds collected in the form of share investments. The need for additional funds is usually for acquiring long-term assets, better productivity, better quality of product or services, better technology of operation and so on. Long-term permanent assets are new generation machineries, latest technologies, new or added infrastructures and so on. However, the company should be careful about the availability of cash to meet the regular and running expenses. For example, the liquidity ratios of the company should be kept on actual required level. For a manufacturing company, RM are needed to make FG through the machine process. It needs to involve labour and supervising managers. The company obtains FG in the form of finished inventory to sell them in the market. The stock of goods in the form of RM, WIP and FG combine to make the total inventory of the company. Once FG are available, the company may like to make sale of these goods in the market either through cash or credit. While cash is available through cash sales, for credit sales, the goods are transferred to the buyers but the company does not receive the payment, this is known as receivables.

In the short term, the manufacturing company deals with two broad components of things. Usually, these two components are termed as current assets and current liabilities. The day-to-day running of the company is done at the strength of the working capital of the company. Usually, working capital of the company is considered as the indicator of liquidity for the company. However, it should be maintained at an optimum level so that the company is in positions to assert and expect maximum benefit out of the investment in the working capital. Let us take a broad view about the matter of liquidity measurement using the concept of working capital and some other indicators. Broadly speaking, working capital of a company is the excess of current assets over current liability held by the company. Therefore,

Working capital (WC) = Current assets (CA) – Current liabilities (CL)

Major components of CA are as follows:

Stock or inventory (RM + WIP + FG)
Receivables (or sundry debtors)
Cash (in hand + in banks or near cash instruments)

Major components of CL are as follows:

Bills payable (sundry creditors)
Wages, salary and so on
Bank overdrafts (OD) and so on

$$CR = \frac{CA}{CL}$$

This is widely accepted as the first major indicator of liquidity of a company. For a general manufacturing company, CR should be 2:1 approximately. However, it varies from one industry to the other and changes with respect to the market conditions.

ATR
or

$$\text{Quick ratio (QR)} = \frac{CA - Stock}{CL - OD}$$

This ratio is considered to be around 1:1. Again, this ratio of 1:1 cannot be considered universally applicable. It varies, again, based on nature of the business of the firm, condition of industry and economy.

Both the indicators, CR and QR, vary among various factors, such as the nature of business (whether it is a manufacturing, trading or service provider company and whether it is in social sector, non-profit making company), the condition of the market or the economy and the overall objective of the firm. A measure of CR and QR together, along with the position of working capital of the company, talks about the liquidity status of the firm in the economy.

Let us take the example of a company's position of short-term finances. Let us assume that the company has currently the following financials:

Inventory (stock)	= 400 ($ million)
Sundry creditors (payables)	= 400 ($ million)
Sundry debtors (receivables)	= 400 ($ million)
Cash (in hand)	= 400 ($ million)
Bank overdraft (OD)	= 200 ($ million)

In order to assess the true liquidity position of the company, we need to group the items according to their nature.

Thus, CA = Stock + Receivables + Cash
CL = Payables + Bank OD

In this example, CA = 400 + 400 + 400 = 1,200 units

CL = 400 + 200 = 600 units

So $CR = \frac{CA}{CL} = \frac{1200}{600} = 2:1$ This ratio is considered as ideal for most organizations.

$$CQ = \frac{CA - Stock}{CL - OD} = \frac{1,200 - 400}{600 - 200} = \frac{800}{400} = 2:1$$

The figure of QR as 2:1 is not a standard ratio. The ideal ratio is expected to be 1:1.

Managerial decision: In this exercise, we find that CR is normal but QR is unfavourable. The management decision should aim at making changes in the parameters through changes in the initiatives that are essential in this context.

If we look at the figure for QR, the numerator is 800 which contains 400 units of cash and 400 units of receivables. If we want to bring the ratio to 1:1, then we need to have some managerial actions. In this case, the managerial actions require two steps.

Managerial actions: Step 1. Work on receivables account. Sales which have been transacted to the extent of 400 units but not paid back as yet need to be coordinated with to get the payment back. Company should put proper initiative to recover those 400 units.

Step 2. Once the receivable of 400 units is collected, then cash reserve of the company grows into 400 + 400 = 800 units. Now, the company should take initiative so that these additional 400 units are not made to add to the cash stock of the company. This means that the company should make suitable investment of these 400 units in the business and see that this money of additional units brings forth adequate or more than adequate returns from the investment.

Once these two steps are accomplished in the right manner and results are realized as mentioned, the QR value becomes 1:1 as the numerator of the ratio is brought down to 400 units of value.

Risk and return are connected in the core financial decisions. The problem of risk is the problem of uncertainly of outcome. Households want to avoid investing into the activities of the companies because of the perceived risk, that is, the uncertainty in the expectations of returns from those investments. However, households across the globe are joining in larger numbers in the process of investing in the shares of the companies. There are two broad ways to invest in the equity share of the companies. These are as follows:

1. Invest at the point of issue of share (primary market)
2. Invest in the share which is on the market lists through the market force and instruments.

An investment in the shares of a company attracts two types of incomes for the investor. These are:

1. Capital gains
2. Dividend yields

Capital gain is the additional money that the investor obtains through selling the share held by him over its purchase price.

Dividend yield is the dividend obtained from the company per unit share of the company.

While capital gain is a one-time gain to the investor through selling off the shares held, the dividend yield continues for over a long period of holding the shares. As long as the company makes good business and earns profit, it pays dividend to the shareholders. Usually, companies wish to have large number of shareholders in their fold. This helps the company in two ways. One way of help is the fund that comes upto the value of stock in the market through exchange of hands of the shares ownership, which is to enhance the gross value of the company. So the company's market value increases along with the increase in the share price in the market. The other is the broad base of ownership which increases the brand presence and enhances valuation with the added support from the large number of shareholders of the company. This helps the company and its brand have higher market share and in many cases enhances the market growth of the company. Each company, in its pursuit to draw additional strength of support from the market would welcome strong supporting voices in the market. Being an owner of the company whose equity share is held by an individual, the person would always be a favourable voice in the market of products and services to hand hold the company and the brand. Consumer broad basing is thus one of the direct effects of larger number of retail shareholding of a company. Although an investor normally wants to avoid risk out of uncertain outcome, when the market of shares shows a positive movement, they wish to join in the market force with a view to skim off some part of the gains available in the market. There are long-term investors who wish to see that the gains on a horizontal scale of forward years are much higher than the usual gains in creating a risk-free sector; investors tend to invest more often in the company shares.

Stock Market Awareness

Stock market reflects the level of investor acceptability of the share, with the rise of the share price the market value of the company rises. In the books of records, the book price per share makes the book value of the company. Whereas with the rise and fall of the shares in the share market, the effective market value of the shares is calculated on the basis of the average market price per share multiplied by the number of shares held by the company.

Let us take a look at the concepts of the book value as against the market value of the share. Let us assume a situation as follows: Mr Epic has in his possession shares of two companies—A and B. Both the companies have convened their respective AGMs on the same day at the same time. Mr Epic wants to take part in AGMs of both the companies. He is interested in the gains through dividend yield as also through capital gains. Some specifications about the companies are as follows:

Company	Book Price of Shares	Market Price of Shares	Likely Dividend Rate to Be Announced through AGM
A	10	12–10	10%–20%
B	10	800–850	20%–25%

Mr Epic can attend only one of the two AGMs happening simultaneously. Since he is holding a significant number of shares, his presence and voice in the meeting may influence the decision. Choice alternatives are as follows:

If he attends Company A's AGM, he can best influence the dividend decision from 10 per cent to 23 per cent. At 10 per cent dividend, his income per share may change from ₹1 per share to ₹2 per share. Capital gain in this case is very poor. So the investor needs to bank upon dividend yield only. However, if he joins that of Company B, he can influence the dividend decision from ₹2 per share to ₹2.50 per share that means in the first case the dividend gain is ₹1 per share expected and in the second case the same is to the extent of ₹0.50 per share. The chance of capital gain is high at Company B and the chance of dividend yield is high on the Stock A. Since he cannot influence the capital gain directly, his choice should be to take part is AGM of Company A.

Prices of share change in the share market because of two broad reasons: fundamentals and technicals. Fundamentals of a company change with the physical conditions such as productions, sales and profit. However, technicals represent the historical and predictive position of the company based on the perceptions of investors, customers and market operators. Technicals are done basically on the historical position of the company. This is attempted to understand a pattern, if any, in the system. Also to understand the factor that leads to various changes in the factors of the company.

Companies publish their financial data through their annual reports. A ratio of the gross return and net return each with respect to the capital investment is an indicator that can be used to understand the position of the company. An investor can take a decision either in favour or against investing in the company. This is done with help of a simple ratio of ROI. If we wish to consider tax charges separately, then the ratio of ROI is recommended to work out as:

$$\text{ROI} = \frac{\text{EBT}}{\text{Total investment in the company}} \times 100$$

Investor would always verify the rates available with banking of financial sector returns as against ROI obtained. If the expected ROI is favourable, then only the investment is available.

For a single independent project, the test of the value of ROI can be used as the direct indicator to either accept or reject the project.

The mutually exclusive multiple projects banking on ROI alone may not yield the right decision for investment. The NPV approach would be a better technique for this. Let us take an example of two mutually exclusive projects to see how the selection of a better project can be made to make an investment.

Project P_1 requires investment of 1,500 units ($1,000) and yields annual expected cash flows of 500, 800 and 1,000 units, respectively, from Year 1 to Year 3.

Project P_2 requires investment of 1,900 units and expected cash flows from the project from Year 1 to Year 4 are 500, 800, 1,000 and 700 units, respectively.

The investor has to identify the better project. The NPV method requires estimation of the future cash flows and discounting rate is needed to calculate the present value and then NPV of both P_1 and P_2.

The future cash flows are needed to convert to the current value. This requires a discounting rate to be taken up appropriate for the situation based on the market and economic conditions.

$$\text{Present Value (PV)} = \frac{\text{Future Value (FV)}}{(1+\text{discount rate})^{y}}$$

$$\text{or } PV_y = \frac{FV_y}{(1+r)^y}$$

For P_1:

$$PV_1 = \frac{500}{(1+0.10)^1} = 500 \times 0.9091 = 456.55$$

(Assuming $r = 10\%$)

$$PV_2 = \frac{800}{(1+0.10)^2} = 800 \times 0.8264 = 661.12$$

$$PV_3 = \frac{1{,}000}{(1+0.10)^3} = 1{,}000 \times 0.07513 = 751.30$$

Cash inflows as total (PV)	= 1,866.97
Cash outflow	= 1,500
NPV for P_1	= 366.97

Similarly, for P_2:

Cash outflow	= 1,900 units
PV_1	= 500 × 0.9091 = 454.55
PV_2	= 800 × 0.8264 = 661.12
PV_3	= 100 × 0.7513 = 751.30

For

$$PV_4 = \frac{700}{(40.10)^4} = 700 \times 0.6830 = 478.10$$

Total PV of inflow = 2,345.07

So NPV for P_2 = 2,345.07 – 1900 = 445.07

Comparison between the projects P_1 and P_2 shows that

$$(NPV)\ P_2 > (NPV)\ P_1$$

Therefore, the investor shall choose the project P_2 if his investment fund permits to make investment of $1,900,000.

In this analysis, two factors are very important. These are as follows:

1. Estimation of future cash flows.
2. Identifying the appropriate discounting factor.

While estimating the future cash inflows and cash outflows, we adopt normally three market conditions: boom, normal and recession. For each market condition, expected cash flow figures are estimated. On the basis of these figures, we calculate the optimum cash flow for the year.

If we assume that for any year,

Cash Flow	Market Condition	Probability	Expected Cash Flow
C_1	Boom	n_1	$C_1 \times n_1$
C_2	Normal	n_2	$C_2 \times n_2$
C_3	Recession	n_3	$C_3 \times n_3$
then $\sum_{i=1}^{3} ni = 1$,		Expected cash flow (total) $\sum_{i=1}^{3}$ ci ni.	

In the case of mutually exclusive projects, no replacement decision is made. This means that the projects are isolated and do not form a part of the chain of replacements, if any. The project needs to be taken forward up to the end of its life. Early detection of the functioning of the investment in the chosen project may be cross-checked with the estimated future cash flows against the actual achieved.

A better method adopted nowadays in most of the project investment is the internal rate of return (IRR). This is seldom done in the context of corporate decision-making. While estimating this, focus on the market and economy is needed to understand basic risk-free rate. Usually, sovereign investments are considered risk free.

Risk is actually associated with most kinds of returns. When a business is run, we have two broad types of risks: business risk and financial risk. Financial risk is the indicator of the debt or loan taken by the company, whereas business risk is something which we have to take care of when we invest in the fixed assets of the company. A direct measure of risk is usually focused on the area of financial prudence for the company. For a capital market linked assessment, we have systematic and unsystematic risks. Systematic risk pertains to the inherent risk factors that are inbuilt in the market system, whereas the unsystematic risk is unique to the company. If we expect a return from stock investment on J_{th} stock as $E(\gamma_j)$ and if the market offers a risk-free rate (usually from government investments) as γ and 'γ' is assumed to be the relative term measuring risk then,

$$E(\gamma_j) = \gamma_F + \sigma_j \tag{10.1}$$

where σ is the standard deviation of the expected outcome on the 'J_{th}' stock in the market.

This relationship helps a fund manager to suitably choose his investment plan in a market and within the market in the chosen securities, either single stock or a mix of securities having composite presence of stock from one or more industry categories. The term 'γ' can be assessed as:

$$\text{Market price of risk, } \lambda = \frac{E(\gamma_m) - \gamma_F}{\sigma_m} \tag{10.2}$$

where 'γ' is the indicator of the surplus the investors can earn over their investment in the market indices. This shows how the market behaves with respect to the general stocks and what is the impact on the chosen share by the market. However, this concept needs to be further expanded to take care of certain relationships, particularly, that between the market or industry and the particular share. This is explained through the expended relation for return as:

$$E(\gamma_j) = \gamma_F + \gamma . \sigma_j . \rho_{j, m} \tag{10.3}$$

where $\rho_{j, m}$ stands for the correlationship between the J_{th} stock and the basic market indicator. $\rho_{j, m}$ may have value from 0 to 1.

Equation (3) can be rewritten as:

$$E(\gamma_j) = \gamma_F + (E[\gamma_m] - \gamma_F) . \tfrac{\sigma}{\sigma m} . \rho_{j, m}$$

or

$$E(\gamma_j) = \gamma_F + (E[\gamma_m] - \gamma_F) . \beta_j \tag{10.4}$$

where β_j is the relative risk measure

$$\beta_j = \frac{\sigma}{\sigma m} \cdot \rho_j, m \tag{10.5}$$

'β' is a very important indicator. It is the risk calculated for the investment stock or portfolio with respect to the market risk adjusted with the correlationship between the specified stock and the market.

CHAPTER 11

CORPORATE MANAGEMENT: MANAGING FROM THE FRONTIERS OF BUSINESS

Preview

Thoughts and practices of management have undergone huge changes and transformations during the period of human journey from the classical or ancient period to the current period of human life. Management is actually a decision about the conduct of life in the context of the moving wheels of the world. Not only is the world of humans absolute in this globe but it also forms one of the most important components of the cosmic presence on this globe. The world of humans has passed through a long way for several millennia, creating huge landmarks in its journey. Human beings have already created empires of choice, taste and preference, creating ease of life for the periods of their existence. The human society has forwarded the goodness of existence for the benefit of the next generation in a series of contributions for the future of human life.

Over the course of several periods and millennia of human activity, the knowledge and expertise gained so far have collectively benefitted human beings at large. With human knowledge spanning thousands of disciplines, the accumulated knowledge and expertise have spread to broad and diverse aspects. Management as an area of thought and practice has effectively caught hold of and included all these and has presented in a way that touches almost all such diverse areas of knowledge and expertise and yet has presented them in a way that benefits human life the most. Therefore, 'management' as a subject of study and as an art of practice combines all available thoughts and practices relevant to the human society.

The areas of coverage and scope of management are thus huge. Management plays a dominant role in running and managing the following.

- *Scientific enterprises:* Whatever be the invention or a discovery, guidance on 'management' is essential to make it fruitful and paves the way for making the output available to the people who would use the products. For example, a new medicine developed by scientists needs managerial support to (a) produce the product in a financially optimized way, (b) market the product through a proper marketing channel using marketing methods and (c) make the CF cycle vibrant for the company so that the business cycle operates with an optimum resource utilization principle in a given market context. 'Management' would always keep track of market developments in order to locate competitions and other restrictive market factors. New product development, based on the demands created in the market, is essential to the creation of a strong competitive advantage for the company. 'Management' would find continuous options to create a wider presence with the existing range of products and services. A pharmaceutical product always follows the medical advice of the doctors. Therefore, whenever there is scope for a new set of medical remedies for a health problem, there is scope for the introduction of a new range of products. The world is now horrified by the emergence and spread of a deadly virus called Corona. Any pharmaceutical company that is able to develop remedy for this will have a huge global market. Diabetes, cardiac remedies, stomach remedies, remedies for diseases of kidneys, lungs, bones, muscles, brain, nervous system, eye, ear, nose, throat, skin, trauma and so on, each has its own scope in the pharmaceutical market. There are areas of market growth with new specifications in products, creating more effectiveness in the products that gives a competitive advantage to the products.

- *Product companies:* Product companies are classified across various identities of goods. Personal (male–female) products, household products, electronic products, industrial products, mineral products and activities, mining activities, automobile products, heavy goods vehicles, oil tankers, water tankers and liquid food items, fashion products, health products, cosmetic products, health supplement products, food supplement products, kitchen aid products, textile products, household engineering products, baby care products, medical engineering products, general daily need products, electronic products, handicraft products, agro-engineering products, bioengineering products, education technology, garments, chemical products, biodegradable products, bio-nondegradable products, animal origin products, consumer goods, consumer durable products, drinks (hard and soft), vegetable oils, fruit extract juices, drinks for human consumption, safety products and so on.
- *Services organizations:* Health services, hospitality services, travel–tourism services, healthcare services, medical services, hospital services, educational services, consultancy services, financial services, household services, community services, technology support services, networking technology services, telecom services, news media, entertainment media, commercial social sites, IT services and so on.

- *Logistics and supply chain companies:* Global logistics, courier, online supply companies, online food chain, online stores, online home services, e-commerce, e-transport, e-entertainment and so on.
- *Government and public services:* Municipal services, urban services, transport services, logistics services, health services, educational services, special services to backward class of people, agricultural products and services, food and distribution services, calamity care services, trauma care services, infrastructure activities, social care services, women and childcare services and so on.
- *Infrastructure activities:* Road construction, bridges, railways, aircraft, aviation, communication networks, safety networks, defence and defence use items, aircraft, ships, submarines, satellites, arms and ammunition, dress and defence costumes and so on.
- *R&D activities:* R&D infrastructure, R&D companies, R&D in different areas of activity and transactions, and so on.
- *Social and spiritual activities:* Services associated with faith and related activities and so on.

Management is essential for a better and more efficient way of running enterprises.

Traditional views have pushed management knowledge and expertise aside from governments of any form and kind. Over the past two centuries, the rule of administration has been processed across the globe through the minds and hands of politicians. Whether it is a democratic nation like the USA or India, an autocratic country like China or North Korea, religious dogmatic countries such as Pakistan and Iran or so-called liberal countries of Europe, politicians with popularity and dominance have gone to the core of governments and driven the respective national economies in the way they visualized their gains in terms of their holding perpetuality of power and interests. Ideas of management, if applied through government infrastructure and machinery, the world would have seen and experienced much better results so far. The fundamental problems of human society have not yet been resolved.

Poverty, illiteracy, ill health, economic and social discriminations have not yet been resolved through eradication in human society. The nations have failed to offer solutions to the problems mentioned earlier. Resource utilization could have been much better with a more prudent application of national resources, and better allocation of benefits to the real deserving could have created better redistributive justice for those who deserve it. The result would have been much better with the proper management knowledge and expertise applied to run the governments than with the current set of politicians and administrators. Each activity of an organization should be based on a proper management analysis.

Basic Analysis

Strengths, weaknesses, opportunities and threats (SWOT) analysis is one of the most basic analyses for each entity in practice.

Strength: Identify the core strengths of an enterprise. Core strength could be in any area of corporate and individual activity. Product strength, brand strength, technological strength, collective strength of manpower, financial strength, knowledge strength, inheritance strength, connection and networking strength, situational strength, R&D strength, unity strength and so on.

Weakness: Any business and process gap, weak minds, lack of adequate inputs in the business cycle, lack of proper connections and networks, lack of proper knowledge, lack of wealth and resources, inadequate manpower, lack of fiscal support, adverse economic and financial environment, adverse political and social context, lack of certain inputs in the supply chain and so on.

Opportunity: New opportunities in the market and economy, fiscal advantage, situational advantage, advantage of networks and data analytics, R&D advantage, advantage of new discovery and innovations, opportunity arising from global context, new knowledge, new technology in possession, drawing advantage from negatives of others, competitive advantage from failure of competition in the market, added and acquired knowledge and so on.

Threat: Sudden adverse situations, new powerful market entrants, globalization of the local economy, new technology in the possession of competitors, sudden changes in the fiscal set-up, new and adverse legal framework relevant to the organization or people concerned, political and social chaos in conflict with the business cycle, unwanted threats from anywhere in society or markets and so on.

Effects of SWOT Analysis

The SWOT analysis indicates the following:

- What to do as a company
- Where to do business
- When to do business
- How to do business

By using this analysis, an entrepreneur can, if any, find a new way out of a business problem. It is very essential for a new enterprise or a start-up to apply SWOT correctly. This would give a clear idea of what the company can and cannot do, such as proper location of business, proper elements of business, proper mix of business elements and proper business cycle for better fulfilment.

Management as a subject of learning and practice, thus, includes a wide range of knowledge and expertise, but capsules all these in a way that benefits human society most effectively. Management is the only discipline that includes many other streams of thought in a small and compact space of mind and creates effective utilizable value for the human society at large.

Purpose of Management

The purpose of management is to create, maintain and perpetuate entities formed with a view to doing something that effectively brings things in a way that is incomparable with any other form of human activity. Management basically creates entities that give shape to the output of any stream of knowledge crafted to a human purpose.

The Vedic Thoughts

The vision of life was presented to the world by ancient India at the dawn of human civilization. Vedic thoughts and ways of human life, based on spiritual truth and practices, offered the concepts of collective living. The view and practice of 'creating one mind' among people to deliver the best for human society have been emphasized by Vedic thoughts spread throughout the world.

Vedic thought mentioned by the sages of Vedas are as follows:

Sam Gacchadham Sam Vadadham
Sam vo Manamshi Janatam
Deva Bhagae yatha purve
Sam janan upasatae.

Create the same goal of a journey in life and work. Speak the same tongue among all to deliver the finest output. Achieve commonness of mind among all to create one mind. As the Gods always urge people to develop the same.

Having a collective mind is the most effective way considered in the modern forms of managing enterprises. It was actually initiated during the Vedic period of India. The concept has been tested over several millennia and presented in a modern way through a modern language during the current phase of managing enterprises. In any context, the collective mind works most effectively. Coordinated actions require oneness of mind and a unified thought for the desired work to be carried out in the most efficient and effective way.

Any scientific discovery or invention does not take shape in the human society unless it is presented to the human society in a way that is helpful to improve the living condition of human beings. 'Management', as a stream of thought and practice, reigns over and above all the areas of activity available in human society. All discoveries are futile if they do not gain acceptance in human society. As an integral component of learning, 'management' seeks to learn and understand human behaviour as a consumer, as a viewer or as person in a society.

Basic Tenets of Management

One of the basic tenets of 'management' is to discover the following:

- People's behaviour with respect to business in general and to a particular business in focus
- General and specific ideas about the tastes and preferences of customers in particular and segments of people in general
- New set of opportunities that are available or created in markets and the economy
- Identify ways to gain market advantage in the process of doing new things for business
- Identify new business opportunities in the domain of business or related areas of activity
- Identify opportunities in any field or field of activity in the world
- Identify opportunities for business to grow through enhanced or engineered products, diversification, market developments, a new range of products or services, new discoveries, new market and economic situations, new global opportunities and so on.

New Age management relies more on the softer dimension of people and organizations than on the harder aspects. All organizations wish to engage the most competent persons in their functions and activities.

Scope of Management

Management involves generating or collecting effective ideas, putting them into practice through coordination, interactions, communication, implementation through the effective and efficient use of all resources to achieve the maximum fulfilment of the objectives in a given context and created situations.

Management thoughts have passed through various phases in the current world scenario. If we were to classify companies across major types, there would be three major types as follows:

- Bricks-and-mortar companies (BMCs)
- Technology and services companies (TSCs)
- Mixed form companies (MFCs)

BMCs are the companies that are engaged in manufacturing and distribution. These companies have high levels of investments in the following:

- Land and infrastructure
- Plant and machinery
- Technology and process for large or mass production
- Competitive advantage through better business processes
- Logistics as appropriate for the business
- Enhanced value in the value chain
- Process re-engineering
- Distribution
- Branding
- Product–price–place–promotions emphasized
- Advertising, promotion and so on

TSCs are more into the following:

- Investments in specific manpower, development of manpower
- Human orientation in business
- Create knowledge bundles
- Technology with a human-supported face
- Identify talent for acquisitions
- More focus on human interactions
- Continuous technological improvements
- Competitive advantage through better services supported by better technology and systems, and so on

MFCs are basically a combination of BMCs and TSCs.

Traditional View of Management

Traditionally, during the modern period, management principles and practices have followed the following functional divisions and classifications (Figure 11.1):

- Planning
- Organizing
- Coordinating
- Communicating
- Leading
- Controlling

Different forms of organizations have different approaches to manage their enterprises. The basic objective of an organization plays a very important role in the development of its style and mode of functioning.

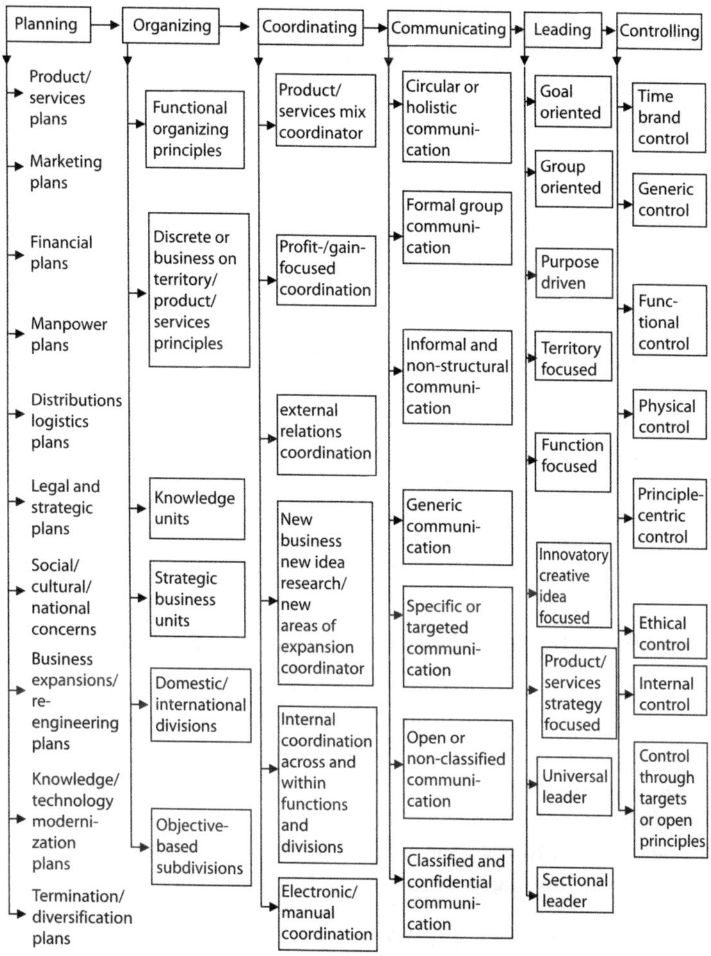

Figure 11.1 Scheme of Corporate Management

Planning for Making Decisions

Planning is needed in order to take a decision as to what needs to be done with respect to the company. The management process begins with the generation of an idea and the objective of the promoters to create and form an enterprise. However, once the idea and objective have been formed, management needs to make plans for the implementation of the idea. Decision-making on ideas requires a rigorous process to select the best or most optimal form of activity and enterprise. However, each area of decision-making may have its own means of selecting the most optimal one and of drawing up plans accordingly. The variables of decision are important. Before arriving at a decision, a manager must identify the variables that are important for arriving at the right decision. Let us take the case of a start-up decision criteria. Possible variables are discussed further.

Decision-making for a Start-up Business

- Primary ideas for projects to be undertaken as a start-up
- Identify the criteria for decision
- Allocate the weights to the criteria chosen
- Design choice alternatives
- Analysing the efficiency and effectiveness of the alternatives
- Select a couple of alternatives for trial run in sequence
- Finally identify the best alternative
- Implement the alternative in real time

Once the decision is arrived at, the implementation process may begin.

However, while selecting the correct alternative, identify appropriate criteria and allocate proper weights to the variables.

Start-up Selection Criteria

Certain sets of variables are important in selecting the appropriate project alternatives for an effective and efficient result from the new entity.

The first step for a start-up is to develop an idea of what to do. Since this is a question, the answer should be made available to the promoters in clear terms. In a situation where the promoter has multiple ideas, a proper analysis should be done to select the best idea for implementation. The process is known as total due diligence (TDD). TDD has two components:

- Financial due diligence (FDD)
- Non-financial due diligence (NFDD)

Financial Due Diligence

This basically implies testing the following aspects of the company or project.

- *Profitability analysis:* This is done to examine whether the company or project is likely to yield profit over the next 3–5 years. Profit making should be enough to support the shareholder and other stakeholder expectations of the company or project.
- *Liquidity analysis:* This is done to examine whether the company or project has the ability to maintain liquidity in real time and in real

terms over the entire period. If there is any seasonality at all, what is the basis of the seasonality and how to address seasonality issues for effective liquidity in the business?

- *Solvency analysis:* Apart from the analysis of profitability and liquidity, solvency analysis plays a very crucial role in the selection of a project for investment or a company to be acquired. Solvency measures the ability of the company to sustain changes and threats of the economy and the market. It examines the sustainability aspects. Whether or not a company is likely to exist and grow in the market depends on whether or not it has the proper solvency. It examines, on the one hand, the debt intake habit and the capacity of the company or project and, on the other hand, the intrinsic ability to serve it or not.

Non-financial Due Diligence

It is also very important to identify the growth potential of a company or project. The NFDD basically includes the following:

- Quality index of the management of the company or the promoters.
- Banking and financial transaction history of the promoters or the management of the company.
- The sociocultural profile of the promoters or the management of the existing company.
- Historical data on the management of the company or the promoters in order to understand the characteristics about them in terms of their business attributes and cultures.
- Credit scores and credit intake compatibility of the management of the company or the promoters as per the records available in the market and business history available in any way.
- Risk behaviour of the management or promoters.
- Attitude and record of transaction of the management or promoters towards and with the employees, workers and other stakeholders and probable stakeholders of the company or the project and so on.
- Any legal issue involving the promoters or the management of the company. If at all, the nature of such issues is explored in order to understand any element of fact that supports the behaviour of the promoters or the management that indicates a departure from the fairness of things in business or otherwise.

Total Due Diligence

This is actually the combination of the FDD and the NFDD as stated earlier.

Further analysis is essential in order to assess the effectiveness of the investment in the project or company. This set of analysis may be termed as investment analysis for the company or project. Although the investment analysis is conducted on the basis of separate parameters, the result of due diligence works mostly in qualifying the tests of investment worthiness for a project or a company. The pattern of investment analysis varies from one company to another. It may be considered as a truth based on the available parameters. The most important among the parameters is the estimated revenue used in the CF analysis. Unless the estimated revenue is reasonably correct, everything else in the analysis shall prove to be imaginary. The company or project should make the prudent estimates of revenue forecasts for future periods.

The term 'management' here refers to the members of the board of directors of the company, that is, directors with executive authority or somewhat connected with the execution of company policies. However, the role of non-executive directors must also be examined in this context.

Investment Analysis

- CFs for a future period of three years or, more rigorously, for five years
- Investment and financing opportunities
- Identifying the sources of revenue
- Market alternatives
- Profitability in all alternatives
- Analysing technology and process alternatives
- Suitable manpower for new business
- Fiscal and legal impacts on the new project
- Social standards and norms vis-à-vis the project
- Fulfilling the objectives of the promoters through mission and strategy

1. *CFs:* Projected CFs for the next three years need to be ascertained. While calculating CFs, the enterprise should take into consideration (a) CF from the core business and (b) CF from other and allied areas.
2. *Investment and financing:* While assessing the investment that is worthy of the project, the enterprise needs to apply the NPV and IRR approach together. This will show the real outcome of the project in real terms. Investors will put emphasis on investing in the project when they find that the project yields higher returns than the gains from investing in the financial instruments of the banking and financial organizations.
3. *Revenues:* The project should be chosen in such a way that it creates revenue options on a continuous basis.

Cash Flows

CFs are of two kinds:

1. Cash inflows
2. Cash outflow

While calculating CFs, we need to have an idea about the income and expenditure of the company or project. In both cases, this estimation depends upon a lot of internal and external factors.

Internal factors include the impact of any significant item of fixed asset, such as machinery, installations, structures, other fixed assets, funds invested in various forms and liquidity position over an average period of time.

External factors include the factors that impact and influence the up and down movements of markets. Condition of the market in general and demand for the product or services, which the company or the project is into, in terms of visible aspect of the market are also very important elements to consider. These have a huge impact on the flow of revenue into the system.

Estimates of Using Assumed Numerical for Revenues

Cash Flow, Net Profit, Depreciation and Shareholder Gain

Let us take an example of a company, using the assumed figures but applying the same tool as is required in a real-life situation to see how CFs occur.

Total revenues (R) = 40,000,000 (from core business + other areas of business)

Total cost (C) = 20,000,000 (cost of goods sold + promotion + distribution + other incidental costs associated with marketing of the product)

GP = R – C = 20,000,000. This is also termed as EBDIT.

Suppose the company has bought equipment and installed machines by paying ₹20 million. Assume the life of these equipment and machines is expected to be 10 years. Depreciation is expected to be ₹2 million per year on a linear scale.

$$\text{So EBIT} = \text{EBDIT} - D = 20{,}000{,}000 - 2{,}000{,}000 = 18{,}000{,}000$$

In order to calculate the interest component, we need to add together all interest payments. This would include interest on long- and short-term loans. Assume that the total interest payment during the year is 3 million.

$$\text{So EBT} = \text{EBIT} - \text{I} = 18{,}000{,}000 - 3{,}000{,}000 = 15{,}000{,}000$$

This amount stands for earnings before tax or pre-tax profit.

Assume that corporate tax is charged at 20 per cent.

$$\text{So I} = 0.20 \times 15{,}000{,}000 = 3{,}000{,}000$$

Therefore, EAT = EBIT – I

$$= 15{,}000{,}000 - 3{,}000{,}000$$
$$= 12{,}000{,}000$$

EAT is also known as the NP of the firm.

This amount is available to the owners of the enterprise. They may recycle the entire amount to further grow the business through additional investment in the company, which may be for higher technology, renovation, diversification or any kind of business expansion. Alternatively, the owners may decide to distribute a part of this business to shareholders and the remaining may be retained for the business. The second option is usually followed by the companies.

NP is utilized in different ways, as discussed in the chapter.

- *The entire amount of NP is reinvested in the business.* This is usually done when a company has strong market demand for a certain range of products or services that require higher level of investment to create additional facilities to ensure and support the additional demand; alternatively, this may be done to acquire new property and to create new infrastructure for the long-term growth of the company.
- *Owners decide to take the entire surplus and utilize the same for a different purpose.* This is usually known as 'repatriation'. Repatriation is usually used as an option when a company finds a market alert on the future of an existing business. Usually with the rapid change in technology in use, new market opportunities may arise before investors, which owners may like to take advantage of. Other reasons may also be there. MNCs may like to skim off NP earned in business in one country to another when new opportunities are opened up in those countries.
- In a normal situation, companies take a middle path, which means that companies distribute a part of the NP to shareholders and recycle the remaining for the purpose of business re-engineering of the company.

Assume that the company decides to retain 50 per cent with the business and to distribute the remaining 50 per cent to the shareholders.

This means that ₹6,000,000 is available for reinvestment in the company and another ₹6,000,000 is to be distributed among shareholders.

Assuming that the company has issued 60,000 shares with a book value of ₹10 per share. Each shareholder shall receive an amount of ₹100 per share in the proportion of the shares held by the person.

In this context, the CF of the company will be as follows:

$$\begin{aligned} CF &= EAT + D \\ &= 12{,}000{,}000 + 2{,}000{,}000 \\ &= 14{,}000{,}000 \end{aligned}$$

Thus, *CF analysis* is very important in the life of a company. Once CFs are properly estimated, the company is in a position to assess and plan additional activities and increased role in the corporate growth and continuation.

Although CFs are visible indicators, they do not express the total health condition of a company. They do, however, give a fair picture of the running health in the current period of the company.

The estimation of a company's future CF depends primarily on the market conditions and the pattern of market demands.

The predictive market analysis depends on the revenue estimates for the future period. Future revenue depends on the expected market conditions. While estimating the market, three situations are usually taken into account.

- *Situation 1:* Assume that the market would be very optimistic (R1).
- *Situation 2:* The market is likely to remain normal as of now (R2).
- *Situation 3:* The market is likely to be either adverse or depressive (R3).

Companies usually assume probabilities; however, there are proper statistical methods to assume the probability of each occurrence.

Let us assume that the probabilities for the next year are p1, p2 and p3. The resultant revenue would then be:

$$R\,(Y1) = R1 \times p1 + R2 \times p2 + R3 \times p3$$

Similarly, revenue for the second and third years can be estimated using the same pattern. This gives the company a better idea of the revenue model and estimates of the profitability, liquidity and solvency of the project or company.

Recession: The Best Opportune Time for Growth Plans

When a recession occurs, the first impact will be on the availability of resources and the utilization of resources in an appropriate manner.

If we analyse the impact of the recession, the impacts could be classified as shown in Figure 11.2.

Figure 11.1 describes the recession triangle using incidents and impacts of the incidents of companies of various shapes and sizes. The incident could be of two kinds: (a) global and (b) local.

The impacts of companies may be global or local, or both, as shown in Figure 11.1. Any major incident of a global nature may have an impact on the company via the national economy and the market. The force G→L may be referred to as type X force, G→C as type Y force and L→C as type Z force.

All these forces have got their areas of unique emphasis. For example, type X force acts via the economy located at L and reaches the company at C via type Z force. Therefore, C experiences either force Y directly or as a result of force X and Z.

If a national company is globally connected in terms of the market, products and services, then the route G→L→C will be most appropriate for the company to consider. However, in the case of an MNC working in another national territory, the route G→C is most appropriate. For all public sector undertakings in the country that fulfil the conditions of a multi-product, multi-location, export-oriented company, the route G→L→C is most applicable. The issues before every company are as follows.

1. *Run:* Recession as an opportunity
2. *Sink:* Recession as a threat
3. *Sleep:* Recession—a period of indifference

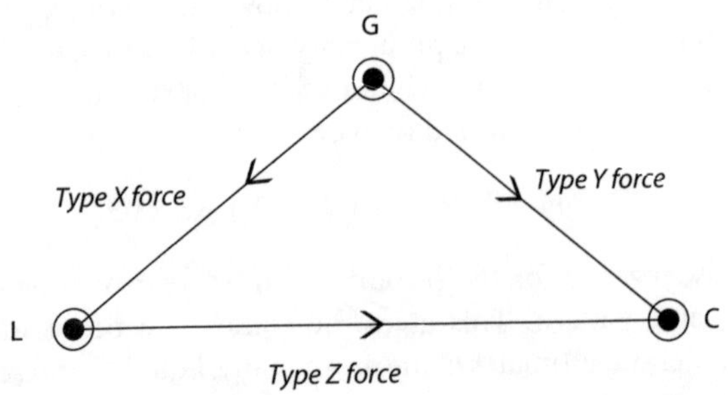

Figure 11.2 Recession Triangle

Note: G = global incident; L = local incident; C = company impact

HR Strategy

1. Run HR
   - Grab the opportunity.
   - Grow faster than others.
   - Try to induct more knowledge inputs into the company at better and more competitive prices.

     These result in superior intellectual density in the company leading to major sustainable competitive advantage in the immediate and longer term.
2. Sink HR (obsessed by fear of a drastically declining market may infuse the view of):
   - Sharp downsizing
   - Gradual downsizing
   - Planned for downsizing, action awaited
3. Sleep HR
   - Be indifferent to incidents and the resultant effects across.
   - Look at the scenario as a distant observer and try to create a view when the situation demands so.

Recession: An Opportunity for Corporate Management

Whereas chaos and crisis make normal living ridiculous, systems, structures and plans re-establish the normal fabric of an institution. The journey of a human being in a society has created the path for others to follow the trails of legacy. Through the process of coining ideas and activities, a fresh human being has been destined to take cues from the paths curved by the forerunners.

Historicity has dominated us, so far, in our posterity thoughts and practices. Whereas we are tuned to the rhythm from within, in most cases, we are dominated by the impacts from outside. Institutions have developed new ways of survivals, taking inputs mostly from the outside. The history of organizations in human society is a history of individual endeavours cumulated to the level of collectives. The traits and properties of the collective are mostly tainted by the essential impacts of history. Human being is quite often referred to as a needy animal, as if needs are the sole input to create a person's identity.

Real Essence of Growth

We need to ponder over and discover the real essence of growth.

The question remains: What is the growth factor?

- Is it the abundance of resources?
- Surplus ideas?

- Profuse opportunity?
- Something else?
- What makes a person an individual?
- What is the essence of a person's identity?
- What is the worth of a person in the context of society?
- We need to discover the essential force which makes life, which guides life to the logical and sequential end.

Awareness of Conscious Being by a Manager

The *conscious spirit* of a human being, which is invisible, intangible, unnoticeable, needs to be explored. The issue is:

- Can we unleash it?
- Can we make it grow?
- Can we make it the guiding factor of life?
- Can we assimilate the individual consciousness of many and apply that in the context of the collectives?
- The answer to all these questions is: yes, we can discover the spirit within, make use of the spirit for the benefit of society and civilization. We should cultivate new ideas for the transformation of institutions and society and, finally, transformation of a person into a divine identity suited to the empirical requirement.

Postmodern civilization will need new human species. Management by consciousness would pave the way for that. Managing enterprises by consciousness would establish a link to this phenomenon with society, which would certainly initiate the process of transformation of the person as well.

Manager with Mother's Attributes

A manager is expected to be the mother of the company/department/function. As a mother in a family takes care of individual and collective emotions, the personal well-being of every member of the family, priority is always given to the overall growth and well-being of the family, taking into account the special needs of an individual in their organization. They are compassionate and caring yet result oriented. A manager is expected to manage their organization in the same manner.

A manager is expected to possess a comprehensive development of their personality through the cultivation of motherly values in an organization. Whereas the intellectual content of personality matters a lot, the practical orientation of values is considered more important than the former. In practice, a manager expects conceptual, experiential and experimental content. In short, a person should develop an inclination towards perfection; then, success in the corporate world becomes obvious.

Scaling high without any limits in the mind is what is called *unbound aspiration*. There are certain aspirations which are truly, purely based on a material component of fact and rationality. There are others who do not like to look at the material component of facts and rationality.

Human civilization has reached a very high level at all stages of its revolution. Look at the Vedic social weather where the ancient sages had dreamed of a society based on truth and realization of the divine. The truth was universal in their realizations and perceptions. They were living on this truth and wanted others to be the same. The Vedic sages had discovered the fact that 'your mind, your heart, your senses are built on the truth, try to realize that, understand it in your own way and shape it.'

Business should inherit both visions of truth. Business practice is to have a dimension of universal truth and visualization of our ancient sages, and to involve the truth lying in the material content of the universe, a good manager will make a synthesis between the two. The best sensation is one that can accommodate the perennial and the empirical, and make the best sense of it. Look at the most successful company/ enterprise in recent times. The experiments of the combination of the universal and the empirical have been carried out by these enterprises and are therefore successful. The best achievers in the field of business and industry are those who have been able to do so.

Manager on the Face of a Crisis

Response on the Global Financial Crisis of 2007–2009: View and Observation of a Global Manager

With the world in the midst of the worst financial crises since the Great Depression era, the boundaries between markets and governments have receded. The stock market crash starting from 1929 had led to a series of bailout actions from the government of the United States, which continued till the end of the Second World War. The $700 billion rescue package offered by the US government, followed by a series of rescue packages offered by the governments of France, Germany, Australia, the UK and the Eurozone authorities, has prompted a new thinking in the minds of market makers and market leaders. Economic liberty in particular and liberalism in general are under attack by market forces. The era of market forces seems to have begun, which may lead to a complete transformation of the structures and modes of the current system of capitalism. Increased intervention by governments that had erstwhile believed in capitalism has adopted a new mechanism to address the market threat.

Whereas each market had its market makers bouncing up and down the capital market throughout the world, the scope of market making has declined drastically. Taking Nikkei 225 as an example, having decreased by 17 per cent and bounced up by 14 per cent on the following day is beyond the scope of any risk management mechanism. The basic theory of risk management, market making and capital market restructuring is all under massive threat.

The correction by the combined intervention of the market and the government seems not only illegitimate but also inadequate. Doses of $700 billion and $360 billion in bailout money, as mentioned by other governments, put together are in no way sufficient to compensate for the damage already caused to the financial markets of the world. The magnitude of the damage so far has been estimated at somewhere between $35 trillion and $50 trillion. This cannot be remedied by the meagre funds pumped in by the governments, as mentioned earlier.

A prudent manager, who is aware of global markets, would find that an individual correction was needed in the current structure of the global financial system.

The corporate world needed to look at transforming, or at least taming, certain forms of markets. To list down, a few of the observations are as follows:

1. The structures and mechanisms of consumerism need to be properly reviewed and structural transformations need to be made in the patterns of relations between markets and consumers. In a way, it is necessary to transform the pattern of consumerism in the light of spiritual values inbuilt in individuals.
2. Limited market intervention through a regulatory mechanism in such a way that consumers and investors are given priority over governance, that is, restructuring the market governance pattern.
3. Flow of funds from larger entities to smaller entities in a continuous process, so that the control of the funds and the velocity of the movement of the funds are partly in the hands of consumers.
4. The cohesive mechanism of administering financial markets by non-financial forces needs to be developed in a planned manner.

The relevant statement in a Nobel Committee Lecture in 2008 by Professor Paul Krugman, a Nobel laureate in economics, can be squarely contradicted by saying that 'it's neither the era of end of capitalism nor an era of "come back of socialism", it's but an era of enforcement of the "collective objective" on the "individual" while maintaining the economic liberty of the individual.'

Markets beyond Crisis

It has been predicted by many heads of nations in the world, regarding the pandemic from a virus called Corona, that because of chaos in the societies across the globe, disruptions have been throughout the world, leading to a huge crisis in the global economy and national economies. A manager has a learning component of the facts of the crisis and, at the same time, a manager has to adopt proper policies and strategies to ensure that the company thrives on the crisis and, at the same time, see if any fruitful gains can be made from the situation.

Historically, markets are the places where economic and commercial activities are undertaken by diversified forces under the influence of known and unknown factors from around. Markets behave in a normal fashion through trails of ups and downs in most cases; however, there are occasions and cases of disruption, catastrophe and crisis. Historically, markets have experienced catastrophe and crisis at certain intervals of decades or centuries. From the prehistoric period till date, markets have shown performance on the expected lines and, at times, beyond the expected ones. Whereas every operator in the market wants to make a profit from the transaction undertaken by them, each market, during each period of its existence, denies and baffles the expectations of most people. Again, markets that have survived for longer periods or ages are very successful in infusing attractions through increased expectations of gains or rapid gains. Therefore, markets throughout the world have nurtured the very basic elements of human greed and desire. Our needs are many and diverse, but every item and element of need has a limited identity and can be defined and described in rational terms. However, desire and greed can never be described and defined in purely rational terms.

It has been mentioned by the great thinkers that the desire is effective in giving a shape to the market through increased expectations from market operators; without the existence of a desire, the markets are said to be monotonous and linear.

When the desire of many individuals accumulates in the marketplace, normal trading and exchange forces in the market are disrupted by the impact of those accumulated desires. The reason behind this is the undefined nature of the direction of desires. Manu, one of India's most prominent sages, gave the classical definition and interpretation of desire. According to Manu, desire is endless and multiplies for the next level of fulfilment of the previous level. Manu said, *Na Jatu Kamah Kamanam Upabhogenah Samyati* (desire is never quenched with the fulfilment of it, rather it increases further). This is a perennial truth and is probably more effectively applicable during the modern era.

Markets driven by desires lead to the performance of activities which would strengthen the forces of desire, and therefore, where there is a conflict between 'ends' and 'means', there is an inherent tendency in most of the people to follow the 'ends' rather than to consider the 'means' of achieving those 'ends' to be important. Executive corruption, corporate malpractice, public malfunction, narrow choice and utter selfish behaviour in the marketplace are all the results of an intrinsic drive towards the 'ends' without emphasizing the 'means' of achieving those 'ends'. The collapse of all markets in recent times has one common thing to blame, which is the aggressive selfish nature of consumers and utter 'ends' concern of market operators. Let us look into the housing crisis that has taken place in the USA over the last two decades and the consequences of that. At the root of this is the aggressive desire to reach a height in our lives, a standard that our purse does not really support.

Let us take an example, Mr X has a monthly income of $100. In the following way, he plans his family out:

$15 goes to his insurance including medical insurance, $20 goes to his food and pocket expenses, $10 goes to his travel and entertainment, and $50 goes to his home loan payments.

Now, Mr X is hardly left with any surplus in effective terms. He has promised to carry forward and maintain the life. The promise comes from his employment of $100 in earnings and some expectation that he will increase his earnings in the future. The problem arises with a slight change in the market structure. For example, inflation conditions, employment conditions and any other exigencies that may come in. The person is not only neck-to-neck in CFs but is also faced with a situation of encountering and managing crisis. The moment structure in the personal and market front changes, he will be unable to fulfil his commitments.

When the exigencies come from a personal front, they have a local effect and do not affect the market as a whole. However, if it is driven by a change in the market structure, many people are affected simultaneously, thereby accumulating problems and developing these forces into a macro-problem.

Exteriorization: The Way of Modern Living

This is a market crisis situation. The US financial crisis of 2007 onwards and the subsequent spread of the crisis in the world during 2008 onwards have a common root in the way of living and the pattern of expectations of living a good human life. The civilization that we have created so far has made us believe in externals more than anything else.

We are exteriorizing the forces of civilization, which is making us drive through the forces of exteriorization more and more, day by day. Ultimately, there is no contentment, we are never satisfied and happiness has gone. The belief is more on the external possession than the intrinsic development. Civilization has made us believe in the growth and expansion of tangible, visible, measurable, quantifiable and so-called rational parameters. We forget about the inner truth of human existence.

This civilization has taught more about the external truth than the intrinsic ones. We have made ourselves more of a 'needing' and 'desiring' entity than an entity with a different kind of potential. The classical Indian view of civilization was the opposite—a life to live within and without simultaneously.

Indian civilization has believed in four aspects of life that are of proportionate importance to it. They are as follows:

1. Dharma
2. *Artha*
3. *Kama*
4. *Moksha*

Life should begin with the principle of righteousness. Children are taught the eternal principles of truth, the eternal principles of integrity, the principles of goodness and noble attributes. *Satyam* and *ritam* are considered to be the foundation of life. Our civilization has taught *Satyam Vadishyami Ritam Vadishyami* (I will always speak the truth and be true in my activities). 'Dharma' or the principles of righteousness infuse the very basic noble attributes of life. These persons cannot behave in a way that deviates from the principles of honesty and justice for their personal gain.

This civilization also taught us the pursuit of wealth; *artha* infuses the pursuit of wealth. We need to create wealth and maximize it. While doing this, we need to keep in mind the fact that creating wealth and maximizing it should be based on the principles of 'dharma'. Again, human life needs some kind of desire to be fulfilled. Desire should not be allowed to grow unbound. The human difference from the animal lies in its ability to manage desire through the exercise of superior consciousness. Desire, nurtured at the level of superior consciousness, would always impart an effect of taming the desire. This would only make a desire equivalent to need. Human need should be fulfilled, the need for desire should be fulfilled. There will be no room for aggressive desire beyond the limits of need. All these activities in life should be moulded in such a fashion that the ultimate goal of life to attain *moksha* is fulfilled. *Moksha* is liberation from the clutches of desire and exteriorization. When we try to attain *moksha* that we look within, we barely look within our inner world and try to discover the divine sitting there. This inner world is the world of divinity. It is present in every human being. When we try, with emphasis, to achieve balance in our life and focus on the inner world, we observe significant external impacts. People of this kind, people with this kind of mindset would make the market a different place—a place where more of thou and less of me would be nurtured, a place where a component of your mind would always be bleeding for the cause of others.

We need to restructure the market and the economy in order to get away from the impacts and abrupt disasters that lead to massive agonies in global society. Let us redefine our civilization in terms of the eternal principles that apply in the current context. It would surely bring more happiness to people in human society. This should remain a fundamental issue in the minds of the New Age manager. Future managers should resist the influence of currents events and introspect into the fundamentals of the reality of life. The manager who can do that transcends from remaining just a manager, in the usual sense of the term. That person transcends to become a sustainable corporate leader.

CHAPTER 12

MANAGER ECONOMIST: ULTIMATE IDEALS TO REMEDY ECONOMIC EVILS

Poverty: The Menace of Human Civilization

Poverty is an age-old menace for human civilization. It has many facets starting from the following:

- Economic poverty
- Poverty of wealth
- Poverty of skill
- Poverty of resources
- Poverty of mind

The poverty of human civilization is a combination of these or some of these factors, as mentioned above. Any attempt to remove or reduce the spell of poverty has to go along with the concurrent attempt to remove or reduce it in the respective segments.

The other way of understanding poverty is the lack of well-being and happiness in human beings. The society represents the collective standards of happiness and well-being. However, individuals sometimes deviate from the concept and requirement of collectiveness of well-being and happiness. The standards which the society sets for itself and promotes as a required standard of living a good life are essentially the standards or benchmark to identify the span and scope of poverty. The ideas, ideals and dreams which the society cherishes for it predetermine the scale with which it sets the standards and target for it. The moment the ideas, ideals and dreams undergo a specific change, they transform the standard for the society.

The progress of civilization has brought in changes in the expectations of a good life and thereby changes in the standards and contents of the ingredients and components of a good life. The perception of a good life has been so widespread that anything which glitters in the world becomes an item of hunger to the modern life. This hunger is to possess things which appear to a modern man as something that elevates life to a standard hitherto unattained by anybody else. Any combination of things would not actually suffice. It is actually the chosen combination of goods, services, standards and colours of life that is acceptable to the modern mind. It is not one standard that the modern mind aspires to have alone.

Rather, it varies over a period of time or most of the time. Thus, nothing remains as minimum demand. It turns into want. The minimum need for certain sections of people on earth is very much understandable, which is regarding the issues of the following:

- Food
- Dress
- Shelter
- Health
- Education or skill
- Peace and protection
- Self-fulfilment

These are the issues combined together for a large number of people on earth. However, once the first three get fulfilled, the remaining ones become the focus, not in sequence, but as and when they come up to. The issue changes abruptly once the first three gets satisfied. The individual choice starts playing an increasingly higher role as we proceed beyond the first three. The economic solution then gets mixed with the mind and psyche of individuals. Emotions, tastes, preferences, attitudes, choices, ideas and so on play very complex but crucial roles in economic choice.

The entire set of complexity needs to be included in the focus for the economists to search out the real solutions to economic problems of the world. So far, the human society has experienced many doctrinal efforts towards economic remedies. Each one of them has proved short of the right remedy to the problems. Many varieties of the socialist pattern and many faces of the liberal democratic market-driven patterns have already proved their huge shortcomings. Repeated approaches to use a mixture of those patterns through democratic, quasi-democratic, authoritarian and other methods have gone waste mostly. The quantum of natural and national wealth that has gone waste is really enormous.

Although the world has so far tested so many approaches, it has failed to look into the most reliable economic models which India has lived not for a short period but a very long period—several thousand years providing happiness and peace to lives. The Vedic era of India had lived on the spirit of spirituality. It was spirituality, lived in empirical lives, that provided profuse happiness and enduring peace to human beings. Modern life has allowed certain attributes in life that go against the spirit of spiritual living. Greed has the most important role in shaping the mental framework of a modern man. Greed takes on many hues. Greed for money, fame and power and recognition are some of those endless items which the human society loves to nurture. Greed breeds in dissatisfaction. Nothing actually satisfies a modern mind for a long period. If someone says that they are satisfied, it is just for a brief period.

Satisfaction evaporates off and on. Even unprecedented gains do not have the power to maintain human satisfaction for a long period unless it is reinforced with similar things to happen again. Sense of deprivation is one of the most common sentiments among young and growing minds. Modern attitude proves that they have so much potential with the treasures of intellect, qualities and intrinsic worth, but the world has not opened up proper opportunities for them. The spirit of life is thus constrained by the spirit of hunger. This hunger is hardly physical; it is mental hunger which bites the mind of most people. Thereby the world is left with the identity of the economic problem as something driven by chaos and confusions of life. Hunger, all profound, makes the man a true representative of the modern society. No amount of resource is going to satisfy this hunger. A person, rich in wealth, is actually a beggar in mind. Continuous hankering on the things not possessed yet bites the inner mind, even though the person seldom reveals that as a fact. Jealousy comes forward as the next bullet in the mind of an accomplished person to fire in the world of happiness, jeopardizing the impacts of the attainments of the human society so far. The remedy cannot come from the history lived during the past few centuries; rather, it lies in the several millennia-lived Vedic principles and practices of spirituality. If the human society has to live happily and in peace, Vedic principles have to be adhered to. Vedic principles cannot be lived the same way as the sages had lived. It should be translated into the post-modern form keeping the principles constant. A manager can play a strong role here to make that happen. Economists of the current profile can seldom get a chance to do the same. Managers can do if they want. It is the solemn role of managers to carry the mantle of Vedic economy forward to offer a proper remedy to the problems of economic evils of the modern world. A manager–economist should emerge as a new breed of human face having solutions in hand of the long-term economic issues.

It is in this context that a manager must be through with the proper view of economy of the globe.

Analysing the Facts

Basically, the agrarian mode of civilization had a mere expectation of simple living and good thinking of living a good life. A square meal for the day, minimum clothing for a human look and a reasonable shade over the head are used to be considered as a standard of a good life. With the change and progress of civilization, particularly, at the advent of industrialization, the requirements and ingredients of a good life started changing with gadgets added on to the agrarian standard of a good life. To take an example, the standard of living at the agrarian level of satisfaction was mostly natural and things were tested based on the living experience of the elders and the forerunners. There were hardly any measuring instruments to measure the worth of content and the spread of content.

The industrial mind wanted to become scientific in its own nature and measures the calories, vitamin and mineral or the other contents of food and accordingly create a basket of food to be treated as a balanced content of food for a good life. However, this view of balanced content keeps changing over a period or a short period. The level of satisfaction in an industrial society goes beyond a minimum position to survive and grow rather had spearheaded the concept of multiplied want and demand to be considered as the basis of living a good life that hardly gets limited to the want and demand fulfilled. Economists who have received stamps of excellence in the modern world have their skewed views. One such skewed view is as follows:

The first requirement of the concept of poverty is of a criterion as to who should be the focus of our concern. The specification of certain 'consumption norms' or a poverty line, may do part of the job; 'the poor' are those people whose consumption, standards fall short of the norms or whose incomes lie below that line. If society feels some responsibility for providing to all persons an established measure of well being beyond mere existence, for example, good physical health, then it will add to its list of necessities the resources required to prevent or cure sickness. At any given time a policy definition reflects a balancing of community capabilities and desires.... (Sen & Drèze, 1998, p. 15)

Poverty is a fact of deprivation and a sense of deprivation as well. However, we have to measure the standard for identification of poverty; the fact of deprivation has to be taken care of. On the other hand, a source of deprivation is persistent in people with an abundance of economic resources. The global purchasing power standard of $1 per day and the next level of standard of $2 per day are considered as the minimum requirement of a good life. It takes care of the minimum fund required. The minimum health and hygiene that are required for a marginal living in some cases and good living in other cases define poverty. The poverty of mind persists at each level of attainment. A sense of deprivation living to and urge to come up to a particular standard according to the mental framework is perceptive poverty. Though accordingly recovered from the first level, the advance economies are suffering from the form of perceptive poverty at each level of their collective and individual living.

The cause of poverty has been differentially described; one such description, stands as mentioned below:

There are three main fronts on which progress must be made if we are deepening our understanding of why poverty occurs, and significantly improve the effectiveness of poverty reduction policies. First, poverty research needs to focus on poverty dynamics – over the life cause and across generations.... Second, there is a need to move efforts to measure poverty dynamics beyond mere income and consumption to more multidimensional concepts and measures, of poverty - This is increasingly common in static analysis but is rare in work on poverty dynamics. This might involve assets or, more ambitiously, using concepts of human development or well being. Third, a thorough understanding of poverty and poverty reduction requires cross - disciplinary research, using strengths of different disciplines and methods, and quantitative and qualitative approaches to poverty analysis. (Addison et al., 2009, p. 3)

Although we need to address the issues of economic poverty in general, there is an urgent need to identify and take care of the issues of perceptive poverty as well. But global society has taken into account the issues of economic poverty for a large section of the population and thereby tries to solve the issues of perceptive poverty in the process of its accomplishment.

Perceived Objective of Work

Although technology drives the means of production, so far it has failed to drive down a significant change in the mode of human involvement in the productive system. One of the very old companies which are present in almost all countries in the world and have survived threats, the resilience of global market situation, withstood the First and Second World Wars, onslaughts and many more cross-currents in the global scenario for a long period of close to two centuries, remain still on the top of the world trying to be present in the mind of consumers across the globe with their own intrinsic value offered through the brand, product and services everywhere, 'Procter & Gamble (P&G)' still maintains its name, from its very inception. The journey for nearly 200 years could have been a journey succumbing to the pressures and threats from the gallops in technology, productive system, human behaviour, the spread of knowledge in a new era and the rapidly changing pattern in consumerism on the one hand and the changing faces of global relations, cultures and political identities and occasional devastations by nature, on the other.

Individuals are not calculating automatons. Rather, people are malleable and emotional actors whose decision making is influenced by contextual cues, local social networks and social norms, and shared mental models. All of these play a role in determining what individual's perceive as desirable, possible, or even 'thinkable' for their lives—. (World Bank Group, 2015, p. 3)

This is not the single example of a company for durability, sustainability, continued re-engineering, adaptability, inclusiveness and growth through providing intrinsic value and connecting with relevant people throughout the world, there are so many other examples as well spread in most of the continents of the world. Certain attributes pursued by core individuals have an enduring value. The attributes that have been practised are very worthy to mention here in terms of their absolute values. These are as follows:

- Truthfulness
- Honesty
- Cooperativeness
- Sincerity
- Simplicity
- Integrity in character
- Positive intention
- Positive values
- Universality in approach
- Supportive to global minds
- Positive spirit
- Urge to transform
- Strong commitment to work and organization

The above-mentioned attributes are the fundamental aspects of the character of an ideal person who can drive the organizations to the levels of success and achievements. Apart from the example mentioned, the great Indian corporate group of Tata has consistently followed almost all those principles which are mentioned above. The issue is that one, two or even a few enterprises following a certain set of good principles will not suffice, the world needs a large mass of corporate houses and the societies coming forward together. This is where the role of a corporate manager to become a manager–economist, the way it is prescribed here, is of utmost importance. A manager–economist shall create the environment for a spiritual economy in the world to foster forward the remedies of economic evils. Foremost, they shall create a perceptive environment that is conducive to make spiritual managers in society.

Mental models and social beliefs and practices often become deeply rooted in individuals. We tend to internalize aspects of society, taking them for granted as inevitable 'social facts'. People's mental models shape their understanding of what is right, what is natural, and what is possible in life. Social relations and structures, in turn, are the basis of socially constructed 'common sense', which represents the evidence, ideologies, and aspirations that individuals take for granted and use to make decisions – and which in some cases increase social differences. (World Bank Group, 2015, p. 12)

Let Goodness Prevail

Technology has gifted us instant communication, cosmic travel, non-human and robotic activities and re-engineered organism on the one hand and created a human intellect in a non-human context on the other. However, in all the situations, technology has failed to transform the intrinsic attributes of the human being in any way.

The bad and corrupt remain bad and corrupt. Moreover, with the power of technology in hand, the bad and corrupt find better penetration in the global context to create an edge for them and perpetuate more aggressively to defeat the goodness of the world society. However, the technological change has favoured the most productive firm in each industry and helped reallocation of the resources towards growth across the potential markets. At the beginning of the 20th century, most firms in the world used to harp on the domestic boundaries more than the overseas places. It was at the beginning of 21st century, in general, and the recent period in particular, the firms have chosen wider boundaries taking advantage of trade agreements, fiscal permissibility, cross-border trade, contractual trade and free trade agreements, globally.

Emergence of Superstar Firms

The emergence of electronic commerce and the business-to-business functioning on a wider scale on the one hand and business-to-consumers on the other have actually provided a better solution to ease the barriers to trade, distribution, reach out, demographic identities and other restrictive elements in the business process. The world has gone in favour of two extremes: on the one hand, the world has paved the ways to create 'superstar firms', but on the other, technology has eased out the access of knowledge to the business process as a whole and scale the business without a significant component of 'resource-mass'. The economic doctrines which were usually followed during the 18th, 19th and early and mid-20th century have all taken a back seat with the capital market indicators coming up in a big way to determine the industrial prospect of nations and enterprises. The World Bank, in its survey on world development, published in the *World Development Report 2019*, has identified the role of superstar firms in a big manner which reads as follows:

Large firms dominate the global economy: 10 percent of the world's companies are estimated to generate 80 percent of all profits. Superstar firms shape a country's exports. One study of 32 developing countries found that, on average, the five largest exporters in a country account for a third of its exports, nearly half of export growth, and a third of growth due to export diversification. (World Bank Group, 2019, p. 37)

The large firms have a beneficial effect on two aspects:

- The large firms can accelerate domestic economic growth through enhanced capacity of pulling resources, replacing the fatigued and old technology with the new one, upgrading the skill unfolding potential of manpower and creating a new business process.
- The large firms are accelerators in the economic chain, wherein instead of limiting their thrust on the direct productivity or the direct business system, they create multiple platforms for a large number of new generation activities and entrepreneurship.

The World Bank study has supported the view and importance of large firms from another point of view which highlights the emergence of the latest technology. Digitalization, automation, robotization and creation of machine intelligence and machine-neurons have actually changed the focus of the world business from mere brick and mortar to a knowledge-centric, continuously innovative and competitive and throughout the emergent business design. The job market thereby has focused on two broad categories with respect to the quality and nature of the job as follows:

1. Brand-seeking jobs
2. Jobs on creative platforms

As jobs are the focus of every economy, creation of the same depends on the factors of consumption, distribution, production, innovations, quality of manpower and resources.

'Spiritual economy' assumes that resources are of three types:

- Knowledge resources
- Value resources
- Spiritual resources

A self-contented economy is the economy that is free from factors of greed, aggressive ego and utter selfishness and is cooperative in nature, takes care of all, oriented to the spirit of sacrifice and goodness.

Emergence of Super Consumption

The brand-seeking jobs are supported by the existing brands who are present in any domain and who can operate from any geographical context whereas the other one is available to a person of any description to adapt and move for a job design nurtured and created through the active intervention of potential knowledge. Physical presence in the context of the job is gradually getting replaced by the virtual presence of relevant people backed by certain types of physical identities brought through the combination of material, financial and human resources. A classical economist, Adam Smith, has put the value on an individual's pursuit of selfish interest which contributes to better human good, though, by default. Smith has favoured the individual selfish tendencies as an autonomous measure to solve certain economic problems, as many of those interests would find competition from the stomachs of the markets to settle down many of the erratic tendencies of the collective transactions in the floor of the market.

Market God: Extends Invisible Hand to Settle Things

The produce of industry is what it adds to the subject or materials upon which it is employed. In proportion as the value of this produce is great or small, so will likewise be the profits of the employer.-- But the annual revenue of every society is always precisely equal to the exchangeable value of the whole annual produce of its industry, or, rather is precisely the same thing with that exchangeable value....

By preferring the support of domestic to that of foreign industry, he intends only his own security; and by directing that industry in such a manner as its produce may be of the greatest value, he intends only his own gain, and he is in this, as in many other cases, led by an invisible hand to promote an end which was no part of his intention. Nor is it always the worse for the society that it was no part of it. By pursuing his own interest he frequently promotes that of the society more effectually than when he really intends to promote it. (Smith, 2003, p. 572)

As the markets move forward to a higher number and degree of different faces of start-ups, the competition in the market rises higher and higher. The start-ups require supportive ambience and congenial market parameters. However, a higher degree of competition thrown open by a new range of start-ups redefines the market realities, in most of the cases, in favour of consumption. In the process, the market experiences a phenomenon of redistributive resources and the creation of a new range of value for the society and nation. As the World Bank has observed, the process of facilitation offered by technology has to be garnered by a search for continuous receptivity in the society by way of creating a new horizon and connecting it with different shades of consumers through new pathways.

According to the World Bank,

Technological progress leads to the direct creation of jobs in the technology sector. People are increasingly using smart phones, tablets, and other portable electronic devices to work, organize their finances, secure and heat their homes, and have fun. Workers create the online interfaces that drive this growth. With consumer interests changing fast, there are more opportunities for people to pursue careers in mobile app development and virtual reality design. (World Bank Group, 2019, p. 20)

At one point of time, the population was argued as a negative factor towards economic growth and the world was not ready in the proper sense of the term to accommodate everybody in the process of growth which used to occur in certain sectors and some parts of the globe and also some sections of the population within the national boundaries.

However, during the middle of the previous century, it came to the understanding of the thinkers and practitioners that the human being can be considered as a resource, and proper utilization and management of the said resource could lead to an expansion of the global economic standard and distributive development of the economies of the world. This, however, has been further fine-tuned through different ways and different aspects and levels of technology. This has been provided by converting human power into a more resourceful element in the chain of business in the world. Culturally, the pattern of economic management has a broad divide between:

- Dominant rationale
- Dominant intuitive

The *dominant rationale* has always banked on the externalities such as tools, technologies, in hard and soft form, with applications through systems, structures, procedures and formal agenda, whereas the *dominant intuitive* have backed on the creative, perceptive, intuitive and sixth sense of doing things.

At least since the time of Adam Smith, competition has played a central role in economics. It is because of competition that individuals and firms, pursuing their own self-interest are led, as if by an invisible hand, to do what is common good.... Markets work partly because of competition and partly because of the advantages that result from decentralization. Competion is important because it provides incentives.... There is no strategic corporate policy to outwit rivals. To be sure, profits are maximized if firms minimise their costs of production. But to get customers as many as the firm could possibly want – all the firm needs to do is charge ever so slightly less than the 'market price'. (Stiglitz, 1994, pp. 109–110)

Economic leadership transcends with a combination of these two with the emergence of two major global economies in the Asian continent, namely China and India, the need to look at economic leadership from a different perspective has become urgent. The Western model emphasizes more on the first category and has pushed the global business from a 'people-friendly' to a 'profit-friendly' process. The new reality of the world demands a new kind of leadership based on traditional approach of the past millennia and tested wisdom. The wisdom-centric attitude to life, as ancient India had lived on during its Vedic period, has strong relevance for the future state of the economy in the world. This process will not only tend to develop leadership with a balance between the two varieties but also shall attempt to inculcate the ancient wisdom in the developmental process for the real survival and growth of the economy in a holistic manner in future.

The Poor, the Rich and the Global Man

The total global wealth has reached around $200 trillion in 2010. In 2020, this is around $300 trillion. The dollar millionaires have crossed the size of the Australian continent by number. The Gini coefficient is far away from the mark of global equality, zero. The dollar millionaires are far away from getting the happiness; they were otherwise expected to have drawn from the wealth that they have amassed. The economic pyramid still persists. The pyramid of wealth has a wide base and sharp apex signifying the higher degree of concentration in the hands of a few and leaving the vast majority between the space of frying pan and fire. The richest 1 per cent of global adults control around 45 per cent of the global assets. The wealthiest 10 per cent have around 85 per cent of that. However, the bottom 50 per cent of the global adult population has only 2 per cent of the global wealth to their command. The current estimate of nearly 5 billion global adults which show the per cent average wealth to their command have also risen significantly. The major magazines, listings, richest persons on earth do now consider those having $1 billion as the minimum size of the par.

If we look beyond the twentieth century and adopt a very long term view, the idea of a stable capital-labour split must somehow deal with the fact the nature of capital itself has changed radically (from land and other real estate in the eighteenth century to industrial and financial capital in the twenty-first century). There is also the idea, widespread among economists that modern economic growth depends largely on the rise of 'Human capital'.... The truth is that economics should never have sought to divorce itself from the other social sciences and can advance only in conjunction with them. The social sciences collectively know too little to waste time on foolish disciplinary squabbles. If we are to progress in our understanding of the historical dynamics of the wealth distribution and the structure of social classes, we must obviously take a pragmatic approach and avail ourselves of the methods of historians, sociologists, and political scientists as well as economists. (Piketty, 2013, p. 33)

Yet profuse cries are in the air. Sumantra from India, Nasir from Bangladesh, Haris from East Europe, Hof from the Nordic, Elzen from South America, Wilson from Africa and many other from across the globe have their cries unheard but echoed through the winds of change swiping through the barriers of cultures and countries.

Story of Sumantra: A Lotus on Garbage

Sumantra lives alone in a shanty shelter to park the bicycles for the traders, customers and others visiting the market in Salt Lake, Kolkata. He hopes to take pleasure in a wonderful bed to go to sleep in the night, but in reality, he sleeps in a rotten and torn mat picked up from the garbage. Some of his clothes are made of banners of some political parties and thrown-away jute bags rejected by the shoppers for being cut 100 places by the rats. For breakfast, a tea seller gives him half a cup of tea in an earthen small jar which is already used by a customer and thrown in the rags. Sumantra gives a smile with this morning hot half-full cup of tea. For the biscuits, he has to fight with the dog and pick up one or two broken thrown away by some 'good-hearted' householders visiting the tea stall after completing the stretch of morning walks.

Sumantra is allowed to take the shelter as he provides an essential service of looking after the bicycles from the backside of the store and guard it against those interested in stealing away of bicycles parts. The lunch for him is at times available and most of the other times not. Sumantra has a source of water after everybody gets their jars and containers filled in from the public place of water supply by the side of the market; he gets a few drops to fill in the same empty earthen jar to quench his thirst for water. He fortunately was getting thrown away by the 'good hearted' householders and others for having bits and pieces of food residuals for his consumption. Sumantra's dinner is however secured. The owner of the bicycle parking place is gracious to offer him two pieces of thin handmade bread and some pickles or other items to get a part of his stomach filled in for his dinner. Sumantra goes to his bed. He has immense pleasure in going for *reviews of his life.*

He used to live in a village far away from the place where he is right now and also had his parents. Sumantra, now aged around 45, looks back for those days when he was 4 or 5. His mother, Laxmi Devi, was very kind to him. Sumantra, the fifth child of the parents was so profusely cared for. They had a small piece of land with a yield of one crop a year. The yield was not insufficient for them to fill in their belly for a period of 4 months a year. Sumantra's father, Narayan, a hard-working person, was so stout, confident and responsible that he hardly troubled his children to garner the earnings for the family. Narayan used to work in the field of others as an agricultural labourer. He could work beyond the normal hours of time and earn higher than others in his category. Narayan never cared for his personal health. He was always keen to see himself managing and fulfilling the needs of the family. However, Laxmi Devi was not idle, she used to work in the household as a housemaid and whatever little amount she could earn would always add value to the stream of income for the family. Laxmi Devi wanted her children to grow as a good citizen and a good person, and at the same time, she wanted to establish them economically to live a good life. She wanted to get her children educated. All the children were sent to a free school slightly away from their cottage at the other end of the village.

The school used to open and close every day but for the teachers. Students who are most eager to learn used to come and go back home empty every day after taking mid-day meals whenever it is available. Classrooms were mostly broken and dirty which could make anyone wretched. The library was mentioned on the door of it but the books in the library used to remain at the same positions throughout. The door lock has caught deep rust for not being touched for a long time. Only one attendant of the school, who lived in the school premises with the family, used to open the outside gates forthwith for willing students to come in and go back. Biju Sardar, the gatekeeper, used to advise the students to come to the school on the last day of the calendar month and the first day of the calendar month only to have the benefit of meeting the teacher in the classroom for a while. Laxmi Devi's children had a moment of meeting the teachers, occasionally on the first working day of the calendar month, when the teachers used to visit the school to complete formalities for their salaries. Laxmi Devi was truly illiterate. She had developed the conviction that her children would grow with intellect and rank with others enjoying the benefits of the world by virtue of the power of their intellect.

Laxmi Devi had a dream that each child would grow to be an intellect and have a position in the world like others. She knew the new rule of the world, 'If you want to have a position in the world, you need to be strong in either intellect or capital, or both.' In the absence of both of these, you have a grand position in the dark path and horizons of the world where you will have hardly a span of good life led by many others. In the race of life, you need to understand what makes you grow up and up on the ladder to finally get a foot on the horizontals of the average economic plate. Laxmi Devi and Narayan together with their children were just maintaining a life of happiness with a standard of living far below that of a global standard. Sumantra recounts the occasions when his mother had offered exclusive love and affection to him. Once or twice a week, Sumantra hardly had a chance to get the mother free from her works and duties. They had a single-room cottage and a cot inside that. The cottage shed was covered by long leaves of palm and coconut trees fitted on a framework made on bamboos and tied with knots given by ropes made of coconut fibres. It used to give a cool and pleasant living during the hot summer, relatively like the one lived during the winter. The walls of the cottage made of a special type of mud had made the inside of the room counteractive to the external temperature.

Narayan could not do the repair for the house for last five years because of the paucity of the fund required for it. The disaster came on a day. It was a massive cyclone. The room cover got blown away and was flying in the air getting smashed and dropped at a place untraceable. The village turned into shanties. Trees, homes and all the other structures were broken and washed off to the lakes, and it rained heavily thereafter. It continued to rain for the third day inviting a massive flood. The barrage authority nearby had no other options but to open the locks of the gates and allow the rush of water towards the areas populated by human beings.

Sumantra along with others was carried away by the waves of the flood. He got his senses back in the district hospital under the care of semi-doctors. The eyes could not trace any known person. Sumantra, lost in the woods of the world, cried. He later got a shelter near the hospital at the mercy of a person running a small tea stall. He grew over there and learnt many things in life. He learnt to make tea, get the breads toasted and offer it on a plate with butter and sugar added to it. He also learnt to clean the stall, to speak to the people and to collect the money. Till then, Sumantra was on his knees contributing effectively to the stall owner and making him earn. In the process, he earned his living in the form of kindness. The stall owner gave him the food and shelter for living till the time he was contributing labour. As he grew further, Sumantra started facing severe problems with his knees and the joints of hips. People had advised to visit the hospital for the remedy. With the permission from the stall owner, he visited the hospital 4–5 times but got the chance to meet the doctor only once. The hospital belonged to the government and offered free outdoor treatments for poor patients. Sumantra belonged to that category as per the definition of the term.

Sumantra was not wearing the right kind of dress to be chosen for the doctor's crew, nor he was having any connection with the person collecting ₹10 for a quick visit with the doctor. Finally, when he could reach the doctor's table on the last day, the doctor was ready to go out and gave a prescription to him for some medicine for his problems. The hospital store did not have the medicines prescribed for Sumantra. The only option remained was to buy those from the open market. Sumantra tried hard to get some support from the stall owner for the medicine but failed. He talked to many customers at the tea stall about the issue. Finally, he got a person working at a medical shop assuring him to get a few samples collected from the medical representative for him.

Sumantra got some medicine through the same person and consumed them. Till that time, Sumantra was walking, doing his work even though in a lot of pain, but after the course of medicine is over, Sumantra found that his knees were unable to bear the load of the body and getting folded. Sumantra cannot stand up now. He walks sitting. Can he continue to work sitting? No, get lost! The stall owner proclaimed. I can't bear with you further. Find your own way. Sumantra had an acquaintance with a helper of a bus of a long-distance operator. The bus went to Kolkata and was finally parked near Salt Lake.

Sumantra came to the final destination Salt Lake with the helper of the bus riding a long distance. Now, Sumantra is 'disconnected' from his own past, heritage, relations and connections. The nearest market is his next phase of life's destination where he is now residing. His earning is two pieces of handmade bread in the dinner through his contribution of work to the bicycle shed owner. He works while sitting and cannot get up straight. Some people consider him as a mad person as he is always in scabies. However, there are others casting compassionate eyes on this silent man, Sumantra. He never utters a single word with anybody but always mumbles to himself.

The Endowment Effect on Man

An object is worth more to you if you already own it. Researchers found that some Cornell students who would choose a chocolate bar over a coffee mug start to prefer the mug once they have been given one. This 'endowment effect' has been spotted with all sorts of things, from basket ball tickets to shares and petrol vouchers. The question that has puzzled economists is just why a supposedly cleaver species like Homo sapiens should fall a prey to something so irrational. Now scientists may have provided an answer. The ***endowment effect*** *has been seen brain imaging studies in people and in chips, which suggests it is an evolutionary adaptation. Trade was risky when there were no contracts, law or language. The bird in the hand was worth even more when bushes were dangerous.* (The Economist, *April 2008, p. 18)*

Is Sumantra really poor? What kind of poverty he is residing in? If you go by the standards of defining poverty, Sumantra is nowhere close to the lowest level of the poverty line. The purchasing power of $1 a day is far above the upper limits of Sumantra's estimation. Look at the components of Human Development Index:

- The basic requirements for the purchasing power of $1 per day
- Basic education for a proper understanding of world and life
- Facilities for basic health for survival
- Fundamentals of living condition
- The facilities for sewerage and sanitation
- Thriving on the issues of sustainability through keeping parity with the requirements of the green earth
- Minimum calorie requirement for survival and proper growth of body and mind
- Hazard-free boundaries of life

Let us look into the case of Sumantra for examining the points mentioned above.

The Basic Requirements for the Purchasing Power of $1 a Day

Sumantra has reached an age of 45 years. According to the estimation of population science, the maturity and fulfilment of life should begin within the age bracket of 25–45. If someone has been able to create something for their own life, they have to have a seeding within that period of life. However, there are a good number of exceptions in the world who have gone beyond or started before this age bracket and gave the exceptional fulfilment and contributions for the world. In the Indian context, Mohandas Karamchand Gandhi, generally called Gandhiji or Mahatma Gandhi, identified as the Father of Indian Nation, started his stigma after he crossed 50 years of his formative life in different parts of the world. For Mahatma Gandhi, the span between 50 and 80 years was the most active and effective span. Another Indian, Swami Vivekananda had made a mark in the global and national context at a very young age starting his teens. His earlier name was Narendranath Datta. Swami Vivekananda was a disciple of Sri Ramakrishna, considered as God embodied on earth.

Vivekananda had carried a message of his master Ramakrishna to spread across the world for the salvation of humanity. He was a voice with a form—considered a voice without a form by many contemporary thinkers of the world. He had finished his journey of life at 39 years only, creating a huge impact on the entire landmarks of India among all segments of populations and many corners of the world. Swami Vivekananda's mission was to spread the idea of divinity in human being and arousing the downtrodden of the country and the world. His idea was to uplift the economically deprived people from their conditions of economic deprivation to a situation of significant economic identity. The special situation of India is properly taken care of by Vivekananda. The social divide across cast, religion and other identities were the prime focus of him. He wanted to bring up to par all downtrodden people and make them join the mainstream of the social and economic life of the nation.

Vivekananda's heart used to bleed at the cry of a human being at any part of the world. He was the messenger of salvation for humanity from a deprived crying and downtrodden condition to a condition of a new understanding of life and proper positioning of life in the emerging context of the world. Swami Vivekananda tried to finish his global duties in the span of around 20 years, between the age of 20 and 40. On the other hand, Gandhiji was slightly different. He had two parallel initiatives for his movement. For the first time in the history of the world, a large scale of mass movement arose and Mahatma Gandhi had again focussed on rejuvenating the lives and aspirations of the weaker sections of the societies. He used to call them by the term 'Harijan' (men of the God).

Those who were backward in social class and economic activities and had received deprivation of any kind for long were otherwise unacceptable by the upper state of the society were termed as 'Harijan'. Gandhiji used to work on behalf of them in social and political front to liberate them from the clutches of the menace of life. It was indeed his unique contribution that a movement for political freedom and needs, massive participation of people, in general, and thereby, garnered a collective strength to throw out impositions on the system.

Happiness

Neither in the case of Swami Vivekananda nor the case of Mahatma Gandhi a quantified definition of poverty was mentioned. Poverty is an index of mind relating to the expectations of the same person. Let us look at the case of a person resided near the temple of Lord Viswanath (Lord of World) at Varanasi, India. The person, Manickram, was a shoe mender. He was a beautiful shoe mender. He was very perfect in his work. He knew the art of mending shoes properly. He had the skill to mend any kind of shoe at the quickest interval of time given to him. The person used to sit at his designated place by the side of the road which runs towards the main gate of the temple. Manickram used to sit in the morning hours for a brief period and again in the afternoon hours for a short period. The man used to charge a very nominal and reasonable rate. He did not speak to anybody except for a few words for communicating the requirements related to the works. He was thoroughly engrossed in his works but always had a fresh smile on his face. Very surprisingly, many of the days, the man was not visible in the afternoon. Sometimes, he is, and sometimes he is not visible.

A sage, a regular visitor to the temple, had observed Manickram, shoe mender, doing his work in a particular method but disappearing many a time in the afternoon hours. The shoe mender was really very popular. Most people requiring the mending of their shoes would come to him for the best remedy of their problems. Even then, this man was not continuing his work beyond certain limits in most of the days. Why? The sage was curious to know. What makes him remain away from such a high-demanding work? How come this man refrains from charging higher when others are freely charging much higher? Manickram's demand was the highest because of the quality of his work, the sincerity in the service and the exact payment, which was very reasonable and nominal.

The sage could not restrain himself but had asked Manickram some questions, 'Why don't you continue this work every day in the afternoon hours when the demand is so high? Why don't you charge higher? Do you have any other thing to do during that time? Where do you stay?' The man had only one answer with a smile saying, 'I am happy'. He did not want to indulge in these kinds of discussion beyond this. The sage thought he would see what this man does other than this work. The sage wanted to follow this man down to his destination. For a few days, he had followed him thoroughly and found the same thing happening. Manickram used to count the coins earned and bagged them and journeyed back walking by the side of the road down to his destination near the river Ganges. He was staying in a small space of less than 40 square feet or 200 cubic feet. It was by the side of the footpath beneath the extended ground floor balcony of a house with a hand put stone piece as the door cover. The man had to creep inside in. He had a small idol of Lord Rama. Reaching the small space of his residence, he kept the idol open before him, puts the stone piece as the barrier at the entrance door and started his works there. The stone piece was not adequate to cover the length and breadth of the opening to enter that small space. Therefore, a sound from inside comes out and even visibility of the inside from the footpath is there if someone peeps in. The sage was following this man and wanted to understand the other stream of work.

To his surprise, the sage found the shoe mender chanting the holy name of Lord Rama with an idol of Lord Rama by keeping it in front. As the chanting continued for long, the man got into a deep ecstasy with tears rolling down from both eyes and fully absorbed in the bliss of realization. The name of this shoe mender was not known to him till that point of time, but the sage found the shoe mender far superior to many sages who are otherwise known. Once the sage tried to talk to him and got to know his name. The sage had understood the living style of Manickram that he worked for his daily need but did not work beyond that. He worked till the time he is in a position to acquire the money needed for daily survival. The shoe mender considered the time available with his life as God's time. He took away some time from God's time which was essentially required for his survival only. He did not work beyond that limit. Manickram considered the fulfilment of life lies in the realization of the divine. He believed that this life is blessed with the faculty to realize the divine; therefore, it is imperative for humans to thrive on the process identified for the realization of the divine. and this is what he did. The shoe mender, Manickram, was blessed with happiness. How much did he earn a day? Probably, his earning a day accumulated for close to a week would come closer to the purchasing power of $1 a day. On the one hand, the shoe mender was extremely poor, but, on the other hand, he was extremely happy. Manickram considered his life as a life blessed with God's boon. He used to visit the Lord Viswanath (Shiva) and chant before Lord Rama every day, and on top of it, he contributed his service towards the devotees of Lord Viswanath through mending the shoes of devotees requiring that. The shoe mender was happier than most of the happy people on earth.

The Hydrogen Economy

Nothing ages faster than the future. A few years ago, there was general agreement that if the internal combustion engine ever was replaced by something clean, that something would be the fuel cell. A fuel cell is a way of reacting hydrogen and oxygen together in a controlled way and extracting electricity from the processors. It was to be the precursor of what was known as the ***hydrogen economy****, in which that gas would replace fossil fuels and power almost everything. (*The Economist*, 2008, p. 60/17)*

Sumantra is not that much happy. Sumantra is not unhappy either. He has lost his physical abilities. His eyesight is very poor and he cannot see far objects. His entire body carries patches of infections oppressed by the realities of the world, Sumantra is living a self-content graceful life. 'Sumantra, do you want some money? Only tea, half a cup in a small size earthen jar.' Sumantra does not have any expectation from the world nor does he have any revolt against the world. He feels the world as it appears to him. He can see the morning sun rising in the east. Sumantra prostrates before the sun offering him the highest regard. Is it that he has seen his life having been extended by one fresh day? Will he be able to carry the smile he exchanges with the rising sun, down the hours and minutes of the day? Probably yes, at times, and probably not.

—We are poor, not demigods. —We have plenty to be sorrowful about, and are not emerging into a golden age. —We must concern ourselves with justice and see right prevail. —And all this, only this, can enable us to become peacemakers. (Schumacher, 1973, p. 131)

Sumantra does not differentiate between the eating pot for him and that for a street dog. He still survives as many street dogs do. Sumantra has developed a unique friendship with these street dogs. The nights belong to the street dogs, the days to Sumantra. He watches the parked bicycles throughout the day from the corner where he sits. His friends, the street dogs carry the mantle of watching throughout the night allowing Sumantra to take a rest in the small place designated for him at the back corner with a small shed above.

When it rains small Sumantra is safe. However, when it rains profusely, Sumantra has to take shelter at the back of the boundary wall of the market having a better shed on top and getting enough comfort. During winters, Sumantra has plastic bags to cover with and get protection from winter chills. Sumantra is not unhappy nor is he very happy. He is thankful to the world for providing him with the basic sustenance as considers whatever he has in his possession as the best that could be for a man like him.

'I do not have any money. I do not want any money. What do I do with this winter jacket? My friend, Bitu, the black-coloured street dog, needs it more than me. If you give it to me, I will give it to him.' Sumantra does not beg to anyone. He does not beg for money. He does not beg for anything else required for life. He maintains his life and thinks that as a good life.

All the Indians are free and no one of them is a slave. The Lakedaemonians, how ever, hold the Helots as slaves, and these Helots do servile labour; but the Indians do not even use aliens as slaves, much less a countryman of their own. (McCrindle, 2015, pp. 211–213)

How do we define this life? Is this life of Sumantra a poor man's life? An unfortunate life? Life of a person who needs caring and nurturing by the world? An underprivileged life? A backward life?

The conditions which reign in the realm of this type of people would need the experience to understand the fallout. Let Sumantra survive the way these people are maintaining their lives in the earth till the time a new messenger brings in the holy message of divinity for everybody and turns their lives up to get the gifts of the world. Till the time, the wealth of the world will be open to flow across and flood every deserving place.

The earth does not have the providence for around a trillion billionaires in the next 50 years' time. However, the earth has got immense ability to create happy lives everywhere at every corner of it, long and short, even if the number surges to tenfold of the existing.

The inhabitants, in like manner, having abundant means of subsistence, exceed in consequence the ordinary stature, and are distinguished by their proud bearing. They are also found to be well skilled in the arts, as might be expected of men who inhale a pure air and drink the very finest water. And while the soil bears on its surface all kinds of fruits which are known to cultivation, it has also underground numerous veins of all sorts of metals, for it contains much gold and silver, and copper and iron in no small quantity, and even tin and other metals, which are employed in making articles of use and ornaments, as well as implements and accountrements of war. (McCrindle, 2015, pp. 211–213)

Let all the economic evils be chased by the essential humanistic happiness of life. Let all the yields of society be swayed by the waves of divinity considering everyone the embodiment of the divine. Considering everyone has a proper share of the cake of global wealth, it should be devoted to the benefit and satisfaction of those souls.

Let all Sumantras and Manickrams stand up, have their health hazards parked away, get a glowing face and be in a position to tell, 'Oh the world! What a nice place to live in. What a nice place to grow across. What a nice place to experience. What a nice place to share the unconsumed bread with the next.'

Basic Education for a Proper Understanding of World and Life

The millennium goal as spelt out by the global organizations, such as the World Bank, the UNESCO and other regional institutions, has moved forward to make people educate across the globe. Target 2C of the World Bank has mentioned the promise to ensure that by 2015 children everywhere, boys and girls alike, will be able to complete a full course of primary schooling.

The goal of educating every child at least through primary school was announced in 1990 by 'Jomtien Conference on Education for all' (Thailand, 5–7 March 1990). This conference was really the first one to have created global initiatives towards the need for education for everyone. Education for all (EFA) was co-convened by five global institutions. These are United Nations Educational, Scientific and Cultural Organization (UNESCO), United Nations Children's Fund (UNICEF), the World Bank, United Nations Development Programme (UNDP) and United Nations (UN) Population Fund. Though the first decade did not yield good result, after Dakar Conference in 2000, it really took off as a movement globally. The progress has been not only significant but also very satisfactory for all. Till 2000, Europe and Central Asia, Latin America and the Caribbean, East Asia and Pacific had shown three distinctly different trends on the same. EFA has created awareness apart from sensitizing all nations on this. This has been a significant move forward by global institutions towards human development. Education creates initial sensitization towards making dormant human potential get surfaced. Indeed, it has helped a lot in creating somewhat better understanding for making things happen in the best possible manners. Intrinsic human wealth does not fully surface through empirical education that the world is providing now, but it helps surely towards the betterment of human life.

The Wealth of a Country consists of two elements—the value of tangible assets located in the country and the net total of claims on overseas residents ... the Wealth of an economic unit within a country, such as an individual or a household can also be seen as consisting of two elements—the value of tangible assets owned by the individual household and the net total of the individual / household's claims on tangible assets, the second element comprising financial assets net of liabilities. (Revel, 1965, p. 368)

There has been a sharp increase in enrolment rate in schools in Sub-Saharan Africa, despite a strip rise in the population growth. As of 2010, an estimate of 100 million children worldwide had lost the chance of getting into schools for proper education, and nearly 150 million children had lost the chance to complete their first length of the primary education. The situation has not drastically changed even after a decade. About half of this total number has faced the perils of economic disadvantage as the first barrier to getting them enrolled for introductory education. East Asia and the Pacific and other parts of Asia have experienced scattered disadvantages for the children of their homes.

There are various ways to define literacy. Experience of life teaches a person the most. A person having never visited a formal institution of learning can have wise assimilation of knowledge of life. We call it wisdom. Let us try to understand the formal definition of literacy as advocated by global institutions first.

Literacy comes closer to a general measure of the outcome of educational initiative. The first spell of outcome for any educational initiative should process through various steps of literacy, starting from the basic language, understanding and being adept in communication, basic sciences, culture and art, realms of commerce and transactions, understanding nature and its various footfalls and understanding the biomass and the inert objects scattered around. The laws of nature discovered at various phases of our evaluation and the laws of the world as imposed by human institutions do contribute to the assimilation of knowledge in the process of education. The views about education differ widely from one civilization to the other.

Gnōthi seauton—'know thyself'—was uttered by the great philosopher Socrates long back in the Western hemisphere of the world. Even a few millennia years before that *atmano viddhi*—'know your true self'—was uttered by the Vedic sages of India in general and the sage 'Yajnavalka', in particular. Discovering the world within the person has been advocated in the Indian civilization as the true intent of education. Swami Vivekananda's view about education stands as 'education is the manifestation of perfection residing already within'. 'Perfection within' needs realization of the true self within through spiritual process. The ways have been described in chapter:

Human Brain: The Most Powerful Resource

The most important of all resources are obviously the initiative, imagination, and brainpower of man himself. We all know this and are ready to devote very substantial funds to what we call education. So, if problem is 'survival' one might fairly expect to find some discussion relating to the preservation, and, if possible, the development of the most precious of all natural resources, the human brains. However, such expectations are not fulfilled. 'Sinews for Survival' deals with all the material factors—minerals, energy, water etc.—but not at all with such immaterial resources as initiative, imagination, and brainpower. (Schumacher, 1973)

The idea is that humans, by virtue of their inherited intrinsic qualities, do carry the same perfection throughout. Realizing the divinity within creates the psychological basis of growing into perfection. It is the art and science of unfoldment of the inner divine spirit that makes the person liberate those intrinsic qualities which are dormant and lying beneath the material scales of life. The view further says that a process of self-identification and introspection would facilitate getting hold of the inner dimension of the person and liberate the person from the unfortunate impositions of the externalities of the world.

The concept further argues that this life is blessed with the presence and touch of the divine, and therefore, all the best qualities coveted for life do reside within. Consistent and persistent endeavour can truly make it exhibit before the functional ingredients of life. Your thoughts, actions, perceptions, beliefs, imagination, ideas and ideals have the chance to raise their heads out of the impositions of the material desire and want.

A normal human self would always be driven by the material instincts and desires. The more you try to put the fire of desire down by fulfilling it, the more it becomes vigorous. One particular level of desire having been quenched by the provision of it would encourage the multiplication of the same in a different form with different attire. The view suggests that this life is like a chariot which is being driven by the intellect of a human person, whereas the divine is residing silently in the back. Till the time you give unto him, the driving force of life, imagination and thoughts and actions are left in the hands of the worldly intellect and knowledge. The sages of Upanishad in India had identified the connection in a nice manner as follows:

Atmano Rathinam Viddhi, Shariram Ratham Eva Tu
Buddhi Tu Sarathi Viddhi, Manah Pragraham Eva Cha

Know that this body is like a chariot, the supreme self resides within in the form of Atman. The life is being lived at the instance of the human intellect, whereas the mind acts as a connecting cord between the human driving force and the divine seated within.

Through persistent endeavours, the unfoldment of inner self is absolutely possible. The person then acquires knowledge which is universally applicable both for material conduct of life and its spiritual quest. Let us take an example from the recent events in India.

Conspicuous Consumption

As seen from economic point of view, leisure, considered as an employment, is closely allied in kind with the life of the exploit: and the achievements which characterize a life of leisure and which remain as its decorous criteria have much in common with the trophies of exploit. The decay which the (ceremonial) code has suffered of the hands of a busy people testifies all depreciation apart—to the fact that decorum is a product and an exponent of leisure-class life and thrives in full measure only under a require of status. (Veblen, 1899, p. 31)

Here are a few highlighting lines about a person who was considered a godman by a great European thinker Romain Rolland. His name is Sri Ramakrishna, the spiritual master of Swami Vivekananda whose name has appeared before.

Ramakrishna did not have any formal education from any formal educational institutions. He had no chance to learn a language, mathematics, basic sciences, rationality and reasoning, philosophies, scriptures, literature and any other significant piece of knowledge of the world. The person did not have any tutor to teach him the elements of knowledge required to live a modern life. Yet Romain Rolland finds in Sri Ramakrishna the 'highest wisdom' a human person can content on earth. A man who had never studied the scriptures and works of literature could spell out the highest intrinsic truth of nature and the universe by being absolutely one with it. In the process of his being absorbed in the universal consciousness, he used to unfold the untold truth of human existence. 'God was real to him, as real as an individual identifying the next person sitting in the sequence.'

The divine light which had emanated out of him was full of empowerment and strength for those believing in him, and among many others, Swami Vivekananda was the most prominent of this category. The burning fire of belief that Vivekananda had carried throughout, made him accepted in the world as a prophet of the new era. His addressal at the Parliament of the World's Religions at Chicago, USA, held in 1893, had conveyed an electrifying spiritual spirit among the sensitive minds of the Western world.

The best thinkers, scientists, technologists, personalities of art, culture and literature of the world have empathized with all with great eagerness. To take a few names, Madame Kalve from Europe, Leo Tolstoy from Russia, Romain Rolland from Europe and a large number of dignitaries from the USA and other parts of the world started considering this man as the prophet for a new civilization. Vivekananda used to consider a noble and value-based character as the first intent of education to which literacy and knowledge would follow. If a person understands intrinsic divine qualities, well understanding the cries of the deprived souls becomes omnipresent in them, though the global institutions have taken a different route.

That which divides two people most profoundly is a differing sense of degree of cleanliness. Of what good is all uprightness and mutual usefulness, of what good is mutual good will: the fact still remains—'they cannot bear each others odor!' The highest instinct of cleanliness places him who is affected with it in the strongest and most perilous isolation, as a saint: for precisely this is saintliness— the highest spiritualization of the said instinct. To know an indescribable pleasure in bathing, to feel an odor and thirst which constantly drives the soul out of night into morning, and out of gloom and gloominess into brightness, into the glittering, profound, refined—: such an inclinations is distinguishing—it is a noble inclination—but it also separates.—The saint's pity is pity for the dirt of human, all too human. And there are degrees and heights at which he feels pity itself as defilement, as dirt. (Nietzsche, 2019, p. 539–540)

The objective of education has gone to the sedimentary granules of understanding life on earth. A person is expected to acquire and garner information available across. Application of the knowledge becomes more important than knowledge itself. The Socratic view of 'pure knowledge' has been replaced by the concept of 'effective knowledge' as advocated by Xenophanes, Descartes and other Western philosophical thinkers. This school of thought has influenced the minds of global institutions more than the other schools.

Education has a great impact on economic transformations. Proper EFA individuals in the world would create an ideal place for all humans in this globe creating a homogeneous and happy environment for all to live happily.

We would classify the objective of education as follows:

1. Education driving towards the height of wisdom.
2. Education driving down the lanes of life. This may be called a practical school.

Whereas the wisdom school includes the driving motive of Socrates, the Indian sages, universal godman Ramakrishna and the prophet of modern era Vivekananda and the like.

The practical school considers formal education as its goal. Assimilation of information of various qualities and imperatives becomes the ultimate objective of this school. The idea for a person is to acquire intellect and knowledge such that it can earn a benefit in exchange. The intellect has to be accumulated in such a fashion that it gets a proper market value at an appropriate point of time. This form of education has failed to remove anxiety from life. Contentment is absent as life is full of those seeking which actually matter less in an individual's journey towards realization of inner truth.

Age of Anxiety

Welcome to the age of Anxiety over the past year, fear, betrayal, and confusion have railed investor confidence, leaving stomachs queasy and unsettled. Every day, it seem, some giant bank or Wall Street Titan discovers a few billion dollars more in troubled assets it did not realize it owned and now has to write down. Whether it's been the immolation of Bear Stearns, the descent of home prices, or the credit frute— weren't even going to talk about sky-rocketing price for food and energy—the news has been wrenching. With all that turmoil, perhaps, its surprising, then, that the major stock indexes haven't sustained more calamitous decline. (Fortune, *2008, p. 8)*

The knowledge and intellect acquired as such are considered as the sellable commodities in the world. One develops knowledge and intellect to get the monetized equivalent of it. The idea goes further, wherein knowledge is equated to wealth. If knowledge has the power to create new ideas, tools, technologies and processes, it will be rated higher than other inputs which are otherwise unable to do the same. As a tradable commodity in the marketplace, the knowledge of a person should dress up in a fashion so that it would be rated higher by the takers in the market.

The knowledge should find effective and matching avenues to carry the essential elements down to the place appropriate for its final application. A scientific discovery or an invention which fails to fetch a market value is a waste in the eye of the world. Any item of thought and idea has to get its own client to have its position on earth. If the idea or the elements of knowledge fails to get a client, it does not have any value, material or otherwise.

The knowledge should blend itself with the elements of application contributing to the enhancement of value for life. If the knowledge is replaced by an idea or an ideal that fails to garner a client, it will find a place in the garbage of human society. The global institutions have developed this pattern of educational framework throughout. This may be branded as a process of 'exteriorization'. Value of life is estimated through the value of the things in possession of life.

Ideas and ideals contributing to the spread of noble thoughts and practices of living do not have a significant place to pace up. The global institutions have chosen the process of exteriorization as it has the following attributes:

1. It is measurable.
2. It is quantifiable.
3. It can be separated from the clout of the many.
4. It has got an individual identity separate from others.
5. It is disconnected between the past and present time.
6. It has a chance and prospect to grow big individually and become unique and distinct in its features and outlays. UNESCO advocates this through the institute of statistics and other fora. It addresses the issue of literacy to read and write with understanding a short and simple sentence about everyday life. Pushing the objective of life down to the level of day-to-day mundane, elements and parameters.
7. It identifies the philosophy of life as 'appearance first, quality next'.

Although the wisdom school is unfit for the apparent practicality of life, the practical school fits in. The wisdom school has identified the goals of life on a very long term, whereas the practical school wants to have it in the short run. Let us look at a comparison of the two in Table 12.1.

Table 12.1 Comparison between Wisdom School and Practical School

Sl No.	Description	Wisdom School	Practical School
1	Measurable	It tries to understand a person through the broadness and vastness of his/her mind. It wants to see the concept that this life is for 'me' and for 'many others'.	It considers that achievements are always measurable in terms of external possession and personal achievements. The person's intrinsic content proves secondary to external possession, achievement and recognition.
2	Quantifiable	The view says human beings are an embodiment of the infinite divine soul. Hence, they are essentially infinite in quality and potent. Quantifying people reduce them to a minute granules of their ultimate potentials.	Quantification is judged as the ultimate credential of the person. A dollar millionaire is rated low with respect to a dollar billionaire. Right at this moment, a vast number of dollar millionaires are more than the number of people residing in the Australian continent. Quantification is a feature of rating the countries on their development. Gross domestic product (GDP) and the rate of change in it is being considered as one of the ultimate parameters to judge the position of a country. Even the state of happiness is being measured in quantified terms to understand how happy people in the country or region are.
3	Separable	Human life is inseparable from the universal existence. This life is essentially the focus of consciousness and not a bundle of a material composition comprising it. The consciousness which makes and drives this life has a connection with the universal consciousness. If separated out of life, it loses the ultimate chance to grow noble and great.	Life should be lived to extract the best enjoyment out of the world. An interesting observation can be mentioned here. Millionaire parents of children meeting other parents in public schools in the USA are seen bewildered at the sight of billionaire parents over there. The comparisons are sometimes visible, sometimes dormant. People do compare on their possessions and achievements because of their focus on the externalities of their life alone.
4	Individuality	The wisdom suggests that an individual is an integral component of the whole. Not only that the whole represents through the individual but also essentially makes the individual the embodied face of the whole. The supreme consciousness not only travels through but also remains in synthesis always.	Individuality makes the person different from others with the continued satisfaction of his/her human ego. Each individual considers his/her entity as distinctly different from others and expects a unique achievement and recognition valued by the rest.

India's Position: Current and Prospect

There are two aspects to this point:

1. *Revealed campaign:* I call it media myopia. The journalistic view of the Indian economy would create ripples reverberating upon the points that it is all sinking. It is like sinking to the doom, and this has been continuing by them since a couple of months back.
2. *Realistic position:* However, if we take a realistic look at the economic point of India vis-a-vis the world, we find new prospects emerging. The results of which are as follows:
   a. Changing locus of investments from one region to the other within the Asian continent.
   b. Reinforcement of investments into the new set of technology built up in traditional industries.
   c. Investors such as Blackstone, BlackRock, Abubakar and some midsize investors from the USA, Europe and Japan who are investing into equity participation in Chinese manufacturing have been facing problems with the recent repatriation rules empowered by the government of China making their net surplus non-relocating from Chinese territory. This has already strained the relation between their equity investors, fund providers and industrial enterprises in China. Many of these equity investors carry the fund portfolio participated by Japanese, European and American bankers, and they are in lookout for alternative destination to put in the investment fund with equal or enhanced growth potential. Many of them have chosen India and are planning to relocate their investment destinations. The result of the spell of investment is economic prosperity for the people of the nation.

India's Economy in the Recent Past

The first physical symptom was the Sensex and Nifty dropping down a little bit. However, both Sensex and Nifty have bounced back. With the rationalization of corporate taxation, better repatriation norms, cases of cross-industry penetration, rationalization of labour laws, better bankruptcy norms and wider flexibility in mergers, acquisitions and take over norms, India has really positioned itself as the investment focal point in the world. Media looks at the matter from a short-view angle and identifies that India has Sensex of 36,000–40,000 and has a crash point. Forecasts about the Sensex is that it shall go well beyond 50,000. Media has also mentioned that certain sectors in the Indian economy have reached the irrecoverable position. This mention is being given to the automobile sector.

Sensex, from the beginning of 2019 till today, has been hovering around the 35,000–40,000 since 21 January 2019. Let us look back 10 years ago. The Sensex was below 10,000. In January 2014, Sensex was still hovering around 10,000 to a little bit more of 10,000. In June 2014, Sensex suddenly grew up to 15,000. In 2020 mid-January, Sensex was around 42,000. Now, there is a significant drop in Sensex as an impact of Coronavirus has occurred.

From 2014 onwards, the Indian economy has grown not only steadily but also fabulously for the last six years.

In September 2019, India's position was still on top of the world's major parameters. If we look at the changes in the capital market indicators, the way the capital market indicators have shown the resilience has been very strong, which reveals certain intrinsic possible factors created in the economy.

Intrinsic Factors

The possible intrinsic factors are:

1. The major spread of the medium and small sector in the economy.
2. Growth of new factories and start-ups.
3. Tenured investment implemented at the bottom level of the economy both in the agricultural industry and business.
4. GDP and its percentage were considered as a major economic determinant by the economic thinkers in the early part of the last century.

After the Second World War was over, the world had seen three different phases of oil crash in: (a) 1969, (b) 1978–1979 and (c) 1998–2000.

Now each of these has actually transformed the global technology in the industry, business and distribution.

The first transformation had occurred immediately after the Second World War on the process of technology. Manufacturing globally had undergone massive changes from a manual-driven to process-driven manufacturing across the globe, which was first adopted in the automobile, shipping, aircraft making, electronics, consumer durables and home appliances industry.

Some important impacts of the post-Second World War initiatives were in medicine and medical technology. Cancer detection, positron emission tomography (PET) scan, magnetic resonance imaging (MRI) all these types of technologies have emerged during this period globally. So there is a massive transformation from manual to process. And in the economic parlance, the meaning of this is a change from labour-intense to a technology-intense economy.

The moment there is a labour to technology transformation, the indicators which have been considered as GDP-centric indicators fail to catch hold of the reality. Focus gets shifted to the role and condition of the capital markets and their indicators. The moment there is a transformation in the process technology, we have hardly a few factories run by 20,000–30,000 people, but a better factory can be run by a few thousand people. For example, Tata, traditionally, have been doing steel. In one of the plants, for a particular level of each metric ton output, the number of the labour force which was needed and which is being utilized made almost 1/20 by the managers with better quality, speedy production, more output and better finishing. The advent of computers and the massive spread of computers in the 1980s and 1990s and subsequent period, then the next phase, created a knowledgeable economy. The world had gone for knowledge economy, computer-driven things everywhere with an emphasis on manufacturing in the large scale initially then the entire 1990s and 2020s onwards shifting the manufacturing from mega to mini.

As seen from economic point of view, leisure, considered as an employment, is closely allied in kind with the life of the exploit : and the achievements which characterise a life of leisure and which remains as its decorous criteria, have much in common with the trophies of exploit. The decay which the (ceremoinial) code has suffered of the hands of a busy people testifies all depreciation apart—to the fact that decorum is a product and an exponent of leisure-class life and thrives in full measure only under a require of status. (Veblen, 1899, p. 31)

Given the background of this, immediately after the Second World War, mega-industrialization was the process in the entire world. If you look at India, during India's previous five-year plan period, the first three plan periods consistently emphasized on large-scale industries. But it underwent changes thereafter. India could not catch hold of global trade. The 1980s, 1990s and remaining period the global trade was more of from mega to mini, the emergence of small and medium enterprises (SMEs). During this period, the world has witnessed changes in the academic portfolio also. The industry was supported by thoughts from academics.

Emergence of Behavioural School of Managing Societies

If we look at the thoughts for running the world, human psychology leading to consumer taste preferences had dominated the scenario during the 1890s and subsequent period in the world, and therefore, we have got a behavioural school of thought for managing enterprises wherein organization behaviour plays a major role.

Declaration of the Rights of Man and Citizen of 1789—

The representatives of the French people, organized in National Assembly.... recognize and proclaim, in the presence and under the auspices of the Supreme Being, the following rights of man and citizen: 1. Men are born equal and remain fee and equal in rights .... 2. The aim of every political association is the preservation of the natural and inalienable rights of man; these rights are liberty, property, security and resistance of oppression;... 4. Liberty consists of the power to do whatever is not injurious to others; thus the enjoyment of the national rights of every man has for its limits only those that assure other members of society the enjoyment of those same rights.... (Adler & Pouwels, 2012, p. 437)

Consumer behaviour plays a major role in consumer dynamics. We have behavioural finance to identify global finance, and finally, the behavioural school of economics to see how psychology impacts the economic process. If we look at the value created in the market of an enterprise, it has got two different aspects, one is physical-material and the other one is perceptive-psychological, added together to the total value. The physical-material is determined through the fundamental analysis of the company or the market, whereas the perceptive-psychological keeps on changing rapidly in the market. Capital markets globally thrive on a portfolio and a mix of both. A segment of the price comes from the physical-material value, whereas the other segment perceptive-psychological is normally ignored by people who do not penetrate deep into the subject.

Although a company does not change its profile overnight normally, the perception of the company's position in the market keeps on changing, which is called volatility factors of the market. Product markets show a steady pattern for a while, but the share markets do not. However, if you take a look at the steady return from the share market, we get the pattern. This is what we understand from the global financial market as of now.

India has proved edge over many other economies in terms of growth in participation by the consumers, depth and breadth of consumer involvement in the market and thereby enhancing the potential value of the market significantly. That is the reason why the Indian capital market has gone beyond many leading economies in growth parameters during the last five years. Major economies such as the USA, China, Japan, France, Germany and England have tried to focus on India's emergence of the capital market and its vast and continuously growing consumption base. Consumers are drawn from all sections of the economy.

Agricultural workers, industrial workers, people belonging to lower-middle class, people in the midsegments of the middle class and those in the higher class, all join the process of consumption at varying degree. The strong basis of legal safeguards for people have restrained the markets and the economy from what was observed by many scholars and political thinkers long before. The observation made by Karl Marx long back is no longer valid in the current world in any way except for any narrow political reason by some people. However, a manager–economist should have proper respect for all different thoughts which have played significant roles in the pre-modern and modern world, at least.

The bourgeois cannot exist without constantly revolutionizing the instruments of production and thereby the relations of production and with them the whole relations of society. Conservation of the old modes of production and unaltered form was on the contrary, the first condition of existence for all earlier industrial classes. Constant revolutionalising of production, uninterrupted disturbance of all social conditions, everlasting uncertainly and agitation distinguish his burgeois epoch from all earlier ones. All fixed, fast frozen relations, with their train of ancient and venerable prejudices and opinions are swept away, all new formed ones become antiquated before they can ossify. All that is solid melts into air all that is holy is profaned and man is at last compelled to face with sober senses, his real Conditions of life, and his relations with his kind. (Marx & Engels, 1978, pp. 473–479)

The USA and most of the leading economies have the Indian market of consumption as the most attractive place on earth now. If we take the purchasing power parity (PPP) in the global economy, at a PPP level, India has already attained a close to $10 trillion on 30 June 2019. However, the way IMF and World Bank calculate and the media focuses on India's economic size is less than $3 trillion as of now. India is close to reaching out to the target of $5 trillion within the next few years and poised to go beyond. The coronavirus debacle for the world shall halt everything for some period; however, the world shall get out of it and get back to its wheeling forward.

This will have a tremendous amount of impact during the next two decades. The target that India has fixed for $5 trillion within the period of a couple of years or three; this will not only be fulfilled but there are also chances of making it double in a period shorter than a decade. Two reasons are important here to keep in mind:

1. The West European model of SME development (particularly Sweden, Denmark, Norway and Scandinavia)
2. Participation of educated youth in the process of the industry in a larger number in the years to come.

The Walled General Theory and after

J. M. Keynes made a remarkable contribution to the thoughts of national and global economies of the world by introducing his thoughts known as General Theory of Economics, largely accepted due to its widespread and it is transformed in various forms with significant influences in the economic thoughts during the world war periods and post-Second World War period as well. The General Theory, however, had a wide focus on creation of wealth and distribution of the same in the interest of global humanity.

The emergence of a new mode of business post-technological revolution of several generations up to the fifth generation up till now, the economic thoughts have travelled to the grassroots shifting the focus basically from the general to the specific. Although the general approach of economic theory values the intermediaries as a secondary form of capital, the new technology has connected the primary capital to tertiary capital through direct distribution of manufactures and proceeds from the origins to its consumption end. The world has chosen medium-less or intermediary-less connectivity for economic distribution assuming it to be a better way out for creation and proper distribution of wealth across the globe.

During the last 50 years, the world has driven itself towards massive globalization creating connectivity among people and organization providing direct access to benefits of connectivity to the individuals. However, during the same period, the emergence of similar phenomena of sticking to the local prerogatives and individual aspirations have shown prominence in the world.

The World Bank has observed very recently in its *World Development Report 2020* that creating a value chain on a global scale has become important in transforming the economic conditions of people in the societies of the world. The focus of the global value chain (GVC) has been on the new technologies per se and the impact of new technology in the life and activities of the people in the world. This talks about the impacts of new technology in creating new manufacturing processes and systems, distribution on a global scale for a local person, creation of wealth through different modes and allowing access to the wealth to everyone wherever it has potential to get parked in and progress to fulfil the agenda of societies and economies.

The role of individual labour has been marginalized by technology. Also, the role of a human being as a potential source of knowledge, skill and expertise has been growing sky-high. A man is no longer considered a burden on the corporate and business, rather, a man is a resource, an innovator, a creator and contributor of value. As a person in the chain of production, distribution, in providing services, a consumer and customer providing inputs towards better qualities, better utility, better the service or product, a man stands as a real resource.

There is one sort of labour which adds to the value of the subject upon which it is bestowed: there is another which has no such effect. The former, as it produces a value, may be called productive; the latter, unproductive labour.– Though the whole annual produce of the land and labour of every country is, no doubt, ultimately destained for supplying the consumption of its inhabitants, and for procuring a revenue of them, yet when it first comes either from the ground or from the hands of the productive labourers, it naturally divides itself into two parts. One of them, and frequently the largest, is, in the first place, destined for replacing capital, or for renewing the provisions, materials, and finished work, which had been withdrawn from a capital, the other for constituting a revenue either to the owner of this capital, as the profit of his stock, or to some other person, as the rent of his land. (Smith, 1776, p. 161)

The issues of poverty, illiteracy, ill health require thinking in a manner that would connect and involve individuals in a way hitherto untouched upon by human society for offering solution to economic problems of nations.

Collaboration, Cohesion and Collectivity

The spiritual orientation of society and the human system would enhance collaboration, cohesion and collectivity among people on earth. This may be created through segments of the global system and later on uniting the segments on a global scale to contain everyone and create homogeneity. Initiatives made by us are actually creating a homogeneous world through homogeneous Asia as the initial step towards that.

An Asian initiative towards creating a homogenous Asia focused on a combination of scope and potential of technology, the impact of resources—natural and created—the role of organizations and nations and the overall role of an individual. The song of Asia as it reads below reveals an integrated approach among all towards creating an agenda that would finally resolve the economic, social and cultural problems of the world. The Song of Asia attempts to stimulate the concept of oneness among the Asians. This was developed with that hope of creating one Asia in due course of time.

Song of Asia

A

Asia...............Asia...............Asia
Chariot of Asian Sun enters the horizon
Infusing the path of earth with illuminations
Divine wisdom spreads
In the minds and hearts
Realizing the Blissful Supreme Brahman within.

B

For the building of new one Asia
Let's put our strength
of brain and minds
Together we combine our strength
of innovation creative potential and dreams
Into the reality of making Finest products and services

C

We grow together endlessly
We grow continuously
We win the world.
Asia emerges on top of the globe
Integrated Asia holds hands
of the people of the world
Asia now all set to create

D

New Global Man
To make
World free from poverty-illiteracy-ill health
A new world of happiness
World of harmony

Sarve Vavantu Sukhinah
Sarve Santu Niramayah
Let all be happy and wellAsia calls.........Rise Unite.

Homogeneity in an economy requires total involvement of the individuals in a wholesome manner. An example of the Indian economy in 2019, until the beginning of 2020, is a remarkable pathway of some ground thoughts of the economy. The points to consider are:

1. The capital market indicator surging very strongly up from nearly a BSE Sensex point of around 33,000 up to 42,000 during the middle of January 2020. This analysis excludes the drastic fall of the index as an

impact of coronavirus starting in March 2020. Also, the GDP growth index sliding downs from around 7 per cent to around 4.95 per cent during the same period.

2. The hue and cry raised by some people, the media and some political forces about the Indian economy saying that it is collapsing. On the other hand, the government's thrust to make from less than $3 trillion to $5 trillion size of economy posing a very high hope on the economy and focusing on certain areas which may not appear to be directly leading to provide economic benefits.
3. Large impact of unofficial economy in the nation wherein, the value created over a long period of time through unofficial means without having its contribution to economic agenda and estimation, thereby failing to impact on the GDP growth index for the nation, has created this kind of doubtful situation.
4. A strong liquidity in the capital market by creating an impact on the sensitivity indices of the market is basically receiving contribution from both end of the economy (the white economy and the parallel black economy).
5. The evils of parallel black economy reduced or eroded would immediately push up the economic indicators of nations. It holds more goodness for an economy like India.

Sir Keynes has observed and mentioned about the global economic positions in general terms while formulating the General Theory. A highlight of which is as follows:

The Classical Economics presupposes that the factors of production desire and receive as the reward of their efforts nothing but a predetermined share of the aggregate output of all kinds which they can produce, both the demand and the supply of each factor depending upon the expected amount of their reward in terms of output in general.

It is not necessary that the factors should receive their shares of the output in kind in the first instance;—the position is substantially the same if they are paid in money, provided they all of them accept the money merely as a temporary convenience, with a view to spending the whole of it forthwith on purchasing such part of current output as they choose.

It is necessary that current output should comprise the whole of wealth;—the position is still substantially the same if the factors of production swap their wage in respect of current output for other forms of wealth, provided that those with whom they swap intend to employ the whole sum forthwith to purchase some part of current output. It may even be the case that the supply functions of a factor, in terms of what it can produce in terms of something which it cannot produce.

The essential point is that by whatever roundabout methods every factor of production ultimately accepts as its reward a predetermined share of the expected current output either in kind or in terms of something which has an exchange value equal to that of the predetermined share.

Several thousand years ago the Indian Sage Kautilya had formulated Arthashastra called 'Kautilya's Arthashastra'. This was basically based on the thoughts, beliefs and philosophies visualized and realized by Indian sages during the entire Vedic period in India. Kautilya's principles of the economy were the first in the history of human civilization where the economic thoughts had embraced all aspects of human life considering a human being as an integral one. Kautilya believed in the following:

1. An individual human being is the unit of all economic activities.
2. An individual has to combine with other individuals to create and form institutions to engineer collective activities.

   The belief in the formation of this collectivity lies on the Vedic principle of collective mind which reads as,

   Samgachhadhawam Sambadadhwam Sam vo Manamsi Janotam.
   Deva Bhage Yatha Purbe Sam Janana Upasata.

   Combine your minds together with all others as because all minds are gifted by the divine. Pure minds so united will create collectivism as it is there in the divine world.

   Therefore, individual minds with purity connecting with other individual minds with purity desist from anything evil to occur, and thereby the question of the parallel black economy will not arise at all.

3. Kautilya had considered individual belief, way of life, an individual's practised culture, social norms, social structure, condition of health, level of knowledge earned through education or practice are very important in giving a shape to the economy.
4. Kautilya wanted that the leaders of economic zones, called the 'raja' or king have to be a fully spiritual-oriented person. He has mentioned that the 'raja' should be *Brahma Gyani*— a person who has realized the wisdom of supreme lord. It means when people attain a state of *Brahma Gyan*, they are above all discriminations, is very simple, dedicates his/her life to the cause of others, serves the world first before thinking of serving himself/herself, and he is concerned for everyone in the nation or the world.

This is the basic tenet of the spiritual economy. The spiritual economy creates a person free from greed, anger, gluttony, envy, jealousy and so on. The person should be a giver, not a grabber. They should have acquisition only for the minimum maintenance and fairness of living, not for piling up the wealth and depriving others. A person should never try to deceit, cheat, betray, disregard and abandon anybody in the world. Also, they should try to contain embrace, establish cooperation, offer care and support, consider that the supreme self is present in every individual. Therefore, every individual is important.

...So what does the process of integrative thinking look like? How do integrative thinkers consider their options in a way that leads to new possibilities and not merely back to the same inadequate alternatives? They work through four related but distinct stages. The steps themselves are not particular to integrative thinking everyone goes through them while thinking through a decision ... the first step is figuring out which factors to take into account--

In the second step of decision making, you analyze how the numerous salient factors relate to one another... Integrative thinkers do not break down a problem into independent pieces and work on them separately or in a certain order. They see the entire architecture of the problems, how the various parts of it fit together, and how one decision will affect another.

Just as important, they hold all of those pieces suspended in their minds at once. They don't parcel out the elements for others to work on piecemeal or let one element temporarily drop out of sight, only to be taken up again for consideration after everything else has been decided... All these stages lead to an outcome. A leader who embraces holistic rather than segmented thinking can certainly resolve tensions that launched the decision-making process.... (Martin, 2007, pp. 64–66)

Kautilya came forward with the doctrine that the king should have the primacy of the interest of the citizens. A leader should have the primacy of the wellbeing of people. 'Thou first, me next' is the fundamental view of Hindu economy. This 'me' is a realized and liberated self who considers everyone in the earth as equal. This view of life should be the guiding and governing view for the economies and societies of the world.

Spiritual economy stands for that and advocates the same for the entire world to make the world free from poverty, illiteracy, ill health and all kinds of discriminations that have prevailed over during the several millennia of human civilization. Economic evils can only be resolved fully by appropriate application of the Hindu economy. Kautilya's

Arthashastra provides a highlighting dimension of the Hindu economy. This particular work is based on the principles garnered by Kautilya, drawn from the thoughts and realizations of Vedic sages. This economic principle can offer solutions to the economic problems of any kind that prevails in the modern world in different parts of the world. Let this be applied in the context of the nations and the world.

References

Addison, T., Hulme, D. & Kanbur, R. (2009). *Poverty dynamics: Interdisciplinary perspectives*. Oxford University Press.

Adler, P. J., & Pouwels, R. L. (2012). *World civilization*. Cengage Learning.

Fortune. (2008, 23 June). *Fortune*, p. 8.

Martin, R. (2007). How successful teachers think. *Harvard Business Review* (June), pp. 64–66.

Marx, K., & Engels, F. (1978). The communist manifesto. In R. C. Tucker (Ed.), *The Marx-Engels reader*, pp. 469–500. Norton.

McCrindle, J. W. (2015). *Ancient India as described by Megasthenès and Arrian*. Creative Media Partners, LLC.

Nietzsche, F. (2019). *Beyond good and evil: Prelude to a philosophy of the future* (1st ed.). General Press.

Piketty, P. (2013). *Capital in the twenty-first century*. Harvard University Press.

Revel, J. (1965). *Changes in the social, distribution of property in Britain during twentieth century*. Third International Conference of Economic History, Paris.

Schumacher, E. F. (1973). *Small is beautiful*. Blond & Briggs.

Sen, A., & Drèze, J. (1998). *The Amartya Sen and Jean Drèze omnibus: Comprising poverty and famines, hunger and public action, India: Economic development and social opportunity*. Oxford University Press.

Smith, A. (1776). *The wealth of nations*. W. Strahan and T. Cadell.

Smith, A. (2003). *The wealth of nations*. Bantam Dell.

Stiglitz, J. E. (1994). *Whither socialism*? MIT Press Cambridge.

The Economist. (2008, 21 June). *The Economist*. p. 18.

The Economist. (2008, 21 June). *The Economist*. p. 60/17.

Veblen, T. (1899). *The theory of leisure-class: An economic study of institutions*. Macmillan.

World Bank Group. (2015). *World development report 2015: Mind, society and behaviour*. The World Bank, Washington. https://www.worldbank.org/content/dam/Worldbank/Publications/WDR/WDR%202015/WDR-2015-Full-Report.pdf

World Bank Group. (2019). *The world development report 2019: The changing nature of work*. http://documents.worldbank.org/curated/en/816281518818814423/pdf/2019-WDR-Report.pdf

CHAPTER 13

BRAND MANAGER

Brand Management: The Most Sustaining Role of a Company

Understanding the mind of consumers has been the focus of companies throughout the world amid doubts, confusions, challenges, difficulties, problems, prospects and victories in the market space of the world. Companies have been doing their marketing in the manner they have seen others doing the same but always with a difference. The difference becomes essential as the changes that have taken place, as also the kind of changes taking place in the continuity of the journey of life, are gradually growing apart from each other. As the structure of markets is changing, the world would need a differential approach in presenting its products and services across the globe.

The basic approach in marketing was identified as the art and science of understanding the minds of the customers with regard to the habit and practice of consuming things of material products and enjoying the offered services from the entities having their expertise in the same. The art and science of this understanding of the consumer mind are actually focused on the expressed behaviour of the consumers as recorded in the process of data intake from the persons in place. In the journey forward to market things, the companies need to understand what those things are for which people would be ready to shell out some money from the stock of the same. It is actually reciprocated in nature also. On the one hand, companies need to find the appropriate number, quality and flow of customers, and on the other hand, the consumers need to find out the entities from whom they can source their products or services with a reasonable degree of satisfaction and, possibly, to be happy in.

Customers want to reduce the degree of uncertainties while buying a product or a service for use and consumption. Products and services offered by entities, thus, require developing a certain standard in the quality, quantity, price, frequency, availability and so on. Companies are, thus, required to create a proper identity. This identity is in the form of a certain name, symbol, structure, culture, values, promises, identity and so on created through certain mechanisms for a purposeful journey of existence. It becomes easier for the customer to accept the product or the service which comes with a chosen or accepted level of identity.

The brand creates that identity for the company and the product or the service as well. A manager, in the function of marketing for a company, or more specifically for products, needs to understand the customer's expectations for identity and should try to satisfy the expectation by suitably developing the same. The customer's choice towards identity has diverse but effective meaning in the context of the market for the company and the product. The customer wants to be sure about various aspects of the product before actually attempting to use it. It is in this context that the proper understanding of the company offering the product or the service becomes very important while making some kind of analysis of the company in the context of the market and at a particular mix of conditions prevailing around. Customers want to develop some kind of faith in the company or the identity of the product thus provided to be satisfied with the concerns about the value for money spent on the product or the service thus attempted to take in exchange of money spent.

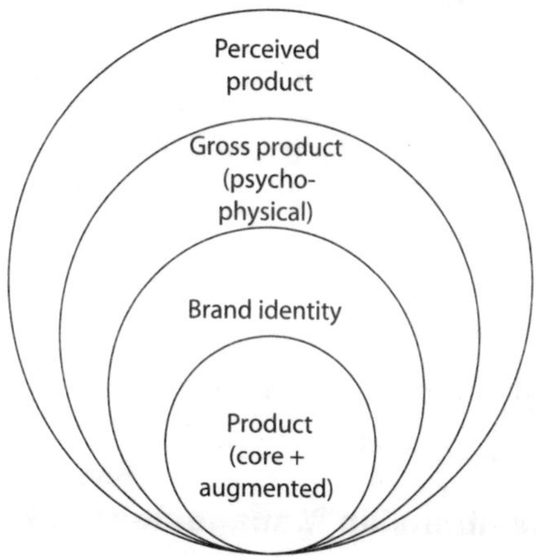

A customer wants to have the offer from a brand to be convinced about the following, among many other dimensions of understanding:

- *Quality of the product or service:* Customers want to see the consistency in the maintenance of the quality by the company, and for this, they would examine the process of the offer and its depth of connection with the offer for the product or the service over the life of the product or the duration of the services offered.
- *Compatibility of the price, quality and other features of the product or the service:* The customer wants to understand whether the price offered as such is the right one or not. The validity of a customer's understanding is usually drawn from the market and the understanding usually developed in the context of the conditions prevailing

across. Although all the customers are not sensitive to the levels of prices, the manager should structure things assuming that market is, in general, price sensitive.

- *Place of the offer for the product or the way to possess the product or receive the service:* It is important that the product of the service should be made available to the reach of the customer when the need arises for the same. Availability at ease or with least trouble is, thus, one of the most important concerns of the customers in the markets across the globe, in general, and certain specific categories of markets, in particular.
- *Promotions that are done by the company verified against the actual offers of the same in physical terms:* Strategic decision for promotions in the context of the prevailing conditions of the market and the economy are essential for optimizing the revenues and bringing in home the host-of-benefits promotions which are supposed to have. The company needs to identify priorities and fix the strategy in accordance.
- *Kind of people that are available in the process of its offer in the market and usually interact with people in the market:* This involves the in-house and external people for the same. In-house people include the salesforce, service people, revenue people and the people involved in fiscal and regulatory functions.

4Ps of Marketing

The 4Ps involved in marketing are price, place, people and promotion (Figure 13.1).

Customer Relationship Management (CRM)

Companies need to develop a unique way to structure customer relationship factors into CRM. The basic philosophy of CRM is fundamental in

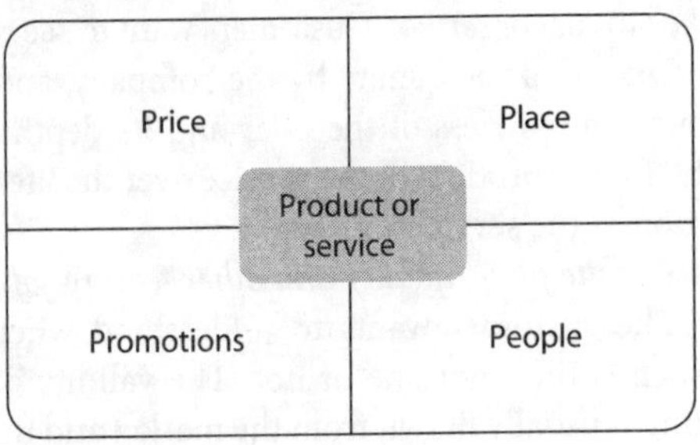

Figure 13.1 4Ps of Basic Marketing

7Ps of Marketing

Basic Elements	Attributes	Description
Product To see that the product conforms to the expected attributes of quality, size, features, appearance, dimension of the core, fitted to the changing needs of the customers and the assurance of the brand in the context of market	• Core product or service • Augmented product or focus of service • Product/service brands • Gross product/service • Perceived product/service	• Depends on the customer tastes, preferences, choices in the context of the market • Depends on the perceptions about the quality of life and the values of life.
Price While doing the pricing exercise for the product or the service, the company needs to be careful whether the price charged justifies the contents of the product. Also, it should conform to the conditions of the demand for the product, the competitions available in the market, supply of identical or replacement products by the other operators, sustainability and profitability of the company.	• Cost of goods to sale • Policy on the profit and profitability of a product • Price being charged by the competitors • Available scopes in charging a different price per unit • Special prices, including discounts and rewards in the purchases • The economic condition of the target market	• Price strategy for the product or the service to offer in a particular condition of the market and economy • Making a new strategy for the product or the service to make a long-term strategy towards maximizing revenues for the company • To identify components of the price for the best gain by the company
Place The company should be ready to process the delivery of the product to the doorsteps of the buyers in conditions of maintaining the goodness of the product and have assured services whenever needed.	• Nearest to the customer's place • Least cost of distribution • Longer life of the product in possession of the customer	• Drawing benefit of the proximity of supply of required product • Availability of the chosen brand with quality assurance • Customer value optimization

(Continued)

(Continued)

Basic Elements	Attributes	Description
Promotion Basic objective of promotion is to create awareness, enhance the depth of understanding and create interest in the product or services offered by the company. It attempts to create a business climate for the organization wherein the products or services receive welcome by most customers, either individual or cluster of people forming trade associations. This, apart from the usual sales in the market, attempts to create favourable sentiment in and across the market and expand in the minds of the customers. Frequency and depth of promotions depend on the expectations of the customers in general.	• *Advertising:* To reach out to the potential customers. • *Sales promotion:* Consumer, trade, salesforce promotions. • *Personal selling:* Face to face with the customer by people from the company. • *Direct marketing:* Reach out to the customer directly. It requires the data by, offer and creativity of the company. • *Public relations:* To build the brand and maintain direct relations with groups of people who matter or the influencer. It is developing and maintaining relationships across the potential and actual market.	• Cost–benefit analysis (CBA) for advertising • Facing the challenges of any kind of offensive marketing by other operators in the market either directly or indirectly • *Ethical position in the market:* To create and maintain through advertising • *Earth consciousness:* Helping out the society on certain vital issues and focusing on the protection of the environment • *Effectiveness of sales promotions:* Business to business transactions are given higher importance • Context of personal selling • Direct marketing keeping brand value
People People working for the brand or the company are required to be involved with the culture of the company in such a way that the responses from their end become autonomous. Mission, vision, goal, the short-term and long-term objective of the company should be properly known and made available to the people at the frontiers of the company. Any functional identity of the person should make the person develop clarity about the corporate policy as applied to the function and behave accordingly.	• Salespersons • Personal selling executives • Field coordination managers • Direct marketing executives and managers • Frontline executives • Customer service executives • Networks and data store executives • Revenue executives • Front office executives • Public relations executives and managers	• Some of the general features of the salespeople are very important as these are the features which are representative of the company, in other words, they are the ambassadors of the company • People who are at the interface with the market have to be well versed in the core policies, philosophies and values of the company in the context of the market and the society

Basic Elements	Attributes	Description
Process Process-driven companies are oriented to develop faceless work units. Because of the identical nature of the work units, process-driven companies become impersonal in certain spheres of business. In the era of digitalization, the business process gradually adopts the faceless options. It is indeed very important for any company to fix the style of the functioning, cultural face of the organization, mode of transactions and communicate the same to the functionaries and the markets. Marketing process could be physical, digital or any combination of it. Companies may want to generate proper data about the buyers and users of the products and service. It is in this context, it is advised for a structured business process to involve process technology so that the functions become standardized for a given background of the market and the economy. Managerial decision-making in the context of the changing scenario of markets can be properly coordinated with the help of chosen variables for that kind of business in a particular market condition.	• The functional and managerial process • Cost efficiency in the process is essential from the company • The business process of the company should be standardized in such a way that partners in marketing or the channel members should be conversant with the same • Whenever the business faces any difficulty or any kind of challenge from the market there should be an autocorrection in the system—this implies that the frontline persons should be oriented to the options of business process reorientations • Parameters connected with the governance of the company • Appropriate technology should be in place to fit in the requirements of the market and the society • The process technology be fitting into the requirements of the company and be tuned to the emerging trends of the markets	• Managerial process conversant with the organizational structure is prone to pressures from the market. Business exigencies may push the frontline managers to take decisions on the spot with some amount of divergence from the core policies of performance in the company. • Process divergence is expected to be in tune with the changing pattern of the functional identity and pattern of governance of the company • Inter-functional discord in the business process needs to be resolved through the managerial inputs of dispute settlement or direct negotiations • Technology for the process needs investments. Cost benefits for the induction of technology to upgrade the process needs to evaluate on an ongoing basis • Business process should support the long-term perspective of the company

(Continued)

(Continued)

Basic Elements	Attributes	Description
Physical evidence Physical evidence is one of the best ways to build a relationship with customers. This helps in developing clear pathways for developing a chain of customer relationship management (CRM), towards creating long-term value for the company. This helps in product re-engineering of the company, where the design, shape, signs and attributes of the core products are modified keeping in mind the impact of the changing patterns of the consumer psyche and skimming off value from the business.	• Consumers want to be convinced by seeing only • Something which is justifying may be supported by physical evidence • Physical evidence makes the marketing effort of the sales executive more successful • E-commerce activities focus on the concept of physical evidence while dropping the product at the doorsteps of the buyers through the exchange process • Features of the product shown in the digital visit are better appreciated by the customers of the product or the service	• Once the matter of physical evidence comes in place, companies get the opportunity to present and push to the customers' products of different price range and specifications. It is a gateway to penetrate the psychological domain of the customer—an opportunity for the marketer to bridge the gap, if any, between the marketing manager and the consumer of the company. It is in a way a kind of business forces which may help the manager to establish networking with the customer and get the advantage of active customer data for the business.

the management of an enterprise. While managing CRM, a manager should be aware of the underlying philosophy that

- Each customer is a unit of value for the organization. This is termed as customer-skimmed value (CSV).
- Customer value is reciprocating. The rule of commerce prevails, which stands as: give value to get value (GVTGV).
- Customer value is psycho-physical in nature. It is a combination of the material value achieved by the customer and the psychological value as perceived.
- Process of enhancing the CSV is a mix of physical benefits provided and the psychological value.
- CRM changes dimensions and characteristics with the change in the context of the market and the prevailing socio-economic conditions.
- Customer retention, customer profitability and customer mobility depend on the depth of the relationship among the representations of the company and the influencers on the customer choice and decision-making process. A manager's role should be efficient enough to manage the same.

Matrix of CRM for a Market-driven Company

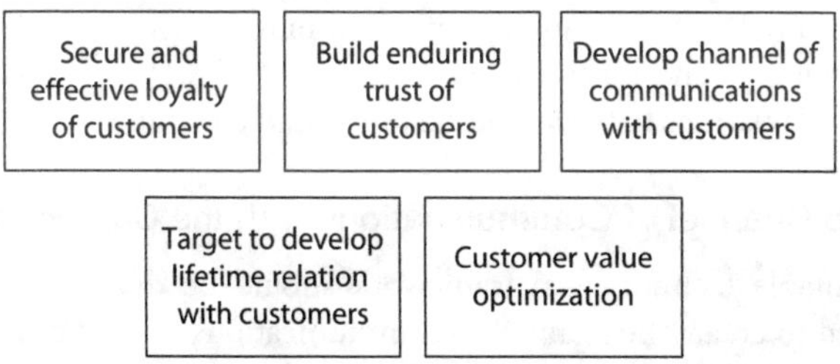

Develop Customer Loyalty

- To create an effective sense of loyalty among existing customers
- Target new set of customers with a view to develop a sense of loyalty among them
- To make the customer understand that the company not only listens to regards as an important view of the customer
- To develop loyalty programmes as such, so that the company tries to make the point of being with the frame of mind of the customers
- To make sure that there is an end result of the CRM agenda so that customer's loyalty is ensured in the process

- Creating customer friendship with the brand and make the customer supportive of the brand in a non-commercial forum or social context in the current period
- To be in the continuity of touch with the customer

Earn Trust of the Customer

- Develop trustworthiness of the company by proving to be trusted with corporate activities
- All doubts to be removed between the customer and company
- The company should be alert enough to see that any departure from the corporate assurances be immediately taken into account for correction
- Any related or connected matter of concern should be analysed properly to see the impacts of that on the choice of the customer
- To understand directly from the customers the factors influencing customers' decisions on the purchase of products or speak for the brand in the sphere of influence
- Analysing financial and non-financial parameters with a relative degree of importance in the framework of company–customer relationship
- Transforming customer relations from any kind of person-specific to impersonal and company-specific flow of relations
- Developing long-term relations out of the short-term and smaller span of relations between the customer and company

Develop Channel of Communications with the Customer

- A suitable technological framework should be developed or possessed to create the channel of communications in such a way that it is maintained with a reasonable degree of reliability.
- Relation with the customer on a shorter scale should be carried forward to develop a long-term channel of communications.
- Elements of the channel of communications should be nurtured in the right spirit to make customer encouraged enough to connect and remain connected with the channel of communications.
- Along with any formal channel of communications, a non-formal channel of communications should be developed to carry forward the relations through the non-formal route if the formal route becomes less effective.
- The channel of communication should be rewarding to the customer and at the same time provide value to the company.
- The channel of communications should not be a tradable property of either the company or the customer.

Lifetime Relations with the Customer

- Through a continuous process of managerial interventions and supportive technologies, the relationship developed with the customer should be nurtured for a long-term focus of the same
- Connections with the customer would require some space in the minds of both so that the connection persists for a long term
- As long as the product survives, the relationship should be maintained
- To carry forward the relationship to the context of any new product or a replacement of product so that the customer is aware in advance about that product and takes interest in that as well
- For a brand repositioning or brand re-engineering, the role of CRM is very strong, and the manager should be into the depth of it to take it forward

Customer Value Optimization

- The manager should be convinced that customers are value-conscious
- Each transaction of the customer should bring home a satisfaction of the concern for the superior value of a product or service offered
- The material value of the product or the service proves to be most important in the design of the company
- Apart from the physical material value, the concept of the ethical value of the company creates a difference in the market
- A customer feels elated when the uniqueness of the brand brings home the perception of having gains from the transaction with the company
- The pride of having the association with a coveted brand delights the customer
- The company keeps on ensuring the enhancement of the brand which means the customer would go along as well
- If the company can enhance notional value or the intrinsic value of the brand, it would do great service to the customer and the society

Digital CRM

In the era of digital dominance, the customer has the fate of getting identified as a piece of data in the stock of the company. Consumer data enhances with the rising trend of the people trying to occupy space in the urban flow of lifestyle. It is actually the technique of collecting data of the probable customers and the set of existing customers to make use of the same in the journey of the corporate functional activities.

Customer data is now available in the private markets throughout the world on sale. However, various social sites and different forum of activities are there to take care of somewhat details of the customer data. Purposeful use of data is possible when it goes into the activity of one kind and somewhat has a connection with the other. So data is collected from one source can be made applicable for the other. The extent to which one data is made applicable for a purpose can have some kind of commonness for many other functions of life.

Companies across the globe have become used to the set of data analysis through their own ways. Analysis of data requires a structured mechanism to understand people of various types as identified by people. Now, it comes on the system that so much of activities are involved in the spirit of analysis of personal data. A digital system can take care of the process of the entire range of data inputs for the purpose of the company.

Digital framework of the customer data analysis can take care of the different aspects of human being. The broad classifications include:

- *Customer demographics:* As per usual norms, customers are classified into categories of: high, middle and low income; highly, moderately and poorly educated; skilled or unskilled; age groups of relevance: upper-age, middle-age and lower-age group; living pattern: own or hired accommodation; possessions: house, apartments, cars or other vehicles; profession: entrepreneur, senior and junior executive; net worth identity: high, middle, low and so on.
- *Customer psychographics:* These include tastes, choices, preferences in consumptions and so on.
- *Customer lifestyle:* As indicated through the habit of using certain basic products such as white goods and possessions.

Methods of Intelligent Research for CRM

A smart and intelligent system is required to be in place for storing, analysing, selecting and using the data for the purpose of the organization. Marketing strategy requires having customer data in place for the appropriate functional activities of the company. Big data requires a total analysis of the data frame for the use of marketing choice. The classification of the customer is possible only when the attributes are properly chosen and identified for each functional requirement of a company.

The analysis can be on the spirit of multi-tier classification of the customer features. For a multi-product, a multi-location company's opportunities could be found in many ways through analysing customers.

CRM basically depends on the existing set of customers. By definition, it has to limit within that framework. However, TNCs and MNCs are constantly in the lookout for a new range of customers for the existing business or extension of the existing into new areas of business.

Any communication which the manager wants to send across requires the support of the framework for the design of the organization and the new perspective of a set of new products or services to be offered. It is in this context that certain designs of the new business are tried where the kind of customers that would fit in offers through the new products or services in the series of the offers by the company are decided.

Once the data is made available, analysis is made possible. The basic premise is that a human being lives in dynamic and continually changing environments. The corporate world needs to cope with the pace of changes in a way that attempts to consider all the possible and required parameters relevant for the purpose. The human context needs to be kept in mind to develop that kind of smart system.

Basic Human Trend as Sensed by Knowledge Technology

- Humans live in dynamic and continuously changing environments.
- Humans can still keep pace with the changes in the broader environments and carry life forward with their own agenda.
- Humans are adaptive to situations around them and can take care of the challenges of the situation to a great extent.
- The memory system of the new situation should be made adaptive to the changes that occur in the process.
- The smart system should be able to add new knowledge to the existing set of knowledge continuously.
- The knowledge that is more important for the new system should be poised to throw a new challenge to the context and should continuously deplete the previous knowledge.
- Any organizational scheme chosen should facilitate the memory of the smart system and be in a position to locate the right data at the right time and context of the business and its environment.
- Human memory system should be replicated in the computer memory system to a great extent to make the system thoroughly intelligent.
- The organization should be in a position to recognize similar and dissimilar types of data for maintaining analytic in a way that directly feeds into the requirement of the CRM.
- Episodes, incidents, symptoms, requirements and classified need of the function should be automated into the smart system.
- Levels of activity should include conceptual cluster, related cluster, associative relations, focused relations and enduring relations.

CRM Process

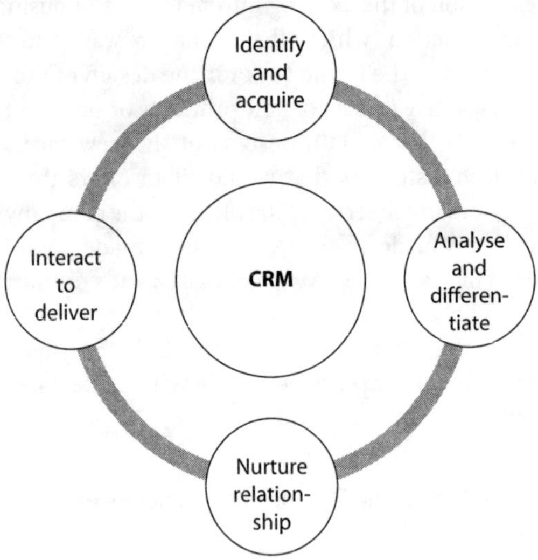

CRM is basically complied through certain functional steps involving the data of existing and potential customers within the scope of the market and the company. It is not an easy process to get consumer data. In fact, consumer data is very premium. Market-driven economies are mostly consumer focused. The consumer is considered as the king of the market. For each of the market segment and consumption category, the consumer data makes the basic source of strategy and decision-making on behalf of any organization, product or process.

The marketing research group of a company should focus on consumer data in the most unbiased way. Impersonal search gets the most effective personalized data and its culminating analysis.

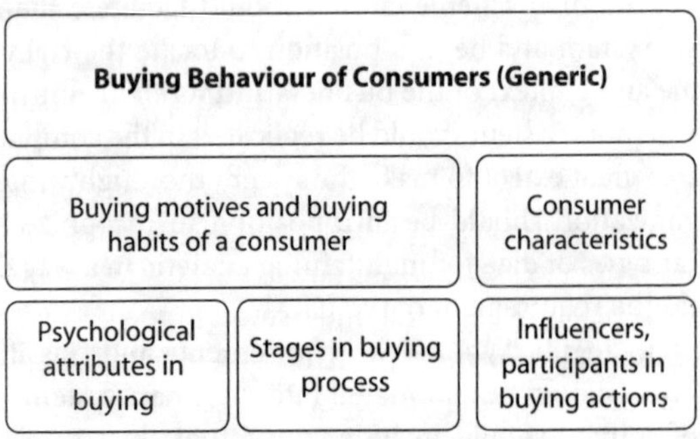

Identifying Consumer Behaviour

A typical process involving this includes the following steps:

- Identify and acquire data of existing or potential customer
- Analyse and differentiate customer data across demography, psychography, and sociocultural and technology knowledge
- Nurture relationship with each existing or potential customer
- Interact to deliver customer value for delighting

The most important aspect of framing strategy for marketing is to identify the 'consumer behaviour' for fixing strategy.

Factors of Importance for Developing Buying Behaviour of Consumers

The buying process can be complex and distant from the usual plans and actions of marketing. A company should be aware of the fact that the consumers are human beings with psychosomatic features in the characters.

Customers are intrinsic and extrinsic in their approach. The buying behaviour of a consumer arises from the core aspect of the being, particularly from the characteristics of the person. Consumer data is thus very important input to the development of the features of the consumption, and thus, to identify the specific aspects of the choice, taste, preference and thereby the decisions of the person. As mentioned above, the customer's profile is important for the manager to know and understand properly. Some of the highlighting points are as follows:

- A customer's characteristics with respect to the living of life and maintaining the standard of living in a society.
- A customer's buying habits are important aspects of the person particularly the way people behave in buying things of common with those that are being offered by the company.
- Why buy? The reason why the person wants to buy is it to satisfy a need, greed or some other reasons. This would reveal the buying motive of the customer in the previous buys. As a result, the future attempt to make a buy would be open and the company would approach closer to the actual motive behind the person buying things in the current context of the market and the society.
- *Emotional, rational or flexible nature of the buyer:* Psychological attributes of the buyer needs to be understood in the best possible way.
- *Customer buying process:* Steps involved in the usual buying process are important to understand.
- *Customer influencers:* Identifying the set of influencers for purchase decisions, particularly for big buys, is important. Buying behaviour of

individuals for personal use differs from that for the family needs or organizational needs. Consumer research needs to establish that.

Highlights of the Research Process

Consumer data is available with various sources, the organization can possess it through acquiring the same from the market or by doing direct and primary research. While designing the research program, some of the following points can be considered as relevant are:

- Customer is the first person to give responses to the relevant points as mentioned against the points of concern. From the viewpoint of an observer, the response of the customer may be obtained.
- The perceptual approach may lead to understanding the nature of customer behaviour as understood through the process of thinking, judging, paying attention which are related to the connection between consciousness and the object of awareness.
- Individual differences to identify through the uniqueness of responses of various persons and the justifiable aspects of subjectivity in the organization.
- Social relations of the person including the impact of stimuli on the responses of others make a unique aspect of the customer psyche with respect to the market.
- Self-confidence and autonomous responses create a category in the personalities of the related combination of attributes.
- Customization is not to rush too quickly into the scenario of the customer-driven activities and the context of the organization for the benefit of understanding the process of customization.
- To use a minimal set of attributes in the process of elevating the scenario of transactions in the market and economy.
- Sequencing the customer interactions in such a way that it contributes to the benefit of the organization and focus on the process of customer research to understand the purchase behaviour of the customer.
- In the process of the research, it is very important to understand the process of change and transformation in the context of the market.

There are various ways by which consumer research can be performed in the best possible methods.

The highlighting aspects of consumer psychology as applied to consumer research process are as follows:

- *Based on the grounded theory of qualitative psychology:* It remains positive in approach and adopts interpretive elements. It emphasizes the use of systematic techniques to study the output of mental framework in the context of the possession of things for life. However, the approach remains consistently positive.

- *Based on the procedures of narrative psychology:* It is composed of a unique sequence of events, mental states and happenings involving people as the main characters or identified actors in the stream of life in the world of commerce or life in general.
- *Based on the conversational analysis:* It is essentially naturalistic—observation based. It is known as a part of the science of actual behaviour. In the process of this analysis, the respondents are seen in the actual context of verbal or non-verbal transactions where intersubjectivity of common and shared understanding are actually taken into account to understand the flow of attributes and dynamism in the behaviour of people in the actual context of their life and activities in a particular scenario. Certain kinds of actions, such as a greeting, placing questions, interactions, complaints, accusations and invitations amid many people or alone are important in the conversational aspects.
- *In the pathways of discourse analysis:* Using language as productive and unambiguous tool to understand the way transactions are made to occur may lead to productive inputs for the identification of the trend of the personality in the context of the market.
- *Focus group study:* It is required to analyse the objective perception of reality in the sense of the utility and requirements of the market and society. The focus group needs to be identified and chosen in a way that actually determines functional dimensions of the research designs and the ultimate utility of the same in the context of the market and the factors exerting influences on it.
- *Cooperative inquiry:* It is done to identify the pressing issues and their impacts on the scenario of the market. Communicative space is determined in this context for a better understanding of the value dimension, and the objective function is required to be in place. It focuses on the cooperative dimension of the people in the community of clusters as relevant to the people concerned in the society. Essentially, it includes the impacts on the people in the society and enhances the logical attributes and determinants in the system and organization.
- *Thematic analysis:* It is based on the inputs of the market and the scenario and the context in which the organization and production process are designed for the success of the product and the portfolio of the company which has been in place for understanding certain intrinsic dimensions. The thematic analysis may lead to three different dimensions and different approaches.

- *Analytical approach in thematic research:* The analytical divisions include essential views, contextual approach and constructive or relative approach. The categories thus imply different behavioural patterns for life and activity.
- *Segment analysis:* This is typically based on the kind of products, type of the customers of the product, the usual choice pattern of the customers and the buying approach of the customer in the context of the market and society. Markets are required to be segmented to get across the flavour of the markets.
- The focus of marketing research should be gross to subtle.

The markets are segmented based on the following:

- Requirements of the company
- Competitive forces of the market
- General nature of the market

Markets are segmented for certain functional benefits to the company and market. Some of the highlighting benefits are as follows:

1. Better administrative control over the business
2. Fine-tuned approach in functional control
3. A better approach in managing operating and financing costs
4. A higher degree of hold on the market and distribution costs
5. Better in managing manpower across the company and its brands spread across different parts of the world
6. High capacity in establishing a network with customers and other stakeholders of the company
7. Better chance to have closer interactions with existing or potential customers
8. Better in managing basic 5Ps of marketing
9. Superior customer service through closer interactions and customer involvements in the product, process, distribution and promotional approach of the company
10. Superior customer value is offered
11. Higher value generation by the company

Some of these parameters for market segmentation are as follows:

- Ethnicity
- Lifestyle
- Family life cycle
- Household consumption
- Income

- Age group
- Personal attitudes in consumptions
- Any specific benefit sought
- Calculative in value judgement
- Perceptive utility seeker
- Elegance seeker
- Legal and regulatory compulsions
- Market challenges through forces of competition
- Cultural differences of conflicting proportions
- A corporate choice about segments
- Corporate choice based on the future projections of business
- Technology-driven segments for better business operations
- The economic or financial choice for segments of the business
- Process-driven segments for better business dynamics and flow of goods and services
- Fiscal classifications of business in a nation
- Stakeholder impacts on nature and characteristics of business segments

Focus of Marketing Research

In order to incorporate the rational dimension of a business into the business process, companies do carry out periodic research on the factors of a business. The factors of a business include product decisions, distribution dynamics, fiscal decisions, nature of competitions, types of economic forces in place, local-made challenges for branded products, retail pressures from products of low specifications and prices and forces active in the sales market of the product and services. Research activities are usually carried out for each of these factors of the business and in many other areas of business activities for satisfying better profitability from the business.

Marketing research is ideally targeted at the main point of marketing. This is actually a matter of focusing on the consumer or the customer in general. At times, we need to have a general understanding of the gross

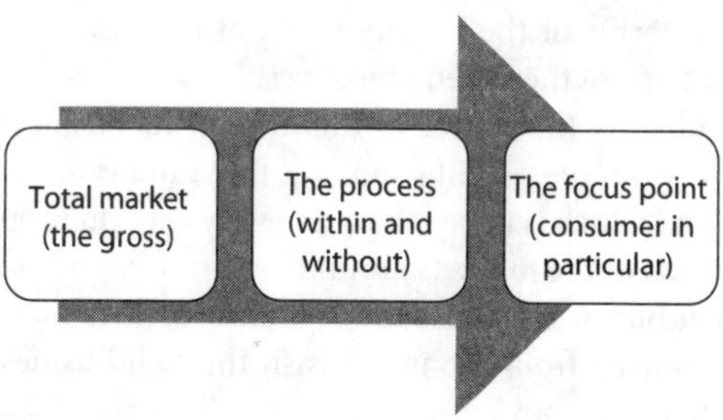

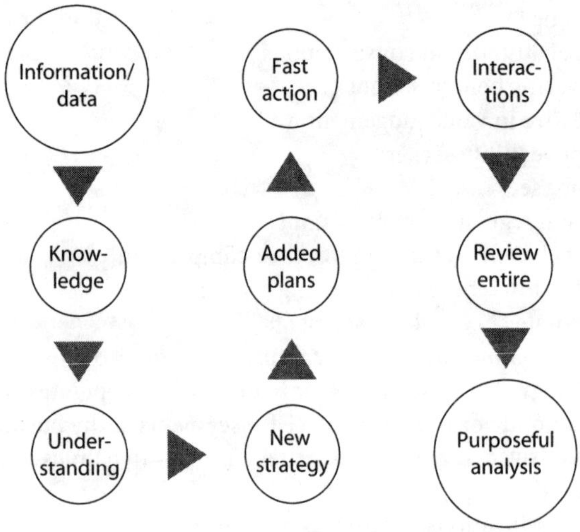

Flow of Research Activity and Analysis for Creating Action Agenda to Proceed with the Research Design for Consumer Behaviour

market. Also, the internal characteristics and external factors of the market are essential knowledge that marketers should have logical interests in.

Customer Knowledge: Creating SBU

Managers should find out ways—mostly the digital one—to communicate with the customers in different perspectives and gather ideas about them in real terms. For a large-sized company or companies present in many distant territories with diversified products, splitting the business activity into various 'SBUs' is essential. Each such SBU shall be self-complete in terms of its revenues, investments, sales, profitability and acceptability in the system of the business.

An SBU works on the following principles:

- It develops the idea of business and the relevant objectives of the business in terms of the requirements of business and its effective utilization to fulfil the stated objectives.
- It should identify the source of funding for its business. If it has to draw funds from the parent company, that fund is to be identified as the loan fund which is to be repaid squarely with due appreciations as per the trends of the markets around.
- It is set in its business process and operating cycle to make the process complete in itself from the initial cash through business operations and back to cash again.

- It turns in profit for the organization. Depending upon the policies of the company, the SBU may reinvest the earned profit to expand and create a new prospect for the company. It may also wind up facilitating the onset of a different SBU in the company.

Normal Operating Cycle (OC) of SBU

SBU Investment

Normally, the short-term investments are the focus of an SBU. However, long-term funding is quite often expected in the maintenance of various types of SBUs. While developing the long-term plan for the SBU, the company should explore options of the external sources and that of the internal sources to identify the optimum investment plan for the same. Once the optimum investment plan is developed, the cost of the investment has to be carried forward to assess the profitability involved in the investment.

An SBU operates under the overarching cover of the mission and objective of the organization. The SBU should develop a plan for the actions to see that the mission converged to objective and strategy should get properly implemented.

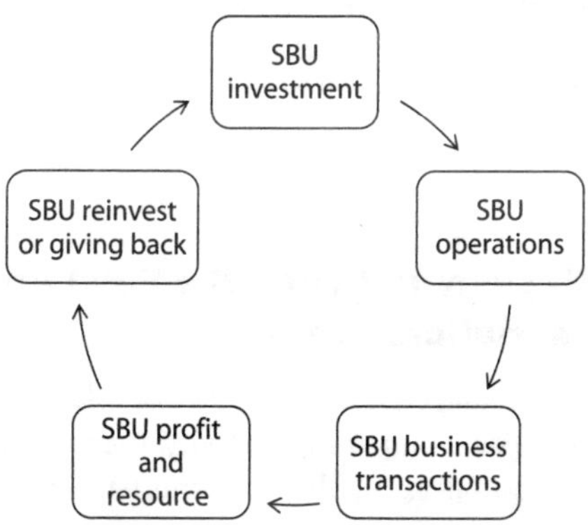

Business operations of an SBU consist of an entire range of activities with an emphasis on the customer. It looks at the horizon of the market to take care of the matters relevant to the customers. SBU manager should focus on the following:

- Special needs of the customers or very special category of customers.
- Gaps in the market, in the form of contents, quality, distribution dynamics, added features of the products and so on.
- SBU funding from internal or the external sources be identified on a competitive scale with a view to optimize the cost and enhance the scope for profitability.

- Internal customization is introduced within the company. This means the SBU functions as a market entity for the transactions to take place as it is done in the market.
- SBU is fed with manpower drawn from the company, primarily. However, it should create connections for external human resource in just the number needed and strictly as per the requirements of the emergence and growth of the SBU.
- SBU should be in use of such technology which positions it on the frontiers of the business in a particular condition of the market.
- SBU should strive to create its own identity in terms of reaching the position and height of a brand of its own or else, a special identity within the parent brand.
- Any proposition for a value-added feature of the product.

This would help the company identify the most growing unit and differentiate the other sluggish category. Usually, the customer data is classified basically on the premise of the strength of one or the other functional or financial strength as understood by the market. The markets, thus, classify the customers among the high-net-worth income (HNWI), middle-net-worth income (MNWI) and low-net-worth income (LNWI) categories.

For high-end products, HNWI is the most relevant group. However, for the other categories like mass consumption items, MNWI and LNWI are more relevant.

Manager's Strategy to Reach the Final Point of Business Destination: Profit

The main focus of managerial action is to see whether the plan is for short or long range. For a short-range activity, the focus could be on creating current assets and utilizing that on a short-term period in terms of business gains.

'The art and tools of working capital management are applied here' to maintain short-term investments and lead the same towards the point of success. However, long-range plans would involve market funding or internal funding or a hybrid funding which is a mixture of both. A broad guideline for revenue management applies here. Implementing the plan requires rigour marketing action. Professionals of SBU marketing take the business forward. The business flow then reaches out to the customer in real terms.

Strategic Vision and Positions of a Company

In order to win a desired position in the market, a company has to create its strategic move by developing a strategic vision in the pathways of life. Corporate vision lacks the strategic vision in most of the cases. Hence, the company should be focused on the ultimate objective of doing the business.

Companies rushing along with frenzied activities over time would always be inclined towards continuing the activities year after year without any clear vision and strategy for the business in operation. Issues of the current period may involve the company into focused activity on a short-term basis. This will create a companywide trend of short-sightedness into the system wherein the company fixes its focus on the activities in the short-term period than in the long-term. The forward focus of the company lacks in this, both in the context of the business and society.

Companies may have targeted somewhat gains and would try to achieve that in the short term. But for the long-term focus for periods of three years or beyond, it is always a chosen dynamics that the company needs to create. With a long-term focus in place, the company can go for longer period activity with a renewed vigour for the activity. It is in this context, the company always pitches for the renewed target and shall attempt to reach a position that is close by.

Functional Myopia: The Myopic Finance and Myopic Marketing

The usual choice of the finance function is to assess the things of the current period in the context of the historical performances in the markets and economy. The finance function is usually oriented towards the needs of the business and the returns from the business. However, it lacks a proper instrument to take a position on the future based on the trends of the market.

Competitions in the market arise from each operator having the urge to create short-term gains through the business. While facing competition in the market, the company needs to have positions in the future. This would involve investments in activities of the future.

Parameters used by finance professionals identify the profitability, liquidity and solvency of the company based on the achieved data. The efficient analysis would require the following factors to be explored:

- Return on sales (ROS) on a particular periodicity and the impact of that on the business outcome
- ROCE for SBUs and new investments made for business growth
- ROI of marketing and expected ROI for prospective sales are some of the tools that could signal caution on the trend of business as per the value generated through the business and contributed to the society as such.

ROS reflects the cost per unit of delivering customer value. This also highlights the company's position in terms of accessibility in the mind space of the customers and the degree of awareness created by it in the context of business.

Sales growth indicates the company's share in the market amid other operators. Once the volume of sales picks up to reach the pinnacle of the market height, it is likely to be one of the significant market operators. With a significant position in the market, the company should focus on the market growth in such a fashion that it makes a clear inroad into the perception of value gained by the customer. The market share of the product should be measured in terms of a mixture of volume and value.

Global Marketing Matrix for Products, Services and Brands

Investments in Marketing: The Missing Dimensions of the Role of Finance

When it comes to the tangibles, such as land, buildings, plants, types of machinery, equipment and properties of some sort, the finance professionals are good at the depictions of them in the financial statements of the company. However, the future value of investments is just perceptive estimates based on certain parameters of the market. Probabilistic estimate from the operational data is dependable in many cases but may lead to the wrong position of the company in most others. This is so because these activities depend on non-finance interventions. The finance professionals pick up data from there and use that data to suggest the final position of the company. Things are mostly left out of the purview of those finance professionals.

Impact of the Concept and Practices of Marketing on Finance

Once the domain of finance sets the tune of the corporate agenda, the strategic move of the company continues to move further. Some of the highlighting areas of activities where marketing functions should provide the guiding edge for financial investments are actually segments of the marketing agenda. Sometimes, the ROI for a group of products and services may require repeated investments to actually become a significant player in the market.

A manager should gear up with the idea and knowledge of the new mixture of things to win the market, which also describes the impact of such marketing actions on the overall performance of the company.

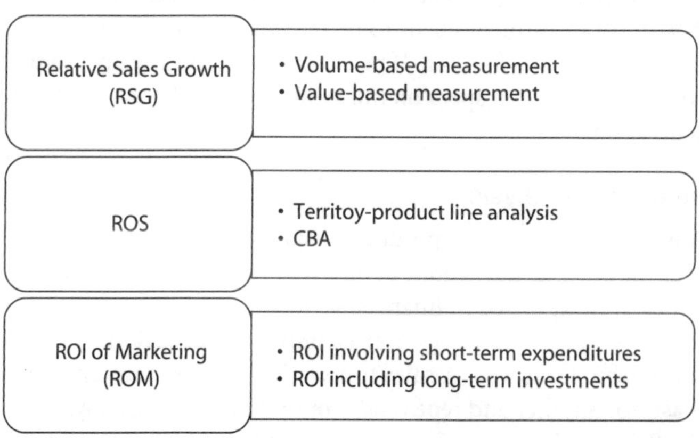

Relative Sales Growth

RSG is a time-based study where within the period of focus, the total volume of sales is assessed. Volume-based growth is actually assessed with respect to the entire range of product offtake by the channel members, the buyers in the cash and credit market and the inventory of finished goods in transit at the point of consideration for the same. It should be measured product-wise, product line-wise or cluster of product and service factors together.

The value component of RSG is to be calculated at the current prices. Entire value of the sales made and the cost component for that is required to be assessed on a constant price basis. Value of the RSG reflects in actual terms the amount of revenue actually collected through sales of products and services.

Return on Sales

ROS has to be assessed based on the impacts on the process of making sales and the actual sales transacted in the market. Sales actually take place with the acceptance of the customers in the market in a given situation of the surroundings.

All expenses involved in the process of transacting sales are to be made in such a way that it always takes care of the basic and underlying objective of the company, its philosophies and values. Input, processing, promotional, opportunity, overhead, distribution, manpower, third-party activity and the opportunity cost of the money invested for a short-term period in the business are combined to understand the extent of the cost involved in this business.

While doing a straight calculation of the ROS, the company needs to identify the specific aspects of money invested in real terms. Any amount of short-term investment needs to be segregated from the total expenditure made in the act of selling. If promotions are specifically product oriented, then the amount spent on the promotions of the same is taken into consideration.

Cost–benefit Analysis

CBA is applicable to all the products having a significant role in the total sales of the company. It is done at different functional levels of corporate activities. It is expressed in financial terms.

However, each promising transaction has the option to offer non-financial benefits as well. A sales transaction for the moment may create the basis for another and repeat sales option for the company.

In the paradigm of sales, various elements of costs are incurred. Certain items of costs are directly related to the process of making sales and certain other categories of costs are only remotely associated with it.

Costs are classified into direct and indirect costs. Direct costs include the cost of goods sold (COGS), cost of making sales and sales promotion costs while indirect costs include part of branding costs, part of R&D costs, part of manpower and similar kind of costs. Benefits include short-term and long-term aspects of the contributions from consumer values.

- If the buyer is just satisfied, they develop a positive view of the product.
- If the buyer is happy, they shall keep on mentioning whenever the reason for that occurs.
- If the buyer is delighted with the product such purchased, they will become a non-engaged ambassador of the brand and of course for the product.
- The benefit of the company is maximized whenever the sales stimulate delight in the customer through the product quality or overall buying experience, the non-financial benefit of this kind would mean to the person a relationship on the chain of value and attributes, that stays for a longer period.

Pyramid of Customer's Perception of the Brand and Company

How Marketing Can Contribute to the Value Enhancement of the Company

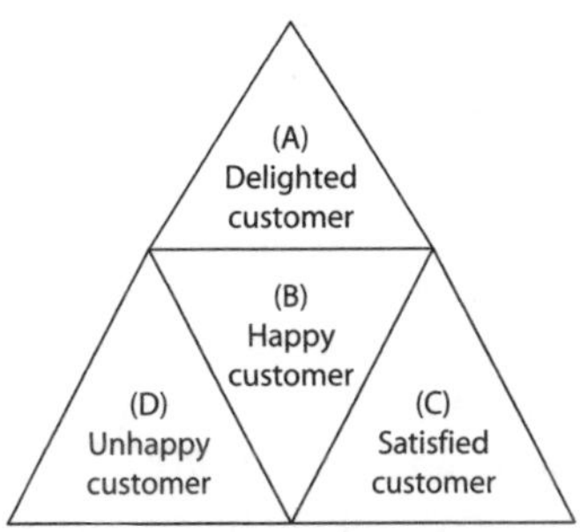

Customer Perception about the Brand and/or Company

[(A) to (B) to (C) to (D)]

The corporate objective is required to reach D. However, many companies have to thrive at the level of C. Companies need to work on developing customer perception along with A, B, C and D. A delighted customer is a long-term resource of the company. That customer enhances the value of the brand and company both on the physical and perceptive scale. Both have a strong impact on the commodity and service market on one hand, and on the stock market on the other. A company with high customer value is always perceived as an excellent investment option in the capital market. Once the investment takes place, the overall attractiveness of the company increases in the capital market. It creates a good situation in the capital market. Highlights of which is as follows:

- Higher share price because of the high probability of profitability of the company.
- Higher volume and value of stocks traded in the capital market.
- Higher trading frequency in the stock market.
- Impact of the strong position in the capital market goes to the financing market in general.
- Better terms in the investment funding for the company for any kind of expansion project, diversification project and corporate restructuring funding from the banking and other funding sources.
- Financial management of the company may obtain impetus for running the enterprise 'funded by distribution channel members' in the overall business process (the company is in a position to take advance from the channel partners for such a period which it requires to produce and send across the product to the distributor). For example, if the working capital cycle (raw materials + work-in-progress + finished goods + distribution time together) of the company is two weeks, the company will take advance of two weeks. Also, if working capital required is half of the product price per unit, the company may charge only half amount in advance and run with zero working capital. The higher the amount of advance, the higher is the profit from the branding activity of the company. Thus, a strong brand does impart huge financial value to the company.
- With higher brand image, the company enjoys a higher degree of attractiveness from qualified and efficient manpower for recruiting in different strategic positions of the company.
- In the case of technological transformation, a company requires high-calibre scientists and technologists. A company with strong brand presence and perception in the market attracts those kinds of people for the functional activities, R&D activities and other strategic activities.
- The board of the company finds relatively easier to source top executives, such as CEO, chief marketing officer (CMO), chief financial officer (CFO), chief technology officer (CTO) and similar other top-level functionaries for the company when its brand has attained strong market preference through delighting customers.

Therefore, to summarize the impact of delighted customers and thereby strong brands, we get strong benefits in the following areas:

- Strong brands help in product diversification.
- Strong brands are likely to get better terms for their presence in supermarkets, malls, distribution hubs, retail stores and in the markets of wholesales.
- Strong brands enjoy better terms from the distribution companies; particularly, the e-commerce companies for the wider scale of distribution within an economic zone or on a global scale.
- Strong brands help in short-term financing of the company.
- Strong brands facilitate in getting best professionals for the upper senior and top positions of the company.
- Strong brands influence the perceptive value of shares in the capital markets attracting higher volume, value and frequency of stock investments in the share market, thus enhancing the overall corporate value in the market and the economy.
- Strong brands make a company strong enough to become an active operator in the process of mergers, acquisitions and takeovers.
- Strong brands are always greeted with a welcome note by the nations and economies in the global context.
- Presence of strong brands with their work process is always a matter of political attractions by the governance of the countries/regions/provinces of countries and any place in the world.

The way to transcend from being just a manager to a corporate leader is to be consumer oriented. Some of the following aspects need to be taken care of:

- Always think in terms of the consumer
- Dream the position of a consumer
- Put yourself in the shoes of a consumer
- Develop the mind of a consumer within yourself
- Become a person with consumer mind first and manager next

Make Your Customer Delighted and Be Delighted as the CEO/CMO/CFO/CTO of a Company

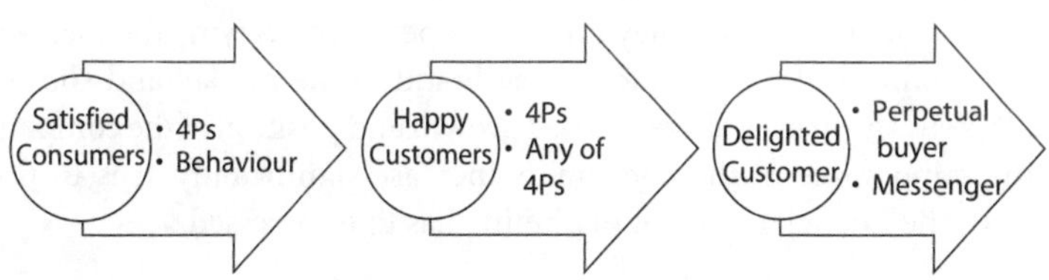

It is to keep in mind that for any product or service, the consumer is the most important person to help the company create, develop, maintain, sustain its value or erode or destroy it totally.

The unhappiness of a consumer is the most important factor than anything else in the journey and life of a company. Consumer perception is the intrinsic factor in the customer choice for acceptance or rejection of the product/brand/company. It acts as a poison pill for the company/brand or the product. Until a quick redressal is done, the brand or the company would land up in a self-annihilating position.

The happiness of the consumer is good. It helps the company and the brand to move forward with the impetus drawn from the market of happy consumers. However, a consumer being happy may not last long. In the short-term period, it is strong and good; but in the long run, a consumer's happiness may erode. Happiness is sometimes enduring in nature but not always.

Most managers want to make their consumers satisfied. It is a mental position which is like single incident response. A person who is satisfied for now, may change or even transform the mind based on the perceptive understanding about the product/brand or company; or when the consumer gets the feel and presence of a competitor product/brand.

Consumer satisfaction cannot be considered to last-long unless the market receives new operators and become relevant with their whole set of offers through the product or the service.

Dissatisfied customers are required to be approached to understand the cause of dissatisfaction and how to make a turnaround of the perception and response on the company and the brand.

The company and the brand garner the highest value with the product, and the brand makes the consumer delighted.

If a satisfied customer contributes a customer value of 'P', then a happy consumer contributes 'n P', where n is a low-value multiplier. However, if the consumer turns delighted, the consumer value would be 'n P', where 'n' is a large multiplier.

That means a delighted consumer would contribute a high value per unit to the company.

While calculating the brand value of the company and its brand, customer value occupies a very important role.

A delighted consumer may turn into a person conveying the message of the goodness of the product or the brand to the market and society, and thereby the market share, market growth and position of the company in the mind space of the consumers increase significantly. It is in this context, the financial value of marketing has to be assessed.

ROI of Marketing

ROM is usually done companywide at the end of the financial year. However, for large companies with many products, spread in large territories, it is advisable to be on toes of changing plans for better profitability.

As the context of the market has been identified, it is better to segment it into product groups, or product categories to understand which product is doing how. ROM helps in identifying the core strength of one product or a category of products as against other product or other groups of products.

A combination of all these analyses contributes to the idea of customer value growth, as depicted here.

ROM is actually required to be evaluated periodically. The measure for ROM has two broad components:

1. The revenue
2. Cost and expenditure

Whereas the future trend of brand revenue component can be estimated through the probabilities of brand sales in a particular business zone by assigning probabilities of sales in each category of customers at a particular condition of the market. The probabilistic estimation can be identified based on past performance with added dimensions.

Investments made or to be made in marketing activities are normally taken in the usual sense. But for a company in a competitive market with free flow of information available, the companies should do promotional activities to strengthen the marketing of the company, usually, under a brand for the benefit of the overall growth and stakeholder value of the company.

While considering the stakeholder value, the manager needs to consider the 'consumer' as one of the most important stakeholders along with usual others.

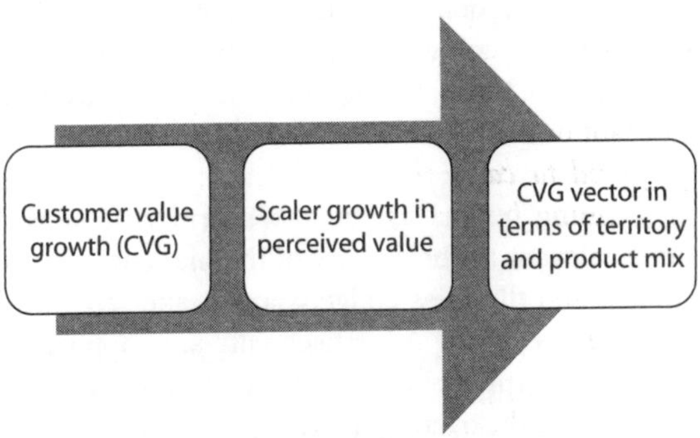

Let us see how the estimate of future brand revenue can be done using the probability of occurrence.

Future brand revenue can be measured using simple binomials as:

$$(x+a)^n = \sum_{k=0}^{n} \binom{n}{k} x^k a^{n-k}$$

Where x stands as the historical average of sales as on current period;

a is considered as the added dimension of sales or the increased components of sales; k is the periodicity of the estimate; and n stands for the period up to which the estimate is being done.

Apart from this simple summation, ΣRi can be made. Where 'R' is the revenue measure and 'i' is the suffix for the respective measure of probability.

Both estimates are based on past trends. This needs to be corrected through multiplier model. Multiplier index can be identified by the company based on the specific branding initiatives by the company.

Financing Marketing Activities

- *Brand promotions:* Usually, direct breakeven point in the marketing investments is expected to be around three years. However, its result would influence the expansion of the company's market share and market growth. It is an investment in the long-term gain of the organization. However, short-term objectives may be fulfilled through brand promotions as well.
- *Branding:* It takes place normally through promotions. However, other options have also proved a strong success. Branding is a continuous process which does not occur through just advertisements and other modes of promotions. Branding through the cultivation of 'faith' is also a proven fact of huge success.
- *Advertising:* Advertising for product and services is usually needed for registering the uniqueness of the product or service in the mind of consumers in a specific context. Choosing the right medium for the advertisement and developing the right content as the message is very important in the case of advertisement.
- *Money required to carry the advertisements:* This normally comes from the running budget as the short-term cost of business and expenditure relevant to the activity of the marketing function. Marketing budget and the sales budget should take care of the requirements of advertisements. Advertisements are supposed to finance from the working capital of the company. However, it can come from the sales budget or the overall marketing budget.

- *Advertisements*: They are normally targeted at creating the stimulus for actions by the consumers. However, creating awareness and interests are important objectives of advertisements. In order to develop awareness in the mind of the target consumers, the company needs to carry on the advertisements up to certain benchmark levels.

  For effective advertisements, the company requires that the marketing functionaries are careful about the actual target, the quantum, cost, expected revenues from and contributions of advertisements to the long-term image or the branding, brand maintenance and brand development of the company.
- *Launching new brands:* This could be an initiative for 'brand splits' or 'brand diversifications' to create a multi-brand conglomerate and become more visible in the market. New brands can create their own pathways in the markets and sometimes can become more penetrative in the mind space of the consumers. It may create potential value for the company, either in the current period or for the period in future. It could place itself in the same market or may push it for the magnitude, frequency and depth of the advertisement.
- *Focused R&D:* It is actually required not only for product development but also many other aspects are important in this. R&D becomes a very important principle for continuity in the market and capturing better and more space in the marketplace. Principle of '*Kaizen*' refers to the continuous improvement made in the content, production, shape, features and utility of the product. It applies to the process, technology, distribution and value-added component of the product or service offered by the company.
- *Target market research:* This is actually a continuous process which usually includes the following:
  - Acquisitions of the target group of customers (domestic and international)
  - Developing special competency to meet the challenges of competitions
  - Survival and growth in special situations of the market and society
  - Investing in marketing and distribution technology to operate beyond the limits of current markets
  - Investing in the probable business loss in the market because of the unethical forces of the market
  - Legal and regulatory implications of any change in the setup and structure of the governance of a particular market

The objective of financing marketing activities is to enhance the net earnings of the company. A segmented analysis can prove the effectiveness of the marketing activities with respect to the investments made into the same.

Company is required to identify the items of cost and investments into marketing activities, and the relevant revenue earned because of the marketing activity. With the costs, revenues and investments are identified, the assessments may made following the standard procedures.

Financial Objectives of Branding in Marketing

Marketing ROCE (MROCE)

The MROCE can be estimated by the ratio:

$$\text{MROCE} = \text{EBIT (M)/NA (M)},$$

where EBIT (M) is the earnings before interest and tax, NA is the net value of assets involved in the entire business transactions under the focus of the marketing activity and NA (M) is the net asset of the company that is tuned to the business operations through which these earnings have been generated.

A segmented analysis can make this exercise easier, as follows:

$$\text{MROCE} = \text{S (M)/NA} \times \text{GP/S (M)} \times \text{EBIT/GP}$$

Here, S (M) is the number of sales made through marketing and branding activity, and GP is the gross profit earned through the process of branding and marketing.

If the company has gone for utilizing external debt fund for branding and promotional activities, it has to prove before the equity holders that the initiative would ultimately benefit the equity earnings of the company and obviously impact the market to increase the share price on the market floor and create a favourable position for capital gain for the investors in the share of the company.

The best and most suitable indicator for this is the measure of return on equity (ROE):

$$\text{ROE} = \text{Operating performance} \times \text{Leverage factor}$$

This reflects the combined efficiency of the marketing function and provides vital for the long-term growth of the company.

$$\text{ROE} = \text{(Sales/NA)} \times \text{(GP/Sales)} \times \text{(EBIT/GP)} \times \text{(PAT/EBIT)} \times \text{(NA/NW)}$$

Here, PAT is profit after tax, NW is the net worth and ROE reflects combined impacts of major business indices of the company.

ROE from Branding

This measures the following aspects of the business of the company:

- Operating efficiency for the marketing function
- Financing efficiency for the company
- Shareholder value creation for the investors in the company

Operating performance is indicated by EBIT/ NA,

whereas the leverage factor id is indicated by PAT/EBIT × NA/NW.

Retention ratio = RE/PAT,

where RE stands for the retained earnings.

Leverage factor is the product of PAT/EBIT and NA/NW.

Calculation of customer value is based on the customer's buying habit, process, volume and frequency.

However, the financial parameters can be calculated as follows:

Profit margin = EBIT/Sales
Assets turnover = Sales/NA
Return on net assets (RONA) = EBIT/NA
Financial leverage = PAT/EBIT
ROE = PAT/NW

Competition Analysis within the Industry

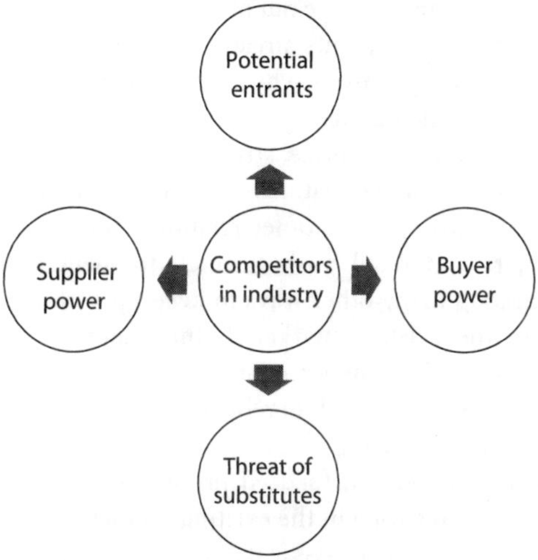

Michael Porter's Five Forces Model

Five forces model of Michael Porter has gained wide popularity among concerned people in marketing. It talks about the types of forces which are active within the industry and relevant for the company and brand. Five forces model of Michael Porter gives a good idea about the positioning needed for a company in a particular condition of the market and the economy.

Force 1: Industry Competitors

Existing companies within an industry face challenges from new entrants when the segment of the industry proves itself very lucrative. The fate of the new entities depends on the shape of things within an industry.

The relevant issues are as follows:

- The number of important operators within the industry
- Identity of the existing operators in terms of their magnitude and volume of business
- Investments circulating within the segment
- Revenue and profit significant within the segment in the industry
- A segment is attractive with a large number of buyers having strong buying power
- Any scope of making high gains in terms of successful business operations within the segment

Companies with high investments made in the immovable properties and high fixed costs cannot move out of the segment easily because of the exit barriers of high investments already made into the business operations. This is one of the reasons why existing operators sometimes lose their competition in the market.

Frequent concessions on price, strong promotional mix, quick addition of new products, added features in distribution, personalized solutions in big sales, stronger customer relations, additional incentives to channel partners and retail push through frequent retail promotion schemes are among many other ways to keep up with the challenges of competition in the existing market. If the major companies' performances show the good business outcome, the industry segment becomes attractive to the customers, and thereby new companies find it attractive to invest within that segment.

Constant innovation and focused promotions could, among many other options, remain strong in the existing segment.

Force 2: Potential Entrants

Low entry barrier High exit barrier (D)	High entry barrier High exit barrier (A)
Low entry barrier L ow exit barrier (C)	High entry barrier Low exit barrier (B)

Combination B: It is the most attractive position of the industry for existing companies. In this combination, since the exit barrier is low, those companies which are unable to perform in that segment of the industry can easily move out of its domain. Those who are doing well are reluctant to invest further to make a company more agile to face challenges of the markets, particularly, new entrants with a different or better mix of things on offer to the customers. At this position, the earnings and revenue potential of the companies are moderate and cash flows are expected by the existing operators at the same moderate rate.

Combination A: In this case, since the entry barrier is also high as the exit barrier, the number of operators would constrict to a few. High entry and exit barriers mean that the business is such that it would imply a high or very high level of investments to do the setup. Also, it should be into the kind of operations which means that the investments in manpower, into the process, in the entire range of technology, in the distributions and customer service setup, all put together, make a huge project, and the company needs to make such a high level of investments to enter into and remain in the business in that particular segment.

This combination offers the highest potential for gains from the business, provided the market accepts the products and services of the new company into the segment. However, with the high potential that lays here, companies having intent and capability of investing to that extent would rush to the segment making the segment highly competitive. This segment of business would provide the highest profit and the highest level of cash flows from the market, provided companies can skim off profit in the usual manner after fully taking care of the responsibilities involved in. Competition being high, companies would have to prove the competency to win the market.

'Combination A gives the highest potential of profit in a given context of the market.'

Combination D: Low entry barrier and high exit barrier may create chronic overcapacity at the time of bad market condition. This combination allures the companies when the markets are stable and attractive for a while. In search of profits and good business, companies do rush as the entry barrier is low. But the involvement of the company becomes such that it can hardly exit from the business as the company has to meet many obligations in case it wants to do so. This may occur in manufacturing, distribution, services companies as also in case of companies into personal care, electronics, telecommunications, airline, shipping, fleet carriers and so on.

Combination C: Low entry barrier and low exit barrier make an easy way in and out for companies in a segment of the market or the entire market. In this case, companies enjoy some returns to sustain. Returns remain low and through a random process of entering and exiting the market tends to maintain somewhat equilibrium across the prospects of the business.

Forces 3 and 5: The Buyer Power and the Supplier Power

The buyer's bargaining power increases if they are organized among themselves, or they have some common ground to assert power over the companies. Similarly, the suppliers can become constrained in terms of supplies if they are drawing from a set of closely connected and organized sources.

Buyers become particularly more demanding when the product or the process involves their share of finances as well.

The buyer's power is higher when:

1. The buyer's switching cost is low.
2. The buyers are more organized to create a body of power and assert with that on the market.
3. The product is undifferentiated.
4. The buyers are price sensitive because of the low or undefined margin of profit in the purchase.
5. The buyers can integrate their buying or process in the upstream.
6. The company lacks the power to make superior offers compared to others in the same segment of the market.

A company can withstand the buyer's power through:

1. Creating a higher degree of product differentiation
2. Superior branding such that the buyers would have intrinsic pressures to remain faithful to the product

3. Taking the buyers into the product advisory such that they feel more involved in the making and the process of the product or the service
4. More offers and superior benefits which the competitors in the market does not make
5. Involving buyers more into the process of the company through non-financial coordination
6. Making the selling process such that the switching costs of the buyers become high

The supplier power is high when:

1. The process is more into the supply side of the economy.
2. The suppliers are able to raise the unit price or the overall price of the supplied materials.
3. Substitutes are only a few, and the dominance of the flow of supplied materials is high.
4. Suppliers have the chance and valid interest in combining themselves into some kind of coordination to assert pressure on the supply.
5. Supplied material is unique or critical in nature and availability of alternatives to the company is poor.
6. The suppliers can integrate downstream.

A company can protect its interest against the supplier power by:

1. Creating alternatives to the existing suppliers in the same range of the materials of supply
2. Developing the power to make alternative arrangement of the same quality and at the price that is around the same as the existing
3. Creating alternatives to the existing flow of business in the same range of costs and the same standard of quality
4. Maintaining multiple supplier networks and asserts its dominance in the process of its doing business
5. Maintaining win-win situations with legal networking with the suppliers in real-time
6. Making strategic and critical inputs in the supply replaceable in the business process of the company, thereby reducing the importance of the company in the gamut of the business

Force 5: Threat of Substitutes

Companies are likely to face the threat from substitute products in the market. Ongoing markets are full of similar threats from around the operators in the market.

Substitutes usually come as a threat from the rise of technology and its specific applications in the domain of the business the company is in.

Michael Porter's five forces have played a favourable role in the evaluation of corporate strategies by many. It also helps in understanding and designing corporate strategies. Michael Porter has most rightly suggested managers to be aware of the forces of competition and the market.

Reviewing Michael Porter's Five Forces

Digital era management is sharper, more focused and principle centric than before. It is in this light, the factors of five forces cannot be just taken for guidance towards managing corporate enterprises in the current period, particularly for those having eye and valid projections for the future.

A comparison between the digital era compulsions and characteristics of the companies would actually put the required strategies for the maintenance and growth of the brand and the company.

Five forces need strong recasting to fit into the emerging business realities of the digital era. The focus of the five forces model has been the company. Digital era management needs to change the focus to the consumer.

The role of buyers and suppliers and the industry competitiveness become important once the fundamental fabric of the business is properly cemented. Companies need to be tuned to the fundamental spirit of the business through analysing the scenario of the consumers in a given context of a market and society. Although it is assumed that the digital era is fully tuned to the machines and is mechanistic in nature, in reality, it has lots of similarity with the ancient Vedic spirit of living in India.

Digital Era Management Resembles Spiritual Living

Digital management philosophy has unique similarity with the classical Indian spirituality. Some of the connected philosophical principles are:

Philosophical Basis of Management in Digital Era	Philosophical Basis of Classical Indian Spirituality
• Machine drives the process and systems. • All activities are based on principles of impersonality and non-specific identity of human context and combinations.	• The mind drives the process of life and living. • All activities are based on the principles of impersonality as every entity is an embodiment of the universal truth.

Philosophical Basis of Management in Digital Era	Philosophical Basis of Classical Indian Spirituality
• The machine needs the most intense involvement of human minds to perform and multiply for future growth for the benefit of human society. • Although oriented to business in the ultimate analysis, the focus should be to prioritize the interest of the consumer before that of the company. • The man and machine should marry the concerns with every initiative to progress further to take the power of the machine to the superior most height for human society. • Power of machine would be multiplied to infinity to serve the management process, systems and structures with an unending efficiency and effectiveness over a reasonable period of time. • The mind of a digital manager is creative with respect to the truth behind the functional and operational world and tries to contribute always to the creation of new and advanced capabilities of the human world.	• Minds to combine across a cause which is universally oriented to the welfare of everyone as every person is the same embodiment of the divine. • Spiritual realization is a factor of the individual, but collective welfare is possible through the cultivation of the collective consciousness. • The mind of individuals to marry the minds of the collective to create a concern for all and create the conscious basis of human oneness with the cosmos. • The spiritual practice would help the individual to look within and discover the divine self within to draw the energy and drive to be oriented to the world in the best possible way. • Mind engrossed in spirituality is a mind that gradually proceeds towards a condition of dissolved mind where the individual mind is merged with the super cosmic consciousness and draws the spirit of goodness for the creation on earth.

Therefore, digital era corporate management needs to maintain core philosophy as 'consumer first, company next'.

Brand and Product Strategy in the Era of Digital Economies

There are five promises that are predominant with respect to the emergence of digital management to be sustainable in the human society.

As mentioned in the cosmic design above, a digital manager has to maintain the five promises in managing enterprises. These are:

1. Always take care first the consumer benefit and welfare, before being concerned about anything else
2. Understand the consumer preference on a constant basis and fulfil the same

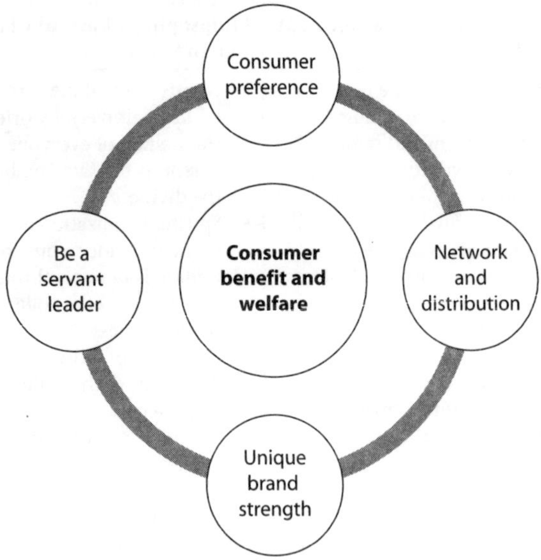

3. Establish network among consumers and distribute happiness to the consumers
4. Create uniqueness in the brand and constantly develop it through the managerial initiatives
5. Try to become a servant leader in the context of the company and its consumers

Consumer Benefit and Welfare: Highlights of a Remarkable Case from India

This is a unique reference from the Indian corporate context where the emergence of a new entity in the market has dramatically transformed the market scenario. This is about the company launched by Baba Ramdev almost two decades ago. With the spread of his message of yoga, thousands and millions of people started practising his yoga throughout the country. While yoga practice took up the proportion of a massive force drawing millions within the fold, the issue of human health and good life came in very prominently. Ancient Indian sages had a long life, because of certain factors of which some aspects relevant now are:

- A man used to live an honest life.
- No hatred, greed, jealousy, envy, harm to others were the pathways of life.

- Faith and truth were the basis of life's philosophy.
- The man used to live in the context of nature. Food was always naturally organic and fresh.

These are the basis of the organization formed by Baba Ramdev, in the brand name of 'Patanjali'.

The Patanjali challenge in the Indian market became such that all the companies who are leaders in doing business in most areas are heavily influenced by the 'Patanjali' wave. It has affected companies into:

- Personal care items
- Health products and food supplements
- Basic food items and food derivatives
- Soft soluble and soft drinks
- Fast-moving consumer goods (FMCG) products of an almost entire range
- Household items and commodities
- Natural herbal products
- Baby products
- Ladies products
- Beauty products
- Ayurvedic products for medical and health remedy
- 'Aarogya Kendra' or the designated health centres destined to help people free of charges to offer an organic remedy to various health and hygiene issues of people belonging to all age groups
- E-commerce activity
- IT and ITES

Distribution Points of Patanjali

Patanjali Ayurveda Ltd uses a totally different mechanism for the purpose.

Patanjali in the Indian market has become a real business threat to all the relevant operators (most of them are established MNCs with prior huge market share and dominance) in similar categories.

Faith in the tradition as triggered by Baba Ramdev has become a phenomenal force in the design of things, and the market has been deluged with the flavour of 'Indianness' and the spirit of 'natural organic' product, and 'no harmful chemicals' have actually deluged the Indian market.

In the context of the Indian market, this has already been tested and found grand success. There are many mid-sized brands which have gone the way to prioritize the customers before the company. However, the trendsetter and leader of this category have been a company which in common parlance is made known by the name of a famous Indian monk, Baba Ramdev.

Story of Patanjali: The Company of Baba Ramdev

Patanjali Ayurveda Ltd, an organization formed at the onset of this century, was started at the base of the Himalayas, near the holy city of Haridwar.

The philosophical objective of the company is *upkar* not *byapar*, meaning 'welfare' not 'commerce'.

Core Policy of the Company

- Product of nature
- No chemicals
- Pure as divine
- Same kind of product with the difference that it contains no harmful elements
- Moderate pricing which makes it affordable to the middle-class and lower-middle-class people
- Products are presented in the most modern shape, design and medium of logistics to reach the customers
- Durable and affordable
- Uses the latest technology in the final making of the product and its delivery

Product Strategy of Patanjali

- Emphasizes the natural and ayurvedic range of products
- Shape, feel, packaging, look remain the same as the existing operators in the market
- Understands the behaviour of the consumers, consumer taste, preference and so on and also goes by the impetus of the market
- Product names are given similar to the existing. Product innovations are seldom on the augmented features of the product
- All products carry a tag: 'Contains no harmful chemicals'

Distribution Strategy of Patanjali

- It distributes the products through its own centres called Patanjali Chikitsalaya, meaning centres for health recovery. Several thousands of the same centres are spread across the country. At each place of Patanjali health centre, Patanjali health consultants are there to offer free counselling to consumers for any kind of health deficiency or difficulty. A large number of products of natural origin are available at the centre at very reasonable prices. Consumers are given recommendations for suitable combinations.

- Also it is done through the usual system of channel members in the chain of distribution as adopted by others.
- E-commerce mode of distribution is also in place.

Brand Strategy of Patanjali

1. Yoga Guru (Master of Yoga) Baba Ramdev is the brand himself, reflecting faith, spirituality, freedom, health, nation-first are the main issues of Patanjali vision and conviction.
2. Yoga for life is supported by the products facilitating the yoga for life and vitality
3. 'No celebrity' strategy of promotions to make the brand vibrant and grow in the market for a long period
4. 'Swadeshi advantage', the advantage of having nations own product, is projected before the public. 'India's own product helps keep India's financial resources within the nation'.
5. 'Pick our product, it is the same with no harmful chemicals within, rather carries herbal and organic essence for your health'.
6. Baba Ramdev is the main icon. Millions of people have developed faith in him as they follow him in the open house mass meditations as also on the screen of television channels. Followers of him are active multipliers of the products of Patanjali.
7. 'Patanjali, the brand for *upkar*—the welfare of everyone.
8. Organic lifestyle by consumers transforms society.
9. Product Quality high, price less than the most in the market.
10. Own your health product and be safe and grow.

CHAPTER 14

TECHNOLOGY MANAGER

Technology-driven Product Life Cycle (TPLC)

The depiction of the product life cycle (PLC) through a figure (Figure 14.1) is the usual way of understanding a company's position from the marketing point of view. The marketing manager needs to understand the factors influencing the stages of growth and possibilities through corrective and augmentative actions in the life of an organization throughout. At every stage of the organization, there is a lot of scope for examining the features of it and then getting into the re-engineering or corrective initiatives for making the organization competitive enough to come up to the level of forefront of the business.

The features as shown in Figure 14.1 are normal in the sense that these have been followed by companies across the globe so far. This is actually relevant for large-scale production of manufactured goods. These could be mass consumption items of household need or needed for industrial or other purposes.

PLC alone cannot justify the business and economic trends in the modern world. Combined with the relevant aspects of technology, the concept of PLC can be applied in the case of modern enterprises now. This combined approach can be named as TPLC.

TPLC applies to the products which have been branded as 'FMCG', 'fast-moving consumer durables' (FMCD), a product in the range of personal care, automobile (cars, light/medium/heavy vehicles or their ancillaries), pharmaceutical (drugs, medical consumables and so on), civil-engineering, medical-engineering, heavy products, large manufacturing (aircraft, ships, defence equipment and so on), infrastructure developments (roads, bridges, railway lines, trains, stations, added facilities, highways, river bridges, sea-coast links and so on), telecommunications (towers, cables, station units, distribution points, boosting points and so on), electricity (generation through thermal plants, atomic plants, hydro-plants, green electricity, etc.), agricultural technology (agro plants, bio-farms, organic farming, horticulture, bio-medical farms, natural-medicine plants and so on), public utility materials firms and any large-scale project that caters to the economic development in general.

Any project oriented to the space science (space station, spacecraft, propellers, lander, landing stations, etc.), nuclear plants, airways, satellite

	Initial Position	Growth Phase	Peak Period	Decline Phase	Review
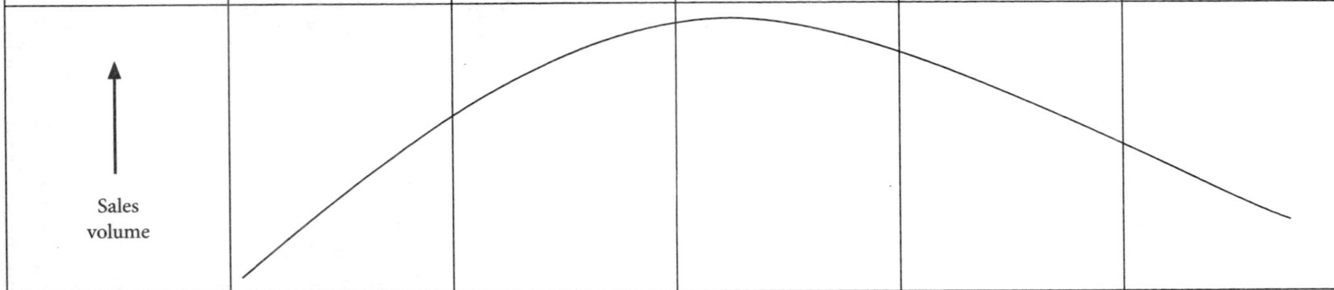					
Demand condition	Initial demand	Growing demand	Peak demand	Declining demand	Steep fall-off in demand
Nature of technology	Low capacity utilization and rapidly changing techniques	Mass production methods and incremental change	Mature technology, process-driven production run. Emphasis on innovations and search for new market segments		
Investment intensity	Long term—high Short term—low	Reinvestments on short and long terms		High replacements of equipment and channel maintenance	
Nature of industry	Few competitors, high prospect and low entry barrier	Growing number of competing firms and increasing vertical integration	High investment needed and number of firms starts to decline	Stability gets gradually questioned, followed by exit of some firms.	
Essential factors	Competence, skill, connectivity and clear objective of business.	Leadership, access to financial resources and control.	Supply of moderate cost manpower, less resistance in market and more extension of market reaches		

Figure 14.1 Product Life Cycle (PLC) in General for a Product

launchers, space observatories and so on is specifically oriented to technology.

Technology shapes the nature of competitiveness for any kind of products and services. With the incremental changes in the technology of production and distribution, the company can create a short-term competitive edge over others in the market. However, a major breakthrough in technology gets a rapid advantage in the markets, globally. It hardly matters whether the customer is a resident of a less advanced country or region of the world or in an advanced country, as customers have become global in nature in most of the areas of product usage. Certain areas of focus are basically technology driven, whereas others are influenced by the impact of technology.

Technology management is dominant in the field of the defence industry. It is also leading the organizations which are developing a more advanced instrument, guns, machines, combat aircrafts (with higher speed, accuracy of targeting, escaping the enemy observatories, night combat capacities, high fuel capacity and so on), drones for civil and military use, robots for industrial, medical, commercial, mining and R&D activities use (particularly for hazardous chemicals and so on), nanotechnology instrumentation and research activities, atomic research, communication instruments, communications systems, tanks, mortars, missiles, explosives, bombs, ballistic missiles (short-range, long-range and intercontinental ballistic missiles and so on), textile, garments, iron and steel machineries, food and fruit processing, computers and allied industry, computing sets (laptops, desktops, palm tops, iPads, chip making, digital instruments, consumer digital appliances, consumer electrical appliances, consumer electronics, mobile phones, medical engineering tools, hospital, process automation, automation in delivery and distribution and so on.

However, with the changes that have already occurred in the world so far, there is a pressing need that a corporate manager is thoroughly aware of the impact and consequences of technological changes on the management strategies and system. From this point of view, the role of a manager as a technology manager is of utmost importance. A manager with the knowledge and at least awareness of the impact of fast-changing technology shall help the organization thrive and rise above the turbulence of the market dynamics.

Technology Manager as an Entrepreneur

Technology contributes to the making of a new enterprise that has the vital for the future shape of things including the challenges that may come in the context of the business and economy. Understanding and developing a competitive position in relation to competitors and competitive advantages in resources and capabilities are fundamentals for the growth and sustainability of the company. Proper analysis of the market forces and elements of market structures is important from the point of view of an organization.

In their endeavour to identify new strengths and vitality for facing competition and market uncertainties, organizations need to explore and find out new opportunities for the future. It is essential to focus on, at this point, developing and continuously crafting a strategy for the organization should help a lot.

'Technology drives a manager to serve the organization, basically as an entrepreneur.' As product development becomes imperative in general, the product cycles have been becoming shorter. This pushes a higher degree of pressure on firms to develop new products or to acquire them from other firms. Continuous changes in the products quality, design, specification, packaging, pack sizes and an intense touch of technology are essential both for products and services.

The three major ways in which a product's sales may be maintained or increased are mentioned as follows:

- To try out and introduce a new product as the existing one becomes obsolete so that 'overlapping' cycles occur
- To involve innovative knowledge and expertise of the company and try to extend the cycle for the existing product, either by making minor modifications in the product itself to 'update' it or by finding new uses
- To adopt more advanced technology so as to make changes in the production technology itself to make the product sharper and more competitive.

However, product innovation alone is inadequate as a basis for a firm's survival and profitability. Firms must strive to produce their products as efficiently as possible. Continuous developments in the process orientation technology with a higher degree of involvement of computerized techniques, especially, as ICT have profound effects upon production processes in all sectors of industry and economy.

Productive forces combine to make significant progress in the new era of technology. There is a close relationship between the progress of a product through its life cycle and the technology used and the methods from which it is made. In the production cycle, each stage has a particular production characteristics. Products of modern era follow the feature in general, as the cycle proceeds, the emphasis shifts from product-related technologies to process technologies in particular to minimize production costs. In this respect, the relative importance of labour costs, especially for semi-skilled and unskilled labour, increases. More generally, different types of geographical location are relevant to different stages of the product cycle.

'In the life cycle of products, four factors have to be kept in the mind of the manager/entrepreneur always.' These factors could be summarized in the following way:

- *Factor 1:* Cost of the goods manufactured (COGM; including the fixed costs and variable costs) and COGS together become beneficial to the company (entrepreneur/manager should also focus on the stream of expected cash flows at different conditions of the market (if the market booms, if it remains normal or if it becomes recessionary with appropriate probabilities assigned to each to obtain most optimum cash flow for each month or periods in the future)
- *Factor 2:* Investments to be made into the entire process to adopt and upgrade technology (optimal portfolio of investment funds to be obtained from the investors and shareholders in the market. Risk and return factors of the fund need to be analysed to ensure that the fund procured in such a way satisfies the 'value optimization' principle. The new-age manager would, thus, be a prudent analyst of combined factors—drawn from the market and those drawn from within, and take the agenda forward based on that.)
- *Factor 3:* Market analysis is needed very rigorously to understand whether the existing set of products yield the expected set of revenue and profitability on getting new shape through new technology or not. This analysis requires testing of the expected results after the introduction of the new technology against other options. The manager requires to see the quantum and rate of the net revenues from the technology-driven changes or transformations and see if that can support the efforts of market development, product development or even proper diversification. Product–market matrix would throw light on this aspect, and the manager can take decisions accordingly. However, if the manager finds inadequacy in the quantum and flaw in the speed of net revenues from this strategy, it is prudent to decide on a new product, which may or may not belong to the same product line to benefit the stakeholders of the organization in a better manner.
- *Factor 4:* The right kind and mix of human force to satisfy the requirement of technology and fit into the objective of the company, competitions from the market, general economic conditions, sociopolitical climates of the markets and global standards of business and economy becomes essential.

If we observe closely the changes that have taken place so far in the global context, we find that systematic changes have occurred in the production process as a product matures. The idea of systematic change has an appealing impact in the industry circle and strong validity. There, undoubtedly, are important differences in the nature of the production process between a product in its very early stages of development and the same product in its maturity. But the linear and sequential notion of change is overly simplistic and deterministic. At any stage, the production process may be 'rejuvenated' by technological innovation. There may not necessarily be a simple sequence leading from small-scale production to standardized mass production.

Adoption of New Technology in the Production Process

With new technologies in place, the production process shall involve a new set of things as input factors in the system. Factors 1–4, as mentioned above, should be considered by a new-age technology manager as important for making things easier and more acceptable by the stakeholders of the company.

The production system becomes more flexible yet lean and straight. With the new and developed technology in place, most technological developments in production processes have become gradual and incremental. On the one hand, we have the result of 'learning by doing' and 'learning by using', and on the other, we have applications of R&D on an ongoing basis into the system and adopting the same in the new phase of production. But periods of radical transformation of the production process have occurred throughout history. Over the long timescale of industrialization, the production process has developed through a series of stages, each of which represented increasing efforts to mechanize and to control more closely the nature and speed of work. This is actually applicable for enhancing the shareholder value of the company.

The two features of the technology-driven production system are very important. These are:

- Mass production of items as components and finished products
- Flexible features of the finished products

Both of these features are dependent upon the demand from the customers. Mass production of items as components is dependent upon the large-scale demands from the customers in the markets. This may induce the manager to explore different types of markets. These are:

- Domestic markets
- Foreign markets

Large-sized countries with a large number of the domestic consumer base, like India, may satisfy the need for large-scale customer base within the country. However, with the emphasis given more on value-added products, companies may have to explore foreign markets as the best measures of getting into expanded markets.

Let us explain the combinations in a two-by-two matrix with the technology-changing mode of local to global along the vertical axis and the horizontal axis growing from local to global production. An MNC ideally faces the sociopolitical and economic challenges from various nations on the issues of products of global scale technology but actually produced within nations. Thus, a product developed with a foreign technology, but produced within the country, induces the nostalgic notion that the product is from own nation. However, the ultimate benefit of the production goes to the parent company. Yet an MNC manager has to look into this psycho-social–political perspective of the target economy and finally arrange to get into the choice matrix from the mix of matrices as depicted below:

Production–Technology Matrix: Local–Global Choice

Global technology Local production (B)	Global technology Global production (A)
Local technology Local production (D)	Local technology Global production (C)

It has been observed in the market studies of some domestic markets in advanced economies and some developing economies that wherever the basic technology is drawn from, nations expect the same to be produced in their own countries and draw the satisfaction of the foreign technology produced within the domestic economy.

Combination A: With the global technology and production system, the MNC has to have the support of mass purchases from the customers of the target markets. Gradual process of changes in the strategy of the MNC is essential. Global technology and production mix may pose issues. Some of which are as follows:

- Logistics, as identified by the MNC, has to be in place favourable to the transportation of the company.
- Distribution of the finished products across the spread of the markets distorts the aesthetics of the finished goods.
- Logistics and distribution costs of the finished products become very significant in certain cases compelling the companies to review the strategic choice for a better business process.

Combination B: With the advent of favourable economic, political and market conditions in the destination country, companies decide on bringing the global technology to local areas. Thus, the location of production is changed and moved to the country of consumption. This satisfies the fiscal and economic objective of the destination country. Obviously, the 'made-in-home country' tag attracts domestic customers more. The combination of global technology and local production is a unique mix, which usually attracts customers. This process proves better to the shareholders and other investors as it is likely to reduce the cost of operation, cost of distribution and expand the market base. The result of these mix of benefits is a higher flow of revenue to the destination country and interests the country more and more. This strategic move continues until there is any fiscal, legal or repatriation problem created in the destination country.

The fiscal problem could be any kind of targeted taxation or financial duty, levied at any stage of production, distribution, marketing or administrative initiative. The adverse fiscal condition may induce the company to withdraw from that market, and the company may look for any other country as the alternative production–market setup, if it has enough capacity to consume the output.

Combination C: There are ample cases where a domestic innovation into a product or service has attracted global customers towards the product and service. Usually, this refers to the specific areas of activity where product–market mixture requires a review of the marketing strategy of the organization for a particular product line or the entire range of products.

Combination D: A large number of small- and medium-sized companies follow this combination with a view to optimally utilize the resources and continue with domestic flavours of productions and marketing. However, many companies have made very good wealth through this combination as the core business strategy.

The manager should be aware of the dynamics of the market and proceed with the next level of choice regarding the customization for the products within the territories identified. The good idea of product–market matrix makes it feasible for the manager to strike the right choice.

Product–Market Matrix: Issue of Diversification

Market Extension Existing product New market	**Diversification** New market New product
Static Mixture Existing product Existing market	**Product Extension** New product Existing market

This product–market matrix is applicable for each of the four combinations mentioned above.

General Understanding of Business Process

Development of Business Process (Phase 1)

Industrial Regime • Manufacture of durable goods and items • Manufacture of consumer goods • Decentralized manufactures • Agro-industry and agro-based business and industrial units • Governments into business and industry with identity as 'public sector' to provide and fulfil social objectives	• Manufacturing involving large manpower, called workforce • Labour, supervisory and managerial staff identified through a hierarchy • Unity of command and chain of relations identified • Role fixing along with responsibilities connected with • Division of labour, collecting together of labour into workshops and the division of the labour pool into specific tasks • Connecting through the human chain and extend distribution to a larger horizon • Value for labours and resources • A man acting as the power unit of output
Machinofacture Regime • Machines to mega-machines • Hand finished to uniform products	• Machinofactures involving the application of mechanical processes and power through machinery in factories together with further division of labour

Development of Business Process (Phase 2)

Scientific Management Regime • Taylorism in place • Effectiveness of managerial actions • Divisional and functional coordination • Divisional and functional control • Identity and accountability of all with respect to the desired output	• Work study—objective of work identified • The subjection of the work process to scientific study in the context of the industry and business • Enhanced fineness of the division of labour into specific tasks • Enforcing control and supervision • Segregated output measures against each role identified • Accountability enforced for workers and managers

<table>
<tr><td>Fordism
• Mass production
• Assembly lines of production, storing and distribution
• Product standardization
• Large volumes of output</td><td>• The development of assembly-lines of production to take care of the need of the time bound production
• Product standardization to create impersonality of human intervention in the production process
• Creating engineered processes that controlled the pace of production
• Mass production
• Large volume of output</td></tr>
<tr><td>Technology-driven Output
• Flexibility in the production
• Mega-production regime
• Customized output
• Less labour and a higher degree of automation
• Robotics in productions, distributions and value engineering
• Continuous improvements
• Design engineering, product engineering and process development for higher market share and revenues</td><td>• Flexible Production methods suited to the sudden need of the markets
• Extra large-scale production for the entire period divisible among various components and splits
• ICT supported production methods
• Competent system to respond positively to quick feedback from the markets and redesign production and distribution accordingly
• Knowledge-based process connecting and synchronizing man-machine dynamics
• Smart system and smart product through the application of digital methods in all major areas of business and process satisfying the customer's real-time need and expanding into the markets</td></tr>
</table>

'Industrial regime, machinofacture regime, scientific management regime, Fordism and technology-driven output are the broad phases of the growth of the production system in the context of the global industry.' Whereas the level, pace, nature and strength of industrialization differs widely from one nation to the other. It is incidental to the companies that the economic cycles are understood properly.

'These stages map fairly closely on to the long-wave sequence, which can have the approximate resemblance with the Kondratiev wave.' The transformation associated with the transition from manufacture to machinofacture is actually a kind of revolutionary change in the system.

The application of scientific management principles to the production process emerged in the rising phase and developed more fully in the next phase. The bases of Fordist mode of production were established during this phase but reached their fullest development during the phase of peak performance.

The Fordist mode of production system was epitomized by very large-scale production units, using assembly-line manufacturing techniques and producing large volumes of standardized products for mass-market consumption. It was a type of production especially characterized for particular industrial sectors, suited to the requirements of automobiles. Not all sectors, or all production processes, lent themselves to such a system, but it was seen to be the main characteristic of the last phase.

The Fordist mode of production gave a huge cost advantage and allowed companies, particularly the automobile companies of global scale. However, the abnormal rise in the global petroleum prices during the early 1970s and the late 1970s of the 20th century imposed a compulsive transformation in the pattern of automobile engines, and thereby the entire automobile industry and all other machines using petroleum fuel had to transform their technology from 'least fuel concerned' to 'most fuel concerned'.

The traditional automakers, rather the giants in the field from the West, had to take back seats in the global markets. The emergence of new leaders from the East was phenomenal. It got spread to all industries. Fuel-efficient cars and engines became the driving force of the industry. Kondratiev wave actually became distinct with the Fordism which had dominated the markets for a long period of close to six decades.

Technology became the core driving force henceforth. Global economy became fuel concerned. With this change in the economic model, the focus of global society got shifted to the development of new technology that suits the requirement of new age.

Age of computers, electronics, telecommunications, IT, biological technology, nanotechnology, microsystems, robotics, AI, digital transactions, e-commerce, e-transmissions, e-education, cyber society and so on emerged replacing the old and previous mode of production, and thereby the human living underwent dramatic changes.

Flexi-production System and Process

The production system has been given elemental flexibility which depends on the intrinsic capacity of the system to keep the entire productive forces and elements in mind and to have the same utilized once the objective function of the productive system is required to undergo change. The desired change in the production system could be based on the pattern set for the production before the onset of that production lot or the same could be because of the sudden change in the competitive factors of the markets compelling the brand to make adjustments with the new trends of the markets for the same.

Indian consumer market had to readjust and reorient itself because of the strong wave of Ayurveda-based concept emerged from the Indian soil. The impact of this Ayurvedic wave was so powerful that almost all companies of multinational or transnational origin had to adopt some version of the similar inputs of Ayurvedic concepts in some way or the other.

Daily necessity items or household goods, personal care items, food replacements, staple food items, consumable fluids, home furnishing, designs, small appliances, household utilities and so on are just a few among the plethora of such items and product categories that had to be adjusted with Ayurvedic elements added to them. Natural herbal origin of ingredients into medicinal and paramedical products became elements of strong sentiment and belief. Companies needed to explore those aspects and find out through product innovations how to develop them and finally to actually integrate them into the production system.

R&D of companies need to explore and find out the product mix in such a fashion that it allows respective companies to reorient their production process to include these influences of the markets. MNCs and TNCs could make these quick readjustments to hold the fort of the market, at least, partially, as their production system had the inbuilt flexibility involved in it.

The key to production flexibility today lies in the deep and extensive use of ICT, which provides more sophisticated control over production.

Two particularly important processes are as follows:

- The science and technology of flexible specialization
- The process of flexible mass production

The potential of these flexible technologies is immense, and their implications are enormous. They involve three major tendencies:

- *Information intensity:* This is a trend towards information intensity, rather than energy or materials intensity, in production. Therefore, the current position is that of a *diversity* of production systems where the relative importance of specific processes is changing. In fact, no single production system is ever completely dominant. Even during the heyday of Fordist mass production, there were firms and sectors in which small-scale, more craft-based production persisted.
- *High velocity and volume of production:* This is much-enhanced flexibility of production that challenges the old best practice concept of

mass production in respect of the process and output of production. A high volume of output is no longer necessary for high productivity; this can be achieved through a diversified set of low-volume products.

- *Risk-return trade-off through continuous optimization:* Since rapid technological change becomes less costly and risky, the 'minimum change' strategy in product development is less necessary for cost-effectiveness. Also, the new technologies allow a profitable focus on segmented rather than mass markets; products can be tailored to specific local conditions and needs.

A major change in labour requirements, in terms of both volume and type of labour, occurs.

This involves certain new-age practices in the corporate strategies with respect to the manpower involved:

- Shift towards multi-tasking rather than narrow labour specialization
- Greater emphasis on teamworking
- Individualized payments systems

Even when all the emphasis is on flexible production, there is still a good deal of mass production and indeed of craft production. This summarizes some of the mixed behaviour between the major systems of production.

The five features of the evolved patterns of organizations, as mentioned above, indicate the varieties which ideally present a new form of organizations with everchanging features and specifications. Entities having presence across the globe are those who have gathered the best abilities to garner the resources towards the best and most optimum utilization of the strengths and transform the intrinsic worth into the corporate value in material and financial terms.

Mode of production that affects and impacts the basis of organizations are those elements that actually contribute to market extensions and further deriving of utility from the markets. A true achiever enterprise should be the one the world looks for.

The Composite Organization in Global Markets

The Internets and Intranets of Global Corporations

A network of communications becomes very important in the management process of a TNC. TNCs are usually very large. TNCs are present in many countries with senior executives drawn from many countries. They create a global environment within the organization. There are many TNCs which are larger in the magnitude of business than the economy of

Multiple Factors of Production

Technology • Types • Patterns • End use • Features • Focus • Relation with corporate objectives	**Craft Production** • Simple and flexible tools • Non-standardized components • Inheritance of expertise • Customized production to suit customer preference of uniqueness	**Mass Production** • Complex but rigid machinery • Standardized components • Averse to switching production frame • Heavy time loss & cost incurs for switching production pattern	**Flexi-production** • Highly flexible production methods • Modular components and systems • Ease of switching to different production system • Quick adoption of new product and new process
Labour Force • Skill set • Professionalism • Impersonality • Polyvalence • Teamwork • Adaptability of new technology	• High skill • Professionalism in production process • Continuous improvement of skill • Adopting new knowledge • Adopting new technology and process	• Lack of personal colours to production • Interchangeable labour utility • Uniformity in the production system • Impersonality in the labour usage	• Multi-skilled labour • Polyvalent worker • Teamwork • Spirit of work synchronized with the

(Continued)

(Continued)

Supplier Relationship • Personal • Functional • Connectivity • Quantum • Proximity • Preventive	• Very close contact between customer and others • Supplier having direct impact on the production and process • Proximity of suppliers being located within close connectivity	• Distant relationships with suppliers • Both functionally and geographically oriented • Large inventories held at assembly plant just in case of exigency • Back up for Supply Disruption	• Very close relationships with Suppliers • Functionally tiered system of suppliers • Use of 'just-in-time' delivery systems • Encourages geographical proximity between customers and suppliers
Production Features	• Relatively low batches of production	• Extremely high-production lot	• Extremely high quantum
Product Variety • Range • Features • Market requirements • Modifications • Adaptability • Standardization	• Extremely wide range of products • Each product customized • Product suited to specific requirements of the Market	• Narrow range of product differentiation • Set of standardized product groups • Diverse designs with only minor modifications • Narrow product modifications	• Increasingly wide range diversity • Set of large number of differentiated product categories • Production process with adaptability to modify at the external features of product

many countries. TNCs thus provide huge support to the global professionalization and creation of value.

Although TNCs come in all shapes and sizes, there are two basic characteristics apply to all of them, whether they are involved in manufacturing, services, agriculture or resource exploitation.

- TNCs are connected to the world through networks and with their own organization present in other countries through a unique system called networks within networks. They are structured through a myriad of complex relationships, transactions, exchanges and interactions within their own internal corporate network and between that network and those of the other key actors with whom TNCs must interact.
- The fact that a TNC's networks are spread across and embedded within different national jurisdictions and contexts means that coordinating and controlling its internal and external networking activities are vastly more complex than a purely domestic firm.

There are unique sub-organizations within a TNC. Some of these are as follows:

- The CEO Council
- The CFO Council
- The CMO Council
- The Chief Knowledge Officer (CKO) Council

The CEO Council is the formation of a top association of the CEOs of the TNC based at different countries. This is usually considered as the highest policy and strategy evaluation and strategy re-engineering combination of the TNC. The communication network among the members of this CEO Council is considered as the core guiding element for a TNC. Some of the specific tasks the CEO Council undertakes are:

- Strategic interventions within the territories and collaboration with the transnational entities for better business opportunities
- Benefits available in one of the country-specific entities to embrace and spreading the effects across
- Networking on business process and connecting the business prospects through collaborative enterprising or initiative of business
- Cross investments in the shares and cross holding of shares of one country unit with the other with a view to prevent any kind existential threat like hostile takeovers
- Co-sharing of knowhow, expertise, knowledge, specific skill, excerpts of innovations and so on

- Allowing R&D to flow forward and share the results among the national entities
- Collectively taking care of any global challenge arising out of political, social, cultural, economic and climatic issues
- Networking with the global institutions and organizations with regulatory implications for facilitating business across the globe
- Any kind of disaster and catastrophe of global scale to manage collectively under collaborative communications among the national units across the world

The CFO Council plays a very important role in terms of the following very important aspects of global business:

- Relocation of funds from firms within a country
- Repatriation of net profit from one country to the other or from one market to the other
- Procurement of optimum funding options from the most feasible source
- Expanding the investor base through the share participation
- Maintaining share prices in the stock markets
- Enhancing corporate valuation through an optimum investment portfolio
- Investment risk and solvency management within the territory
- Hedging against the currency risk and risk of international funds movement
- Financing options in each domestic region for constant liquidity at an optimum level

The CMO Council coordinates among them on the issues of marketing. The major issues are:

- New influences in the existing markets in a region of the world
- Developing marketing spread of a new product and services and spreading the mix of new set of products and services to new markets to create proper global diversification
- Changes in the basic structure of demand in one region may be supported by the providence of a matching variety from the other
- Developing and creating global trends to facilitate the marketing process of national entities
- Co-branding with relevant partners in other nations and within nations to enhance the market share and have market growth in place
- Cost and time efficiency in the promotion strategies
- Creating long-term global competitive advantage in the strategic positioning of the products and services

- Sharing of the excerpts of marketing research for the benefit of understanding by counterparts in different nations of the same parent company

The CKO Council coordinates among the members on the issues of knowledge management. Important issues are:

- Cross-cultural values to exchange and interchange among the members to create cultural competence across the TNC throughout the world
- Integrated R&D to create intellectual property rights (IPR) and benefit the technological development and process augmentation of the national companies spread across different locations of the world
- Sharing of specific knowledge which is unique to a region with other members in other nations to create a knowledge pool among the members of human force spread across the nation
- Sharing of unique technological process among the member nations
- Manpower loaning among the national entities on deputation or assignments for a specific period
- Creating a global knowledge pool and drawing competent people from various locations to act as a team of experts to provide support or consultancy in deserving cases
- Manpower enrichment academy to benefit the entire TNC from all relevant aspects of business and corporate management

Unbounded Organizations of TNCs

TNCs have a unique feature of broadness. They are ever expanding. Any new opportunity found anywhere goes to the advantage of TNCs. It is actually made possible because of the features that are made autonomous in the system of the TNCs. They bank on the relational network of the national enterprises in their respective regions.

This relational network practice of a TNC raises the issue of the boundaries of the organizations. Questions may be valid as to where its organizational boundaries begin and also where they end.

In a legal sense, of course, the boundary of a firm is clear; companies have to be registered in the jurisdictions in which they operate. National regulations and laws apply to them in most situations. However, in some cases, the issues of international law may come into place. If the national entities maintain their respective legal and regulatory obligations, then chances of getting into international legal conflict are reduced significantly.

The firms that operate across national boundaries have to follow the rules of the destination country with respect to the trade process that is undertaken. In all possibilities, there is a very less international legal framework for business in general except for the restrictions and guidelines maintained by the global institutions relevant to the field of trade.

Nevertheless, at a TNC's core is a set of formally organized rules and conventions, regulated and institutionalized through the firm's own internal mechanisms. But in a functional sense—especially when we see them as networks within networks—a TNC's boundaries are much less clear. The distinction between what is going on inside and outside is not only very fuzzy but also continuously in a state of flux. We need to explore these complex internal and external relationships of TNCs in order to show how and where their operations are coordinated, controlled and configured.

The organizational boundaries of TNCs are usually identified through the following:

Network of relations outside and network actions inside:

- TNCs set out the basic framework for network analysis. It shows that different parts of a TNC have network relationships both inside and outside the firm's boundaries. The important point to note is that a subsidiary is not solely embedded within a rigid hierarchical corporate structure but may have business relationships network outside that structure that are specific to its operations.
- The configuration of a business network is specific to each individual subsidiary. Some subsidiaries may be embedded in relationships that are both externally and internally connected with the TNC. This may be, let's say, applicable in the case of a subsidiary while other subsidiaries may have external business relationships only.
- This can be a distinguishing factor between the external and corporate process.
- Individual business relationships can range from the proximity of connection to a high degree of mutual exchange of resources and procedures.
- For a high degree of mutual exchange that involves mechanistic resources, it is treated as a high degree of involvement between the parent company located in one nation and the subsidiary located in another.
- There may be cases when a subsidiary is dominated by highly involved relationships of external in nature and somewhat internal relationships within the broader boundary of the global organization or both.
- Some other cases may be prevalent where, other subsidiaries, in contrast, may have only relationships consisting of close exchanges between external internal or both.

- Within the sphere of the same industry, since every relationship has its own specific features and background, it is always expected that a high degree of variation occurs as regards involvement both within the individual subsidiary and between the different subsidiaries in a TNC.
- The nature and complexity of the broader industry environments in which the firm operates, including the nature of competition, technology, regulatory structures and so on make it more flexible than others without that element.
- The firm's specific background and physical position, including its culture and management style are considered as a kind of accepted practices built up over a period, producing a particular and unique identity of its own in the context of the business and economic environment.

TNCs and MNCs Culture Contaminations

Although they are separated from each of their segments or subsidiaries from the other, MNCs and TNCs are usually considered by many social activists located in different countries as the polluting agents of national culture.

The head office location is considered as the home country; both MNCs and TNCs have received this kind of identity from various countries of their new expansions. A home country influenced by these enterprises is considered alien in many cases, creating social resistance of different kinds. This influence is identified as something foreign in nature and draws more attention from many national or local groups.

It is a matter of concern by many management strategists why quite often it is assumed that TNCs are all much the same, regardless of their geographical origin. This is actually not the case.

TNCs are created through a legal and structured process of combining many elements where the cognitive, cultural, social, political and economic characteristics of the national home country continue to play a major role in the functional orientation of the company.

It appears from the functional attitudes of many TNCs and MNCs that even if many of them may have the investments and shareholding patterns as same, they do not have the same functional pattern.

From a particular, regional or national origin enterprises may have somewhat identity in the style of management but are hardly identical in their economic, commercial and managerial attributes. This is evidently the case almost always. Within any national context, there are distinctive corporate cultures, arising from the firm's own specific corporate history, which predispose it to area-based systems. Because of many such reasons,

Features	MNC or TNC	National, Local or Domestic	Globally Integrated
Management structures and philosophies: • Nature • Process • Attitude, approach and limits • Defined objectives • Jurisdiction of operation • Span of control • Business portfolio • Nature of control • Global to national • Management pattern • Diversity and homogeneity • Goal	• More of a decentralized pattern of command and control • Decentralized decisions for implementing the plans to fulfil the defined objectives of the corporation • Business units as portfolio investments to satisfy the concepts of costs and profit centres • Responsibility centres across investment units or asset bundles • Informal connections with formal process of activities to fulfil each objective • Headquarter control to deliver as per the objective function and the declared values of the corporation globally	• Domestic control • National law and regulatory implications • Centralized across national jurisdiction • Unity of command, unity of purpose • Hierarchy or functional distribution of authority and responsibility • Core corporate philosophy to match with the industry imperatives • Regionalization within the national jurisdiction • Domestic socio-economic-political impacts on business • Driven by core objective divided among functions	• Global hub to coordinate all resources across the regions of operation in the world • Shared asset utilization across the places of operations • Sharing of strategic human resources • Divesting among partner units of other countries the overall global responsibilities to fulfil global commitments • Decision-making in domestic regions but made compatible with the pattern and core elements of decisions of the global headquarter • Data sharing through process integration • Simulation of resources and activities • Networking among all on real time

Features	MNC or TNC	National, Local or Domestic	Globally Integrated
Management communication, control and policy objectives: • Profit-making from business • Optimization of resources • Value integration • Perspective providing • Leadership values • Norms and practices • Network within and across • Fulfilling objectives	• Financial independence of enterprises across each national boundary • Cross holding of shares by the other entities belonging the same group • Investment sourcing with mutual credibility and global strength • Headquarter to National Unit Control made informal yet formal • Global objective, local perspective • Homogeneous and purposive coexistence	• Financial decisions taken within the territory in an integrated manner • Long-term investments made through centralized decisions • Short-term financing decisions left to the scopes of the organization at its regional headquarters • Formal intra company network of communications using standard or specific routes and networks to work for the organization and reach out to all	• Controlled communications • Flexibility in the speed and process of communication • Management control remains open ended • Versatility and focused intent of the corporate leadership • Invisible yet very clearly understood norms and practices • Mutual understanding is the basis of transactions among people
Attitude and response to the global dynamics, administrative control: • Planning • Organizing • Coordinating • Communicating • Management Control • Adaptability • Resource and Competency Policies • Brand Equity • Cultural Sensitivity • Decision Making Trends	• Formal Management Structures followed in terms of • Formal Planning • Structured Organization • Formal and Informal Communication • Management Control • Adapting and Leveraging Parent Company Competencies • Leveraging the Brand Advantage Globally • Functional Control spread across territories.	• Culturally, more sensitive to the local traditions, customs, traits, social norms and socio-economic patterns generally accepted by most people in the regions concerned • Management control having impacts from the local or the national administrative focus • Remain stick to the policies adopted. However, flexibility in terms of accommodating customers allowed running, enhancing business volume and value	• Global in magnitude and local in interactions • Network of leaders from all destinations • Shared views and attributes given priority in the decision-making • Accumulating elemental coordinates • Resource sharing • Optimizing human expertise • Flexible process • Core values remain in focus

(Continued)

(Continued)

Features	MNC or TNC	National, Local or Domestic	Globally Integrated
Issues of technology, process, manpower, knowledge and resources: • Approach to R&D • Knowledge orientation • Methods of production • Adaptability • Management research in different functional areas • Standardizations • Strategic objectives • Core values • Cost behaviour • Manpower policies • Cultural impacts • Outlook to world	• Global range of technology • Expanding into local requirements for technology • Emphasis on continuous improvement of technology used in the production, process, distribution, communication, product research, consumer research and normative technology • More of a strategic concern than the plans in hand • Quick in adaptations of new methods and practices in managing enterprises	• National range of technology • Less of R&D but emphasize on the incremental changes in the existing set of things • Labour intense mode of production to benefit the society and remain committed to the social and national needs • Connected with the national considerations • Resource optimizing on national issues and national perspectives • Cost advantage through finance and manpower optimization.	• Global range of R&D • Global standards in management process and functions • Global specifications of products • Quality control utmost importance • Benefitting from the scales of production • Catering to demands arising from any region of the world • Mechanistic approach in the management process to draw cost advantage and provide value maximization • Universal values.

some of the largest TNCs have adopted sophisticated global network system containing elements of demographics, product, place, culture, structures and involving dual reporting links. Now companies are using their own cloud technology, big data store, supercomputers, the Intranet and Internet and integrated ICTs, among many other methods or devices.

Concerns of the Technology Manager

When in a new territory, the company usually faces certain issues which are concerns of the local societies and people around. Among many such concerns, some are the tip of the icebergs. These are as follows:

- What is newly brought in by the new transnational or multinational enterprise?
- What is the visible benefit the local and national society can expect to derive from the presence of the transnational or multinational corporation?
- Is there any significant long-term benefit to the nation in terms of technological development or economic impact of its presence?
- Is it poised to offer any significant value to any social or economic segment of the national region?

Successful TNCs and MNCs have always proved helpful to the destinations from where they have targeted their operations. Unless the products or the services are adequately accepted by the local society, and a sufficient number of customers chose the company for its products or services, it cannot operate from that territory.

The TNCs and MNCs have consistently provided prominence, as large entities, to the local market sentiments. They have given prominence to understand the set of consumer demands and specific sentiments. As global corporations, these organizations have expanded overseas to capitalize on their firm-specific assets of technological leadership or marketing power.

The ideal type of organizing involves far more formal coordination and control by the corporate headquarters overseas. The transnational and multinational organizations have, in effect, created a portfolio of subsidiaries of quasi-independent businesses. These organizations see their overseas operations as linked units to their controlling domestic corporation. Thus, the corresponding units present in the respective national domains are more dependent on the centre for the transfer of knowledge, and the parent company makes greater use of formal systems of control. TNCs and MNCs are better equipped to leverage the knowledge of technology and capabilities of human resources of its parent company, but its particular configuration and operating systems tend to make it more responsive than the national-level companies.

The Technology Manager's Awareness Required on Areas That Are Critical in Success or May Lead to Failure in the Business

- A manager needs to understand that a match is required between the functional climate within and the prevailing environment around.
- Lack of proper understanding of consumer behaviour or customer characteristics may lead to disaster for the business.
- Inappropriate plans or poorly defined plans for the functional agenda, investments, resources, risk-taking decisions, undertaking projects, financial budgets, operating budgets, marketing strategies, technology choice, client relationship, promotional inputs and social and environmental commitments may lead the company to a position of risk and uncertainty.
- Failing to convince the executives on the objectives of the company and functional objectives of the functions, the executive is attributed to cause damage to the cause of the function.
- Allowing inaccurate data to persist and influence the decision-making process may prove fatal in the performance indicators of the company.
- Lack of development of 'trust factor' among all functional managers and not being able to trust managers and people on the floor may lead to erosion of motivation among the important manpower and finally lead to loss of business value.
- Overestimating resource competencies and poor capacity planning are destined to dislodge the functional objectives from their core focus and likely to lead to organizational distress.
- Unable to be on to the path of change—in technology, process, system, management style, outlook to the people and society—may lead the company to the limits of proper existence.
- Unable to develop employee commitment may lead to the loss of precious human energy and thus affect the profitability of the organization.
- The inadequate communications among the members of the organization, customers, coordinating government officials and other relevant stakeholders may erode the solvency of the company.
- Inadequate and inappropriate idea of time and cost management may risk the revenues of the organization.

- Wrong induction of manpower in strategic positions may prove hazardous and disturbing for the organization.
- Failing to understand the nature and magnitude of the organizational change in the face of changes happening in the society and market may lead to the bankruptcy of the organization.
- Lack of appropriate corporate leadership may fail to infuse energy into the system.
- Departure from ethical practices may pollute the work environment of the organization and in the long run, pushes the organization down in ranking and erodes its own brand value and future prospect in the market.

Technological Revolutions

The world has witnessed the Himalayan transformations in the technology of human usage, since the last half a century. The invention of the computing system and computers as the tool in the hands of human beings have actually made so much change in the human life that has been very rare in human history. The journey of 50 years has brought in so much change that was not possible during the last two millennia of the human journey.

The kind of things that modern society has provided was never found before in human history. However, the human condition and the life of human being had a remarkable level of achievement in ancient India only. Nowhere in the world was such advancement, or even a tiny fragment of that present. The ancient Indian way of depicting thing was through human knowledge. This knowledge of the material or the empirical world was considered equally important from the point of view of holistic Indian philosophy.

Technological artefacts, tools and products were in use in ancient Indian civilization. It all started during the Vedic period when the Vedic sages developed their realization of the Supreme, God, through their meditation and devotion. A large number of the masses were absorbed in the consciousness of the divinity and used to maintain a simple life without any external elemental dependence. But a class of people, who were known as a kingly class, was into developing art and science of living superior life. The technology was developed to a height that is a matter of awesome view even now, at this age of supercomputers and nanoscience. On the one hand, extremely small in the scale of micro of micros, and the other hand, large sizes as the mega-machines and very large magnitude of things have embraced modern living.

Some of the amazing things that ancient India had in its possession were wonders. Aeroplanes used during the period of the Ramayana and the Mahabharata were approximately sometime in between 4,000 and

6,000 years before the birth of Christ. The ballistic weapons used during those periods were actually sharper than that of the current ballistics. Powerful nuclear bombs or hydrogen bombs which have huge destructive powers are actually less in their magnitude and accuracy destructions than the 'Brahmastras' which was in the hand of human being and made use of as well during that period. Stem cell research is yet to reach a point of success where most dead cells which are just expired can be brought back to life through transplanting living stem cell from a living person and properly positioning that in the dead body. However, this miraculous expertise was available with ancient Indian physicians who had actually revived life into the dead. Lord Lakshman, who lost his life in war, was brought back to life through the application of proper medicine. Wish technology is a field where a large number of scientists have been trying to develop to proceed to the next level of technology for the world.

The ancient Indian society had lots of pieces of evidence created where wish had its physical applications through certain means not visible actually. The wish was more of a biological blend of technology than a device-based variety. The ancient Indian thoughts were oriented towards the process of synchronization with the human system. In the modern world now, the actions of the range of biometrics and bio instrumentations together are trying to have a reach of that. The neural network used in the capital market for the predicting the stock prices in future or natural algorithms using the biometrics are some of the areas the modern world is trying to catch up with that of the ancient Indian achievements on the scales of primary science and applied science.

Magic of the Ultra Small

The foundation of the modern form of nanotechnology was actually laid by Professor Richard Feynman, a famous physicist, during his lecture series hinting at the amazing options available at the bottom end of dimensions. Just before the sixth decade of the 20th century, Feynman had urged upon the scientists to look into the small to super small. Feynman's advice of 'there is plenty of rooms at the bottom' had pushed the scientific attention to the realm of small to very tiny. Gradually 'nanoparticle' and 'nanotechnology' came in place by the early 1980s of the 20th century. Now, this nanotechnology has gone into a wide range of applications in human society with its strong and very decisive applications in the following areas among others:

- Energy
- Medicine and drugs
- Nanodevices
- Nanobiotechnology

- Optical engineering
- Defence and security
- Bioengineering
- Cosmetics
- Nano fabrics

Synthesis of Nano Materials

This can be understood as having two approaches:

- Bottom-up
- Top-down

When the elements in the atomic structure form cluster through recombining with each other, a new type of formation is generated that leads to the creation of a new identity in terms of the material components of the new formation. These formations are usually done by atom-by-atom and particle-by-particle formations leading to very tiny crystals in the scale of the same nanoparticles. Some of the wide range of applications are:

- Scanning tunnelling microscope (STM)
- Atomic force microscope (AFM)
- Transmission electron microscopes (TEM) and scanning electron microscopes (SEM)
- Dynamic light scattering (DLS)
- X-ray photoelectron spectroscopy (XPS)
- Ultraviolet visible spectroscopy (UVS)
- Nano-dimension, usually termed as nanometre, is one billionth part of a meter

Other important and direct applications are:

- Nanoparticle can easily penetrate through ultra-thin membranes of small cells. Thus, it is helping a lot in the detection of cancer or predict the chances of cancer in a human cell.
- This analyses the genetic features and attributes of an individual and can do many penetrating analysis of human and animal gene.
- With this technology, the environmental cleansing of pathogens is possible.
- Nano coating of the membranes of different types of cells can be used in the treatment of cancer in certain parts of the body.
- Being used profusely in genetic engineering, this has actually many dimensions—correcting the genetic code towards genetically modifying some of the features that would help human being to correct any of the unwanted aspects.

Nanotechnology offers various scopes of various positive benefits to human beings in maintaining human health and various other ways to support human activity positively.

The Mega and Magnificent

Apart from the ultrasmall technology, modernism has in its scope the super large as well. NASA has been doing outer space observation during the last half a century or more periods. NASA's observatory is not only the largest of its kind in the world but most magnificent as well. It is now in a position to catch hold of the truth of the physical presence of stellar bodies in the space. A human space mission to various destinations in the space on one hand and exploring the nearby planets and the solar system on the other has a strong potential to unfold huge opportunities to human society towards a better life for all.

Large systems are required to manufacture large aircraft carriers for naval use on sea, exploration of seabed resources such as fossils and planktons and so on. Large systems are required for installations of manufacturing processes and delivery facilities for aircrafts, ships, submarines, integrated plants for nuclear capacities and wide infrastructures, such as seashore bridges and long river bridges.

The European Organization for Nuclear Research, known as CERN, machine in Switzerland is one of the largest projects with the sophistication of very tiny nanotechnology inbuilt inside and time fragments of tracing particle movements brought down to the level of micro—a micro fraction of a second. A combination of super-large dimension, capacity and span on one hand, and ultrasmall in dimension and time fragments on the other are the features of the research installation at such experimental capacities in the world. Rocket propellants, space stations, shipbuilders, submarine builders, defence production stations and many other facilities which at present require a combination of ultrasmall and super large scales together to produce very effective and utility things.

The Emergence of AI

Now, the world is heading towards a new revolution in the form of accelerating the wheels of change through powerful synthetics, called AI. This is not only going to provide a massive and very fast pace of change but also transformations in the form of the patterns, pace, faces, motives, goals, attributes, dynamics and results of human expectations and living. It has already developed powers in decision-making science and technology.

Decisions based on multi-layered algorithms lead to a set of decision matrices offering the best choice among other suitable alternatives. AI has been in use for a few years in various fields with a reasonable degree of effectiveness and efficiency. Many questions have been raised against the role of AI in future.

The fundamental issue is whether AI shall produce the ultimate good for profitability and sustainability of companies in future. Whether its application absorbs into the process the investments made and costs incurred or not. However, once it takes off properly in larger scales of applications, the amount of investments required would be spread across the points of usage pushing off the profitability and solvency of each enterprise applying this in the decision-making and application process.

As of now, the world has experienced a wide range of activities using AI-based decision and functional enterprises. These range from agro farming, crop harvesting, banking to customer service and so on. AI has a widespread use with a generic approach and specific choice. AI requires basic things for the enterprise and the functional applications in decision science and its application base in the form of its growing into the super brain and million appendages of functions in its making of things and adequate impacts on the zones of applications.

Enabling AI

Technological process that enables AI to come up has certain layers of identity fixing and making. Some of the core aspects of this are as follows:

- Development platform (static, dynamic, rotational and end-use oriented)
- Analytic platform matched with business reality and needs
- Data architecture, data lakes, data mines and so on
- Vast processing power (multi-trillion factor multiplications)
- mix of ultrasmall (nano) and mega (super large) in versatility and capacity
- Big data and data governance
- Building AI solutions architecture
- Vast data storage
- Ever-expanding memory
- Plasticity in formations and usage
- Identify quantified objectives for AI in terms of the current business and the future requirements of it

- AI to comply with national laws, rules, social norms and ethical implications
- Business complexity to ease out through deployment of data scientists, data engineers, user interface designers, visualization specialists, graphic interpreters, building AI sensitivity to partial responses in traditional business portfolio

Issues in AI That Require Focus

- Proper knowledge set in the organization for AI analytics.
- Compatibility of AI with the business objectives and core values
- Industry-specific, economy-specific, region-specific, product/service-specific, culture-specific analytics for AI (in fact, the AI architecture refers to its enabling use in areas of core activities of corporate or social organizations. Each of these has to be considered important in contributing to the factor of shaping the business strategy and the follow-up actions to fulfil that).
- AI in the long-term spectrum that includes the issues of the short term. (However, the relations between the long-term spectrum and that of the short-term need to be ascertained continuously so that the goal-oriented functions are less affected by the divergence in the progressions of the company either).
- Data algorithmic bias, data authorization, data transfer into a visible format in packages of use.
- Cost and value match for AI. (For every activity of an organization, the cost and value propositions are cross-checked. Each element of the activity of the organization, in general, and specific activity, in particular, requires the associated cost and value data to assess its implications. Cost data has two splits: direct and indirect whereas, the value data is considered on its implicit terms. Both cost and value data are subject to the conditions of the market and the economy prevailing, on one hand, and the features of the company, on the other. Both depend upon the level of investments made, capital of the enterprise, the brand equity developed and the overall corporate climate of performance. If the enterprise can make a continuous synergy between the cost and value of the works within the entity, it can reach the corporate goal with better results)
- AI-based performance matrices for senior executives. (For the group of people working in the functional or administrative domain of the manager, generalized and specific performance matrices can be developed to use in the process of the business for getting the performance indicator of the persons contained in the team and then it

vouch for this against the actual work done in terms of the magnitude and the quality of the delivery of the person. Same can be applied against a group of people or a large group in an organization.)

- Cross-functional knowledge exchange towards building an interdisciplinary team of people to remain as a strategy focus group and assist the big data and analytic run forward fast with the given purpose.
- AI—profitability set up and AI—solvency set up to offer constant guide. (These could be the guiding architectures to understand readily the direction of the business—whether the business is heading towards profitability or not, and whether in the long term, the solvency of the business is protected or not. The guiding notes thus obtained, could be any way to redress the condition of the business and then to get back to it with further agenda of progress forward).

Managerial Implications of AI

AI has a growing impact on corporate management. Basically, in the areas of decision-making and then in the management process, the impact of AI has been growing steadily. The traditional ways of managing enterprises are gradually getting replaced by the decision science as ordained by the factors of AI.

AI transforms the decision-making process from a traditional system of hierarchy-based decision matrix to a different type. The transition may be structured as in the following table.

Advantages of AI-based Decision

Markets and economies create situations anew always and keep on changing the relevant factors of influence, making the corporate journey risky in most of the situations. The AI-driven management system has a better capacity to thrive through the relatively riskier segments of the market. Even though AI-powered organizations have the advantage of skimming better revenue and profit from the market yet have superior safety architecture to create the risk-return trade-off in favour of the organization. The AI-based decision support system is agile and has the risk appetite to test the power of risk and extract better value from the market for the benefit of the stakeholders of the company.

With the replacement of the decision tools from complex manual exercises to the algorithmic process of generating decisions amidst the existing corporate culture, it requires to gather the strength of operations from the new system in terms of the participation of people in the organization without any element of hesitation in the process. Most mega corporations and businesses are continuing for a long period, they are not born digital,

Traditional Pattern of Organization	**Dominant Types**	**Hierarchy in Patterns**	**AI-driven Organization**
• Top-down decision variables. • Leader as a father. • Legends drawn from the top to drive the engine of movement and growth. • Carrot and stick as the major approach to work. • Experience counts more than the current knowledge about things. • *Senpai* and *kōhai* (Japanese) or *agraja-anuja* (Indian; the senior in age to junior): Seniors to obey first, both maintain interdependence. • The junior to listen to the senior first and then act • Revenue and cost should go hand in hand. Any investment made now has to maintain its efficiency to pull revenues and proceed towards making profit in real terms. • Justice always refers to the attitudes, efficiency and effectiveness of the person in the organization.	• Scientific knowledge as the spirit of work. • Decision support system involving models on manual and machine supports. • Work creates the ways to receive rewards. • Experience counts but for new developments in the technological advancements • Experience and knowledge interdependent with mutual support for organizational achievement. • Shorter ways of gain are welcome unless that contravenes the established norms of business and the industry. • Subjective orientation in the functions and actions becomes important in the face of the changing scenarios of the market and the economy.	• Top executives create the culture of functioning within the organization. • Senior executives create their own domain of resource mobilization and proper utilization of the same. • Senior is the person experienced in life and work and hence the junior has to receive knowledge and guidance from the junior. • Adoption of new technology is on the scale of expertise on that technology in terms of its applications in real work situation. • Seniors are mostly sceptical about final outcome of the new technology. Technologist has to satisfy the points raised by the seniors. • Job enrichment and multi skilling is also recommended for the seniors.	• Data-driven system • Algorithms in each stage of the data science to drive the inputs to a decision. • Scheduling of events with AI systems. • Each employee can produce a set of data based on thoughts, perceptions, preferences, ideas and considerations. • Corporate leaders need to provide vision that can motivate people in the organization to rally around a common goal. • AI-oriented culture needs to receive proper justification from the top management so that the workers and others in the organization develop a peace of mind about job security.

Traditional Pattern of Organization	Dominant Types	Hierarchy in Patterns	AI-driven Organization
• Culture of centripetal tendencies. • Wish drives the wheel of intent. • Individualization of the attributes. • Centralization of ownership and control. • Workmanship precedes the concerns of others. • Relevance of society and the environment understood in philosophical terms only.	• Discrete focus on the issues of corporate culture by individuals. • Rationale in the work and the process. • Objectives properly. communicated in collective terms. • Result orientation in the pursuit of the work and combinations.	• Responsibility follows from the identity. • Cultural norms follow the hierarchy of layers in the organizations. • Focus is laid on the achievement of the identified domains of assignments. • Mix of the result and the approach to the culture matters most. • Society and world identified as relevant based on the utility of the same.	• Experience-based or leader-driven decision-making rests a while. • Inputs to decisions and ingredients for decision comes from the general employees at large with diversified views. • Everyone has to trust the decision-making algorithms skimmed off from the data made available for taking decision.
• Command and control • Individualized approach in the systems and processes • Warmth of a family • Inputs to decision-making provided on personal notes • Rewards on personal scale • Duties override the rights of the individuals in the context of the organization • Personal and professional values to synchronize as both are supposed to contribute towards the overall growth of the organization.	• Functional activities presuppose the tuning of the functions across the core objective of the organization. • Colourless association of people discharging the assigned responsibilities. • Duties and rights match with each other within the boundaries of the organization. • Technology can be used as an added tool to service the functions and actions based on the chosen strategies and decisions.	• Decision flows from the top. • Compliance at the level of executions. • Feedback to tune the decisions mostly. • Decision variables drawn from the market as endorsed by the hierarchy • Permissible rights in the midst of plethora of duties to perform. • Rewards based on the volume of work and its quality. • Technology outputs are quite often argued against referring to the experienced outcomes.	• Vast range of scheduling permutations. • Hundreds of millions of options are distilled using the first level of algorithms. • Another algorithm to boil down those millions into just hundreds of relevant decision options based on data. • Final decision is made by planning managers and experienced people to select the optimized model for decision matrix.

so in these cases, the possibility of conflicts arises in the culture and traditions of the companies. Then, one of the most important tasks is to introduce a new digital culture that involves and recognizes the act of accommodating the existing pattern and cultural milieu of the company.

AI transforms the pattern of decision-making from the hierarchy-based, leader-oriented, experience-based, composite form of decision-making to impersonal and data-driven decision-making.

AI's approach is then to collect all relevant data with its degree of association with the core objective of business, to assimilate a vast pull of data, create the first level of decision algorithm to analyse the data and then to expose the data to the next-level algorithm for further fine-tuning suited to the need of the organization. After these steps are through, the AI scientists then present this shortlisted data to the relevant people in the corporate decision-making and choice closing to take a final call on that.

This approach is a mix of the AI system with the leading choice of the company. Obviously, this combination is a mix of the subjective choice and the objective—data-driven choice matrix.

Role of AI Analytics Translators in Business

Analytics translators are people who have knowledge of the business process and the relevant knowledge of the AI system and its implications. Analytics translators can bridge the business gap by pulling business people from the areas of operations, logistics-supply chain, distribution, marketing—sales, manufacturing, finance, investments, risk management, manpower, acquisition, motivation, development, retention and so on. AI has a strong potential into the ways of effective marketing on large-scale customer base—both current and potential. AI has actually a strong use in the following areas:

- Core analytic to match with the business objectives
- Aligning the corporate strategy with the AI outputs in the relevant aspect of business
- Talent recruitment, skill induction, training, talent development
- Performance management
- Big data—storage, assimilation, continuous scanning, data streaming and data support in the objective fulfilment
- Change management, new project adoption—scanning appropriation and so on
- Purposive codification of data
- Appropriation of business units, product units, territory units, functional units, project units, composite units

- Business control—oversight facilities and oversight analytics
- Overall Strategy making and dynamic strategy evaluation
- Policy objectives for profit maximization and wealth creations
- Shareholder value optimization for a higher level of transactions in the capital markets
- Branding and brand equity

AI-driven Superstar Firms

Globally, economies with reduced trade barriers are continuously attracting super-large firms to accommodate higher value and grow in overall national value. Growth is particularly strong in markets undergoing accelerated technological advances.

Large firms actually dominate the global economy by holding almost more than two-thirds of the global economic value. It has been reported by the World Bank in its *World Development Report 2019* that 'about 10 percent of the world's companies are estimated to generate 80 percent of all profits.' These are superstar firms. These firms shape the country's exports. Also, another segment of the study reported by the World Bank in its *World Development Report 2019*, says,

---

Study of 32 developing countries found that, on an average, the five percent largest exporters in a country account for a third of its exports, nearly half of export growth, and a third of growth due to export diversification' are due to these SUPERSTAR FIRMS. (World Bank Group, 2019)

Scale without Mass

Large firms contribute immensely towards providing a new shape to the domestic economy. This is particularly very dominant in developing economies. The digital economy has helped firms of very large scale to grow at a rapid rate. The digital market provides new opportunities for firms to stifle their competition. Technology has facilitated some of these superstar firms to rise to the top by way of crowding out their competitions across the global markets, and many others in the range of competitions have been dwarfed by these superstar firms. The World Bank has observed that 'Growth is particularly strong in markets undergoing accelerated technological advances.' (World Bank Group, 2019)

When the business creates value by way of combining the networks of idea generations, productions, marketing spread across globally, it becomes difficult to understand, locate and determine the actual source of value creation for the nations to assess the impacts of the fiscal value

for the revenue to the governments. Thus, through the process of diversification and spread of business across economies, the superstar firms generate additional revenues globally for themselves through applications of powerful tools of technology.

AI plays an important and sometimes the most important role for the superstar firms to ascertain the value optimization from the global business through spreading across the global business. As the *World Development Report 2019* has estimated that 'The top one percent of exporters in rich countries account for a large share of exports—on average, fifty five percent—than those in poorer countries.' The same report of the World Bank has echoed the strength of the technological transformations in economies as, 'Technological Change favors the most productive firms in each industry, incentivizing the reallocation of resources toward them. Digital technologies allow for fast scaling.—Platform-based business are on the rise across the globe, providing new opportunities to trade goods and services.'

It becomes clear that a global scale manager should be technologically conversant and proceed along with the growth of knowledge in the field of technology to draw and create competitive advantage in the marketplace to become the winner and achieve goals.

Reference

World Bank Group. (2019). *The world development report (WDR) 2019: The changing nature of work.* http://documents1.worldbank.org/curated/en/816281518818814423/pdf/2019-WDR-Report.pdf

CHAPTER 15

MANAGEMENT: THE CONCERN FOR SUSTAINABILITY

Sustainability is a major focus of management. This has to be viewed from various aspects as discussed under the following issues.

- Elements of sustainability in cosmic system
- Philosophical basis of sustainability
- Concerns for creating sustainability
- Creating sustainable enterprise
- Sustainable market
- Sustainable enterprise in business
- Technology, resource and process for sustainable business and market
- Concerns for sustainability in new enterprises
- Issues of sustainability for economic and social benefits
- Role of social systems and norms in maintaining sustainability

Sustainability: Compatibility with Cosmic Nature

A modern view of life and society is fundamentally connected with short-termism. The concern for now is dominant in the concerns of life. Although education and social learning add certain elements that are advancing attentions towards future, organizations and individuals rely on achievements and gains for a short period rather than for the long period. In the journey of life of organizations and individuals, the short term plays a major role, most of the times, much higher than the long term. Living now with all kinds of satisfaction in life has actually become primary in the design of life and the world. The animal world also relies on the 'living now' motive. The wide similarity is observed in the approach to life of wild animals and the major dynamics of the human society. Because of the dominant short-term orientation of life, most civilizations of the ancient world have perished, except the Indian civilization. The Indian civilization has survived through more than 30,000 years because of its fundamental inclination towards university and divine truth.

Philosophical Basis of Sustainability: The Role of Indian Civilization

The ancient civilisation of India differs from those Egypt, Mesopotamia and Greece, in that its traditions have been preserved without a break down to the present day. Until the advent of the archaeologist, the peasant of Egypt or Iran had no knowledge of the culture of his forefathers, and it is doubtful whether his Greek counterpart has any but the vaguest ideas about the glory of Periclean Athens. In each case there had been an almost complete break with the past. On the other hand, the earliest Europeans to visit India found a culture fully conscious of its own antiquity—a culture which indeed exaggerated that antiquity, and claimed not to have fundamentally changed for thousands of years. To this day legends known to the humblest Indian recall the names of shadowy chieftains who lived nearly thousands of years before Christ, and the orthodox brahmin in his daily worship repeats hymns composed even earlier. (Basham, 2004, p. 4)

The Indian civilization in the ancient period was the only one of its kind in the entire world which adopted universality as the way of life. The life and system developed in the ancient period in India were based on the spirit of universality. The Indian spirit was in favour of doing, thinking, wishing and visualizing goodness and well-being of all. Every human being was considered as unique and, at the same time, someone embodying the divine spirit within. European scholars talk of 'monotheism' and 'polytheism' to differentiate between the only form or representation of god and denying god's presence in any other form. This has been formed as a monotheist view. One god principle is based on the theory exclusion first and then compulsive inclusion by adopting the mechanism and forces of the world. The Indian belief that every human being possesses the same divinity within themselves makes the ideal true and universal. Indian sages of the ancient period had pronounced in their own context and invited the world to join the quest for truth and universality in life. Universality was formed in the faith. The supreme divine, in the abode, is god with a form. The same supreme is present in every life and organism as a vital spirit. This is invisible and does not have any tangible form or structure of any kind. This divinity is present in a subtle and minute entity within the living system. The sages had discovered the seabed of this supreme divinity at the inner core—the cave of human cardiac system. Deep inside the heart, a dark cave is imagined and the supreme centres its presence in human beings as the *atman*—the divine soul. This *atman* or the divine soul is situated in the human context but embodies with the spirit, potent and power of the supreme. The supreme is almighty. As he is almighty, he has the power to take any form whatsoever, can manifest himself as tangible, can reveal through any form and in many ways and is considered to have revealed through the forms of gods with differences in gender, look, emphasis and prominence. With a world population of 330 million or 33 crore, it was considered that god is present in 33 crore forms. The widest choice is because of India's spirit of individual freedom of choice and thought and at the same time honouring the choice and thoughts of all other individuals.

At most periods of her history India, though a cultural unit, has been form by internecine war. In statecraft her rulers were cunning and unscrupulous. Famine, flood and plague visited her from time to time, and killed millions of her people. ..Yet our overall impression is that in no other part of the ancient world were the relations of man and man and of man and the state so fair and humane. In no other early civilisation were slaves so few in number, and no other ancient lawbook are their rights so well protected as in the Arthashastra (of Kautilya). No other ancient lawgiver proclaimed such noble ideals of fair play as did Manu (in Manu Samhita). In all her history of warfare Hindu India has few tales to tell of cities put to the sword or of the massive of non-combatants. The ghastly sadism of the kings of Assyria, who flayed their captives alive, is completely without any parallel in ancient India. There was sporadic cruelty and oppression no doubt, but in comparison with conditions in their cultures, it was mild. To us, the most striking feature of ancient Indian civilisation is its humanity. (Basham, 2004, p. 9)

Collective Identity of an Enterprise

The Indian society has never opted for living in isolation. Never in its history, India has proved as an aggressor nation, but it has tried to convey the message of universal truth and divinity to the people of the world. India's spirit of divinity is actually the mindset of acceptability of individual liberty and the scope of individual potential. When European society was busy in witnessing the slave trade in general and slave fight in the arena, Indian society, guided by the sages, was busy in the realization of the divine truth. Roman citizens had the occasion of witnessing fun in the arena. They had to buy an entry ticket to enjoy the fun. A large number of citizens used to gather there. The fight was actually between a lion, kept hungry for two–three days and a slave who wants freedom. The slave would be freed if he can survive the light with that hungry lion. In the arena, a protected place, citizens used to enjoy the fight. The result was obvious, devouring of the slave by the hungry lion.

Some historians have observed some kind of soft slavery in certain cases in India as well. This may have been with a handful of landlords or certain bad kings, but never a phenomenon. India has never endorsed such inhuman in its history, but the spirit of truth and eternity has been lived on, and the idea and living experience have been spread across by sages and people of India. Winning was never a priority through any means in India. Rather in its quest for perfection, India has won in all ages. Winning in India spirit has been an automatic subset of the spirit of perfection, highlighted and upheld by Indian society always. Indian society had its inbuilt spirit of democracy which allowed everyone to enjoy the uniqueness in life on one hand and the spirit of collectiveness, on the other. Truth and its application in life created a bent of mind in India that has always created a focus in life that focuses on universality.

The inhabitants, in like manner, having abundant means of subsistence, exceed in consequence the ordinary stature, exceed in consequence the ordinary stature and are distinguished by their proud bearing. They are also found to be well skilled in the arts, as might be expected of men who inhale a pure air and drink the finest water. And while the soil bears on its surface all kinds of fruits which are known to cultivation, it has also underground numerous veins of all sorts of metals, for it contains much gold and silver and copper and iron in no small quantity and even tin and other metals, which are employed in making articles of use and ornaments, as well as the implements and accoutrements of war. ..It is accordingly affirmed that famine has never visited India, and that there has never been a general scarcity in supply of nourishing food. (Schwanbeck, 1877, p. 40)

Message from the Vedas

The sages of ancient India, in general, and during the Vedic period, in particular, had always taken initiatives towards maintaining truthful life. *Ritam vadishyami, satyam vadishyami*—I will always speak and maintain truth in life and apply the same truth in life—was the basic spirit of living by the truth. This is actually the spirit of eternal truth; the truth of our empirical living is always a subset of this truth. Eternal truth is that truth which one realizes through his living of life in eternity. That means the aspect of life which focuses on the spirit of god and tries to understand that spirit through the process of realization. Eternal truth is constant at its core but transforms over the passage of time. It cannot be changed through any impositions. Eternal truth is constant, that is why it is said to be immutable. This cannot be changed at its core. However, with the constant flow of life that moves forward, the eternal changes its structure and form. Life, at its current of things, always picks up new elements of truth from the flow of things in this creation. This flow is also the flow of truth. Thus, truth is self-embodying in its reservation. When life makes efforts in the process of its survival to the measures of eternity, then the elements of life connect with the elements of creation. The cosmic system of having things in its own lap and creating a flow of things in the position of nature make certain changes in the process of human understanding of the creation in its perspective. Over the passage of time, the essence of cosmic nature shifts its meaning. But it maintains a constant identity in the flow of the spirit in life. Thus, with the passage of time, the true identity of the spirit changes at its outer structure. The society which can maintain and uphold this spirit in its process sustains itself better than others.

The social process and the process of life are combined to maintain the flow of things in such a manner that attempts to widen the view of life. The life that embraces the truth of god is wide enough to cover the concepts and concerns that have emerged out of the original bent and combination of things. This earth system attempts to maintain the eternal truth in its progression towards the attainment of complete unfoldment of the truth in life. The truth reveals itself through the realization of god. However, it has the patent to embrace everything in the creation. The scientific view of creation of this universe has undergone many changes and transformations, making the cosmic dynamism revealed to all. The scientific view of the creation has always attempted to unfold the truth of the universe in its perspective to make it accessible to all.

Leaving aside the issue of creation, which remained a difficulty for both models (standard model and big bang model), cosmologists focused their attention on the only other issue that was problematic for the big bang model. It was not clear how a universe created from Big Bang could evolve to form galaxies. As Hoyle had once pointed out; 'If you postulate an explosion of sufficient violence to explain the expansion of the universe, considerations looking at all like the galaxies could never have been formed'. In other words, Hoyle was complaining that the Big Bang was absurd because it would have blown apart all the existing matter to create a universe containing a thin and even smattering of substance, as opposed to a universe with its matter concentrated in galaxies. (Singh, 2005, p. 442)

Scientific View of Collectivism

There have been several modifications of the standard model. Professor Hoyle and Professor Narlikar had raised certain pertinent issues which lead to questioning the validity of the Big Bang Theory. Research output coming out of pieces of research and testing applications are gradually placing and establishing the view of continuity. The view of a sudden occurrence of things and incidents leading to the entire creation lacks in reason and rationales behind the entire creation. A new theory of the sudden explosion leading to the formation of this universe does not explain the presence of anti-matter, black holes, quasars, pulsars and so on. The creation has continuity through rise and fall; appearance and disappearance; and birth and death. Even the cyclic emergence of the opposites maintains continuity through the essence of existence. Human context is also like that. Like seasonal changes in the appearance of nature, trees take on new green leaves in place of the ones which have ripened enough to fall from the body and branches of the trees. With the newly grown green leaves in place of the dead leaves that have fallen from the branches of the trees, the growth of trees continues till the tree itself grows old and reaches the end of its vital. The natural selection finds options for alternatives removing the scene of the old to get a new one in its place or elsewhere or otherwise. Nature always attempts to maintain its continuity.

Amidst all the changes and transformations, there remains a constant factor. Material science has gone into the depth of the cosmos to understand the reality behind. However, the scientific view and understanding have gone into the subject of vastness. The universe was considered to have only our solar system. The vastness of the universe was considered as the limited vastness. The view has undergone massive changes. Now, the view has changed to numerous solar systems. Instead of one seen in the universe, there have been millions of suns. The view of vastness has been fixed on vastness that is beyond all limits of thoughts and understanding. The creation is so vast that at the human scale, it will require thousands of years to reach out to one end of this vastness. Infinite is that which cannot be reached out to. It is unbounded at both ends. The infinite is unbounded on the scale of time as also on the scale of space. The infinite is beyond all kinds of identities and forms.

Few greater concepts have ever been formed in the mind of thinking man than this one. Namely that we, the microbe inhabitants of a minor satellite of one of millions of sums which form our galaxy, may look out beyond its confines and behold other similar galaxies, tens of thousands of light – years in diameter, each composed, like ours, of a thousand million or more suns and that, in so doing. We are penetrating the greater cosmos to distances of from half million to a hundred million light years. (Singh, 2005, p. 193)

The vast infinite has all strengths and power. The vast can be contained in any dimensions. The vast infinite can reveal the supreme through any form or size. It is the free will of the supreme to be revealed through any dimension yet remains in the vast and the infinite in terms of spirit. The vastness of the universe is gradually getting revealed more and more. The tiny human capacity of understanding and grasping the cosmic vastness cannot be actually based on direct facts. However, human capacity has been multiplied by the tools and supportive technology developed to aid human knowledge and activity. Different categories of the light waves and rays have helped in understanding roughly things that might be there at any corner of the cosmos. One Sun and several stars, planets, steroids were considered to be the total physical combination of this universe. In this, the role of earth system was very minuscule. The cosmic view is, therefore, the observational view of a tiny eye comprising all tools and technologies available in the human context. NASA's observatory is engaged in this process of observation among many others with either lesser or different powers to focus on. Power of observation and the power to analyse the observed phenomena makes the human spirit enable to have a somewhat better perspective view of the earth system and cosmos.

Certain assumptions are fundamental in developing theories of this universe. The accepted theory of the cosmos is based on perspective assumption. The Big Bang theory assumes the presence of a small object originally. This very small object, a minuscule matter of some composition, was very unique. It was an extremely condensed form of some kind of existence. It was a matter with the basic properties of matter contained in it. This assumption supersedes the limits and boundaries of all kinds of perceptive assumptions prevailing in tribal or forestry societies. The presence of this vastness makes no idea vibrant that human capacity, even engineered with high technology and various appliances, is unable to discover the ultimate reality which is so enormous that understanding it would leave puzzles to capture things or to relate things to the horizon of man in the universe. The scientific understanding of the universe is also founded mostly on the same kind of guess or super guess to relate to the micro findings.

As Hoyle explained about the Big Bang theory of creation, one of them (two theories—the steady state model and the Big Bang model) is distinguished by the assumption that the universe started its life a finite time ago in a single huge explosion. On this supposition the present expansion is a relic of the violence of this explosion. Now this Big Bang idea seemed to me to be unsatisfactory.... On scientific grounds this Big Bang assumption is much the less palatable of the two. For it is an irrational process that cannot be described in scientific terms.... On philosophical grounds too, I cannot see any good reason for preferring the Big Bang idea. (Singh, 2005, p. 352)

Although it is said to be based on the findings through different physical tests and experiments, the factors related to creation have been considered through a social mechanism of 'supporting the louder'. There are sociological principles to mention social dynamics in a discrete manner, but at the base of it, the social process comes to a principle orientation through the voices which are most prominent and strong in their potent. 'Supporting the louder' is actually the principle which makes the majority of the voice acceptable. If it fails to justify the quality, the focusing principle of giving a higher degree of importance to those elements of knowledge which have a higher impact is expected to have larger dominance in the human design.

The Big Bang theory has been adopted through the process and mechanism of supporting the louder. Maximum number of scientific papers voicing in favour of the Big Bang theory made the theory acceptable in the scientific community. However, each one had to begin with the same fundamental assumption that 'the universe started its life a finite time ago in a single huge explosion'. How was the original mass of things developed and how did it become so extremely or infinitely condensed in its composition remain an untouched area of probing, as these are beyond the human scope.

Not only the sudden appearance of an infinitely strong material object is in the question, but also the related issues are of utmost importance as well. If a mass of things has to be somewhere in space, then it cannot be in the condition of zero. Space itself had originated before. Also, the mass of matter was such that it could create a life after the big explosion. The entire universe does not have lives but some parts of it, particularly this earth and maybe some other place may contain lives. So the mass of matter has not only spread to make life originated but also created the conditions sufficient enough to have different sets of lives in different forms altogether. Although the Big Bang theory does not have the power to explain these fundamental issues, most of which have been raised by highly established scientists, it is in a position to explain many other issues subsequent to the creation of the universe. That is why this theory has been accepted as the guiding theory towards the origin and progress of the universe.

Scientific ideas, thus, take shelter in the sociological methods of recognition and application. The core mechanism of science lies in the lack of rational or non-rational ways to look into things. When this paucity of rationality is considered in the core of scientific methods, it can be said that scientific truth has much to hear from the perspective truth. Belief, as a function of the causes of existence, make this aspect of organizational or human behaviour as unique, and thus, perception as a scientific method has to be taken in the human preview as a valid scientific method of our quest into the truth of the universe.

Functional Reality

The functional reality, thus, makes the scientific way to have its continuity into charted or somewhat uncharted paths. The same principle has been applied in the areas of the study of micro science as well. While studying human science, human life and its functional realities, the basics have been fixed on the about of the existence. Life and its pattern of growth are understood through the functional attributes of a human organism. The human brain is the central force and central entity in a human organism. Only a minuscule of brainpower has been explored so far. The cause, type and specification of life are all known only partly. Based on the historical data of human functions and human attributes, the steps for corrections in the human context to correct the ailments are continued. Whenever the experiment enters a new area to combat a diseased force or to take care of the health problems in the human context, the experiments approach in the human context has been affected. Medical remedy for a major ailment mostly leads to some kind of reaction. One organ gets remedy from a disease but passes a different inflict on a different organ.

Perception and subjective understanding of things and facts of the world make the basis of reality. The factors of reality can be partly visualized through the experimental and tested truth on one hand and the perceived and intuitive truth on the other. The complete truth may be seen either way. However, the integral truth is a combination of all these. The two-factor understanding is a combination of experimental and perception dimensions of truth. However, perceptions may not be the right kind of it in the context of a particular phenomenon and a particular context. It can be made better by way of knowledge providence. With a higher level of knowledge of the thing or context, the power of perception is enhanced. The perceptive capacity of a person enhances through enriching the contents of things and a better understanding of the behaviour of individuals, material objects and transactions of incidents and finally the realization of the context of the object.

In-depth realization is best possible through the consciousness of the person attempting to have the said realization. It is possible through a spiritual understanding of the context and the matter. The spiritual process acts through the depth of consciousness of the individual. This depth of consciousness is achieved through spiritual process. The spiritual process could be any. There are wide and diversified approaches towards understanding certain aspects of or the transaction in the context of the world. Spiritual understanding is penetrating. The penetration occurs both on the physical plane and on the functional context. Physical context requires a kind of insight that develops out of the call for universal concerns. The spiritual approach in life tries to make open the basics in such a way that it can open up its doors for the realization. Realization is not transforming the context or the situation; rather, it is the transformation of the consciousness of the person. Through this process of transformation, the person develops a renewed view of life. Power of understanding of a person changes. It changes in such a fashion that there develops a board basing of the perceptive power of the person. These provide a superior understanding of cosmic reality. The cosmos thus develops super cosmic approach to the view of life in such a way that makes things understood before the conscious mind in a way that keeps up with the emerging aspect of physical reality. Physical reality and the nature of the earth system keep on changing. Likewise, the mental and psychological aspects also transform in a way that helps lives to grow in a manner conducive to the principle of sustainability.

The amazing mystery of human life has been explored through the opening up of the unexposed dimension of life. Life is thus a composite of various aspects of knowledge. Science has discovered many of the secrets. Genetic science has exposed a process on the basis of whatever is contained within. Genetic code reveals the basics of the formations and potentials of life. With the exposure of this genetic code in life, the probability of many good things in life has opened up. Originally, the probabilities or chances of having all the good points of life were present. Genetic science is basically information science as applied to human life. However, now, transformation in the human system is being transformative in the human context. However, genes help in advancing knowledge.

New technological and scientific developments will provide us with new metaphors, new ways of understanding how life works, and new approaches to manipulating molecules. That future will inevitably contain opportunities and challenges. Systematic life may enable us to resolve major economic and ecological problems or it may in advertently threaten the human race and the ecosystem. We way find ourselves able to manipulate aspects of our behaviour or anatomy by deliberately and precisely changing our genes and those of our offspring. This might open the road to health, fulfilment and pleasure, but it will also pose major ethical dilemmas. By revealing and cracking the genetic code, science has shown itself capable of revealing life's greatest secret. But science cannot tell us what to do with that secret, nor ensure that the knowledge and technology that flow from it are used for the greatest good of the many and with the least damage to the planet. (Cob, 2015, pp. 313–314)

The secret about the formation of life at the micro-cosmic level and that of the creation and dynamism of the macro-cosmic entities are getting explored with human scientific initiative. Whatever be our discovery or inventions towards these two ends of the universe, the great question remains as to how it happened, what are the causative factors and attributes and what factor makes and continues to make continuity in the journey of life. Human endeavour is now focused on creating synthetic life. Now, the trend and progress of the genealogical science show that genealogical transmutations are not far away from now. Genetic engineering is attempting to identify attributes contained in the codes of life. Genetic code is actually the code of life. Qualities contained in that code are the qualities the life is expected to develop at the grown upstage of a human. At the embryonic stage, if those fundamentals are known and if we have the ideal or desired set of these attributes known, then we can think of making corrections at this embryonic stage. This is expected to create and develop a future life which is comprised of a set of qualities desired of an ideal person on earth. However, this would require that human scientific endeavours reach out to the innermost aspect of this journey in life and its mechanism to continue in the stream of life, which is beyond human limits.

Drawing from Scientific Perception

Whatever is there contained in the genetic identity can be deciphered. But making those contents happen is beyond human reach. Our endeavours are to understand how it happens. With a certain mix of elemental and molecular contents, the final outcomes are understood through the exposition of those lives on earth. The method is observational. The core scientific process is influenced or guided by the results of observational outcomes. Certain trends observed from the historicity have been adopted by these sets of experiments and initiatives in the genetic sciences. As it is urged upon, the focus of these studies has been to understand the historical trends of functioning as a scientific trend. Once these trends have been identified, the process of genetic engineering catches up to take on the spirit of movements and to see that the engineered input—combinations take on the desired embryonic combinations.

Describing the content of genes as information, and viewing the activity of cells and organisms as involving the movement of information, puts all levels of life into a single framework. As crick put it, life is characterised by the flow of energy, the flow of matter, and the flow of information. Information flow involves the activity of specific molecules and at the level of a whole organism of cells, or group of cells. Conceptualising the whole process is having an underlying unity in terms of information provides a context that helps explain how molecules, cells, organs and organisms interact and are coordinated. (Cob, 2015, p. 306)

Basically, the initiatives undertaken in the genetic science are focussed on the imperatives and combinations allowed through the decisions on the basis of historical study. Observations identify the right mix of genetic attributes leading to the desired combinations of developed qualities in a human organism. Thus, it is at this level any correction or a process of correction adopted is to fit in the desired qualities through the creation of a mix of nano-attributes at the genetic level. The objective is that it should be grown into the desired character of the grown-up person.

Ancient civilization in India had a superior way to make the same outcome happen. The objective of modern genetics is to create the desired type of a person through understanding the genetic code and applying corrective steps on that so that the desired combination of a person is created. Ancient Indian sages had developed a better scientific method of creating a better man through the method of lineage. Lineage is something that combines factors pertaining to the goodness in life. These attributes of goodness developed through living lives transmit down through series of lives to the generations and create an era of civilization with certain dominant attributes in it. 'Satya Yuga' or the era of truthfulness was an era created through this 'living good' principle. Life based on 'righteous spirit' can make a civilization happen this way. A righteous principle in single individual life makes the spirit of life sustainable. Similarly, the same righteous principle adopted by everyone in a corporate context can make the corporate journey truly sustainable.

References

Basham, A. L. (2004). *The wonder that was India*. Pan Macmillan.

Cob, M. (2015). *Life's greatest secret: The Race to crack the genetic code*. Profile Books.

Schwanbeck, E. A. (1877). *Fragments of the Indika of Megasthenes, in ancient India as described by Megasthenes and Arrian, by J. W. McCrindle*. Trubner.

Singh, S. (2005). *Big bang*. Harper Perennial.

CHAPTER 16

ORGANIZATIONAL PLANNING

In order to do the best for the organization, the manager has to develop an understanding of the best management practices for the type and kind of organization they are managing. The affairs of two major requirements of a manager are efficiency and effectiveness. The manager has to develop high level of efficiency and effectiveness to be successful in the context of the company. Efficiency can be developed in various ways by the managers on their own. But in order to enhance effectiveness, they have to understand the situation prevailing around.

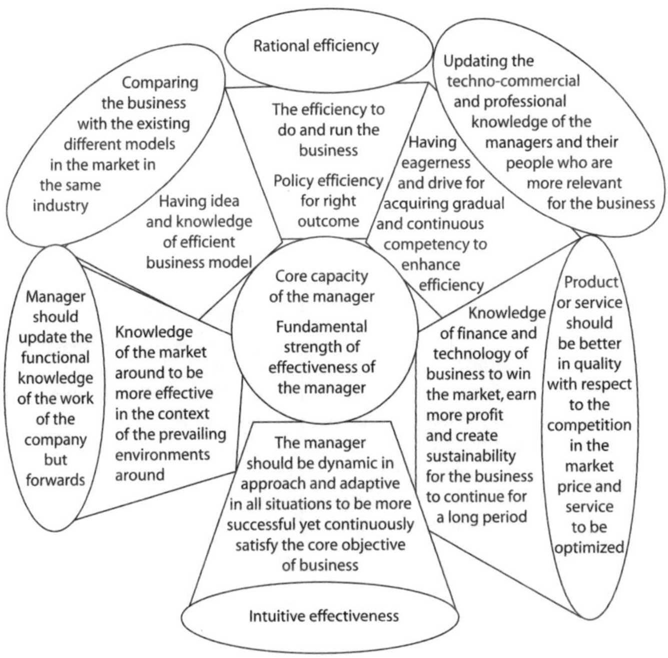

According to Mr Ratan Tata,

Today's leadership skill set, Gopal observes, has moved away from the mere analytical, aggressive and thrusting, towards human, inclusive and intuitive. Good leaders, he advocates, overlay the known facts with their gut feel and instinct, which they consciously develop through keen listening (to a company's infra sounds as he calls it) reflection contemplation and mentoring. Manager, who neglect this side of their personality end up becoming 'bonsai managers', as Gopal labels them somewhat ingeniously.

Good mentoring is so very important for creating leaders, and the book rightly urges the companies to create structures to initialize mentoring. I have often said that I wish that the close relationship I developed with Mr. J.R.D. Tata in his later years had happened sooner, so that I could have been a wiser manager. (Tata, 2016, pp. 7–8)

The Intuitive Effective Manager

The intuitive manager may be of three different types:

- The intuitive normative manager
- The intuitive onlooker manager
- The intuitive achiever manager

The intuitive normative manager relies more on the philosophical dimension and remains relatively indifferent to the affairs of the organization.

Supports business course Attitude To business	**B > The Rational Manager** Depends on: • Measurable and quantifiable dimension of the business • Understand the market and competitions from the point of view of the physical material value of perfect business • Behaves formal, acts formal and expects formal interactions	**A > The Mother Manager** The ideal manager: • Achieves in the long run • Understands business perspective better • Leads business to sustainable future • Caring yet efficient in getting best result
Indiffer-ence Weak Mean Strong Intuitive faculty	**D> Average Manager** • Indifferent to business requirements • Hard and rigid in attitude and mind • Knows the rational parameters but cannot act on them • Weak in ethical and moral rectified and delivers weak results	**C > The Intuitive Manager** • A thinker with prophetic vision • Understands and acts on the soft more than the hard • Ethical rectitude having priority over others • Philosophical view of life dominates material concerns • Intuitive faculty dominates and guides the rational faculty

The intuitive manager may function under different roles. Those are basically the differences that arise out of various mix of identities. The manager has to follow certain principles to perform. According to Peter Drucker,

---

A philosophy of management what the business enterprise needs is a principle of management that will give full scope to individual strength and responsibility, and at the same time give common direction of vision and effort, establish team work and harmonize the goals of the individual with the common weal.

The only principle that can do this is management by objectives and self control. It makes the common weal the aim every manager. It substitutes for control from outside the stricter, more exacting and more effective control from the inside. It motivates the manager to action not because somebody tells him to do something or tacks him into doing it, but because the objective needs of his task demand it. He acts not because somebody wants him to but because he himself decides that he has to he acts, in other words, as free man. (Drucker, 2006, pp. 135–136)

The objective of a company is best understood by a person having a strength of perceptive understanding. Rational parameters of business are always essential to understand the factual realities to do business. Factual details of business need to be oriented and tuned to the objective of the business. The objective of the company should branch up to the functional details of the company in the activities of different functions. Each function needs to tune the activities to the applications for each functional detail of the departments which always needs to be harnessed and pruned to the effective culmination of the agenda of the division or the company. Each functional area has to be developed and restructured into a mechanism and strategy that would best fit in the objective of the company.

The rational manager shall follow the steps of formal planning and craft strategies in accordance. Various aspects of planning include the functional and process planning, whereas each aspect of the company's life and existence requires its segment.

Before the manager gets into designing strategy or making a plan of action, an effective and factual understanding of the situation prevailing around is essential. This requires a careful understanding of the following contexts which have a direct or indirect impact on business:

Scenario Analysis for Business (SAB)

In order to start a new business or to continue with the existing business or for expansion, reorientation, re-engineering of an existing business, changing business process, adopting new technologies or changing the product mix or re-orienting the manpower and talent management policies, the manager needs to have a proper understanding of the scenario. This can be depicted into the following steps:

- Analysis of a different set of options to identify the right and effective opportunity.
- Selection of the most appropriate option for effective execution but maintain other option as possible alternatives, in case, the need for such arises.
- Continuously evaluate the scenario to assess the potential of doing new business, adding new dimensions to the existing business or changing technological, economic, political, cultural or social environment.
- Implementing the right option that arises out of the situation or the alternatives.
- Monitoring, coordinating and controlling the activities of the business towards effective completion of the agenda of the business. The business requires to be focused on its core objective and try to fulfil it continuously.

Scenario analysis requires to be properly done, and then its execution needs to be done through the application of the same, based on the given objective of the company.

Scenario analysis has to be based on the required factors for the company. General understanding requires an assessment of some highlighting factors such as economic, market, political, cultural, social and environmental.

The economic factor: To identify the long-term and short-term orientation of the company, it is always advisable to do the economic analysis. This involves analysing the macro-environment on one hand and micro-environment for business on the other.

The macro-economic factors offer opportunities for business from around, whereas the micro-economic factors would harp on the input factors and factors of continuity of the business. In order to drive the business down through the cycle of time, the elements of support for the business are drawn from the scenario around.

The market factor: The market factors are closely associated with economic factors. A business requires a combined look into the factors of the market and economy. Market orientation of the company is best possible by the customer orientation of the company. Clearly, the functional approach of the company is possible through customer focus in every aspect of the company. Some of these are as follows:

Usual Approach of Most Companies Particularly in Less Developed Economies	Desired Approach for Customer Focus Company for a Successful Management Practice
• Reception area having priority to the members or staff and senior employees. • Opening hours of the company's work day begins with socializing among members of staff and employees. • Permissibility to less-focused staff and employees makes the organization detached. • Company listens to customers' relevant issues, comments, complaints and suggestions but acts partially or delays the issue or acts in fragments or does not act at all. • A group of individuals, having a long-term personal or collective interest, harps on the policies or influences the company's policies from political, cultural, social, linguistic or national identities. • Customers' tastes and preferences are prioritized over the perceived tastes and preferences on the compositions, quality and distribution. • Usually, companies follow a marketing mix comprising 7Ps as follows: • *First four Ps:* o Product o Price o Place o Promotion • *Next three Ps:* o People o Process o Physical evidence	• Welcome for customer first. • Priority is given to the customer than any member of staff or any junior or senior employee. • Socializing options to be kept open for the customers of various colours. • Customer-focused companies would make customer at the centre of the business paradigm—understand the need to have these values installed in them and understand the need of customers. • A company should give most priority to: o Customers' suggestions/ observations o Customers' feedback on individuals' systems, process, products or services o Address customer complaints promptly o Corporate policies should be designed, maintained, governed and enforced in such a way that these are free from – Political influences – Social group influences – Cultural influences – Linguistic or national influences • Company needs to formulate plan and develop strategy to satisfy and go beyond the target set based on the objective of the company. • By following 7Ps of marketing mix companies, they give indirect support to the customer's

	preferences. However, it would be better to: o Create unique in offers of products/services o Maximize customer perceived values (CPV) $$CPV = \frac{\text{Benefits derived from the product/service}}{\text{Cost of acquiring the product/service}}$$ o Create uniqueness in brand perception o Create customer's identity in product/service o Create strategies through customer involvement

The composite factor: A combined view of all the relevant factors of the world put together consider different conditions of the market and mix of different situations of the economy. At three stages of the economy, confronted with three different situations of the market, nine different combinations of the market economy do emerge as a result of the scenario analysis. A company has to design the corporate standard with respect to the actual position of the market economy combinations as specified in the scenario analysis below:

Market–Economy Scenario Analysis for Corporate Positioning

It is worth to hear from Peter Drucker on the spirit of an organization. According to him,

---

It is the purpose of an organization to make' common men do uncommon things' – this phrasing is Lord Beveridge's. No organization can depend on genius; the supply is always scarce and always unpredictable. But it is the test of an organization that it make ordinary human beings perform better than they are capable of that it bring out whatever strength there is in its members and use it to make all the other members perform more and better. It is the test of an organization that it neutralizes the weakness of its members.

Management by objectives tells a manager what he ought to do. The proper organisation of his job enables him to do it. But it is the sprite of

<table>
<tr><td>Strong</td><td>ME–13
• Develop sustainable model
• Capture ideas
• Sustainable models
• Outstanding
• New product line
• Review product mix
• Review service contents
• Long-term investments
• Create intangible value of the company through brand enhancement</td><td>ME–23
• Higher magnitude of share participation
• Optimum level of operating and financial leverage
• Working capital investment optimization
• Looking for fiscal benefits
• Functional integration
• Marketing focus to drive business forward
• Strategic management outlook to craft medium- and long-term profit strategies</td><td>ME–33
• Triple bottom lines
• Revenue management
• Total quality management
• Joint venture—domestic and international
• Create durable assets
• New business start-up
• Expand brand crate brand satellites
• New technologies
• Argument core competency
• Review, reorient and expand
• Risk management for corporate wise, product wise, function wise centre wise
• Participative leadership</td></tr>
<tr><td>Economic Conditions ↑
Emerging</td><td>ME–12
• Ethical business
• Teleological view of business
• SBU
• Profit centre
• Activity-based costing
• Focus on per capita productivity
• Performance arrival
• Grassroots participation in productivity services</td><td>ME–22
• Higher customer focus
• Emphasis on cash flows
• Talent acquisitions
• Emphasis on innovations and creativity
• Expansions of business through scale up production delivery of services, output maximization
• Business diversification
• Motivational programme for employees
• Customer integration
• Working capital management</td><td>ME–32
• Focus on entrepreneurship
• Idea generation and concept development
• Strong financial management
• Role clarity
• Leadership development
• Performance transparency
• Employee growth option
• Focus on increased product/service usage
• Identify talent for effective contribution
• Value-added product/service
• Market orientation</td></tr>
</table>

	ME–11	ME–21	ME–31
	• Aware of possible risks • Scope for acquisition of product line, spectrum of services • Short-term investments • Business process re-engineering • Bankruptcy assessment and prevention • Cost centre approach • Conservative marketing • Business status quo • Explore rich business opportunities • Review business process • Look for short-term prospects	• Product development • Service argumentation • Higher market duration • Focused promotion mix • Personalized customer focus • Caring business • Liquidity- and profitability-focused business • Equity-driven projects • Project selection by internal rate of return • Fiscal integrity • Cover development option for employees • Social options	• Niche market focus • Customer orientation • Enhance brand loyalty • Greater penetrator • Business re-engineering • Sales orientation • Salesmanship • Business with negative working capital take business advance to prepare and deliver • Take care of supply chain and logistics • Value engineering • Wealth maximization
Weak	Poor	Rising/satisfactory	Strong
	→ Market conditions		

the organization that determines whether he will do it. It is the sprit that motivates, that calls upon a man's reserves of dedication and effort that decides whether he will give his best or do just enough to get by. (Drucker, 2007, p. 144)

Once the scenario analysis is done properly, the company should proceed forward with the idea of identifying appropriate connections of the corporate objective with the functional objectives of the department of function which the department is supposed to perform. Each manager should develop a proper understanding of the steps towards achieving full-scale objectives.

The companywide objective is normally coined in philosophical terms. This overall objective requires to be spitted among the divisions of the company in practical terms. Each employee and worker of a company should be convinced of the given objective. Some of the common questions, that a company should provide answers to the workers and employees, should be understood by their terms. Questions which haunt the minds are usually:

- What am I supposed to do as a worker or an employee?
- Why is this role important in the overall task of the company?
- What purpose of the company do I fulfil by doing this job?
- Am I doing something that provides a direct or indirect benefit to the company and the society in general?
- Do I need to be duty-bound to perform this assigned role?
- Do I have the right to offer my idea towards doing the same work in a better manner with benefit to the company?
- Can I become a unique role—identity—by doing the assigned work in the best possible manner?
- In case, there arises a conflict between myself and the assigned role how best can I resolve that?
- Have I been able to maintain my integrity and honesty as an employee of the organization?
- How do I contribute better to the betterment?

The *Harvard Business Review (HBR)* Observation on Decision-making

A manager has to make a decision that is appropriate for the company in a given situation. The amount of money invested and are required to be invested has to be recovered first, and then, on top of everything, the company needs to earn additional revenue and profit in such a way that returns to the initial investment proves more attractive than any other investment opportunity available in the relevant market. But the tools for making decisions are changing rapidly. A strong and suggestive yet based on the most happening global pattern of decision-making has been observed by a team of decision advocates through direct interaction with leading decision scientist. Ram Charan has been interviewed by Melinda Merino, senior editor of the *HBR* on the art and science of decision-making by the senior managers of global corporations. Mr Ram Charan has spent close to four decades on the corporate scenario observing, advising and guiding a large number of global corporations. Melinda Merino, the senior editor of *HBR* wanted to know his response on what has changed the most over the years about how executives make a decision. Mr Ram Charan answers saying:

Getting to the right answer is tougher these days, it's not just the greater number of variables to consider; executives also need to make subjective judgments about highly ambiguous factor that are moving targets. The usual competitive analysis does not work well when technology keeps crashing industry boundaries and the pace of change is so fast that you can't wait for things to stabilize.

So you are wrestling with more quantitative factors, with no conventional methodology, under the real threat that part of your business has peaked or could become irrelevant. Meanwhile enormous opportunities that require big bets arise and vanish quickly. And any decisions you make will be judged in the court of public opinion. You have to take into account potential consequences for a range of constituencies who may have no direct long term economic interest in the business regulators, shareholder activists, social watch dogs, the media. These conditions were beginning to emerge ten years ago, but now they are dominant. (HBR Staff, 2013, p. 73)

Business analysis, the set of data inputs and intuition help in the process of decision-making. The best performing chief executives try to collect a lot of information from various sources. The information does not make a decision, rather the information and analytics are inputs to the structuring of decisions. Among the ingredients of decision-making, the elements which are considered more important and more relevant are taken into account for the decisions. The manager tries to develop various alternatives for the decisions. From all the available alternatives to choose, the one which is best suited to the objective of the company is selected.

The CEO tries to be true to companywide objective and each manager has to identify the divisional objective and satisfy each of these in the context of the company.

A manager has to develop a set of alternatives before taking final choice for the business. Different alternatives and options are required to be kept in mind for continuous display of the right inputs through the different alternative options available. Actually, broad strategic options should be continuously crafted in the minds of the senior executives. Chief executives themselves collect the relevant business data from all areas and corners. The aspects to which the company puts the highest emphasis are then combined. The top management has to understand this and pass it on to the functional departments and people coordinating the departments. Alternatives and options require certain attributes, some of which are:

- Competence
- Credibility
- Power of perception
- Data analysis and interpretation
- Combining the internal with the external strength
- Taking lessons from past and present
- Prophetism for future
- Values

The manager's responsibility stands as:

- Look out into the external environment for:
    - Strengths of the market in terms of consumption
    - To identify opportunities available in the related field or any other field
    - To understand the risks available or potential risks that may crop up as a logical culmination of the business process
    - To find out the ways to grab the opportunities that have been identified or those other opportunities that may figure out or surface in the course of doing business.
- See through the complexity and the factor of business through the lens of the current reality of the corporate. Identify the right level of a decision based on the right mix of variables selected from a large number of decision variables.
- Creating impacts in shadows or impact imaging based on the various sets of alternative decisions to examine or focus on the alternatives to select from those alternatives the best one based on the outcomes and perceived results of the ongoing set of events.

- Develop a decision option which proves to conform to the business objective. The complexity of the situation to be brought down to straight and simple format for the right choice to be exercised to implement in the right manner.
- A good decision would involve the spread of goodness among people of the organization. This would create a good internal environment or good internal society through the creation of an informal social network in the context of the company and its business. Goodness in thoughts should reflect through managerial actions.
- The manager has to good trustworthy before the entire internal environment and people of the organization. The manager should prove trustworthy before the customers, the traders, the trade connections, stakeholders, people inside and outside. By being trustworthy the manager can command trust from the entire community and the market society.
- While developing the decision alternatives, the manager of any category, particularly the CEOs, should try to blend the rational variables with factors that arise through perceptions of reality past and forward.
- An effective manager will rank the decision alternatives among first, second and third. Prioritization of the alternatives should be done based on the strength of the outcomes and scopes for perpetrating on the lines of business may be in the same domain or a different domain.
- The manager should try to build credibility in the areas of business through building support among the members, shareholders, members of the board, employees, customers, business process support people, those who have invested or financed the activities of the company, people in the society at large, people in the media and people who are relevant in the corporate, social and national life of a nation.
- The manager needs to be oriented across performance and maintain transparency in the process and programs identified and adopted through the decision-making process and take all efforts to implement the decision elements.
- While implementing a decision, the manager is required to see that resources—material, financial, human and technological—should be utilized properly for the best idea towards making the best choice for the organization.
- The amount of capital invested in the organization should be linked to the range, content, quantum of activities and also to connect and explore new opportunities for the business to expand into.
- A manager should acquire the courage and mental strength to accept and face risks and problems the business may face.

Managers' World of Decision Tree

A manager becomes successful with an effective and efficient focus on the various aspects of the decision tree, as mentioned below:

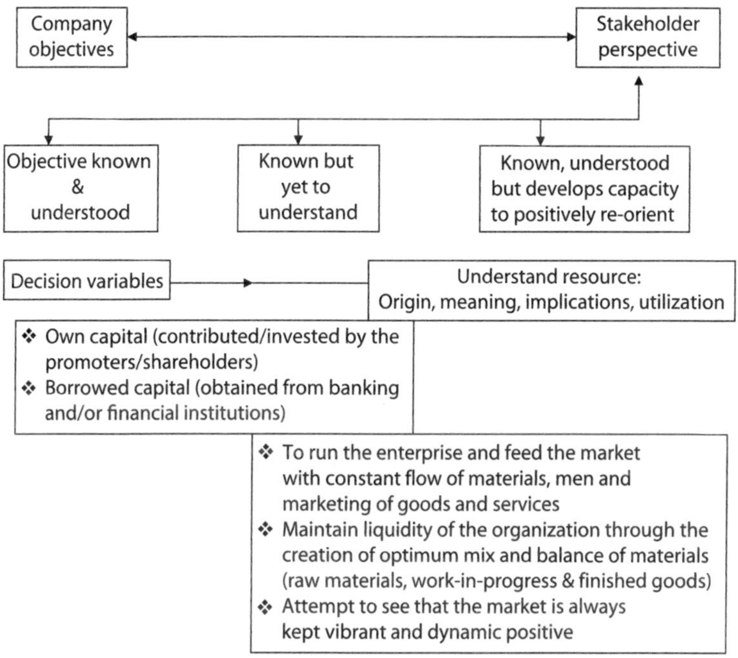

- Investment and capital needs assess the utility and apparition through capital budgeting and support tools (net present value, internal rate of return and so on).
- Maintain the level of working capital in such a way that it keeps and mentions a balance between the receivable and payable on a continuous basis; also, the new requirements of the markets should be continuously maintained.
- Information aggregation and re-engineering
  - Quantitative models—statistical/mathematical/simulation/Monte-Carlo methods/computational algorithms/random sampling and so on.
  - Decision analysis using various options and the selection of final option through the triangle of risk–return–market growth matrix.
  - Information–aggregation tools:
    - Market and customer information
    - Financial tools and techniques

  - Manpower and personal dynamics
  - Fiscal and government rules/regulations
- Maintain and attempt to enhance market share always
- Constantly look into market competitions and wining over these competitions and see that whether the company is capable of making market growth
- Keep track with the changes in the process in technology, how the restructuring of markets is taking place and repositioning the products and services
- Opportunity and facilitation matrix of the market
- Real market and potential market matrix and analysis
- Market forecast on existing products/services
- Customers' need/taste/preference and dynamics to kept track on
- Local and global market dynamics

References

Drucker, P. F. (2006). *The practice of management*. Harper.

Drucker, P. F. (2007). *The practice of management*. Butterworth-Heinemann.

HBR Staff. (2013, November). You can't be a wimp—Make the tough calls. *Harvard Business Review*. https://hbr.org/2013/11/you-cant-be-a-wimp-make-the-tough-calls

Tata, R. N. (2016). Forward. In R. Gopalakrishnan (Ed.), *The case of the bonsai manager: Lessons for managers on intuition* (pp. 7–8). Penguin.

CHAPTER 17

GLOBAL MARKET AND GLOBAL BUSINESS

Decision Matrix: Global Economic and Financial Concern (GEC) versus National Economic and Financial Concern (NEC)

Strong

Explorative GEC	Euphoric
• Global relation matrix • Product/services matrix • Market development matrix • Value matrix • Investment optimization • Incremental value gains • Seeding in new options Weak	• Market integration • Market penetration • New market development • Product/services development • Diversification • Creative contribution • Innovation • Evaluating global relation • Global investment opportunities • Global market niche Strong
• Cost advantage • Expense optimization • Incremental value addition • Potential analysis • Process restructuring • Process reorientation • Content reengineering Sustenance	NEC Domestic Competition • Volume competition • Value competition • Creative competition • Advantage competition • Core strength competition • Positioning matrix • Corrections and evaluations Competitive

Weak

Analysis of Global Domestic Policy

Konosuke Matsushita, the founder of Panasonic Corporation, created a success story of being a humble apprentice in a bicycle company and later, at the age of early 20s, getting a job in an electrical designing lamp parts' company. In 1917, at the age of 27, this man started making a two-way light socket. His initial investment fund was $100 of which $50 was his own and the remaining $50 was borrowed by him on personal capacity.

Panasonic Song
For the building of a new Japan
Let's put our strength and minds together
Doing our best to promote production,
Sending our goods to the people of the world
Endlessly and continuously,
Like water gushing from a fountain.
Grow, industry, grow, grow, grow!
Harmony and sincerity!
Matsushita Electric.

Considered the god of management by large sections of Japan, Matsushita believed in the role of a manager as a practitioner of all functions in his company, be it assembly lines, accounts office, cleaning trash or all.

The Untrapped Mind
The 'untrapped mind' is open enough
to see many possibilities.
Humble enough to learn
from anyone and anything
forbearing enough to forgive all,
perceptive enough to see things
as they really are,
and reasonable enough to
judge their true value.
(Konosuke Matsushita: Matsushita words of wisdom)

The Way
Every person has a path to follow.
It widens, narrows, climbs and descends.
There are times of desperate wanderings.
But with courageous perseverance and
Personal conviction,
the right road will be found.
This is what brings real joy.

Choice Matrix for MNCs

SWOT analysis to identify the appropriate locator for the organization refers to the comparative and competitive position of the industry and business concerned. This analysis can be applied to the factor of the company and to the factor of the market or the economic region as well.

Organization Factor Analysis

Factor	Trend (Past Yearly)				Projections (Forward Yearly)			Remarks
	Y-4	Y-3	Y-2	Y-1	PY1	PY2	PY3	
Domestic factors GDP								
Rate of change of GDP 1								
Stock market index: Sensex								
Nifty								
Industrial production index								
Fiscal environment 2 Corporate tax								
Tax exemptions 3								
Employment trend								
Household savings trend								
Bank profitability 4								
Central bank interventions 5								
Basic interest rate								
Organizational data business volume								
EBIT								
GP								
NP								
ROI								
Market price of equity share 6								

1. Rate of change of GDP calculated at constant prices
2. On a Likert scale of 1 to 5; 5 being the most favourable, 1 the weakest
3. Exemptions on numerical percentage
4. GP earned year on year
5. On a Likert scale of 1 to 5; 1 is the best; 5 is the weakest
6. Trend of changes of average share prices over daily, monthly and yearly

While the market factors are those that primarily identify the demand and supply of products and services in a particular market, the depth of understanding goes beyond the concept of the known demand.

The traditional view of demand and supply considers the expressed need for products or services. However, the expressed need is not only the source; organizations should understand things in retrospect and in prospect. A team of researchers conducted continued research on the importance of some important strategies for global organizations and found the importance of purpose in designing strategies for effective enterprises. According to the research group, each organization is required to identify a purpose of the organization for the best effective management of the enterprise. In their words,

---

Eight years ago we launched a global study of high growth in companies investigating the importance of three strategies known to drive it creating new markets, serving broader stakeholder needs, and changing the rule of the game. What we found surprised us. Although each of those approaches did boost growth at the organisations we studied, there was a fourth driver we hadn't considered at all; purpose.

Companies have long been encouraged to build purpose into what they do. But usually its talked as on adds on—a way to create shared value, improved employee morale and commitment, give back to the community, and help the environment. But as we worked with high growth companies in our study and beyond, we began to recognize that many of them had moved purpose from the periphery of their strategy to its core—where, with committed leadership and financial investment, they had used it to generate sustained profitable growth, stay relevant in a rapidly changing world, and deepen this with their stakeholders. (Malnight et al., 2019, pp. 72–73)

Most organizations do not have a clearly designed purpose for their being present in the marketplace. Purpose-driven organizations are mostly oriented towards their philosophy of being and that is how and why these organizations develop the capacity to thrive better than the others. Certain issues identified by a team of professors contributing to the idea of developing purpose-driven organizations have been noted here in philosophical terms but tested in terms specified in certain organizations, particularly organizations with Indian origin and operating primarily in Indian context and American context. The issues are diverse and span across the organizations' perspectives of established stability in the market and the issues of growth across, apart from the other issues of stakeholder expectations to fit in the process of purpose-driven organizations.

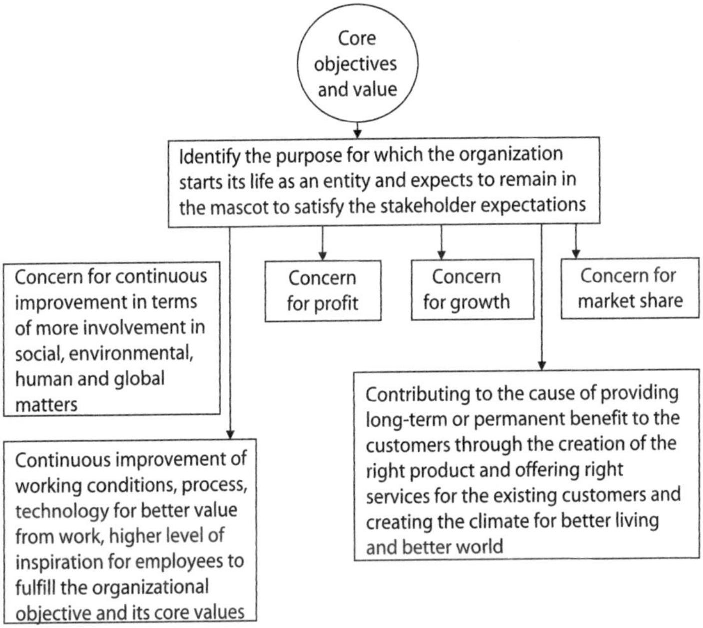

Features of a Purpose-driven Organization

The issue stands as the core concern for the basis values and core objectives for which the organization stands as known in the market and the economy. It is this core concern which the purpose-driven organizations are expected to keep in mind in effect for the growth of the organization. Markets and societies do benefit from the companies in terms of their offering in the market as the offering does share the life of people in the society. The *Harvard Business Review* paper identifies the process to develop a purpose of an organization in two different ways: retrospective and prospective. According to them,

---

The retrospective approach builds a firms existing reason for being. It requires that you look back, codify organizational and cultural DNA, and make sense of the firms past. The focus of the discovery process is internal. Where have we come from? How did we get hare? What makes us unique to all stakeholders? Where does our DNA open up future opportunities we believe in? These are the kind of questions leaders have to ask....

The prospective approach, on the other hand, reshapes your reason for being. It requires you to look forward, take stock of the broader ecosystem in which you want to work, and assess your potential for impact in it. The idea is to make sense of the future and then start gearing your organisation for it. The focus is external, and leaders have to ask a different set of questions: where can we go? which trend affect our business? what new needs, opportunities, and challenges lie ahead? What role can we play that will open up future opportunities for ourselves that we believe in? (Malnight et al., 2019, pp. 76–77)

Some of the Indian companies have done their purpose in the making and running of the organizations. Organizational psyche and certain types of ethnographic study have led them to develop the process and culture within the organizations that have offered them continuity and growth in marketplace.

Although the purpose of being of the companies is going to decide on the direction of the company's pathways, productivity plays a critical role in organizations. Technology may drive productivity to a higher level; however, manpower plays most importations role.

Unless the productivity of service workers is rapidly improved, both the social and the economic position of that large class—as large a group as people making and moving things ever at their peak—must steadily go down. Real income cannot for any length of time be higher than productivity. The service workers may use their numerical strength to get higher ways than their economic contributions justifies. But this only impoverishes all of society with everybody's real income going down and unemployment going up, or the incomes of the unskilled service workers are allowed to go down in relation to the steadily rising ways of affluent knowledge workers, with an increasing gulf between the two groups, an increasing polarization into classes. In either case service workers must become alienated, increasingly bitter, increasingly bitter, increasingly see themselves as a class apart. And the escape hatch—the productive and therefore well-paid jobs for poorly educated and poorly skilled people is making and moving things—is closing rapidly. (Drucker, 1992, p. 94)

Productivity for an organization is next to no other factor. It is the most important aspect of managing an enterprise. Productivity depends on several factors. Technology is one such factor which makes productivity the core agenda. The emergence of machines has several phases. Hand tools were initially used for the process of work. Using hand tools was equal to using multiple hands for a piece of work. From hand tools, small machines emerged. Small machines to large machines and mega-machines thoroughly revolutionized the process of productions. Even until then, the role of large number of labours was instrumental in the production. Excavating earth in scratch of mines was a very old approach. Gradually, once the mines were identified, minerals from beneath the earth surface were constantly rigged and thus mines came up and large number of workers were actually employed in those mines. The productivity of these entities depended on the availability of all the right machines to extract the required elements in mineral substance and convert that into a required texture, shape and size of the material in demand. Mega-machines are normally process driven. There remain certain varieties of mega-machines which require large number of human participations in the manufacturing process. For example, blast furnace required to convert ferric oxide iron or as to raw iron through different intermediate steps. Grinding the ore is done, which comes in the form of stone ingot, to make it into near dust size then brings in the process consumable to convert the ferric oxide to the level of ferrous oxide. A process of deoxidization continued to bring this to the level of molten iron. While the main productive machine is automated, the entire process used to involve a large number of workers. Mega-machines involved human participation in a large amount. But as the technology transformed further, a fully automated system involved much less manpower in the core production.

Management as a process may be adopted in any way that the owners or promoters of the business may think proper about it. However, a variety of standard processes is there to have management functions under control. Important aspects of the company that need to be brought under control are as follows:

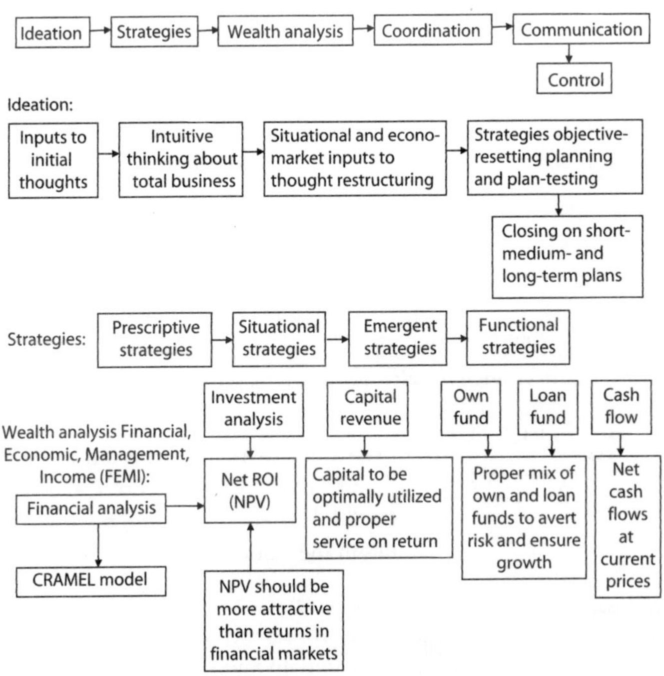

C → Capital → To see that capital is only adequate, neither more nor less. The relative position of debt taken with respect to the equity invested in the company by the promoters and equity capital taken up later on to support the enterprise. Adequacy of capital may be examined in different ways of which the most important is DER. Debt taken for the company is a better way to fund the company's growth, expansion, diversification, modernization, automation, market presentation, market share, market growth, manpower welfare, greening the functions–processes and other ways to grow. Debt, though provides a relief to the business, in terms of availability to fund for development and growth, it costs the company at the market rate. Disproportionably, high level of debt makes the company liable to pay higher rent of money in the form of interest to be paid every month. If this liability is disproportionably high, then the company at times faces the risk of inability to pay for the rent and service the debt fund. Although the standard of DER depends on money factor, usually the debt intake should not go much beyond twice the equity level. However, for expanding business having high prospect and potentials for doing more business, acquiring access to new technology, new market, new areas of business and expansion, at times higher input cost or investment fetches even much higher returns.

Risk → Usually two types of risks are talked about in corporate and market-driven enterprises. These are business risks and financial risks. Leverage is considered as the indicator. By efficient use of leverage, management control can be asserted to avert risk. One should apply the tools of leverage to contain risks within manageable and reasonable level. There are three different ways to examine the risk-taking ability of the company in order to prevent risk. These are as follows:

1. DOL
2. DFL
3. DWCL

$$\text{DOL} = \frac{\%\text{ change in operating profit}}{\%\text{ change in sales volume}}$$

$$= \frac{Q\,(P-V)}{Q\,(P-V)-F}$$

(The value of this is expected to be more than 1. With higher level of F, the value of DOL is higher. The control parameter here lies in the value of 'F')

Here,

P = Price per unit
Q = Break-even quantity of sales

F = Fixed cost
V = Variable cost

$$\text{DLF} = \frac{\text{\% change in EPS}}{\text{\% change in (EBIT) operating profit}}$$

$$\text{Operating profit (EBIT)} = Q(P - V) - F$$

$$\text{EPS} = \frac{(\text{EBIT} - \text{I})^{(1-t)}}{\text{N}}$$

Where, I = Total interest
N = Total number of shares
T= Tax rate

So $$\text{DFL} = \frac{\text{EBIT} - \text{I}}{\text{EBIT} - \text{I} - \text{I}}$$

This shows that in the absence of 'I', the DFL is 1. DFL is thus more than 1 for any company having taken debt in crateful. Higher the value of total interest, higher will be that value of DFL. 'I' acts as the 'gear' of finance for a debt financial company. Companies can draw the benefit of higher leverage through the position of geared companies. However, if this level is extremely high, the highly geared company faces the risk of the liability of the debt servicing through business operations. At times, wrong induction of debt for the company may push it for obtaining further debt to service the liability arisen out of debt. Liability-conscious companies can prevent this work.

WC leverage is the percentage change in ROCE as a result of 1 per cent change in WC.

$$\text{DWCL} = \frac{\text{\% change in ROCE}}{\text{\% change in WC}}$$

$$C_T = C_W + C_F$$

Where, C_F = Investment in net fixed assets (fixed asset values net of depreciation)

$$\text{CE} = \text{EBIT}$$

Let C_W = decrease in WC
Then the percentage change (decrease) in WC

$$= \frac{\Delta C_W}{C_W} \times 100$$

With the change in the WC, there occurs a corresponding change on the total capital in the system.

So $$\text{ROCE} = \frac{\text{CE}}{\text{CT} - \Delta\text{C}_\text{W}}$$

This means there is an increase in ROCE.

$$\text{So the increase in ROCE} = \frac{\text{CE}}{\text{C}_\text{T} - \Delta\text{C}_\text{W}} - \frac{\text{CE}}{\text{C}_\text{T}}$$

$$= \frac{\Delta\text{C}_\text{W}}{\text{C}_\text{T} - \Delta\text{C}_\text{W}} - \frac{\text{CE}}{\text{C}_\text{T}}$$

$$\text{So the percentage change in ROCE} = \frac{\text{CE} \cdot \Delta\text{C}_\text{W}}{\text{C}_\text{T} - (\text{C}_\text{T} - \Delta\text{C}_\text{W})} \times 100 / \frac{\text{CE}}{\text{C}_\text{T}}$$

$$= \frac{\Delta\text{C}_\text{W} \times 100}{\text{C}_\text{T} - \Delta\text{C}_\text{W}}$$

So $$\text{L}_\text{W} = \frac{\%\text{ change in ROCE}}{\%\text{ change in WC}}$$

$$= \frac{\Delta\text{C}_\text{W} \times 100 / \text{C}_\text{T} - \Delta\text{C}_\text{W}}{\Delta\text{C}_\text{W} \times 100 / \text{C}_\text{W}}$$

Or $$\text{L}_\text{W} = \frac{\text{C}_\text{W}}{\text{C}_\text{T} - \Delta\text{C}_\text{W}}$$

This means WC leverage

$$\text{DWCL} = \frac{\text{Original investment in WC}}{\text{Changed amount of total capital employed}}$$

If we assume that $\text{L}_\text{W} = 1$, then $\text{C}_\text{W} = \text{C}_\text{T} - \Delta\text{C}_\text{W}$

Or $\text{C}_\text{W} = \text{C}_\text{W} + \text{C}_\text{F} - \Delta\text{C}_\text{W}$ or $\text{C}_\text{F} = \Delta\text{C}_\text{W}$

This means the break-even condition for WC leverage is to have a decrease in the WC by an amount equal to the fixed capital.

Let us examine this control condition. Let the change in WC be a fraction, say *x*, of its original level.

Then $\Delta\text{C}_\text{W} = x \times \text{C}_\text{W}$

And let *y* be the ratio of net fixed assets to gross WC.

Then, $CF/C_W = y$ or $CF = y \times C_W$

$$\text{Now } L_W = \frac{C_W}{C_T - \Delta C_W}$$

$$= \frac{C_W}{C_F + C_W - \Delta C_W}$$

$$= \frac{C_W}{y \times C_W + C_W - x \times C_W} = \frac{1}{y+1-x}$$

Thus, if $\boxed{L_w > 1}$

$$\text{Then } \frac{1}{y+1-x} > 1$$

Or $1 > (y + 1 - x)$

$$\boxed{\text{Or } x > y}$$

In case, $\boxed{L_w = 1}$

$$\text{Then } \frac{1}{y+1-x} = 1; \text{ or } 1 = y+1-x$$

$$\boxed{\text{Or } x = y}$$

Also it $\boxed{L_w < 1}$

$$\text{Then } \frac{1}{y+1-x} < 1; \text{ or } 1 < y+1-x$$

$$\boxed{\text{Or } x < y}$$

This analysis shows that if the change in the WC is more in magnitude than the ratio of net fixed assets to WC, we can have a positive leverage. The result shows that when the change in WC as a ratio of the original level of WC is more than the ratio of net fixed assets to WC, then we expect to get ROCE at a rate higher than the rate of change of WC.

One per cent change in WC under the condition of $\boxed{x > y}$ results in more than 1 per cent change in ROCE in the business.

The WC leverage analysis proves to be very important for marketing strategies. Industries requiring less investment in fixed assets would be more responsive to the positive leverage of WC. Thus, service industries, hospitality industry, trading, plantation industry, metal fabrication, agro-industry and so on are more responsive to WC management than heavy industries, such as steel, cement, automobiles, electronics, television, mobiles sets, refrigerators, shipping, aircraft making, defence production, naval production, space stations and major infrastructure. For any product of services in the consumer-driven industry, the test of WC leverage is very essential. Managers of marketing and strategies should be conversant with the concept and application of WC leverage and should apply that in the executive functions.

References

Drucker, P. F. (1992). *Managing for the future*. Butterworth-Heinemann.

Malnight, T. W., Buche, I., & Dhanaraj, C. (2019). Put purpose at the core of your strategy. *Harvard Business Review* (September–October), 72–73.

CHAPTER 18

ETHICAL MANAGER: ROLE OF ETHICS IN CORPORATE MANAGEMENT

Definition of Ethics

Ethics was first practised in India during ancient Indian Vedic period as a part of the 'righteous' way of living. The concept of 'ethics' began rolling down the lanes of knowledge in the West after several thousand years of India's having lived life of righteous values. Actually, the practice of ethics is of Indian origin, but the term 'ethics' was coined in Europe. This term has been coined from the Greek term *ethikos*, which means character.

Ethics as an attribute was considered a noble value in ancient India. Most probably, this was the first of its kind in human history, a thought, a spirit and a practice of life. In the entire ancient India, goodness in spirit and practice in life was inbuilt in people's lives during the Vedic period. This is why the other way to describe this period was 'Satya Yuga' or a millennia-long period of truth-based living of life. Ethics was automatically inculcated as a part of life during this period of human history.

India's spirit of truth-based living of life got spread through different types of trade and commercial routes to other parts of the world. In most parts of the world, thereafter, people gradually started to develop the views of goodness and wholesome truth in their lifestyle. Historians, philosophers, sociologists and other similar categories of people have coined their ideas primarily influenced by colonial advocacies of few scholars of the European and Western grooming. These sets of people have assumed everything to have emerged from the Western soils and Western locations of the world. It is indeed true that they were advanced in the acts of snatching things of valued possessions from others by applying muscle power of savage kind. Whenever it required them to have strategies of submitting to get some better valued possessions, they did that. Invading to grab others' resources was considered an act of heroism in the West. Hardly any ethical concern remains here, except for the concern for their selfish gains. But hardly, in most cases, the noble souls have emerged with the spread of the universal noble acts to impact life in general.

Religious calls from the West have preferred to get restricted to faith-based goodness. 'Inclusion in faith first, general goodness next' can be mentioned as the modus operandi of most of them. Vedic sages were people who not only thought but also prayed for the goodness and well-being of all in the world, regardless of their caste, creed and religious faith. Once they developed the spirituality within, Vedic sages uttered the realization of truth in their terms.

They used to follow two major principles in life: *satyam* (eternal truth) and *ritam* (applied truth). Throughout the Vedic period, the practice of *ritam* was prevalent in public life in India. In fact, the Vedic era lasted for more than five millennia, and its influence partially lasted for another period of almost five millennia—spanning up to a period of 3,000 years before Christ. During this entire period, life was structured across four objectives: dharma (righteous principle of life), *artha* (material intent of life), *kama* (honest needs of life) and *moksha* (fulfilment of life). People in India used to live righteously during the entire Vedic period of nearly 10,000 years.

A basic set of attributes of this righteous living comprised of:

- Truthfulness
- Honesty
- Caring
- Compassion
- Priority of organizational concern to personal interests
- Duty oriented to the roles of work and society
- No harm in any way to others
- Self-giving for a good cause
- Cooperation
- Concern for the world and mankind
- Honouring others' right
- Friendliness

As we have understood from the discussion above, the concept and practice of ethical living were in place in India from ancient times. However, the term 'ethics' has been derived from the Greek word *ethikos* which pertains to character. When applied to business, this means having a character for the business or the corporate organizations. There is a similar term that prevails and many times considered synonym of ethics, which is 'morality'. But, essentially, these concepts are quite different.

The term 'morality' has been derived from the Latin root *moralis*, which means behaviour. Ethico-moral actions thus pertain to set of actions engineered orchestrated by the characters and expressed through behaviour. As is understood, behaviour is relatively external—the response one gives to interactions with the others at the interface. This means that purity of behavioural responses is a reflection of the character of the person. The idea might prove too subjective, because a person's actions could also be anything independent of their character.

A basically honest person may act as dishonest or vice versa under stressful circumstances. Similarly, an unethical being might act ethically too. 'Strategies' could be many for different managerial situations in the corporate contexts. Strategies, in most of the cases, are irrespective of the characters of the individuals. For example, an air hostess is required to smile before and in any interaction with the passengers. There may be occasions that restrict her from smiling, but the job specification demands a smiling face, so she has to develop appropriate strategies to prove that she has a happy smiling face in all situations.

The behaviour is obviously as per the requirements here, but that does not emanate from the core of the being. Examining this situation from a behavioural point of view would yield a result that could contrast with that from a consideration of character. Ethics has both long- and short-term aspects. For creating a long-term ethical basis, an individual or an organization has to develop a character that is conducive to fairness for everyone within and around the entity.

An individual should, in all respects, prove fair to all of the company's stakeholders on the one hand as well as to their own context. Any conflict that arises from it must be resolved on the basis of fairness towards all concerned, using a principle called maximin. This principle highlights the objective to provide maximum goodness that will cause minimal damage to the system and the world.

Ethical Rectitude: Company Imperatives

For companies to follow ethical practices in the respective organizations, certain commonly perceived actions are advisable. Each company has its own prerogative of having a clear 'ethics' policy. There are companies that have defined ethics as a separate department, but there are many that adopt ethics as a generic policy that is included in the company's different functions.

Therefore, the marketing policy of the company includes aspects of ethical marketing; finance follows ethical financial system; and the human resource department (HRD) follows ethical policy in managing manpower.

Some of the common practices advised for a company are as follows:

- Establish ethical norms and practices for corporate activities.
- Prioritize organizational concerns over the individual concerns.
- Control mechanism on a dynamic scale to see that the ethical norms are properly adhered to in all cases of corporate practices.
- Evaluate deviations from the prescribed and accepted standards of the organizations and record it properly.
- Initiate renewed actions to correct deviations from the prescribed norms.

- Universalization and generalization of the norms and principles adhered to by various organizations belonging to the same industry, same trade, same range of activities.

Examples of this concept could be cited as the initiative taken by a particular industry. American defence industry initiative is one of these kinds. A lot of allegations are made on the modus operandi of transaction, payments and so on for the defence industry. American defence industry was under observation from various quarters regarding the initiative of the industry. Defence is one of the most important areas of activity in many multinational corporate and business transactions. Defence deals, it is alleged in many cases, do involve a lot of cut money and other informal and unofficial behind-the-curtain deals and arrangements.

Redressal mechanism may also begin with a generalized initiative of business associations and industry or nation-specific characteristics, including certain types of international arrangements or initiatives. Value maximization, then boils down to maintaining integrity in the system in such a way that it dynamically maintains the consistency of the purpose and programs.

Effects of unethical acts as understood in the cases mentioned earlier are felt by the organization as a whole, affecting the entire set of stakeholders of the organization. The effect on the economy of the country could be seen as the sum total of this form of effects. As in the case of municipal corporation, the effect of unethical action percolates down to all participants of the system. When summed up, it gives the total picture of the corporate world. Ethical rectitude, as mentioned already, is the way to come back to be placed on the track of integrated activities. Ethics plays a great role in shaping the characters of the organizations.

Organizational growth could be achieved through the adoption of any means including unethical ones. But every method or system has reactions or backlashes of its own. A short-term grassroots orientation is sure to breed short-term character at the aggregate or macro-level.

Denied corporate objective results in the organizations ultimately collapsing and crippling. A short run could make long-term loss obvious. In the case of organizations, short- and long-term orientations are the prerogatives to choose from. As already mentioned in the beginning, short-term profit orientation may prompt organizations to do things that violate the generally accepted ethical norms of the corporation, industry or the country.

Accepted ethical practices, in most of the cases, derive their origin from the normative concepts of ethics that do prevail. Normative approaches to ethics could be of various colours, concepts and views.

Ethics would obviously be in favour of universalizing the organizational attitudes.

Analysis of some dominant philosophies of thought on normative ethics would clearly identify this.

Rawl's Theory of Justice

While discussing 'rights', there were no discussions on duties. There are certain positive rights which remain enforced till the duty of not to breach them is observed. All fundamental aspects of human virtue are the rights to privacy, property, work, individual dignity, non-discrimination, humanitarian behaviour, life and death.

The right to serve the deserving with their required things is also considered as the pertinent right. For example,

- The right of the job seeker to get a job
- The right of the shareholder to get full information about the company
- The right of the auditor to access the relevant details of the transactions
- The right of the baby to get personal care and affection of the parents
- The right of the student to get the best lesson from the teacher
- The right of the consumer to get the best product at the optimum price
- The right of the citizen to get the civic care
- The right of downtrodden to get the social care
- The right of the underprivileged to get privileges
- The right of the wife to get due attention and love of the husband
- The right of the reader to get a smooth, eye-friendly, proper reading stuff
- The right of the elderly to get respect from the young
- The right of the employer to get proper services from the employed
- The right of the worker to get the recognition for their work
- The right of the teacher to get respect from the taught
- The right of the taught to get proper imputes at the most appropriate time
- The right of the sun to get due recognition for the solar rays that humans receive
- The right of the beggar to get alms
- The right of the convict to get adequate opportunity for self-defence
- The right of the appellant to get quicker justice
- The right of the women to get due position and respect in the society
- The right of the minor children to get proper support and care from the parents
- The right of the author to get value for their writings

- The right of the creator to get due recognition and value for their intellectual property rights
- The right of individual human being to get the lease of life to have an honourable existence

Rawl's principle ***of justice is based on*** fairness and equality. According to this principle,

1. Each person has an equal right to the most extensive scheme of basic liberties compatible with a similar scheme of liberties for all.
2. Social and economic inequalities should meet two conditions:

   They must be:

a. To the greatest expected benefit of the least advantaged
b. Attached to offices and position open to all under conditions of equal opportunity

This school of thought believes in the dominance of the 'veil of ignorance' in the lottery of life. One does not know what is happening or going to happen to them, their family, their people, their organization and their entity of concern.

In the lottery of life, things are uncertain so any kind of ethical choice people make would be based on the partial knowledge that they have. Based on the part of the fragmented knowledge, if any choice is made, the choice is most likely to make a fragmented outcome. According to this school of thought, social and economic opportunities having been prevalent on a free and fair basis, social and economic inequality might stay in the society without affecting the social framework.

Once the veil of ignorance is lifted, the social and economic inequalities disappear through the safeguarding of their interests. Justice allows the least advantaged in the society have the proper share of the social cake and live a preferred life through the desired level of liberty.

Rawl's support of individual liberty goes a long way to bringing about a balance into the fabric of the society that brings harmony for all.

Utilitarianism versus Individual Liberty

As mentioned in the doctrines of Kant, utilitarianism could be judged on the grounds of social justice.

Extension of Kantian doctrine on ethics could be read as follows:

- Utilitarianism could be supported in the framework of a set of activities when maximization of utility is possible even at the cost of individual liberties and rights.

- Utilitarianism does not support the Kantian maxim of 'respect for all' because the person having the highest utility in the society can command highest respect. In the presence of a disproportionate respect for all, the Kantian model of equity in respecting all gets denied.
- In a society, the inequalities among the equals are created when utilitarianism is considered as the pivotal ideal within it. This obviously tends to create an imbalance in the society which separates good from individuals rights in the short term. Things that are good in the short term may not be good in the future. Drinking 'neem (a medicinal plant-leaf from India) juice' can prove useful and may be forced on a patient for its physical utility. A patient may be reluctant to drink such an unpalatable juice, but they are still forced to drink it. This could violate the right of the individual to choose the food and drink. An individual can find juice more palatable and might accept neem as they are forced through a deviation in the rights thereunto.

The issue of an individual's right could be resolved in a situation where the individual is confronted with the situation where rights are progressively denied based on their utilities.

Ethical Dilemma: Indian Ways to Transcend

The history of human race is full of conflicts and struggles. Human life leaves hardly any scope to withdraw from the hassles of life without being involved in. In history, dialectics of life involves every soul in a struggle for a cause or conflicts between good and bad, ought to and naught. Indian civilization has waged wars throughout its phases to uphold the cause of the good and the rights against those who are indulged in unethical and non-righteous acts. There has been a ceaseless conflict between dharma (righteousness) and *adharma* (unrighteousness), among the moral, idealistic, spiritual forces and the unregenerate forces of darkness, lust and evil in which dharma always wins.

In the struggle between good and evil, even good people have undertaken the paths of personal sacrifice for the common good of many. Life is construed on the basis of the righteous principles (also called dharmic principles) elaborated by Lord Krishna in the Bhagavad Gita as fearlessness, purity of the inner world, disciplined pursuit of knowledge, ability to give, control over the outer dominated senses, educating oneself, meditation, simplicity, non-violence, sticking to the truth, ability to overcome anger, giving up unnecessary possessions, inner peace, refusal to discuss other's faults, compassion, lack of greed, softness, repentance, lack of fickleness, talkativeness, inner strength, forgiveness, patience, cleanliness, lack of feeling of enmity and not feeling puffed up or egoistic.

These qualities that are called *daivi* qualities are the basic ethical values according to the Indian ethics.

Dharma in Public and Private Lives

Whereas the *daivi* qualities as propounded earlier are most relevant for the private life as also for the individual, some of the attributes that are advocated for the collectives include the following:

Dana (D): To give others their due share of things
Daya (D): To be compassionate to one's fellow creatures
Dama (D): To restrain one's passion and sensual emotions

The three Ds form a cardinal value called 'ahimsa' or non-violence. Participation in ritualized cycles of activities of 'karma' (action) is *samskar* (repeated births that do not hold core values). In a collective situation, a network of reciprocal activities is established with varying degrees of intensity among the individual elements. In many cases, institutional dharma rules over personal dharma. For example, King Yudhishthira playing dice. The 'Kshatriya dharma' (attributes of the warrior-kings class) was to honour and win any kind of challenge. Yudhishthira was committed to playing dice with Duryodhana and his team by wealth and personal hypothecation. He pursued that. King Yudhishthira, when defeated, started losing his material resources, and then his people one after another. He lost his four brothers and finally his wife. Till he himself turned into a lone person dispossessed of material and men, he had to continue as it was the imperative of the secular ethics or bare principles of institutionalized righteousness. His belief may be explained as institutions predominating over individuals. As the common understanding goes: groups and not individuals carry on exchange, make contracts and are bound by obligations; the persons included in the contracts are moral persons. Groups not only exchange material or economic values or goods and services but also exchange courtesies, entertainment, gestures and other relevant attributes of which market is one parameter of the wide and enduring contract.

Kautilyan Ethics

After discussing the ethical dilemma between individual ethics and collective ethics as mentioned in the dilemma between Arjuna's initial views and Lord Krishna's, an in-depth view of institutions such as the statecraft is required. Kautilya shows the applications of a long-term viewpoint and objective into a short-term objective-based action programme.

Arthashastra of Kautilya discusses various elements of real politics. Book 11 of *Arthashastra* suggests the following:

Let those of a higher rank be discouraged from eating at a common table with, and marriage with those of lower standing. The lesser should be provoked to claim equality of status in family, proven, and change of place. On all occasions of conflict the king should support the weaker party with army and funds, should help them 10 annihilate their opponents. If they all remained together in one place, they might be capable of taking up arms. (Arthashastra, *2.1)*

Here, the king is asked to formulate his strategy, but in the final accounts the king would support the weaker sections of the conflict or the weaker arms. The king's objective here is the unification or cohesion between two groups to form a larger organized, disciplined body with less conflicts and more cooperation and cohesions.

Kautilya's View of Providing Public Goods

Kautilya's *Arthashastra*, as edited and translated by Ganapati Shastri and R. Shamasastry, respectively, describes the ideal *janapada* (the place of domiciles of the collectives):

Free from swamps, salt impregnated lands, uneven lands...well furnished with waterways and roads, with trade goods of great values and varieties, able to bear the army and the taxes...with peasants who are dutiful, lords, that are childish, a population mostly of the lower castes, and with men who are loyal and clean-lived. Such is the perfection of the Janapada. (Arthashastra, *6.1)*

In the case of conflict between the momentary and the sacred, Kautilya sets the priority to support the eternal principles or the long-term views in the following words: 'Whenever there is a disagreement between history and sacred law or between evidence and the sacred law, then the matter shall be settled in accordance with sacred law. But whenever sacred law is in conflict with rational law, then reason shall be held authoritative.'

Kautilya wanted to form a powerful and benevolent bureaucracy to safeguard eternal interest against the short-term cross-views. King Asoka later supported the idea of all-powerful bureaucracy supervising the trade and administration with a righteous view. Asoka's belief turned the weaker section of the society into a safety net. He wished all inanimate beings to have security, self-control, peace of mind and joyousness. Asoka's later belief turned into a pleasure in patience and gentleness and the conquest not by arms but by piety. He thought about the joy in the cooperative effort and the retreat for the vanquished.

Case 1: Trot's Fortune

Trot, a small entrepreneur, was engaged in the business of supplying computer parts and replacement parts to Sonada Municipal Corporation. Trot's turnover grew at a slow pace: From a meagre sum of ₹2.5 million, it grew to ₹3.3 million in a period of three years ending in 1998. The growth for his business was perceived by Trot as sacrificing and enduring. Suddenly competition had set in with other suppliers occupying a significant share of the business from Trot and earning good image also. Trot's objective was either to remain in the same business or to be with the same company. He looked for other opportunities. Suddenly an opportunity came through the corporations launching of new road construction programmes. Trot got involved in that. He developed an insider link of being able to change his quotation papers on the bash, knowledge of other quotes, municipal expectations and other relevant factors for which he paid 5 per cent cut money to the insiders helping him in this game. Trot established link with the top and influenced people including the selected few trade union heads in order to receive quick payment when there was a cash-rationing system prevailing. At each stage, the amount informally levied varied in percentages; it was however the highest at the top where a politician or a public representative happened to be the highest person. Most interesting part of Trot's story is that he had to quote the lowest amount in order to be the L1 (the lowest bidder) and win the business. Now, this necessitated Trot to quote such a low price that it compromised the quality of the work.

The effects in objective terms are shown in the following table.

Corporation Expectations	Trot	Causality/Result
Superb quality road made by using best grade stone chips	Provided decent looking (for the time being) road using a polish over poor quality stone chips	Weak fabric of the road, less durable
Use of heat-resistant pitch for road	Used poor quality material to complete the work quickly	Repeated expenditure from the public exchequer making the road durable for the same purpose
Minimum repair and maximum growth	Maximum number of repairs	Caused fiscal deficit

The aforementioned analysis shows how the satisfaction of personal motives of a few could jeopardize the ultimate objective for the growth of corporations.

In this case, Trot was prompted by the prevailing circumstances to choose an easier path of winning corporate battles. Growth objective of the municipal corporation demanded getting the best value for money spent on activities. But that was denied by a power nexus emanating from the unholy link that Trot established to get the contract sanctioned to him, to be satisfied with whatever quality he offered in his work and in return for a few personal gains in the chain. This signifies the unethical practice on the part of Trot as well as those who were the managers of Sonada Municipal Corporation. At the instance of fulfilling the gains of a few, the greater interest of the municipal corporation was getting sacrificed. A more general observation of the scenario could lead to the following conclusive effects of Trot's variety of acts.

Bending of Ethics

- Reducing the long-term framework to a shorter term
- Poor quality of public work
- Too much and repeated pressure on public exchequer
- Dominant minority extracting benefit at the cost of the vast majority
- Lack of integrity of the managers
- Organization losing focus and control
- Organization's existence is questioned by the actions it upheld

This is a glaring case of corrupt practice which in a sense is a definite violation of ethical norms. The municipal corporation as an entity has failed to protect and uphold the interest of general citizens who are the residents under its domain. It denied residents the following rights:

- Having a good civil infrastructure
- Getting good civil amenities
- Proper development
- Appropriate pace of growth
- Living a quality life

The most important concern, obviously, would be the spoiling of the public resources for the benefits of a few. Private consumption, here, overweighs the public considerations. The municipal corporation's obvious failure is to get into such a system. A way out of this would involve ethical initiative on the part of the organization. When public fund serves the dominant minority interest, it fails to satisfy its declared objective. The maximization linear programming model mentioned earlier proves this.

Matters that are elements of the core pertain to the character of individuals.

Whereas those surface factors pertain to behaviour, in the example of the air hostess, when smile is spontaneous, when it emanates from within, it is a character factor, while responses fall under behaviour, through method and act of a strategy. If one examines the scope and purviews of one against another, one obviously finds that the scope of behaviour is not a long-term one. Behaviour is focused for a shorter term. Character is for a longer term. Character defines the course of action, while behaviour gives it an immediate shape. The course of action that character defines is ethical, whereas those that behaviour sets are moral. So an ethical and moral course of initiative has both short- and long-term perspectives. While the long-term perspective defines and determines the course of action, the short-term perspective follows and maintains it. Quadrant B in Table 18.1 is the desired attribute combination in a personality.

Table 18.1 Character–Behaviour Matrix

A. High character, low behaviour	B. High character, high behaviour
C. Low character, low behaviour	D. Low character, high behaviour

In social and organizational contexts, the relationship between character and behaviour can make things more logically clear. Strong behaviour and character are revealed through personalities like Gandhi. On the other hand, personalities who have done atrocities in the world to make their own agenda happen reveal a strong character and weak behaviour. These are savage and demonic type of personalities. Persons with very weak character and behaviour are avoidable. However, all areas of weakness in the character–behaviour matrix can be augmented through an analysis of values–skill matrix given further.

M. K. Gandhi (Mahatma), the father of Indian nation, had been a person with a high standard of character and high behavioural instinct/responses. Gandhi, in national context, or J. R. D. Tata, in the organizational context, are people with certain set of qualities, which are as follows:

1. Honesty
2. Sincerity
3. Transparency
4. Integrity
5. Truthfulness
6. Generosity
7. Cooperation

Table 18.2 Values–Skill Matrix

F. High values, low skill	E. High values, high skill
G. Low values, low skill	H. Low values, high skill

In Table 18.2, the combination reflected in Quadrant E is the right mix of attributes. Quadrant H requires training in values, whereas Quadrant F requires training in skills. Quadrant G requires training in both areas.

Qualities of this sort form the basis of social and organizational ethics. An individual nurtures and grooms up their character based on the philosophy which they begin with. The first question that arises here is whether one can be ethical, yet successful, in corporations?

Long-term success and sustainability are possible only through being ethical at the individual and collective context of organizations.

Unethical entities cannot remain in the business and societies for long term; they are for short-term gains only. The unethical entities are destined to invoke pains and destructions in their tenure.

Doctrine of karma (laws of work) advocates 'like cause, like effect'. Any wrongdoing is destined to invite pains and destructions.

Becoming successful in personal, social or organizational contexts is a great thing. No doubt almost every individual, whoever they may be, thrives on becoming successful in their own areas. Successes could be perceived either in the short term or long term or both. This discussion obviously triggers a related discussion on the sanctity or purity of the ends of means. There are multiple ways to achieve success.

One can be successful when they target achieving the ends. While doing this, they could either maintain the sanctity of the means or not. An ethical means may or may not prove successful. For this, success would be measured against the target's backdrop or the ends. While trying to achieve integrity of the means, ethical objective can be maintained or not. In the event of maintaining integrity at the cost of achievement, the organization loses its focus and ultimately invites a question mark on its existence.

When survival is at stake, the company can hardly hold back its ethical decision in case of its day-to-day or future activities. Purity of means may not be very easy to maintain; if observed, the quality of work and life enhances greatly. Corporate concerns could be based on various combinations of the ethical positions for the means and ends. There could be situations where the context created might have several combinations or ethical alterations, which are as follows:

Ends	**Means**	**Objective**
Pure	Pure	Long term
Pure	Corrupt	Short term
Corrupt	Corrupt	Fragile and aimless

Long- and short-term concerns differ widely. When one wants to remain on the longer path, one certainly has to follow a certain set of principles which one adhered to as a general principle to be honoured by all. The matter could be better understood if the reverse situation is discussed. Let us take the combination of pure ends and corrupt means. Say, a company A has an end value of reaching a 50 per cent market share in the areas of FMCG products which are required for the organized sector. The following situations could be of interest and importance.

In the absence of integrity of means, the corporate competition turns into a battle of the jungle. The strategies showed clearly talk about this. In combination, the business with target company is won through an arrangement that the company has made by paying, say, bribe and so on. In this case, it is not the power of the product, service manpower or the technology that the company uses but the power to bribe.

While doing this, company A projects that awarding bribe should be considered fair instrument for business and in the long run, it is the unethical financial strength of the company that works, not the other areas of corporate activity.

If the corporate action boils down to fighting for business by paying bribes in financial terms, it reflects short-term orientation and is likely to pollute the corporate environment. The approach has a strong chance of getting back to the corporate climate and is likely to create a persistent unethical series of behaviours and actions in the organization.

Combination	Initiator Company	Target Company	Strategy	Outcome
C1	A	T	Off-screen	Win the business skimming with T
C2	B	T	Offensive	Defeat A off-screen, with T activity
C3	C	T^1	Counteroffensive	Defeat B, with T^1, win T off-screen
C4	D	T^1	Enhanced offensive	Defeat A, B and C, win T^1 and T

Once this rule has been upheld, the one in a position to offer more bribe will more effectively secure the business. That is what happened in the case of C2, C3 and C4 combinations as shown in the table. While winning T^1 pays the bribe and invests heavily in the company's activities, investments which boost the company's activities are of a long-term nature and greatly affect the company's prospects. Just because the company is unable to enhance the bribing base, it does not get market and hence faces problems.

Rational–quantitative view may be used as a guide to follow ethical path of decision and actions in many cases. One such approach is depicted further.

Maximize W and V, subject to I greater than or equal to R and W is less than equal to 1.

Where

W = Fraction of investment made in the division or activity under consideration
V = Fair values of the division as calculated, based on the standard and accepted norms of finance
I = Power of bribing or the informal investments made to promote and carry forward the activity under consideration with a view to fulfil the company objective
R = Revenue allocations to carry forward activities and promote business

The objective situation mentioned earlier is a linear programming problem which could be solved given the adequate data for that. Maximization of company value is a dependent function of the revenue allocation for the activities which the company wants to uphold. As and when the company wants to maximize the value of R, fund available in other areas of corporate activities will fall short of the respective expectations. A company faces two conflicting situations:

1. Maximization of R leads to the gradual reduction of the capacity of a company to meet contingent financial obligations.
2. Enhancement of value through R maximization would be an obvious deviation from the mission and principles of the company creating long-term problems.

Objectives of Ethics Practice

If I is defined as the scope of bribing in the organization, as because the scope exists, then the organization suffers a setback and V suffers to the extent I remains active. V depends upon the nature and scope of I; one should keep in mind important human factors when commuting the scope of I.

Power Distance Index

The factor, as indicated, sounds important based on the category of people involved and also the nature of involvement. V: maximization demands; I: minimization demands subject to other factors remaining constant. V could be considered as company specific, organization specific, situation specific or context specific.

It is, at the same time, perceived as a dependent function for the accomplishment of the objectives of the organization. I, as mentioned earlier, depends upon individuals in the system. It obviously impacts the power distance index (PDI) of the organization as also the persons involved in the chain and other people in the system.

Power distance may be the physical distance in power fabric of organization. It might be the informal power that rests in the organizational context within the individual. Therefore, power distance varies from one individual to the other, based on the informal and formal power they enjoy in the organization. The remedies that could be suggested here should begin with ethical rectitude of the organization and the relative position of the individual within the organization. A framework for ethical rectitude shall rest with the objective, mission and version of the organization.

The aforementioned analysis tries to prove a point that the usually uttered notion of 'ethics indifference brings success,' can be greatly disputed. Unethical practices can contribute to immediate gain, but at the cost of future prospects always. So it pushes the company to the realm of the short terms and promotes and upholds the schemes to survive and multiply in the chosen areas of its growth.

Unethical actions have another dimension also. If one puts their hands in fire, it is obvious that they would get burnt. Similarly, when another hand is put inside the ice cubes for a fairly long period of time, it will be cold. If both hands are engaged simultaneously, the one inside the fire and the other inside the ice cubes, the other will neutralize the impact of one. The effects of both shall only remain based on the nature of initiated causes.

Similarly, if an organization or an individual follows the corrupt means of achieving pure ends, it might achieve the purpose, but the net result will be the corruption of the entire system. One good act cannot neutralize a host of bad acts. One might argue about the sanctity, relevance and relativity of good and bad, but still a vast majority would definitely agree on one thing that the importance of it in individual and organizational dynamics cannot be ignored. No matter whatever be the amount invested in activities, unless the processes and functions turn ethical, it will be very hard to hold back the process of growth for enhancing it.

Government sanction of 100 units of currency for a particular activity reduces nearly to 10–15 units only for the proper activity; the rest is consumed by the intermediaries. The reduction in sanction value automatically reduces the activity's size, volume and quality. This has been a phenomenon throughout the world which reduces the scope and potential for the economies to grow and develop. The ethical functions of continuity indicate a normative relationship between the degree of unethical means and the fruits of development as an impact of the unethical means.

Other things remaining constant, in the absence of unethical means, effectiveness of an investment is maximum, but if the corrupt practices set in the benefits that might accrue from the activity dilute to a great extent and ultimately pull it down to the level of no development or static state. This is a resultant, effective condition which shows how material resources and energy dissipation takes place to take care of the players' concerns of the entire process. Those who are the economic games managers and organizers also consume the benefits of the entire process.

It is suggested by many Western scholars that a debate on philosophical basis of ethics is essential for constructing a developing opinion for the organization. There exist various approaches to ethics in business or management.

The broad divisions could be interpreted as shown in Table 18.3.

Table 18.3 Normative Ethics in Management

Holistic School		Teleological School		Deontological School	
Eternal ethics	Empirical ethics	Ethical egoism	Utilitarianism principle	Rights principle	Justice principle
(a)	(b)	(c)	(d)	(e)	(f)

As mentioned earlier, various schools of thoughts offer various points of view to look into the dimensions of ethics that give a shape to the different points of view and apply it to the respective organizations or scenarios. The philosophical basis of an organization goes a long way to get the approach to managing the means to achieve the ends in organizations. It is known to us that a particular habit is formed by an organization by the act it initiates based on the thoughts or thought waves that it had. Habit then finally determines the organization's destiny.

Doctrine of Karma (Law of Cause and Effect)

This has been explained by the following:

Sow a *thought*, reap an *act*.
Sow an *act*, reap a *habit*.
Sow a *habit*, reap a *character*.
Sow a *character*, reap a *destiny*.

Each and every bit of thinking prompts actions to initiate which fit the thought. It is therefore believed that in order to have a good act undertaken by anyone in an organization, a set of good thought waves is required to be cultivated. Culture of good thinking then becomes a prelude to good acts. This is true for all kinds of organizations and collective bodies. Thoughts are primarily cultivated on a very personal level by the individuals, depending on the consciousness levels of the individual. Thoughts initiated by many individuals thus combine to produce a collective thought. This aspect could be better understood, if an example from physical science is given. This integrative relationship is shown by wave–particle dualism.

Light flows in photon bundles—the basic particle which causes illumination. To give the effect of light, the light particles flow in continuity. This turns into a continuous wave as the time and space gap between two photons movement is minimum and tends to be zero. That means at a frequency of ejection, which tends be to infinite, particles of light combine in a collective to form waves.

It is this relationship between the individual and the collective that makes the individual an integral part of the collective. Also, the characteristics of the collective are formed at the instance of the individuals. It is the sum total of the individual characteristics corrected at the congregation level. So any decided thought or any kind of reworking of thoughts essentially requires mending or correction at the individual level and then the integration of the individual effects into a collective bracket. Obvious question may arise that if the collective has no homogeneity, then how will the dominant attributes of the collective be dependent on the dynamics of the majority or the influence of maximum parameters.

Chosen thoughts of the individuals thus constitute chosen characteristics of the collective. Thoughts of the collective then lead to collective action. Repetitions of the collective actions thus help to form a collective habit; the collective habit then forms a collective character, which in turn makes the destiny for the collective. Be it an individual or an organization, destiny at the collective level becomes utmost important. Ethical decisions in organizations depend on such ethical choices.

An ethical choice is an extension of the character of the entity. It is the prerogative of the organization that wants to pursue ethics or not, but the effects that the organization breeds in through that are very important and spectacular. An organization may take the decision to leave aside the question of ethical choices or otherwise to the individuals, unless the organizational character proves ethical at the collective level, the very purpose behind the organization's survival might be at stake.

On the topic whether ethics should be left to the prerogative and judgement of individuals, different schools of thoughts possess different opinions. Certain schools are of the viewpoint that ethics is a personal attribute and the involvement of organizations in that is not encouraged. Only at the individual level, ethical norms and practices are considered relevant. There is a certain other school which believes that at the collective level ethics should be encouraged. This school thinks that one cannot perform as ethical being unless the collective supports ethics or creates an ethical environment.

The environment creates an atmosphere congenial to ethical acclaim and rectitude. This school believes that ethical environment is the prerequisite to individual ethics. In other words, individuals cannot remain ethical unless a supportive environment is created.

The holistic school offers an integrated view of ethics. This primarily takes care of the concerns of either side of ethical ingredients. Discrimination on anything (age, gender, social class, economic class, ethnic origin, racial origin, religious origin and any other demographic parameter) is considered as violation of ethical principles. In this case of discrimination, one has to step into the other's shoes. In the case of other schools, discrimination is tackled in other ways.

Case: Karna, the Great Warrior

Basically, a person of noble origin gets burnt because of an unethical companion. Karna was born of Kunti, later known as the mother of five Pandava brothers: Yudhishthira, Bhima, Arjuna, Nakula and Sahadeva. The birth of Karna was not socially acceptable, as he came through an unusual route to see the light of the earth.

The story runs as follows: Once, the virgin girl Kunti got the chance to feed and serve the great sage Durbhasa. Sage Durbhasa was known for his one-pointedness. He used to reward people with great boons if he was pleased but a displeasure in Sage Durbhasa was definitely a matter of fear to people as he used to curse heavily. Sage Durbhasa was very powerful with a very high spiritual acclaim; both his boons and curses used to be highly effective and held good accurately as per his verbal assertion.

Being highly pleased with virgin girl Kunti's service, the sage rewarded Kunti with a great and unusual kind of boon. He said, 'Kunti, I give you the great power of being able to get a son of his own kind from any god you like at any point of time. You just have to utter the mantra (hymn) to the God of your choice.' Kunti became unusually thrilled. The young girl had wanted to see the efficacy of the sage's boon.

She offered the mantra towards the Sun God. Surprisingly, the Sun God blessed the virgin girl with the embryo of a son of his own kind. Son of the Sun God, besides all the divine qualities, had an extremely high potential and vigour. It was but an unusual scenario and socially unacceptable at that point of time in history. Kunti had no other alternative but to part with the newborn.

The boy was perfectly put on a raft, so that he could survive the river's normal onslaughts and floated in the water. The raft floated along the river current and when it reached the other bank, washermen saw it and it was picked up by a man who did not have children. The baby was brought up by that man. This is Karna's birth story. Karna, Kunti's son, is now known as Suta's son, the person whose care had made him survive and grow.

Karna gained knowledge of all kinds, including warfare. He had special privilege to learn warfare from a guru (teacher) of the magnanimity of Parashuram. He flourished into the full bloom of a sun being expert in all areas of knowledge. But since he was known to be the son of Suta and not belonging to a kingly family or a Kshatriya (the warrior class), he was denied entry from guru Dronacharya, who used to teach the Pandavas and Kauravas (the two streams of the princely family of the state), into the princely practice of learning warfare. He was even denied entry into the princes' performance show before the congregation of Bharata's royal family. The show had been witnessed by Dhritarashtra, king of the state, along with the court and the families. The performance of Arjuna, the third brother of the Pandavas, was the most spectacular. Karna learned all the fighting arts of excellence that Arjuna had exhibited. The family of origin created a differential treatment to them—Karna against Arjuna. This created a great revengefulness in Karna. Karna was eventually considered by Duryodhana, the eldest son of the blind King Dhritarashtra, as an extremely high and resourceful person.

Gradually, the feud in the princely family took a clear shape. The blind king Dhritarashtra denied the Pandavas their due share of power. Strictly speaking, Karna was the eldest among Kunti's children, but as nobody knew Karna's real identity, Yudhishthira was denied his right over the throne. Blinded by his affection for son Duryodhana, Dhritarashtra slowly transferred to the latter an effective mantle of power and denied its share of power to the sons of his brother Pandu. Karna became the closest and the greatest friend of Duryodhana—the effective head of the state.

Duryodhana and Karna had organized a game of chess. The defeated prince, Yudhishthira, was taken as bounded prisoner along with his brothers and wife Draupadi. Even in a broad daylight, Draupadi, the wife of Pandavas, was grossly insulted in the court having been prompted and enjoyed by Karna and Duryodhana. A lot of other incidents happened like that where Karna, as a trusted friend, either took an active part in or supported Duryodhana's gross mischievous and unethical acts. Everything Duryodhana used to do, Karna was an involved partner.

Finally, the Kurukshetra war came to be known as the inevitable war of righteousness with the unjust, unscrupulous and unethicals. Lord Krishna, the embodiment of God on earth and a friend of Arjuna, was always on the side of Arjuna and the Pandavas, who fought for their minimum right and for the establishment of righteousness in public and private life. Karna's objective in the Kurukshetra war was to prove that he is a superior match against Arjuna, and to defeat and kill Arjuna. Finally, Karna and Arjuna got a chance to face each other after the war had set in. Between them it was a terrible war but still deterministic. Just before the war broke out, Karna was stripped of certain essentials of his existence.

Known for his giving habit, Karna was approached one day by his mother Kunti. Kunti had shown him her motherly affection; Lord Krishna had revealed to him beforehand the fact that he was born of Kunti. Lord Krishna had advised Kunti to take away a protective gem which Karna had around his neck. Although surprised by his mother's request for the protective gem, Karna gave it to her knowing full well that this would endanger his life in a direct war before Arjuna. The divine arranged for this to protect the righteous. Karna, though noble, by his personal character and attribute wrapped up his sins perpetually by being supportive to, and in many cases showing strong affiliations for, Duryodhana, the symbolic figure of unjustness, cruelty, unrighteousness and evil.

Another problem for Karna was a curse he had got from his guru Parashuram. Parashuram was under the impression that Karna was a Brahmin. He made a vow to clear the world of the warriors by making the Brahmins victors. Karna was found by him as not belonging to the Brahmins but to the Kshatriyas because of a certain variety of habit which the latter possessed by contrast against the former. Parashuram had cursed Karna saying that when the right time comes for the application of the knowledge that he has gained, it will be forgotten by him in the field of war and his chariot will also be stuck up by the earth preventing its movement.

In the background of these, Karna faced a terrible war with Arjuna, the archer par excellence, in the Kurukshetra field. Karna had always been the supporter of the crimes committed by Duryodhana. By his association with the unrighteous, Karna was tainted with co-actor in evil schemes, while Arjuna, on the other hand, had the superiority as he was one of the main protectors of righteousness; therefore, the Lord was with him.

The war began with Arjuna and Karna fighting each other with dreadful weapons which crashed each other in the air or on the ground. After that, Arjuna intensified the war. Arjuna had waged a war on the principles of traditional war.

So far, that principle had never been violated by Arjuna. If someone does not possess arms at any point of time, the rule suggests not to use any weapon to assault or kill them. Arjuna's war intensification required Karna's matching which he tried but now the curse fruited itself. Karna had forgotten to use those weapons which were the need of the moment. The problem intensified when his chariot's wheels also got stuck in the ground arresting his mobility. Arjuna, at the instance of Lord Krishna, had utilized this moment when Karna was trying to make the chariot wheel run, putting his arms aside, urging Arjuna not to use weapons against him at that moment. Arjuna had fired the appropriate weapon on Karna, which put an end to the latter's life. Heavily hurt Karna immediately accused Arjuna of killing him unarmed and thus described this as an act of cowardice and against the principles of the morality and ethical principles of war.

Ethical Issues in the Case of Karna

- The usual allegation was that Karna, otherwise a good man, was killed by Arjuna in a way that violated the war principles that were otherwise properly observed by Arjuna throughout.
- The second allegation was that Kunti, Karna's real mother, knew full well that she would put her first and virgin-born son's life in danger by taking the protective gem from him.
- The third allegation was that Karna was deprived of the right opportunity to grow and establish his worth in the world because of social discrimination.
- The fourth allegation is against the Lord. It is said that Lord Krishna, who knew everyone's background, had weakened Karna's mind by revealing him the fact that he was born of Kunti, and that the Pandavas were his younger brothers. When he came to know that he was supposed to wage a war against his younger brothers, he might have reduced his aggrandizement and effectiveness in the war accordingly.

Responses Using the Holistic Viewpoint of Ethics

Holistic view of ethics looks at things in its totality. The empirical wing of it looks at the immediate causes and effects. From this point of view:

- Arjuna can be blamed for violating the war morality.
- Kunti can be blamed for violating the principles of motherhood.
- Lord Krishna can be blamed for gross violation from divine qualities.

Empirical ethics examines things at the point of its occurrence. It considers things in isolation. From an empirical point of view, every incident is considered in isolation and examined in its own light. An incident in itself is complete and autonomous, and requires a sort of self-test. The incident being ethical or not is proved through its attributes. While considering the empirical ethics, the background and surrounding relationships are not considered at all. Empirical ethics, judging every incident by its own quality, obviously comes to the conclusion that the actions of Arjuna, Kunti and Lord Krishna were unethical.

From a holistic point of view, eternal ethics takes a fresh look at the ethical dimension. Look back and place things at the stream of flow of incidents over a longer period of time. The purpose of being ethical or not comes out very clearly. The essence of the entire Mahabharata War has been a struggle consistently done for and in favour of righteousness. Arjuna was pivotal in carrying the war of righteousness forward under the divine instruction and guidance of Lord Krishna. Karna, though a nice person at his individual level, was always a part of the crimes committed by the king and the prince. In fact, Karna was considered one of the most important heroes by King Duryodhana to protect him for whatever the degree of crime he committed.

Karna considered himself as an integral component of the Kauravas, the wrongdoers, and took the reign not only to protect Duryodhana but also to establish his right as superior. Thus, the existence of Karna was a real threat to dharma or righteousness; by choice, he was a criminal as such in his act.

And as it was not really possible to kill him while he had the protective gem on, Kunti did the right thing by collecting the protective gem from him and putting him into a threat of life. By protecting dharma, Lord Krishna really performed the divine act. He offered everybody the clues and showed ways to finish Karna straightaway, who sided with the demons and gave them muscle and nerve power. By actively protecting dharma, Arjuna did the right thing too. Besides, as a husband, Arjuna had every right to take revenge on the result Karna and Duryodhana had inflicted on his wife Draupadi. In the Kurukshetra war, Karna was a real threat to the victory.

Karna needed to be killed as quickly as possible. The concern for righteousness is much above the time-bound concerns for morality in the affairs of war. Arjuna really upheld dharma and protected ethical values by taking the chance to kill Karna.

We are presenting two cases here to make the lines of difference between the empirical and eternal principles of ethics clear. The first case has been taken from a major set of interactions in Mahabharata, the world's greatest epic, and the other has been taken from a set of practices, views and visions of a modern corporation that occupies a significantly honourable position among global corporations.

Ethical Analysis of People: Production Concern in the Background of R. R. Blake and J. S. Moulton Model

Country Club (1,9)	**Team Management (9,9)**
Production is incidental to lack of conflict and good fellowship (ethically sensitive—fragmented)	Production is from integration of task and human requirements Ethically sensitive (integrated)
Impoverished Management (1,1)	**Dampened Pendulum (5,5)**
Effective production is unobtainable because people are lazy, apathetic and indifferent (ethically poor)	
Middle of the road, push for production, but do not go all out. Be fair but firm (moderately ethically sensitive)	
Task management (9,1) People are a commodity, just like machines (Ethics Neutral)	
Production-oriented	

Source: Blake and Moulton (1962).

Teleological Ethics

So far, we have discussed the concepts and cases of the holistic school of business ethics. We have also discussed various approaches to that. As explained earlier, the eternal and empirical aspects of ethics carry a set of different meaning. As mentioned, eternal ethics differs widely from the empirical one on the scope, purview, expanse and dimension of it. In nature, the eternal view of ethics could be considered as holistic. It tries to integrate all aspects of life and activity in order to find out the form of ethics. An incident according to this model of ethics cannot be considered in isolation. This requires an overall discussion and analysis of things pertaining to any incident/occasion.

An incident takes place on the basis and standing of its background, legacy and tradition. It involves many players and operators to look into things, who have different viewpoints and even different angularities. One person's point of concern may not be the same as the others. In fact, the response each one gives is unique in nature, and differs significantly from the other person's response. Holistic outlook demands that the positions as reflected through different participants of the system have to be honoured and taken care of. It is a sort of totality in the outlook and vision and pruning actions accordingly.

The holistic school of ethics cannot remain indifferent to the means while achieving the ends. It cannot be even like becoming cautious of the means as the ends deserved it. The holistic school also highlights the importance of ends, but always in the background of the means that have been adopted to reach the ends. The basic assumption here lies on the belief that people like David Bohm have advocated. David Bohm suggests that a complete and total view of any object is only possible when the observer, the observed and the instrument of observation are on the same level of consciousness. Observer may have a definite point in their mind and some motive in the back of it, but from a holistic perspective the whole thing dawns on the person.

Teleological ethics focus on the end result and then relate the end result to the process of achieving the autonomy of individual 'teleo' which means a consequence. One who is consequence conscious and still is ethical becomes teleologically ethical.

Teleological, as we have already mentioned, may have two different aspects of it: ethical egoism and utilitarianism. While both are concerned with 'should' and 'ought', and are concerned with the study or values and standards, they try to supply and justify a coherent and consistent moral system and lead to a hierarchical system of norms and rights from which second- and third-order rules could be evolved. Teleological is normally connected to the quality of consequences, whereas deontological concerns about the quality of one's intention towards that.

'Ethical egoism' is based on the concept of ethical relativism. Ethics does not have a universal standard according to this school of thought. Things, incidents and interactions at the time of occurrence, place of occurrence depending upon the entity involved in that have to be measured on the merit of their quality. Things and interactions could be judged on the quality of them as against the quality or the standards and potentials of similar things, activities, interactions and so on. Ethical egoism derives its origin from the relativistic aspects of ethics.

Companies behave ethically on two grounds, which are as follows:

1. Ethics helps develop credibility.
2. Ethics is essential to sustain.

This shows that companies reckon with their own standards and the standards and norms of the recommendable in order to ascertain that there is no gap in credibility. Companies either abide by the market standards or adhere to their own standards. The process starts with companies being able to come out with the following:

1. Mission statement
2. Objectives to perform
3. Objective standards to achieve with a view to fulfil the mission

The steps involved in this are not really out of the track of the company's doing a business so far. The enterprise, in its pursuit to take the business ahead, might consider those aspects of doing the business as the elements and ingredients of being sustainable on longer terms.

Case: Ethical Egoism

Edward's Cries

David and Fran visited the rear part of Amazon along with their kid in their weekend. Fran, a caring mother of unusual upcoming, was always prepared to sacrifice her comfort with a view to taking care of the baby. When the proposal came from her husband, David, to spend a week in the deeper part of Amazon, Fran was really excited. To a great extent, Fran's immediate excitement was because of the opportunity to take her one-year-old son out to visit one of the nature's plantation areas. Fran's baby boy, named Edward, was a crying baby who was always under medical care. Edward always felt peace only in David's lap. Both the parents were highly affectionate to the child and found a scope to delight Edward in the Amazon tour.

Being a dense forest, Amazon was heavily infested with deadly animals and cannibal tribals. Also, man-eating cannibal tribals were especially fond of the flesh of crying children.

David drove his limousine deep into the forest before the resort for halt and rest. It was a cloudy day and they fell in love with the pleasant surroundings. The gentle breeze, a cloudy contour, upright forest with a tremendous degree of intrinsic attractions almost dragged the couple with their child down the unsealed paths that were hardly traceable deep inside the forest. They were enjoying the trip so much that the child also took a stride to get up in the wakes of the forest.

The trees greeted the dignified visitors through their blooms. They were cheered over by floral feed. Herbs were hushed at David's walking. The air smeared at the ear and faces of the minor and the pair of adults. It proved so charming to them that it really defeated all spreads of their lives. Fran recalled her first days of love for David. It was so soothing and tough at the same time. A simultaneous blow of hot and cold relations reckoned through the medium of nature. It seemed that the entire amount of happiness and bliss that could have been there in a lifetime was present for them at Amazon rainforest and David, Fran and the young Edward all enjoyed that to the full brisk.

While everything went so fine and enjoyable, the situation suddenly got a dramatic turnaround. David, who had gone farthest, saw a group of a few forest men approaching. While David and others were on the top of one of the cliffs, they found the man-eating tribals running down the other hill. The glacier which ran in between separated the two. The forest was partly on the hills and partly on plains. On the hilly side was the rest house where tourists like David came and stayed. The hilly area that David was exploring was constantly being protected from deadly animals and man-eating tribals through the iron nets and by security guards. Every half an hour, security guards gave a round to the jungle interiors with a view to protect the tourists who ventured into the jungle for a thrilling personal experience.

Within the jungle, there were safety caves at definite intervals that could be used as a sort of protective places. Jungle tribes who were the deadliest used to run around and break in the caves only when they were in groups with a good number. Man-eating tribals were very much fond of the child flesh. Whenever they got a child to devour alive, they celebrated a feast in groups. The usual norm as followed by them had been that whenever there had been some occasion for them to celebrate with child flesh, they excused the adults and others through remaining indifferent with them.

When David saw the group of man-eaters rushing from the other hill towards them, he became frightened. David called Fran and Edward, and started running to the guest house. They were under the impression that the tribal team will take more time than required by them to reach the safe enclosure. But to his surprise, David soon realized that the group was getting closer. There was no way out except a safety cave nearby. David rushed to Fran and pulled them inside the cave with a safety net being given over the cave. David, Fran and Edward, afraid of being taken by the man-eating tribals, embraced each other. Fran prayed to the divine, 'Oh Lord, see that my beloved Edward and his father are saved to life.' David also prayed in his mind urging the Lord 'to save Edward and Fran'. Shocked by the knock of death, inside the safety cave the couple and the child trembled in fear, hoping against all the lost hopes of seeing the faces of the armed security guards on the ground.

Security guards gave a round at certain intervals inside the jungle for the rescue of tourists in danger. Minutes went on; the security guards had not been seen at all. Time had already come for the man-eating tribals to search them out. Man-eaters, in search of the team, came down to the area where David and his family were actually hiding, but were unable to trace them out even on a longer search. At this stage, the real problem started. Suddenly Edward spurred loud cries, usual to his nature. It created real danger for the entire team. David and Fran became really shocked. It was a great moment of danger for all of them. Fran put in all possible efforts into persuading the baby to stop crying. Fran's solace did not stop Edward. The child now reckoned to more violent cry. Vigorous as it was, it now gave man-eaters the chance to trace their food. Once they were out into the jungle, the man-eaters would be in an advantageous position to pick up the chosen item, the baby Edward. Edward had real difficult times all the more so when the danger had been dragged to the door by him. Fran and David's desperate bid did not stop Edward from crying so loudly. Now it was not only the objects' smell but also the indications received through Edward's loud cries that the man-eating tribals could trace the family out. Facing death, David was now thinking deeply about the options left with.

The following thoughts flashed in his mind:

- All of us should stay together and face the slotted fate.
- I should try to stop Edward from crying by applying force, beating him, even beating him to unconsciousness, if required. If Edward stops crying hopefully, we might have some time for respite and if the security people reach by that time, we would all be saved.
- A rational approach would be to take the advantage of the custom of man-eating tribals who do not touch others when they get hold of a child. If they are offered with a child's life, delighted tribals will go away leaving aside others untouched. In this case, they will save two lives out of three. The maximum injury inflicted on them would thus be minimized.

David thought but did not find a way out. Fran thought it was her ill plight and insistence that Amazon was selected as the tourism and adventure spot. So she thought she was responsible for the likely loss of all three lives. God knew what was going on in the mind of Edward and he cried with the same, if not higher, veracity making all known of their presence in a particular place.

Discussion on the Case: Edward's Cries

Edward's Prerogatives

It is certain that Edward put his parents and himself into trouble. Edward had no intention of doing so. It was only a matter of childish habit that made him cry all the time. The prerogative of Edward was to communicate in his usual pattern, which here were loud cries. The question may arise as to why this habit? Edward, a lone child of David and Fran, did not receive due personal care and importance from the parents. Both David and Fran were busy professionals and had little time for their son. Even though they were trying to give Edward their individual time, giving him time together was a very rare occasion. Both the parents found hardly any occasion to delight the child with their personal presence.

A sense of deficit accrued in Edward and got released through the loud cries. Edward, a child, did not have the capacity to safeguard himself. His parents, his natural custodians, must take care of him at the right moments for the right set of things. If something happens to Edward, it means a neglect or inefficiency on the part of his parents. Edwards's prerogative was to be at the custody and complete refuge in his parents. Edwards's parents must have had the courage, conviction and capacity to protect the intrinsic and extrinsic interest of Edward in all situations.

The Parents' Concerns

Having understood the prerogatives of Edward, it remains to be mentioned that the parents of Edward would like to have the personal concerns also, in addition to their concerns for their son. It is true that Edward occupied a great part of the parents concern, suffice it to say that Edward's getting due share of case had been the primary concern here also. The parents, because of their nature of professional involvements, did not find personal time to be given to the pleasure of Edward. This made them decide on a special occasion for the delight of Edward; Amazon had been chosen because of its unique ruggedness, the thrill of experiencing the shadows of peril and above all being away, deep in the jungle to mingle with the deadliests with a view to have an everlasting experience that was prolonged in the memory for quite a longer tenure.

The Ethical Concern

While in this context the concerns of the son and parents are clearly understood, ethics has its own demands and ramifications.

Teleological ethics look into the problem with a view to either

1. Maximize minimum benefits available or
2. Minimize maximum problems

As the argument given earlier, if two out of three lives could be saved at the cost of one, it is advisable to do so. Now, it could be mentioned that the man-eating tribals got delighted with a human child at their midst as an item of food. They do not just kill and devour it, rather they celebrate the incident in a big way assembling in a place, renunciating other food and prey items for the day and enjoying with tribal cultural demonstrations. Supposing that David knew this special custom of those man-eating tribals and supposing they had opted for a consequential concern, it could have been the right choice on the part of David to offer Edward as a gift to the man-eaters to delight them and at the same time to save the lives of Edward's parents. This could prove to be a cruel act on the part of a parent to offer their child to death with a view to survive. This act of David could mean minimizing the number of casualties from three to one.

The general argument that could be put forward here is against the calculations and result-oriented decisions. Since the man-eating tribals do normally see a child as their target in a group of people, they do not stop until that target is fulfilled. So, in the absence of supportive security, it was not possible for David to save Edward by sacrificing either of the parent's lives. The other alternative would have been to emotionally force them and crush them to death all at once. This, of course, fulfils David and Fran's parental obligation but is not helping Edward anyway. Because, so far as Edward is concerned, in both the cases, the end result remains the same total annihilation. Edward could sense cruelty in the parents in the first case, and in the second case, their greatness, dedication, love and affection for him. The aspersions are on the parents, not on outcomes.

Business Similia

Having discussed the various aspects of the case from the point of view of the result, one may extend the discussion to the business. Supposing the business is in crisis. The crisis could be financial, technological, managerial and so on or anything of this kind. The result of the BPR suggests a 50 per cent cut in the human force for survival.

The decision might take the enterprise to the re-emergence threshold. In a system of hire-and-fire philosophy, this of course is no problem at all. But those economics where social concern is among the basic concerns, the firing of people could create problems, particularly in unionized organizations and regimes. It is mostly seen in developing countries where the social safety net is yet to emerge and take shape, a lot of resistance comes from the society against winding up or seating down business activities. In most of the cases, free flexibility in scaling up or down is missing.

Normative Ethical Views

The Holistic School

The holistic school believes that there are two different approaches to ethics—eternal and empirical. The Bhagavad Gita has set the tone for this as follows:

Dwabimou Purusha lokae Ksharaseakshara eva cha ksharah sarvani bhutani Kutasthakshra uchyatae I.

(Bhagavad Gita 15.16)

The world consists of the empirical and the eternal beings. All the worldly things come under the empirical self, whereas the timeless, space-less dimension comes under the eternal.

The principles of eternal ethics believe in the core divinity of individuals. Man is not only potentially divine but also divine in all-out behaviour and actions. It is this intrinsic divinity that takes humanity to the height of divinity. Growth takes place not only in human dimension but also in other dimensions. Man is considered as an embodiment of the divine. It is the divine who thinks and acts in man's garb. Biodiversity is then the diverse revelation of the same divine in different directions and proportions.

An individual's true identity could be better understood through one's set of self-identity introspection.

'See who you are' through a set of questions which are addressed to you. The selection alternatives are discussed further.

Self-identity: Selection Alternatives

Set A	**Set B**
I am a body	I have a body
I am a mind	I have a mind
I am senses	I have senses
I am body–mind senses combined	I have a body, mind and senses

Selection alternative, according to the holistic school of thought, would suggest Set B for it. 'I', the factor, which talks about an individual, is surely the revelation of the eternal in the empirical. The relationship would be as follows:

Set C	**Set D**
I am the instrument	Thou art the player
I am the chariot	Thou art the charioteer
I am the outer	Thou art the inner
I am the extrinsic	Thou art the intrinsic
I am the worldly	Thou art the spiritual
I am the mundane	Thou art the eternal
I am the fragment	Thou art the integral
I am petty, small, mean	Thou art the dignity, greatness and vastness

The relationship could be extended to infinite series encompassing all aspects of our existence. Sets C and D coined to each other in apparent reciprocity, but these are intertwined in closed circuits and are either side of the same coin to express coin fully.

Every form of revelation is but a form of the intrinsic truth. Person is the subtle form of the intrinsic.

Cause and Source of Holistic Bliss

It is the eternal bliss that makes the created create, survive and perpetuate. 'Bliss', according to Vedanta, could be both eternal and empirical. Eternal bliss takes various forms and is expressed through emotions such as happiness, pleasure, satisfaction and fulfilment. Happiness and pleasure are the direct derivatives of bliss. Man is satisfied when bliss takes root in reality in the personality. Therefore, he mostly draws satisfaction from the world.

Business world runs on the derivative of bliss also. Take the case of marketing. Be it a product or the case of service marketing; personal or impersonal marketing; contact of cyber marketing, the intrinsic rules, always, are to satisfy the customer, if not delight them. A customer gets pleasure of being delighted only through the fulfilment of desired objectives and fulfilling the concerns for things. Delight and satisfaction, as mentioned, are again the derivatives of bliss. Bliss, the driving force of the living world, the essentiality of all interactions, is expressed through various forms of revelations.

This gives rise to the quality between one that resides within and the one that is seen. The first could be considered as the inner person, while the second as the outer person. As long as the outer person dominates and rules over the inner person, we are in the extrinsic or exteriorized world. The moment there is a change in it, the symmetry starts setting in. It is the harmony and symmetry that is established and makes the system perfect. Exteriorized person loses contact with the inner person. The inner person loses hold over the outer person.

Vedanta again establishes the relationship through a network of different levels of consciousness. According to the Vedantic doctrine, every living entity is a reflection of the consciousness that they represent. Depending upon the levels of consciousness, the behaviour of a person is determined. The five layers of consciousness are considered as five different sheaths (*kosha*). The sheaths are called:

- *Annamaya kosha* or the material sheath
- *Pranamaya kosha* or the vital sheath
- *Manomaya kosha* or the mental sheath
- *Vijnanamaya kosha* or the knowledge sheath
- *Anandamaya kosha* or the blissful sheath

The sheaths determine the quality of personality and also its scope to perform. For example, when *annamaya kosha* or material sheath dominates, it is the primarily the material instinct of life which rules. Human beings at the *annamaya kosha* could be described as the persons with endless hunger, endless thirst and endless lust for sex. *Annamaya* is after the material objects and always wants to remain in that. *Annamaya* personality analyses every incident in the light of its own material identity. Considerations are hunger, sex and so on.

Once hunger is satisfied, it gives rise to another need. Stomach calmed means the next need becomes vibrant. The need for sex then usually multiplies manifold and vice versa. When the personality progresses further on the scales of consciousness, it shows a dominant vitality. Vital sheath shows the dominance of vitality. One is how much potent is a futile question but more futile is the question how much energy one can maintain and exude. Vital sheath is the sheath of action. It shows the kinds of actions that are needed. Vital sheath talks about actions all around. At this stage of consciousness, work dominates—it is but the amount and pace of dynamism that becomes very important. Vital sheath takes care of the vital and applied vitality of human being. Consciousness makes a person go for multiple actions with renewable sources of energy at each spark of thought and action.

Any movement incorporates the vitality and takes care of the vital entity. In the corporate world, the usual dynamism that sets in could be described as being mentioned in corporate dynamism.

Corporate Dynamism

- Breeding conflict, eroding cooperation
- Less harmony, more divergence
- Gratitude and respect being shifted from intrinsic qualities to money and position
- Concern for the short term at the cost of long term
- Soft values of existence being sacrificed to harder objectives
- Fragmented mind being given overdue importance over integral mind
- Noble qualities being subdued for lollipops
- Status consciousness overwhelming the divine consciousness
- 'Success' becomes the keyword replacing 'perfection'
- Competition leads to the war of nerves
- Work context becoming stressful
- Grabbing, not giving, becomes the rule

Vital creates the dynamism but through the other levels of consciousness the end effects are smoothed out.

As it is seen, vital sheath leads to certain levels of actions which prioritize the ends and not the means. Both *annamaya* and *pranamaya koshas* would tend to prioritize the concerns for ends and forget about the means to achieve the ends. It is the definite concern for means that makes one ethical. Ethics demands a continuous awareness for the means to begin with and then to see that performance conforms to the standards set for it in terms of the purity of means. *Annamaya* and *pranamaya koshas* in that respect stand basically divergent from ethical standards. Consciousness does not remain static at these outer sheaths. Its journey is always towards the inner core which is the blissful sheath.

Manomaya kosha, or the mental sheath, becomes important at the immediate next layer of consciousness. Mental sheath talks about the dominance of mind. *Manomaya kosha* dominates when the mind takes over and shows the path to the individual to set the tone for the personality. Psychosomatic, as individual human being is now called, is basically a reflection of the *manomaya kosha*. Mental sheath is the medium of corroborating the outer with the inner, the external with the internal. *Atman*, it is said to be fertile, is related to the body through the *manomaya kosha*.

The role of mind here is that of a link. Mind links body to self. *Atman* or the self is connected to mind and the body. So there is a continuity of connection between the body and the self through the action and impulse of mind. This shows that mind can augment the quality of consciousness in one. Through the engineering of mind, an individual could be transformed from one with animal habits and orientation. According to this school of thought, it is a level of consciousness of *annamaya* and *pranamaya koshas*. Mind can bring in the required changes in material as well as the vital sheaths and bring in the level of confidence that establishes their divine identity, that is, human self is no less than the divine.

Mental sheath takes you to the next inner level of consciousness that is *vijnanamaya kosha*. *Vijnanamaya* and *anandamaya koshas* jointly form the psychic self or psyche. Psyche represents the divine in individuals. Psyche of one should be identical with that of another. *Anandamaya kosha* brings the joy of fulfilment. As mentioned already, human actions are prompted by the concern for *ananda* in any form (happiness pleasure, joy and satisfaction). *Anandamaya* state of consciousness is the supreme human state wherein humans identify themselves with the divine.

Divine identity is difficult to establish but once this is through, human beings tend to forget about personal considerations, at least prioritization changes. 'It is thou first, me then' becomes the imperative of human being. Grabbing gives way to giving. Society stands on the giving principles. Psyche is universally self-seated in human being. It is the embodiment of the formless, changeless and immutable. At this level, truth and light prevail in all signifying the unity and oneness of all. As mentioned earlier, Vedanta offers the idea of universal personality which is common in all; therefore, one cannot harm others. One cannot do wrong to the others. An individual that realizes the divine in themselves is an integrated one, holistic one. As already mentioned, a holistic being only realizes the concern for others and then the concern for the means becomes automatic and spontaneous.

Ethikos

Greek Root of Ethics

Ethics, by definition, pertain to the character having been derived from the Greek term *ethikos*. Character, unlike behaviour, is an intrinsic factor which derives from the innermost. Vedanta suggests *atman* is an intrinsic man. It is the level of experience that *atman* gathers and it is symbolic of the level of consciousness that one is in. A mental sheath which is at the transition can rule over the body and the empirical system. Mental sheath tunes the vital and the material towards the consciousness of the psychic. This is a condition to formation of the integrated personality. According to Vedanta, an integrated personality is one which is essentially an embodiment of the divine and knows that everything is divine or everything rests in the divine. It is the divine that manifests in all and therefore being slave to the senses is not wise. It is better to behave like automated system and personality.

This shows that an integrated personality would go for revelation of divine through the acts of it. Therefore, when it comes to consuming many things and be satisfied with that, the integrated personality goes for a renounced consumption, a set of consumption that depends upon the degree of renunciation. Renunciation is then the spirit of ethics. A renounced soul realizes the concern for others through the understanding of the dominant factors that we have become servants to.

Desire

Desire is fundamental in the creation of need and demand for consumption of things in the market. Desire at the individual level is an element of the collective demand. A society and a market which are devoid of desire lack in the speed of growth of the market demand. However, the excessive and arrogant nature of desire could jeopardize market equilibrium and poise.

Desire, as is the experience of the most, shows that since it does not have limiting factors, it cannot make a system which is responsive. A sort of response to others would require the understanding of the problems and concerns of others. A competitive market can turn into a cooperative one and yet do the best for the individual enterprises. Enterprises would expect maximization of revenues and worth through maximization of sales or other revenue-generating activities. The maximization principle would obviously expect an out-and-out command over things and resources with a view to have an indiscriminate pattern of consumption.

Unlimited consumption always brings in a set of war of nerves among the participants of the system. Ultimately, it turns into an order of win-lose wherein one's win is obviously another's loss. One mounts on resources at the cost of the other. In the absence of the concern for others or the realization of others' problems, the competition turns into war. This had been the observation of Sage Vyasa, the author of the world's greatest epic Mahabharata, as expressed in the *svargoroham parva* (the section on the ascension to heaven) which is discussed further.

Righteousness and the Social Concern

Urdhvabahur viraumyscah na hi Kascit cchrunati mam
Dharmad arthasca kamasca Sa kim artham na sevyate.

(Mahabharata)

I cry with arms uplifted, yet none heeded from righteousness flow forth pleasure and profit. Why then do you not follow righteousness?

Sage Vyasa is crying out for a righteous life and society with his arms raised. Righteousness should be the basis of life. If individuals start becoming righteous, then that reflects in the collective. A collective righteous also offers the context for the organizations to perform ethically. When the concerns for anyone else are important to an operator, ethics becomes an automatic variable of the society.

Organization performing in a righteous manner would also induce others for making a righteous decision and action. Righteousness forms the basis of life and of society. The righteous society also provides the conditions for progress and skimming profits to grow. Growth is an obvious offshoot of righteousness through profiteering.

According to the school of thought, righteousness flows from the core personality who has turned divine. Divine lives and works inside and through them makes their thoughts, actions and choices righteous always.

This concern for others is again reflected in terms of social actions or desired actions which prove harmless and not obstructive to others.

Taming Consumption for Sustainable Order

A limiting condition on the consumption pattern is very essential for a sustainable world order that affects the weaker in the society and the system. When hunger predominates, fulfilling the demand of the stomach proves to be the most urgent and important one. Everybody has the right to satisfy their hunger through the means they want to adopt. Accumulation of the resources and wealth leads to social discrimination which, according to the principle of goodness, is a punishable crime. The arrangements of a free society contradict this principle. When competition becomes the rule of the society, one cannot put a barrier to the vertical growth of that.

Darwin's 'survival of the fittest' theory makes it all the most difficult to contain anybody to a desired limit. It is these limits which are self-imposed that can only work. In order to create harmony for the existence, self-imposed limits can go a long way to bringing social harmony and any other sector. Although the global society talks about this harmony, it goes a long way to create turbulence in that. Harmony establishes peace unto all. In all spheres, harmony is established from the inner urge to be with others and to remain in the social front for the sake of future growth with perspectives that talk about the harmony for all kinds of organizations and efforts. Peace and harmony unto all become the doctrine for humanity. Vedanta believes in the doctrine of wholeness. Human beings are considered as the embodiment of the whole that they are part of.

This is a wonderful postulate to honour and highlight the wholeness in life and actions. Wholeness is the basic character of the entities. Whatever be there, essentially it be whole. Whole reveals him as the fragment and creates problems being the fragment. The implications in the society could be charted as follows.

Wholeness	**Fragmentalism**
• Independent, self-starter	• Dependent, requires prompting
• Autonomous, self-sufficient	• Impulsive, deficit driven
• Dignity, generosity, giving	• Pettiness, meanness, smallness
• Transcends the barriers of space and time	• Contained by space and time
• $W = f(T, E)$ Where W stands for wholeness T stands for time span of life of the entity E stands for eternity	• $F = f(t, h)$ Where F stands for fragments t stands for the short span of zero to infinite h stands for the human which is the essence of divinity. Essence of excellence

The view of wholeness is congenial to forming an implicate order that takes care of the whole system. Divine personality proves to be eternal, integrated and full. In it, the implications on the corporate organizations could be felt at different degrees. This is primarily felt at the level of personalities. An integrated personality can help bringing in holistic ideas and practices in organizations.

Identifying the fragments in the organizations is the task to be undertaken at the individual level. Collective composition of these individuals forms a collective personality for the enterprise. A collective personality behaves like fragments when the individuals in the group are fragments; on the contrary, majority of the individuals in the collective are integrated beings, it reflects in the group dynamics. Group behaviour then becomes the behaviour of people with a holistic mind.

Decision-making and Problem-solving through Holism

1. Decision-making
    - Take the views of all to arrive at a decision.
    - Merit the strength of views only.
    - Be consequence oriented. See that maximization objectives are fulfilled.
    - Weak, lower in hierarchy should not be ignored.
    - Be proactive in views and actions.
2. Problem-solving
    - Take a helicopter view of the problem.
    - Put yourself in the shoes of the conflicting parties.
    - Understand the depth and spread of the problem.
    - Try to understand the problem on the basis of its legacy and potentials.
    - Take a long-term view of the problems, offer long-term solutions.
    - Involve yourself as a detached observer also.

Holistic personality analysis starts with identifying certain ranges of qualities or attributes of those personalities. According to this view, there are two classes of personalities:

1. Divine personality (*daivi purusha*)
2. Demonic personality (*asuric purusha*)

Divine Personality (According to the Bhagavad Gita)

Attributes of divine personalities are such that they make those personalities look like the gods in the heaven. The Bhagavad Gita has laid down certain ranges of qualities for that. Demonic personality also follows certain other sets of attributes. Both are inherited from the same source. The gods and demons are believed to be related as brothers to each other. They belong to the same gene and tradition, parenthood and habitat. Socially accepted and good qualities are attributed to the devas, while the other sets belong to the *asuras*, opposite in character to the former one.

The Bhagavad Gita outlines the divine attributes in the following verses:

Abhyam Sauwasamshudhir jnanayoga vyabasthiti Danam domashca
yajinagshca swadhyastapa arjabam Ahimsa Satyam Krodhastyagah
Shantih apaishunam Dayer bhuteshu loluptwam mardaba hriracapalam
Teja kshama dhritih shoucam adroha natimanata
Bhabanti sampadam daivim abhijatsya bharata.

(Bhagavad Gita, 16/1-3)

Fearlessness, purity, committed to divine knowledge; giving, disciplined senses, respectful studies, asceticism; simplicity; non-injury to others, truthfulness and forbidden anger, peace. Not being a fault finder, compassion, non-greedy, non-cruelty, not involving in bad works, calmness, courageous, forgiveness, patience, cleanliness, cooperative, non-egoistic—these are all the attributes of a divine personality.

Ethical Analysis of the Budget Motivation Model of V. H. Vroom

Motivation = (Valence × Expectancy)

Budget Motivation = (Valence of attaining budget × Perceived influence on results) + (Valence of other effects of actions × Expectancies of these other effects)

Motivation	:	The force to perform a certain act
Valence	:	The orientation (preference of attainment over non-attainment) of a person towards a certain outcome of their act
Expectancy	:	The degrees to which a person believes a certain outcome of their act to be probable
Ethics postulates	:	Budget for maximization of minimal through honouring of rights
Information society:		Ethical, social and political issues

E_S stands for ethically sensitive, E_N stands for ethics neutral.

$E_S > E_N$ for a transition from E_S to E_N. $E_N > E_S$ for a transition from E_N to E_S.

Paths to Motivation: The Ethical Dimension

Fred Herzberg:	Achievement, recognition E_S work itself
	Responsibility company policy and administration
Supervision, technical salary	E_N interpersonal relation working conditions
Hygiene factors (E_N)	Motivators (E_S)
Abraham Maslow:	
Self-esteem	Self-actualization
	Esteem from others E_S affiliation safety physiological

David McClelland: Needs that are required to be discerned are as follows.

- The need for achievement identifiable with one's own effort ($E_S < E_N$)
- The need for power including power over one's own liberty of action
- ($E_N < E_S$) ethics proposes that human being is potentially divine
- An individual can master their fortune through karma.
- E_S stands for ethically sensitive.
- E_N stands for ethics neutral.

$E_S < E_N$ for a transition from E_S to E_N. $E_N < E_S$ for a transition from E_N to E_S. (Therefore, human being is potentially divine and not a needing animal.)

Reference

Blake, R. R., & Moulton, J. S. (1962). The managerial grid. *Advanced Management Office Executive*, *1*(9), 12–15.

CHAPTER 19

SPIRITUAL MANAGER: MANAGE YOURSELF TO MANAGE THE WORLD

Victory of Virtue

Raise your head, oh the soul of truth. Establish a civilization based on truth. Virtue wins. Vices get washed away. The problem of human civilization has been the virtue that has been forced into exile in most times of human journey on earth and embracing vices in place. During the historical period of human progress so far, the marching of human intellect has been miraculously great. Man has progressed in his capacity to make life better and more comfortable progressively. Advent of the skies has led the human world come closer from the previous pieces of existence which are scattered in isolation throughout the geographical boundaries of the world. Human intelligence has brought the minute nano to books on the one hand and the largest mega on the other. Deep inside the oceans bed is how human initiative focuses within action on the one hand and limitless skies on the other, having some kind of cosmic and stellar arrangements. The seabed is considered, on the one hand, as the source of plenty and powerful resources, and, on the other, as a convenient destination for human comfort. The human space explorations have shown that there are many places that await human contact and developments towards the same. Human interventions have been able to make fundamental changes in the process of life within the realm of the living entities, engineering the existing pattern to create a turnout for the next level of generation. The journey has been whole vast and profound, covering all aspects of life and possibilities.

Even then the virtue of being human is being forced into exile. If it must come back, virtue needs to wage a war against vices in order to make a headway and finally dominate for a shorter reign. Virtues as well as vices are profound. Abundance of both, through the fundamental reality of the universe and visible and tangible forces of vices, acquires quick adrenaline propulsions towards asserting itself. Sometimes in the garb of virtue and in other contexts, vices progress; it raises its nails to prick through directly into the heart of the noble and simple. In the process, virtue remains an awesome observer. However, vices cannot withstand the power of virtue when the latter asserts through consolidation.

Human journey in this universe has not been confined only within the externality factors. Noble people took many initiatives to spread across the message of noble minds, goodness and truth. This civilization has gifted the human beings with many great souls to push through the forces of virtue. However, the consistent dominance by the vices has actually pushed waves of shocks through virtuous veins, making a virtuous feeble, simple and self-confined. That is how the greedy and the selfish have overruled all others. Anger, gluttony, envy, sloth along with the forces of greed and covetousness have invited jealousy and untruth into the forces of life across defeating the fundamental intent of creation.

Kingdom of Untruth

Human initiatives, so far, have gone around creativity paradise of individual and collective ego. Ego has dominated the activities so far. It has expanded to the extent of making things happen in such a way so as to create things which are hitherto new to civilization. Heroism and urge to win have dominated the minds of prominence, whether we proceed to make things happen in such a manner that the benefit accrues to a dominant few, or if it is such that the benefit is not immediate the matter has less importance in the eyes of those who try best to achieve.

Winning for a cause and winning in the path of life cannot happen at the same scale. Winning for self-enjoyment or even winning to satisfy egocentric drive makes life's path rough. Those who could garner the forces for a cause in the history of nations have to a certain extent been denied the true spirit of universal dynamism, but they eventually benefit from it. Thus, the invaders of the world have always found parallels to the supreme in them, embodied with the basic contents to human aspirations and expectations.

Those who have garnered the spirit, dynamism and valour of greatest powerful animals have won the fights in the human world. In most of the human journey, the animosity that determines the scales of its power and strength has acquired victory. Two cases of victory, as depicted in the great Indian epics, the Ramayana and the Mahabharata, have established the world's spirit of righteousness by defeating forces of untruth and evil. The forces of untruth and evil were crowned with all aspects of sins; they embodied greed, covetousness, lust, hunger for power, wealth and enjoyments in life, jealousy and enmity. They do not adhere to any principle centrism. They do not follow the path of honesty, sincerity, simplicity, integrity and purity. Rather, they have always banked on the issues of ego satisfaction. One of the most remarkable developments of a series of incidents has been depicted in the most reputed epic, the Mahabharata. The cardinal flow of incidents in the epic is based on an aggressively greedy prince and his blind father emperor who was blind not only physically but also from his affection for his eldest son, Duryodhana.

The Prince of Untruth

Duryodhana, one of the most remarkable characters of human race, was very unique in symbolizing almost all aspects of the untruth in life. Not only untruth is a departure from truth but it is also unique in its exposition and dominance. Highlights from the story are as follows: Duryodhana was the eldest son among hundred sons of the emperor king Dhritarashtra. Dhritarashtra was born blind. After their father's death, his younger brother Pandu became the king. Pandu was the father of five sons—Yudhishthira, Bhima, Arjuna, Nakula and Sahadeva. After the sudden death of Pandu, the authority of kinghood was vested on Dhritarashtra, a true blind man. Yudhishthira had the identity of a prince, but with the set of ill tricks and ill politics, finally the logical claim of Yudhishthira for prince hood was denied. Ill tricks and ill politics had finally made Duryodhana the prince. Duryodhana had based his attention on Bhima, Pandu's second son, from his very early age. This was because Duryodhana was really afraid of Bhima's physical and mental strength. Together, Duryodhana and his brothers had poisoned Bhima to the apparent state of death and pushed him into water of a vast lake. But destiny brought Bhima back to life, also with added strength of body and mind. Prince Duryodhana applied many tricks, ill-winged intent and strategies to kill all five sons of Pandu, finding them his future competitors. Those five sons, called five Pandavas, were sent into exile and made to be housed in a specially constructed palace that had an attractive royal look but was built with highly inflammable materials. Getting a sense of that, the Pandavas created an underground passage to escape the spell of fire and enter a distant forest. As per the original conspiracy plan, people appointed by Duryodhana had set fire to that house of combustible materials. However, the five Pandava brothers safely exited through the underground way created into a deep forest. Later on, knowing that the five Pandavas were alive, Duryodhana tried all possible ways to kill them anyway. Incidents had rolled down to a situation where a dice play competition was arranged to punish them further. This finally led to an unpleasant situation in which all the five Pandavas were imprisoned by Duryodhana and at the same time Duryodhana caused a huge insult to Draupadi by pulling apart her dress from her body in the king's court room. This event, and a series of subsequent events, led to a massive war called the Kurukshetra war. The Kurukshetra war was fought with a purpose to establish the principles of righteousness. The fierce battle was fought between the armies of Duryodhana and that of the Pandavas, with Lord Krishna on the side of the Pandavas. The Pandavas finally won the war with the best hero Arjuna at the forefront.

The war of righteousness was actually conducted and guided by lord Krishna and his disciple, Arjuna. The norms and principles of justice were established after the Kurukshetra war but achieved through a massive casualty of millions of people and resources both natural and created. Massive destruction, common to a great war, usually leads to various types of crisis, particularly economic ones. But in this case, the resultant effect was not a distressed society, but a new society full of blossoms and nature responding positively. Under the leadership of King Yudhishthira, head of the five Pandava brothers, it was a slow but steady convergence towards a just society with happiness and well-being spread around.

The camp of Duryodhana had adopted all sorts of vices and resorted to primitive animosity with all sorts of wrongdoings and all varieties of vices in them. Duryodhana, symbolic among them, was a unique representative of all sorts of untruths, he was hungry for power and did everything he could to have the power, the authority of the state and be on top of it. Being a king of vices whatsoever, he was inclined to grab things and beauty at any cost. In due course of time, Duryodhana paid the highest price.

Perfect Deviates from Perfection

The facts stated in the Mahabharata support a point that for periods longer than the span of virtues, vices remained ruler of societies having established their principles in the society and governed the societies for periods after their victory. The span of control of untruth goes far beyond the effective span of control by the elements of truth. Although the victory goes into the hands of truth at the end of each cycle of time, it is the primary problem of the human universe that the oppressions of untruth always reign longer. Let us look into the set of facts as laid out in the Ramayana, another great Indian epic.

In this epic, the Ramayana, the sequence of events centres around crown prince Raam. A descendant of the Ikshvaku dynasty, Raam's father Dasharatha was a pious and generous king. Having extended his kingdom wider and covering a large landmass inhabited by huge population, Dasharatha was able to establish the rule of law and equity in empirical needs of life by common people. Sage Valmiki, the author and collator of facts about Raam's life works and destiny, has made certain descriptions about his country's people's state affair, economic condition, social and cultural status. People were happy in their lives. They had proper food, homes and clothes. People had hardly any need to go for debt, though debt providence as a system existed, particularly for traders, meaning that the inhabitants did not face any financial crises. The presence of collective rituals, pujas including sacrificial fire, was all endowed with the system with active participation by public treasury. King's endowment for education and health was so widespread that the state's participation was deterministic in any event of a social cause. People could perform their spiritual activities and religious rites freely. All this continued on the basis of a social structure that made the elements of truth and cultivation of truth in life a priority. There were a large number of sages who had built large or small monasteries across their own habitats. The sages used to live a hermitage life, yet they had their families and children, apart from having a large number of disciples and followers around them. The sages used to worship the supreme lord, called the Brahman, the formless, timeless, eternal, omniscient, omnipresent, transcendental being who by formlessness could undertake any abode or get revealed in the same. The sages were in their unique ways to discover and unfold the fundamental truth of this universe and that by existence. Truth hitherto was so deep and profound that it could be fasted in any way. Sages were inclined to discover for themselves the same fundamental truth of this cosmic creation in ways that each could explore. The Vedas were created in this way. Vedas are direct revelations of the Supreme to the aspirant of truth. The revelations lead to the creations of four Vedas called Rig, Sama, Yajur and Atharva. Although the fundamental truths discovered by the sages were divided among four Vedas, they were all the same—only experiencing them in different ways.

One common act of life among the sages was that they used to meditate, led an ascetic life and performed meditation before sacrificial fire. The fire created in front to glow and flame is the same fire that is present in all creations in the form of *teja*, life's energy and strength. This act of sacrificial fire, known as *yajna*, symbolizes the pure truth which resides within an individual. Thus, *yajna* was both symbolic and empirical at the same time. Sages used to give it a very high level of importance as each of these *yajnas* had a purpose. However, a person stands in all of these sacrificial fires as an impersonal being with the intention of spreading the message and vibration of truth across. The sages had an underlying common faith in the cosmic universe. They were non-discriminative in their approach and wished to spread the nectar of realization everywhere for everyone. This is how they used to perceive. This was the way to make things happen in a way that would vitalize the human context by fully immerging in the spirit of the supreme.

King Dasharatha took an oath to take care of the state in this context with the promise to 'protect, provide and propel'. Under the oath, the king was bound to provide health and welfare to all of his subjects—the people. There was the promise of a rule of law. Into the deep realm of forests and caves of hills, the unlawful, arrogant demons, who believed in the reign of might, used to harm the sages. Such demons were normal inhabitants of deep forest and used to kill animals and eat their roasted meat. The demons used to intentionally disturb the sages while they performed their sacrificial fire. The demons knew that grabbing, killing, snatching away were true pyramids of life. That is one of the reasons they used to disturb the sages when they were performing the *yajnas*. The demons used to throw dirty contaminating elements and filthy fluids over the sacrificial fires that the sages created. This is how many demons used to make consistent efforts to totally destroy the context of the *yajnas*. Since the sacrificial fire had a primary role in the making up of the sages' society, they were annoyed and wanted remedial measures from King Dasharatha.

Sage Vashishtha was one of the greatest sages and was considered the most profound and regarded by the community of sages. He was the sage of all sages. Vashishtha was King Dasharatha's advisor and spiritual master, and his entire family. Viswamitra, another profound sage, came to visit the king with the message of the sage community requesting to protect the sages from the onslaught of the demons. Having met the king, Viswamitra urged him to allow Raam, his eldest son, to be taken with him for protection against the demons. Since Raam was dear to King Dasharatha, his heart bled profusely when the great Sage Viswamitra's request was granted. Raam, now a warrior, however, accompanied Sage Viswamitra, and went with him to places where demons used to appear to foil the rituals performed by sages. Although at that time Raam was very young, he was still very powerful in conquering and finishing the demons easily, so that the sages could continue their acts of worshipping God, the supreme.

After returning to the palace, Rama was to become the king. Kaikeyi, the second wife of King Dasharatha, was very greedy, and wanted her son Bharat to become the crown prince instead of Raam. The king had once promised to grant her any three wishes she desired. She demanded that Rama should not get the throne and be exiled, and that Bharat should be crowned. This, however, led to troubles within the royal family. Raam, meanwhile, had married Sita, the daughter of King Janaka, another auspicious king. Sita was a pure lady, said to have been born of the grace of supreme mother, and she was very happy to have Raam as her husband.

The journey began here. Raam and his wife Sita set off to live in forests. King Dasharatha's third son, Laxman, accompanied Raam and Sita into the forest. Sita's remarkable beauty and elegance with purity became a point of attraction for many. Later, a demon king named Ravana forcibly kidnapped her and took her to Lanka, crossing the ocean. Ravana flew in an airplane called *Pushpak Rath* (chariot of flowers). This *Pushpak Rath* could take off in a short space and land in it. With a very high speed, it could travel and cross over one bank of a sea to reach the other. Ravana, the demon king, was excessively covetous about Sita. The demon king was not only greedy but proud of his strength, valour and wealth. He was an enemy of gods in the world of heaven. Sita's rescue from the demon kingdom became Raam's primary agenda. He established an alliance with the monkeys. With the help of the monkeys, Raam built a floating bridge on the sea that linked Lanka and invaded the demon kingdom to rescue Sita from there. Raam rescued Sita after a long and eventful terrible battle and killing the demon king Ravana and his aides. Sita was taken back to Raam's palace on board the same plane, the *Pushpak Rath* which, apart from Raam himself, was also boarded by many others.

Raam became the king after returning to his palace, and he started a happy life. Sita became pregnant, and Raam and others became very happy. The detailed accounts by Sage Valmiki of this phase of Raam and Sita's life have been precisely portrayed and pointed out by the great poet Kalidas in his great epic-based work called *Raghuvansham*. Kalidas has narrated a conversation between King Raam and his army chief, Bhadra. Glimpse of the conversation runs as follows:

Raam: Bhadra, tell me, 'what are the views of my subjects about me?'

Bhadra kept quiet. On repeated persuasion only, the army chief, Bhadra, opened up:

Nirvandhaprishthah sa jagadah sarvam
Stubanti poura charitam tat deyam.
Anytra rakshah bhavana sitayah nah
Parigrahan manaba deva devyah.

My Superior Lord, the public is all full of praise for you and for your deeds.
However, they do not approve of your acceptance of the queen who had lived in the captivity of an *asura* (demon).

Kalatra nindaa gurunaa kila evam abhya ahatam kirti viparyayena.
Ayogha anenayah iva abhitarptam vaidehi bandhoh hridayam vidare.

The serious allegation that slandered his wife broke Raam's heart, just as a piece of iron heated in a furnace split by the strike of a hammer.

Raam, considered as embodiment of God on earth representing supreme variety of dignity, did not consider that it required probing the point. Whether the information gathered by the army and security was just hearsay of few wrongdoers in the society or people of society at large having developed an opinion of that kind to blame the king or voice their sentiment against the queen. Rather the situational description given in the Ramayana by Sage Valmiki shows that people were happy. So much so that there were lots of public celebrations at Raam and Sita's return together. People did not think or consider Raam in isolation.

Sins of Civilization

Together, Sita and Raam had become the symbol of their love, respect and choice at both individual and public levels. It is therefore a painful sequence of seed to think and act on what Raam considered from the security chief's point of view. This view did not have any kind of mandate from the public. Rather the public, in general, were happy in having welcome Sita and Raam together.

From this crossroads of history and prehistory, serious and painful blunder of civilization began. Without examining any allegation, and without even having a single trace of indirect evidence, King Raam accepted the security chief's view with so much importance that he took his decision on the basis of just one person's opinion. Agitated in mind, Raam took up a decisive position about throwing away his wife, even though he knew in his mind that Sita was innocent.

Avaimi cha enaama nagheti kintu loka
Apavaadah balvaana matah me.
Chaayaa hi bhoomeh shashinah malatwena
Aaropitaa shuddhimatah prajaabhih.

Raam says, 'I am aware that she is innocent. However, in my view,
a libel is more powerful than the truth.
People call the shadow of earth falling on the spotless moon,
a blemish.
Everyone believes it to be true, though it is a lie.'

This again is a magnanimous tragedy of human civilization. Raam, considered as the incarnated God, could do such an injustice to a lady whom he knew for certain that she was pure and absolutely sinless. It was not a blunder. The king knew that it cannot be a fact in any way. However voice of protest persisted throughout.

Tasya apanodaaya phale pravrittau
Upasthitaayaama api nirvgapekshah.
Tyanshyaami vaideha sutaam purastaat
Samudra nemim pituh aayya eva.

Although Sita is soon going to deliver,
Yet in order to wipe out this blot,
Overcoming my attachment
I shall give her up as I had relinquished
The earth bound by the oceans,
When ordered by my father.

Apparently, the rule and expectations of broader boundaries of the cosmic system had dominated the mind of king Raam.

The series and sequence of events in both the epics—the Mahabharata and the Ramayana—reveal a fundamental difference in the position of the vices. In the first case, the Mahabharata, it was a visible demon-like person who did all sorts of mischievous activities in the abode of crown prince, prince and finally performing the role of an emperor, denying the principles of fairness and honesty at every interaction and action. Duryodhana attained the symbolism of all sorts of wrongdoing in human context. He wanted all powers in his hand by annihilating anybody who was opposed to it. Duryodhana was extremely greedy. He wanted to capture all sorts of properties and own them. In Duryodhana's mind, the urge to rule, acquire and possess became fundamental. He was also covetous about things of speciality. Duryodhana always used to assert that he was the king of earth; therefore, all properties essentially belonged to him. He thought that he was the master of everything, master of landed properties, master of all business possessions and above all master of all beauties of the world. That is why he lacked in having respect for women and ordinary people on earth. Symbolic of the highest consolidation of demonic qualities, for a long time, Duryodhana could even overrule the truthful and honest group of people. The war of righteousness as guided by Lord Sri Krishna and mainly waged by lord's friend and disciple Arjuna was finally owned by the group of people representing the spectrum of truth. In this case, a remarkable point to observe is that untruth and basket of falsehood had ruled this society and country for periods much longer than the trustworthy, just and righteous forces.

Emergence of Godly Man

History and prehistory of civilization have gone that way. The Vedic sages had created a different form of civilization. The rule and dominance of state was so low that it appeared almost as a non-entity. Sages had things that they had in common. Those who had their hermitages in the forest areas, on the hills, in the Himalayas, inside deep mountain caves, river banks or the seas or spread in the societies—in the midst of human habitat—had one thing in common that they lived their lives to unfold the divine spirit and experience the divine intent in the form of truth. The sages experienced the truth through their own ways of meditation, sacrificial performances with fire or service to mankind, or even a combination of both. The general call voiced and echoed by the sages was *Srinvantu visve amritasya Putrah* (oh, the sons of eternity, the men, listen). They used to point out an individual's real and intrinsic identity. The intrinsic identity is that an individual represents the supreme Brahman, the supreme divinity and, thus, all good qualities of truth, honesty, integrity and so on are present in an individual. An individual cannot play the beast-like role, rather they are godly. All godly qualities are present in every individual. The issue is to unfold those and bring those in the active and performing thoughts and emotions of an individual.

Chariot of Truth

It is now time for those concerned to board and wheel it forward on the chariot of truth. We are all descendants of the divine heritage; God's sons on earth will discover their true identity. Ask yourself, 'Who am I?' and obtain answers from the realm within. Let your inner voice open up. Let the intrinsic find its ways forward. It is you who proceeds forward in the journey of life. Until now, you have been searching for peace, wealth, fame, satisfaction, happiness, dominance over others, superiority, uniqueness, importance and accordingly consuming resources and emotions. Now is the time to look forward and have it in our affirmation that:

No delusions
No swaying away by empirical objectives
No relations with untruth

Rather our affirmation let the vibrant to discover the true identity and tell people on earth to endeavour towards discovering true identity. Let affirmation echo:

I am not this mind, intellect, memory or the empirical identity.
I am not this organ of senses—vision, audibility, touch, smell or taste.
I am not this void, the soil, the earthly energies or the blowing wind.
I am that Shiva, always full of bliss and truth.

Human condition is like a lion that considers itself a lamb. We need to reengineer our understanding. A person on earth is actually sent by

God. The pains, agonies, life's sufferings are the result of consistent departure from truth by one and many. We make the blunders of creating departure from God to such an extent that our world is deluged with thoughts and facts defeating our own potential. As a true descendant on earth, we are constrained by the problems and situations that are occurring now, but the huge potential domain remains unexplored. Let us all explore that potential.

Truth alone has the power to drive through. We have encountered so many aspects of truth in this world to live with—the world and the thoughts of science and technology have put forward truth in some way.

The world of literature tried to unfold the aesthetic view of truth, the philosophical questioning again unfolded certain types of truth in the philosophical way, the social and cultural beliefs of people in the world tried to open up truth to the contentment and happiness of people concerned in their own way; historically, human has tried to understand and unfold truth also. In history, political ideologies and economic doctrines have their own idea of truth.

The way human civilization has progressed, it has considered the scientific spirit as the cultural sprit. The emergence of scientific spirit has embraced the rationales of life in all phases of its development. It has been depicted in a summarized form by the great physicist of our age, David Bohm, in the beginning of his 'wholeness and implicate order'—a great idea of connecting the reality of fragments with the whole—the invisible supreme, David Bohm (2012), has put it as follows:

The notion that all these fragments are separately existent is evidently an illusion, and this illusion cannot do other than lead to endless conflict and confusion. Indeed, the attempt to live according to the nation that the fragments are really separate is, in essence, what has led to the growing series of extremely urgent crises that is confronting us today. Thus, as is now well known, this way of life has brought about pollution, destruction of the balance of nature, over-population, world-wide economic and political disorder, and the creation of an overall environment that is neither physically nor mentally healthy for most of the people who have to live in it. Individually there has developed a widespread feeling of helplessness and despair, in the face of what seems to be an overwhelming mass of disparate social forces, going beyond the control and even comprehension of the human beings who are caught up in it.

It is indeed a truthful observation of a holistic variety and is very unlikely of a scientific mind. Still, like Albert Einstein, David Bohm has effectively applied his inner vision to look beyond the visible and noticeable. Those life factors that play across our human race are so oriented towards externalities that life oriented towards the outer world feels pain in trying to understand those things inside the being. The inner world dooms down to dormancy when the waves of externalities do flag off in our orientations.

Looking within is searching something around which are seldom noticeable. Even though these are noticeable, the factors that are always responsible for our existence should be drawn towards that control force which governs through a series of activities with new horizons having charted for. Thus, an individual realizes the impact and importance of certain aspects of life that are not otherwise understood.

Rational and logical dimensions provide us with tangible understanding of the universe, though there remains a huge gap in the complete understanding. Once that is done, there will increasingly be scopes for understanding the real self. Gradual discovery of the inner truth brings a huge amount of inflict on the person unless the extent realized is made to absorb in the ongoing process of life, the goodness or essence of divine spirit would not develop maturity by itself. It requires a character of goodness.

Goodness

Goodness comes out from a divinely inclined and immerged personality. It must be intrinsic in an individual and needs to get spread across for the greater good of a human being. Basically, an attribute pertaining to human character, goodness occurs when a person understands the limits of individuality and attempts to go beyond that. It is thus a set of attributes and combination of different sets of things that would otherwise make a person inclined to deliver things to the world and involve themselves in such a manner that they attempt to hart at least when connected with the world around them.

Goodness of a man develops in the environment of good and profound set of attributes. Lord Sri Krishna narrated the factors of divine attribute in an individual through the elaboration of 26 special and unique attributes that make a man godly. The attributes thus combine to make human journey on earth different from that which has been pursued differently. The scope and importance of a single attribute among these are so profound that the span of translation of the attribute into a set of actions will be very vast once a person adopts and sets forth these. Thus, the emergence of a true vibration of goodness will be automatically felt as soon as the spirit of diversity is touched upon through a series of actions in life that often occur in a similar manner. While mentioning the divinely qualities to Arjuna, Lord Krishna maintains a sequence and chain of those set of human attributes that otherwise make things brighter and smoother for human existence. As he narrates the attributes, Lord Krishna brings in the issue of the context in which a person lives and grows. The context is again the sum total of the emotions and intrinsic energy individuals used to forget as well.

Intrinsic can be noticed only when the focus is within, and the individual consciousness is drawn within. Inner looking is interiorization; it is an individual's consistent endeavour not to be swayed by the elements of desire and want. Profound hunger for things of work is caught in a particular plateau of human consciousness which would otherwise drive the person down to adopt any means or ways to win or achieve.

Winning the way becomes winning the same way as in the world of animals. Goodness begins with affirmation—positive attitude towards life and the world. Goodness spreads its impacts through distributive welfare for all who deserve the welfare. Goodness is an act, a habit and a character with the bottom line of giving away. Goodness is distributed in nature. Bhagavad Gita has highlighted the following 26 attributes as elements of *Sattva Guna* or qualities of goodness:

1. Fearlessness
2. Purity
3. Wisdom-seeking
4. Giving
5. Discipline of senses
6. Sacrifice
7. Self-study
8. Ascesis
9. Simplicity
10. Non-injury to others
11. Truth
12. Non-anger
13. Giving up
14. Peace
15. Resisting low tendencies
16. Mercy
17. Feeling ashamed of doing bad things
18. Against attitude of gluttony
19. Feeling shy of thinking bad of others
20. Discipline of words
21. Energy
22. Forgiveness
23. Tolerance
24. Cleanliness
25. Cooperation
26. Egolessness

Lord Krishna described these 26 attributes as characteristics of a divine personality. A person rises above the domain of ordinary manhood by any of these qualities present in them.

With these attributes of divinity in place, a man becomes equivalent to a godly character. The godly character thus makes it prominent for an individual to act, behave and characterize in the world.

Fearlessness

Animals in the forest or demons also can become fearless. However, this fearlessness applies to empirical activities and things pertaining to the world. Fear appears in life for two major reasons: first, the fear to lose things of possession and, second, the fear arising out of sense of deprivation. Things of possession may be properties, resources, assets, money, precious things or similar objects. Things of possessions are otherwise intangible also.

Elements of name, fame, pride, recognition, getting established in a unique manner, creating and developing speciality across are certain things which would create moments of dedication. Fearlessness should transpire to not be afraid of losing whatever is possessed be properly equipped with the strength of mind and not be hungry for things not possessed as yet. Be content at the moments with whatever is attained and possessed, let the work be befitting to achieve more, let the work be so energized as to have the logical deficits of life. Whatever be the sense of deficit, judge it to see whether the same is properly justified or not. Strive hard for things that are just and justified, push hard so that the same can be achieved without much agonies. Fearlessness is a spirit that allows a person to stand up against the evils of human civilization. Never be afraid of the evils of society and the world. Let the evil vanish from our organ of memory and mind. Let it flash our lives with lots of strength from within for resisting the waves of delusions of life. A fearless person knows that God is their father and friend who is always with them.

Purity

The belief that God is with all as father and friend makes a person's mind pure. So one has to be pure in mind and heart to live divinely. The act of purity is both extrinsic and intrinsic. One has to be in the realm of the divine, the supreme form of purity. When one makes food that is to be offered to God, the thoughts of God should embrace the mind of the person who prepares food.

When a person does a work, the principle of purity states that one should endow the work to God and do it in the first possible manner that shows that work is no longer just a work with the application of force on an object leading to a tangible change in the position, configuration or the time coordinate of the objects, rather it proves to be an element of worship by the person undertaking the work. Thus, the person no longer acts as just a doer. The person becomes a doer under the command of an invisible supreme. This invisible supreme is always with the doer when the doer thinks of him, invites him in the context of the work that the doers have initiated for.

Principles of purity comprise the act of purity, thought of purity and the concern for that invisible supreme through actions of life.

Principles of work thus converse to the following:

- Work I do belongs to the invisible supreme.
- Work has to be performed with the highest energy and the best possible ability of mine.
- Work is my responsibility in totality.
- I have to drive the work to its culmination with all efforts and make it successful.
- I am a doer for the work alone.
- I do not have an iota of inclination towards craving for or enjoying the spirit and resultant outcome of the work.

Work becomes the best of its quality when the performer is convinced that the work will be carried out as the work belongs to the supreme. 'It is God's work and I am the doer'—this conviction makes the best of work. Work becomes a tool of deep worship; whatever be the context and description of work, it remains worthy to remember God in all phases of work. Work becomes an intrinsic tool of God's meditation. Whenever one works in this way, with this conviction, the context of work becomes non-discriminative. Work then remains pure and purifies the doer's heart and mind.

It is this background of purity that dawning of divine spirit happens in the core of our heart, through which God reveals.

Wisdom-seeking

Knowledge is associated with every life. Although at the stage of potential, the entire set of knowledge remains stored and unexplored. Gradual learning process is what makes knowledge heard. There are two broad components of knowledge: learned and given. Learned knowledge is based on a process called outward in which the given one remains dormant, until the unfolding process remains open. Learned knowledge requires self-initiative of all sorts so that the learner absorbs inputs of knowledge acquired from outside through proper participation.

Participation becomes wholesome when the learning tools, learners' psychic and the context of learning get synchronized throughout. Julian Huxley has highlighted an evolutionary process in learning. As mentioned by Sir Julian Huxley, in his introduction to the great work of

Charles Darwin, *On the Origin of Species*, an individual is in a phase of evolutionary consciousness. As Julian Huxley puts it:

It further emerged that man constitutes the latest dominant group, and in today, thanks to his new method of evolving by the cumulative transmission of experience, the only type capable of realising important new possibilities and of achieving further major advances in the future. Thus, in the light of science of evolutionary biology which Darwin founded, man is seen not just as a part of nature, but as a very peculiar and unique part. In his person, the evolutionary process has become conscious of itself, and he alone is capable of leading it onto realizations of possibilities. A century after Darwin's modest statement that light will be thrown on the origin of man, we can truly say that, as a result of Darwin's work in general and the origin of species, in particular, light has been thrown on his destiny.

An individual's descent is actually an individual's ascent. Charles Darwin applied scientific method to identify evolution of human capacity to realization. Julian Huxley has rightly identified this as human consciousness. As identified by Huxley, the journey is essentially of human consciousness. It is thus the context of human understanding where the empirical ways of acquiring knowledge get confined within the limits of usual capacity. Beyond this begins the act of human journey which talks about the usual act of looking intrinsic.

In other words, exploring the world of human consciousness through a method of introspection and meditation would unveil a separate world—the world that is not visible through the external organs, rather it opens up through the process of inner vision before our eyes. Thus, the inner vision for our cognizance unfolds a different world. This means that the world otherwise invisible opens up a different set of truth for a person.

Depending upon the quality and condition of our mind, the unfoldment occurs. With the help of our external organs, knowledge is acquired, whereas wisdom is intrinsic to a person. A person in their journey and quest for goodness would undertake initiatives for their spiritual journey. It is this endeavour by a person when they seek the realization of God, the process they undertake that leads to wisdom-seeking, and ultimately wisdom sets in.

Giving, Discipline of Senses, Sacrifice

As it is a general undertaking by many, those with big hearts can only perform the role of a giver, whereas self-seeking is usual for people with normal mindsets and sometimes grabbing is also the ultimate face of it.

Giving is a very special quality which can be adopted by a dominant few. Giving comes out of a surplus store of love, concern, emotions which would enable a person to do things which go beyond the limits of personal and individual selfish interests.

Giving stands on the opposite of self-seeking or grabbing. Giving goes beyond the understanding of individual capacity, sense of selfish seeking can be offset only when the urge to give comes in our consciousness.

The principles of giving should be based on certain basic views and convictions:

- Giving is a one-way transaction, there is no expectation of anything in return
- Giving is best when even a recognition is not expected in return
- Giving is best with a non-identity of the giver

Giving should be an integral spirit of character of the person. Giving as a spirit is always divine in nature. This requires an individual to rise above the realm of being under the control of senses such as selfishness, lust, greed, anger, delusions and egocentrism.

Senses require disciplinary action. Discipline is an act of control through an autonomous way. Autonomous control does not come in place unless it is built in as the unique element of individual character. Sense control turns out to be automatic as the personality grows into self-giving and earns wisdom of life.

Wisdom is realizing the divine spirit or divinity itself. That divinity has to be spread across in the entire entity. The entity has to be viewed from the perspective of life, and works and activities which are connected to the world. Disciplining senses is actually most cardinal in the process of the journey in life. The journey must take root in the design of the spirit of people. The design has its most emerging context in the human situation. If the senses remain constant and rule the life in its perspective of the people on earth, these are coordinated on the basis of certain types of hunger. Most penetrating among all types of hunger is the hunger for sex, money and fame. These are major elements of desire which even if one tries to coordinate and control, they may fail in their approach whenever it becomes imperative on them. The best option is to develop a *spirit of sacrifices.*

Sacrificing materials or materialistic demands is not the way. Sacrifice must be planted as a root in life while the person wishes or develops the wish to be one with the divine. *Om appyayantu mama angani, vak, prana, chakshu, shrotram athah balam indriyani cha sarbani—Sarbam Brahmah Upanishadam* (I invoke your presence to take even the control of all my senses—the words, the respirations, the version, the audibility, the strength of life. Oh, the supreme, Brahma, be with me always—this in the spirit of sacrifice). Sacrifice is thus giving up the ownership and control of existence to the hand of lord—the supreme.

Self-study, Ascesis, Simplicity, Non-injury to Others and Truth

Vedic sages have put across the concept of *pancharin* (fivefold debts) that human beings are embraced with. These elements of debts are as follows:

- Deva *rin* (debt to the godly sources)
- *Rishi rin* (debts to the sources of wisdom or sages)
- *Pitri rin* (debt to the forefathers, the lineage)
- *Nri rin* (debt to human society)
- *Bhuta rin* (debt to subhuman species). We are indebted to all these sources. The debt to godly sources is visible if we look at human life and its emergence.

A life having born on earth immediately gets endowed with plenty of cosmic and worldly providence of light, air and support. The sun is offered respect by the sages who call it Sun God and thus personify this cosmic source of light for human life. Similarly, the infinite source of air brings in the 'prana' which is vital for human life. We do not have any role in this, rather we are at the recipient end.

The sense of fairness implies that if you have taken anything from anyone, you are indeed indebted. This summarizes the fact of our being bounded by deva *rin* or being indebted to the Gods. Similarly, we are endowed with already available pool of knowledge. The creators and inventors of knowledge are true sages. We are indebted to them as well. This is *rishi rin*—our indebtedness to sages. If someone wants to repay, then they have to do *swadhyay* (self-study) and *avysha* (practice). Self-study is the process through which we learn things on our own through our own efforts.

Self-study requires meditation and ascesis. When we meditate, the power of our mind is enhanced manifold. It is this enhanced power of mind that enables a person to realize the vast truth which remains outside our cognizance. On the one hand, the visible and tangible world is perceived by our biological organs and, on the other hand, it is perceived by our capacity to document, examine and prove the same through other means.

The vast invisible and transcendental world does not reveal itself in the mechanistic process of understanding or even biologically by using our biological organs, rather it requires thriving through the pool of consciousness that we are merged in. To have this in place in our human consciousness, we need to bring down our personal character to simplicity. *Arjaban* (simplicity) is the divine quality.

The art and capacity of seeing things with a simple mind avoid complexities of all sorts. Simple and straight faith is the way. One must resolve not to inflict any kind of injury on anyone's physical or mental make. No injury to others should always be maintained in thoughts and in deeds. We need to train our minds to think good of all and hopefully to do good to all, if possible. Thus, the transcendental truth dawns in the core of our being.

Truth thus emerges as the central choice of the being. The central choice becomes truth in perception. Truth in belief and truth in action may differ. Truth in perception and action are those which are partly visible and may be either tangible or intangible. However, the vast truth of eternity reflects through everything, every entity—the sky, Milky Way, galaxies, nebulae on the one hand and the cosmos, the world system, the earth system on the other.

Truth is all embracing, all profound, omnipresent, omniscient and also empirical. This life, the facts of the world, the visible dimensions, those invisible ones and so on, all are revelations of the same vast truth. The sun in the sky is true, the flora and fauna are all true, this mortal life and lives are true and the words, thoughts, interactions and transactions are true. Things are also true which a sage realizes only through his meditation for God. The material truth comprises a segment of wholesome truth. Spiritual truth and truth of God combined with the Supreme make it a complete truth. Material truth alone is not total truth—it is only a fragment. The spiritual truth which has been learned and experienced through realization makes it wholesome.

Non-anger, Giving Up, Peace, Resisting Low Tendencies, Mercy, Feeling Ashamed of Doing Bad Things, Gluttony, Feeling Shy of Thinking Bad of Others, Discipline of Words

Anger is a killer. Anger brings in delusion, loss of rationales and finally has an impact on the character of the personality. Anger may drive down to a situation where the options to think bright and fair go to dooms. Lord Krishna says,

> *Krodhat bhabati sammohan, sammohat smritibibhramah*
> *Smritibhramsad buddhinasho buddhinashat pranashyati.*
>
> (Bhagavad Gita, 2/63)

Anger creates delusion in the context of intellect. In this condition of delusion, the person gets detached with the memory of their integrity in the past. A person loses their rational intellect with disconnect from the core of memory. Once the rational intellect is lost, the disaster leads to destruction.

Anger finally leads to the destruction of the person. Lord Krishna urges Arjuna for non-anger, not to get involved and deluged in anger. Anger should be abandoned; non-anger is thus one of the most important attributes of a divine self. Anger is the usual associate of animals. It should be avoided and kept away by people with goodness and having divinely orientation.

Giving up is possible only when the mind is ready for that.

When a cause of anger arises, one should adopt certain immediate steps in mind to overcome it.

- Do not get swayed by the cause of anger.
- Wait, think separately, review the entire situation from all possible angles and then decide only.
- Prioritize patience and tolerance before being reactive to the cause of anger.

Anger needs to be given up. Give up all other low-driven emotions like anger. A noble personality is founded upon the principle of giving up. One should give up anger, greed, selfishness, lower instinct and desires. When we learn and practice the habit of giving up, we obtain peace of mind. In his brilliant work, 'The Waste Land', the great poet T. S. Elliott has used the concepts of giving. Elliott has used the concept put forward in Brihadaranyaka Upanishad by the great Sage Yajnavalkya.

Sage Yajnavalkya identified the concept of giving in terms of Da-Da-Da which is *Damyata-Datta-Dayadhvama*. *Damayata* means preventing a person from envying the goodness which a person grants to them as the goodness. They need to remove this ego of goodness. *Datta* is the art and act of giving. This applies to the human consciousness. Once an individual adopts the art and act of giving, they attempt to move above the limits of human understanding and realization. There are three different strata of consciousness: divine–human–demonic. Sage Yajnavalkya suggests *damayata* for those with a godly character, which means freeing oneself from ego of being special, good and unique. A person needs to cultivate egolessness. For human being, the *danam*, meaning giving, makes the character free. The sage has advocated *dayodhvama* for the demonic people. *Dayodhvama* is to offer mercy to other. Mercy, which is applicable to those who have surplus of emotional possessions, is universal. But those with demonic tendencies, such as arrogance, jealousy, anger, enemy, utter selfishness and egocentrism, should look back to review and correct. It is actually an act of correction for them. They need to be merciful to themselves. Mercy is actually trying to understand their real positions on earth vis-à-vis the demands of fairness and goodness. Demonic, arrogant diminishes when they become merciful on themselves to free them from the clutches of all sorts of evil intents, evil thoughts, evil habits and thereby cleanse their characters of all evil prints on it.

The impact of greed is not only primordial but also penetrating in nature. Greed is to fulfil the hunger that has been rooted inside. Hunger that is intrinsic for maintenance and growth of biological system is universal. But the kind of rational and irrational hunger modernism has pushed in our mind is one of the most fundamental elements responsible for creating imbalance in the lives of people.

Driven by hunger, sometimes madness, an imbalanced behaviour sets in. Greed becomes profound, making the person blind of the world. The rationales, morals and ethical positions of life disappear when greed takes violent pushed inside. An item of greed provided does not make the journey of greed stop over there. Greed and desires are making the journey of greed stop over there. Greed and desires are continuous; a part of it fulfilled does not stop the hunger over there, rather it is like adding fuel to fire.

The spirit of Vedas is thus an invocation of the awareness and intent in an individual to derive peace from giving. Possessions are essential for life, but the intrinsic cosmic sprit is giving. It can be observed in the facts of general nature of the earth system.

A flower knows its purpose of being in the universe, which is to offer whatever possession it has (fragrance and beauty).

The sweet scent of the sweetest form of fresh honey is prepared, preserved and nurtured by the plant life to offer through the flower. The sweet fragrance is for others, for the world to experience and consume from. Flower gives it away for others in the world. It does not consume the same on its own.

A flower creates a unique beauty which it does not experience itself. The beauty of a flower is created and generated through being with the plant life and is consumed and experienced by the world, not by itself. The spell 'giving as a matter of habit of a person' must be imprinted in the character of the individual. Peace and being non-greedy and to be dynamic in life.

As a part of the cosmic principle, the eternity of life is its being formed from the values of selfless giving. William Shakespeare nicely observed:

Oh that you were yourself! But love, you are
No longer yours than you yourself here live.
Against this coming end you should prepare,
And your sweet semblance to some other gift.
So should that beauty which you hold in lease
Find no determination; then you were
Your self again, after your self's decease,
When your sweet issue your sweet form should bear,

As truth and beauty shall together thrive,
If from thy self to store than wouldst convert.
Or else of thee this I prognosticate;
The end is truth's and beauty's doom and date.

(William Shakespeare, Sonnets 13 and 14)

William Shakespeare has identified resonance between the cosmic truth and individual truth. Truth of life has to be found in accordance with the truth that lies spread in the cosmic system. William Shakespeare has explored the connection oneself has with the universe. Transactions that have occurred in the world and that are likely to be will remain in the context of human wellness.

The sweetness of the honey of life and the beauty which life has developed, groomed and nurtured do belong to the life. However, the best essence and worth of life reach its Himalayan apex once they have been understood by life as the sum total of the process of life. This life is dedicated to the cause of the universe and creates the flow of the Ganges, endlessly gushing through the plains, hills, forest lands and meadows past human habitat. The worth of life magnifies with the undertaking of the spirit of the universal system.

An individual is mean-small-pretty entity till they find themselves confined within empirical boundaries. In words and communications, the spirit of non-anger, giving up, peace, respect for others, mercy, non-greedy, being dynamic, feeling shy of ill thoughts and doings, and sense of discipline make a person holy by themselves. The holy nature makes one understand the worth of life in the real sense of the terms.

Energy, Forgiveness, Tolerance, Cleanliness, Cooperation, Egolessness

Once the human consciousness rises above the human limit, it understands and unfolds the inner power, and the dormant energy that remains within starts unfolding. The unfoldment occurs across the passage of consciousness upward from the material state of its remaining at *muladhara* (the seat bed of spiritual energy with every individual) that starts releasing eventually. This is primarily based on the intent of an individual.

Energy in the cosmic system gets rooted in the individuals who aspire for the great cosmic energy system. The energy system has three major classifications, which are as follows:

- The creative energy or volition, called *ichhashakti*
- The preservative energy of action, called *kreashakti*
- The discriminative or distractive energy of wisdom or cognition, called *jnanashakti*

These three forms of energy are present in all individuals. The energy of volition, energy of action and energy for *jnana* or cognition has to be understood in the proper perspective. Proper initiative undertaken by the individual creates a situation within the individual.

As in the yoga aphorism of Patanjali, if an individual follows certain principles, they can attain the situation and create the context for unfoldment. These are as follows:

1. Personal discipline attempting to quiet and pacify the body.
2. Engineered consciousness that positions the person to calm and peace of mind and body together. Inner consciousness establishes connect with cosmic consciousness, whereas the subconscious conducts the work of life.
3. Attempt to master over the habits and tendencies so that all aspects of habits and tendencies are coordinated towards creating a homogeneous journey for convicting with the supreme objective.
4. Visualizing inner illumination and focusing on that to understand and experience freedom from all lowness, desire and hunger. Being in touch with the flames in life's actions and processes so as to bring elements of wisdom and be driven by the wisdom generated from realization of God.

Tasya Saptadha Prantabhumih Prajnana

(Patanjali, 2/27)

When a person follows the steps mentioned earlier, the process of unfoldment of the cosmic energy into the individual starts with seven different steps of earning wisdom in life. The imperative of these seven steps of wisdom is that which helps in liberating the person's consciousness into seven steps of wisdom through two different categories for the same.

Two broad classifications are as follows:

• *Karya bimukti* [or liberation created from the outcome of work]	(Liberating from the bondage and delusions by the result of works and actions undertaken by the person)
• *Chitta bimukti* [liberation from delusions and bondage of mind]	(Liberating from the bondage of the mind from getting clung to the attachment of the factors of bondage)

Karya bimukti has four aspects: *Tajya, heyah, niroddha* and *vivek khyati.*

1. *Tajya* (or understanding of the things that are not conducive to realization of divine).
2. *Heyah* (or things that are not essential for our initiatives for realization need to be abandoned)
3. *Niroddha* (or the attempt to stop things which flow down with spirits opposing to the process of realization)
4. *Vivek khyati* (or the rewards and glories in life that attempt to obstruct the flow of realization in the person who has followed the entire process of realization of divine)

These four are essential to take care and remove in a person attempting to reach the highest level of realization of the divine in their personality. The obstruction and bondage are result of the ability, action and the works of individuals. Even when the *karya bimukti* or liberation from the results of work accomplished, we need to have *chitta bimukti* or be liberated from the bondage of mind.

The following steps are explained here. *Girishikhara, Eta byabasthayam guna dambandhya atita and prajnamand aposhyan purusha.*

1. *Girishikhara achyuta mukh* (or understanding that the person has attained and achieved things for and attempted to)
2. *Eta Samya byabasthayam guna sambandhya atita* (or understanding that noble qualities emerge from within and gets supported by the descend from the cosmic sources and finally gets absorbed in the personality)
3. *Prajnamano aposhyan purusha* (or on being able to follow these seven steps of *karya bimukti* and *chitta bimukti* combinedly marks the dawning of wisdom in a person)

The essential culmination of the process of earning wisdom in a person is to get immerged in the consciousness of the supreme.

This consciousness of the supreme rests in an individual always and in all situations. Supreme is in his formless form of omnipresence and omniscience, as the invisible formless form of God. Be he named in any way, be he worshipped in any way, be he realized in any way, it is always the spirit of divinity which would embrace the consciousness of a person. The process of attainment has to be a process that is the result of endeavours of the person. Virtue sets in an individual's personality who would undertake the journey towards the realization of divinity in the person, which otherwise remained dormant within.

The process undertaken for the attainment depends on the initiative. One of the most prominent initiatives is that of a process named *pranayama*, which means bringing in the essence of vital.

Reengineering the vital is effectively creating a new identity for life and taking the spirit of life forward. *Pranayama* is the process of breath control which acts on the mind and gradually collects all functions of mind towards a single point. Sage Vaisampayana has categorically explained this in Swetaswatara Upanishad as follows:

Pranan Prapidya iha Samyukta Chestah
Kshinal panae nasikaya uchhasitah.
Dustashva yuktan iva baham enam
Vidwan manoh dharoyetah pramattah.

(Swetaswatara Upanishad 2/9)

A wise person always regulates their breathe skilfully.
When the prana becomes feeble, it should be let off through
the nostrils in a regulated way. When one thus gets used to gradually
holding the breath, the wind, like a chariot drawn by unruly horses
which represents various kinds of senses becomes fixed and fitted for
the wisdom of Brahman (Brahma *jnana*).

The process may be summarized in clear terms as follows:

Step 1: *Asana* (sitting posture), either squatting position on a cushion placed on floor or on a chair. Sitting erect on chair, feet placed on floor, parallel to each other, hands on respective knees, eyes closed.

Step 2: Breath coordination through the following three steps:

1. *Puraka* (drawing air through nostril)
2. *Kumbhaka* (holding breathe)
3. *Rechaka* (releasing air through the other nostril)

Step 3: Normal breathing with the same sitting posture and the eyes still closed.

Step 4: Apply the approach of 'willed imagination'—take the awareness along to the top of head.
Step 5: Try to imagine the full moon in a clear blue sky at the centre.
Step 6: Attempt to establish communion with the illumination of lunar glow and maintain this connect.
Step 7: Gradually pull the consciousness down to the cardiac centre.
Step 8: Absorb the consciousness within the cardiac centre and get immerged in.

Mind liberates from other tendencies and gets concentrated across the spirit of divinity.

Atmano esho pranah jayate
Yatha esho pusushe chhaya.
Etasmin etat aatatam
Mano kritena asmin sharire aayati.

(Prashna Upanishad, 3/3)

This life has actually derived its origin from the supreme divine. The soul seated within the form of *atman* contains the seeds of life. It is coordinated by the mind's initiatives to reposition the roots of life to different entities, thereby getting life seated in and revealed from the body formed through mental activity on the biological process.

This life force, called prana, maintains the continuity of life from birth. The life force needs to be coordinated to draw energy from the entire system. The air of life force acts on the living system effectively and perfectly through the process of *pranayama* as mentioned earlier. We need to understand different facets of this air of life force. Known as *pancha vayu*, this is spread among five different yet connected vital air of life, which are as follows: 'prana', *apana*, *byana*, *samana* and *udana*.

Prana Air

The air drawn inside travels through the entire mouth, through the nostrils, reaching the eyes, ears and finally entering the brain and the nervous system. This prana air performs the role of the central vital air or *mukhya* prana. The central vital air controls the overall movements of the air drawn in and released. Both the functions of inhalation and exhalation combine to form *mukhya* prana.

Payuh Upasthena Apanam
Chakshu Shrotrae mukha nasikavyam pranah swayam pratishthite.

Madye tu Samanh esha hi bhutam annam saman nayati.
Tastat etah sapta archisna bhabantih.

(Prashna Upanishad, 3/5)

This central vital air, called *mukhya* prana, has positioned the *apana* air to the excretion and creation organs. It helps to release the excreta from the body and also plays its part in the creation process.

Samana Air

Samana air is situated in between the *mukhya* prana and *apana* air. Its centre is at the naval, called the *manipura*. This *samana air* is meant to sustain the biological process of the digestion and assimilation of consumed food and fluid. The purpose of this *samana air* is to help transform the eaten food and the fluid taken to the essential body fluid, blood and other forms for creating vital for existence. That means *samana air* does the digestion and assimilation process.

Byana Air

Byana air is distributed across the entire body and existence; it supports the functioning of life from all perspective. *Udana* air creates the *teja*, the fundamental energy of life. As long as life exists, *udana* air remains active with all energy. With the end of life, *udana* air merges with mind and *atman* for a new life.

Realization of the inner world requires proper understanding of the functioning of the human vital or prana *shakti*. Five different types of air (prana, *apana*, *byana*, *samana* and *udana*) represent the factors of vital energy within an individual and similar pattern of the arrangement for the cosmic system—the solar system.

With the sun bringing in illumination for the world, the organs of vision of creatures get activated squarely. Energy system for the world centres around the basic concept of prana and *atman*. This *atman* resides in all creatures within the centre of earth or in the centre of human heart. The cardiac centre is full of love and devotion of individuals. Within the core of the heart centre resides the inner sun that enables life to glow on strength of divinity.

Aadityah hi vai bajhah pranah
Udaya twesha hi enam chakshusham pranam anugrihnam.
Prithibyam ya devata sa esha purushashya apana ashatyabhya
Antarah yat akashah sa samano vayuh byanah.

(Prashna Upanishad, 3/8)

The sun in the global cosmic order is vital for the whole universe.
This sun infuses the impulse of life through providing vision in our
eyes. The cosmic order brings *apana* air downwards and rests there.
Samana air is established in between the lowermost and the upper skies.

Byana Air

Byana air spreads around the universe and also within the individual. The space within and the space outside resemble *samana* air.

Inner journey begins with the onset of the idea of vitality within and without. The cosmic system evolves and sustains lives on earth.

When we learn the sequence of things, we understand the ascendance of cosmic energy within the biophysical system on the one hand and the entire world system on the other.

Hridi hi esha atman, atra etad ekshatam nadinam
Tasham shatam eka eka shyam
Dwasaptatih dwasaptatih bhavanti
Prati shakha nadi sahasrani, aasu vyanah charati.
(Prashna Upanishad, 3/6)

Atman resides in the heart centre. There are total 101 biological
channels inside, called *nadi*. Each of these channels have hundreds
of subdivisions and each of these branch channels further
lead 72,000 branches of the channels.

With deep concentration in mind through the process of *pranayama*, one can get the illumination revealed through the cardiac centre to all the minutest, smallest and largest biological channels and cells of the body. *Byana* air passes through and touches all these channels and cells of the body. *Byana* air also moves inside out everywhere.

Byana air coordinates circulation of blood and vascular system, transmission of nervous force, performance of the works through *sapta dhatu* or 'seven metal planes' of biological system, which are as follows: bones, bone marrow, blood, semen, skin, muscle and the juice of life—vascular system.

The Spiritual Being or the Science of Human Spirituality

The spiritual being, a formless yet comprising of a shadow form, made of light remains and resides along with the empirical body. Formlessness of light depicts the essential truth underlying every personality. It does not get revealed unless one follows a sacrificial way to discover the same. *Pranayama* is one of those tested methods which attempts to open up the dormant spiritual quality and functions undertaken by a person. The concepts of unfoldment go deep into the understanding of the dimensions that are not visible or appear tangible with our organs of senses in the context of the world.

The human organs of senses—power to see, hear, taste, touch, feel, perceive, think—are all constrained by the limits of empirical identity. Spiritual process makes it open for the person who has initiated the practice. *Pranayama* makes the gateway to spirituality open.

The following fundamental concepts brought into practice would unveil the spiritual being and make it open for integration into the system of the person. Highlights of the concepts are as follows:

- *Pancha vayu* (five kinds of air)
- *Pancha kosha* (fivefold sheath of spiritual identity)
- *Shatchakra* (six plexuses of spiritual realization)

Pancha Vayu

As narrated earlier, *pancha vayu* are prana, *apana*, *byana*, *samana* and *udana*. These are the functional identities of the air drawn in from the open air. Usual normal breathing process covers all functional identities in a feeble way. However, the process of *pranayama* makes it clear, direct and effective to the extent that reveals the spiritual self, remaining thereto dormant within.

To begin with, the functions of prana *vayu* and that of *apana vayu* are to together make the breathing process continue and happen. In the *pranayama* when we draw deep inhalation, volume of air drawn in increases. Thereby this air gets properly distributed across the physical organs of the body. The functional divisions of *pancha vayu* are discussed further.

Prana *Vayu*

This draws and releases air. This stimulates the upper parts of our body—head, brain, nervous system, bone marrows, vision, hearing, sensing, thinking—setting on a central controlling and energizing organ, called mind, in different contexts of our living. Prana *vayu* thus stimulates and maintains the functions of life from a wholesome perspective. With the process of *pranayama* continued for a reasonable period, the functions of organs in the upper part of the body, such as the head, the brain and the sense controlling mind get coordinated strongly. Thereby the power of mind and power of our entire process of thinking, conceptualizing, decisions and initiatives for actions get coordinated for each one's enhanced power and scope.

Apana Vayu

This sustains the lower part of the body. *Apana* helps prana *vayu* complete the breathing process through finally absorbing the air within and thereby creating the perspective for drawing in fresh air over and over again. The process of *pranayama* enhances this scope. This helps boost the functioning of the kidneys, urinary system, excretory processes and gender-specific biological functions. *Apana vayu* always sustains the organs along and below the body's naval regions.

Samana Vayu

This sustains the entire middle part of the body. The functional scope includes the digestive system, cardiovascular system, cardiac centre, lungs, liver, spleen, gall bladder, stomach and intestine and organs only.

Byana Vayu

This sustains the entire cellular functions of the body, nervous coordination, vascular coordination, coordination with all organs via the nervous system and the vertebral column, endocrine functions and coordination among different psychological functions of the body.

Udana Vayu

This maintains the *teja* or energy level of the entire body. The warmth and heat of the body are very important to maintain work–thought–dynamism balance of human system. *Byana vayu* makes us connect with the entire cosmic system on the one hand and the *atman* or the pure sole residing within the core of our heart on the other.

The span and scope of *pancha vayu* become stronger and very clearly effective once the functioning of human organism is made to streamline a steady progress forward. The journey of life becomes better by this *pranayama* having regularly adopted and practised to unfold the vital potentials of an individual. The scientific quest to understand and capture of the effects of this process of coordination of breath called *pranayama* has been set off intensely.

The scientific explorations have considered the human brain as the central focus from where the conditions of mind can be partly understood. In fact, the breathing process cannot impact the brain and stimulate functions that lead to change of the mental environment otherwise involved in the process of normal breathing alone.

The concept can be seen getting echoed by the leading scientific research on mind. Scientific analysis of mind actually explores different segments of the brain, assuming brain as the seat bed of mind. Similar such research which is still getting continued identifies the role of mind as the most vital in a human system.

While apparently simple functions like pain are showing themselves to be more complex than might be expected, some seemingly imponderable qualities of the mind are starting to look surprisingly mechanistic. Morality, altruism, 'spiritual' and religions experiences, aesthetic appreciation—even love—have generally been thought of as being beyond scientific exploration. (Carter, 2010, pp. 12–13)

Mind stands as a messenger in a human system. Mind stands as an invisible organ but coordinates with all biological functions of human system. The Vedic sages have identified the role of mind in human organism. Sage Vaisampayana has presented a conversation between Nachiketa, an aspirant to learn the truth about *atman*, the Supreme self, and Yama, the lord of death as follows:

Atmanam rathinam viddhi
Shariram ratham eva tuh.
Buddhim tu sarathim viddhi
Manaha pragraham eva cha.

(Katha Upanishad, 1/3/3)

Know for certain that the supreme self called *atman* is seated in the chariot of body. The human intellect drives this chariot down the paths of time and the mind acts as the connecting cord between the chariot and the connected supreme soul seated on that chariot.

Now, the spiritual journey is to transform the mind. The process of *pranayama* with its engineered impact on the vital system makes the mind shift to the supreme spirit, so that the characteristic features of mind would transform into the broad elevated mind that has adopted the qualities of goodness and the spirit of divinity.

Spiritual realization occurs in life through the process of attaining a properly focused mind. Mind that is above all kinds of desires; mind that is free from anger, gluttony, envy, greed, hatred, jealousy and egocentrism. This mind is liberated enough to understand, maintain and take forward the values of life which are good for society and the world.

The idea of spiritual journey centres on the mind. That is why purifying mind of the impurities of the system has been the central focus of life. The impurities are the attributes of non-divinity or demonic types. These are actually the common objectives of all methods of realization. *Pranayama* makes it happen.

Annam Brahmah iti byajanat
Annyat eva khalu Imani bhutani jayante
Annena jatani jibanti
Annam prayanti avishambishanti iti. Tat vijnaya.
(Taittiriya Upanishad, 3/2/1)

Anna or the food for life or material form of consumption is a form of Brahman. Life is sustained by the consumption of food and finally all elements of life converge to one or the other form of food for consumption by some.

Pranah Brahman iti byajanat,
Pranat eva khalu Imani bhutani jayante.
Pranena jayanti jibanti
Pranam prayanti avishambishanti iti. Tat vijnaya.
(Taittiriya Upanishad, 3/3/1)

'Prana' or vital existence is the form of Brahman.
Life emerges from the cosmic vital existence or *mahaprana.*
Life converges to the *mahaprana* at the end of its span.

Manah Brahman iti byajanat,
Manaso hi eva khalu Imani bhutani jayante.
Manaso jayanti jibanti
Manah prayanti avishambishanti iti. Tat vijnaya.
(Taittiriya Upanishad, 3/4/1)

Mind is the form of Brahman where he is seated also.
Mind creates the causative factor for life and continuity.
Life converges to the cosmic mind once its span is over.

Vijnanam Brahman iti byajanat,
Vijnanayat eva khalu Imani bhutani jayante.
Vijnanena jayanti jibanti
Vijnanam prayanti avishambishanti iti. Tat vijnaya.
(Taittiriya Upanishad, 3/5/1)

Wisdom represents Brahman.
Lives emerge out of the presence of divine wisdom.
Life grows on strengths of wisdom.
Life converges to the supreme self and divine wisdom at the end of its span.

Anandah Brahman iti byajanat,
Anandyat hi eva khalu Imani bhutani jayante.
Anandena jayanti jibanti
Anandam prayanti avishambishanti iti. Tat vijnaya.
(Taittiriya Upanishad, 3/6/1)

Ananda or bliss is the form of Brahman.
Life emerges, maintains and grows out of the bliss in life.
Life derives its strength to move forward on time on strength of bliss.
The culmination of life is convergence to the supreme bliss also.

Pancha Kosha (Five Sheaths)

Scientific understanding of human diversity and human unity has been nicely depicted by the genetic scientists, as mentioned in post-gene account.

A gene is the basic unit of hereditary information, It carries the information needed to build, maintain and repair organisms. Genes collaborate with other genes, with inputs from the environment, with triggers, and with random chance to produce the ultimate form and function of an organism.

The genetic code is universal. A gene from a blue whale can be inserted into a microscopic bacterium and it will be deciphered accurately and with nearly perfect fidelity. A corollary; there is nothing particularly special about human genes. (Mukherjee, 2016, p. 480)

The natural position of life is such that difference among human beings are just a small fragment of the potentials of life. The Vedic view of life is the unity of life so much so that every life is the same as each one is directly derived from the supreme and wholesome. Life is derived from the *mahaprana*—the supreme cosmic source of the potent of life. The supreme cosmic system distributes the seeds and elements of individual of life. Every living entity is thus one or the other form.

As identified by Vedic sages, the truth about life is whichever life has arisen in this world or the universe so far, whatever living entities remain on earth now and whichever living entities are awaited to seed and growth on earth in whatever form, are Brahman's revelations, the supreme self. Each form is unique and at the same time each form having derived from the same supreme as origin is essentially identical or close to the same. The sages of Rig Veda, Sama Veda, Yajur Veda and Atharva Veda have proclaimed unanimously the truth of oneness in creation. All the great Vedic sages, such as Sage Vashishtha, Sage Atri, Sage Yajnavalkya, Sage Vaisampayana, Sage Jaimini and Sage Sumanta have realized the uniqueness of the truth of life.

Yatoh vai imani bhutani jayante
Yena jatani jibanti
Tat pranah pravishanti iti. Tat Brahmana Jatah.

So far, the lives that have been generated in this cosmic creation, lives that are awaited to appear in future and all forms of lives that exist now are all derived from the same supreme Brahman (that means being originated from the same source, they have commonness and oneness in their existence. They share the same supreme potential in life).

The genealogists' scientific understanding of life identification represents almost similar kinds of perceptions. Initially put across by the Ukrainian and American scientist Theodosius Dobzhansky and subsequently many others who contributed to further development of the science of human genome, the genetics similarly among creatures have been tested widely leading to the conclusion that though each person is different from the other, the dissimilarity is close to almost nil or negligible.

The scientific understanding has been summarized by the genealogist in the following words:

Variations in genes contribute to variations in features, forms and behaviours. When we use the colloquial terms gene for blue eyes or gene for height, we are really referring to a variation (or allele) that specifies an eye colour or height. These variations constitute an extremely minor position of the genome. They are magnified in our imagination because of cultural, and possibly biological, tendencies that tend to amplify difference. A six-foot man from Denmark and a four foot man from Demba share the same anatomy, physiology and biochemistry. Even the two most extreme human variants—male and female—share 99.688 percent of their genes. (Mukherjee, 2016, p. 480).

The concept of oneness is perceived only when we can attain that supreme consciousness through the path of realization of Brahman. Scientific rational mind has wider tendencies to discriminate and differentiate. General human intent is to harp on those small factors and issues of differences which are actually trifling from the holistic perspective of Brahman.

The theory of *pancha kosha*, or five sheaths of existence, marks the right position to analyse conditions and general qualities of mind conducive to the growth of the mental perspective of too much differentiation to close to oneness of the spirit of existence. Thus, the best-known person and the worst-known person in the world comprise two states of identities which have close similarities to those which were considered dissimilar before. Theory of *pancha kosha* is a matter of realization only. Descriptions in words may not be well communicative; however, they can initiate the realization.

The five sheaths are as follows:

1. *Annamaya kosha* called material sheath
2. *Pranamaya kosha* called vital sheath
3. *Manomaya kosha* called mental sheath
4. *Vijnanamaya kosha* called wisdom sheath
5. *Anandamaya kosha* called the blissful sheath, or the Supreme soul

Each sheath is a functional coordinating system from biological, physiological, anatomical and spiritual point of view. The quality of mind keeps on changing with the scope of the functional coordination both at elemental and system levels. Brief description of the sheaths is given further.

Annamaya Kosha

This is the identity of a person through their desires, wants, greed, mental habits influenced by anger, jealousy, envy, covetousness, backbiting, doing–thinking ill of others, evil aspirations, evil thoughts, dishonesty, clinging to all kinds of untruth and hunger.

A selfish, arrogant mind always looks for personal gains, most of the times, ignoring the virtue of the world and thereby attempting to process by all means. The possession of wealth, money, materials does not quench the hunger of the person. The greed continues to glow fire within. A fire to acquire anything that this mind attempts to do or does undertake continues to fulfil a part of the sense of deficit but continues to maintain the deficit in a renewed form.

Mind driven by the material sheath puts very high degree of emphasis on the factors of difference and discrimination. This mind looks at the world from the negative perspective. Thus, the person carries forward a sense of deprivation. Emotions and sentiments push the understanding that their life is less fulfilling because of factors external to them. These are the factors which would make a person feel their insignificance.

According to the realized understanding of the sages of four Vedas—Rig, Sama, Yajur and Atharva, *anna* is food. This is not only the food which we eat for our survival and growth but this is also an endowed blessing of the divine. He is present, invisible, undetectable, inaudible, untraceable in all those elements which we consider as having and in its getting transformed from any form to a new host—the human body. It works at the level of the human body and system. *Pancha vayu* acts on the different aspects of *anna* to convert this to the energy level of the individual and collective group of them. Thus, sense of deprivation or the sense of deficit or even the deficit-driven tendencies of world disappear from their mind. A new idea of oneness emerges.

Pranamaya Kosha

'Prana' or vital provides the energy of life. Energies required for life are infused by the 'prana' in combination with *vayu* or air. Out of *pancha vayu*, or five air, the *udana vayu* contexts energy for the life. *Udana vayu* assimilates, stimulates and energizes the entire body system. This becomes further figured when a concentrated mind wishes to move forward the dormant energy in the empirical biological system. *Pranayama* maximizes the energy configuration and release of the patent energy.

Pranamaya kosha is a functional system that maintains the biological energy in life. All human functions require some amount of energy. For example, the cardiac functioning needs at least six microvolts for smooth rhythms. The human brain, particularly certain lobes, which are responsible for thinking, rational impulse, autonomous actions and actions of contemplation and volition, is all propelled by the *prana vayu* in general and *udana vayu* in particular. *Pranamaya* rejuvenates the mind by generating the process of concentrated consciousness; a person finds inspiration to create an ambience of life that actually goes beyond the limits of existence. It helps the transcendence of mortal energy to be fulfilled and to take hold of the touch of cosmic energy in life. The cosmic energy is actually the divine impulse that is present in life. *Pranamaya* thus concentrates the *pranic* force on to the spirit of the divine light.

Manomaya Kosha

Man has been defined as a mix of the mind and materials of the body—psychosomatic entity. The human form, basically structured around the skeletal of the body, is covered by the impact of the seven different structural inputs, called *sapta dhatu*. These include bone, bone marrow, blood, semen, skin, muscle and fluid (blood vascular system).

All of these collectively moderate, carry and foster forward the spirit of a living entity. A living entity needs to perform all of its biological functions and activities, generate thoughts, have ideas, make plans and strategies—all of which are actually coordinated by the mind. The organs of the senses can perform only if the mind is added to the respective biological functions. Thus, the eyes cannot see when the mind is withdrawn from the functional focus of vision; the ear can hear only when the mind is in the function of hearing. If the mind is absent, the strongest body would fail to apply its strength to any activity. A strong individual would be reduced to an ordinary frail person.

Material functions can be performed independently of any kind of mental support in a mechanistic way. However, mind is added to make it vibrant. The mind has a super imposing dimension. Yet it is the quality of the mind that determines the quality of the function. Mind is basically restless. The metaphor of the nature of the monkey is properly applied to the human mind. Generally speaking, the conditions of the mind can be explained in the following ways, with the conditions categorizing in each class.

The states of mind are as follows:

1. *Kshipta* (restlessness like the nature of a monkey)
2. *Vikshipta* (turbulence, a monkey bit by a scorpion)
3. *Ekagra* (drawn in and concentrated on one point)
4. *Niruddha* (cessation of mind or a liberated state)

Mind prefers to remain restless on its own habit. Basically because of its understanding or perception, the world or this nature has denied a person of their due possessions and attainments. A sense of deficit develops, sometimes, not in a conscious manner. Rather it develops in a way that silently captures the mind and acts of it in invisibly.

When a person is confronted with some immediate cause of concern or expectation, they become more intensely oriented towards having possessions of those not yet attained—may be material possession, may be resources, may be money, may be name and fame, may be relative achievement compared to some others and so on.

Restlessness and turbulence of the mind are actually controlled by the process of *pranayama*. It helps in collecting different forms of elementary presence of the mind, scattered here and there, and thereby to turn it to the central purpose of life. At this stage, it is the responsibility of the person to identify and determine the purpose of life. The central purpose of life should be somewhat broader and longer than the canvas of life. This broader perspective is actually transcending.

The leader of one's own world has to transcend. General tendency of human being is to be one of the 'me too' lot, and be swayed by the current of life's desires and expectations. The restlessness of the mind shows the unfulfillment of any kind and the search for options, ways and means to make that good. Restlessness, because the mind does not feel pleasant or comfortable in the present state of things, thereby expects many more things (material, financial or intangible) to be done and possessed. Seeking is begging, but winning is achieving. A person who wants to become their own leader should turn away from seeking or begging. Rather the person has the option to win. Winning demands capacity building and identification of things that would contribute to creating a basis for winning through an honest and fair way.

Self-leadership

Human mind creates constraints or liberates the same. *Kshipta* and *vikshipta* states of mind are basically because of the presence of desire, the sense of deficit, jealousy, greed, envy and selfishness; essentially, all these are driven by human ego. The psychologist's view of the ego is different. Ego makes one perceive their dominance, prominence and uniqueness, though all of these can be converted into good quality by changing or transforming perspective.

The spiritual process of the journey of consciousness reveals a different state of mind in the different states of our mind plexus, coordination of all these can make the mind attain the state of *ekagrata* or one-pointedness. Finally, the mind should be drawn to a state of *niruddha*. Whereas *ekagrata* is a state of affairs where all functional tendencies and propensities are drawn in and around a single point. But the fundamental approach of that is to build a state of mind where the former mind has disappeared and a new mind has taken in the position thereon. It is because of the fundamental transformation of the mind. This is cessation of mind, and an illuminated golden mind is in place. Sage Yajnavalkya has identified this mind as *Suvarna Jyotirmaya Manoh* (the illuminated golden mind). A mind free from the clutches of desires, deficits, greed, anger, lust, discrimination, hatred, gluttony and covetousness, hungry for the possession of money–material–fame and devoid of personal ego.

Vijnanamaya Kosha

Knowledge can be acquired, but wisdom is present within each individual. It is just waiting to be unleashed. Unleashing the intrinsic content of knowledge, understanding, perception, realization or acquired learning inputs together with other inputs from outside the environment or the world makes it vibrant to reveal the factors of wisdom in the quest of truth in life. Knowledge is the external layer of wisdom. Knowledge takes into cognizance the spirit of work, the energy of work and the inspiration needed for accomplishing the work. *Vijnana* is the special variety of work that contributes to the wholesome perspective, the context of work, the objective of work and, finally, the resultant drive to which the work contributes. *Vijnanamaya* thus embraces the entire stream of work, the thoughts behind the work and the resultant effect of the work.

Vijnanamaya state of the consciousness opens the gateway to wisdom and transforms life to the extent that it makes the mind think good of all. The basic objective of this state of mind was unanimously described by the Vedic sages as *Sarve Bhavantu Sukhinah, Sarve Santu Niramaya* (let everyone be happy, let the well-being be distributed to all). This mind does not depend on any material advantages or gains, but rather the mind wants all to be good and happy for all. Wisdom is born when a person is free from the impacts of the ego.

Anandamaya Kosha

Whereas the sheath of wisdom still has the causes of differentiation, when consciousness touches the core of our existence, it finds the vast pool of blissful condition and immerses itself in the spiritual view of understanding. Human beings are classified as having three different forms from of a mixture of empirical and spiritual understanding. They are the material body, the subtle body and the causal body. The material body is the physical body as we understand it from a rational–physical and biological perspective. The material body has been profusely described in various ways through biological sciences, the branches of medical sciences—anatomical, physiological, anthropological and so on. Human existence has also been described in environmental, social and other ways. The material body, though in form and appearance, has still proved impenetrable in terms of the knowledge of the system of the material body. Mind is the central organ that coordinates and controls everything in the physical body. Some scientists assume that the human brain is the seat of the mind. However, the spiritual analysis shows that the mind resides at all seven spiritual plexus with seven different identities.

Attempts to map the contents and activities of human brains have shown and demonstrated that our knowledge and capacity affect only about a few million segments of a grown brain organ.

One of the most prominent scientific understandings of the human brain as depicted by neuroscientists maintains:

In normal brains incoming sensory stimuli follow well-worn neutral paths from the sensory organ to specific brain destinations. As the stimulus passes through the brain it is split into several different streams which are processed in parallel by different brain modules. Some of these modules are in the cerebral context...others are in the limbic system. Every brain constructs the world in a slightly different way from any other because every brain is different. The sight of an external object will vary from person to person because no two people have precisely the same number of motion cells, magneta-sensitive cells, or straight line cells.... An individual view is formed both by their genes and by how their brain has been moduled by experience. (Carter, 2010, pp. 175–178)

The scientific analysis of the brain shows and depicts the difference in the biological composition of the brain to a very small extent. Most of the partial and functional tendencies are the same. Thus, the difference between a good man and a bad man is very small and can be removed gradually over a slow process. This difference can be made good by efforts of the kind of *pranayama*. With effective control of this act and practice of *pranayama*, the person gets the *pranic* force stimulated forward so much that, on the one hand, the goodness of habit and character is revealed and, on the other, the creative faculty of the person is unfolded. As the latest idea of neuroscience has mentioned, our consciousness is stimulated on a positive scale either because of its genealogical position or because of the experience gained in life.

A person is considered to be divine if they have all the good qualities that have been spelled out before. A spiritual seeker would develop certain qualities that are divine. They should be a person with full of simplicity like an ordinary child, mildly modest, honest, sincere, sweet in their words, with a unique level of consciousness of noble being and at the same time realize the identity of one's self and see the same self everywhere, perceiving oneness with all and thereby bearing in mind that the same supreme, the Brahman, resides in all personalities, the same way as they are. With the process of *pranayama* going on vigorously, the vital energy within which microcosm comes into contact with, or connects with, the outer, the microcosm.

With the connection between the microcosmic and the macrocosmic, the super-cosmic union takes place and the realization of the supreme, the Brahman, takes place and thus the consciousness attains the highest abode, called the divine plexus or the *sahasrara*. Communion makes life blissful, *anandamaya*, where the person who aspires to spiritual attainment is merged into the godly bliss of life. *Brahmavid*

Brahmaiva Vavati (the person who realized the spirit of Brahman attains the spirit of Brahman).

Shatchakra (Six Spiritual Plexus)

Spiritual attainment occurs in the course of our experience of the journey of consciousness and in the process of the gradual transformation of consciousness from the usual human attributes to the divine identity of a person.

The spiritual identity of a person and the gradual experience are stored in the consciousness. This gets revealed to the person who actually initiated and actively engaged in the process. Realization is actually self-experience and self-discovery. It is a continuous process. The plexus acts at six different points and connects the body to the invisible inner dimensions. The inner dimensions are viewed from the following angles:

- Physical material body
- The subtle body
- The causal body

Spiritual realizations take place at the level of the subtle body, which is the invisible existence remaining present within this existence. The causal body contemplates, delivers and fosters forward acquired experience translating the earned experience into the wisdom of life. The main messenger of the spiritual impulse is the set of paths that have an inbuilt presence in human existence. The channels that contain, transmit and help transform are subtle yet empirical.

The following are present in the composition of human body:

- *Susumna* (this refers to the notochord—the vertebral column that runs from the tail end of the vertebral column to the skull. The bone marrow of the central column passes through the vertebral column).
- *Ida* (this is a channel that runs from the base of *susumna* and paves its way from the left to *susumna* up to the upper end of the throat level and converges to the left of the nose).
- *Pingala* (this is a channel that runs to the right of *susumna*, the central column, and runs to the upper end of the throat level and converges to the right of the nose).

The chakras or plexus are as follows:

1. *Muladhara*: This is the root chakra located at the end of the spinal column. Human self-consciousness rests here in the form of a serpent with three and a half coils. It is in a sleeping state. The purpose of the

aspirant on the spiritual journey is to invoke the conscious from sleeping in the form of a serpent. This self is the seat bed of *shakti*—primordial energy and energy released by the *pranic* forces revealing the condition for the awakening of the spirit of the coil. With the invocation, the coil begins to unfold, and ultimately this indicates upward movement through the spinal column of *susumna. Muladhara*, a storehouse of biological and spiritual energy, opens its flow through *susumna* channel with the touch of the prana *vayu* in general and *apana vayu* in particular.

The action of *apana vayu* extends from the naval region to below. It combines the physiological functions of the entire excretory process, the kidneys and regions, or the functions that support and are associated with it. Also, this *apana vayu* has direct action on the genitals and all related functions. The mental habit of lower instincts, different varieties of lower properties, can be coordinated and controlled through the *pranayama* process.

The channels or *nadis* of *ida* and *pingala* are connected by alternating nasal respiration. *Ida* is governed by the left nostril, while *pingala* is governed by the right nostril. The serpent that remains almost sleepy at the base of *susumna* at *muladhara* completely blocks *susumna* channel. *Ida* and *pingala* are making the first crossover at this point. When a spiritual aspirant is into the process of alternate nostril breathing, the air inhaled passes through the either of these and reaches the lowermost channel and exchanges its pathway of passage. *Ida* is considered to be feminine in nature and lunar in character; whereas the other, *pingala*, is considered to be masculine in nature and to be the sun in life. In order to make effective use of the functioning of alternate nostril breathing, it is suggested that the process be initiated with *pranic vayu* (drawn out of the atmosphere) first drawn through the right nostril while keeping the left nostril closed. Repetition of the process would allow the person to carry the *pranic vayu* drawn through the right nostril down to the level of *muladhara*. As mentioned earlier, the *pranic vayu* splits into five characters.

- Prana *vayu* which covers the areas above the level of the throat.
- *Apana vayu* which goes down to the naval region and the entire position below.
- *Samana vayu* which extends from the regions below the throat to the naval region.
- *Byana vayu* which covers the entire endocrine, nervous and vascular systems.
- *Udana vayu* which generates and distributes (vital) energy to all cells.

Thus, it remains with the *apana vayu* to take care of the regions of *muladhara*. The *pingala* channel opens gradually with the movement of the *apana vayu* down to the junction of *muladhara*. Sufficient flow of it with the mind properly attached to it makes the *pranic vayu* reach the lowermost end of the *pingala*. Now is the time to stimulate the *shakti* serpent (energy in the primordial state) to awaken and raise its head forward, releasing the *pranic* air through the *ida* up and up to the left nostril to be released in the open air, on the one hand, and *susumna* to gradually move upwards with all its contents on the other. The process is not going to happen just as it is. It calls for sustained practice, mental attention and total devotion. Once the journey of *susumna* takes place, the energy flow meets different levels of the plexus with different objectives. The visual effects of each plexus are different.

Ida and *pingala* do cross over at certain points. It is like two or three rivers coming together and flowing up or down. Like the presence of *triveni* (three streams) rivers, the Ganges, the Yamuna and the Saraswati crossover meeting, each of which is a plexus. This plexus is named as follows: (a) *muladhara*, (b) *svadhisthana*, (c) *manipura*, (d) *anahata*, (e) *vishuddha*, (f) *ajnaa* and (g) *sahasrara*. This central column starts with *muladhara* and ends up with *susumna*.

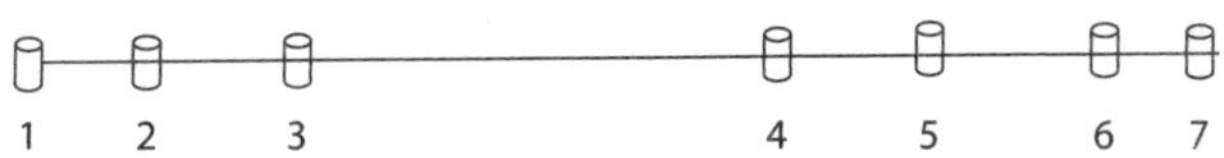

Note: The vertical column with 1 as the basement is shown here horizontally.

In fact, the descriptions of plexuses are subjective. This spiritual process is an experiential one. The experiences of the seeker on this journey are unique to the person. However, there are things in general that will be in common with everyone. Certain visuals, like lotus with different colours and the number of petals seen in most cases, are briefly mentioned here. The basic nature of each plexus has a common understanding.

Muladhara

This is situated at the base of the spinal column at the sacral or pelvic plexus as one understands while taking medication. The colours appear red, which are revealed by a clear or somewhat depicted lotus with four petals. In fact, *muladhara* is the base plexus. It is considered to be the storehouse of all physical, mental and spiritual energies for both empirical and spiritual functions. *Chitta-manas*—these two states of mind reside here. *Chitta* is the seat bed of memory, and *manas* is the mind's thinking organ. *Muladhara* is considered to have elephantine nature—profuse, but reserved, energy.

Here, the shape of an elephant carrying four petalled lotus is meaningful. Four petals represent four different goals of life: dharma, *artha*, *kama* and *moksha*. 'Dharma' is righteousness, *artha* stands for the meaning of life established through possessions or, in some rare cases, giving up. Possessions could be material, money, resources, fame, establishments and so on of a different nature. *Kama* is desire. It refers to fulfilling desires of any kind. Usually, this refers to the desires for instincts of a lower nature, which is actually meant by it. *Moksha* is considered a liberation. This is the view of liberation from all kinds of material bondage. *Moksha* is the spiritual attainment of the wisdom of the supreme self—'Brahman'.

Persons with a dominant intention to enjoy life and be deluged with pleasures of material nature would always have their consciousness bound and moved within the limits of the first three plexuses—*muladhara*, *svadhisthana* and *manipura*. However, the other few individuals who intend to have a superior quality of life are able to overcome the barriers of *manipura* and move up the seventh plexus called *sahasrara* because they have the potential to reach the top.

At all the levels of *muladhara*, the quality of mind is such that all non-divine qualities such as greed, anger, jealousy, lust, covetousness, envy, sloth, untruth and evil-mindedness become the basic make-up of the mind. Mind, at this level, is dominated by selfish tendencies and always carries the message of selfish gains at any cost. The mental drive of being non-divine conditions at *muladhara* is such that the governance of life is exteriorized or externally oriented.

With the mind drawing inputs from the outside, *muladhara* mind is completely selfish and evil thinker. The mind propels an individual to do anything that offers them a personal gain at any cost that might be. Mind at *muladhara* is basically dominated by a person's ego. It is revealed by selfishness, greed, desire and tendencies which are considered to be lower in nature. This individual can do any kind of evil work, and they can always think evil. This mind can also be opened up to the spiritual process, even if it is imposed upon it.

Svadhisthana

Svadhisthana (one's own place—the origin of birth and creations) has a reference of being based at the vertebral column located at the place of genitals in the lower part of lower abdomen. Furthermore, the biological position between the coccyx and the sacrum can be estimated. Its colour is that of fire. This level shows a lot of activity—joy, happiness, hope, self-confidence driven by either positive spiritual energy or neutral, biologically driven energy. *Svadhisthana*—considered to be a place of its own—makes the general motive of work vibrant. With pranic energy added to the subconscious, the process of change and transformation at the level of *svadhisthana* chakra also joins.

This plexus requires direct control through *susumna* impulse. As *susumna* wave rises, our intent at this plexus purifies. Getting rid of impurities at this stage, the *svadhisthana* level understanding of spiritual intentions develops, and thereby the urge for the lower instincts and desires, which are primordial in nature, gradually diminishes, allowing the noble intent of life to grow deeper and larger. This life force helps the flower of life to blossom into its full potential. Thus, a person reaches the height of purity but is guided by a vehicle of dynamism to cover all activities of life in one place.

Svadhisthana plexus is thus a very important part of an individual's spiritual journey. *Ida* and *pingala*, which are logically masters of feminine attributes and masculine attributes, cross over and meet at the level of *muladhara* and then at the higher plane. So *svadhisthana* gets *susumna* flow through this plexus and the *pranic* force through the prana *vayu*.

The *svadhisthana* chakra has six vermillion-coloured lotus petals.

These six lotus petals represent six attributes of vices, which are as follows:

- *Kama* (desire)
- *Krodha* (anger)
- *Lobha* (greed)
- *Moha* (delusions)
- *Mada* (jealousy/addicted)
- *Matsarya* (chaotic)

These are attributes that lead to the creation of a negative personality for the advancement of spiritual energy. That is why these attributes are considered enemies of a spiritual aspirant. These are the attributes that, collectively and singularly, create an obstacle to a person's progress.

The *pranic* force that is being associated with vital energy remains at *svadhisthana* and creates wonder. One who can overcome the impacts of these negative attributes has the strength to move quickly and forward. *Svadhisthana* creates or destroys the pathway. One who falls prey to or is attracted to the pleasures of this plexus is thrown out of the paths of inner spirituality. Inner spirituality must be rejuvenated by avoiding and rejecting vices or six negative elemental attributes. Thus, *svadhisthana* makes the process forward for goodness and divine attributes in life for a spiritual seeker.

Manipura (The Naval Plexus)

This plexus is known as the solar plexus. *Manipura* is the centre through which the journey of life continues. At the level of gradual formation within the mother's being, all vital energy is used to be infused into the new life through the naval cord. After being cut off at the naval root, the naval cord remains a very important plexus of the continuity of the genealogical factors. *Manipura* plexus is, in fact, a transitional junction between the material orientation of life and the spiritual orientation of life. The naval plexus is a place where one can get the light of life.

The question is what kind of life a person would prefer to choose from. If the dominant desire for life is to seek material comfort, biological pleasure, social recognition in terms of name and fame, it can finally create relative position of advantage in terms of life gains. *Muladhara* is a plane where human consciousness can reflect and move down to *svadhisthana*. This is going to happen in most cases. However, if, by means of any inspiration, motivation or sensitization, the human mind develops a certain attraction towards the spiritual path, it paves the way for the journey of spiritual energy through the column of *susumna*. With the mind opened to the spiritual path, the upward passage of spiritual energy begins. This moves towards the next higher plexus, called *anahata* (throat 'chakra').

Every condition that is conducive to the spiritual journey, the conscious energy meets the plexus in the throat and merges with the elemental consciousness. At this level, the spiritual aspirant visualizes 10-petalled lotus representing the *dasa mahavidya* (10 great spirits). These are the forms of Goddess Kali. *Dasa mahavidya* are the different forms of appearance of the supreme mother Mahadevi Durga. The forms are as follows: Mahakali, Tara, Bhairavi, Chhinnamasta, Chandi, Bhubaneswari, Bagala, Kamala, Katyayani and Durga. These are all different revelations of the same supreme mother Durga (also called Devi Parvati, Devi Vaishnavi and so on). Depending on the condition of the mind of aspirants, the form of Devi appears in the realization that is appropriate to an individual.

In fact, the *manipura* plexus is like a city of jewels. It has got so many parts and other precious elements. When the elemental value of the plexus is achieved, the direction and quality of the movement of spiritual energy is important. Wisdom, rationality, emotions, principles, values and concerns are all contained at this level. When the journey upwards is allowed, all these qualities are set in a finer way. And, on the other hand, if the spiritual energy is reflected down, the attributes that dominate the person are opposite in nature.

At the level of *manipura* plexus, *ida* and *pingala* cross over. This is where the *pranic* forces meet, carried by *samana vayu*. Known otherwise as a fire of life, it helps in metabolism, digestion and functioning of organs in the pelvic region, as well as in the abdominal region—the major organs in the abdomen and the lower regions are facilitated by a fire that is stored and generated in the naval region. It also helps to maintain the physiological balance of the diaphragm.

The spiritual idea of crossing the naval region over this level is a purely experiential effort. Being mostly subjective in nature, the *manipura* chakra offers the power and energy to transform individual experience into collective understanding through collective consciousness.

The awakening of our spiritual self occurs first in *manipura*, and gradually, through meditation, the same will be added to the impetus from the subsequent plexuses.

Anahata (The Cardiac Centre)

Anahata means unhurt. It lies within the central spinal column of the cardiac region. The lotus of this *anahata* plexus, composed of 12 petals, looks like the sky in its colour and invites the openness of the vast universe and the atmosphere. *Anahata* is symbolized as two inverted triangles—of which one points upwards and the other points downwards. Even at this level, the spiritual aspirant may be attracted by the lowness of life which is depicted by showing the lower, directed triangle. The triangle that points upwards indicates the upward journey of our consciousness. This is connected to the cosmic system. *Anahata* plexus generates the goodness of life. It enables us to experience the goodness of the cosmic system. The vast presence of the supreme being here opens the door of experience.

Anahata plexus vibrates with the super-cosmic original *om* sound pronounced as 'o-u-m' in a rhythm. In fact, this unheard-of sound is a soundless sound that helps to elevate our mind to *bhuma* (the cosmic whole). Once the sensitization of *bhuma* touches our cardiac centre, we begin a journey in *bhakti*, or devotion to God. The meditation at *anahata* chakra makes one devotee. However, the unconcentrated mind may fall down, and instead of moving upward, the consciousness of the aspirant may be considered empirical. Material identity is more attracted to unconcentrated mind. As a result, aesthetic vision and emotions are revealed in the spotlight.

The aspirant, in this case, considers the material context of love and happiness dearer to them. Also finds this clearly dear and thereby consider this to be the essential truth in life. At this level, these 12 petals represent 9 stages of devotion, called *nababidha bhakti*, and three stages of energy called *trayee shakti*. Bhakti elements are *shravana, kirtana, vishnu smarana, padasevana, archana, vandana, dasya, sakhya, aatma nivedana* or hearing God's message, chanting, remembering God, service to the Lord, offerings, dedicating spirit, Gods, servanthood, friendship and self-concentration. Whereas the *trayee shakti* are *kreya shakti, guna shakti* and *jnana shakti*, or the energy of dedicated work, values divinely in character and wisdom and knowledge of God.

This cardiac plexus allows the realization of the supreme to be unfolded in one and the absolute, the infinite.

This is referred to as *bhuma*.

Yoh vai Bhuma tat sukham,
Nah alpe sukham asti, Bhuma eva sukham...
(Chandyogya Upanishad, 7/23/1)

Whatever is one with the vast greatness then it brings the happiness for the person. Lesser elements of happiness do not imply happiness, the vast, the infinite has to get registered in our consciousness for bliss—the super joy or intrinsic happiness of life.

Yatra na anyat pasyati na anyat pasyati na anyat shrunati
Na anyat vijanati sah bhumah...
(Chandyogya Upanishad, 7/24/1)

Whenever one is focused on the supreme oneness of this cosmic creation and not an anything else is viewed or heard and known as then they are deviated from the path of realization.

The vast reality of the supreme, the *bhuma*, when perceived is, in fact, the underlying and prevailing identity. The process of realization is the process of entering into the realization of the supreme. *Anahata* is opening up the spirit of realization.

Meditation at this level of the *anahata* chakra invokes the open sky and the vastness, the clarity of the vast and open sky. After the alternate nostril breathing, concentrating at the level of heart centre and trying to visualize the clear blue sky at the cardiac centre makes the journey upright, leading it upward.

***Vishuddha, Ajnaa, Sahasrara* (The Plexuses at Throat Centre, Forehead and Top of Head)**

A journey of consciousness to the level of the cardiac plexus is better to bring into discussions. When devotion comes to the cardiac centre, the force of devotion pushes the consciousness upwards to deeper levels of spiritual realization. At the stage of the *vishuddha*, the 16-petalled lotus, that at the *ajnaa* chakra or the forehead plexus four-petalled lotus, and finally, when the process of realization is complete or near completion, the 1-000 petalled lotus is unfolded. These three are deeply spiritual in nature, and the process is totally experimental. The learners of these should have a pure mind and a pure heart—a mind that is absolutely detached from all kinds of gross or subtle desire, completely free from the effects and influences of the ego, and largely and solely directed to divine realization. A person usually develops a spirit of detachment from the impact of the world. It leads to the disconnection of all relationships and attachments to the world.

The final journey within begins with the process of self-mastery, when mind and intent have become pure and the person realizes the essence of their being.

Chit anandam rupah shivoham aham
I am the supreme blissful self; I am embodied with the spirit of ever blissful consciousness—Lord Shiva within. This journey requires self-initiative towards self-realization. Alternate nostril breathing through *puraka*, *kumbhaka* and *rechaka* creates a basis to push the consciousness up from the condensed centre at *muladhara* upwards to the top of head for deeper and intense realization.

The required quality of the person for this self-realization is to make the mind simple, arjaban, or a simple mind would always create the basis for understanding the divine consciousness. The simple and steady intention of divine realization facilitates the inner journey. As Patanjali concludes yoga at the 'Kaivalya Pada'—oneness:

Purushartha shunyanam gunanam pratiprasavah kaivalyam
swarup pratishtha va chiti shaktih iti.
(Patanjali Yoga 4/34)

When we have forsaken all other tendencies in life, and all attributes are made to cover up the spirit of divinity, the consciousness of the supreme begins in people's lives.

Self-realization alone leads to self-mastery and self-governance.

A realized person achieves the quality of true self-leadership. This person is the fittest king, the right personality to make the right choice in life and activity. The appropriate person, who is capable of leading their own internal domain, can establish leadership in such a way that the entity takes the right path of progress. It is therefore the spirit within which a person realizes the supreme within, brings in and combines the knowledge and expertise of the world to guide and lead any kind of organization in any context. This person becomes a true leader of themselves and the organization.

Thus, a self-realized person creates an internal environment full of divine qualities. They become the leader and messenger of noble qualities in the world, gradually creating a society and a system in the world dominated by these noble qualities, and thus leading to the creation of a new society and a new civilization in the human world. This new civilization will regard every person as equal. The view of life will be one such that divine qualities would be present in every person. Every person, therefore, would be potentially divine. An individual would be free from greed, desire, anger, envy, gluttony, selfishness and ego.

An individual will regard goodness as essential to life and will adopt goodness. Truth, integrity, cooperation, selfless work, devotion to the divine, unattached to the desires of life, free from meanness, compassionate, caring, friendly to others, helpful to all and supportive of life in the world and the universe.

This individual is going to create, maintain and foster forward the oncoming divine civilization. Whether a person is in the household, a corporate manager, a member of a monastery or a member of any kind of institution, if a person takes part in the process mentioned earlier, they shall be a part of a new civilization.

The onset of divine civilization shall remove all kinds of poverty, all evils, all vices and shall clearly establish the victory of virtue on earth.

Virtue shall win.

Ideal of a New Civilization

Spiritual Manager Lays Foundation of a Noble Business Civilization

The Basis: Condition of Civilization

the history of human civilization has been that of rising and falling consciousness. Human journey had begun with a set of promises that were mostly unfulfilled throughout its path. At the beginning, the promise was undeclared. Attraction to something good, however, has always created attractions. Good attracts, on the one hand, while the pull of bad things overweighs the store of good things on the other. The condition of this earth system has undergone periodical changes and transformations through human interventions. In fact, developments in the field of scientific knowledge and its application through technology have transformed human thought, life and society. The standards and processes of human activity and life have been profoundly influenced by the gradual progress of scientific thinking and its impact on the human world through appropriate technology has actually changed, rather than transformed, the socio-economic system on a periodic basis. The latest study of the impact of technology on human society shows its direct influence in changing the course of human life. A special report on the impact of technology on the world economy reads as follows:

Most people are discomfited by radical change, and often for good reason. Both the first industrial revolution, starting in the late 18th century, and the second one, around 100 years later, had their victims who lost their jobs to Cartwright's power loom and later to Edison's electric lighting, Benz's horse-less carriage and countless other inventions that changed the world. But those inventions also immeasurably improved many people's lives, sweeping away old economic structures and transforming society. They created new economic opportunity on a mass scale, with plenty of new work to replace the old.

A third wave of invention and economic disruption, set off by advances in computing and information and communication technology (ICT) in the late 20th Century, promise to deliver a similar mixture of social stress and economic transformation. It is driven by a handful of technologies including machine intelligence, the ubiquitous web and advanced robotics capable of delivering many remarkable innovations; unmanned vehicle; pilotless drones; machines that can instantly translate hundreds of languages, mobile technology that eliminates the distance between doctor and patient; teacher and student. Whether the digital revolution will bring mass job creation to make up for its mass job destruction remains to be seen. (Avent, 2014)

Technology has reshaped the living standards of society. It has had an impact on the thoughts of individuals in general. Technology has created a space for society. Physical proximity in terms of living in a society of shared values has been replaced by a web-based space where web proximity through different media has transformed the world into a village, while the next-door person has become an unknown, unconcerned one. Physical society is gradually being replaced by a virtual society. New society is in vision that will depend on the virtual networking of relationships. Social bondage through physical contagion is gradually losing its charm, and non-physical, web-based existence and networking has taken root.

Human Reality

The human condition depends on perception and understanding in the context of the exploration of ideas. Each idea has its natural impact on the conditioning and streaming of society. Observation by the historians through the human journey has revealed that the idea can lead to the identity of the person, the human understanding of the dignity of an individual and the distinction between human consciousness and animal consciousness. The world's greatest historian, Arnold Toynbee, has observed through the study of human civilization that human dignity, revealed through conscious human values, forms the basis for differentiating parameters between human and subhuman species. According to Toynbee and Ikeda:

Man finds himself in the awkward and embarrassing situation of being an animal who is also a self-conscious spiritual being. He is aware that the spiritual aspect of his nature gives him a dignity that other animals do not possess, and he feels that he ought to maintain his dignity. Therefore, human beings are embarrassed by those physical organs and functions and appetites that are common to them and to non-human animals and that therefore, impugn human dignity by reminding us of our physiological kinship with brute beasts. Non-human animals are not embarrassed by the functioning of their physical nature because they are not self-conscious. Embarrassment caused by the fear of losing dignity and the humiliation of actually losing it, are specifically human troubles.

(Toynbee & Ikeda, 2013, p. 3)

Perceptions depend on the state of consciousness. Human effort has been to stay away from bondage and the clutches of appetites to quench the thirst of physical organs. Subhuman species do not have the spiritual values that humans can adhere to if they want. It depends, however, on the levels attained by a person on the journey of life, on the consciousness that stands as a potential within an individual.

Actions through individuals or the collectives have always seen their reciprocating responses or reactions on the work plane that form the revealed component of consciousness.

Sri Aurobindo focused on the primacy of consciousness in shaping people's lives on earth. His culminating work, *Savitri*, begins by asserting that the temple of eternity is to be lit by eternal light.

It was the hour before the Gods awake.
Across the path of the divine Event
The huge foreboding mind of Night, alone
In her unlit temple of eternity,
Lay stretched immobile upon silence' marge.
Almost one felt, opaque, impenetrable,

In the sombre symbol of her eyeless muse
The abysm of the unbodied infinite;
A fathomless zero occupied the world.

(*Sri Aurobindo, 1940, p. 1*)

The dawn of civilization seems to have been blessed by the divine touch. The supreme truth has the consent for a journey through human conditions and grows into the blossom of a composite truth that combines empirical experiences with glimpses of divine revelations. Human journey has been blessed by the divine intent to take place through the paths of realization based on whatever consciousness has been achieved. This is this basis on which the potentials were enormous and the journey of Savitri began. This journey, though having a voluntary choice, could lead to the ultimate realization of the supreme truth.

At the beginning of the journey, consciousness was as if sleepy or dormant to the core. Revelations required the unfolding to show the release of divine events in life-taking stock of all and sundry of empirical events. The vast span of silence, as a gift of the divine, was likely to have the mixture of voice and silence together. Thus, the realization of life could lead to an understanding of the basis of eternal silence and make it audible revelation of the words that are conceived to emanate from God. Word uttered, piercing through the ocean of silence, thus creates a new horizon, where the word constitutes a form, an image, a unity of consciousness or a formlessness, getting into the shape of the ideas formed within. The symbol thus makes an entry into the realm of infinite divine presence, where an individual has their first opportunity to merge with the eternal presence in the outer season for the next phase of truth. It is thus released into the vast void to be diluted and deluged into the infinite void. The basis of the journey in Savitri's life was, therefore, the unfolding of a continuity that never ended in time and space.

Search for New Life

Empirical life, however, is confined within the boundaries of space and time. While the bounded reality counts on its fragments to bring together a wider span of space on the one hand and that of combining time fragments into a wholesome spirit of time on the other hand, that matches with the unbounded space. Thus, human mind gets a pathway to open up, either through physical communion or through its vast sense of connectivity via intuitive network or the par psychological perceptions on empirical scale. An account of the human history would thus talk about the relevance in the framework of consciousness.

As A. Toynbee and D. Ikeda say,

> *I believe that all observable phenomena are normal phenomena. As I see it, the so called supernormal phenomena that are the subject of so-called par psychological study are, in truth, normal phenomena of kinds that are either rare or else are common but have been overlooked and neglected in the west till recently. I myself have been a firsthand witness of telepathic communication that was, I know, genuine. I suppose that all living things have always communicated with each other telepathically and that, even since the invention of human speech, human beings continue to communicate with each other telepathically as well as by word of mouth or by writing. (Toynbee & Ikeda, 2013, pp. 18–19)*

The historian's observation of human mind dynamics must be in a collective context over a period of time. Collective mind dynamics may not contain specific elements of mental features. The psychological features of human mind quite often derive their roots from the practical positions of the world. Human condition is described, on the one hand, by its empirical features and, on the other, by its eternal features. Whereas the empirical feature speaks loudly about the visible, rational, measurable and quantified dimensions of the object, its intrinsic nature would reveal only a part of the true feature of the intrinsic as it exists in the context of time and space.

Empirical truth is thus seen through countless features of the visible world. This, in turn, brings out the features of life that have a wide impact in the lives of others within the considered boundary of understanding. Life, in its flow of events, should embrace things that are not related in any way. The understanding of reality begins with the understanding of the material that contains the earth system and the universe. This should continue on an ongoing basis and face questions that really confront the eternal questions of life and combine the understanding of both.

Sri Aurobindo has discovered the true contents of the substance of matter as a form of consciousness that truly constitutes a part of the understanding of the whole truth.

Seeker's Journey

Life is a series of events, interactions and facts that are apparently unconnected but have meaningful associations that lead to a final understanding of the meaning of life. Life, in its flow of events, leaves the opportunity to garner an abundant element of truth. In the quest for our understanding and intrinsic search, the spell of an individual's ignorance begins to leave the space for the light of life take its position. Wisdom has to dawn in the context of life in order to take shape as a whole. Sri Aurobindo has stated this condition of an aspiring individual in *Savitri* as follows:

A random series of inept events
To which reason lends illusive sense, is here,
Or the empiric Life's instinctive search.
Or a vast ignorant mind's colossal work.
But wisdom comes, and vision grows within;
Then Nature's instrument crowns himself her king;
He feels his witnessing self and conscious power;
His soul steps back and sees the Light Supreme.
A Godhead stands behind the brute machine.
This truth broke in in a triumph of fire;
A victory was won for God in man,
The deity revealed its hidden face…

(Sri Aurobindo, 1940, p. 21)

The symbol of new eminence, as seen in the journey through the paths of aspiring souls, has its gift in the revelations of the supreme truth through thought and work. In his endeavours for the same, he let the trajectories reveal a new way of understanding by always absorbing the shocks and thrusts of the world and trying to discover intrinsic truth from within.

Intrinsic truth can be properly understood when it fits into the design of the universe. Nature's instrument is thus given its total spell by supporting the new basis of understanding. Empirical involvement of life on earth is considered natural, but this span of being natural does not include any other aspect of the natural branded through the supernatural context of living in the universe.

When the soul joins the journey of life in totality, its association and touch in life renders human consciousness a lease of life that can invite the source of light to open up and construct a mechanism of truth that fits into the design of life. Godhead, in an individual, peeps his face up to a new realization of life.

Earth consciousness desires the material fulfilment for growing higher in material content and the urge to combine materiality with patches of consciousness. The material urge to grow to its full content makes the appearance of the world complete. The quest of life should culminate in the quest for eternity. In the stage of the human world, the eternal entity has opted for different forms that are cherished by nature in its limits and realms. Within their limits, the persons reveal the conscious boundary of aspiration. This aspiration has been revealed in *Savitri* in the following words:

A world's desire compelled her mortal birth.
One in the front of the immemorial quest
Protagonist of the mysterious play
In which the unknown pursues himself through forms.
And limits his eternity by the hours
And the blind void struggles to live and see. A thinker and toiler in the ideal's air,
Brought down to earth's dumb need her radiant power.
His was a spirit that stooped from longer spheres
Into our province of ephemeral sight,
A pointing beam on earth's uncertain roads,
His birth held up a symbol and a sign;
His human self like a translucent cloak
Covered the All-wise who leads the unseeing world...

(Sri Aurobindo, 1940, p. 22)

Human understanding of nature is a knowledge of nature through physical or psychological networking, where the expectations of the human can be fulfilled on the material plane. In the world of consciousness, this may not be corroborated. Human pursuit must lead to a struggle to realize a broader truth that awaits manifestation.

An individual is a thinker and a toiler in the empirical air. This earth system assimilates all these thoughts and toils to create opportunities for progress on the path of ideals. A spirit that originates from an individual's biophysical limits can find liberating dimensions beyond the horizons of the perceived or physical limits of an individual. In fact, the passage of spirit and light from the world of immortality is the divine touch in human abode. The conditions of an individual thus find ways to be released through wider transformations.

Beyond Human Limit

In the spell of uncertainty that surrounds the living world, the impacts of the senses are gripping an individual's life. Greed dominates the overall activities and thoughts. On the other hand, greed has an overarching effect on the living conditions and conditions of present civilization.

Demand and need are supposed to give shapes to the products and services in an industrial civilization. However, it has been observed that human need and demand have been constantly shaped and reshaped by greed. Greed, by its very nature, has an unending impact on people's decisions. Historians' finding comes to the conclusion that greed is suicidal. As Toynbee and Ikeda observe:

My conclusion is that private competitive economic enterprise is condemning itself to death because all parties fail to restrain their greed. The ethical or, perhaps, unethical postulate of the ideology of competitive economic enterprise is that greed is a virtue, not a vice. But this postulate in contrary to truth and falsehood brings nemesis. Unrestrained greed is self-destructive, because it takes suicidal short views. I believe that, in all industrial countries in which maximum private profit is the motive for production, the competitive economic system will become unworkable.

...Human nature is greedy, and greed leads to disaster if it is not restrained. In economics, as in all other human activities, self-mastery is, I believe, the only way to self-salvation...

(Toynbee & Ikeda, 2013, pp. 113–115)

The passages of events in history are pieces of evidence as real times during the period. Historical events clubbed together form continuity. However, discrete segments of history always talk about the general and specific features of the mind. Products and services are sold and, if the demands hype, produced the most. With increased demands, there are requirements to make more things happen.

Aggressive rise in demand may happen through new product adoption or increased use of the same. Widespread demand may be fostered with greed to possess a market centre stage. If greed can be made the driving force, commercial gains from existing products and services can be maximized. Techno-commercial civilization banks on the nurturing of greed in the marketplace in different ways. Toynbee and Ikeda have actually echoed that the spiritual greed leads to self-destruction. Self-mastery, the remedy, can be possible by spiritual belief and practice in place for individuals.

The conditions of the individual minds are created by social conditions. When the mind tends to restrict the impacts of the senses or, more particularly, greed, it creates the basis for superior understanding of life. This basis for superior understanding opens up opportunities for higher levels of understanding. An upward journey in the layers of consciousness would actually transform reality in the background as well. In the absence of divine touch, this unfolding has barely taken place. As Sri Aurobindo put it, mind discovers its limits on this journey.

In God's supreme withdrawn and timeless hush
A seeing self and potent Energy met;
The silence knew itself and thought took form;
Self-made from the dual power creation rose.
In the still self he lived and it in him;
Its mute immemorable listening depths,
Its vastness and its stillness were his own;
One being with it he grew wide, powerful, free.
Apart, unbound, he looked on all things done...

(Sri Aurobindo, 1940, p. 284)

A journey on the planes of consciousness actually leads to an understanding of the limitations of the mind. In the absence of the touch of the timeless, the supreme God, there is no liberation of the mind. When the endeavour begins in this journey, a gradual urge to receive the divine touch makes thing happen in the art and content of the endeavour. God's grace appears to be the most potent energy on this journey. With God's grace in place, the unlimited faculty of the mind's limited horizon gets opened up.

When the mind joins the journey of ascendancy in the valley of consciousness, the world's murmurings are coined in the vast ocean of silence. The power of creation, having its eternal seed sown in the bed of mind, must grow and see the face of light, not only the empirical light but also the rays of eternal light. This pierces through the paths and depths of accumulated darkness. While the touch of eternal light removes the spell of darkness, the ocean of silence captures the inner layers of the mind.

While this journey is underway, mind urges further progress in the vastness of the infinite. Mind grows wider and powerful in order to understand its futility and finally to abolish the mind.

The Divine Person

Replacing the mortal mind, a new mind dawns. This new mind is endowed with truth and light. It is beyond the boundaries of worldly thoughts, aspirations and mental constructions. This new mind gives birth a new form—divine embodied. Divine mother takes up on a new form, embracing this new mind and spreading the rays of her truth and light for the natural reincarnation of the divine. Sri Aurobindo has shown this to be the context of appearance of Savitri.

A mind daring heavenly experiment,
Growing towards some largeness they felt near,
Testing the unknown's bound with eager touch
They still were prisoned by their human grain;
They could not keep up with her tireless step;
Too small and eager for her large-paced will,
Too narrow to look with the unborn Infinite's gaze
Their nature weary grew of things too great.
For even the close patterns of her thoughts
Who could have walked the nearest to her ray.
Worshipped the power and light they felt in her
But could not match the measure of her soul.

(Sri Aurobindo, 1940, p. 363)

So far, Savitri is seen as a symbol of divinity on earth—a mystical symbol that has taken up the truth in its totality. However, Savitri is a true persona of the supreme, who appeared on earth to remove the limits and boundaries of earth's consciousness and embrace true divine consciousness in its mortal abode. Endowed with a lease of long life as a blessing, Savitri truly transformed the potentials of the earth into perpetuity in the context of earth's consciousness. Savitri was a personified truth. Her mortal act actually combined the truth of existence with the truth of the potent. Human existence can thus be determined either by the perceived truth of the human world or by going beyond it. Whereas the former gives rise to only a small fragment of the truth, the latter would be supplemented with further exploration of the truth.

Savitri sees positive things all around. This creation and the divine intervention in creation have always been seen as a mixture of good and bad; a mixture of light and vast holes of darkness around. Human observation has highlighted darkness more profoundly than the light that is visible.

Fate, nature and, most of all, the lord of nature have been blamed for the presence of such darkness. This view is based on the mind that reads it. Savitri sees all the acts and potency of creation through the eyes of positive reckoning. Her reading of the universe is that of a broad mind that can go beyond the limits naturally imposed. Her soul goes beyond all perceived boundaries. A broad soul capable of perceiving and realizing the truth that unfolds only at the point of realization of the broader truth.

Savitri considered the continuity of consciousness both in the empirical form of matter and in the touch of eternal presence as components of same supreme truth. *Satyavan*, the truth in empirical life, has his re-emergence as the embodied truth back in life. Observing the truth in life is actually living in the context of material reality while still living on the principles of truth. *Satyavan* brought back to life depicts the same features of truth as it is. But Savitri replies to the vague power in the following words:

If the eyes of Darkness can look straight at Truth,
Look in my heart and, knowing what I am,
Give what thou wilt or what thou must, O Death.
Nothing I claim but Satyavan alone.
There was a hush as if of doubtful fates.
As one disdainful still who yields a point
Death bowed his sovereign head in cold assent.
I give to thee saved from death and poignant fate
Whatever once the living Satyavan
Desired in his heart for Savitri...

(*Sri Aurobindo, 1940, p. 363*)

The material world is guided by the principles of matter. Savitri wants to transform this rule. Her urge is to change the world from material centric to God centric. Material-centric life gets the impact of matter and therefore life begets the urge to have enhanced association of matter.

Penetrating within matter at its elementary form, she could discover the spirit that resided within the core of matter. Matter, as a form of spirit, unveils its identity when its spirit is touched upon. With spirit as the starting point, matter is seen as equivalent, in its essence, to the fundamentals of spirit. Together, it comprises the wholesome truth.

Journey of Savitri has paved the way for a new civilization where matter is seen as important as the spirit and together making the dynamics of life happen. Material world thus would lead to a new context of spiritual understanding in life, in order to live a life with God at its centre and, always, everywhere, across its horizon.

Spiritual Orientation of Human Mind

Review of Civilization

Chaos and conflict are the normal orders of the day. Most of us are going through these one way or the other. People are armed with their words, actions or weapons to wage wars and initiate conflict. Even the Lord of

Earth, too, is carrying arms. It is not just to wage war, but to establish the rule of 'dharma' or righteousness in human society. Lord Rama very categorically mentions this point in Ramayana in the following words:

Satyena Ayudhyam alabhe
neyam mama mahi saumaya durlabha sagarambara
na hi ceheyam adharmena sakratvam api Lakshmana

I am carrying arms for the sake of the truth. It is not difficult for me to gain this whole universe, but I do not even want the suzerainty of the heavens if it is through unrighteousness.

The dawn of civilization saw wars and contradictions in the human system that tended to bring the waves of chaos into order. Divine dominance having been countervailed by demonic avalanches, the process of war did not stop, but only changed its pattern. In a sweeping change of pattern, the modern age has called war a competition, trying to contain both sides through a philosophical description of the event as 'laissez-faire'. As Ivan Alexander (1997) put it:

If competition were only a form of battle then victory for one side, and surrender by the other would mean victory for the monopoly of the victor. It would bring order, but not desirable order. Such is the case: that which makes competition work as a social mechanism is not the pitched battle but the voluntary truce. Competition is a form of compromise. Almost, every act in business is a reconciliation of warring probabilities.

Although competition is described as a process of reconciliation, it is a war of entities for the possession of resources. The war that Lord Rama initiated was a war determined to establish righteousness. A close look at the Ramayana, the great epic written by Sage Valmiki, shows how holistic the process of war was.

A glimpse of it is discussed further.

Concerns for Righteousness

Ravana, the demon king, had heard of Sita, a lady of incomparable beauty, and had become extremely eager to possess her. Sita, the wife of Rama, was living with her consort deep in the forest. Ravana, a demon with the power to change his face and his appearance, took the form of a Brahmin, begging alms from the householder. Ravana took the opportunity when Rama and his brother–follower, Lakshmana, were away from home for hunting. While giving alms to a person with the look and appearance of a sage (Ravana, the demon taking that form through illusory, magical power), the pious lady was kidnapped by Ravana and taken to the air-plane to get her to his own place in Lanka (now Sri Lanka) across the Indian Ocean. Ravana did his job like a true demon, while Rama did not reciprocate with a similar strategy to get Sita back.

Hanuman, the great devotee of Rama, with more magical but divine power, visited Lanka to find Sita. It was easy for Hanuman to take her back and return her to his lord.

In fact, Hanuman expressed his intention to take her back, to fly across the stratosphere and tropopause, crossing the Indian Ocean, back to his lord. But Sita refused to do so. Her sense of divine dignity wanted the lord to rescue her on his own, to wage a war against the unrighteous, not by adopting escape strategies—a reconciling compromise—but to confront and win her. That is why the lord carries arms. Business observes quite a contrasting scenario, asserting the power of Ravana and ridiculing Rama.

The result is often ridiculous.

Business Mind of the World

In contrast to the popular impression, business develops a kind of mind. The general feature of a business mind is to try and take things by any means. Motivational force is a perpetual success observed by Whitehead (1993) as a deviation from the mind of the society.

The motive of success is not enough. It produces a Short-sighted world which destroys the sources of its own prosperity. We must not fall into the fallacy—Thinking the business world: in abstraction of the Community is largely dominated by the business mind.

Business mind is the one that creates an ambience for newer social settings and leads to changes in newer orders. Is this compatible with the changes? The legacy of the West in the Roman system of enjoying the live show of a slave, given the opportunity to fight the hungry lions in the arenas in their bid to free themselves, is worth mentioning here. The view of this live fight between the slave and the lion, and the obvious devouring of the slave by the lion, could give the maximum pleasure and release a lot of adrenaline in 'civilized' Romans. Do we, the business lords and slave intellectual traders, find an appropriate heritage in that?

Whitehead's observation could be supported by the following fact.

Obsessive shoppers, who risk bankruptcy in order to buy things they do not really want or need, can be saved by a pill already used to treat other compulsive behaviours. A preliminary study suggests that compulsive shopping or buying could affect about 1–6 per cent of the American population. According to a doctor, the problem appears to be more common in women, who mostly buy clothing, shoes and makeup products, than in men, who tend to purchase electronic equipment and clothing. Most patients think about buying all the time. They arrange their lives around shopping. But their euphoria in the store is followed by guilt and disgust when they think about what they have done. The urge to shop can be so powerful that people go bankrupt or lose their jobs because they were too busy shopping to show up on time.

Shopping syndrome has been found to be reduced by the use of the medicine (Fluvoxamine) at least to 50 per cent. The report highlights a very important aspect of civilized existence. We keep on buying without even knowing the purpose. The so-called techno-commercial civilization is based on buying instincts or buying facilities. Unless there is a boom in terms of horizontal and/or vertical use of goods and services, the objective of profit maximization cannot be fulfilled. In the purism of enhancing the consumption base and increasing the depth of consumption, the reckless war of advertising and promotion efforts seldom address real needs, but bank on illusory needs. As the obsessive shopping habit report suggests, buying takes place irrespective of whether or not there is a real need. Always thinking about buying sometimes turns people into patients. The disease, being a buying syndrome, enhances the worth and bottom line of the corporation, but at the cost of the health of human mind. What prompted buyers to follow a course of their lives to abnormality is a matter of serious concern.

Before exploring this problem further, let us look at another aspect of the present civilization. Again, that is the contemporary behaviour of consumers. PTI (the *Times of India*) reports that the Chinese had become fond of taking the powdered flesh of the human foetus in their morning soup. The report (PTI, 1995) states:

Aborted human foetuses intended for human consumption are being sold for as little as one pound in the Chinese city of Shenzhen. At private clinics, aborted foetuses could be obtained for between one and 1.75 pound. Zou Zin, a doctor working at the Lus Hu Clinic in Shenzhen, is reported to have said that the foetuses are 'nutritious' and claimed to have eaten 100 herself in the past six months. She said the best were the first born males from the young women. If not eaten, the foetuses would be wasted. A woman doctor from Shenzhen said that the foetuses were even better than placenta in nutritional value. They could make your skin smoother, body stronger and are good for the kidney.

Is this the tragedy or the glory of the human civilization? The Shenzhen foetus-soup is considered to be one of the extreme varieties of the chosen consumables where a human being prefers to consume the flesh and blood of their own species in a nascent form.

As a cosmic tendency to maintain balance, human society now intends to establish a balance through its aggressive consumption habits: on the one hand, the dominance of physical sex and, on the other, the devouring of the nascent offspring. Do we see a trend emerging in the current pattern of consumption? It is obvious that the current pattern of consumption is based on desire. With the desire occupying the centre stage of life, individuals try to find ways and means to fulfil it. One desire that has been fulfilled gives rise to another. In the course of fulfilling their desire, individuals continually miss happiness and satisfaction. Desire cannot be satisfied with its service. Manu, the great social and behavioural scientist of ancient India, foresaw this problem.

Na jatu kamah kamanam upabhogena samyati
havisa krishnavartmeva bhuya evabhivardhate

(Manusmriti, 11.94)

Desire is never satisfied with the pleasure of the objects of desire.
It grows more and more like the fire to which fuel is added.
Not only does the fire of desire keep burning but is also
flamed thoroughly.

Desire has been the central focus of human existence. Desire for the things that are necessary for existence is very much important. But who is going to measure and set the benchmarks on the desires? The question is: to what extent and not beyond that? Can there be any conditions for limitation and boundary?

It is obvious that corporations, in their pursuit of getting into things, forget about boundary and limiting conditions. Controversies prevail over the ideal of corporate governance. Is it just profit maximization or something else? Is profit maximization the goal of corporate existence or the means of corporate progress? These are the various questions frequently asked by the company's stakeholders.

Corporate progress has been shifted to corporate selfishness with the aim of profit maximization. In the absence of any kind of softening instrument, the aim of profit maximization culminates in a situation of war in the marketplace. Indiscriminate war in the marketplace could lead to a social situation that is, again, conducive to a perpetual war of nerves in the human system. Consumption instinct, which has been already been mentioned, will surely lead to a fatal kind of nerve war in society.

Direct or indirect consequences are as follows:

1. Breeding conflict, eroding cooperation
2. Less harmony, more divergence
3. Honour for an individual is being replaced by honour for money and position
4. Concern for the short term at the cost of the long term
5. Soft values of existence are sacrificed to harder objectives
6. Fragmented mind has been given an overdue credit over an integral mind
7. Noble quality being subdued for lollypops
8. 'Status consciousness' overwhelming the 'divine consciousness'
9. Worship of the divine being replaced by worship of money and ego
10. Existential outlooks being reduced to myopic views, putting aside the views of holism

Invited to these consequences, individuals working in organized activities get more stress on their work-life than others who do not.

Human Happiness (Story of an Individual Bounded by Perils)

A man was chased by a tiger while walking through a dense forest. Somehow, he was able to run through and climb a small banyan tree. The tree was leaning towards the ditch on its side, and the bed of the ditch was full of weeds inhabited by wild snakes. In his effort to be safe, the poor man had climbed up one of the branches of the tree that was leaning towards the ditch. But the branch could not bear the man's weight and broke. Because the Banyan tree was full of various kinds of weeds, the man did not fall from the tree; his legs were stuck in the threaded weeds that covered the branch. But the sudden jerk of the broken branch had alarmed bees that were living inside the beehive on another branch of the tree. Suddenly the bees rushed to the man, chased continuously and bit him thoroughly. The whole incident alarmed the deadly snakes living inside the bushes on the bed of the ditch. On the other hand, the tiger was waiting on the bank of the ditch, hoping to get hold of the man, who was considered a delicious food by it. The climax of the incident, being a man whose legs were tied incidentally naturally to a branch of the tree, hanging upside down, was graced to test the sweetness of life. The beehive was on another branch just above the tree trunk, the honey was leaking drop after drop and as a sort of grace started falling on the lips and lower jaw of the man. The sage sees a person's taste buds enjoying honey, testing the sweetness of life.

This story tells exactly what the human situation is like. Surrounded by the elements of destruction, he is absorbing the continuous biting of the bees and then getting satisfied with the drops of honey, even when snakes and tigers are around. What is the future of this man? Can he get out of this trap? Can he come out as an individual free to move and live? Constrained by the conditions, we get enjoyment even through the subtlest of means.

Through his advocated dominance, Whitehead's 'business mind' has created a hell of a problem that ridicules the noble, the gentle, the honest and the truthful. It is against this context that the lord would like the re-emergence of a new weapon—a weapon of values, a value-based system.

Response of the Modern Mind

Ivan Alexander is of the opinion that the marvels of technology are only wanted if they sustain and promote acceptable values. People continue to cherish the old ideals of peace, liberty, fraternity and order. The question is whether the business mind is creating wider gaps in global society and more and more sectors of economic and social disparity. Is that ethical? A value-based mindset would contribute to value-based business management practices. The West's talk about values and ethics has been a teleological or consequence-driven approach. John Rawl's 'maximin condition' would go a long way to protecting and enhancing justice as a social contract in which he emphasizes the following.

1. Each person has an equal right to the most extensive scheme of basic liberties, which are compatible with a similar scheme of liberties for all.
2. The following conditions must be met by social and economic inequalities. They are as follows:
   a. To the greatest expected benefit of the least advantaged
   b. Attached to offices and positions open to all under the conditions of a fair opportunity.

Robert Nozick, a critic of John Rawl, supports individual rights in the 'entitlement theory' he propounded.

While the assertion of rights has been the most generalized view of the Western experts, the oriental view has been quite different from that. The orient, particularly India, asserts human duties. Adam Smith's 'invisible hand' tends to correct the market by its macro assertion that it considers all aspects of the market to be important on a variety of scales. Market potential is enhanced by a free flow of various inputs and flows with varying intentions, as well as a variety of dynamics. Thus, the market is destined to curb or tame the illogical demand or expectations of one participant on the other. The market tends to correct the unethical practices of an operator or a group of operators through a process of mutual conflict, hegemony, and synthesis.

The existence of multiple forces is the character of a market, but, according to Adam Smith, the process of getting and ordering would be a multiplied assertion of individual selfishness, thereby sensitizing an individual's infinite expectation. Logical and illogical expectations confront us with a similar set of things and finally get the market to correct the result. The basic input for the market would be the utter selfishness of everybody. Maximization of selfish tendency would be instrumental in getting the maximum drive out of an individual's existing potential.

The rule, however, is going to be an orderless order. Gradual fragmentation of the consciousness of the being has been the rule. Both the inter-organizational and intra-organizational contexts are changing rapidly because of the infinite expectation that is propelled by utter selfishness. Uncertainty is the order of the day. Even though we do possess a lot of tools and techniques to learn the present and study the future, we do not know exactly what the situation around us could be to provide for a course of action based on certainties that tend to establish a global society that satisfies the rights and maintains distributive justice. The message for us is to learn how to live in chaos and uncertainty. And not be in a hunch for certainty at a point where it is hardly traceable.

Fine, it is going to be a self-doers society with incipient and emerging uncertainty and chaos. Then, what is the invisible lever that is going to hold back and keep the collective going?

In a decentralized system, as advocated, is it not the collective mind that keeps entities spread across boundaries and supra boundaries? Is it not a simple, genuine, honest trust that would be a must to hold the system back against the odds and onslaughts of disruptive forces?

A sound mind can go a long way towards establishing genuine trust on the basis of which a future society that could be identified as value-based could emerge. This leads us to an introspective visit to the realms of mind.

Mind Speaks

The importance of the mind in human existence has been felt so much that there have been millions of interpretations of the mind. Poets tend to discuss it in one fashion, scientists in another. The endowment and acceptance of minds have been the focus of worldly love. A disciplined mind gives rise to one result, an unrestrained mind gives rise to another. The mind does not stay in one place. Essentially kinetic, it now resides in one place and then a thousand miles away. The mind is shapeless, but it takes the shape of the object to which it is devoted. Intrinsically, colourless, the mind can take the colour of the context of its matter. There has been a lot of research on mind. It has been accepted by poets and scientists as a matter of research. Scientists are trying to scan it and then correct the irregular mind. The aim of the scientists is to bring back a normal mind through the use of various medicines, tools and techniques. There has been a great deal of effort to get back a clean and healthy mind for which a variety of efforts have also been made. We should discuss the various aspects and dynamics of the mind.

Aspects of Mind

Much has been devoted to the mind in the ancient scriptures of the Hindus. Upanishad, a landmark in the wisdom of human civilization, talks eloquently about the mind. In Kathopanishad, while answering the questions raised by Nachiketa, Yama, the lord of death, describes the nature of the relationship among body, mind and the *atman*.

Atmano rathinam viddhi, shariram ratham eva tu
Buddhi tu sarathi viddhi, manah pragraham eva cha.

Know the *atman* as the lord sitting on the chariot, the body as the chariot, the intellect as the driver of the chariot and the mind as the connecting cord that links the *atman* to the body.

If the chariot representing body is required to be pulled forward, then one would act on the mind. With a kinetic and inspired mind, one takes forward the entity, satisfying the divine in every respect. It is the process of inspiring the mind that helps to establish a permanent link between the empirical entity and its divine spirit.

The Upanishad used the beautiful metaphor of a monkey to explain the actual nature of the human mind in general. The metaphor is as follows: the human mind is like a monkey bitten by a scorpion, which has been made to drink intoxicating liquor and, finally, a demon entering it. By using this metaphor, the Upanishad wants to uphold the real nature of the human mind.

The restlessness of the human mind is like a monkey's restless nature. It is never in a definite place or context. The mind is now in Calcutta, the next moment in Belgrade and the third moment in Bombay. Now the mind is enjoying a sweet memory, suddenly it rushes into a sour one and, in the third moment, a tasteless one. The amount of burning that a scorpion injects into the monkey is important. The constant biting of jealousy is always distracting. In good spirits, we cannot take the good of others.

A friend or a person belonging to a peer group makes an individual jealous of their success or achievement. The constant biting of jealousy has been a major dynamic of the human mind. Like a monkey drinking intoxicating liquor and becoming intoxicated, a human being suffers from a continuous intoxication of desires. Under the wrong impression of buying peace by satisfying one element of desire, we invite a larger element of desire by fulfilling it.

The desire of a lower order grows into a higher order with its fulfilment. Intoxication with desire multiplies the usual restlessness of the monkey.

Finally, when the demon enters the monkey, it reaches the summit of its ego and its actualization. It is the state of self-actualization that satisfies the undiscovered or unidentified dimensions of the human ego ('I am so special' and so on). In an effort to find out and establish uniqueness, a person forgets about the context of others, builds empires around the false notion of individuality. Ego misleads the individual, distracts them and binds them to the periphery of their own world. Egocentrism is taking the human beings to the brink of total destruction. With a demon entering it, a monkey can only foresee complete destruction in the near future.

In the gospel of Sri Ramakrishna (Gupta, 1990), the embodiment of the lord, there is a story told by the lord. The story is as follows:

There lived a frog in a small ditch. This frog was a little bigger in size than the other member frogs living there. That is why all the frogs used to consider the biggest one as their king. Once the king frog saw a subject-frog rushing in and trembling in fear. Having been asked by the king, the subject said, 'Lord, today I happened to see an elephant, a huge animal. Somehow I was able to come away with my life.' In utter disgust, the king asked 'Is the elephant's size bigger than mine?' 'Yes lord, he is much bigger.' King then had swelled its body by taking in air and asked, 'Is he even larger?' 'Yes lord,' Then agitated in mind, the king tried his best to expand his body more and more in order to prove his point, but finally the king's body burst. The condition of man is almost the same.

Aspects of Mind

In the ancient Hindu psycho-philosophy, a thorough and very rigorous study mind was carried out. Most initiated by the great psycho-philosopher Patanjali, a series of postulates and explanations of the mind are given. Patanjali's 'Yoga Surra' mostly deals with the mind. According to Patanjali, there are five different stages of development in the mind.

These are *mudha* (inert or dull), *kshipta* (turbulent), *vikshipta* (scattered), *ekagra* (concentrated) and *niruddha* (cessation of mind).

The *mudha* mind is dull and less active, but it fabricates all sorts of ill things. At this stage, the individual is occupied by the ill thinking of others. *Mudha* does all sorts of low, ill thinking, but cannot translate them into action.

The *kshipta* mind is wild. It is always in an angry mood, always running helter-skelter. There is no patience. A wild mind nurtures all negative emotions and activates many of them. A wild mind leads to destruction.

The *vikshipta* or scattered mind is always dissipated. It crosses the harmful stages of the *kshipta*, but then gets scattered completely. It cannot focus on things to uncover reality. A scattered mind cannot have peace and happiness. With its characteristic digression, the scattered mind does not help to maintain the link between *atman* and the body. It is not congenial to unfold the talent or genius of an individual. With the scattered mind, an individual loses the fervour and spirit of the inner essence. Unless the scattered mind is disciplined and made to concentrate, the individual will not be able to unfold the inner potentialities.

The *ekagra* or concentrated mind is capable of concentrating on one single point. A concentrated mind can help to win in life in the truest sense. No ill thoughts come into a concentrated mind. A concentrated mind cultivates only the positive values of life. Noble thoughts are reflected in it. A noble thought leads to a noble destiny through noble action, noble habit and a noble character. Patanjali's concept of the theory of cause and effect is as follows:

Sow a thought, reap an act.
Sow an act, reap a habit.
Sow a habit, reap a character.
Sow a character, reap a destiny.

Human destiny is created only by human beings. We are reaping the fruit of the seeds that have basically been seeded by us. A concentrated mind helps to unfold and sows noble seeds that lead to noble destiny.

The *niruddha* or the cessation of mind talks about a stage where the mind ceases to exist in its present form. Divinity induces at the point at which the mind ceases to act and exist in its present form. Divine grace begins to flow when the concentration of the mind is reached. But this is not all of it. With a new form a structure, the mind induces divinity and reflects all kinds of divine emotions. Divine grace is the ultimate reward and achievement. Lord Sri Ramakrishna says, 'Bondage and liberation are both in mind.'

The mind that ceases to exist in the usual form liberates individuals. The mind is all there is. A person who visits many holy places makes many verbal repentances within their mind and always repeats the name of God, but whose mind is engrossed in elements of desire, will not receive divine grace. Let us read the story of two friends told by Lord Sri Ramakrishna (Gupta, 1990).

The story is as follows: On a weekend, two friends are walking down a road. One of them joined the prayer gathering of a temple where a Swamiji (a monk) was reciting and explaining Bhagavat (the story of Lord Krishna). He asked the other friend to join the Bhagavat gathering, but his friend refused. He had other plans and said, 'Excuse me, I am not a fool to waste my weekend like you by joining the Bhagavat, rather I am going to visit a brothel and enjoy the flesh with all my senses.' But after a while, it happened that the second friend developed a strong sense of disgust in mind. While deeply involved in pleasure, his mind was surrendered to the Lord at the Bhagavat gathering. The inner voice in him began to repent vehemently this act of pleasure. He thought to himself, 'Hell this life which is so engrossed in sex and senses. My friend is so great! He is immersed in the divine bliss at the Bhagavat gathering, if I were like him, Oh God!'

On the other hand, the first friend, sitting among the spiritual aspirants, joined the chorus *bhajanam* (prayer song), but his mind was continuously stationed at the sex worker's house where his friend was. He thought in his mind, 'I am a fool doing all this nonsense of praying to God and listening to Swamiji. My friend is so lucky that he is enjoying the flesh!' The story concludes with the fate of these two friends at the end of their lives. For the person who joined the Bhagavat gathering, the representations of 'Yama', the lord of death, had come to punish. On the other hand, to the friend with the empirical body in the house of sex worker but the mind approaching the lord of Bhagavat came the representations of Vishnu. Mind is the central indicator for all of us. What one does, with whom one works, is not important. If the mind is surrendered to the lord, and is pure, the person is liberated and attains the divine realization.

Beyond Mind Consciousness

Sri Aurobindo has offered a unique concept of the supramental. The supramental is divine. Human beings have three states of conscience: animal, human and divine.

In the animal state of the triad consciousness, a person behaves like an animal. They are prone to jealousy, envy, crookedness, heating, stealing, anger and lust. They cannot rise above the dictates of the senses.

They take pleasure in the sufferings of others; they are always agitated in their mind. The first three states of mind—*mudha*, *kshipta* and *vikshipta*—symbolize animal consciousness. At this stage of understanding, all empirical relationships are based on reciprocation. Love becomes an instrument of trade. Arrogance and primacy of a person in all affairs become the dominant attributes of this type.

With the evolution of consciousness, one reaches a 'human' state with a concentrated mind, one's appearance later reveals the reality. A person learns to stand and face with dignity and confidence. They continue to be in the empirical activities, but they are no longer a slave to their senses. Their life is bound by the righteous principles. At this stage, qualities such as caring, compassion, fellow feeling empathy and honesty are revealed. They rise above the law of retaliation and reciprocity, which are the dominant attributes of the animal world. 'Human' in consciousness, a person rises above utter selfishness and desire which lead to the state of divine consciousness.

Divine consciousness is the highest. In this state of being, life is consecrated to the divine. A person does things, gets involved, but the mind is always surrendered to the lotus feet of the divine. Lord Sri Ramakrishna gives examples of a maid taking care of a child in the house of her employer lady. The maid does everything for the child, loves the child and gets involved also, but all the time her mind focuses on her own child whom she has left uncared for. Like this maid, we are expected to do everything reasonably required, but the mind is always in the divine world—in the company of the divine. This is the state of divine consciousness. In this state of consciousness, a human being is perfectly in unison with the divine. They do work, but on the basis of the principles of renunciation of the fruits.

In their view, a divine person becomes holistic and helps to establish a holistic society. A liberated mind or supramental state is a prelude to a holistic view. Holistic management practices are only possible when leaders and operators cultivate divinity and unearth inner divinity. They are the best managers and leaders who transcend the realms of mind and are one with the divine. With a liberated mind, they can help liberate the myopic selfish paradigms of business management.

Spiritual Mind

A liberated mind makes an individual great and helps to build order in the system. With the liberation of individuals, the collective is influenced, and the collective mind emerges from the bondages of desire.

The free collective mind, supporting 'elevated, collective consciousness', helps to establish a value-based order.

The aforementioned analysis shows that a value-based order can be achieved in three steps:

1. Understanding the past and the present properly in the light of the value requirements
2. Understanding the role of the mind in the entire process
3. Mind engineering to achieve the goal of a value-based system

The findings of the European Science Foundation's research on the impact of values, by Van Deth and Scarbrough (1995), show that there has been a sustained drift in collective values through changes in individual values throughout Europe. Researchers have shown that there has been 'an increased emphasis on non-material and emancipator goals; shifting away from tradition, respect for authority, and material well-being towards self-fulfilment, independence, and emancipation'.

The gradual drift of modern man from the process of fragments must have a converging culmination. The point of convergence, however, is not at all a person, a symbol or a system; rather it is a set of attributes that symbolizes divinity. Swami Vivekananda (1995a) addressed this view in a post-lecture discussion on civilization in America in 1894.

According to Vivekananda (1995a),

Religious thought should be directed at developing Man's spiritual side. Science, art, learning and metaphysical search all have their proper functions in life, but if you seek to blend them, you eliminate the spiritual, for instance, from religious altogether. You Americans worship what? The dollar. In the mad rush for gold, you forget the spiritual until you had become a nation of materialists. Even your preachers and churches are tainted with the all pervading desire. Show me one person in the history of your people; who has led the spiritual lives like those whom I can name at home have done.

It is this observation that shows the extent of materialism that has engrossed the minds in the West. The European Foundation study shows the process of drifting away from the basis of rigid materialism. The survey of values mentioned earlier refers to the progress towards spiritual values. According to Banerjee (1997a), 'the ordinary rational mind as well as all human activities are anchored in what could be termed as apparent individuality (to discover the true individuality) the scientific materialistic mind should find ways to have a feel of the divinity within himself'.

The search for true individuality could be made through an engineered mind that finds a role model. Banerjee (1997b) suggests that this is the role of a mother or, more precisely, of a motherhood in individuals.

'Motherhood is the heart of a mother which the country needs so much.' Society is confronted with an emerging situation in which a motherly heart is gradually withering away. We need to have a motherly heart.

Many others have felt the need for a motherly heart, albeit in a different way. Vanourek (1995) questions the underlying value system of the dollar. He says:

The management said, 'It's really only the bottom line that counts' makes the dollar its value system. This bottom line values system does not guide typical daily decisions. If we say it is only the bottom line that counts, what might the shipping clerk do at the end of the quarter when a defective product is noticed? He ships it. Without this value system, what might a vice-president do at the first sign of a business slow-down? He lays off the factory workers without exploring other options first.

The dollar-driven ultra-individualism, according to Adams, will find its way, more profound in nature in the future. The Dilbert principles put forward by Adams (1997) state: 'The predictable result of the Dilbert principle is that skilled professionals won't put up with the indignity of being managed by idiots.' He goes on to say, in his 31st prediction, 'In the future skilled professionals will leave their corporate jobs and become bosses themselves in ever-increasing numbers.' The sheer impact of individuality is on certain dimensions of the mind, making an envious person boastful of things of oneself. A system dominated by self-aggrandization is definitely going the opposite way in the liberating mind, and hence according to our observation against a value-based system. Future society can benefit mostly from the liberation of the mind.

Mind liberation can be based on two approaches:

1. The yoga method
2. The surrender method

Process of Concentration of Mind

Shri Anirban (1988), a great yogi, explains the basis of yoga in the following words:

In the depth of my being, the subtle substance of mind appears in the form of tiny points or rays of electric light. It is this light, spreading outward, that creates my world—my outer as well as inner world. But in both these worlds, disturbing movements of various kinds are constantly taking place.

The outer is always disturbed by the extraneous, in most of the cases the inner follows the same way. Yoga disciplines the inner realm and gives new shape to the outer realm. It is also congenial to the birth of inner divinity. According to Patanjali, this could be established by means of eight-limbed yoga, with the limbs as follows:

1. *Limb I, Yama:* This means restraint. Non-injury, truthfulness, non-stealing, continence, non-covetousness and so on are the attributes of Yama, which purify character through moral self-control.
2. *Limb II, Niyama:* This pertains to disciplined habits of austerity, the study of noble things and devotion to the supreme.
3. *Limb III, Asana:* This means posture. While seated posture is generally recommended, other postures are also acceptable as long as the internalization process is not disturbed.
4. *Limb IV, Pranayama:* It manages breathing. The alternate nostril inhalation and exhalation with holding breath for a brief period of time in between comprises the process of *pranayama*, which is to vacate the mind of objects and to cleanse it, the ultimate goal is the extreme concentration of the divine.
5. *Limb V, Pratyahara*: This is renunciation or withdrawal. A mind, concentrated on the divine, withdraws from things contaminated with desire.
6. *Limb VI, Dharana:* This is conceptualization. The conception of the divine comes after the withdrawal takes place.
7. *Limb VII, Dhyana:* This means meditation. In the condition of meditation, things are revealed in proper reality: the realization takes place.
8. *Limb VIII, Samadhi:* A state of unlimited bliss through a sense of identity with the divine.

Eight-limbed yoga, as outlined earlier, is a matter of long sincere practice. Through effort and practice, one can raise the consciousness to such a height that the mind becomes divine from its original materialistic condition. A divine mind exudes the divine qualities of character reflected through behaviour.

Surrender to God

The same effect or, in many cases, a far superior effect could be achieved by surrender. Surrender demands an identified entity of the divine. Once that is done, surrender works out marvels. The idea and outlook are, 'I am insignificant, you are all.' 'Thy Will be done.' A unique example of this is available in the being of Swami Vivekananda. Vivekananda had gained global fame and established his supremacy, but his supremacy was based on a surrendered attitude. He used to consider himself to be the most insignificant and attributed all successes to his mentor, lord, in the form of Sri Ramakrishna. The hymns dedicated to Sri Ramakrishna by Swami Vivekananda (1995b) are as follows:

Orn! Hrim! Thou art the true, the imperturbable One, transcending three Gunas and yet adored for their virtues! In as much as I do not worship day and night, with yearning, Thy compassionate lotus feet which destroys all ignorance, therefore, Thou friend to the lowly. Thou art my only refuge.

A surrendered mind creates personalities humble enough to cultivate a well-cemented collective consciousness. This is perhaps, the most dependable way to have a Stress-free and value-based order.

With this self-realization, a manager proceeds in corporate and social life to invite the dawn of a new civilization where a person is free from poverty (of body and mind), ill health and lack of wisdom.

References

Adams, S. (1997). *The Dilbert future.* Boxtree.

Alexander, I. (1997). *The civilized market.* Capstone.

Avent, R. (2014). Special report on the world economy: The third great wave. *The Economist.* https://www.economist.com/sites/default/files/20141004_world_economy.pdf

Banerjee, R. P. (1997a). Vivekananda's concept of individuality in the context of teamwork in organisation. In P. Bharata (Ed.), *Centenary of Swami Vivekananda's return to India* (pp. 97–98). TISS.

Banerjee, R. P. (1997b). In search of a mother: The missing motherhood in a liberalised economy. In Atmanand (Ed.), *Globalisation and dimensions of management in India* (p. 28). Shipra Publications.

Bohm, D. (2012). *Wholeness and the Implicate Order.* London and New York: Routledge.

Carter, R. (2010). *Mapping the mind.* Phoenix.

Darwin, C. (2003). *The Origin Of Species.* Signet.

Gupta, M. (1990). *Gospel of Sri Ramakrishna.* Advaita Ashrama.

Mukherjee, S. (2016). *The gene: An intimate history.* Penguin Books.

Soros, G. (1994). *The alchemy of finance: Reading the mind of the market.* John Wiley & Sons.

Sri Anirban. (1988). *Inner yoga.* S. N. Chatterjee (Trans.). Voice of India.

Sri Aurobindo. (1940). *Savitri: A legend and a symbol.* Sri Aurobindo Ashram.

Swami Vivekananda. (1995b). *The complete works* (Vol. 8). Advaita Ashrama, Mayavati.

Toynbee, A., & Ikeda, D. (2013). *Choose life: A dialogue*. I. B. Tauris.

Van Deth, J. W., & Scarbrough, E. (Eds.). (1995). *The impact of values*. Oxford: Oxford University Press.

Vanourek, R. A. (1995). Servant leadership and the future. In L. C. Spears (Ed.), *Reflections on leadership* (pp. 298–307). John Wiley & Sons.

Whitehead, A. N. (1993). *Adventures of ideas*. Cambridge University Press.